THE BIBLE
AND
MODERN LITERARY
CRITICISM

THE BIBLE
AND
MODERN LITERARY
CRITICISM

A Critical Assessment
and Annotated Bibliography

Compiled by

MARK ALLAN POWELL

with the assistance of
Cecile G. Gray and Melissa C. Curtis

Bibliographies and Indexes in Religious Studies
Number 22
Gary E. Gorman, Series Adviser

GREENWOOD PRESS
New York • Westport, Connecticut • London

Library of Congress Cataloging-in-Publication Data

Powell, Mark Allan.
  The Bible and modern literary criticism : a critical assessment
and annotated bibliography / compiled by Mark Allan Powell with the
assistance of Cecile G. Gray and Melissa C. Curtis.
      p.   cm.—(Bibliographies and indexes in religious studies,
  ISSN 0742-6836 ; no. 22)
    Includes indexes.
    ISBN 0-313-27546-7 (alk. paper)
    1. Bible as literature—Bibliography.   2. Bible—Criticism,
interpretation, etc.—Bibliography.   I. Gray, Cecile G.
II. Curtis, Melissa C.   III. Title.   IV. Series.
Z7770.P68   1992
[BS535]
016.2206'6—dc20   91-38128

British Library Cataloguing in Publication Data is available.

Library of Congress Catalog Card Number: 91-38128
ISBN: 0-313-27546-7
ISSN: 0742-6836

First published in 1992

Greenwood Press, 88 Post Road West, Westport, CT 06881
An imprint of Greenwood Publishing Group, Inc.

Printed in the United States of America

The paper used in this book complies with the
Permanent Paper Standard issued by the National
Information Standards Organization (Z39.48-1984).

10 9 8 7 6 5 4 3 2 1

CONTENTS

FOREWORD

Sometimes a traditional view of the authority of the Bible is still kept; it is the divinely inspired, authoritative guide to Christian conduct and belief, containing a timeless oracle from God . . .

-John Bowden, *Who Is a Christian?*

The English Bible, a book which if everything else in our language should perish, would alone suffice to show the whole extent of its beauty and power . . .

-Thomas Macaulay, *Essays*

These two statements exemplify the commonly held, traditional misconception that the Bible is *either* scripture *or* literature. Those who view the Bible solely as scripture treat the literary equation as nothing less than heresy, while proponents of the literary approach regard scripturalists as idolatrous worshippers of a mere book. We see evidence of this polarity almost daily--one of the most startling manifestations in Australia having been public reaction to a Lenten television program on the Sydney University academic, Barbara Thiering, and her interpretation of the content and meaning of the New Testament. A biblical scholar in the liberal Protestant tradition, Dr. Thiering attracted an unprecedented backlash from the viewing public, who contacted the broadcaster in significant numbers to complain of its callousness in scheduling such a "destructive" program during the holiest season of the Christian calendar. For them, the Bible is a sacred document not to be tampered with, while for Dr. Thiering it is a literary document susceptible to the same kind of analysis as any other ancient collection.

To the "faithful," literary critics of the Bible ought to be classified as pariahs, misguided scholars with a penchant for "stirring the possum"--they undermine faith, introduce doubt and confusion among honest believers. In this respect little seems to have changed since the foundation of modern biblical criticism in the seventeenth century by Richard Simon (d. 1712). Upon publication of his *Histoire Critique du Vieux Testament* in 1678, the book was suppressed and he was ejected from the Oratory in Paris. Today, many modern opponents of literary criticism of the Bible wish the same fate on its more outspoken advocates.

Despite such continuing opposition, there is emerging, in some sectors at least, a gradual convergence of these two poles. Until relatively recently, study of the Bible as scripture has been confined to the seminary, while study of the Bible as literature has been the preserve of the university. As Mark Allan Powell states in his Preface to the present work, "the new convergence of biblical and literary studies destroys this dichotomy. The most recent studies attempt to examine the Bible as literature and as scripture at the same time." Particularly satisfying is the ecumenicity of the growing awareness that literary content, analysis and criticism are crucial to genuine understanding of the meaning of biblical texts. Thus Protestantism's James Barr asserts with typical vigour that ". . . story is an absolutely essential aspect of the Old Testament; it cannot, however, be too simply identified, indeed it cannot be identified at all, with history. Story belongs to literary form and cannot be removed from it without danger."[1] Almost simultaneously, Catholicism's Hans Küng reminds us that "the Bible in the metaphors and analogies of its time answers questions that are infinitely important also for people today--in metaphors and analogies, it must be noted. The language of the Bible is not a specific language of facts, but a metaphorical language of images."[2]

If we thus recognize that the testaments are story at least as much as history and scripture, and that this story employs metaphor, analogy, and other literary devices, it is essential that we now heed the insights of literary critics. In their various guises and from without their various schools these critics are able to help us understand the literary forms, imagery and language of the biblical texts. Concerned as it is with qualities of language, structure of plot, use of symbolism, and the author as poet, literary criticism of the Bible has at least as much to contribute to biblical understanding as the long established areas of form criticism and redaction criticism. From the standpoint of belief this contribution may be especially important, not least because of the apparent trend among some movements and denominations to arrange and interpret the biblical story to suit their particular needs. For example, one group may wish to emphasize God's punishing wrath rather than his liberating love: "It may be possible to clothe such stories in doctrinal propositions which keep them within the bounds of theological orthodoxy. Yet, such stories are hardly compatible with what appears to be the central or privileged story of implacable, death-defying love, which is the privileged story of the Christian heritage."[3] In such an instance literary criticism may have a role to perform in helping believers to understand the real meaning of the story and thereby avoid grotesque misinterpretations. Perhaps this is an as yet unarticulated function of biblical literary criticism?

Whatever its functions, literary criticism of the Bible is a growing force in theological circles, just as it is a field of increasing activity among secular scholars of literature. As Powell rightly indicates, "exegetes and critics . . . are producing, at an astonishing rate, study after study that applies methods derived from modern literary theory to biblical texts." To the extent that this is occurring, biblical literary criticism has become part of the fabric of scholarship and therefore warrants study in its own right.

It is especially for this reason that we approached Dr. Mark Allan Powell, Assistant Professor of New Testament at Trinity Lutheran Seminary in Ohio, to prepare a volume that would document the development and trends in biblical literary criticism. While his particular expertise lies in literary criticism of the Gospels, Dr. Powell is also widely read and thoroughly knowledgeable (how often these two attributes fail to appear together!) in all aspects of literary criticism as applied to the entire Bible. The validity of this assessment lies in the following pages, which I am pleased to commend for a number of reasons. First, the introductory essay, "The Bible and Modern Literary Criticism: A Critical Assessment," maps in a most interesting and clearly written manner the geography of this largely uncharted field; any student seeking to understand the subject will find this discussion of benefit. Second, the bibliography succeeds in covering, in an unusually logical manner, all key components of biblical literary criticism--the development of modern literary theory, methods for literary study of the Bible, literary studies of specific biblical texts, and evaluation of biblical literary studies. Third, Powell has tenaciously and objectively annotated a fully representative range of the most important works in this field of study. More than that, in his listing of literary criticism of particular books of the Bible (Part Four) he has come close to achieving comprehensive coverage; this feature will be of special value to scholars.

Putting all of these attributes together in a single volume has been no mean feat, yet Dr. Powell has done so without hesitation. The result is a careful and judicious survey that is both accessible to the student and useful to the scholar. It is commendable not only for its broad treatment of all aspects of biblical literary criticism but also for its logical arrangement and clear-headed assessment of the most important publications in the field. In short, this work establishes a high standard for future bibliographic treatment of biblical literary criticism. As such, it is a worthy companion to Arland Hultgren's 1988 contribution to Bibliographies and Indexes in Religious Studies, *New Testament Christology*.

1.   James Barr, *The Scope and Authority of the Bible* (Philadelphia: Westminster Press, 1981), p. 11.

2.   Hans Küng, *Does God Exist? An Answer for Today*. Trans. by Edward Quinn (London: William Collins Sons, 1980), p. 639.

3.   Andrew M. Greeley, *Religion: A Secular Theory* (New York: Free Press, 1982), p. 90.

The Revd Dr. G. E. Gorman FLA FRSA
Series Editor
Charles Sturt University, Riverina

PREFACE

The focus of this book is on the convergence of two fields, biblical studies and modern literary criticism. In the last quarter of a century, these two fields have come together in a manner that has caught many by surprise. The validity of using literary criticism as an approach to Holy Scripture is still debated in theological circles, and the merit of the Bible as a work of literature is still questioned in literary ones. Exegetes and critics, however, are not waiting for their respective academies to resolve these questions. They are producing, at an astonishing rate, study after study that applies methods derived from modern literary theory to biblical texts.

One purpose of this present volume, then, is simply to document this phenomenon. We have assembled here the most comprehensive list ever published of works that draw on modern literary criticism for a scholarly study of the Bible. The number of the works listed and the diversity of the authors represented are indications that biblical literary criticism must be accorded a significant place in the history of scholarship.

We also hope that this work will assist both theological and literary communities in their ongoing assessment of these interdisciplinary developments. A truly critical assessment should avoid simplistic generalizations regarding either field, but should remain cognizant of the inevitable contradictory impulses that occur when such complex and varied disciplines are brought together. Knowledge of the literature included in this bibliography will provide the best foundation for making such an assessment.

A final purpose is more practical: We hope to provide interested persons with a useful reference tool that will enable them to find particular works on fairly specific subjects. The following explanatory notes regarding the bibliography's organization, scope, and special features should help to facilitate its use in this regard.

Organization. The bibliography is organized into six major sections and the logic of this presentation is explained at length in the introductory essay. Basically, the subject matter of each section forms the logical foundation for that of the section that follows.

Part One ("Basis") lists works that have been instrumental in laying the foundations for the development of modern literary theory. These works present insights from other fields (philosophy, sociology, anthropology, linguistics) that have helped to establish the intellectual framework within which literary theorists work.

Part Two ("Theory") lists works representative of the several different schools of literary theory that are most influential today. The items included here are not by and large the work of theologians or biblical scholars but, rather, are the work of scholars whose primary interest is general or secular literature.

Part Three ("Method") lists works that represent an intentional effort to devise methods for a literary study of the Bible. Most of these works are written by biblical scholars, though they draw heavily on the insights of their secular colleagues listed in Part Two.

Part Four ("Criticism") lists studies in which methods such as those described in Part Three have actually been applied to biblical texts. This section is really the heart of the bibliography, encompassing more than half of the total listings. Studies on any particular book of the Bible are grouped together, and these groups are then listed according to the order in which books appear in the English Bible. This format should make it easy for readers to pursue research on the particular biblical writing that interests them.

Part Five ("Evaluation") lists works that offer critical evaluation of the kinds of studies found throughout Part Four. In fact, many of the items here are reviews of studies listed elsewhere in the bibliography. Others offer more generalized comments concerning the literary-critical enterprise as a whole.

Part Six ("Implications") lists a few works that point out the impact that this new approach to the Bible is having on other, related fields, such as homiletics and theology. Finally, the bibliography comes full circle by citing a few examples of how biblical literary criticism affects a theological apprehension of literature in general.

Scope. The listings in Part Four ("Criticism") are the only ones intended to be comprehensive. In the other sections, I have selected representative works that appear to be the most important and accessible, but I have tried not to allow my own prejudices to govern that selection process. For the most part, the works listed in these sections are the ones included most often in the footnotes and bibliographies of the items included in Part Four.

In Part Four itself, I have included practically everything that I could find, and any omissions here must be credited to my own lack of resourcefulness. In general, a 1990 cut-off date was enforced, though occasionally I was able to get advance copies of material published later than that. The majority of the listings are in English, but several other languages are represented as well. To increase foreign language listings still further than what I have been able to provide, German readers may wish to consult the journal *Linguistics Biblica* on a regular basis; French readers should do the same with *Sémiotique et Bible;* and readers of modern Hebrew, with *Beth Mikra.*

Finally, a number of the works listed contain bibliographies of their own that may be more expansive in a specific area than what is included here. See especially items, 0117, 0244, 0265, 0280, 0343, 0353, 0438, 0480, 0490, 0503, 0509, 0523, 0526-0527, 0530, 0551, 0561, 0565, 0574-0575, 0588.

Special Features. Two special features should help to make the bibliography useful: cross-references and indexes.

The cross-references are of two types. First the annotations themselves make extensive use of cross-references to other items in the bibliography. Works about a particular author are cross-referenced to works by that person, and so on. These references will be especially useful when a work discusses or comments on a study that is listed elsewhere.

Second, lists of cross-references are included under many of the headings and subheadings of the various sections. These references will lead the reader to works that might conceivably have been placed in that section but that, for some prevailing reason, are found elsewhere. For example, the reader who is interested in literary studies on the Gospel of Mark might be directed via the cross references under that heading to a book on the method of structural exegesis that includes a chapter on the

Gospel of Mark as a case study.

Three indexes are included. The first two are alphabetical listings of the authors and titles of all the works included here. The Author Index includes references to authors of forewords or prefaces, and to authors of individual chapters of works that are otherwise referenced by their editors. The Subject Index is also quite extensive, providing lists of the most significant references to over 1000 topics.

Corrections, additions, and inquiries concerning supplemental updates should be sent to Mark Allan Powell, c/o Trinity Lutheran Seminary, 2199 East Main Street, Columbus, OH 43209-2334.

ACKNOWLEDGMENTS

I could not have completed this work without the two assistants named on the title page. Cecile Gray, English Professor at Capital University, helped immensely with the research, writing approximately 500 of the annotations. Melissa Curtis, computer specialist and secretary to the faculty at Trinity Lutheran Seminary, did all of the work of preparing the camera-ready manuscript, including production of the indexes.

In addition, Joyce Klayman and the library staff at Trinity Lutheran Seminary were invaluable in obtaining materials for our review. Douglas Gray typed and edited many annotations and offered his spouse patient support as she became completely absorbed with the project. Kristin Gallagher, Karen Jewell-van Buskirk, and Amy Kroninger served as research assistants and proofreaders.

We believe the work has been worthwhile. We are grateful to Trinity Lutheran Seminary for providing us with the resources and the atmosphere necessary to complete the project, and to G. E. Gorman and Greenwood Press for bringing it to publication.

Finally, I wish to thank my own family--my wife, Charlotte, and my sons, David and Michael--for their love and affection. I treasure the joy that you bring me every day of my life.

THE BIBLE AND MODERN LITERARY CRITICISM: A CRITICAL ASSESSMENT

One of the most significant developments in biblical studies in recent years has been the appropriation of insights drawn from various schools of modern literary criticism. It has become commonplace to speak of the *plot* of Ruth or to identify David as a *character* in 1 Samuel. The voice that comments on the life of Jesus in the Gospel of John is now more likely to be called "the *narrator* of the Fourth Gospel" than "the Fourth Evangelist."

In some cases, such borrowing of terms may be merely cosmetic, but an increasing number of biblical scholars are employing literary-critical methods and concepts in ways that demonstrate a secure grasp of the discipline. This dexterity is all the more impressive when one remembers that most of these scholars are primarily students of religion or theology and have had to learn literary criticism as a "second language." The secular field of literary criticism, however, has been accommodating: A number of literary critics have themselves gotten in on the act of biblical interpretation.

In short, Bible scholars are turning to literary criticism, and literary critics are turning to the Bible. Such a convergence should not seem strange. The Bible, after all, *is* literature and, in some sense, has always been studied as such. No method of exegesis bypasses the essential act of reading (or hearing) the text. Until recently, however, professors of religion have not been primarily interested in the Bible's literary qualities *per se*. They have shown more interest in the Bible as a compendium of theological insight or as a record of significant history. Many colleges and universities have offered classes on "The Bible as Literature," but such a title usually implies that the Bible is to be examined as literature *instead of* as scripture. Aesthetic evaluation is emphasized as distinct from theological interpretation. The new convergence of biblical and literary studies destroys this dichotomy. The recent studies attempt to examine the Bible as literature and as scripture at the same time. Literary criticism becomes the means but theological interpretation remains the end.

Thus, the trend toward literary criticism of the Bible is in some sense revolutionary. Some observers have even described the trend as a "paradigm shift," comparable in importance to the development of the historical-critical method. In future years, they say, Bible scholars will by definition be persons trained in literary, not historical, modes of analysis. Is this an exaggeration? Perhaps. But the bibliography contained in this book shows that scholars need to take literary criticism of the Bible seriously as a major new force in theological studies.

As an introduction to the bibliography, this essay intends to provide a foundation for understanding and evaluating the developments to which the listed works attest. We will begin with a brief consideration of the *basis* for modern literary theory, of the intellectual prolegomena from which that field derives its key assumptions. Then, we will present an overview of modern literary *theory* itself, with special consideration for its various systems and approaches. Next, we will examine *methods* for biblical study that have been developed with reference to these approaches. We will also consider how these methods are applied in the *criticism* of actual texts. Finally, we will offer some *evaluation* of this new convergence of disciplines and consider its *implications* for theological and literary studies. The six parts of the essay correspond to the six principal parts of the bibliography itself. Parenthetical references are to enumerated items in the bibliography.

BASIS

Literary theory has not developed in isolation from other intellectual movements. The diverse theoretical approaches to literature that will occupy our attention shortly are all dependent on developments in other fields. The bibliography cites a few representative works from three fields that have been especially significant: philosophy, sociology/anthropology, and linguistics. A fourth--modern psychology-- has been influential in the development of reader-oriented theories and is subsumed under that category (see 0334-0427).

Philosophy. Since much literary theory seeks to discern meaning, literary theorists are often influenced by philosophical conceptions of what meaning is and how meaning can be discerned. The work of Charles Sanders Peirce (0015) has been significant in some circles. A nineteenth-century American Pragmatist, Peirce approached philosophy as a science and attempted to develop set rules of logic whereby meaning could be determined. More influential over all, however, has been the phenomenological strain of thought initiated by Edmund Husserl (0008) and refined by Martin Heidegger (0007). Heidegger, in particular, focused on the ontological and existential concerns that determine modern understandings of literature and its relationship to life. The implications of Heidegger's ideas for criticism have been articulated most notably by his student, Hans-Georg Gadamer (0003). Another influential philosopher for recent literary studies has been Paul Ricoeur (0016-0021), a philosopher of hermeneutics, who has devoted himself intentionally to studying processes of interpretation. Ricoeur sometimes engages in literary criticism himself and is explicitly interested in hermeneutical questions involving the nature of scripture or "sacred texts" (0558, 1687, 1717).

Sociology and Anthropology. To the extent that literary theory is concerned with the relation of texts to contexts, modern ideas about the nature of human society become significant. Claude Lévi-Strauss's structuralist studies in anthropology (0036-0038) became the basis for at least one branch of structuralist literary criticism. René Girard's theories about the origin and inevitability of violence in human society (0031-0034) have also been significant in studies of conflict as a basic literary motif. Likewise, Frederic Jameson's views on the essentially political character of language (0035) are often cited by various ideological schools of modern literary theory (Marxist, feminist, and so on).

Linguistics. Developments in twentieth-century language analysis have proved even more significant for modern literary theory than have the less direct connections to philosophy, sociology, and anthropology. Literature is intrinsically related to language, and recent studies into the nature and function of language form the background for almost all contemporary approaches to literature. The field of modern linguistics owes its current stature largely to the work of Ferdinand de Saussure (0048, 0067), who offered a now classic distinction between *langue* (the language system that people use to generate discourse) and *parole* (the actual utterance of language produced through speaking and writing). By demonstrating the possibility of studying language at the level of *langue*, Saussure transformed linguistics into a systematic field of research. In one way or another, Roman Jakobson (0055-0058, 0072, 0263), Noam Chomsky (0044-0045, 0059), John Austin (0042), and John Searle (0068-0069) have built upon and/or reacted against Saussure's basic insights. Their work--and that of others like them--has produced different models for describing how language works. These models, in turn, have led to the development of different theories for understanding literature.

Whatever differences may exist among the various schools of modern literary criticism, almost all view literature as an act of communication. Literature, like language, can be said *to mean something*, that is, to communicate. This apparent truism should not be taken for granted. As we shall see, literary theorists differ widely in their opinions of *what* literature means and *how* it achieves that meaning. Some theorists are even willing to say that literature can mean *any*thing or even *every*thing. But only the most radical of the modern theorists would say that it means *no*thing.

The relationship between literary analysis and philosophy of language is natural but not exact. As one scholar of both language and literature, Walter Ong (0061-0065, 1622), continually points out, significant differences exist between the dynamics of oral communication and written communication. These dynamics come especially to the fore in the analysis of literature that was produced in a predominantly oral culture. Since all of the biblical writings fit into the latter category, Ong's insights have proved especially relevant for scholars trying to develop an appropriate literary approach to the Bible.

THEORY

General. A newcomer to the field of literary theory is greeted with a vast array of systems, many of which bear strange-sounding names like Formalism, Imagism, Aestheticism, Stylistics, Decadence, and Deconstruction. A system of categorization devised by M. H. Abrams helps to bring some order to this chaos (0076). According to Abrams, all the different schools of literary theory may be understood as representative of four basic types of literary criticism:

(1)   *Mimetic* types of criticism view a literary work as reflective of the world and evaluate it in terms of the truth or accuracy of its representation.

(2)   *Expressive* types of criticism are author-centered and evaluate a work in terms of the sincerity and adequacy with which it expresses the views and temperament of its writer.

(3)   *Objective* types of criticism are text-centered, viewing a literary work as a world-in-itself. Evaluation of a work depends upon analysis of intrinsic criteria, such as the interrelationship of component elements.

(4)   *Pragmatic* types of criticism are reader-centered and evaluate a literary work in terms of the effects that it has on its readers.

Literary theorists also sometimes distinguish between two functions that a work of literature may serve. Abrams's first two types of literary criticism (mimetic and expressive) are interested in the *referential function*. The literary work serves as a means to an end--it is valued primarily for its ability to point beyond itself, to tell us something about either the world in which it was produced (mimetic) or about the person who produced it (expressive). Abrams's last two types of criticism (objective and pragmatic) are interested in the *poetic function*. The literary work serves as an end in itself--it is valued primarily for its own sake (objective) or for the effects it achieves on those who receive it (pragmatic).

Although in its broadest sense literary theory includes approaches to literature representative of all four of Abrams's types of criticism, the field of *modern* literary theory emphasizes the latter two types: objective and pragmatic. In other words, modern literary critics seem to be more interested in the poetic function of literature than in its referential function.

The model that undergirds these categories and distinctions is linguistic theory. As indicated above, one feature that most varieties of modern literary theory seem to have in common is their conception of literature as an act of communication. Roman Jakobson has suggested that every act of communication encompasses at least three elements, a sender, a message, and a receiver.

Sender --> Message --> Receiver

In literature, the sender may be identified with the author, the message with the text, and the receiver with the reader:

Author --> Text --> Reader

The relative significance of these components in the process of interpretation is debated by various schools of literary criticism. What Abrams calls expressive types of literary criticism emphasize the role of the author, whereas objective types of criticism emphasize the text, and pragmatic types, the reader. Hermeneutically, the expressive types of criticism assume a theory of communication in which speakers or writers give meaning to language. The objective types of criticism assume a theory of communication in which language possesses meaning in and of itself. Pragmatic types of criticism assume a theory of communication in which those who hear, read, or otherwise receive a message are the ones who determine what that message means.

The only type of criticism not represented in the communication model described here is mimetic criticism, which views a literary work as a reflection of the real world and evaluates it in terms of the accuracy of its representation. This type of criticism, related to what Jakobson calls "context," is the least practiced in contemporary literary studies. The conception of literature as an act of communication has moved literary theorists away from a purely mimetic assessment of texts.

In fact, the recent history of literary criticism can be understood in some sense as a shift from the left to the right side of Jakobson's paradigm. At the beginning of the twentieth century, literary criticism was dominated by expressive modes of criticism that emphasized the role of the author in the creation of meaning. Around the middle of the twentieth century, a revolution in thought brought about a new dominance of objective types of criticism that located meaning in the text itself. By the end of the twentieth century, however, yet another revolution had brought pragmatic, reader-oriented approaches to the fore.

In compiling this bibliography, we have decided that the term "modern literary theory" should be defined broadly enough to include the text-centered approaches that became influential around the middle of this century, even though they are no longer attracting the most attention in secular circles. We have not included, however, the mimetic or author-centered approaches that most literature scholars now consider to be outdated and no longer worthy of the designation "modern." In short, we pick up the development of literary theory at the moment of its first revolutionary shift: from expressive criticism to objective criticism and, hence, from interest in referential functions to poetic ones.

Text-Centered Approaches. The notion that texts contain meaning seems obvious at first. Most people find it natural to talk about "what a story means." But such an expression can be a short-hand way of describing how an author intends for a story to be understood. Do stories really have meaning in and of themselves? Can a story mean something that its author did not intend for it to mean?

Early in this century, literary critics usually spoke of meaning with reference to the intentions of authors. The best way to know what a story meant was to ask the author. In practice, of course, this was not always possible. Some authors are not available for interview, being dead or forgotten or simply uncooperative. Still, to the extent that an author's intentions could be determined, these were deemed normative for interpretation. Accordingly, a great deal of attention was devoted to learning as much about authors as possible. Any interpretation, for example, of a novel by Charles Dickens would be expected to take into account the circumstances of its writing: the life and personality of the author at this stage in his career, and his views concerning the condition of English society at the time. Critics might disagree in their construals of an author's intentions, but they were united in the belief that stories meant what their authors intended them to mean.

In the 1940s, this assumption was challenged by an approach that came to be called the New Criticism. New Criticism began by rejecting the proposition that texts must be interpreted with reference to "background information." To say that a certain character in a Dickens novel is based on a landlady that Dickens himself once knew as a child does not help to interpret the story. Rather, such information is a foreign imposition--a distraction that prevents the story's being understood on its own terms. This resistance to background information, however, countered only the excesses of author-oriented criticism, without going against the basic understanding that undergirded that approach. One could argue that identifying characters in Dickens' novels with real people from Dickens' own life is intrusive precisely because Dickens did not intend for his novels to be read in this manner.

But eventually New Criticism went further. Scholars such as Cleanth Brooks (0125, 0144-0146) and W. K. Wimsatt (0125, 0144, 0222) held that meaning resides within the free-standing, public work of literature itself, and can be determined through analysis of the literary features of the work alone. Meaning is determined by form and structure, not by authorial intent. A competent author may, of course, utilize form and structure to make the finished work mean what he or she intends. But from the critic's point of view, authorial intent is irrelevant. Examination of the text determines what the text actually does mean, regardless of whether this coincides with authorial intent. Some texts, as it turns out, mean less than their authors hoped; others mean more. A "classic" is by definition a work of literature that continues to be meaningful in places and times unknown to the author--hence every classic means more than its author could ever have envisioned.

The vigor with which New Criticism attacked what it regarded as "the intentional fallacy" in interpretation has faded and most literary critics now consider total disregard for authorial intent to be extreme. Still, New Criticism left its mark: today, most literary critics would accept as axiomatic the idea that the meaning of literature can transcend the intentions of historical authors. Even E. D. Hirsch (0096-0097), the most outspoken proponent of authorial intent, admits that authors sometimes mean more than they are aware of meaning.

The most influential heir of New Criticism in the modern day is Wayne Booth (0139). Booth, who sometimes tries to disassociate himself with the movement, has in fact moderated the approach of New Criticism in a way that continues to appeal to a wide variety of scholars. He speaks of narratives as embodying an *implied author,* who may be reconstructed by the reader from the narrative itself. Stories inevitably convey impressions about their authors; the totality of these impressions define what may be called the story's implied author. For example, anyone who reads John Bunyan's *Pilgrim's Progress* will no doubt conclude that the author is a Christian. This conclusion can be reached, furthermore, without reference to any background information about the real John Bunyan. According to Booth's approach to interpretation, literary works should be understood from the perspectives of their implied authors. This approach is text-centered because an implied author's viewpoint can be determined without considering anything extrinsic to the text itself. Literary critics can speak of the intentions of the implied author without violating the principle that stories should be interpreted on their own terms. When hermeneutical preference is given to a work's implied author over its real, historical author, the narrative is allowed to speak for itself.

This concept of implied authors has been enormously influential in the development of modern literary theory. For example, if an author produces a work that espouses values at variance with his or her actual point of view, most scholars would now agree that the perspective of the implied author determines what the story means. A critic may recognize by way of an interesting historical footnote that the story's real author did not actually think this way but, nevertheless, the story means what the story means.

The distinction between real authors and implied authors also becomes significant when one reads more than one work by the same person. Although Robert Louis Stephenson wrote both *Treasure Island* and *Dr. Jekyll and Mr. Hyde*, the implied authors of these two books are not identical. Most critics would agree that each work should be interpreted on its own terms.

Finally, the notion of an implied author is significant for interpreting works that have multiple authors or works that are anonymous. Even a work that has no real author--such as a tale that developed over a period of time by being passed down from generation to generation--can be studied according to the perspective of its implied author. Regardless of the process through which a narrative comes into being, it will always evince particular values, beliefs, and perceptions that can be described as representative of its implied author.

At approximately the same time that New Criticism was bringing a new text-centered consciousness to literary criticism in America, analogous movements were generating similar emphases in other parts of the world. One that would prove especially significant for literary studies was Russian Formalism, best exemplified in the work of Vladimir Propp (0202). Propp studied over one hundred Russian folktales and discovered that, although the specific characters and the actions they perform vary, the functions of the characters and the actions remain essentially the same from one story to the next. In all, Propp identified thirty-one constant functions that recur almost invariably throughout the tales. Most impressive, perhaps, was his observation that even the sequence in which the functions occur remains essentially the same from one story to another. Even when certain functions are absent in a story, the sequence of those that are present remains undisturbed. Thus, Propp's analysis indicated that the form of a story may determine its meaning. Stories develop in recognizable ways and so can be interpreted through analysis of the structural relations of the various narrative parts.

New Criticism, Russian Formalism, and other text-centered approaches to literature ultimately found expression in the creation of a new discipline, narratology. Narratologists are essentially observers who attempt to describe how different types of narratives work, that is, how they obtain their meaning. Most narratologies, such as those developed by Mieke Bal (0133) and Gerald Prince (0198), are concerned primarily with fiction. Seymour Chatman's influential study deals with fiction and film

(0150). Adele Berlin (0488), Robert Funk (0513), and Meir Sternberg (0570) have worked specifically with biblical narrative.

Chatman's work may be taken as an example. Narrative, he says, is comprised of two elements: story and discourse. Story represents the content component of narrative (what it is about), and discourse the rhetoric component (how it is told). A story, Chatman continues, is composed of such elements as events, characters, and settings. The interaction of these elements constitutes what we might call a plot: somebody does something to someone at a certain time in a certain place. But stories that concern the same basic events, characters, and settings may be told in ways that produce radically different narratives. For this reason, the element of discourse is of great interest to the literary critic: how is the story told? Discourse entails many factors: the sequence in which events are related, the quantity and quality of explanation provided by the narrator, the use of artistic devices such as irony, repetition, or symbolism, and so on. Attention to factors such as these allows the critic to determine the meaning of the story in light of the particular way in which it is told.

Structuralism. Developed primarily in France during the 1950s and 1960s, structuralism is also a text-centered approach to interpretation. Its unique philosophical basis, however, sets it apart from the approaches described above. This is true even though, historically, structuralism has roots in Russian Formalism.

Like the formalists, structuralists believe that texts are structured in recognizable ways determinative of meaning. But structuralists do not limit their analysis to the study of simple linear arrangements of functions, such as those discovered by Propp. They search not only for the syntagmatic or diachronic (sequential) relationships, but also for paradigmatic or synchronic ones--that is, for associations that exist at various levels of meaning within the text. Three such levels that are often cited are the syntactical level (the words of the literary work itself), the logical level (connections within the work that must be made in order for it to make sense), and the mythical level (assumptions about life or about the world in general that hold true for this work). Thus, structuralists conceive of texts as conglomerates of meaning with layers of underlying significance superimposed upon each other. The analogy of a musical score is sometimes used: in order to be fully appreciated, such a score must be read not only from left to right but also up and down, for individual notes do not just contribute to the melody but also combine with other notes to form harmonic units. In the same way, structuralists are interested in the interrelationships that may be discovered when all of the layers of a text are considered at once. They are generally most interested, however, in the deeper layers, for these may reveal levels of meaning that transcend the conscious intentions of the author. In fact, structuralists tend to interpret the surface level of the text in light of the logical and mythical relations that they discern at deeper levels.

A typical example of paradigmatic associations to be discovered within a text would be what Claude Lévi-Strauss (0036-0038) calls "binary oppositions." Schematic pairs, such as "light and darkness," "good and evil," or "rich and poor" may function at any level of the narrative to provide intrinsic structure. Such schematic pairs also reveal something about the meaning of the work--at the surface level of the text if that is where the pairs are found, or at a deeper level if that is where they are to be discovered. Lévi-Strauss also emphasizes a tendency toward mediation of such oppositions. Mediating elements serve as boundaries between opposed ones, incorporating elements of both. In literature, an island may mediate between land and sea, or the activity of hunting game may mediate between the activities of killing and sustaining life.

A. J. Greimas (0253), focusing on the logical level of signification, expands Lévi-Strauss' notion of binary oppositions to encompass a four-term model. Each term in an opposition, Greimas surmises, presupposes its negative--which is not quite identical to the opposed term. Thus, an apparent opposition of rich and poor actually provides a four-way grid for relationships between rich, not-rich, poor, and not-poor.

Like other modern approaches to literature, structuralism depends heavily upon linguistic theory. We may recall, for instance, Ferdinand de Saussure's distinction between *langue* and *parole*. The former is the system of language, the set of rules and norms that govern speaking or writing; the latter refers to the actual written or spoken words and sentences themselves. The writing on a page or the acoustical sounds of a voice may be described as *signifiers*, but the concept evoked by those markings or sounds are *signifieds*. Structuralism picks up on this aspect of linguistic theory by regarding the surface level of texts as signifiers of deeper meaning. Tzvetan Todorov (0302) attempts to construct a structuralist grammar of literature. The assumption is that there is a fixed system of rules that determine how literature works, and that this system can be apprehended independently of actual literary expressions in particular works. Just as most speakers of a language do not have explicit knowledge of all the rules that govern their speech, so most writers do not consciously follow all of the laws of literature. Nevertheless, as a form of communication, literature does follow certain conventions that cause it to mean one thing or another. By analyzing a text's communicative strategy, structuralists hope to become "fully competent readers" who may understand the work in a way that even its author did not.

Structuralism, then, is a text-centered approach to literature. In fact, there is quite a bit of overlap between items listed in the bibliography under the sub-heading "Text-Centered Approaches" and those listed under "Structuralism," with the narratologies in the former group showing perhaps the most structuralist influence. At least one structuralist, however, Roland Barthes (0224-0231), crosses the line into what we will later describe as "Reader-Oriented Approaches." In his earliest work, Barthes was concerned primarily to demonstrate the constraints that texts place upon interpretation. Meaning is encoded within the texts themselves and the task of readers or critics is to decode these texts to discover their meaning. But ultimately Barthes decided that all readers cannot be expected to decode texts in the same way. The codes may generate a plurality of meaning and the text may mean different things to different readers.

Rhetorical Criticism. Within literary circles, rhetorical criticism is considered to be a pragmatic approach to literature that seeks to understand the means through which literary works achieve particular effects on their readers. The discipline is distinct, however, from the other reader-oriented approaches to be discussed below. For one thing, rhetorical criticism is not new--it is at least as old as Aristotle, who was perhaps its greatest practitioner.

Aristotle identified three species of rhetoric: (1) judicial rhetoric, which seeks to persuade the audience to make some judgment about events in the past--its typical features are defense and accusation; (2) epideictic rhetoric, which seeks to persuade the audience to hold or reaffirm some point of view in the present--its typical features are praise and blame; (3) deliberative rhetoric, which seeks to persuade the audience to take some action in the future--its typical feature is advice. In order to determine how an audience might be persuaded in one or more of these ways, rhetorical critics examine the types of arguments that are used, the manner in which the material is arranged, and the style in which it is presented. They are interested in both the point that a work wishes to make, and in the basis on which that point is established. Sometimes external evidence or documentation is cited or the trustworthy character of the writer is invoked. At other times, an appeal is made to the readers' emotions or sense of logic.

From what has just been said, it may appear that rhetorical criticism is actually more interested in discerning the intentions of authors than the perceptions of readers (and some would say that this is the case). But rhetorical critics insist that the effects of a work must be understood with reference to its intended audience. One must identify *the rhetorical situation* that is being addressed. This emphasis moves rhetorical criticism away from solitary concentration on the text to a concentration on the sort of background information that the New Critics despised. This time, however, the information sought concerns the readers more than the author. As Lloyd Bitzer puts it, "a peculiar discourse comes into existence because of some specific condition or situation which invites utterance" (0310, pp. 5-6). Since the situation is viewed as controlling the response, critics must examine the persons, events, objects, and relations that have called for that response. This view of literature as response is what makes rhetorical criticism a reader-oriented approach--the text is understood from the perspective of those to whom it is addressed.

One might also get the impression from this description that rhetorical criticism is a method for examination of *persuasive* literature--speeches, essays, sermons, and the like. But some rhetorical critics, such as Kenneth Burke (0314-0315), claim that all literature seeks to motivate, that is, to achieve some sort of effect on its intended audience.

Of course, rhetoric itself interests all schools of literary criticism. The New Critics especially enjoyed identifying rhetorical devices, and structuralists regard the rhetoric of a narrative's discourse as one level on which the text must be understood. But rhetorical critics go beyond these understandings of rhetoric as a feature of style (or, as they would say, as mere ornamentation). Chaim Perelman and L. Olbrechts-Tyteca propose in their influential book (0330) that rhetoric is always argumentation. The meaning of a work of literature, therefore, should be understood primarily in terms of the persuasive effect that its rhetorical strategies are expected to have on its intended audience.

Reader-Oriented Approaches. Rhetorical criticism differs from other reader-oriented approaches in that it presumes to interpret literature from the perspective of a historical intended audience. But literature is also read by people for whom it was never intended in circumstances that its author never envisioned. A number of reader-oriented approaches have attempted to discover the process through which readers make sense of texts, regardless of whether those texts were written with them in mind. Reader-oriented critics study the dynamics of the reading process in order to determine the ways that readers perceive literature and the bases on which they produce or create meanings for any given work.

One of the most obvious ways to proceed with such a study would be simply to interview readers and record their responses to various works. Such a procedure is indeed practiced (0377). But most reader-oriented critics would not be content merely to catalogue the reactions of actual flesh-and-blood readers. They search, rather, for some interpretive principle that will allow normative or at least probable readings to be delineated.

Stanley Fish has developed a model called "affective stylistics" (0362), which attempts to describe a reader's encounter with a text in its sequential order (i.e., reading it from beginning to end). At any given point in the reading process, the reader will have formed conclusions about what has been read so far and will have anticipations regarding what is to come. As the reading continues, some of these anticipations will be fulfilled, while others will not be. The unfulfilled anticipations represent mistaken expectations that cause the reader to revise previously held ideas. Thus, through interaction with the text, the reader is encouraged continually to check his or her responses and to revise them according to ongoing developments within the text.

Fish's model describes one predictable manner in which readers might make sense of a text, but it cannot describe the manner in which all readers will receive the text. Some readers may be unequipped to discern all the text's signals; others may be more tolerant of inconsistencies than Fish imagines; still others may "cheat"--sneak a look at the end or ask a friend how the story turns out. At the very least, Fish's model will work only for what he calls a "first-time reader." It cannot describe responses to literature (such as the Bible) that is often read repeatedly.

Another model that describes the interaction of readers with texts is the "phenomenological criticism" of Wolfgang Iser (0389-0390). Iser also views the experience of reading as an evolving process of anticipation, frustration, retrospection, and reconstruction. But whereas Fish focuses on sequential, line by line reading, Iser is more interested in total response to the work as a whole. His governing principle for determining such response is the human desire for consistency. Readers, Iser thinks, will find inherent constraints in most literature against interpretations that cannot be maintained for the work as a whole, as well as incentives for interpretations that can be. Iser realizes, of course, that real readers may not always recognize or respect these incentives and constraints, so he speaks of a hermeneutically defined "implied reader." The implied reader is to be thought of as one who actualizes the potential for meaning that is found within texts. Although the actual responses of real readers will always be unpredictable, Iser holds that one can interpret literature in terms of its effect on an implied reader who, for instance, can be assumed to desire consistency. Such an interpretation, however, will be only partial. Texts also contain what Iser calls "gaps"--indeterminate elements that readers must fill in subjectively.

Still other reader-oriented approaches have attempted to describe the reading process in terms of psychoanalytical theory. Norman Holland (0381) has devised a system he calls "transactive criticism," which seeks to understand interpretation as the product of a reader's typical defenses, expectations, and wish-fulfilling fantasies. He stresses the effect of personality on perception: a reader makes sense out of a text by transforming its content in accord with his or her own identity. Such a theory holds that texts, in fact, have no universal or correct meaning.

Embracing this relativism, some literary critics have decided to renounce all attempts at neutrality and simply describe their particular perspectives. Schools of interpretation have formed around various ideologies (Marxist, feminist, and so on) in which the practitioners attempt to read all texts from their preferred stance, including texts that were not intended by their authors to be read in such a fashion.

Ultimately, Stanley Fish observes, reading strategies lead people to form "interpretive communities" (0361). For reader-oriented critics, who have rejected such standards as authorial intent and structural analysis as determinative for meaning, no interpretation can ever be established as the single correct or "right" one. Still, Fish says, agreement on interpretation can occur among those who share the same basic reading strategy. Accordingly, Fish dubs his own model for "affective stylistics" to be but one such strategy that a community might use.

All of the reader-oriented approaches discussed here share in the belief that readers determine what a text means. This proposition moves away from the idea that texts somehow contain meaning within themselves. The latter concept was itself a significant move away from the idea that authors determine the meaning of the texts that they write. The adoption of reader-oriented approaches, then, represents the second major revolution in literary theory in fifty years.

Poststructuralism/Deconstruction. The movement known as poststructuralism or deconstruction embraces the same kind of subjectivity and extreme relativism found in the more radical forms of reader-oriented criticism, but for different reasons. The reader-oriented critics admit that texts mean different things to different people, but they affirm the role of readers in determining these different interpretations. Deconstruction denies the possibility of determining meaning by any of the means discussed so far--perceptions of readers are no more determinative for meaning than are the intentions of authors or the dynamics of texts.

This approach is favored by scholars who doubt that any variety of literary analysis can ever reveal a work's true meaning. Under the leadership of Jacques Derrida (0439-0446), they have discovered that texts ultimately deconstruct themselves into endless labyrinths of possible meaning. Seizing on Saussure's notion of signifiers and signifieds, Derrida notes the central problem of language and literature: every signified is also itself a signifier. Ultimate meaning is always already deferred.

Derrida further notes that, in accord with Saussure's linguistic theory, the meaning of any term is always determined in reference to other terms. It is only possible to know the meaning of "car" by knowing the difference between "car" and "truck" or between "car" and "cat." Meaning is distinguished by *difference*. For Derrida, then, literary texts can never be considered on their own terms. Texts must necessarily be considered with reference to . . . to what? To *everything*. The starting point for meaning is not a given, but a cultural construct that is itself transitory. Hence the meaning of any given work of literature is always changing.

How, then, do deconstructionists propose to do interpretations? Derrida himself regards deconstructive interpretation as something that must be done "in exile," by critics who know that criticism is, in some sense, impossible. But recognition of the indeterminacy of meaning does not make deconstructionists cynical. Rather, it opens up the possibility of what Derrida calls "a joyful affirmation of play." Deconstructionists invite readers and critics to approach texts creatively and to appreciate fully the capacity of texts to generate an unlimited plurality of meaningful effects.

Paul de Man (0438), on the other hand, uses deconstruction primarily to point out fallacies in existing interpretations. Tensions within texts inevitably develop to an extent that the text's logic is confounded by its own implications. Deconstruction exposes an endemic discrepancy between reason and rhetoric. All that remains when de Man is through deconstructing is the "performative aspect" of the text, which he regards as immune to deconstruction. The function of the enterprise, then, is ultimately to replace interpretation of texts with performance of them.

Another deconstructionist, Michel Foucault (0461, 1598), thinks the point of deconstruction is to demonstrate that discourse is necessarily governed by context, and therefore by rules that are subject to historical transformation. Deconstruction forces critics and readers to recognize that "speaking the truth" means placing oneself within the systems that determine truth at the particular time.

METHOD

For over a century now, the dominant mode of biblical study has been the historical-critical method. Actually a conglomerate of approaches, this method seeks to reconstruct the life and thought of biblical times. The method is essentially the same as that which is used by historians in other fields when they encounter texts that bear witness to the period they wish to study. Source criticism, for example, attempts to delineate the sources that the biblical writers used in the composition of their manuscripts (most scholars think the Pentateuch is a compilation of at least four previous documents). Form criticism concentrates on defining the *Sitz im Leben* (setting in life) that individual units of tradition might have had before they came to be incorporated into the books where they are now found (some material might have been used pedagogically, some for worship, and so on). Redaction criticism seeks to discern the theologies of the individual writers or compilers themselves by observing the manner in which they edited the sources and arranged the individual units of tradition.

The major limitations of all these approaches are at least twofold: (1) They all exemplify what Abrams would call mimetic or expressive modes of criticism and therefore attempt to elucidate biblical literature in terms of its referential function. The poetic function of this literature has been largely ignored by historical critics. (2) They often fail to take seriously the nature of biblical materials in their current form. Hans Frei (1573), for example, has demonstrated the failure of historical criticism to read biblical narratives *as narratives*. The four New Testament Gospels are stories about Jesus, not compilations of miscellaneous data concerning him. Rather than interpreting these Gospels as stories to be read from beginning to end, many historical critics dissect the accounts into separate passages that can be evaluated individually.

Limitations such as these have often been noted by historical critics themselves. In the 1960s, recognition of such limitations led to a strong desire to find alternative approaches. The prevailing sense was not that historical criticism had failed, or that its goals were invalid, but that something else should also be done. The original goal of historical criticism had been to study the Bible in an academically responsible way, the way other books are studied. But by the 1960s, as we have seen, other books were no longer being studied in exclusively mimetic or expressive ways. Text-oriented and even reader-oriented theories were well established in studies of secular literature.

The possibilities of modern literary study of the Bible were demonstrated here and there by various literary critics who ventured into the Bible scholars' domain. One of the first to do this was Eric Auerbach (0128), who challenged traditional assumptions associated with mimetic approaches to the Bible. Auerbach demonstrated that "narrative depictions of reality" can be studied according to the canons of literary criticism regardless of whether those depictions are considered to be historically accurate. The representation of reality in narrative form, Auerbach proposed, is a basic element of literature that transcends distinctions between aesthetic and historical purposes. Eventually, biblical scholars would come to understand this to mean that Bible stories can be studied the same way that fictional stories are studied--even if the scholar does not regard the stories as fictional. Questions of historicity can be "bracketed out" when the texts are studied for their poetic value.

In the 1970s, the need for modern literary study felt in biblical circles and the possibilities for such an approach recognized in secular ones finally came together. Bible scholars, sometimes with the assistance of colleagues in the English department, began to develop methods based on modern literary theory but designed specifically for biblical exegesis. Rhetorical criticism, structural exegesis, and narrative criticism received the most attention during this decade.

Acceptance of rhetorical criticism was natural for Bible scholars because of its close dependence on knowledge of historical situations. As such, rhetorical criticism was a literary method that many historical critics found easy to adopt. The method received official sanction in the 1968 Presidential Address of James Muilenburg at the annual meeting of the Society of Biblical Literature (0541). It came to be applied most intentionally to prophetic oracles and to New Testament epistles. Biblical scholars, however, have shaped rhetorical criticism to suit their own interests. In Old Testament studies, the method is often viewed as an extension of form criticism and is used to highlight particular techniques of composition. In New Testament studies, the method has served as an extension of redaction criticism and is used to elucidate the particular strategies of selected biblical authors. In either case, the focus that rhetorical criticism has in secular circles on the effects of literature upon its intended audience is often ignored.

Structuralism also flourished in the 1970s, being taken over from the secular field with little adaptation and applied directly to biblical (especially Old Testament) texts. The approach was not greeted enthusiastically by many outside the academy, however, for it was thought too difficult and esoteric to be of any practical use, for instance, to parish pastors. This would change in the next decade, when structuralist studies shifted their focus more prominently to the New Testament and also took on more simplified and readable forms for presentation.

Narrative criticism, meanwhile, was essentially a new discipline, tailored specifically for biblical studies out of new critical and formalist models with smatterings of structuralist, rhetorical and reader-response concepts mixed in as well. The eclectic method was only beginning to take shape in the 1970s but it would surface in the 1980s as the most popular literary approach to certain biblical writings, including Old Testament sagas and New Testament Gospels.

Also in the 1980s, reader-oriented models for biblical exegesis made themselves known and, by the end of that decade, deconstruction was "looming up menacingly behind," as one New Testament scholar puts it (1615, p. xxi). The other disciplines just mentioned, however, continued to be practiced as well. By 1990, biblical scholarship had experienced in just twenty years the gamut of new developments that occupied secular literary theory for fifty. If Bible scholars had been behind, they were now up to date, with a greatly expanded repertoire of methodological approaches to texts.

CRITICISM

The section of the bibliography labeled "Criticism" is the most comprehensive portion of this work. Here we list published examples of the application of modern literary methods to actual biblical texts. The listings are organized according to the order in which these texts occur in the English Bible. A quick survey of the listings reveals a diversity of concerns:

(1) A number of the studies are interested in demonstrating the literary coherence of relatively large segments of biblical material. This trend is a response to the atomizing tendency that dominated biblical studies for most of the twentieth century, that is, the tendency to examine material in terms of discernible "units of tradition." Scholars influenced by modern literary criticism prefer to look at texts in their "finished form" rather than in light of their compositional histories. They acknowledge that many of the biblical writings are probably collections of disparate materials, but remain interested in discerning the connections that allow those materials to be read as parts of coherent wholes.

(2) Many studies focus on particular literary aspects or characteristics of biblical writings. For example, a great deal of research has been devoted to identification of the particular characteristics of Hebrew poetry--parallelism, repetition, meter, and so on. Or, again, many biblical scholars have investigated the use of various structural or rhetorical devices evident in biblical literature--the studies on chiasm alone are legion. Such studies are conducted by scholars with varying degrees of commitment to literary criticism as a total enterprise. Even scholars who remain primarily oriented toward historical-critical exegesis benefit from the observations that literary studies offer concerning specific features of texts.

(3) Other studies approach biblical texts in light of concepts basic to the study of literature from any perspective. Literary critics of all theoretical persuasions discuss such matters as plot, characterization, irony, symbolism, and so on--this is the stuff of undergraduate courses in literature analysis. Biblical scholars, however, sometimes discover that even these basic matters have gone unattended with regard to biblical literature. Accordingly, such studies represent an appropriate and necessary place for literary study of the Bible to begin.

(4) Still other studies attempt to interpret biblical writings from a particular theoretical perspective. Works are listed that exemplify every one of the modern approaches to literature discussed in the "Theory" section of this book (see the cross-references given under each of the subheadings in that section). Although the methods are used more purely at some times than at others, the intentional adoption of text-oriented, structuralist, rhetorical, reader-oriented, and deconstructionist modes of interpretation for biblical materials is evidence that the Bible is today being accorded attention that represents the full range of literary scholarship.

EVALUATION

The new literary approaches to the Bible have not been introduced without controversy. The section of the bibliography called "Evaluation" lists works that critique the new approaches and the manner in which they are used in biblical studies. Some of these works review particular efforts, others evaluate the appropriateness of one or another system, and still others critique the literary enterprise as a whole.

Among the objections that are most often raised to literary-critical study of the Bible are the following:

(1) *Literary criticism treats texts as coherent even when they are actually composed of disparate elements.* As we have seen, the observation that lies behind this objection is often correct. Methods that attend to the poetic function of literature show little interest in the compositional history of the literature under discussion. Historically inclined editors and scholars may be interested in asking where Chaucer found the various stories incorporated in his *Canterbury Tales*, but this information would be of little significance in determining, for instance, the effect of the current work on contemporary readers. In the same way, literary critics sometimes seem to disregard the documentary hypotheses and source theories that have been espoused with regard to biblical materials, but this does not mean that they consider such information to be wrong or valueless. They may simply find the information to be less helpful for an examination of the Bible's poetic function than it would be for studies of its referential function.

(2) *Literary criticism of the Bible seeks to impose on ancient literature concepts derived from the study of modern literature.* Some scholars have noted that the very idea of analyzing the Bible from the perspective of modern literary criticism is anachronistic, because the Bible is *not* modern literature. Literary critics, they claim, ignore genre distinctions and ascribe to the biblical writers a sophistication and artistry unknown in the ancient world. The legitimacy of this objection must be tested against the actual work that has been produced. Most biblical literary critics, however, would at least admit that differences exist between ancient and modern literature and would intend to conduct their studies in ways that acknowledge those distinctions. Modern literary theory, they would claim, frequently studies ancient works, such as the writings of Homer or Euripides. In any case, many of the modern literary approaches seek to define universal reading strategies that bring out timeless qualities of literature.

(3) *Literary criticism seeks to interpret the Bible through methods devised for the study of fiction.* It is often noted that the majority of the theoretical works that articulate various schools of literary criticism are primarily concerned with analysis of novels, poetry, or other works that do not intend for their depictions of reality to be accepted as factual. Accordingly, some would say that using these methods to study biblical literature is inappropriate because the biblical writers *did* intend for their writings to be taken as accurate descriptions of what actually happened. Most literary theorists today would claim, however, that the reading strategies they espouse transcend generic distinctions between "history" and "fiction." If secular literary

criticism tends to focus on works of fiction, this merely reflects the particular interests of the practitioners of that field. Actually, there is no reason why narratologists could not study biographies, or reader-response critics could not study political speeches. Sometimes, in fact, they do. The real issue, literary critics would say, is not whether it is *possible* to study the poetic function of most non-fiction in the same way that one studies the poetic function of fiction, but whether it is *desirable* to do so. The majority of literary critics have simply not found the poetic function of non-fictional works (including the Bible) to be sufficiently interesting to merit their attention. Some secular scholars, however, are now rethinking this prejudice with regard to biblical literature--most would now agree that the Bible offers more than they had previously imagined.

(4) *Modern literary criticism ignores the referential function of biblical texts and so undermines the historical witness of scripture.* This objection restates a concern implicit in some of the protests noted above and, perhaps, gets at the heart of the issue. The shift of interest among biblical scholars from the referential function of texts to their poetic function is thought to represent a theological shift away from affirmations of the historical truth of scripture. Theologians who wish to "bracket out" questions regarding the historicity of biblical accounts may be suspected of doubting the authenticity of those accounts. At the very least, literary critics may be accused of seeking to supplement the traditional paradigm of God-revealed-through-*history* with a new paradigm that presents God as revealed through *story*. Orthodox Judaeo-Christian teaching, some say, has always viewed the Bible as a testimony to God's action in history. The actions themselves were pre-eminently significant; the Bible serves only to mediate the significance of those events to us today. The adoption of literary-critical approaches to scripture may be regarded as symptomatic of a new understanding that downplays the significance of the events themselves in favor of unmediated access to revelation found in the encounter of readers with texts here and now. It is difficult to gauge the legitimacy of this objection, since proponents of biblical literary criticism vary widely in their theological perspectives. Some have rejected traditional theology with its historical concerns and have called for a new hermeneutic based on existential reading theories. The majority, however, seem concerned to present literary criticism as a supplement to historical-critical exegesis rather than as a replacement for it. Again and again, we hear literary critics affirming the significance of the referential function of biblical literature for theology and for faith, while at the same time insisting that the Bible's poetic function should not be ignored. Many Bible scholars, as we have seen, have even found ways of applying the literary methods so that they shed light on the historical witness of texts.

(5) *Literary-critical approaches to texts are based on theoretical propositions fundamentally at odds with Jewish or Christian theology.* This objection goes beyond that just cited to fault literary critics not only for ignoring matters thought essential to Judaeo-Christian religion, but also for propagating notions considered contradictory to that religion. Deconstructive approaches are accused of promoting the notion that all truth is relative, and reader-oriented criticism is said, similarly, to affirm subjectivity to a degree incompatible with orthodox doctrines of divine revelation. The philosophical basis for structuralism is accused of being deterministic or of supporting elitism. Rhetorical criticism is attacked for reducing all discourse to the level of argumentation and for denying the possibility of selfless motivation. Charges such as these must be considered individually, each on its own merits. Similar accusations have also been leveled with regard to historical-critical methods, which some opponents consider to be indebted to positivist, existentialist, or humanist notions of reality.

Potential benefits that are often cited for using literary criticism in biblical studies include the following:

(1) *Literary criticism respects the canonical form of the biblical writings*. Some scholars consider the attention to biblical writings in the form in which we now have them to be a major benefit that literary criticism brings to the exegetical enterprise. Historical criticism, they say, has often been preoccupied with the analysis of oral traditions or source materials that may have existed prior to the formation of the writings that we now possess. Such studies may be interesting in their own right, but they have only indirect relevance for teachers, pastors, priests, and rabbis who must interpret the works in their current form. In any case, believing communities have canonized as scripture the writings in their finished form, not the preliminary sources or traditions that may have been used in their development.

(2) *Literary criticism offers important insights not available through historical-critical exegesis*. Most biblical literary critics view their work as supplementary to the task of historical criticism, and so, as contributing at least one necessary component to the full task of interpretation. The communication model of Roman Jakobson is often invoked to describe scripture as a communication between God and humanity. Historical criticism has enlightened us with regard to the "sender" component of this paradigm, concentrating on what the Bible reveals about the actions of God in history and about the beliefs of the biblical writers concerning these actions. To be complete, however, a concept of revelation must assume recipients to whom something is revealed. Literary criticism, accordingly, enlightens us with regard to the "message" and "receiver" components of the paradigm, concerning, for instance, the effect that the biblical writings have on people who read them today. Or, again, some say that, despite the enormous contributions that historical criticism has made to our understanding of the referential function of scripture, that method has failed to enlighten us concerning the Bible's poetic function. By reading biblical stories *as stories* and biblical poetry *as poetry*, literary criticism unleashes the inherent power of these stories and poems for personal and social transformation.

(3) *Literary criticism serves communities of faith*. A number of the studies listed in the bibliography commend literary-critical exegesis as an approach that uncovers insights compatible with the perspectives of believing communities. Historical criticism is sometimes disparaged in these same studies as harboring an inherent skepticism that works against the faith perspective. Regardless of whether this is the case, the idea that literary criticism is somehow better suited for interpreting scripture from a faith perspective will probably hold up better with some literary methods than with others. Text-oriented approaches that concentrate on interpreting the Bible in light of what it says about itself are especially attractive to communities that place a premium on the authority of biblical texts. Approaches that seek to read texts from the perspectives of their implied reader, who in biblical literature will probably always be a person of faith, may inevitably produce readings that are attractive also. Other literary approaches, however, favor deconstructive or ideological reading strategies that may challenge traditional religious understanding in significant ways.

(4) *Literary criticism places biblical scholarship in dialogue with the academic world at large*. Ironically, some scholars claim the great benefit of literary criticism is not that it connects biblical studies to readers within the community of faith, but to readers outside that community. By adopting modern literary approaches, scholars are able to study the Bible in the same way that other books are studied and thus may expect their scholarship to be taken seriously even outside the believing communities. Biblical studies is thus becoming more academically respectable as a field of inquiry. As evidence that this is the case, one may note the large number of Bible scholars who now publish widely in technical and professional journals devoted to the study of literature in general. In addition, numerous "secular scholars," including some who claim no allegiance to any particular religious creed, have recently taken an interest

in biblical literature and have begun to publish their own interpretations of these writings.

IMPLICATIONS

Whether the new literary approaches to the Bible are evaluated positively or negatively, they have certainly made their mark not only on the field of biblical scholarship itself but also on other fields that are related to or affected by biblical interpretation. These include:

(1) *Homiletics*. Obviously, changing paradigms for the interpretation of biblical texts have implications for the proclamation of those texts. Within homiletics, voices are now heard advocating "narrative preaching" or "story sermons." Many homileticians draw on the works of Walter J. Ong, John Searle, and others who have also influenced the furtherance of literary criticism in biblical studies.

(2) *Theology*. A similar movement toward "narrative theology" involving such figures as Stanley Hauerwas (1703), Ron Thiemann (1723), and David Tracy (1724-1726) parallels in some respects the rediscovery of the literary character of the Bible. Also, Paul Ricoeur and other theologians who have been influential in literary studies of scripture have made their mark in the larger field of theological studies as well. Furthermore, a number of theological studies are beginning to appear that address the question of "postmodernism," the challenge to modern thinking of which deconstructive literary criticism is but a single example. Dominick LaCapra (1708-1711), for instance, has considered the implications that modern literary and linguistic theory have for the writing of intellectual history. A number of theologians have found LaCapra's work relevant for theological studies.

(3) *Literary studies*. As theologians and biblical scholars become more conversant with modern literary theory, it is only natural that they will want to contribute their own insights to the ongoing development of that theory. Just as secular literary scholars are beginning to contribute to the field of biblical interpretation, so also an increasing number of biblical and theological scholars are beginning to try their hand at the interpretation of secular works. A debate ensues as to whether it is possible or desirable to speak of "a Christian poetics," or of any approach to literature that is deliberately informed by religious ideology.

CONCLUSION

Modern understandings of literature show the influence of phenomenological and hermeneutical philosophy, of social-scientific theory, and of studies in linguistics. Literary critics today struggle to develop a theory that interprets literature in terms of its poetic function, but they differ on such questions as whether text or reader should be given priority in the interpretive paradigm. Because the Bible is also literature, biblical scholars have recently been caught up in these debates and are now engaged in an attempt to develop literary methodologies appropriate for the study of biblical materials. The methods developed thus far are still viewed by many as experimental, but they are nevertheless seeing much use. The bibliography that follows lists almost 1,000 studies that draw on modern literary criticism for a theological investigation of the Bible (see Part Four: Criticism). As this approach to scripture grows in popularity, the challenges and questions that it poses become increasingly poignant. Theologians, exegetes, and literary critics themselves will want to consider this development and the implications that it has for their respective field.

THE BIBLE AND MODERN LITERARY CRITICISM: AN ANNOTATED BIBLIOGRAPHY

PART ONE: BASIS

PHILOSOPHY

See also 0105, 0233, 0251-0257, 0266, 0343, 0434, 0439-0446, 0449, 0454, 0457, 0474, 0509, 0763, 1573, 1687, 1717, 1720-1722.

0001   Berman, Art. *From the New Criticism to Deconstruction: The Reception of Structuralism and Post-Structuralism*. Urbana: University of Illinois Press, 1988. 344 pp.

A dense, philosophical work, this book focuses on American literary thought. Berman locates the philosophic origins of American literary criticism in Locke and Hume. He sees New Criticism as problematic because it is inconsistent in its philosophical base. His discussions of structuralism and deconstruction show the differences between American and European responses.

0002   Bernstein, Richard J. "What Is the Difference That Makes a Difference?: Gadamer, Habermas, and Rorty." In *Hermeneutics and Modern Philosophy*, ed. by Brice R. Wachterhauser, 343-376. Albany: State University of New York Press, 1986.

Proposes that Hans Georg Gadamer, Jürgen Habermas and Richard Rorty differ more in emphases than in essentials. Bernstein concentrates on the themes of praxis, practice, practical truth, and discourse. He concludes that the common ground of these three is their "nonfoundational pragmatic humanism."

0003   Gadamer, Hans-Georg. *Truth and Method*. Trans. by Garrett Barden and William Glen-Doepel. New York: Seabury Press, 1975. 551 pp.

Originally published in 1060 as *Wahrheit und Methode*, this work offers a major philosophical statement on hermeneutical theory by a former student of Martin Heidegger.   Gadamer adapts and applies Heidegger's thinking with regard to aesthetics and criticism. The first portion of the book is titled, "The question of truth as it emerges in the experience of art."   The second part is, "The extension of the question of truth to understanding in the human sciences." The third part considers, "The ontological shift of hermeneutics guided by language."

0004   Gerhart, Mary. "Paul Ricoeur's Notion of 'Diagnostics': Its Function in Literary Interpretation." *Journal of Religion* 56 (1976): 137-156.

Discusses Ricoeur's appeal to scientific diagnostics in his model for the interpretation of literary texts, with special attention to the implications this has for theological studies.

0005   Güttgemanns, Erhardt. *Fragmenta Semiotico-Hermeneutica: Eine Texthermeneutik für den Umgang mit der Hl. Schrift*. Bonn: Linguistica Biblica, 1983. 347 pp.

A review of six major hermeneutical approaches, each associated with one of the following figures: Barthes, Augustine, Schleiermacher, Wilke, Saussure, and Freud. The author is noted for his own efforts at constructing a hermeneutic that is appropriate to scripture but sensitive to semiotic and literary concerns (0519). His view is summarized in a final chapter.

0006   Hamburger, Käte. *The Logic of Literature*. Trans. by M. J. Rose. Bloomington: Indiana University Press, 1973. 396 pp.

The writing in this book is dense, but it contains a significant understanding of the relationship of literary theory to logic and linguistics and to language and reality. Hamburger's literary theory contains a genre theory, which may be compared to that of Frye (0088).

0007 Heidegger, Martin. *Being and Time*. Trans. by John Macquarrie and Edward Robinson. London: SCM Press, 1962. 589 pp.

Originally published in 1927, this is the *magnum opus* of the German philosopher who is known today as a primary exponent of 20th century existentialism. Heidegger seeks to compel persons to consider the nature of *being*. This most significant of all concerns, he holds, is normally neglected in the affairs of everyday life. Furthermore, Heidegger believes modern humanity is in a state of fallenness due to one-sided technological development that produces a "highly inauthentic way of being." The issue for Heidegger is not the *what* of being so much as the *how*. This necessarily involves consideration of others and of surroundings: a person is nothing apart from his or her surroundings, but being completely absorbed by them also leads to nothingness, to being "nothing in particular." Heidegger's thinking derives in part from that of his senior colleague, Edmund Husserl (0008), but Heidegger is more concerned with ontology.

0008   Husserl, Edmund. *Ideas: General Introduction to Pure Phenomenology*. Trans. by W. R. Boyce Gibson. New York: MacMillan Co., 1931. 465 pp.

An English translation of the German philosopher's classic *Ideen zur einer reinen Phänomenologie*, first published in 1913. Here, Husserl offers his initial presentation of phenomenology, the method he developed for description and analysis of consciousness. Through an emphasis on experience, Husserl hoped to mediate the opposition between empiricism, which emphasizes observation, and rationalism, which emphasizes reason. Also through phenomenology, Husserl tried to give philosophy the character of a science. The fundamental methodological principle was "phenomenological reduction," through which attention is focused on uninterpreted basic experience. This focus leads to a quest to discover the essence of things and to reflection on the functions by which essences becomes conscious.

0009   Joy, Morney. "Derrida and Ricoeur: A Case of Mistaken Identity (and Difference)." *Journal of Religion* 68 (1988): 508-526.

Compares and contrasts the manner in which Jacques Derrida and Paul Ricoeur respond to the relation between metaphor and metaphysics. Joy begins with a summary of Martin Heidegger's thought, to which both Derrida and Ricoeur are indebted. Heidegger says that "the metaphorical exists only within the metaphysical." Derrida seeks to demonstrate, through deconstruction, that metaphysical and philosophical paradigms are agencies of uncertainty. Ricoeur attempts to relate a "poetics of existence," by which reason (however flawed) can provide ground for self-reflection.

0010   Langer, Susanne K. *Philosophy in a New Key: A Study in the Symbolism of Reason, Rite, and Art*. 4th ed. Cambridge, MA: Harvard University Press, 1960. 313 pp.

Attempts to approach the subject of symbolic transformation as a natural activity, with logical rather than ethical or metaphysical interests. Langer notes that, although historically idealist schools of philosophy have been the first to recognize the necessity that study of symbol and meaning must be the starting point of philosophy, this insight need not be restricted to idealist interpretations. The chapter titles of this influential work reflect the wide range of its subject matter: "Symbolic Transformation"; "The Logic of Signs and Symbols"; "Discursive Forms and Presentational Forms"; "Language"; "Life Symbols: The Roots of Sacrament"; "Life Symbols: The Roots of Myth"; "On Significance in Music"; "The Genesis of Artistic Import"; and "The Fabric of Meaning."

0011   Makarushka, Irena. "Nietzsche's Critique of Modernity: The Emergence of Hermeneutical Consciousness." *Semeia* 51 (1990): 193-214.

Traces the roots of postmodern reading strategies to the legacy of Friedrich Nietzsche's critique of modernity. In arguing that "there are no truths, only interpretations," Nietzsche encouraged a redirection of philosophical concern from historical consciousness to hermeneutical awareness.

0012   Merleau-Ponty, Maurice. *Phenomenology of Perception*. Rev. ed. Trans. by Colin Smith. London: Routledge and Kegan Paul, 1962. 446 pp.

This difficult but essential work of phenomenology contains a long introduction, "Traditional Prejudices and the Return to Phenomena." Its three major sections are "The Body"; "The World as Perceived"; and "Being-for-Itself and Being-in-the-World." Along with the work of Edmund Husserl and Martin Heidegger, this book provides crucial philosophical background for readers who are interested in phenomenological approaches.

0013   Michaels, Walter Benn. "The Interpreter's Self: Peirce on the Cartesian 'Subject.'" In *Reader Response Criticism*, ed. by Jane P. Tompkins, 185-200. Baltimore: Johns Hopkins University Press, 1980.

Attempts to correct the American misunderstanding of French structuralist and deconstructive criticism. Michaels provides a detailed reading of Charles S. Peirce's late nineteenth-century understanding of Descartes' notion of philosophy and the self. Michaels says, "For Descartes, the self is primary--it can be known directly, and its existence is the single privileged certainty; for Peirce the self is derived--it can only be known by inference from the existence of ignorance and error." What Peirce tells the literary critic, then, is not only that reading is constitutive for meaning but that readers have themselves been constituted, and hence " the critic's pose of neutrality is as fictitious as the philosopher's."

0014   Palmer, Richard E. *Hermeneutics: Interpretation Theory in Schleiermacher, Dilthey, Heidegger, and Gadamer*. Studies in Phenomenology and Existential Philosophy. Evanston, IL: Northwestern University Press, 1969. 283 pp.

Surveys and critiques the hermeneutical views of the named philosophers. The work is usually cited in literary circles because of its support for the idea of an "intentional fallacy" (cf. 0222). See also 0375.

0015   Peirce, Charles Sanders. *Philosophical Writings of Charles S. Peirce*. Ed. with an introduction by Justus Buchler. New York: Dover Publications, 1955. 386 pp.

A collection of the most significant philosophical writings by the American philosopher (1839-1914) who is known today for developing pragmatism into a method of research. Peirce was also a scientist and mathematician. His specialty was logic, specifically three-value logic, which admits a third alternative between true and false. With regard to philosophy, Peirce spoke of the threefold categorization of Quality, Relation, and Representation (or, sometimes, Quality, Reaction, and Mediation). This system had many applications. Modalities, for instance, could be listed as possibility, actuality, and necessity. Signs could be icons, indexes, and symbols. Symbols, in turn, divide into terms, propositions, and arguments. Peirce's philosophy has continued to be influential in some branches of semiotic theory, particularly as articulated by Umberto Eco (see 0242-0243).

0016 Ricoeur, Paul. *The Conflict of Interpretations: Essays on Hermeneutics*. Studies in Phenomenology and Existential Philosophy. Ed. by Don Ihde. Evanston, IL: Northwestern University Press, 1974. 528 pp.

Contains translations of several essays, with an introduction by the editor. The essays are grouped into "Hermeneutics and Structuralism"; "Hermeneutics and Psychoanalysis"; "Hermeneutics and Phenomenology"; "The System of Evil Interpreted"; and "Religion and Faith." Ihde says that these essays are united by "the question of interpretation." See also 0888, 1689.

0017 Ricoeur, Paul. *Interpretation Theory: Discourse and the Surplus of Meaning*. Fort Worth: Texas Christian University Press, 1976. 107 pp.

This book contains four essays that may "be read as step by step approximations of a solution to a single problem, that of understanding language at the level of such productions as poems, narratives and essays, whether literary or philosophical. In other words, the central problem at stake in these four essays is that of works; in particular, that of language as *a work*." The collection moves from "Language as Discourse" to "Speaking and Writing," to "Metaphor and Symbol" and finally to the dialectic relationship of "Explanation and Understanding." See also 1552.

0018 Ricoeur, Paul. "Metaphor and the Main Problem of Hermeneutics." *New Literary History* 6 (1974): 95-110.

Says that the two main problems of hermeneutics are "that of the status of written texts versus spoken language, and that of the status of interpretation versus explanation." Ricoeur aims to connect the problems raised in hermeneutics by text-interpretation and the problems raised in rhetoric, semantics, and stylistics by metaphor.

0019 Ricoeur, Paul. "The Narrative Function." *Semeia* 13 (1978): 177-202.

Sketches a general theory of narrative discourse, comparing and contrasting historical and fictional narrative. Differences between the two exist "at the level of reference." Both, however, have in common a reference to historicity, to the fundamental fact that we make history and are historical beings. History opens us to the possible, while fiction opens us to the essential.

0020 Ricoeur, Paul. *The Rule of Metaphor: Multidisciplinary Studies of the Creation of Meaning in Language*. Trans. by Robert Czerny. Toronto: University of Toronto Press, 1979. 384 pp.

This philosophic study describes the understanding of metaphor from Aristotle to structuralism. Ricoeur's approach is interdisciplinary and comprehensive, difficult to read, but significant for readers whose concerns are linguistic, aesthetic and literary-critical. See also 0047.

0021   Ricoeur, Paul. *Time and Narrative*. 3 vols. Chicago: University of Chicago Press, 1984, 1986, 1988. 288, 208, 362 pp.

Volume One is divided into two parts: (1) "The Circle of Narrative and Temporality," deals with the theory of time in Augustine, the theory of plot in Aristotle, and the "inverted interplay of concordance and disconcordance" that these analyses engender; (2) "History and Narrative," proposes that even history that is removed from the narrative form continues to be bound to our narrative understanding by a line of derivation that we can reconstruct with an appropriate method. Volume Two contains Part III, and its theme is "the configuration of time by fictional narrative, (which) corresponds strictly to the theme of Part II in Volume One." Volume Three contains Part IV, which brings together "the threefold testimony that is provided by phenomenology, history, and fiction concerning the power of narrative, taken in its invisible wholeness, to refigure time."

0022   Rorty, Richard. *Consequences of Pragmatism (Essays: 1972-1980)*. Minneapolis: University of Minnesota Press, 1982.

Collects essays that explore the thought of a number of writers including G. W. F. Hegel, Martin Heidegger, Michel Foucault, John Dewey, and Jacques Derrida. Rorty differentiates relativism from pragmatism, seeing both phenomena as embracing a number of possibilities. He opposes "realism," both in its philosophical underpinnings and in its consequences.

0023   Rorty, Richard. *Philosophy and the Mirror of Nature*. Princeton, NJ: Princeton University Press, 1979. 401 pp.

Surveys "some recent developments in philosophy, especially analytic philosophy, from the point of view of the anti-Cartesian and anti-Kantian revolution" that Rorty describes in his Introduction. He aims to undermine confidence in "the mind" as something about which one should have a philosophical view; in "knowledge" as something that has foundations; and in "philosophy" as it has been conceived since Kant.

0024   Rorty, Richard. "Texts and Lumps." *New Literary History* 17 (1985): 1-16.

Contends that literary criticism has recently been "seeking help from philosophy" while taking "philosophy a bit too seriously." He discusses Hirsch (0096-0097) in order "to suggest that philosophy of language and epistemology not be taken as seriously as both he and his opponents take them."

0025   Sartre, Jean-Paul. *What is Literature?* London: Methuen and Co., 1950. 238 pp.

Examines writing from a writer's perspective, taking up such questions as "What is Writing?," "Why Write?," and "For Whom Does One Write?" Sartre takes the position that prose writing is the only art form that, by virtue of its meaning (language), is bound to the task of communication. The writer, therefore, is a giver of the consciousness and has an ethical obligation to aid in the project of bringing liberty to all people. This ethical criterion must be the foundation for all literary criticism. See also 0231.

0026 Schweiker, William. "Beyond Imitation: Mimetic Praxis in Gadamer, Ricoeur, and Derrida." *Journal of Religion* 68 (1988): 21-38.

Compares the ideas of Hans-Georg Gadamer, Paul Ricoeur, and Jacques Derrida with regard to the classic philosophical problem of "mimesis." In modern terms, the problem of mimesis involves the question of how we achieve meaning or understanding in an ambiguous world. Gadamer explores the phenomenon of understanding and interpretation with reference to cultic mimesis; Ricoeur, with reference to narrative; and Derrida, with reference to "theatrical mimesis." Taken together, ritual, narrative, and theater provide the best metaphors for "getting at our being in the world."

0027 White, Hayden. "The Question of Narrative in Contemporary Historical Theory." *History and Theory* 23 (1984): 1-33.

Considers the relationship of narrative form to historical reality in contemporary historical theory. White discerns four views: (1) Anglo-American analytical philosophers who seek to establish the epistemic status of narrative as a "kind of explanation" of events and processes; (2) Social-scientifically oriented historians who regard narrative historiography as a non-scientific, ideological strategy; (3) Semiologically-oriented literary theorists (including Roland Barthes, Michel Foucault, Jacques Derrida, Tzvetan Todorov, Gérard Genette, and Umberto Eco) who view narrative simply as one discursive code among others; and (4) Hermeneutically-oriented philosophers (including Hans-Georg Gadamer and Paul Ricoeur) who view narrative as the manifestation in discourse of a specific kind of time-consciousness.

0028 White, Hayden. "The Value of Narrativity in the Representation of Reality." *Critical Inquiry* 7 (1980): 5-27.

Addresses the question of the nature of narrative philosophically: the question invites reflection on the very nature of culture and possibly on the nature of humanity itself. Basically, the problem is how to translate *knowing* into *telling*--how to fashion human experience into "a form assimilable to structures of meaning that are generally human rather than culture specific." White discusses the supposed lack of objectivity in ancient historical annals and chronicles in order to raise the question of whether it is ever possible to narrativize without moralizing.

SOCIOLOGY AND ANTHROPOLOGY

See also 0094, 0100, 0110, 0244, 0258, 0453, 0497, 0500, 0524-0525, 0593-0594, 0663, 0741, 0773, 0882, 0896, 1205, 1217, 1230, 1264, 1304, 1388, 1503, 1557, 1596, 1621, 1690.

0029   Barthes, Roland. *Mythologies*. Trans. by Annette Lavers. New York: Hill and Wang, 1972. 160 pp.

A translation of a 1957 French work in which Barthes uses the method of Ferdinand de Saussure (0067), to examine "pop" or "petit-bourgeois" culture. The book is a collection of brief, often humorous essays which say that myths are created by the political right wing. Barthes opposes them.

0030   Geertz, Clifford. *The Interpretation of Cultures: Selected Essays*. New York: Basic Books, 1973. 470 pp.

Presents "a semiotic approach to culture" by an eminent anthropologist. Geertz regards the analysis of culture as an interpretive search for meaning rather than as an experimental science. He further acknowledges that anthropological writings and ethnographic descriptions are themselves "interpretations of interpretations." The ethnographer *inscribes* social discourse, rescuing it from its perishing occasions and fixing it in persuable terms. Although Geertz regards his book as "a treatise in cultural theory," he develops it by way of a series of concrete analyses, actual investigations of particular organizations and cultural ecologies.

0031   Girard, René. *Deceit, Desire, and the Novel: Self and Other in Literary Structure*. 2nd ed. Trans. by Yvonne Freccero. Baltimore: Johns Hopkins University Press, 1976. 305 pp.

A study of the concept of "mimetic desire" in literature and in society. Girard's theory is that our desires imitate the desires of others and that others therefore serve as both models and rivals with regard to our desires. The point is illustrated in literature, as can be seen in the novels of Cervantes, Dostoevsky, Flaubert, and Proust. Girard's exploration of this theme evidences a sacramental vision profoundly influenced by Christian theology.

0032   Girard, René. *The Scapegoat*. Trans. by Yvonne Freccero. Baltimore: Johns Hopkins University Press, 1986. 224 pp.

The central interest of this book is the anthropological phenomenon of the scapegoat who is chosen as a sacrificial victim to rid society of its problems and conflicts. Girard will not accept Christ as such a victim: it is Christ's proclamation of his innocence that Girard finds to be unique. He uses a number of literary sources as evidence, including the biblical passion story.

0033   Girard, René. *Things Hidden Since the Foundation of the World*. Trans. by Stephen Bann and Michael Metteer. Stanford, CA: Stanford University Press, 1987. 469 pp.

This book is the conversation of two psychiatrists, Jean-Michel Oughourlian and Guy Lefort, with René Girard. It extends Girard's notion of "scapegoat" described in 0032 and of "desire" in 0031. Girard has moved far, however, from the literary-critical focus. This study is a combination of anthropology, mythology, psychoanalysis and theology. It is divided into three books, the second of which deals with "The Judaeo-Christian Scriptures."

0034   Girard, René. *Violence and the Sacred*. Baltimore: Johns Hopkins University Press, 1977. 333 pp.

Expands on a theory formulated in 0031, to the effect that models of human desire must necessarily also be rivals for the attainment of those desires: hence, conflict is inevitable. Communities deal with this inevitable violence through a process of selective victimization, which involves the selection of scapegoats. The paradoxical role of the scapegoat/victim as one who is both savior of the community and accursed by the community is fundamentally linked to paradoxical notions of the divine as both holy and terrible. The theory is formulated further in 0032 and applied to the book of Job in 0882. See also 1051, 1457, 1621.

0035   Jameson, Frederic. *The Political Unconscious: Narratives as a Socially Symbolic Act*. Ithaca, NY: Cornell University Press, 1981. 320 pp.

Jameson's book is based upon Marxist hermeneutics, but is also derived in some measure from archetypal criticism. He writes of the "political unconscious." The text rewrites history and reality, he says, and he uses writings of Balzac and Conrad to illustrate his ideas. See also 0264, 0895, 1710.

0036   Lévi-Strauss, Claude. *Anthropology and Myth: Lectures 1957-1982*. New York: Basil Blackwell, 1987. 242 pp.

A series of annual reports on the teaching of Lévi-Strauss, following "the evolution of his thought through a period of three decades. Part I is introductory and contains essays on "The Future of Anthropology (1959-60)" and "Totemism and the Savage Mind (1960-61)." Part II concerns "Mythologies" and Part III, "Inquiries into Mythology and Ritual." Parts IV and V concern social organization and kinship, and, finally, Part VI provides nine appendices on various topics. This book is specific, detailed and readable. Lévi-Strauss' theories on myth and anthropology are basic to one strain of structuralism.

0037   Lévi-Strauss, Claude. *Myth and Meaning*. London: Routledge and Kegan Paul, 1978. 54 pp.

A collection of lectures from a radio series assembled from a series of conversations between Lévi-Strauss and Carole Orr Jerome. The first chapter describes "The Meeting of Myth and Science," and the second compares "primitive" and "scientific" thought. Chapter three discusses "Harelips and Twins: The Splitting of a Myth." The fourth and fifth chapters discuss the relationships between myth and history, and myth and music.

0038 Lévi-Strauss, Claude. *Structural Anthropology*. 2 vols. Garden City, NY: Basic Books, 1963, 1976. 410, 384 pp.

A collection of essays previously published in French in 1958. Taken together, the essays offer a comprehensive view of Lévi-Strauss' theories. They discuss the relationship between linguistic and anthropological studies, and between language and culture. Particular subjects discussed include shamanism, kinship, myth, and ritual. The significance of such studies for literary criticism is that they provided an essential base for the development of one form of structuralism.

0039 Maranda, Pierre. "The Dialectic of Metaphor: An Anthropological Essay on Hermeneutics." In *The Reader in the Text*, ed. by Susan R. Suleiman, 183-204. Princeton, NJ: Princeton University Press, 1980.

Examines "myths" as semantic characters of cultures and subcultures and declares that "metaphors, unless they are stereotypes, open up new roads in order to connect concepts that would otherwise stay unrelated." Maranda asks, finally, "Is not interpretation . . . a conservative defense by which a society tries to perpetuate itself in the most economical way?"

0040 White, Hayden. *Tropics of Discourse: Essays in Cultural Criticism*. Baltimore: Johns Hopkins University Press, 1978. 287 pp.

A collection of essays that consider how tropes function in the discourses of the human sciences. The term "trope" is derived from literary criticism (where it refers to "figures of speech") to describe the generation of new ways of thinking through variation from what is normally expected. White defines "tropics" as "the process by which all discourse *constitutes* the objects which it pretends only to describe realistically and to analyze objectively." In short, White applies structuralist and poststructuralist concepts of language to literature that is not intended to be poetic but, rather, mimetic, referential, historical, or scientific. For example, he proposes an allegorical reading of Darwin's *Origin of the Species* in one essay, entitled "The Fictions of Factual Representations."

LINGUISTICS

See also 0006, 0017-0018, 0020, 0185, 0238, 0244, 0252, 0258, 0261, 0263-0264, 0266, 0271, 0279-0280, 0288, 0306, 0317, 0341, 0396-0397, 0442, 0445-0446, 0453, 0466, 0517, 0519, 0525, 0554, 0557, 0559, 0583, 0663, 0725, 1114, 1129, 1137-1138, 1302, 1424, 1477, 1561, 1624, 1680, 1683, 1697, 1702, 1710, 1712.

0041 Anderegg, Johannes. *Fiktion und Kommunikation: Ein Beitrag zur Theorie der Prosa*. 2nd ed. Göttingen: Vandenhoeck and Ruprecht, 1977.

Grounds method in the conviction that fiction and fictionality are revealed in the interaction between text and reader, and are to be understood as a specific form of communication. Anderegg attempts to describe the phenomenon of fiction by using models that show the relationship between sender, text, and recipient.

0042 Austin, John. *How To Do Things With Words*. 2nd ed. Ed. by J. O. Urmson and Marina Sbisa. Cambridge, MA: Harvard University Press, 1975. 166 pp.

A collection of essays given at Harvard University in 1955 that laid the foundations for what is known as "speech act theory." Austin distinguishes between "constative" utterances, which are merely descriptive or referential, and "illocutionary" (or "performative") ones, which perform an action. Examples of the latter are promises, vows, bets, verdicts, and ritual words. Since speech is firmly connected to social context, however, all utterances are ultimately produced by illocutionary acts. Austin's ideas were systematized and developed by his student, John Searle, in 0069. As a philosophical theory of language use, his speech-act theory influenced literary emphases on performative speech, which, in turn, led to new understandings of "meaning" as something that literature *does* as opposed to something that literature *has*. See also 0309, 0359, 0462, 0467-0468, 0575, 1211.

0043 Ching, Marvin K. L.; Haley, Michael C.; and Lunsford, Ronald F. *Linguistic Perspectives on Literature*. London: Routledge and Kegan Paul, 1980. 332 pp.

Opens with an essay by the editors on "the theoretical relation between linguistics and literary studies." They conclude that a diversity of models, including case grammar, componential analysis, semantic interpretation, and speech act theory have made significant contributions toward revealing the "language of literature." The essays that follow make use of such models and are divided into two sections. "Figurative Language" includes nine articles by linguistics scholars on metaphor and paradox. "Stylistics" includes nine more articles on narrative grammar, formal devices, and other stylistic features of language and literature.

0044 Chomsky, Noam. *Aspects of the Theory of Syntax*. Cambridge, MA: MIT Press, 1965.

A refinement of certain ideas expressed in 0045, which was widely available in mimeographed form prior to its actual publication. In this book, Chomsky seeks to reinterpret his then unpublished theory in light of objections and misunderstandings that had been raised by it. His concept of the "lexicon" and of "transformations" receive particular attention. Chomsky seeks to develop a "standard theory," which recognizes syntactic, semantic, and phonological components of language, but which sees only the first of them as playing a role in the recursive generation of sentence structures. He speaks of "deep structures," which are generated by the syntactic base and are then given semantic and phonological interpretations. See also 0059.

0045   Chomsky, Noam. *The Logical Structure of Linguistic Theory*. Chicago: University of Chicago Press, 1985. 592 pp.

The principal work by the influential linguist who develops and refines the work of Saussure (0067) in a different direction than that taken by Jakobson (0055-0058). Chomsky focuses on the syntactic aspect of language in an attempt to develop a universal, abstract grammar basic to all language systems. His real interest here is in syntax (formal structures of language), which he studies apart from semantics (the meaning function of language). Chomsky proposes two models in this book, a "phrase-structure grammar" and a "transformational-generative grammar."   By promoting the concept of syntax as a series of recursive rules, he hopes to overcome what he regards as a methodological limitation of structuralism, namely "the restriction to procedures based on substitution, matching, and other taxonomic operations." Despire its publication date, most of the material in this book dates from the 1950s and is further refined in 0044. See also 0059.

0046   Cohen, Ted. "Metaphor and the Cultivation of Intimacy." *Critical Inquiry* 5 (1978): 3-12.

Suggests a function of metaphor which may be considered philosophically, independent of aesthetic character: the achievement of intimacy. This happens because "(1) the speaker issues a kind of concealed invitation; (2) the hearer expends a special effort to accept the invitation; and (3) this transaction constitutes the acknowledgement of a community."

0047   Crosman, Inge Karalus. "The Status of Metaphoric Discourse." *Romantic Review* 68 (1977): 207-216.

Reviews Paul Ricoeur's *La Métaphore Vive* (cf. 0020), which claims that, "unlike 'dead' metaphors, whose meaning is already fixed by usage, 'live' metaphors are semantic 'events,' whose meaning emerges from the individual utterance at hand." Crosman says that, according to Ricoeur, "metaphor cannot fruitfully be studied at the level of words." *La Métaphore* also introduces the notions of metaphorical truth and reality, and by doing so engages in "a philosophic discussion of the status of metaphoric discourse." The review is thorough and helpful.

0048   Culler, Jonathan. *Ferdinand de Saussure*. Rev. ed. Ithaca: Cornell University Press, 1986. 157 pp.

A study of Saussure's theory of language (cf. 0067) that tries to place it within contexts both inside and outside of linguistics, and to interpret its legacy for both structuralism and poststructuralism. Culler hopes that reading Saussure will point up the "facile distinction between structuralism and poststructuralism, which may caricature structuralism and transfer to poststructuralism what is most interesting in structuralist writings."

0049 Dillon, George L. *Language Processing and the Reading of Literature: Toward a Model of Comprehension.* Bloomington: Indiana University Press, 1978. 240 pp.

This work of grammatical criticism discusses the ways that words are grouped, and the effect of our grammatical presuppositions on the way that we read literature. The groupings of words considered are phrases and clauses. Dillon then writes about larger contextual problems like reference and attachment. He considers, for his examples, segments from Spenser, James, Milton, Faulkner and Stevens. A dense but readable book, his work is related to Stanley Fish's ideas.

0050 Fowler, Roger. *Linguistics and the Novel.* London: Methuen and Co., 1977. 145 pp.

This book has two foci: linguistics as a basis for understanding the various aspects of fiction, and linguistics as a way that practical criticism might be carried out. Fowler gives specific examples of practical linguistic criticism by approaching authors like Dickens, James, Joyce, Lawrence and others.

0051 Gasparov, Boris. "The Narrative Text as an Act of Communication." *New Literary History* 9 (1978): 245-261.

Examines the narrative literary text, i.e., the "verbal text which functions as a secondary modeling system in relation to the natural language in which it is written." This dense and rather difficult article uses Bühler's *Sprachtheorie* as a point of departure and is abundantly illustrated from modern literature.

0052 Goodman, Nelson. *Language of Art: An Approach to a Theory of Symbols.* 2nd ed. Indianapolis: Bobbs-Merrill Co., 1976. 288 pp.

Intends to provide "an approach to a general theory of symbols." Goodman, a philosopher, deals largely with visual symbols and includes a number of helpful diagrams. The book has six sections: "Reality Remade"; "The Sound of Pictures"; "Art and Authenticity"; "The Theory of Notation"; "Score Sketch and Script"; and "Art and Understanding."

0053 Grimes, Joseph. *The Thread of Discourse.* Janua Linguarum Series Minor, 207. The Hague: Mouton Publishers, 1975. 408 pp.

Presents the results of major international research in cross-language study of discourse structures. As a contribution to what has come to be called "discourse analysis," Grimes offers a number of observations on models of language structures larger than sentences that appear to be represented in diverse language groups. These include such matters as patterns of thematic placement, genres in oral discourse, and pronominal systems, as well as virtually universal patterns for semantic role structures and rhetorical argumentation.

0054   Hoey, Michael. *On the Surface of Discourse*. London: George Allen and Unwin, Publishers, 1983.   219 pp.

A basic introduction to "discourse analysis," a linguistic-based method of analysis that attempts to define the rules and relationships of communication units larger than the sentence.   Hoey deals with written language only, considering the ways in which discourse patterns develop out of clause relations. Patterns are signaled to the reader by means of lexical signaling and repetition.

0055   Jakobson, Roman.   "Sign and System of Language: A Reassessment of Saussure's Doctrine."   In *Verbal Art, Verbal Sign, Verbal Time*, ed. by Krytyna Pomorska and Stephen Rudy, 28-36.   Minneapolis: University of Minnesota Press, 1985.

Challenges a basic concept of Ferdinand de Saussure's *Course in General Linguistics* (0067).   Saussure opposes language as a system (synchrony) to its historical development (diachrony) as static versus dynamic moments.   Jakobson calls this a false opposition because it excludes the role of time in the present moment of languages and so creates an erroneous disruption between past and present in the linguistic processes.   Although this article was originally published in 1959, it articulates ideas that Jakobson had been teaching for thirty years.

0056   Jakobson, Roman.   "Subliminal Verbal Patterning in Poetry." In *Verbal Art, Verbal Sign, Verbal Time*, ed. by Krystyna Pomorska and Stephen Rudy, 59-68. Minneapolis: University of Minnesota Press, 1985.

Discusses the question of whether the "grammar of poetry" revealed through structural analysis represents consciously applied devices.   Jakobson insists that, while some poets may be conscious of such devices, this need not be the case. Poets, like oral tellers of tales, are usually ignorant of the structural code they follow.   Jakobson's analyses found that poems often exhibit concrete linguistic patterns not only with regard to meter, rhyme, and assonance, but also with regard to such abstract elements as grammatical case, number, person, tense, and verbal aspects.   If some of these patterns lie beyond the threshold of perception for the average reader, this does not mean that they fail to have an effect on that reader.   This essay is followed by a discussion with students on the same subject.

0057   Jakobson, Roman, and Halle, Morris. *Fundamentals of Language*. 2nd ed. Janua Linguarum Series Minor, 1.   The Hague: Mouton Publishers, 1971.

Contains two essays: (1) "Phonology and Phonetics" by Jakobson and Halle, which considers the feature level of language, the variety of features and their treatment in linguistics, the identification of distinctive features, and phonemic patterning; and (2) "Two Aspects of Language and Two Types of Aphasic Disturbances," which draws implications from Ferdinand de Saussure's "radical distinction between the syntagmatic and associative" planes of language for understanding speech disturbances. It is in this latter essay that Jakobson identifies the two operations of linguistic signs as "combination" and "selection," a notion that would later be applied to literature by structuralists. See also 0072.

0058 Jakobson, Roman, and Pomorska, Krystyna. *Dialogues*. Cambridge, MA: MIT Press, 1983. 183 pp.

A series of interviews conducted with Jakobson late in his life. Primarily a linguist, Jakobson also devoted himself to the studies of form and structure in literature. Dialogue topics here that will be of particular interest to literary critics include "The Path Toward Poetics"; "Approaches to Folklore"; "The Time Factor in Language and in Literature"; "The Factor of Space"; "Time in the Framework of Signs"; "The Concept of the Mark"; "Parallelism"; "Poetry and Grammar"; and "Semiotics." See also 0072.

0059 Lawrence, Irene. *Linguistics and Theology: The Significance of Noam Chomsky for Theological Construction*. American Theological Library Association Monograph Series, 16. Metuchen, NJ: Scarecrow Press, 1980. 196 pp.

An excellent introduction to the linguistic theory of Chomsky, which also considers the implications of that theory for theological study. The bulk of the book is descriptive. Chapter One considers "Linguistics Before Chomsky," with attention to the work of Saussure (0067) and to both European and American structuralism. Chapter Two describes Chomsky's revolutionary ideas and Chapter Three discusses the interaction of these ideas with alternative positions. The latter half of the book turns to explicitly theological concerns, discussing the implications Chomsky's universal generative semantics holds for religious pluralism and the problem of "God-language."

0060 Longacre, R. E. *An Anatomy of Speech Notions*. Lisse, Belgium: Peter de Ridder Press, 1976. 394 pp.

A catalogue or taxonomy of "underlying notional categories of language." Longacre starts with the smallest and least complex levels--what he calls predications--which are found in individual sentences. From there he moves to consideration of larger and more complex levels, to what is sometimes called "discourse analysis." Finally, he is able to study "plot structure" as a universal linguistic phenomenon. Specifically, "plot" is analyzed in terms of deep and surface structure.

0061 Ong, Walter J. *Interfaces of the Word: Studies in the Evolution of Consciousness and Culture*. Ithaca, NY: Cornell University Press, 1977. 352 pp.

In a collection of eleven essays, the style of which is conversational and witty, Ong relates "major developments in culture and consciousness" to the "evolution of the word from primary orality to its present state." The book is insightful and wide-ranging.

0062 Ong, Walter J. *Orality and Literacy: The Technologizing of the Word*. New York: Methuen and Co., 1982. 201 pp.

This occasionally difficult book looks at cultures prior to the printed word, at the alphabetical manuscript stage, at the typographic stage, and at the electronic stage, which brings with it a new sort of orality. Ong refers to a number of scholars who have written in the same field, including Jacques Derrida and other contemporary literary critics.

0063   Ong, Walter J. "Orality-Literacy Studies and the Unity of the Human Race." *Oral Tradition* 2 (1987): 371-382.

Differentiates "oral" cultures from "literary" and "electronic" cultures, and sees the present "age of secondary orality" as looking "simultaneously to the past and the future." Literacy made possible metaphysics, which was antithetical to narrative. Ong reminds the reader of the "vast oral tradition" underlying the Bible's text, saying that "the Bible is very likely the most variegated orality-literacy mix we have in the text."

0064   Ong, Walter J. *The Presence of the Word: Some Prolegomena for Cultural and Religious History*. 2nd ed. Minneapolis: University of Minnesota Press, 1986. 360 pp.

Traces three stages of the word (oral, alphabet and print, and electronic) and discusses the implications that transition between stages has for culture and religion. To the extent that religion deals with the invisible, cultures oriented toward the mediums of alphabet and print are less able to deal with religious truth than those oriented toward oral mediums. The current transition to electronic mediums offers a re-vocalization that may also bring a re-sacralization of our culture.

0065   Ong, Walter J. "The Writer's Audience Is Always a Fiction." *Proceedings of the Modern Language Association* 90 (1975): 9-21.

Discusses the role imposed on an audience by a written or printed text as differentiated from that imposed by spoken utterance. Authors "fictionalize" their readers, and the audience in turn is called upon to fictionalize itself.

0066   Pratt, Mary Louise. *Toward a Speech Act Theory of Literary Discourse*. Bloomington: Indiana University Press, 1977. 236 pp.

This groundbreaking work discusses the act of narration. Pratt combines speech-act theory with the idea of natural narrative. She says that there is little if any distinction between "ordinary" and "literary" language. See also 0153.

0067   Saussure, Ferdinand de. *Course in General Linguistics*. Rev. ed. Ed. by Charles Bally and Albert Sechehave in collaboration with Albert Riedlinger. Trans. by Wade Baskin. London: Peter Owen, 1974. 236 pp. Also trans. by Roy Harris. London: Gerald Duckworth and Co., 1983.

The original document in the field of structural linguistics, this work provides both methodologies and categories for semiotic work. The main text of the book is divided into "General Principles"; "Synchronic Linguistics"; "Diachronic Linguistics"; "Geographical Linguistics"; and "Questions of Retrospective Linguistics." Saussure's linguistic theory, as presented here, gave birth to the science of semiotics, from which structuralism and structural exegesis are derived. The book makes a distinction between *langue* (language systems) and *parole* (language acts) that is now basic to linguistic study. It also distinguishes between "signifiers" and "signifieds," and between syntagmatic (or diachronic) aspects of language and paradigmatic (or synchronic) aspects of language. See also 0005, 0029, 0045, 0048, 0055, 0057, 0059, 0226, 0255, 0258, 0298.

0068   Searle, John R. "The Logical Status of Fictional Discourse." *New Literary History* 6 (1975): 319-332.

Explores the difference between "fictional and serious utterances," which terms Searle defines at length. He distinguishes, first, between fiction and nonfiction, then beween fiction and lies, and fiction and drama. He explores the creation of fictional characters. The author of fiction, Searle says, pretends to perform illocutionary acts. As yet, there is "no general theory of the mechanisms by which serious illocutionary intentions are conveyed by pretended illocutions."

0069   Searle, John R. *Speech Acts: An Essay in the Philosophy of Language.* Cambridge: Cambridge University Press, 1969. 203 pp.

Is divided into two sections, "A Theory of Speech Acts" and "Some Applications of the Theory." Searle begins by defining the method and the scope of his inquiry, then discusses "Expressions, Meaning, and Speech Acts," "The Structure of Illocutionary Acts," "Reference as a Speech Act" and "Predication." In the second section of the book he begins by discussing the naturalist speech act, and assertion "fallacies." The two final chapters address "Problems of Reference" and "Deriving 'Ought' from 'Is,'" in which Searle probes the "alleged impossibility of deriving an evaluative statement from a set of descriptive statements. This book represents an attempt to systematize the thoughts of John Austin (0042) and has been extremely influential in giving his ideas wider exposure. See also 0127, 0359, 0462, 0575, 1211.

0070   Smith, Barbara Herrnstein. *On the Margins of Discourse: The Relation of Literature to Language.* Chicago: University of Chicago Press, 1978. 225 pp.

This series of essays develops Smith's theory of the two types of discourse, which she calls "natural" and "fictive." She relates her theory to the use of language in poetry and to other art forms as well. This book is important for readers interested in structuralist theory, reader-response, and psychoanalytic theories.

0071 Uitti, Karl D. *Linguistics and Literary Theory.* Princeton Studies in Humanistic Scholarship in America. Englewood Cliffs, NJ: Prentice-Hall, 1969. 272 pp.

Provides a structural and historical overview of the "hybrid field" of linguistics and its relationship to literary theory. Chapter One reviews "Language, Thought, and Culture" from classical times to the present. Chapter Two focuses on the contributions of linguistics to literary theory, with an emphasis upon New Criticism and structuralism. The book is written specifically for "nonspecialists," that is, for persons who work primarily in other disciplines.

0072   Waugh, Linda R. *Roman Jakobson's Science of Language*. Lisse, Belgium: Peter de Ridder Press, 1976. 115 pp.

Summarizes the most significant aspects of this great linguist's theories regarding language and literature, which would be instrumental in the development of formalism and structuralism. Some key points that Jakobson stresses: the relative autonomy of language itself as well as of its parts; the means-end relationship between code and message; the indissoluble tie between static and dynamic aspects of language; the opposition between selection and combination as two axes on which items operate; and the logical structure of binary oppositions in a hierarchized and mutually implicating relationship.

0073   Wheelwright, Philip. *Metaphor and Reality*. Bloomington: Indiana University Press, 1962. 192 pp.

Begins with a consideration of language in general and then goes on to distinguish between stereotyped language and metaphoric language. Wheelwright studies the emergence of symbols out of general metaphoric speech and the human tendency to concoct myths. He distinguishes classes of symbols: (1) archetypal symbols (such as light/darkness); (2) symbols of ancestral vitality; and (3) symbols of cultural range. Wheelwright's ultimate concern is not with symbols in literature (though literary critics rely on his insights) but with "the characteristics of reality that suggest themselves when . . . the full connotations of tensive, expressive language are taken at face value." See also 1115.

PART TWO: THEORY

GENERAL

0074   Abrams, M. H. *A Glossary of Literary Terms*. 5th ed. New York: Holt, Rinehart and Winston, 1981. 220 pp.

This is a useful, small reference tool. Abrams defines in some detail a number of important critical terms. A brief introduction to "Modern Theories of Literature and Criticism," including the innovations of the 1970s, can be found at the end of the volume. Terms are listed alphabetically.

0075   Abrams, M. H., ed. *Literature and Belief: English Institute Essays*, 1957. New York: Columbia University Press, 1958. 184 pp.

A starting point for thinking about the problem of belief in literature. From a literary-critics' perspective, the problem is occasioned by "the occurrence in the greatest poems of large-scale moral, philosophical, or religious assertions which seem to contradict assertions in other poems of equal aesthetic value, and which sometimes run counter to our own deepest convictions." The volume contains essays by M. H. Abrams, Douglas Bush, Cleanth Brooks, Walter J. Ong, Nathan Scott, and Louis Martz.

0076   Abrams, M. H. *The Mirror and the Lamp: Romantic Theory and the Critical Tradition*. New York: W. W. Norton and Co., 1958. 406 pp.

A classic study of early nineteenth-century English literature, which takes into account the artist's product; the artist's self; the relationship of the product to "the universe," and the effects of the product on the reader, listener or spectator. Abrams' immediate concern is to study Romantic theory in light of critical tradition, but the work is best known today for its typology of "modes of criticism" (objective, expressive, mimetic, pragmatic), which relate, respectively, to the four elements just mentioned. See also 0483, 1609.

0077   Adams, Hazard. *Critical Theory Since Plato*. New York: Harcourt Brace Jovanovich, 1971.

An anthology of literary critical theory through the centuries. It includes writings from ancient times, like Plato's *Ion* and excerpts from *The Republic* and *Laws*; Aristotle's *Poetics*; and Horace's *Art of Poetry*. From the Middle Ages, Adams includes Dante Alighieri's "Letter to Can Grande della Scala," in which the poet defines comedy. The collection also comprises Sir Philip Sidney's "An Apology for Poetry," from the Renaissance, John Dryden's "An Essay of Dramatic Poesy," and Immanuel Kant's first two books from *Critique of Judgment*. Among the essays from the nineteenth century are several by Samuel Taylor Coleridge, John Stuart Mill, Matthew Arnold, Karl Marx, and Sigmund Freud. From the twentieth century, the most influential essays of T. E. Hulme, I. A. Richards, Leon Trotsky, and others appear. Included also are T. S. Eliot's "Tradition and the Individual Talent," and W. K. Wimsatt's and Monroe C. Beardsley's "The Intentional Fallacy" and "The Affective Fallacy" (0222).

0078   Beebe, Maurice, ed. *Literary Symbolism: An Introduction to the Interpretation of Literature*. Wadsworth Guides to Literary Study. Belmont, CA: Wadsworth Publishing Co., 1960. 181 pp.

Is intended as a resource book for beginning college composition and literature students. Both of its major sections are comprised of extremely brief pieces and excerpts. Part one contains brief examples of critical theories about symbolism, some from authors like Charles Dickens and some from literary critics like M. H. Abrams. In the second part, literary works alternate with critical discussion of them. Chapter Four and Part II treat the book of Jonah and several approaches to it. Although this book is dated, it is a useful place to begin for those with little background in literary criticism.

0079   Bloom, Edward, ed. "In Defense of Authors and Readers." *Novel* 11 (1977): 5-25.

Couples two panel discussions from a conference at Brown University. It includes a statement by Wayne C. Booth in defense of authors, with questions from the floor and responses by Frank Durand and Hyatt Waggoner. Speaking "For the Readers" is Wolfgang Iser, with responses from Inge Crosman, Robert Crosman and Roger Henkle.

0080   Brooke-Rose, Christine. "Round and Round the Jakobson Diagram: A Survey." *Hebrew University Studies in Literature* 8 (1980): 153-182.

Says that "modern criticism has moved toward a much greater plurality, and tries, not always successfully, to integrate all the six aspects of communication in (Roman) Jakobson's diagram." Brooke-Rose concludes, however, that the "Jakobson diagram, in fact, has been exploded: no addresser, no addressee, no reference, no message, only (perhaps), a contact and a vast metalanguage.

0081   Cain, William E. *The Crisis in Criticism: Theory, Literature, and Reform in English Studies*. Baltimore: Johns Hopkins University Press, 1984. 336 pp.

Focuses "on the critical, theoretical, and pedagogical concerns of the present--the influence of new 'continental' terms and models, and question of the discipline's 'authority' and 'objectivity,' the relation between theory and practice, and the continuing efforts to move 'beyond' New Critical formalism." In Part One, Cain examines the work of E. D. Hirsch, J. Hillis Miller, and Stanley Fish. Part Two displays an "historical orientation," and Part Three surveys "major books of theory and criticism that were published or reprinted in the 1970s and 1980s."

0082   Chatman, Seymour, ed. *Literary Style: A Symposium*. London: Oxford University Press, 1971. 427 pp.

Collects the papers given at a Symposium on Literary Style held in 1969. The first section, "Theory of Style," includes articles by Roland Barthes, Tzvetan Todorov, and others; the second, "Stylistics and Related Disciplines," has contributions by authors including René Wellek, Lubomir Dolezel, and Karl D. Uitti. Other sections are: "Style Features"; "Period Style"; "Genre Style"; and "Styles of Individual Authors and Texts." Chatman says that three questions can give the reader some sense of the book's persistent themes: (1) "What is style?" (2) "How do style features emerge?" (3) "Is linguistics sufficient to describe literary style?"

0083   De Beaugrande, Robert. "Surprised by Syncretism: Cognition and Literary Criticism Exemplified by E. D. Hirsch, Stanley Fish, and J. Hillis Miller." *Poetics* 12 (1983): 83-138.

Claims that the current state of literary criticism is not "a fragmented or chaotic enterprise." Rather, these disagreements "represent different actualizations within the potential of a unified system." De Beaugrande takes three critical methods: authorial intention (E. D. Hirsch), reader response (Stanley Fish), and deconstruction (J. Hillis Miller) and shows "how they presuppose, rather than exclude each other." Finally he provides a special test "to show the surprising convergence of theoretical statements despite the declared opposition of these critical methods."

0084   Detweiler, Robert. "After the New Criticism: Contemporary Methods of Literary Interpretation." In *Orientation By Disorientation*, ed. by Richard A. Spencer, 3-24. Pittsburgh: Pickwick Press, 1980.

Begins by showing that critical approaches like Marxism and psychological criticism existed alongside New Criticism in its heyday. Hence, pluralism of critical approach is nothing new. Detweiler considers "recent studies of narrative form, of metaphor, and of intertextuality as extensions of formalism that are supplanting the old New Criticism." Structuralism evolves from formalism; and both it and "Soviet semiotics have close connections to Marxist criticism." Both "psychological" and "archetypal" critical models have survived, and phenomenology has remained influential.

0085   Eagleton, Terrence. *Literary Theory: An Introduction*. Minneapolis: University of Minnesota Press, 1983. 252 pp.

This work of socialist criticism studies several post-formalist literary theories, including phenomenology, semiotics, post-structuralism, psychoanalysis and others. Eagleton finds that all of these are lacking, since they uphold contemporary social structures. He would prefer a criticism that was more intentionally political and change-seeking. This work is especially strong in its discussion of Edmund Husserl and Martin Heidegger.

0086   Ellis, John. *The Theory of Literary Criticism: A Logical Analysis*. Berkeley and Los Angeles: University of California Press, 1974. 274 pp.

This study of aesthetics tries to understand the nature of the literary critical discipline. Ellis sees the critical task contextualized by other disciplines. He studies, among other topics, the way that critics approach texts, the way they define literature, and the relation of literature to society.

0087   Fish, Stanley E. "Consequences." *Critical Inquiry* 11 (1985): 433-458.

Concludes a discussion begun with Knapp and Michaels' "Against Theory" (0101). Fish agrees with Knapp's and Michaels' premise. He concludes, "theory's day is dying; the hour is late; and the only thing left for a theorist to do is to say so."

0088   Frye, Northrop. *Anatomy of Criticism: Four Essays*. Princeton, NJ: Princeton University Press, 1957. 394 pp.

Begins with a long "Polemical Introduction" which is an apologia for criticism. Frye refers frequently to the Bible as he describes "Historical Criticism: Theory of Modes"; "Ethical Criticism: Theory of Symbols"; "Archetypal Criticism: Theory of Myths"; and "Rhetorical Criticism: Theory of Genres." Much of his later work, *The Great Code* (0586) will spring from this book. It contains valuable discussions of Aristotelian genres. See also 0006, 0299.

0089   Frye, Northrop. "The Critical Path: An Essay on the Social Context of Literary Criticism." In *In Search of Literary Theory*, ed. by M. W. Bloomfield, 91-194. Ithaca, NY: Cornell University Press, 1972.

Traces Frye's own development as a literary critic, from early encounters with New Criticism which had, for him, an insufficient sense of poetry's contexts. Part II of this essay concerns itself with the Bible, Judaism, and Christianity. The entire essay suggests links between myth, literature and religion, and hinges on "the dialectic of concern and freedom."

0090   Frye, Northrop; Baker, Sheridan; and Perkins, George. *The Harper Handbook to Literature*. New York: Harper and Row, 1985.

Contains an up-to-date dictionary of literary terms and definitions. This handbook provides an excellent companion to Holman's *Handbook* (0098). It also has a "Chronology of Literature and World Events" by Barbara M. Perkins as an appendix.

0091   Gerhart, Mary. "Genre--the Larger Context." In *Art/Literature/Religion: Life on the Borders*, ed. by Robert Detweiler, 19-30. Journal for the American Academy of Religious Studies, Thematic Studies, 49,2. Chico, CA: Scholars Press, 1983.

A historical survey of genre theory that traces: (1) the dispute in classical times over which genre is basic to all others; (2) the effects of New Criticism, which viewed generic comparison as gratuitous; (3) the German morphological tradition, which is preoccupied with genre theory; and (4) the deconstructive critics, who are concerned with genre for purposes of declassification rather than classification. Gerhart also discusses "genre as epistemology" and the larger context of genre in relation to modes of thought.

0092   Graff, Gerald. *Professing Literature: An Institutional History*. Chicago: University of Chicago Press, 1987. 315 pp.

A history of academic literary studies in America from 1828 to the waning of the New Criticism and proliferation of controversies over literary theories that marked the 1960s.

0093   Hernadi, Paul. "Literary Theory: A Compass for Critics." *Critical Inquiry* 3 (1976): 369-386.

Offers four different "maps" of literary theory intended to relate literary criticism to other realms of knowledge. The first map, for instance, diagrams an intersection of two axes: the rhetorical axis of communication and the mimetic axis of representation. The final map interrelates basic approaches to literature as more or less distinct, yet combinable disciplines. See also 1609.

0094   Hernadi, Paul, ed. *What Is Literature*? Bloomington: Indiana University Press, 1978. 257 pp.

Contains nineteen essays that attempt to describe the nature of literature. Many essays in the collection contextualize the study of literature with reference to a number of related disciplines like semiotics and sociology. Contributors include Monroe Beardsley, E. D. Hirsch, Norman Holland, Murray Krieger, René Wellek, and James Wimsatt.

0095   Hinderer, Walter.   "Theory, Conception, and Interpretation of the Symbol." In *Perspectives in Literary Symbolism*, ed. by Joseph Strelka, 83-127.   Yearbook of Comparative Criticism, 1.   University Park: Pennsylvania State University Press, 1968.

Says that the forms of a literary symbol are in immediate connection with the forms of thought and consciousness, and so are subordinate to historical changes.   Theory and interpretation of symbols "go in different paths, since they aim for different objectives."   The bulk of this article uses the modern drama *Die Sündflat*, which takes its plot from Gilgamesh and the Noah story, to consider interpretation of symbols.

0096   Hirsch, E. D.   *The Aims of Interpretation*.   Chicago: University of Chicago Press, 1976.   177 pp.

Takes an anti-relativistic stance, claiming that authorial intention matters and is knowable.   Literature has an ethical thrust as well as an aesthetic one, and that neglected aspect needs to be reinstated.

0097   Hirsch, E. D.   *Validity in Interpretation*.   New Haven, CT: Yale University Press, 1967.   287 pp.

Contends that objectivity is attainable in the study of literature.   Hirsch posits a program for determining whether one interpretation is more valid than another.   Both authorial intent and the concept of genre are important, as are intrinsic logical constraints.   Hirsch also distinguishes between a text's "meaning," which does not change, and its "significance," which does.   See also 0096, and, for broader consideration of Hirsch's views, 0024, 0081, 0083, 0103, 0129, 0354.

0098   Holman, C. Hugh.   *A Handbook to Literature Based on the Original by William Flint Thrall and Addison Hubbard*, 4th ed.   Indianapolis: Odyssey Press, 1980.

Provides a comprehensive and detailed dictionary of literary terms.   An indispensable tool of the trade that belongs on every literary critic's desk.

0099   Jauss, Hans Robert.   *Aesthetic Experience and Literary Hermeneutics*.   Trans. by Michael Shaw; 2 vols.   Minneapolis: University of Minnesota Press, 1982.   359 pp.

Asks "What does the aesthetic experience mean? How has it manifested itself in the history of art? What interest can it have for the present theory of art?"   The book is divided into two volumes because of "the phenomenological distinction between understanding and cognition, primary experience and the act of reflection."   The first volume covers questions about the three fundamental categories of poiesis, aesthesis, and catharsis; about aesthetic pleasure as "the underlying attitude peculiar to the three functions"; and about "the contiguous relationship between aesthetic experience and other provinces of meaning in the world of everyday reality."   The second volume attempts to demonstrate the task of literary hermeneutics.   See also 0335.

0100   Kermode, Frank. "Figures in the Carpet: On Recent Theories of Narrative Discourse." In *Comparative Criticism, A Yearbook 2,* ed. by Elinor S. Shaffer, 291-301 Cambridge: Cambridge University Press, 1980.

Surveys the present state of literary theory, taking into consideration a number of writers including Meir Sternberg, Seymour Chatman, Gérard Genette, Tzvetan Todorov, Wolfgang Iser and others. Kermode theorizes that "the main hope" for literary study "lies in some future combination of semiotics with reception-theory and sociology of knowledge."

0101   Knapp, Steven, and Michaels, Walter Benn. "Against Theory." *Critical Inquiry* 8 (1982): 723-742.

Refuses to ground practical criticism in either a text-oriented or a reader-oriented approach. "Theory attempts to solve . . . a set of familiar problems: the function of authorial intention, the status of literary language, the role of interpretive assumptions, and so on . . . The mistake on which all critical theory rests has been to imagine that these problems are real." The tendency is "to generate theoretical problems by splitting apart terms that are in fact inseparable." Knapp and Michael's thesis is that "the whole enterprise of critical theory is misguided and should be abandoned." See also 0087, 0109.

0102   Krieger, Murray, and Dembo, Larry S., eds.   *Directions for Criticism: Structuralism and Its Alternatives*. Madison: University of Wisconsin Press, 1977. 168 pp.

Contains a long introduction by Murray Krieger and five essays by Edward Said, Hazard Adams, Hayden White, René Girard, and Ralph Freedman. The authors are united primarily by their dissatisfaction with structuralism, albeit for different reasons. White, for example, is interested in poststructuralism theories, and Freedman, in phenomenological tradition.

0103   Lentricchia, Frank. *After the New Criticism*. Chicago: University of Chicago Press, 1980. 384 pp.

Gives an historical account of what has happened "since the American New Critics passed out of favor," offering an evaluative critique of "various forces that have shaped contemporary thought about literature and the criticism of literature." Part I, "A Critical Thematics, 1957-77" contains chapters on Northrop Frye, Existentialism, Phenomenology, Structuralism and Poststructuralism. Part II, "The American Scene: Four Exemplary Careers" discusses Murray Krieger, E. D. Hirsch, Paul de Man, and Harold Bloom.

0104   Lundin, Roger. "Metaphor in the Modern Critical Arena." *Christianity and Literature* 33 (1983): 19-35.

Contrasts contemporary theories of metaphor, particularly those held by deconstructive and philosophical-hermeneutic schools of criticism. Lundin begins with a historical survey of metaphor, from Aristotle, who views it as a displacement of true meaning, to Frank Kermode, who holds that metaphors reveal nothing more than our desire to create a meaning that does not exist. Deconstructive critics and philosophers of hermeneutics both blur the distinction between scientific (literal) language and literary (metaphorical) language, but whereas the former see metaphor as dragging all language down into indeterminacy, the latter see metaphor as raised to the epistemological level of a linguistic reality present in all human knowing. This article is written from a theological viewpoint, with occasional reference to the Bible and to Christian faith.

0105   Margolis, Joseph. "The Threads of Literary Theory." *Poetics Today* 7 (1986): 95-100.

Discusses Geoffrey Hartman, Jacques Derrida, E. D. Hirsch, Hans-Georg Gadamer, Roland Barthes and others from the perspective of a philosophy professor. Margolis says that the recent history of literary theory has exposed the problems inherent in certain lines of argument, but fails to consider that the "underlying conceptual puzzles are basically the same for literature and science."

0106   Martin, Wallace. *Recent Theories of Narrative*. Ithaca, NY: Cornell University Press, 1986. 242 pp.

Provides a broad survey of critical thought after formalism. Martin attempts to show the critical application as well as the theoretical basis for a diverse group of critical methods. His interest lies in both fictional and nonfictional narrative texts.

0107   McKnight, Edgar V. *The Bible and the Reader: An Introduction to Literary Criticism*. Philadelphia: Fortress Press, 1985. 147 pp.

An excellent survey of the historical development of modern literary-critical theories with clear explanations of the principles and methods employed by different approaches. The title of the book is misleading in two ways: (1) although the author is a biblical scholar, the book deals only peripherally with biblical studies; and, (2) a greater emphasis is given to text-centered approaches (formalism, structuralism, and so on) than to reader-oriented approaches.

0108   Michaels, Walter Benn. "Saving the Text: Reference and Belief." *Modern Language Notes* 93 (1978): 771-793.

Says that the "question of belief in poetry and the question of reference in poetry are in fact the same question." Michaels examines this question's "persistence" and explores "some of the possibilities for and consequences of a different answer." Michaels examines the "genuine continuity of Anglo-American criticism over the last half-century." He concludes that "meaning is not independent of belief but bound by it . . . (and therefore) our construction of texts becomes a matter of practical and even political interest."

0109   Mitchell, W. J. T., ed. *Against Theory: Literary Theories and the New Pragmatism.* Chicago: University of Chicago Press, 1985.   146 pp.

Contains essays, by several authors, written in response to Knapp and Michael's essay "Against Theory" (0101). Defenders of theory represent a wide range of theoretical positions, from the interpretive realism and historicism of E. D. Hirsch, Jr., to the textual objectivism of Hershel Parker, to the deconstructionist orientation of Jonathan Crewe. "Pragmatic, antitheoretical" essays are contributed by Knapp and Michaels, Stanley Fish (cf. 0087), and Richard Rorty, whose own stances are far from identical.

0110   Mitchell, W. J. T., ed. *On Narrative.* Chicago: University of Chicago Press, 1981.   304 pp.

Collects papers from a symposium on "Narrative: the Illusion of Sequence," as well as "critical responses" and "rejoinders" added later.   The symposium gathered philosophers, literary critics, psychologists, art historians, anthropologists, novelists, and narratologists to discuss "the ways we tell, understand and use stories." Among those present who contributed articles were Jacques Derrida, Seymour Chatman, Victor Turner, Paul Ricoeur, and Ursula Le Guin. "Afterthoughts on Narrative" are provided by Paul Hernadi, Robert Scholes and Barbara Herrnstein Smith, along with a "Critical Response" by Louis O. Mink.

0111   Natoli, Joseph, ed. *Tracing Literary Theory.* Urbana: University of Illinois Press, 1987.   400 pp.

Presents a collection of essays that Natoli describes in his preface as a "theory carnival." They include: A. C. Goodson's "Structuralism and Critical History in the Movement of Bakhtin"; Eva Corredor's "Sociocritical and Marxist Literary Theory"; Irene Harvey's "The Wellsprings of Deconstruction"; Barrie Ruth Strauss' "Influencing Theory: Speech Acts"; Carolyn J. Allen's "Feminist Criticism and Postmodernism"; and others. The editor's own introductory article, "Tracing a Beginning through Past Theory Voices," is particularly helpful.

0112   Newton-De Molina, David, ed. *On Literary Intention.* Edinburgh: Edinburgh University Press, 1976.   275 pp.

Brings together a number of essays by authors from England and the United States, beginning with W. K. Wimsatt's and Monroe C. Beardsley's "The Intentional Fallacy" (cf. 0222). These writers and others--including E. D. Hirsch, Frank Cioffi, Graham Hough and Alastair Fowler--focus on "the familiar triangle of (i) author, (ii) work, and (iii) reader." The articles consider various perspectives, from New Criticism to reader orientation.

0113   Ray, William. *Literary Meaning: From Phenomenology to Deconstruction.* Oxford: Basil Blackwell, 1984.   300 pp.

Presents four ways of reading, taking into consideration the voices that Ray considers most important to each. These methods include phenomenology; psychoanalytic and hermeneutic theories; structuralism and semiotics; and "Dialectical Criticism, including models conceived by Stanley Fish, Roland Barthes, and Paul de Man." Ray attempts to provide an "impartial paraphrase" of each "theory in question" before making his own comments upon it.

0114   Russell, D. A. *Criticism in Antiquity*. Berkeley and Los Angeles: University of California Press, 1981. 200 pp.

Includes both Greek and Roman critical approaches to literature. In the prologue, Russell treats the reasons for literary criticism in the classical world and something of the nature of its practice, in regard to both prose and poetry. Russell includes three chapters on the historical development of narrative, from its beginnings to the Roman Empire, and two chapters on "The Poet and His Inspiration" and "The Poet as Teacher." He then discusses mimesis, rhetoric, theories of style, classification of literature, and literary history.

0115   Russell, D. A., and Winterbottom, M., eds. *Ancient Literary Criticism: The Principal Texts in New Translations*. Oxford: Clarendon Press, 1972. 607 pp.

Contains the translated texts of numerous ancient literary critics like Plato, Aristotle, Horace, Tacitus and others. It also provides excellent introductions to each critic and indexes to terms in Greek and Latin, to names, and to general topics. An extremely useful reference book.

0116   Salusinszky, Imre. *Criticism in Society: Interviews with Jacques Derrida, Northrop Frye, Harold Bloom, Geoffrey Hartman, Frank Kermode, Edward Said, Barbara Johnson, Frank Lentricchia, and J. Hillis Miller*. New York: Methuen and Co., 1987. 244 pp.

Each of these critics is interviewed on the theme of Stevens' poem, "Not Ideas About the Thing but the Thing Itself." Also, the position of each critic is summarized in order to make the interviews more accessible. The interviews are personal as well as scholarly, and the book is both inviting and revelatory with regard to the diversity of contemporary critical positions.

0117   Schmidt, Siegfried J. "Selected Bibliography on Interpretation (1970-1982)." *Poetics* 12 (1983): 277-292.

This bibliography is thorough, though it is not annotated. It includes books and articles in English, German and French.

0118   Selden, Raman. *A Reader's Guide to Contemporary Literary Theory*. Lexington: University Press of Kentucky, 1985. 160 pp.

Sheds light upon the most important movements from formalism to reader-response criticism. It provides helpful guideposts for the beginning literary-critical thinker. Selden's presentations are clear, brief and accurate.

0119   Singleton, Charles S., ed. *Interpretation: Theory and Practice*. Baltimore: Johns Hopkins University Press, 1969. 247 pp.

A collection of essays from a seminar on hermeneutics (interpretation theory) and exegesis (interpretation practice) in three fields--history, art, literature. Essays included in the latter category are by Paul de Man and Murray Krieger. De Man's article is "The Rhetoric of Temporality, Allegory and Symbol, Irony"; Krieger's is "Mediation, Language, and Vision in the Reading of Literature."

0120   Sontag, Susan. *Against Interpretation and Other Essays*. New York: Noonday Books, 1966. 304 pp.

Contains articles that Sontag wrote over four years. She calls these pieces "not criticism at all, strictly speaking, but case studies for an aesthetic." The title essay concludes, "In place of a hermeneutics we need an erotics of art." She considers many art forms, from serious fiction to science fiction movies, to painting and graphic arts. See also 0472.

0121   Spanos, William V.; Bové, Paul; and O'Hara, Daniel, eds. *The Question of Textuality: Strategies of Reading in Contemporary American Criticism*. Bloomington: Indiana University Press, 1982. 384 pp.

Contains essays on such topics as literary criticism and politics, deconstruction, structuralism and grammatology, metaphor, stylistics, poetics, and semiology. The essays derive from the *boundary 2* "Symposium on the Problems of Reading in Contemporary American Criticism" and they are presented in pairs, the second responding to the first, except in the case of "An Exchange on Deconstruction and History" between Eugenio Donato and Edward W. Said.

0122   Valdes, Mario J., and Miller, Owen J., eds. *Interpretation of Narrative*. Toronto: University of Toronto Press, 1978. 216 pp.

Contains papers read at an international colloqium in 1976. There are three major sections: (1) "Verification of Formalist Analysis," including work by Christie V. McDonald, Michael Riffaterre and others; (2) "Verification of Hermeneutic Criticism," with essays by Cyrus Hamlin, Félix Martínez Bonati, Wolfgang Iser, and Eugene Vance; and (3) "Metacriticism," with papers by Hans Robert Jauss, J. Hillis Miller, and Paul Hernadi. Uri Margolin provides a conclusion, and O. J. Miller, an Epilogue. The first section provides a "demonstration of expert readers concerned with their methodology and its implicit claims." The second brings "to the discussion a fundamental agreement and acceptance of the hermeneutic method and reception theory." In the third section, Jauss brings "the philosophical question of hermeneutics into view," Miller makes "us question the questioners"; and Hernadi provides "a map of the intellectual landscape covered."

0123   Wellek, René. *Concepts of Criticism*. Ed. by Stephen G. Nichols, Jr. New Haven, CT: Yale University Press, 1963. 403 pp.

Originally published in 1942, this volume contains several articles concerned with the methods of studying literary works, with differentiating literary theory, criticism, and history from one another, and with showing how these three areas of study work together for viable critical understanding of literary periods. Finally, Wellek studies trends then current in literary-critical theory and practice.

0124   Wellek, René. *A History of Modern Criticism, 1750-1950. Vol. 5, English Criticism, 1900-1950. Vol. 6, American Criticism, 1900-1950*. New Haven, CT: Yale University Press, 1986. 345 pp.

These two volumes present the early twentieth-century critics in an impressive manner. Especially significant is Wellek's erudite discussion of T. S. Elliot's thought. Wellek's sense of history plays an important part in the writing of these two volumes, which allow the reader a comprehensive view of the English and American formalist critics.

0125   Wimsatt, William, Jr., and Brooks, Cleanth. *Literary Criticism: A Short History*. 2 Vols. Chicago: University of Chicago Press, 1957, Midway reprint, 1983. 755 pp.

A dated study, but it does give the reader insight into the thought of Wimsatt and Brooks, two major New Critics. The wide span of literary criticism from the ancient Greeks to twentieth-century Americans is contained in the volume, which is graciously written and clearly presented.

TEXT-ORIENTED APPROACHES: NEW CRITICISM, FORMALISM, NARRATOLOGY, ETC.

See also 0001, 0014, 0084, 0088, 0103, 0107, 0110, 0112, 0122-0125, 0258, 0260, 0264, 0274, 0279, 0288, 0305, 0407, 0410, 0423, 0482, 0488, 0513, 0539, 0548, 0552, 0570, 0607, 0612, 0624, 0637, 0650, 0679, 0785, 0812, 0819, 0827, 0830, 0881, 0989, 1031, 1065, 1073, 1106, 1147-1152, 1163-1165, 1178-1179, 1126-1128, 1250, 1265-1267, 1314, 1334, 1450-1354, 1372, 1387, 1573, 1594, 1635-1636, 1640, 1666.

0126   Abrams, M. H. "How to do Things with Texts." *Partisan Review* 46 (1979): 566-588.

Rails against the new "Age of Reading" and the "systematic dehumanizing of all aspects of the traditional view about how a work of literature comes into being, what it is, how it is read, and what it means." Abrams critiques the work of Jacques Derrida, Stanley Fish and Harold Bloom in this article, saying that "Derrida is able to deconstruct any text into a suspension of numberless undecidable significations,

Fish can make it the occasion for a creative adventure in false surmises, and Bloom can read it as a perverse distortion of any chosen precursor-text." The result for Abrams is that "we lose . . . access to the inexhaustible variety of literature as determinably meaningful texts."

0127   Amante, David J. "Theory of Ironic Speech Acts." *Poetics Today* 2 (1981): 77-96.

Follows Searle's procedure in analysis of the illocutionary act (0069) to create a series of constitutive and prescriptive rules governing "ironic speech acts." Amante begins with short examples of sarcasm and verbal irony, and then describes the ironic speech act as necessarily having an ironist (or eiron), an observer or observers, and a target.

0128   Auerbach, Erich. *Mimesis*: *The Representation of Reality in Western Literature*. Trans. by Willard Trask. Garden City, NY: Doubleday and Co., 1957. 563 pp.

A profound work of highly original criticism. Auerbach says that literature evolves increasingly toward mimetic, realistic forms of representation. His survey goes from the *Odyssey* and the Bible through Virginia Woolf and Marcel Proust. In the first two chapters, he compares the sacrifice of Isaac to Homeric epic, and Mark's story of Peter's denial of Jesus to Petronius' *Satyricon*. This close textual analysis takes into account philology and politics as well as the sweep of history. Today, this book is thought to have marked a milestone in the development of literary approaches to the Bible. Auerbach's analysis of the "depictions of reality" presented in biblical stories convinced many biblical scholars that these stories can be studied as literature without prejudging whether those depictions are historically correct. See also 0635, 0696, 0839, 1628, 1679.

0129   Bagwell, J. Timothy. *American Formalism and the Problem of Interpretation*. Houston: Rice University Press, 1986. 160 pp.

Proposes a semantic understanding of the notion of "the intentional fallacy" (cf. 0222) and defends formalism. Chapter One attempts to show that the concept of the intentional fallacy is tied up with a concept of literary discourse as distinct from nonliterary discourse. Chapter Two deals with "Validity in Authority: E. D. Hirsch," and Chapter Three with "Stanley Fish: the Reader as Author." Chapter Four attempts "to vindicate the doctrine of the intentional fallacy by demonstrating how the notion of literary discourse can be grounded philosophically in terms of the concept of intentionality itself."

0130   Bal, Mieke. *Femmes imaginaires: L'ancien Testament au risque d'une narratologie critique*. Montreal: HMH, 1985. 281 pp.

A noted narratologist (0133) attempts to revise narrative theory in light of feminist ideology. The theory is illustrated through interpretations of several biblical narratives involving women. A revised version of this book, published in English, reversed the accents--theoretical sections were abridged and exegetical interpretations expanded (0612).

0131   Bal, Mieke. "The Laughing Mice, or: On Focalization." *Poetics Today* 2 (1981): 202-210.

Responds to criticism of Bal's approach to narratology (0133). Bal sees problems that cause misunderstanding about the book's theory: "embedding versus succession, different types of focalization, the communicative and the linguistic status of focalization, free indirect discourse, the relation between pragmatics, and the notion of implied author." Bal discusses "the difference between concepts and entities" in relation with these problems.

0132   Bal, Mieke. "The Narrating and the Focalizing: A Theory of the Agents of Narrative." Trans. by Jane E. Lewin. *Style* 17 (1983): 234-269.

Undertakes an analysis of Gérard Genette's theory of narratology. Bal analyzes and evaluates the basic principles of the theory and suggests modifications where she sees imperfections. Bal discusses "Narratological Figures" and "The Narrating and the Focalizing," using Colette's *La Chatte* as example.

0133   Bal, Mieke. *Narratology: Introduction to the Theory of Narrative*. Trans. by Christine von Boheemen. Toronto: University of Toronto Press, 1985. 176 pp.

Offers "an introduction to all the major elements that make up a narrative and provides a comprehensive theory of narrative texts." The book is divided into three sections: (1) "Fabula: Elements," which includes Events, Actors, Time, and Location; (2) "Story: Aspects," which includes Sequential Ordering, Rhythm, Frequency, From Actors to Characters, From Place to Space, and Focalization; and (3) "Text: Words," which includes The Narrator, Non-Narrative Comments, Description, and Levels of Narration. See also 0519.

0134   Bal, Mieke. "Notes on Narrative Embedding." *Poetics Today* 2,2 (1981): 41-60.

Considers the narratological problem of "embedding," which is Bal's term for what Gérard Genette calls "metadiscourse" in his *Figures* (0247). The term refers to the phenomenon of "discourse within discourse," such as occurs when a narrator or character quotes someone else. Bal is particularly interested in the complexities with regard to point of view that result from this common phenomenon. She presents a typology of different sorts of embedding.

0135   Bal, Mieke. *On Storytelling*. Foundations and Facets--Literary Facets. Sonoma, CA: Polebridge Press, 1991. 352 pp.

A collection of essays annotated to illustrate Bal's approach to storytelling. Part I outlines her method, Part II contains her theory of narrative, and Part III consists of commentary on a wide variety of texts, including biblical ones. Bal's narratology draws heavily on structuralism, though she is also influenced by poststructuralist thought.

0136   Bal, Mieke. "Tell-Tale Theories." *Poetics Today* 7 (1986): 555-564.

Reviews Stanzel's *A Theory of Narrative* (0297), Genette's *Narrative Discourse* (0249) and Brooks' *Reading for the Plot* (0147), seeing them as "examples of a wider-ranging trend." Stanzel is pre-structuralist, Genette is structuralist, and Brooks "claims to go beyond structuralism." Brooks enriches "the views of narrative in a way neither prestructuralist nor structuralist narratology has been able to do . . . but he has not been able to delimit the semantic range of his concepts."

0137   Booth, Wayne C. "Distance and Point-of-View: An Essay in Classification." *Essays in Criticism* 11 (1961): 60-79.

Attempts "a richer tabulation of the forms the author's voice can take." Booth describes both "dramatised" and "undramatised" narrators and points out that there are varying distances among narrators, authors, readers, and characters. He makes his famous distinction between *reliable* and *unreliable* narrators in this essay. The article is included in 0213.

0138   Booth, Wayne C. "'Preserving the Exemplar': Or How Not to Dig Our Own Graves." *Critical Inquiry* 3 (1977): 407-424.

Observes that poems and other texts really exist in many senses, and asks whether or not we are right to rule out at least some readings. Booth believes that we are. The essay was originally presented as one of four considering the topic, "The Limits of Pluralism." Booth identifies a number of "monisms" that pluralists tend to accept, but says that "what we are promised by the new pluralists is an escape from the dead hand of the past--a new vitality." See also 0428, 0459.

0139   Booth, Wayne C. *The Rhetoric of Fiction*. 2nd ed. Chicago: University of Chicago Press, 1983. 455 pp.

A classic study of text-centered criticism, which, in the 1960s and 1970s was considered essential for any student of literature. The work is updated, furthermore, by an extensive afterword written twenty-one years after publication of the first edition. Booth's explorations begin with reading specific texts rather than with abstract philosophical principles. Many of his ideas, including his typologies of narrators (reliable, omniscient, and so on) and his concept of an implied author and implied reader, continue to be extremely influential in narrative criticism, especially as currently practiced in biblical studies.

0140   Booth, Wayne C. *A Rhetoric of Irony*. Chicago: University of Chicago Press, 1975. 292 pp.

A thorough look at the subject of irony. Booth is most concerned with what he identifies as "stable irony," which must be discovered by the reader. He lists four steps through which the reader is expected to recognize what is ironic: (1) rejection of the literal meaning in response to internal or external clues; (2) trial of alternative explanations; (3) evaluation of these in terms of what is believed about the author; and (4) decision based on assumed intentions of the author. In short, irony is treated as a rhetorical device, one that can be not only recognized but also evaluated. See also 0317. For reviews and application, see 0214, 1377, 1461.

0141 Brémond, Claude. *Logique du récit*. Paris: Seuill, 1970. 350 pp.

Reworks the formalist system of Propp (0202) to propose that the fundamental narrative unit is not function, but sequence. Any completed narrative, however long or complex, can be represented as an interweaving of sequences. These sequences are triadic: (1) a situation opens a possibility; (2) the possibility is actualized or nonactualized; (3) if actualized, the possibility ends in success or failure. The book also contains critiques of A. J. Greimas and Tzvetan Todorov. See also 0260.

0142 Brémond, Claude. "Morphology of the French Folktale." *Semiotica* 2 (1970): 247-276.

Furthers the type of research begun by Propp (0202) to develop a model that analyzes narrative in terms of decisions made at key points in the story. Every time a potential objective is presented, either a procedure is developed to actualize that potential or an inertia develops that hinders such actualization. If the choice is toward actualization, the attempt leads to either success or failure.

0143 Brémond, Claude. "The Narrative Message." *Semeia* 10 (1978): 5-55.

An English translation of a 1964 French article offering a review and critique of Propp's *Morphology of the Folktale* (0202). Bremond summarizes Propp's findings, but questions whether a simple sequential listing of functions is adequate. He proposes that the connections between functions are of different kinds--some functions presuppose others necessarily while others are connected only by varying degrees of probability. The true threads of narrative plot are comprised of units or "probability groupings" larger than the functions. The translation of this article for *Semeia*, a journal of biblical studies, is significant: the article has nothing to do with biblical literature *per se*, but its insights on narrative syntax are considered relevant to formalist and structuralist Bible scholars.

0144 Brooks, Cleanth. "The Formalist Critics." *Kenyon Review* 13 (1951): 72-81.

Begins with a formalist manifesto, which Brooks calls "some articles of faith." He declares that "the formalist critic knows as well as anyone that literary works are merely potential until they are read--that is, that they are recreated in the minds of actual readers, who vary enormously in their capabilities, their interests, their prejudices, and their ideas. But the formalist critic is concerned primarily with the work itself."

0145   Brooks, Cleanth. "Irony and 'Ironic' Poetry." *College English* 9 (1948): 231-237.

Defends his use of the term "irony" (cf. 0146). Brooks insists upon the relation of parts to one another within a work of literature. Context renders a line ironic; otherwise, writing may be "merely callow, glib, and sentimental."

0146   Brooks, Cleanth. "Irony as a Principle of Structure." In *Literary Opinion in America*, ed. by Morton D. Zabel, 729-744. Rev. ed. New York: Harper and Bros., 1951.

Offers an understanding of irony informed by New Criticism's emphasis on the internal coherence of texts. Statements may be characterized as "ironical" when they are warped by the context of the text in which they are found. But all ironies are not obvious--any statement made in a poem carries ironic potential in that all such statements are modified by their context. Brooks relates irony to metaphor and to indirection.

0147   Brooks, Peter. *Reading for the Plot: Design and Intention in Narrative*. New York: Vintage Books, 1985.   364 pp.

Brooks says that "this is a book about plots and plotting, about how stories come to be ordered in significant form, and also about our desire and need for such orderings." Brooks draws on the insights of narratology and structuralism, as well as on psychoanalytical theory, in order to examine "the text itself as a system of internal energies and tensions." A number of nineteenth and twentieth-century novels are considered. See also 0136.

0148   Brown, Edward K. *Rhythm in the Novel*. The Alexander Lectures, 1949-50. Toronto: University of Toronto Press, 1950. 118 pp.

A collection of essays on the use of repetition in literature. The first discusses combinations of words, phrases, sequences of incident, and groupings of character. The second deals with a more complex combination: "the growth of a symbol as it accretes meaning from a succession of contexts."   The third shows themes "interweaving, and in doing so repeating and varying in an interactive relationship." Finally, all these kinds of repetition are illustrated with reference to E. M. Forster's *A Passage to India*. The title of Brown's book derives from Forster's comment that rhythm is "repetition with variation."

0149   Chambers, Ross. "Commentary in Literary Texts." *Critical Inquiry* 5 (1978): 323-337.

Says that the two principal functions of commentary within texts are to invite the reader to interpret the text and/or to guide the reader in interpreting the text. Chambers concludes by describing the relationship of extra-textual "interpretation" to intra-textual "commentary."

0150   Chatman, Seymour. *Story and Discourse: Narrative Structure in Fiction and Film*. Ithaca, NY: Cornell University Press, 1978. 277 pp.

A comprehensive approach to the general theory of narrative that synthesizes the work of such critics as Roland Barthes, Wayne Booth, Gérard Genette, and Tzvetan Todorov.   Chatman treats "story" (the "what" of narrative) in terms of events, characters, and settings and "discourse" (the "how" of narrative) in terms of different types and styles of narration. This book has become a standard reference for recent studies of the Gospels and Acts. See also 0183, 0207.

0151   Cohn, Dorrit. *Transparent Minds: Narrative Modes for Presenting Consciousness in Fiction*. Princeton, NJ: Princeton University Press, 1978. 331 pp.

Takes up "Consciousness in Third-Person Context" and "Consciousness in First-Person Texts." Cohn says that consciousness in third-person narrations fits into one of these types: (1) psycho-narration: the narrator's discourse about a character's consciousness; (2) quoted monologue: a character's mental discourse; or (3) narrated monologue: a character's mental discourse in the guise of the narrator's discourse." Cohn discusses first-person narrative in chapters on "Retrospective Techniques"; "From Narration to Monologue"; and "Autonomous Monologue."

0152   Culler, Jonathan. "Defining Narrative Units." In *Style and Structure in Literature: Essays in the New Stylistics*, ed. by Roger Fowler, 123-142. Ithaca, NY: Cornell University Press, 1975.

A classic article that helps to define the problems involved in defining plot structure. Culler insists that whatever model is used should provide descriptions of particular stories that correspond with our intuitive sense of their plots. He finds fault with theories of Claude Lévi-Strauss, A. J. Greimas, Tzvetan Todorov, and Roland Barthes, to name a few, but ultimately must be content with raising more questions than he answers. A successful theory, he decides, will have to offer an explanation for the hierarchical structuring through which we move from the text itself to plot summaries.

0153   Culler, Jonathan. "Problems in the Theory of Fiction." *Diacritics* 14,1 (1984): 2-11.

Reviews Pratt's *Towards a Speech Act Theory of Literary Discourse* (0066) and Lanser's *The Narrative Act* (0177). Culler points out two problems in the theory of fiction: "the role of the notion of fiction" and "the problem of the convergence of narrative studies and speech act theory, where the new emphasis on fictionality paradoxically urges us to treat narrators as if they were real people."

0154   Davis, Walter A. *The Act of Interpretation: A Critique of Literary Reason*. Chicago: University of Chicago Press, 1978. 194 pp.

Attempts to lay out a scientific method for adjudicating multiple interpretations of a text. Following R. S. Crane, Davis suggests that the best interpretation is not the one easiest to apply or the one most congenial to our intentions, but the one most difficult to eliminate. The work is indebted to Robert Marsh and Wayne Booth. It is written in conscious dialogue with fundamental questions of philosophy, and it contains a sustained interpretation of Faulkner's "The Bear."

0155   Dipple, Elizabeth. *Plot*. The Critical Idiom, 12. London: Methuen and Co., 1970. 78 pp.

Traces two contrary ways of understanding plot. First, Dipple describes the standard definition of plot as "a hackneyed mechanical term," a definition that she views as the result of progressive reduction through neo-classicism. Then, she examines the ways in which the idea of plot has been expanded in modern criticism through attention to *poiesis* (the process through which meaning is produced) and through the development of time theories (e.g., Martin Heidegger; Frank Kermode). The happy result is a recapturing of the Aristotelian concept of plot as "action, which is the soul of fiction."

0156   Dolezel, Lubomír. "The Typology of the Narrator: Point of View in Fiction." In *To Honor Roman Jakobson: Essays on the Occasion of His 70th Birthday, 11 October 1966*, 2 vols., 1:541-552. The Hague: Mouton Publishers, 1967.

Begins with a summary of "axioms of the structural theory of the literary works of art." Crossing from structuralism to narratology, Dolezel then opposes texts with speakers to texts without speakers, and finally presents three types of narration: "(1) objective narration, (2) derived forms of third-person narration, (3) forms of first-person narration."

0157   Dyson, Anthony E. *The Crazy Fabric: Essays in Irony*. New York: St. Martin's Press, 1965. 233 pp.

Explores the techniques of irony used by a number of fiction writers, most of them English, from the eighteenth to the twentieth centuries. Dyson's focus is on the individual's approaches to the techniques of wit and satire rather than on abstract theory.

0158   Egan, Kieran. "What is a Plot?" *New Literary History* 9 (1978): 455-473.

Gives a number of conflicting definitions of plot, and calls for a more precise use of the term. Egan believes that "poetics may well gain some rigor by borrowing and suitably transforming some of the definitions, distinctions, and relations that have enabled linguistics to make progress in recent decades." The definition he settles on is this: "a plot is a set of rules that determines and sequences events to cause a determinative affective response."

0159   Forster, E. M. *Aspects of the Novel*. New York: Harcourt Brace Jovanovich, 1927. 176 pp.

This classic little book contains a series of lectures in which the author, also a brilliant novelist, describes the parts of a work of fiction, making important differentiations between story and plot, flat characters and round ones, and various points-of-view.

Forster also asks how a book's merit should be evaluated, admitting that we finally judge by our own affection for it.

0160   Fowler, Alastair. "The Selection of Literary Constructs." *New Literary History* 7 (1975): 39-55.

Says that literary history as a discipline has been devalued, and that formalism and structuralism are forces against it, so that "the old positivistic literary history is no longer possible." Structuralists have been tempted to eliminate relativism and elitism at a stroke, by the desperate expedient of collapsing literature into language." Fowler concludes that "forms in relation to men and their works are the literary historian's proper study."

0161   Fowler, Roger, ed. *Style and Structure in Literature: Essays in the New Stylistics.* Ithaca, NY: Cornell University Press, 1975. 262 pp.

This collection of essays, which proclaims a "new stylistics," considers a broad range of poetry, and serious and popular fiction. The introductory chapter is especially useful because it defines and discusses stylistics itself.   Stylistics resembles structuralism in some respects but is attentive to the broader concept of style rather than limiting its concern to structure.   Still, the new stylistics is flexible and theoretically catholic, drawing on structuralism, formalism, and linguistics. The book contains an important article by Culler, "Defining Narrative Units" (0152).

0162   Freedman, William. "The Literary Motif: A Definition and Evaluation." *Novel* 4 (1971): 123-131.

Offers a description of what a literary motif is and how it functions. Freedman posits five factors to be considered in identification and evaluation of a literary motif: (1) frequency of recurrence; (2) avoidability or unlikeliness of appearance; (3) significance of contexts in which it occurs; (4) degree to which instances in which it occurs fit together; (5) appropriateness of the motif to what it symbolizes.

0163   Friedman, Alan. *The Turn of the Novel.* New York: Oxford University Press, 1966. 212 pp.

This book attempts to differentiate modern "open" novels from older "closed" ones, showing that modern fiction contains more moral ambiguity. Friedman coins the phrases "stream of conscience," and "flux of experience" to describe the nature of modern fiction. Authors considered include Hardy, Conrad, Forster, Lawrence and Joyce.

0164   Friedman, Norman. "Point of View in Fiction: The Development of a Critical Concept." *Proceedings of the Modern Language Association* 70 (1955): 1160-1184.

Traces the development in critical consciousness of the tension between *showing* and *telling* in literature.   Friedman then discusses "Editorial Omniscience"; "Neutral Omniscience"; "'I' as Witness"; "'I' as Protagonist"; "Multiple Selective Omniscience";

"Selective Omniscience"; "The Dramatic Mode"; and "The Canon." The author's choice of point-of-view is critical, he says, having everything to do with rendering the "story-illusion," which constitutes artistic truth in fiction. The article is included in 0213. See also 1030.

0165   Garvey, James. "Characterization in Narrative." *Poetics* 7 (1978): 63-78.

Garvey discusses the attributes of participants in a story, both "structural" and "non-structural." The non-structural attributes are described through "attributive propositions," which in turn arise through "norms" that relate textual details to narrative structure. He defines and classifies "attributes" and uses diagrams and tables to present his argument.

0166   Glicksberg, Charles S. *The Ironic Vision in Modern Literature*. The Hague: Martinus Nijhoff, 1969. 268 pp.

A careful analysis and history of the paradoxical, tragic, and nihilistic aspects of irony. With regard to the latter, Glicksberg says that nihilistic irony is "that fusion of laughter and pity fueled by a vision of mankind lost in a world without meaning." This is a modern concept. In Sophocles' *Oedipus Rex*, people may live in a meaningless world but nihilism is transcended by the notion that the gods, good or bad, know what they are doing and must be obeyed. Modern irony mediates between comedy and tragedy without ever really resolving them. See also 0175.

0167   Goodman, Paul. *The Structure of Literature*. Chicago: University of Chicago Press, 1954. 281 pp.

Works on an Aristotelian basis, understanding narrative as consisting of events which lead to other events based on "probability." Goodman says that when a drama begins, "anything is possible; in the middle things become probable; in the ending everything is necessary."

0168   Harris, Wendell V. "Mapping Fiction's 'Forest of Symbols.'" In *University of Colorado Studies*, 133-146. Series in Language and Literature, 9. Boulder: University of Colorado Press, 1963.

Proposes "a tentative scheme of classification that will reflect the variety of modes of symbolism . . . arising out of the fictional representation of the phenomenal world." Harris defines imagery, metaphor, symbol, and myth, and he discusses the functions of each.

0169   Hartman, Geoffrey H. *The Fate of Reading and Other Essays*. Chicago: University of Chicago Press, 1975. 352 pp.

Has four sections that comprise essays written by Hartman since 1970. The book aims "to broaden literary interpretation without leaving literature behind" (and) "to look inward toward the discipline of literary study itself." In one essay, Hartman comments on "the dangerous liaison between literary studies and psychoanalysis," and in another upon the "equally dangerous liaison between rhetorical studies and literature." The third section explores changes in conventions or habits of reading. The final section contains "four position papers."

0170   Harvey, W. J. *Character and the Novel*. Ithaca, NY: Cornell University Press, 1965. 222 pp.

A general study of the novel that focuses on ways in which art represents reality. Harvey's main contribution lies in his study of characterization, specifically of the facets of literature that make characters seem real or true to life. He isolates four constitutive categories (time, identity, freedom, and causality) and discusses the concept of character with regard to each.

0171   Hochman, Baruch. *Character in Literature*. Ithaca, NY: Cornell University Press, 1985. 204 pp.

This psychological study of literary characters uses Freud's concepts of the dichotomy between the conscious mind and the unconscious. Hochman gives eight pairs of opposed categories that disclose information about characters, like stylization and naturalism, and literalness and symbolism. He applies his theories to a number of specific characters from American, Continental, and British fiction.

0172   Hutchens, Eleanor N. "The Identification of Irony." *ELH* 27 (1960): 352-363.

Finds a need to define "irony" more closely, since at the time she wrote this article the term was being used in so many ways as to be almost meaningless. She takes the *Oxford English Dictionary*'s definitions, the first and third of which seem to follow the rhetorical and dialectic devices known as irony from early Greek comedy through Socrates down to modern times. Hutchens says that in 1833 Bishop Cannop Thirlwall presented a definition of "practical irony," which connects the other two. Finally, irony is something which "makes a sport of human existence."

0173   James, Henry. *The Art of the Novel: Critical Prefaces*. Ed. by R. P. Blackmur. New York: Charles Scribner's Sons, 1962. 348 pp.

A collection of James' own critical prefaces to his novels, with an introduction by Blackmur. James was one of the greatest and most influential novelists of the twentieth century, and he had a great passion for psychological realism in his fiction. His prefaces reflected self-consciously on the literary process, demonstrating an interest in the technical aspects of the art of fiction.

0174   Kermode, Frank. *The Sense of an Ending: Studies in the Theory of Fiction*. New York: Oxford University Press, 1967. 187 pp.

This study was originally a group of lectures given in 1965, using apocalyptic fictions as a focus for deriving a general theory of fiction. In the first two chapters, "The End" and "Fictions," Kermode speaks of apocalyptic thinking, and of how our fictions change in relation to it. He speaks of Renaissance innovations, especially Shakespeare's and Spenser's, in "World Without End or Beginning." Then, he moves on to a discussion of modern literature, shaping his analysis with the theories he spelled out in the initial chapters. This book is useful for anyone who has interest in the apocalyptic thinking of our own time, as well as in the relationship of time to fiction. See also 0189.

0175   Knox, Norman. "On the Classification of Ironies." *Modern Philology* 70 (1972): 53-62.

Reviews Muecke's *The Compass of Irony* (0185) and Glicksberg's *The Ironic Vision in Modern Literature* (0166). Knox concludes that there are problems with both books, in that both limit irony too much.

0176   Krieger, Murray. *A Window to Criticism: Shakespeare's Sonnets and Modern Poetics*. Princeton, NJ: Princeton University Press, 1964. 244 pp.

Uses a parable of a house without mirrors and windows as a basis for showing how a poem mirrors reality but also enriches the reader's experience of the world through its ability to enhance the reader's vision. Krieger calls a poem "both mirror and window," and reads Shakespeare's sonnets accordingly. The parable has been taken up by biblical scholars and is cited repeatedly to indicate that biblical texts may function poetically (as mirrors) as well as referentially (as windows).

0177   Lanser, Susan Sniader. *The Narrative Act: Point of View in Prose Fiction*. Princeton, NJ: Princeton University Press, 1981. 303 pp.

Presents a theory of point of view based upon "a theory of the text, and a concrete poetics of narrative voice." Lanser begins by emphasizing the pivotal role of point of view in narrative and then goes on to discuss the subject with reference to various textual choices: historical author, extra-fictional voice, public narrator, private narrator, focalizer, and character. In Chapter Four, she discusses the significance of "Status, Contact, and Stance," and in Chapter Five she integrates speech act theory with a model for analyzing fictional characters, thus offering one mechanism for recovering the narrator's system of values and attitudes from the text. Finally, she applies her poetics to two short stories. See also 0153, 1204.

0178   Leitch, Thomas M. *What Stories Are: Narrative Theory and Interpretation*. University Park: Pennsylvania State University Press, 1986. 232 pp.

Consists of two sections: "Narrative Ontology" and "Narrative Tropes." Leitch begins by defining narrative, extensively in the second chapter, entitled "Narrative as a Display Mode." Part II contains chapters on "The Narrative World"; "Plot"; "Character"; "Narrative Fiction and Nonfiction"; and "Toward Narrative Aesthetics." Biblical scholars might find the final chapter in Part I, "The Polytropic Principle," particularly interesting, since it deals with an ancient text, the *Odyssey*.

0179 Liddell, Robert. *Robert Liddell on the Novel*. Introduction by Wayne C. Booth. Chicago: University of Chicago Press, 1969.

Combines two previously published works, *A Treatise on the Novel* (1947) and *Some Principles of Fiction* (1953). These two short books help the reader to understand the art of story-telling, and to make judgments about a novel's quality. *A Treatise on the Novel* contains sections relating to critical theory and practice; the range of the novelist; the values of the novelist, plot-making, character-making, and background in fiction. *Some Principles of Fiction* deals with other aspects of the novel, including subject-matter in fiction, summary, and dialogue. A section on "Terms and Topics" may be especially helpful.

0180 Lubbock, Percy. *The Craft of Fiction*. New York: Viking Press, 1957. 264 pp.

A reprint of the classic 1921 study of Henry James' novels and of the realistic tradition in fiction, complete with a new preface by Lubbock and a forword by Mark Schorer. Though dated, the work still bears consideration.

0181 Michaels, Walter Benn. "Against Formalism: The Autonomous Text in Legal and Literary Interpretation." *Poetics Today* 1 (1980): 23-34.

Argues against a particular "account of meaning" connected to formalist criticism. Demanding that study of a piece of literature "be confined to the *text itself*" has a counterpart in the objectivity of contract law. Michaels argues that the phrase "the text itself" is oxymoronic and that therefore formalism is impossible and no one has ever been a formalist.

0182 Miller, D. A. *Narrative and its Discontents: Problems of Closure in the Traditional Novel*. Princeton, NJ: Princeton University Press, 1981. 300 pp.

One of two major narratological studies on narrative endings, the other being that of Torgovnick (0217). Though published the same year (by the same publisher), Miller's work reaches quite different conclusions. His thesis is that novels may build toward closure, but they "are never fully or finally governed by it." Miller finds that narrative endings often leave ambiguities and dangling threads. The attempt for critics to find total coherence between a narrative's endings and the elements preceding it produces forced and potentially erroneous readings.

0183 Mosher, Harold F. "A New Synthesis of Narratology." *Poetics Today* 1 (1980): 171-186.

Reviews Chatman's *Story and Discourse* (0150). Mosher finds its description of narrative to be helpful, and disagrees only with Chatman's definition of mediation.

0184   Muecke, Douglas C. "The Communication of Verbal Irony." *Journal of Literary Semantics* 2 (1973): 35-42.

Considers intentional irony and addresses four questions: (1) How does an ironist communicate the real meaning? (2) On what basis do we infer that what we are reading or hearing is ironical? (3) What has gone wrong when we assume that an ironical message is not ironical? (4) What has gone wrong when we infer that a non-ironical message is ironical?

0185   Muecke, Douglas C. *The Compass of Irony*. London: Methuen and Co., 1969. 276 pp.

Attempts to classify ironies systematically in order to be able more easily to ascertain what sort of irony is operative in particular literary situations. He locates four "modes" of irony: Impersonal, Self-disparaging, Ingénu, and Dramatized. He goes on to classify ironic situations. His approach is both historical and ethical. See also 0175, 1377, 1461.

0186   Muecke, Douglas C. *Irony*. The Critical Idiom, 13. London: Methuen and Co., 1970. 92 pp. Also published as *Irony and the Ironic*. New York: Methuen and Co., 1982. 110 pp.

Shows how concepts of irony have developed and changed historically, from Aristotle through the nineteenth century. Muecke sees irony as contrasting appearance and reality, such that the ironist pretends to be unaware of it, while the victim is truly unaware. He details irony's various elements, including "innocence," the "contrast of reality and appearance," the "comic element," the "element of detachment," and the "aesthetic element." He distinguishes between verbal and situational irony. The final chapter, "On Seeing Things as Ironic," considers general irony and romantic irony. See also 1377, 1461.

0187   Mukarovsky, Jan. *Aesthetic Function, Norm, and Value as Social Facts*. Trans. by Mark E. Suino. Ann Arbor: University of Michigan Press, 1970. 102 pp.

Sees art as synonymous with "dominance of the aesthetic function." Mukarovsky's thought was foundational for the famous ideas of Wellek and Warren as set out in *Theory of Literature* (0220). His position is close to that of the Russian formalists. He differentiates "aesthetic function, which is a dynamic concept" from "aesthetic norm . . . (which) is constantly striving for stability and universal validity."

0188   Oinas, Felix J., ed. *Heroic Epic and Saga: An Introduction to the World's Great Folk Epics*. Bloomington: Indiana University Press, 1978. 373 pp.

A collection of essays on heroic literature, both verse and prose. The literature explored includes Homeric, Mesopotamian, Sanskrit, Turkish and Iranian epics; Insular and Continental epics and sagas; and the African epic. A wide variety of heroic tales are discussed by a broad spectrum of scholars. This book could provide a fine introduction to one of the Bible's genres (heroic analog).

0189   Pascal, Roy.   "Narrative Fictions and Reality: A Comment on Frank Kermode's *The Sense of an Ending*." *Novel* 11 (1977): 40-50.

This article takes up Kermode's question of "the structural fictions of narrative (0174). Pascal criticizes Kermode's "rather indecisive views on the relation of the fictions to reality," seeing them as "shaped out of real features of reality" and also as finding their ultimate source in the changing human arena.

0190   Perrine, Lawrence. *Story and Structure*. 4th ed. New York: Harcourt Brace Jovanovich, 1974. 552 pp.

An anthology of short stories thought to illustrate or exemplify certain points of literary technique. Perrine organizes the stories under such categories as "Escape and Interpretation"; "Plot"; "Character"; "Theme"; "Point of View"; "Symbol and Irony"; "Emotion and Humor"; and "Fantasy." Each section is introduced by Perrine's own evaluative comments. The book is designed for undergraduate courses. Rhoads and Michie refer to it in 1250.

0191   Perry, Menakhem. "Literary Dynamics: How the Order of a Text Creates its Meaning (with an analysis of Faulkner's 'A Rose for Emily')." *Poetics Today* 1 (1979): 35-64, 311-361.

Studies the reader's response to the "reading continuum" of a story, or "concretization" in the reading process. Perry formulates "the principles and functions governing the location of elements relative to each other in the closed continuum of the text, (which) must therefore play a major role in the characterization of a literary text." Theoretical information is followed by an example, a lengthy analysis of Faulkner's short story "A Rose for Emily."

0192   Piwowarczyk, Mary Ann. "The Narratee and the Situation of Enunciation: A Reconsideration of Prince's Theory." *Genre* 9 (1976): 161-177.

Raises several objections to Prince's formulation of the zero degree narratee (0200) and proposes a revised and expanded definition. Then Piwowarczyk re-examines the specific signs which mark the narratee's presence in the text, categorizes the signs themselves, and relates them to "an analysis of the situation of enunciation." See also 0407.

0193   Prince, Gerald.   "Aspects of a Grammar of Narrative." *Poetics Today* 1,3 (1980): 49-63.

Defines *narrative* as "the representation of at least two real or fictive events in a time sequence," and *grammar of narrative* as "a series of statements or formulas" that describe an apparently universal set of intuitions or "rules" about what narratives are like. Prince proposes to establish such a grammar by means of a number of formulae. Then, he tells what such grammar does and does not provide.

0194 Prince, Gerald. *A Dictionary of Narratology*. Lincoln: University of Nebraska Press, 1987. 118 pp.

Gives an alphabetical listing of the terms narratologists used to describe the phenomena of their discipline. Prince, one of the founders of narratology, provides many examples and illustrations of the concepts defined in this book. Useful to anyone who attempts to read narratologists.

0195 Prince, Gerald. *A Grammar of Stories: An Introduction*. The Hague: Mouton Publishers, 1973. 106 pp.

Attempts to show that a finite number of explicit rules can account for the structure of what are generally and intuitively recognized as stories. After an introduction studying the possibility of such grammar and specifying its role, Prince defines a "minimal story" as consisting of three statements, the first and third of which are stative, and the second of which is active (e.g., "John was rich/John lost his money/John was poor"). Prince goes on to show that the grammar of kernel simple stories, when complemented by other rules, can assign a structure to any work generally and intuitively recognized as a story.

0196 Prince, Gerald. "Introduction to the Study of the Narratee." In *Reader Response Criticism*, ed. by Jane P. Tompkins, 7-25. Baltimore: Johns Hopkins University Press, 1980.

Narrators of fiction address themselves to a narratee who may or may not bear resemblance to the reader--for example, the caliph in *1001 Nights*. Also distinct is the "virtual reader," or the readership the author imagines, and the "ideal reader" who could interpret any text. The narratee receives a description mostly from "the narrative addressed to him." Prince classifies narratees according to their "narrative situation," to their position in reference to the narrator and the characters of the narration. The narratee functions as a "relay . . . between the author and the reader," as a part of the narrative framework, and as a mouthpiece for the moral of the work.

0197 Prince, Gerald. "The Narratee Revisited." *Style* 19 (1985): 299-303.

Responds briefly to Mary Pratt's assumption that his work on narratees produces theory to suit interpretation's ends. Prince counters that studying the narratee "constitutes above all an essential component of any general account of narrative and should be investigated and elaborated as such."

0198 Prince, Gerald. *Narratology: The Form and Functioning of Narrative*. Berlin: Mouton Publishers, 1982. 184 pp.

Defines narrative as "the representation of at least two real or fictive events or situations in a time sequence, neither of which presupposes or entails the other," and narratology as "the study of the form and functioning of the narrative." Prince attempts to answer three questions: (1) What are the features of narrative which allow us to characterize its possible manifestations in pertinent terms? (He discusses the narrator-narratee transaction, modes of discourse, events, and such "organizations" as temporal, spatial, and causal relations, character, and setting.) (2) What would a formal model accounting for these features and manifestations look like? (He discusses narrative grammar.) (3) What are the factors that affect our understanding of a narrative and our evaluation of its narrativity? (He discusses codes, constraints, signs, wholeness, orientation, and so on.)

0199 Prince, Gerald. "Notes on the Text as Reader." In *The Reader in the Text*, ed. by Susan R. Suleiman, pp. 225-240. Princeton, NJ: Princeton University Press, 1980.

Says that although texts allow more than one possible answer to some of the relevant questions that may be asked about them, texts themselves often make hermeneutic suggestions. "Reading interludes" in a text show that portions of that text at least are readable in certain more or less straightforward ways. But they may also perform as "counterreaders." They "determine in part the distance between a particular text and a particular reader and play an important but ever-changing role in the way the text is received each time it is read."

0200 Prince, Gerald. "Notes Toward A Categorization of Fictional 'Narratees.'" *Genre* 4 (1971): 100-106.

Distinguishes five major categories of narratees, on the basis of the degree to which they are involved in the events that are narrated. Prince also describes narratees' functions as related to theme, setting, and plot development. The term "narratee," now widely used in literary criticism was coined by Prince in this article. See also 0192, 0407.

0201 Prince, Gerald. "On Readers and Listeners in Narrative." *Neophilologus* 55 (1971): 117-122.

Says that literary "codes" must be familiar to the reader or "receiver." Narratives may be classed according to the types and numbers of signals that they direct toward receivers.

0202 Propp, Vladimir. *Morphology of the Folktale*. Trans. by Laurence Scott. Preface by Louis A. Wagner. 2nd ed. Austin: University of Texas Press, 1968. 184 pp.

A seminal study describing "the structure or formal organization" of folktales. Propp examines the linear sequence of elements in the texts of over 100 tales and compares them to discern 31 constant functions that recur almost invariably in the same sequence. He classifies tales according to both category and theme. This work is definitive of Russian formalism and has been influential in the development of other approaches, such as structuralism and "generative poetics" (0519). See also 0141-0143, 0260, 0539, 0650, 0989.

0203   Propp, Vladimir. "Structure and History in the Study of the Fairy Tale."
Semeia 10 (1978): 57-83.

Propp's book *Morphology of the Folktale* (0203), was rediscovered after WWII. Some
continued to dismiss it as merely formalism, including Lévi-Strauss. This article is a
defense of his earlier work against Lévi-Strauss.   One section contains some
interesting material on plot and on the relationship of myth to fairy tale.

0204   Rabkin, Eric. *Narrative Suspense: When Slim Turned Sideways. . ."* Ann Arbor:
University of Michigan Press, 1973. 216 pp.

Concerned with how the phenomenon of suspense is produced within a narrative.
Rabkin locates the origin of narrative suspense in subliminal knowledge and presents
a theory of genre based on narrative suspense. Although he defines his terms as his
argument progresses, Rabkin's book is so heavy on jargon that it is difficult to follow.

0205   Richter, David H. *Fable's End: Completeness and Closure in Rhetorical Fiction.*
Chicago: University of Chicago Press, 1974. 214 pp.

Discusses "the architectonic principles of coherence, completeness, and closure in a
group of novels whose structure is generated not by plot but by doctrines, themes,
attitudes, or thesis." The first chapter defines "Open Form and the Fable," and the
others each consider a specific work from the eighteenth century. An Appendix
provides an interesting "Selective Checklist of Formally Interesting Rhetorical Fiction."

0206   Rimmon-Kenan, Shlomith. *Narrative Fiction: Contemporary Poetics.* London:
Methuen and Co., 1983. 173 pp.

Introduces the study of narrative fiction, presenting "a description of the system
governing all fictional narratives" and indicating "a way in which individual narratives
can be studied as unique realizations of the general system." Rimmon-Kenan takes
up three major aspects of narrative fiction: Story (events and characters); Text (time,
characterization and focalization); and Narration (levels and voices, and speech
representation).

0207   Scholes, Robert. "Review of *Story and Discourse: Narrative Structure in Fiction
and Film,* by Seymour Chatman." *Poetics Today* 1 (1980): 190-191.

A brief review of 0150. Scholes says the book shows the American critical dilemma
of attraction to new critical methods. He sees Chatman as moving away from New
Criticism and toward Aristotle.

0208   Scholes, Robert, ed. *Approaches to the Novel: Materials for a Poetics.* Rev. ed.
San Francisco: Chandler Publishing Co., 1966. 314 pp.

An anthology of criticism, divided into two major sections: "Theoretical Matters" and
"Questions of Craft."   In the first, Austin Warren and Northrop Frye consider
"Narrative Modes and Forms," and Erich Auerbach, Ian Watt and others address the

problem of realism. In the second section, Mark Schorer and Martin Turnell discuss novelistic technique, and writers like Virginia Woolf, E. M. Forster and Percy Lubbock provide articles on character, plot and point of view.

0209   Scholes, Robert, and Kellogg, Robert. *The Nature of Narrative.* New York: Oxford University Press, 1966. 326 pp.

Seeks to identify the common thread in all narratives--folktales, allegories, realistic novels, and narrative poetry--as being the two elements of story and storyteller. This book urges literary critics to appreciate all forms of narrative, not to dismiss those which are "less" than realistic novels. It therefore makes important reading for scholars who hold up the realistic novel as a touchstone by which to judge biblical stories.

0210 Sharpe, Robert Boies. *Irony in the Drama: An Essay on Impersonation, Shock, and Catharsis.* Chapel Hill: University of North Carolina Press, 1959. 222 pp.

Defines drama as impersonation, and irony in drama as involving a particular perspective on life and mood. Irony is created through artistic techniques by which the director, actors, and playwright put the audience in an appropriate psychological state. Sharpe examines classical and Renaissance dramas, in addition to modern tragedy and comedy.

0211   States, Bert O. *Irony and the Drama: A Poetics.* Ithaca, NY: Cornell University Press, 1971. 243 pp.

Supposes a reader with a good background in critical theory, and uses Kenneth Burke as a point of departure in defining dramatic art as essentially ironic. States analyzes a number of dramatists, from Shakespeare to contemporary writers like Beckett and Ionesco. His approach tends toward structuralism.

0212   Sternberg, Meir. *Expositional Modes and Temporal Ordering in Fiction.* Baltimore: Johns Hopkins University Press, 1978. 352 pp.

Discusses exposition (the process through which readers are introduced to the fictive world of a story) in literature from the *Odyssey* to the modern novel. Sternberg's careful reading of the *Odyssey* could be useful to biblical students, since it keeps in mind the properties of the ancient text. He also observes in detail the author's central concern, rhetorical control.

0213   Stevick, Phillip, ed. *The Theory of the Novel.* New York: Free Press, 1967. 440 pp.

An anthology of criticism that amounts to a poetics of the novel, with essays on genre, technique, point of view, plot, style, time and place, symbol, and the relationship of life and art. Critics included are Northrop Frye, Wayne Booth, Norman Friedman, Robert Scholes and Robert Kellogg. Also, a handful of novelists are represented, speaking about the nature of their craft: Cervantes, Fielding, Sterne, Flaubert, Zola, James, Conrad, Lawrence, Joyce and others. See 0137, 0164.

0214   Suleiman, Susan R. "Interpreting Ironies." *Diacritics* 6,2 (1976): 15-21.

A review article of Booth's *Rhetoric of Irony* (0140). Suleiman describes "two critics in Booth--one the structuralist or semiotician (minus the vocabulary); the other the moralist whose chief concern is with values." She finds, however, that Booth is moving away from a completely text-centered reading and is showing what she considers to be new insightfulness about readers.

0215   Thompson, Alan Reynolds. *The Dry Mock: A Study of Irony in Drama.* Berkeley and Los Angeles: University of California Press, 1948. Reprint. Chicago: Porcupine Press, 1981. 278 pp.

Begins with a description of the nature of irony, which consists of a sort of contradiction that rouses a particular kind of emotional response. Thompson discusses three of its forms: Romantic irony, including both its German sources and modern American writing; comic irony; and tragic irony. The conclusion suggests limitations to ironic discourse.

0216   Tindall, William Y. *The Literary Symbol.* Oxford: Columbia University Press, 1955. 278 pp.

An influential work of its day, this book says that its purpose is not "to survey symbolic parts and wholes but to illustrate them." Tindall uses examples from modern literature, showing the relation of the symbols modernist writers employ to that found in the work of their predecessors.

0217   Torgovnick, Marianna. *Closure in the Novel.* Princeton, NJ: Princeton University Press, 1981. 238 pp.

Discusses the importance of the ending in works of fiction. The term "'closure' designates the process by which a novel reaches an adequate and appropriate conclusion . . . (and) a sense that nothing necessary has been omitted." Each of the nine chapters uses as its example a nineteenth or twentieth century novel. Cf. 0182.

0218   Vellacott, Philip. *Ironic Drama: A Study of Euripides' Method and Meaning.* Cambridge: Cambridge University Press, 1975. 276 pp.

This study of Euripides' plays contains nine chapters, and in the first three, issues of irony and interpretation are discussed. Vellacott's study is sometimes cited by scholars who study irony in the Bible.

0219   Wellek, René. "The New Criticism: Pro and Contra." *Critical Inquiry* 4 (1978): 611-624.

Says that "the New Critics with one voice questioned the assumptions and preoccupations of academic (historical) scholarship and reinterpreted and revalued the whole history of English poetry." Wellek refutes several typical charges against the New Critics, like the supposition that they have no sense of history or want to make criticism a science. He upholds the New Critics' "valiant fight" against "neutral scientism and indifferent relativism" and their refusal to succumb "to the imposition of alien norms required by political indoctrination."

0220   Wellek, René, and Warren, Austin. *Theory of Literature*. 3rd ed. San Diego: Harcourt Brace Jovanovich, 1977. 403 pp.

A classic of text-oriented criticism. First Wellek and Warren attempt to sharpen definitions of literary-critical lingo and to show how to approach texts systematically. Next, they show how critics have looked at literature in relation to other disciplines --like biography, psychology, social climate, "ideas," and other arts. Having completed these critiques, the final portion of the book considers "the work of art . . . as a whole system of signs, or structure of signs, serving a specific aesthetic purpose." They propose an "Intrinsic Study of Literature," which includes attention to "Style and Stylistics"; "Image, Metaphor, Symbol, Myth"; "Literary Genres" and other intrinsic matters. See also 0187.

0221   Welsh, Alexander, ed. *Narrative Endings*. Berkeley and Los Angeles: University of California Press, 1979. 158 pp.

Describes the similarities between narrative beginnings and endings as having "much in common since both are arbitrary disjunctions in a sequence of events that is presumed continuous, extending before and after the events that are narrated." We also have to imagine "a surrounding space for each narrative," so that one narrative is arbitrarily separated from another.

0222   Wimsatt, William K. *The Verbal Icon: Studies in the Meaning of Poetry*. Lexington: University Press of Kentucky, 1954. 299 pp.

This collection of essays includes two famous ones that served as the manifesto of the Chicago School of "New Criticism." "The Intentional Fallacy" (pp. 3-20) and "The Affective Fallacy" (pp. 21-40), both written in collaboration with Monroe C. Beardsley, argue for a strongly text-centered approach to criticism that avoids the perils of determining meaning with reference to intentions of an author or effects on an audience. The other essays undertake an examination of "the relation of evaluative criticism to historical studies, and the relation of literature to other arts, to morals, and more broadly to the whole complex of the Christian religious tradition."

0223   Zabel, Morton D., ed. *Literary Opinion in America*. Rev. ed. New York: Harper and Bros., 1951. 890 pp.

Provides a look at New Criticism, including all its important voices. This comprehensive collection is useful for anyone who wants to understand the critical method that dominates the first half of this century, and which is still influential among biblical scholars today.

SEMIOTICS AND STRUCTURALISM

See also 0001, 0016, 0044-0045, 0055-0058, 0067, 0070, 0072, 0082, 0084, 0100, 0102-0103, 0107, 0121, 1035-0136, 0156, 0160-1061, 0211, 0353, 0388, 0434, 0436, 0448, 0483-0484, 0486, 0489, 0494, 0499, 0503-0504, 0508, 0515, 0517, 0519, 0521, 0525-0528, 0530, 0532, 0538, 0544-0546, 0550, 0565, 0572, 0580, 0593-0594, 0683, 0695, 0720, 0722, 0728, 0732, 0737, 0757-0758, 0763, 0874, 0910, 0995, 1001, 1031, 1048, 1058, 1065, 1069, 1071, 1090, 1092, 1095-1097, 1102, 1108-1110, 1116, 1119, 1135, 1153-1155, 1160, 1175, 1189, 1191, 1195, 1230, 1240-1241, 1259, 1264, 1272-1276, 1284, 1286, 1288, 1319, 1323, 1361, 1367, 1369-1370, 1385, 1388-1389, 1411-1412, 1439, 1460, 1477, 1483, 1499-1500, 1532, 1540, 1542, 1557, 1575, 1581, 1590-1591, 1597, 1602, 1605, 1612, 1623-1624, 1626, 1640, 1653, 1656, 1660-1661, 1667, 1670-1671, 1686, 1702.

0224   Barthes, Roland. *Criticism and Truth*. Ed. and trans. by Katrine Pilcher Keunemen. Minneapolis: University of Minnesota Press, 1987. 119 pp.

This small book responds to Raymond Picard's attack on Barthes' critical methods, the French New Criticism (not to be confused with the American formalist school also called New Criticism). Barthes also states clearly the thrusts of his own work, including linguistic analysis of texts and the way readers read.

0225 Barthes, Roland. "The Death of the Author." In *Image - Music - Text*, ed. and trans. by Stephen Heath, 142-148. New York: Hill and Wang, 1977.

Using an image from Balzac as example, Barthes discusses the way that the author of a text is "removed" and the effect of that removal upon the task of deciphering this text. The essay is based on the claim that "writing is the destruction of every voice, every point of origin."

0226 Barthes, Roland. *Elements of Semiology*. Trans. by Annette Lavers and Colin Smith. New York: Hill and Wang, 1978.

Proposes a "binary structure" with four central themes: "Language (*Langue*) and Speech (*Parole*)"; "Signifier and Signified"; "Syntagm and System"; and "Denotation and Connotation." The work draws on linguistic theory of Saussure (0067) and is fundamental to the development of structuralist theory. See also 0231.

0227   Barthes, Roland. *New Critical Essays*. Trans. by Richard Howard. New York: Hill and Wang, 1980.

A collection of eight brief essays, showing the development of Barthes' thought from 1961 to 1971. Topics include writers like Proust and Flaubert, and many of the essays were originally introductions to translations or new editions of the French works. A good introduction to Barthes' thought.

0228   Barthes, Roland. *The Semiotic Challenge*. Trans. by Richard Howard. New York: Hill and Wang, 1988. 293 pp.

This playful, learned, and difficult book contains an introduction ("The Semiological Adventure") in which Barthes locates his current position, followed by three major sections: (1) "Elements" which includes an "Introduction to the Structural Analysis of Narratives"; (2) "Domains" which has seven essays, including "Saussure, the Sign, Democracy" and "Sociology and Socio-logic"; and (3) "Analyses" which includes 1286.

0229   Barthes, Roland. *S/Z*. Trans. by Richard Miller. New York: Hill and Wang, 1974. 271 pp.

Makes a complete analysis of Balzac's *Sarrasine*, beginning with its title. This book is often cited as the example *par excellence* of structuralist criticism. Barthes dissects Balzac's work into 561 numbered fragments and orders them according to 93 "divagations." Even nonstructuralist and poststructuralist scholars have been impressed by the extent to which he is able to sustain so complex a system throughout.

0230   Barthes, Roland. *Writing Degree Zero*. Trans. by Annette Lavers and Colin Smith. New York: Hill and Wang, 1977. 94 pp.

Originally published in 1953 as *Le Degré Zéro de l'ecriture*, this work defines the nature of writing, as well as the historical, political, and personal forces responsible for the formal changes in writing from the classical period to the present. Barthes' first book, this volume is primarily interesting today for its presentation in seminal form of certain ideas that would later be developed in *Elements of Semiology* (0226). See also 0231.

0231   Barthes, Roland. *Writing Degree Zero* and *Elements of Semiology*. Preface by Susan Sontag. Boston: Beacon Press, 1970. 112 pp.

Combines two early works by Barthes (0226, 0230) in one volume. The book is notable not only for making these works more accessible, but also for the preface, in which Sontag compares and contrasts *Writing Degree Zero* with Sartre's *What Is Literature?* (0025).

0232   Brooke-Rose, Christine. "The Readerhood of Man." In *The Reader in the Text*, ed. by Susan R. Suleiman, 120-148. Princeton, NJ: Princeton University Press, 1980.

Maintains the term "enclosed reader," seeking to reveal encoded structures. Brooke-Rose then divides her material into three broad categories: texts in which a code is overdetermined, texts in which it is underdetermined, and texts in which it is nondetermined. She uses as examples Washington Irving's "Rip Van Winkle," Flan O' Brien's *At Swim-Two-Birds*, E. A. Poe's "The Black Cat" and Drieu de la Rochelle's *Gilles*.

0233   Calloud, Jean. "A Few Comments on Structural Semiotics." *Semeia* 15 (1979): 51-83.

Says that "semiotics proposes a way of arriving at a formal description of what we call meaning, which is immanent in texts and therefore not directly perceptible. This kind of description requires a metalanguage and the analysis proceeds in two stages: a narrative component and a discursive component. Various aspects of these two components are discussed."

0234   Chabrol, Claude. "Problémes de la sémiologie narrative des récits bibliques." *Langages* 22 (June, 1971): 3-12.

Says that the reading of a text always amounts to the constitution of a new object, composed of text and reader but not identical to either. Thus, reading always destroys the text and its meaning, and puts in its place a "subject wishing to know." Chabrol resists Roland Barthes' notion of a hidden or final signified. Rather, there is a "hidden signifier," which is a network of correlations. The article addresses these semiotic concerns with direct reference to biblical literature.

0235   Chatman, Seymour, ed. *Approaches to Poetics*. New York: Columbia University Press, 1973. 184 pp.

Contains a foreword by Seymour Chatman and a collection of papers presented at the English Institute at Columbia University in 1972 on the topic of structuralism, especially under the influence of Roman Jakobson and Roland Barthes. This collection is about poetics, with more emphasis on theory than on examples for practical criticism. The essay by Frank Kermode ("The Use of the Codes," pp. 51-80) is especially intriguing and challenging.

0236   Corti, Maria. *An Introduction to Literary Semiotics*. Trans. by Margherita Bogat and Allen Mandelbaum. Bloomington: Indiana University Press, 1978. 176 pp.

Studies "the system of literature understood as the condition and the place of the literary communication that binds senders and addressees in various eras." Corti investigates "the notion of literature as a system with its own rules of functioning . . . (and) the notion of the text as a hypersign or polysemic message." She sets "side by side the ideas of writers and those of semiologists and critics."

0237   Culler, Jonathan. "Literary Competence." In *Reader Response Criticism*, ed. by Jane P. Tompkins, 101-117. Baltimore: Johns Hopkins University Press, 1980.

This article from Culler's 1975 book *Structuralist Poetics* (0238) claims that to "speak of the structure of a sentence is necessarily to imply an internalized grammar that gives it that structure." A reader, then, must internalize the "'grammar' of literature" in order to be able "to convert linguistic sequences into literary structures and meanings." Poetic conventions form the "basis of literary forms," and literary competence is "a set of conventions for reading literary texts."

0238   Culler, Jonathan. *Structuralist Poetics: Structuralism, Linguistics, and the Study of Literature.* Ithaca, NY: Cornell University Press, 1975. 316 pp.

Presents a poetics that strives "to define the conditions of meaning," based on possible relationships beween literary and linguistic studies. Part I considers the scope and the limitations of linguistic methods, and reviews the various ways in which structuralists have attempted to apply linguistic models to the study of literature. Part II uses linguistics as a model which suggests how a poetics should be organized. Particularly interesting are Chapters 8 and 9 on "Poetics of the Lyric" and "Poetics of the Novel."

0239   Dolezel, Lubomír. "Eco and His Model Reader." *Poetics Today* 1 (1980): 181-188.

Sees reader-oriented criticism as "a manifestation of the *fin-de-millénium* 'democratic' Romanticism which rejects the idea that artistic creativity is a privilege of a few geniuses." But it is also a phenomenon "which threatens to throw literary criticism back into pure amateurism." Therefore, he finds Eco's *The Role of the Reader* (0241) to be refreshing because Eco's "Model Reader has a perfect awareness of his epistemological limitations." Eco re-asserts "the essential control of the text and its code over the reader's interpretation."

0240   Dyck, Joachim; Jens, Walter; and Ueding, Gert, eds. *Rhetorik: Ein Internationales Jahrbuch. Band 9: Rhetorik und Strukturalismus.* Tübingen: Max Niemeyer Verlag, 1990.

This issue of an annual journal is devoted entirely to the subject, "Rhetoric and Structuralism." Articles are devoted to basic concepts of structuralism, but also to deconstruction and to feminist criticism. Especially noteworthy are a piece on "The Rhetoric of Jacques Derrida" by Gonsalv K. Mainberger, and an article on Paul de Man, American deconstruction, and rhetoric (titled "The Melodramatic Science") by Thomas Steinfeld.

0241   Eco, Umberto. *The Role of the Reader: Explorations in the Semiotics of Texts.* Advances in Semiotics. Bloomington: Indiana University Press, 1979. 273 pp.

A collection of nine essays, six of which were written prior to 1971 and before Eco fully developed his Peircean semiotic approach to texts (0243). As such, the collection provides an excellent survey of the development of Eco's thought. Most significant today, however, is the introduction he provides for the volume. Here, Eco lays out his concept of the "model reader," that is, the reader who understands the codes of the text. He also clarifies his distinction between closed texts that assume a particular kind of reader and open texts that seek to generate the reader they desire. See also 0239.

0242   Eco, Umberto. *Semiotics and the Philosophy of Language.* Advances in Semiotics. Bloomington: Indiana University Press, 1984. 256 pp.

Continues Eco's attempt in *A Theory of Semiotics* (0243) to devise a metatheory for literary analysis based on the linguistic philosophy of C. S. Peirce (cf. 0015). Eco insists that Peircean semiosis does not privilege either formalist or deconstructive extremes, but provides for a continuum of connotations to be discerned in the process of interpretation. This book devotes chapters to "Sign"; "Metaphor"; "Symbol"; "Code" and "Isotopy" in addition to considering semiotics with reference to "Mirrors" and with regard to the dichotomy of "Dictionary vs. Encyclopedia."

0243   Eco, Umberto. *A Theory of Semiotics.* Advances in Semiotics. Bloomington: Indiana University Press, 1976. 368 pp.

In his Introduction, Eco says that the "aim of this book is to explore theoretical possibility and the social function of a unified approach to every phenomenon of signification and/or communication." The book is broken into three sections: "Signification and Communication"; "Theory and Codes" and "Theory of Sign Production." Finally, Eco discusses briefly "The Subject of Semiotics," sketching his conclusions. Eco's goal is to construct a metatheory that takes as its starting point communication by means of signs. Cf. the alternative, structuralist metatheory of Greimas (0256-0257).

0244   Ehrmann, Jacques, ed. *Structuralism. Yale French Studies* 36-37 (1966).

This double issue of the periodical *Yale French Studies* focuses on structuralism in its several aspects: linguistics, anthropology, art, psychiatry, and literature. The latter section contains the following essays: "Structuralism: the Anglo-American Adventure" by Geoffrey Hartman; "Structures of exchange in *Cinna*" by Jacques Ehrmann; "Describing Poetic structures: Two Approaches to Baudelaire's *les Chats*" by Michael Riffaterre; and "Toward an Anthropology of Literature" by Victoria L. Rippere. A number of bibliographies are also provided, including one on the works of Jacques Lacan, and one on "Structuralism and Literary Criticism" compiled by Tzvetan Todorov.

0245   Galland, Corina. "La semiotique en questions." *Études Théologiques et Religieuses* 50 (1975): 335-344.

Identifies several questions that semiotics and structural analysis raise concerning theory and practice of interpretation. These questions are organized under the following headings: (1) theory of the text; (2) grammar of the text; and (3) semantics. This article is written for persons engaged in theological/biblical studies.

0246   Genette, Gérard. "Boundaries of Narrative." *New Literary History* 8 (1976): 1-13.

Differentiates narration from description, and finds the boundaries to be indistinct. Genette also examines narrative and discourse, and observes that contemporary fiction tends "to absorb the narrative into the actual discourse of the writer in the act of writing."

0247   Genette, Gérard. *Figures*. 3 vols. Paris: Editions de Seuill, 1966, 1969, 1972.

A structuralist poetics that attempts to take into account the role of the reader in interpretation of texts.   Genette defines "figure" as "a gap between a sign and meaning." Entire literary works as well as their constructive parts function as figures. Genette differs from many other structuralists in his attention to rhetoric and in his view that discernible "laws of literature" are entirely empirical--more customs or habits, in fact, than laws in the strictest sense. The three volumes of this work focus repeatedly on Proust's *Recherche* for their analysis. They have been only partially translated into English (0248-0249). See also 0132, 0134, 0286.

0248   Genette, Gérard. *Figures of Literary Discourse*. Trans. by Alan Sheridan. European Perspectives Series. New York: Columbia University Press, 1982. 303 pp.

Provides an English translation of portions of the three-volume French work, *Figures* (0247). The selections, however, have been rearranged from their original order to fit into two parts ("Theory" and "Practice"). The first part contains three chapters from Genette's first volume ("Structuralism and Literary Criticism," "The Obverse of Signs," and "Figures"), three from his second ("Principles of Pure Criticism," "Poetic Language, Poetics of Language," and "Frontiers of Narrative"), and one from the third ("Rhetoric Restrained"). The second part contains essays from the first two volumes on Stendahl and Flaubert, as well as ones on Proust's *Recherche* that must be supplemented by selections from the third volume previously published in *Narrative Discourse* (0249).

0249   Genette, Gérard. *Narrative Discourse: An Essay in Method*. Trans. by Jane E. Lewin. Foreward by Jonathan Culler. Ithaca, NY: Cornell University Press, 1980. 285 pp.

An English translation of portions of the third volume of Genette's French work, *Figures* (0247). Here, Genette differentiates between "story" and "narrative" (French *récit*; roughly equivalent to what Chatman calls "discourse"--see 0150) with regard to order, duration, and frequency. He also distinguishes between "narrative" and "narrating," and devotes chapters to mood and voice. Much of this study is based on the author's reading of Proust, and provides helpful insights for practical criticism of texts. See also 0250. For review, see 0136, 1204, 1372.

0250   Genette, Gérard. *Narrative Discourse Revisited.* Trans. by Jane E. Lewin. Ithaca, NY: Cornell University Press, 1988. 168 pp.

Updates and supplements the materials presented in *Narrative Discourse* (0249). The first several chapters parallel the presentation of that book precisely: Order, Speed (Duration), Frequency, Mood (6 chapters), and Voice (3 chapters). The rest of the book treats subjects not considered in the first book but which Genette says "today seem to me worth examining, if only to justify rejecting them." These are "Narrative Situations"; "The Narratee"; and "Implied Author, Implied Reader?"

0251   Greimas, Algirdas Julien. "Elements of a Narrative Grammar." *Diacritics* 7,1 (1977): 23-40.

This article has three parts: "Narrativity and Semiotic Theory"; "Elements of Fundamental Grammar"; and "Elements of a Surface Narrative Grammar." Greimas begins with a history of interest in "narrativity studies" and general semiotics and goes on to show the relationship between the two fields of inquiry. The article traces the broad outlines of "the part of narrative syntax relative to the body of the narrative itself."

0252   Greimas, Algirdas Julien. "Narrative Grammar: Units and Levels." *Modern Language Notes* 86 (1971): 793-806.

Asks, "What is the relation between narrative structure and linguistic structure?" Greimas investigates "linguistic models in the study of narrativity," and "aspects of narrative grammar." He postulates an elementary narrative unit, and then attempts to provide for the syntagmatic organization of these units in sequences of such units.

0253   Greimas, Algirdas Julien. *On Meaning: Selected Writings in Semiotic Theory.* Trans. by Paul Perron and Frank Collins. Introduction by Paul J. Perron. Theory and History of Literature, 38. Minneapolis: University of Minnesota Press, 1987. 237 pp.

Contains English translations of essays extracted from three of Greimas' works: *Du Sens* (1970); *Semiotique et Sciences Sociales* (1976); and *Du Sens II* (1983). The articles are presented chronologically and the introduction by Perron offers guidance that makes it easy to trace the development of Greimas' thought from the early influence of Claude Lévi-Strauss and Roman Jakobson to the later development of his own "actantial model" for communication, which has been very influential in structuralism.

0254   Greimas, Algirdas Julien. *Structural Semantics: An Attempt at a Method.* Trans. by D. McDowell, *et al.* Lincoln: University of Nebraska Press, 1984. 325 pp.

Originally published in 1966 as *Sémantique Structurale*, this influential but difficult work develops "a method to analyze and account for meaning" and "attempts to outline a grammar and syntax for signification." This book is both semiological and philosophical and attempts to account for meaning in general. It represents the beginning of a task that would continue in 0253 and culminate in 0256-0257.

Greimas' semiotic theory has been extremely influential for structuralism, particularly as practiced by biblical exegetes (see 1623).

0255 Greimas, Algirdas Julien. "Structure and History." In *Structuralism and Biblical Hermeneutics: A Collection of Essays*, ed. and trans. by Alfred M. Johnson, Jr., 57-73. Pittsburgh Theological Monograph Series, 22. Pittsburgh: Pickwick Press, 1979.

Offers reflection on the relationship between structuralism and historical research by a structuralist who is often accused of being anti-historical. Greimas observes that the solitary focus on synchrony derived from Saussure (0067) is passing, and structuralism is now ready to take account of diachronic transformations. Far from being ahistorical or anti-historical, structuralist methodology is "probably preparing a revival of historical research, because a better knowledge of the general rules of structural transformations is necessary" for drawing conclusions about diachronic transformation.

0256 Greimas, Algirdas Julien, and Courtés, J. *Semiotics and Language: An Analytical Dictionary*. Trans. by L. Crist, D. Patte, et al. Advances in Semiotics. Bloomington: Indiana University Press, 1982. 432 pp.

Attempts to integrate diverse semiotic theories into a metatheory of the production of meaning. The work has been available in French since 1978 and is continued in 0257. The focus is on production of meaning through structures that govern the interrelations of significant features (cf. 0243). On the implications of Greimas' metatheory for biblical exegesis, see 1623.

0257 Gremias, Algirdas Julien, and Courtés, J., eds. *Semiotique: Dictionnaire raisonné de la théorie du langage, 2*. Paris: Larousse, 1985.

A continuation of 0256, not yet translated into English.

0258 Hawkes, Terence. *Structuralism and Semiotics*. Berkeley and Los Angeles: University of California Press, 1977. 192 pp.

Begins by defining "Structuralism," showing its roots in the eighteenth century writer Giambattista Vico and the modern writing of Jean Piaget. The second chapter describes the relationship of linguistics and anthropology, concentrating on the work of Ferdinand de Saussure and Claude Lévi-Strauss. The third chapter takes up the "Structures of Literature," introducing Russian formalism, European structural linguistics and the writings of Roman Jakobson, A. J. Greimas, Tzvetan Todorov and Roland Barthes. The fourth chapter concentrates upon semiology, the science of signs, and the helpful conclusion discusses "'New Criticism'" and "'New' New Criticism." This book provides an excellent introduction to structuralism and semiotics.

0259   Hays, Michael. "Toward a Theory of Semiotics and Reception; or, How Audiences Give as Much as They Get." *Union Seminary Quarterly Review* 35 (1980): 148-156.

Relates semiotics to reception theory, with particular reference to drama. Semiotic interpretation must be related not only to the printed text of a play, but to the metatext of its performance with all that entails--contributions of directors, actors, setting, light, sound, even the participation of the audience become a part of the signifying process.

0260   Hendricks, W. O. "The Structural Study of Narration: Sample Analyses." *Poetics* 3 (1972): 100-123.

Proposes to demonstrate what can be achieved using techniques for the structural analysis of narratives. Hendricks analyzes a segment from a Ray Bradbury novel and a short story by Ambrose Bierce, using Claude Brémond's model (0141), which is derived from Propp's work (0202).

0261   Higbie, Robert. *Character and Structure in the English Novel.* Gainesville: University Presses of Florida, 1984. 208 pp.

Takes a structuralist approach to character, and acknowledges the influences of Sigmund Freud and a number of Freudian thinkers, as well as Ian Watt and others who acknowledge the importance for fiction of "historical and cultural processes." Higbie discusses "the details of characterization" while "seeing them as generated from the same basic structure out of which the whole work rises, relating them to that whole and to other works generated from the same fundamental structure." The first two chapters provide a linguistic and a psychological model of character, and the third discusses the novel's historical context. Later chapters deal with specific eighteenth and nineteenth century works.

0262   Innis, Robert E., ed. *Semiotics: An Introductory Anthology.* Bloomington: Indiana University Press, 1985. 352 pp.

An important anthology that intends to serve the twofold purpose of making available certain classic statements in semiotics and of introducing problems and themes that fall under the purview of semiotics. Important essays by Ferdinand de Saussure, Susanne K. Langer, Claude Lévi-Strauss, Roman Jakobson, Roland Barthes, Meyer Schapiro, Umberto Eco and others are included.

0263   Jakobson, Roman. "A Glance at the Development of Semiotics." In *Framework of Language*, 1-30. Michigan Studies in the Humanities, 1. Ann Arbor: University of Michigan Press, 1980.

Speaks of semiotics as a framework for an interdisciplinary team of specialists. Jakobson approaches the study of signs as a linguist, concerned not only with the similarities but also with the differences between various sign systems. The basic, primary, and most important semiotic system is language, but language is the foundation of culture, and other systems (including literary ones) are concomitant or derivative from language.

0264   Jameson, Frederic. *The Prison-House of Language: A Critical Account of Structuralism and Russian Formalism*. Princeton, NJ: Princeton University Press, 1972. 228 pp.

Understands structuralism in the strictest sense, as "work based on the metaphor or model of a linguistic system." The book proposes to lay bare the "absolute presuppositions" of formalism and structuralism. It is divided into three sections: "The Linguistic Model"; "The Formalist Projection" and "The Structuralist Projection." See also 0035, 0895, 1710.

0265   Johnson, Alfred M., Jr. *A Bibliography of Semiological and Structural Studies of Religion*. Pittsburgh: Pittsburgh Theological Seminary, 1979. 146 pp.

A comprehensive bibliographical listing of works that take a structuralist or semiological approach to religious studies, including some formalist, rhetorical, or phenomenological works that are only tangentially related to structuralism. Also included are so-called "secular" materials that have served the interests of structuralist and semiological studies in religion. With almost 2000 entries, this bibliography is the most complete listing of works on this subject published through the 1970s. Although it is not annotated, it serves as a worthy supplement to the present volume, especially with regard to materials not available in English translation.

0266   Kovacs, Brian W. "Philosophical Foundations for Structuralism." *Semeia* 10 (1978): 85-105.

Intends to clarify for pragmatic American scholars, the foundation of structuralist theories, showing their epistemological basis. The essay concentrates on four issues: the philosophical, psycho-social, linguistic, and theological. Kovacs begins by relating structuralism to science. The article is, in part, a response to Güttgemann's essays in 0519.

0267   Kurzweil, Edith. *The Age of Structuralism: Lévi-Strauss to Foucault*. New York: Columbia University Press, 1980. 256 pp.

A survey of eight figures who have, in one way or another, figured in the structuralist enterprise. The titles of the chapters are instructive: (1) "Claude Lévi-Strauss: The Father of Structuralism"; (2) "Louis Althusser: Marxism and Structuralism"; (3) "Henri Lefebvre: A Marxist Against Structuralism"; (4) "Paul Ricoeur: Hermeneutics and Structuralism"; (5) "Alain Touraine: Structures Without Structuralism"; (6) "Jacques Lacan: Structuralist Psychoanalysis"; (7) "Roland Barthes: Literary Structuralism and Erotics"; and, (8) "Michel Foucault: Structuralism and Structures of Knowledge."

0268   Lane, Michael, ed. *Introduction to Structuralism*. New York: Basic Books, 1970. 456 pp.

Begins with a useful introduction by the author that includes discussion on the contributions to the field by Ferdinand de Saussure, Claude Lévi-Strauss, and Roland Barthes. This is followed by a collection of works by a number of structuralists including those listed above, as well as Seymour Chatman, Roman Jakobson and others.

0269   Lavers, Annette. *Roland Barthes: Structuralism and After*. Cambridge, MA: Harvard University Press, 1982. 320 pp.

This comprehensive, affectionate, and learned study of the development of Barthes' critical theory contains four major sections: "Criticism Begins with Compilation"; "Something Beyond Language"; "A Euphoric Dream of Scientificity"; and "The Science of Literature is Literature." A helpful appendix offers detailed descriptions of structuralism, of semiology, of synchrony and diachrony, and of linguistic units and the way they organize meaning.

0270   Levin, Samuel R. "On the Progress of Structural Poetics." *Poetics* 8 (1979): 513-515.

Briefly reviews developments in the field of structural poetics over the preceding twenty-five years, from the focus on text exclusively to affective stylistics.

0271   Lipski, John M. "From Text to Narrative: Spanning the Gap." *Poetics* 7 (1976): 191-206.

Discusses the disparity between the goals of semiotics and the "current state of cognitive behavior." The tendency of those studying texts from the point of view of linguistic theory has been to apply sentence-level models directly to larger and more diffuse defining units of narrative, often with a questionable degree of success. The "ultimate construction of a true model will have to await further research into the interactions between the human organism and its total environment."

0272   Lotman, Jurij. *Analysis of the Poetic Text*. Ed. and trans. by D. Barton Johnson. Ann Arbor: Ardis Publishers, 1976. 309 pp.

Distinguishes between artistic and nonartistic texts or, more precisely, between aesthetic and nonaesthetic functions. Stated simply, nonartistic texts have the function of transmitting meaning and artistic texts have the function of generating new meanings (cf. 0275). But the boundary between the two is related to culture, and multiple functions can be served by the same text. Artistic texts serve nonaesthetic (e.g., ethical, political, philosophical, promotional) purposes and vice versa.

0273   Lotman, Jurij. "The Future for Structural Poetics." *Poetics* 8 (1979): 501-507.

A letter from Lotman to his colleagues inviting them to consider a "change in the idea of the function of the text in the overall cultural context." Lotman proposes that a vital characteristic of artistic texts is their encoding in a "secondary system" language superimposed on the natural language in which the text is written. The sum total of a text's structural and internal properties combine in a manner analogous to chemical reactions to manifest potentialities that would not be a characteristic of any of the separate components or parts.

0274   Lotman, Jurij. "Point of View in a Text." *New Literary History* 6 (1975): 339-352.

Shows that point of view becomes noticeable when it changes. Then "every one of the points of view in a text makes the claim to be the truth and struggles to assert itself in conflict with the opposing ones." One text used as an example is John 9:1-5, 8-9.

0275   Lotman, Jurij. *The Structure of the Artistic Text*. Michigan Slavic Contributions, 7. Trans. by Gail Lenhoff and Ronald Vroon. Ann Arbor: University of Michigan Press, 1977. 300 pp.

Defines the "artistic text," and sees it as transmitting meanings by "encoding," or placing an overlay of a "secondary systems" upon its language." Thus, there emerges a "complicated hierarchy of strata of meanings." Texts also bring about new meanings, and originality in art has to do with structure. Lotman considers the roles of author, reader, and researcher, and their relationship to one another.

0276   Lucid, Daniel P., ed. *Soviet Semiotics: An Anthology*. Baltimore: Johns Hopkins University Press, 1977.

Lucid's introduction defines semiotics as "the science of signs . . . the fastest-growing and most lively structuralist discipline," and describes the rise of semiotic studies in the Soviet Union. The remainder of the book is divided into six sections: "General Concepts"; "Modeling Systems"; "Communication Studies"; "Text Analysis"; "Art and Literature"; and "Typology of Culture." A number of the articles contained under these headings are the work of Jurij Lotman and Boris Uspensky.

0277   Macksey, Richard, and Donato, Eugenio, eds. *The Structuralist Controversy: The Language of Criticism and the Sciences of Man*. Baltimore: Johns Hopkins University Press, 1970. 345 pp.

A collection of papers and reports on discussion from a symposium on structuralism. The symposium occurred, as the title implies, at a time when structuralism was being challenged not only from without but also from within. The editors note that many of the participants in this symposium (Roland Barthes, Jacques Lacan, and Jacques Derrida) are "structuralists" who now seek to distance themselves from the term. Papers by those scholars, as well as ones by Tzvetan Todorov and René Girard are particularly noteworthy.

0278   Malbon, Elisabeth Struthers. "The Spiral and the Square: Lévi-Strauss's Mythic Formula and Gremias' Constitutional Model." *Linguistica Biblica* 55 (1984): 47-56.

Review's Daniel Patte's attempt to integrate systems for structural analysis proposed by A. J. Greimas and Claude Lévi-Strauss (0545). Malbon believes it is inappropriate to subordinate Lévi-Strauss' spiral model to Greimas' square, as Patte has done. Greimas and Lévi-Strauss raise different issues and offer different insights, and the one should not be accomodated to the other.

0279   Matejka, Ladislav, and Pomorska, Krystyna, eds. *Readings in Russian Poetics: Formalist and Structuralist Views.* Cambridge, MA: MIT Press, 1971. 306 pp.

Aims to acquaint English readers with the methodological struggles in which leading Russian theorists were engaged during the 1920s and 1930s. There are six sections of essays by different theorists: Part I includes "The Theory of the Formal Method" by Boris E'jxembaum and concludes with Roman Jakobson's "The Dominant," which shows formalism's "conversion to Structuralism"; Part II shows "an early structural approach to the problems of oral tradition"; Part III discusses "literary questions related to the language of poetry"; Part IV contains V. N. Volosinov's "Reported Speech" and Mixail Baxtin's "Discourse Typology in Prose"; Part V contains critical analyses of specific works, and Part VI features "Retrospective essays on linguistics and literary study."

0280   Miller, Joan M., comp. *French Structuralism: A Multidisciplinary Bibliography with a Checklist of Sources for Louis Althusser, Roland Barthes, Jacques Derrida, Michel Foucault, Lucien Goldmann, Jacques Lacan and an Update of Works on Claude Lévi-Strauss.* New York: Garland Publishing, 1981. 553 pp.

This large bibliography has three sections. The first covers "General and Introductory Works." The second contains "Works by and about Individual Structuralists," including those named in the title. The third section is about "Structuralism as Applied to Various Disciplines" including "Language and Literature/Literary Analysis"; "Linguistics"; "Literary Criticism"; "Poetics"; "Semiotics" and others.

0281 Pettit, Philip. *The Concept of Structuralism: A Critical Analysis.* Berkeley and Los Angeles: University of California Press, 1975. 117 pp.

A survey and critique of structuralism in four parts (1) an examination of the linguistic framework on which all of the varieties of structuralism are based; (2) a consideration of the range of this model in other semiological disciplines; (3) a critique of the development of the model by Claude Lévi-Strauss; (4) an evaluation of the part that the model can play in the advancement of knowledge.

0282   Pomorska, Krystyna. "Poetics of Prose." In *Verbal Art, Verbal Sign, Verbal Time*, ed. by Krystyna Pomorska, 169-177. Minneapolis: University of Minnesota Press, 1985.

Shows how Jakobson's theory of poetics and analytical method can be applied to prose. Jakobson was primarily concerned with understanding the structures of phonology, though he also applied his semiotic linguistic theory to literature in developing a "grammar of poetry."

0283   Riffaterre, Michael. "Describing Poetic Structures: Two Approaches to Baudelaire's 'Les Chats.'" In *The Reader in the Text*, ed. by Jane P. Tompkins, 26-40. Baltimore: Johns Hopkins University Press, 1980.

Traces analyses of Baudelaire's poem by Claude Lévi-Strauss and Roman Jakobson, noting that their descriptions of the poem's structure do not explain what establishes contact between poetry and reader. Riffaterre himself posits a "superreader" whose response is defined as a composite of readings provided by critics, translators, and students throughout history.

0284   Riffaterre, Michael. "The Self-Sufficient Text." *Diacritics* 3,3 (1973): 39-45.

Explicates William Blake's "The Sick Rose" as a demonstration of the presupposition that "a proper reading entails no more than a knowledge of the language" of a poem. Riffaterre points out ways in which the use of external mythic or philosophic systems of "topoi" can lead to false readings.

0285   Riffaterre, Michael. *Semiotics of Poetry*. Bloomington: Indiana University Press, 1978. 224 pp.

Explains semiotically the exchange of poet and reader. To illustrate his thesis, Riffaterre analyzes a number of French nineteenth and twentieth century poets, as well as Shakespeare and even some prose writers.

0286   Rimmon, Shlomith. "A Comprehensive Theory of Narrative: Genette's *Figures III* and the Structuralist Study of Fiction." *PTL: A Journal for Descriptive Poetics and Theory of Literature* 1 (1976): 33-62.

Maps the field of "the relatively scientific branch of literary study called poetics." Rimmon locates five main points of divergence, which are: *langue* vs. *parole*; deep structures vs. surface structures; *récit* (*histoire*) vs. *discours*; *armature* vs. totality; and paraphrase vs. texture. Rimmon calls Genette's work (0247) "impressive evidence . . . of the benefit both poetics and criticism can derive from a refusal to choose among the various directions of study." His work represents "a skillful combination of almost all of them."

0287   Robey, David, ed. *Structuralism: An Introduction*. Oxford: Clarendon Press, 1973.   154 pp.

Attempts "to give a broad account of the theoretical foundations of the subject and also of its general scope."   Exposition of the topic is presented in essays by John Lyons, Jonathan Culler, Edmund Leach and Umberto Eco.   Then Robin Gandy deals with the question of structure in mathematics, John Mepham takes up the issue of structuralism in the light of the general theory of science, and Tzvetan Todorov presents a chapter on the structural analysis of literature.

0288   Said, Edward W. *Beginnings: Intention and Method*. New York: Basic Books, 1975.   431 pp.

This dense, difficult book describes the concept of "beginnings" in literature, linguistics, and philosophy. Said explores structuralism's contribution to literary study. The section on Michel Foucault is especially informative, as is the discussion of Freud.

0289   Schaff, Adam. *Structuralism and Marxism*. Oxford: Pergamon Press, 1978. 205 pp.

Discusses the philosophical aspects of structuralism in detail, emphasizing the nature of structuralism an an intellectual trend.   Schaff also offers a critical analysis of Marxist structuralism in France, and discusses the philosophical issues in a generative grammar produced by Noam Chomsky.

0290   Scholes, Robert. *Semiotics and Interpretation*. New Haven: Yale University Press, 1982.   161 pp.

A companion piece to *Structuralism in Literature* (0291) that is less theoretical than that work and more concerned with particular texts. The first two chapters, however, try "to situate semiotics in relation to criticism in general and to the teaching of literature in particular" and "to define literature from a semiotic perspective."   Chapter Five looks at irony as a source of pleasure in literary texts. Chapter Eight illustrates the affinity between semiotics and feminism as critical methods.

0291   Scholes, Robert. *Structuralism in Literature: An Introduction*. New Haven, CT: Yale University Press, 1974.   250 pp.

This is a sort of primer on structuralism, which introduces that school's forerunners and major spokespersons.   The first chapter, "What Is Structuralism?", defines "Structuralism as a Movement of Mind" and "Structuralism as a Method."   The relationship of structuralism to literature, especially narrative, is the book's focus. Scholes considers the work of Ferdinand de Saussure, Roman Jakobson, Claude Lévi-Strauss, Michael Riffaterre, André Jolles, Etienne Souriau, Vladimir Propp, A. J. Greimas, Claude Brémond, Tzvetan Todorov, Roland Barthes and Gérard Genette. The final chapter, "The Structuralist Imagination," finds structuralist roots in English Romanticism, takes a look at Joyce's *Ulysses*, and finally at contemporary fiction. Scholes includes a useful annotated bibliography.

0292 Scholes, Robert. "Towards a Semiotics of Literature." *Critical Inquiry* 4 (1977): 105-120.

Attempts to show how the formal qualities of literature are the result of a process that multiplies or complicates the normal features of human communication. These semiotic processes possess an inherent ability to generate and communicate meaning.

0293 Suleiman, Susan R. *Authoritarian Fiction: The Ideological Novel as a Literary Genre*. New York: Columbia University Press, 1983. 256 pp.

This book studies a number of somewhat obscure French writers of the *roman à thèse* (ideological novel), and is primarily a defense of that genre. But Suleiman also discusses contemporary theories of text and reader interchange, especially those of Roland Barthes and Gérard Genette.

0294 Suleiman, Susan R. "Redundancy and the 'Readable' Text." *Poetics Today* 1 (1980): 119-143.

Begins by reviewing Roland Barthes' definitions of "readable" and "writable" texts. This essay studies redundancy, a feature of the "readable" text in realistic narrative, attempting to see "whether redundancy can function as a criterion of genre" especially in the *roman à thèse* or ideological novel. Suleiman makes use of formulae and charts for her explanation.

0295 Segre, Cesare. *Semiotics and Literary Criticism*. The Hague: Mouton Publishers, 1973. 195 pp.

Calls criticism "back within the limits of its traditional function," that is, the interpretation of literature according to its own constitutive values. Interpretation is explication of what is implicit within art. Part One of the book provides theory, and Part Two applies that theory to literary works by Antonio Machado, Gabriel García Márquez and others.

0296 Seung, T. K. *Structuralism and Hermeneutics*. New York: Columbia University Press, 1982. 310 pp.

Explores the nature of the transition from structuralism to poststructuralism. Structuralism has attempted to transform the hermeneutic act of interpretation into a fairly exact science. But today the objectivist conclusions of structuralism must be pitted against Jacques Derrida's theory of signs and his deconstructivism. Seung offers a critique of the relativism and antiscientism that has been provoked by the decline of structuralism. To some extent, the eruption of poststructuralist irrationalism has provided a healthy antidote to naive scientific optimism and dogmatism within structuralist programs. But to exalt this irrationalism as the guiding spirit of a new era is to invite intellectual anarchy.

0297   Stanzel, Franz K. *A Theory of Narrative.* Trans. by Charlotte Goedsche. Cambridge: Cambridge University Press, 1984. 328 pp.

Begins with a diagramatic "Typological Circle," which Stanzel hopes will help graphically to elucidate the relationships and correspondences between different structures of narration. This book refines Stanzel's own earlier work, by incorporating structuralism's recent contributions to literary thought. See also 0136.

0298   Sturrock, John, ed. *Structuralism and Since: From Lévi-Strauss to Derrida.* Oxford: Oxford University Press, 1979. 190 pp.

Contains an Introduction by the editor, followed by five essays: "Claude Lévi-Strauss," by Dan Sperber; "Roland Barthes," by John Sturrock; "Michel Foucault," by Hayden White; "Jacques Lacan," by Malcolm Bowie; and "Jacques Derrida," by Jonathan Culler. All of the subjects of these essays have Saussure (0067) as a common ancestor, although they belong in two opposed categories: "Lévi-Strauss and Lacan are both universalists . . . (while) Barthes, Foucault and Derrida appear as relativists, preoccupied with the historical dimension of thought, its evolution through time, and its implications for given societies."

0299   Todorov, Tzvetan. *The Fantastic: A Structural Approach to a Literary Genre.* Trans. by Richard Howard. Ithaca, NY: Cornell University Press, 1973. 186 pp.

This engaging and instructive work begins by defining literary genres, relying heavily upon the genre criticism of Northrop Frye (0088). Todorov then defines "the fantastic" in relation to both "the real and the imaginary," which hesitates "between a natural and a supernatural explanation of the events described." The reader of such a text should reject allegorical explanations. He continues, differentiating between the uncanny and the marvelous, and between poetry and allegory. Todorov then discusses the discourse and themes of the fantastic in several chapters, including "themes of the self" and "themes of the other."

0300   Todorov, Tzvetan. *An Introduction to Poetics.* Trans. by Richard Howard. Minneapolis: University of Minnesota Press, 1981. 117 pp.

Defines poetics and considers three principal aspects of texts that any competent reader must activate as "templates of organization and meaning": the semantic aspect, the verbal aspect, and the syntactic aspect, which concerns textual structures. Finally, Todorov takes up the question of literary history, with a particular concern for genres and their variations through time. He concludes that poetics may eventually be replaced by "a general science of discourses." For more on Todorov's ideas, see 0027, 0258, 0728, 0737.

0301   Todorov, Tzvetan. "The Origin of Genres." *New Literary History* 8 (1976): 159-170.

Considers "not what preceded genres in time, but, rather, what presides at the birth of genre, at any time." Todorov seeks language forms that, while announcing genres, are not yet genres in themselves, and he asks whether or not literary genres can be differentiated from other speech acts. He concludes that "there is no abyss between literature and that which is not literature; that literary genres have their origin, quite simply, in human discourse."

0302   Todorov, Tzvetan. *The Poetics of Prose*. Trans. by Richard Howard. Ithaca, NY: Cornell University Press, 1977. 272 pp.

Presents as a systematic theory of literature, "an account of the modes of literary discourse and of the various conventions and types of organization which produce meaning in literature." Further, "the goal of literary study" Todorov says, "is to understand literature as a human institution, a mode of signification." The essays in the book are divided into four groups. The first deals with the general nature of poetics, its relation to other critical activities. The second studies the formal analysis of plot structure, and the third, the analysis of genre. The final group calls into question the distinction between poetics and criticism or interpretation.

0303   Todorov, Tzvetan. "Reading as Construction." In *The Reader in the Text*, ed. by Susan R. Suleiman, 67-82. Princeton, NJ: Princeton University Press, 1980.

Asks "How does a text get us to construct an imaginary world? Which aspects of the text determine the construction we produce as we read? And in what way?" The article is divided into sections that address such themes as Referential Discourse, Narrative Filters (including Time and Point of View), Signification and Symbolization, and Construction as Theme.

0304   Todorov, Tzvetan. "Structural Analysis of Narrative." *Novel. A Forum on Fiction* 3 (1969-1970): 70-76.

Offers an abstract description of the structural approach to literature illustrated by the concrete problem of plot. Taking examples from Boccaccio's *Decameron*, Todorov attempts to make general conclusions about the nature of narrative and the principles of its analysis.

0305   Uspensky, Boris. *A Poetics of Composition: The Structure of the Artistic Text and Typology of a Compositional Form*. Trans. by Valentina Zavarin and Susan Wittig. Berkeley and Los Angeles: University of California Press, 1973. 181 pp.

Shows how a "rhetoric of means of expressing attitudes" pertains not only to compositional forms in literature, but to art forms in general. Uspensky explores the ability to vary the structure of language in accordance with the addressee in question, the addressor's role in the situation, the occasion, the topic, and so on. He offers a classic typology of five planes of expression on which point of view may be expressed (ideological, phraseological, spatial, temporal, and psychological) and defines irony as the nonconcurrence of points of view between planes. Uspensky is a structuralist, but his work is written in such a way as to be inviting to readers who have little background in semiotics. See also 0655, 0847, 1162, 1247, 1379.

0306   Waugh, Linda R. "The Poetic Function and the Nature of Language." In *Verbal Art, Verbal Sign, Verbal Time*, ed. by Krystyna Pomorska, 143-168. Minneapolis: University of Minnesota Press, 1985.

Traces the relationship between Roman Jakobson's theory of language and his poetics of literature. Jakobson's semiotic approach to language lay the groundwork for the development of a structuralist approach to literature.

0307   Wittig, Susan, ed. *Structuralism: An Inter-disciplinary Study*. Pittsburgh: Pickwick Press, 1975. 162 pp.

Collects eight essays, the first of which (by Wittig) presents a history of structuralist thought from Ferdinand de Saussure onwards. Two essays are directly concerned with biblical topics (0688, 1109). Also of particular interest is Joseph Blenkinsopp's essay on Gilgamesh. The book also includes work by Barbara Babcock-Abrahams, Evan Watkins, and R. E. Johnson.

RHETORICAL CRITICISM

See also 0088, 0114-0115, 0353, 0486, 0490, 0505, 0514, 0523, 0529, 0534, 0541, 0543, 0561, 0568, 0574, 0577, 0624, 0745-0746, 0759-0760, 0776, 0778, 0810, 0836, 0865, 0903, 0907, 0912, 0918, 0925, 0929-0930, 0944, 0947, 0952-0953, 0960, 0965-0968, 0974-0976, 0978-0979, 0983, 0986, 0994-0995, 0998-0999, 1013, 1018-1021, 1024, 1026-1027, 1050, 1052, 1067-1068, 1071, 1074, 1080, 1082, 1127, 1192, 1251-1253, 1257-1258, 1300, 1315, 1317-1318, 1359, 1420, 1425-1428, 1430, 1433-1438, 1440-1447, 1449-1457, 1461-1462, 1464-1474, 1476, 1478-1482, 1484-1485, 1488-1489, 1492-1498, 1502-1508, 1511, 1513, 1515, 1519, 1521-1523, 1529, 1535, 1537, 1580, 1640.

0308   Baird, A. Craig. *Rhetoric: A Philosophical Inquiry*. New York: Ronald Press Co., 1965. 246 pp.

Not a study of rhetorical criticism *per se*, but an investigation of the philosophy of rhetoric itself. The book tries to be comprehensive in its treatment of causes and results, facts and inferences, such as might be relevant to any field. One chapter is specifically devoted to "Communication in Literature." Here, Baird treats rhetoric in relation to literature; rhetoric and poetic; rhetoric and literature as communication; thought; emotion and language; personality expression; moral content; and language in literature and rhetoric.

0309   Beale, Walter H. "Rhetorical Performance Discourse: A New Theory of Epideictic." *Philosophy and Rhetoric* 11 (1978): 221-246.

Begins by proposing that Austin's distinction between performative and constative (0042) has an application to whole discourses or "rhetorical acts," and that the notion of "performance" thus applied is a principal definer of the category of rhetoric traditionally known as "epideictic." Beale surveys the ancients on epideictic, mentions other rhetoricians' emphasis on its reinforcement of traditional values, and then argues that "the epideictic or rhetorical performative discourse is as much an instrument of social upheaval as of social concord."

0310 Bitzer, Lloyd F. "The Rhetorical Situation." *Philosophy and Rhetoric* 1 (1968): 1-14. Also published in *Rhetoric: A Tradition in Transition*, ed. by W. R. Fisher, 247-260. Ann Arbor: University of Michigan Press, 1974.

A classic article which claims that "a particular discourse comes into existence because of some specific condition or situation which invites utterance." This emphasis on defining the rhetorical situation renews the essential "reader-orientation" of rhetorical criticism and rescues it from preoccupation with stylistic and formal devices. According to Bitzer, "The situation controls the rhetorical response in the same sense that the question controls the answer and the problem controls the solution." See also 0313.

0311 Black, Edwin. *Rhetorical Criticism: A Study in Method*. Madison: University of Wisconsin Press, 1978. 177 pp.

Considers six topics: (1) "The Meaning of Criticism," which Black defines as "a discipline that through the investigation and appraisal of the activities and products of men, seeks as its end the understanding of man himself"; (2) "The Practice of Rhetorical Criticism" which discusses three approaches: the movement study, the psychological study, and the neo-Aristotelian study; (3) "Rhetoric and General Criticism," which draws "some general conclusions about the adequacy of neo-Aristotelian criticism to discharge the general functions of criticism"; (4) "Aristotle and Rhetorical Criticism"; (5) "Alternative Frame of Reference"; and (6) "The Genre of Argumentation," which describes "the process by which, through the medium of language, a private attitude becomes a public faith."

0312 Brandt, W. J. *The Rhetoric of Argumentation*. Indianapolis: Bobbs-Merrill Co., 1970. 288 pp.

Proposes a way of analyzing a certain type of prose--argumentation. The latter includes "essays, speeches, learned articles--in short, all of those modern forms of discourse that have their origin in classical oration" rather than in prose fiction or poetry. Chapters one through three determine the parts of an argumentative piece and their interrelationships, defining and exploring "structural rhetoric." The next three chapters deal with "textual rhetoric," discussing smaller units within the texts (e.g., sentences and paragraphs), and the way that "figures of speech and various logical devices" work. Brandt also considers "defective argumentation" and "reportorial writing."

0313 Brinton, Alan. "Situation in the Theory of Rhetoric." *Philosophy and Rhetoric* 14 (1981): 234-248.

Builds on Bitzer's influential work on rhetorical situation (0310) by addressing three questions: (1) What is the relation between rhetorical situation and rhetorical act? (2)

To what extent is the rhetorical situation a matter of objective facts? and (3) To what extent is Bitzer's account descriptive and to what extent is it normative?

0314   Burke, Kenneth. *A Grammar of Motives*. Berkeley and Los Angeles: University of California Press, 1969. 530 pp.

Attempts to answer the question, "What is involved when we say what people are doing and why they are doing it?" Burke says that any complete statement about motives will offer some kind of answer to these five questions: what was done (art), when or where it was done (scene), who did it (agent), how (agency), and why (purpose). He attempts to clarify the ways in which dialectical and metaphysical issues necessarily figure in the subject of motivation. This volume was intended as the first of a trilogy, the second of which is 0315.

0315   Burke, Kenneth. *A Rhetoric of Motives*. Berkeley and Los Angeles: University of California Press, 1969. 340 pp.

Seeks to write a "philosophy of rhetoric." Burke begins with analysis of texts that are usually treated as pure poetry and tries to show why rhetorical and dialectical considerations are also appropriate. Then he seeks "to mark off the areas of rhetoric, by showing how a rhetorical motive is often present where it is not usually recognized, or thought to belong." Burke's interests in political, ecclesial, and religious issues are never far from the surface.

0316   Burke, Kenneth. *The Rhetoric of Religion: Studies in Logology*. Boston: Beacon Press, 1961. 327 pp.

A study in the persuasive tactics of religion by one of this century's foremost scholars of rhetoric. "Religious cosmogonies," Burke says, "are designed as exceptionally thoroughgoing modes of persuasion. To persuade men toward certain acts, religions would form the kinds of attitude that prepare men for such acts." The final chapter of the book analyzes the rhetoric of the first three chapters of Genesis.

0317   Burks, Don M., ed. *Rhetoric, Philosophy, and Literature: An Exploration*. West Lafayette, IN: Purdue University Press, 1978. 115 pp.

A collection of essays from an interdisciplinary conference featuring linguists, literary critics, and philosophers. Rhetoric, here, is defined broadly as "the rationale of the informative and suasory in discourse." The interest of the writers is not in "digests of devices," but in the mode of "adjusting persons to ideas and ideas to persons." Wayne C. Booth offers "The Pleasures and Pitfalls of Irony: Or, Why Don't You Say What You Mean?," which is essentially a condensation of his book on irony (0140). Other essays include "Rhetoric, Poetics, and Philosophy" by Kenneth Burke; "The Arts of Indirection" by Maurice Natanson; "From Philosophy to Rhetoric and Back" by Henry W. Johnstone, Jr.; "Rhetoric and Public Knowledge" by Lloyd F. Bitzer; and "Literature and Politics" by Donald C. Bryant.

0318   Campbell, Karlyn Kohrs, and Jamieson, Kathleen Hall, eds. *Form and Genre: Shaping Rhetorical Action*. Falls Church, VA: Speech Communication Association, 1976. 189 pp.

A collection of papers by a number of rhetorical critics, focusing on "significant forms" in rhetorical criticism, that is, on "recurring patterns in discourse or action including, among others, the repeated use of images, metaphors, arguments, structural arrangements, configurations of language, or a combination of such elements." An introductory essay by the editors on "Form and Genre in Rhetorical Criticism" is especially helpful. Other contributors include Herbert W. Simons, Ernest Borman, Edwin Black, James Measell, Ronald Carpenter, Michael Halloran, and Bruce Gronbeck.

0319   Chase, J. Richard. "The Classical Conception of Epideictic." *Quarterly Journal of Speech* 47 (1961): 293-300.

Seeks the classical understanding of epideictic to reduce modern scholars' confusion about the term. Chase traces its history in the ancient world, from the fifth century B.C., through Aristotle, Quintilian and "the treatises of the Second Sophistic." He concludes that "epideictic must remain, for all practical purposes, oratory that is dominated by either praise or blame."

0320   Clark, Donald Lemen. *Rhetoric in Greco-Roman Education*. New York: Columbia University Press, 1957. 285 pp.

Not a history of literary criticism in antiquity, but an account of educational methods used by ancient teachers in grammar schools and schools of rhetoric. Still, the various literary theories taught by these teachers of rhetoric are described, so that the book offers insight into different manners of persuasion that were available to writers of this period.

0321   Corbett, Edward P. *Classical Rhetoric for the Modern Student*. 2nd ed. New York: Oxford University Press, 1971.

Concerned with "the strategies of discourse directed to a definite audience for a definite purpose." This textbook, which aims at making students more eloquent, contains four sections after the introduction: "Discovery of Arguments"; "Arrangement of Material"; "Style" and "Survey of Rhetoric." The last section is a history of rhetoric from classical times through the eighteenth century.

0322   Kennedy, George A. *The Art of Persuasion in Greece*. Princeton: Princeton University Press, 1963. 350 pp.

A history of Greek rhetoric, intended for students of classical literature. After an introduction on the nature of rhetoric, Kennedy traces the theory and techniques of rhetoric in Greek literature from the earliest times through Dionysius of Halicarnassus. The book forms the first volume of a trilogy on ancient rhetoric (cf. 0323, 0325).

0323   Kennedy, George A. *The Art of Rhetoric in the Roman World, 300 B.C.--A. D. 300*. Princeton: Princeton University Press, 1972. 658 pp.

The second volume in Kennedy's trilogy on the history of ancient rhetoric (cf. 0322, 0325). This volume covers the period during which the New Testament was produced, although Kennedy does not comment on the biblical texts themselves (but see 0529). The first chapter on "Early Roman Rhetoric" outlines some concepts that are basic for understanding the rhetoric of this period, such as the distinction between judicial, deliberative, and epideictic rhetoric.

0324   Kennedy, George A. *Classical Rhetoric and its Christian and Secular Tradition from Ancient to Modern Times*. Chapel Hill: University of North Carolina Press, 1980. 291 pp.

Observes the development of rhetoric from oral tradition, through Classical Greece and Rome, the Middle Ages, Renaissance and Neoclassical ages. This readable book shows the influence of trends in society upon the rhetoric of each age. Includes a chapter on Judaeo-Christian rhetoric.

0325   Kennedy, George A. *Greek Rhetoric Under Christian Emperors*. Princeton: Princeton University Press, 1983. 333 pp.

The third volume of Kennedy's history of ancient rhetoric (cf. 0322-0323). This volume deals with the period after the production of the biblical texts, but its chapter on "Later Greek Rhetorical Theory" includes discussions on progymnasmata, stasis, invention, and other matters often thought to be important in understanding the earlier texts.   One chapter is also devoted to "Christianity and Rhetoric," giving consideration to the writings of Eusebius, Athanasius, John Chrysostom, and others.

0326   Lausberg, Heinrich. *Handbuch der literarischen Rhetorik: Eine Grundlegung der Literaturwissenschaft*. München: Max Hüber Verlag, 1960.

A basic handbook of literary rhetoric, covering devices, figures and symbols, and other stylistic features that belong to the phenomenon of literary communication.

0327   McCall, Marsh. *Ancient Rhetorical Theories of Simile and Comparison*. Loeb Classical Monographs. Cambridge, MA: Harvard University Press, 1969. 272 pp.

Seeks "through a detailed analysis of . . . terms of comparison . . . to arrive at the ancient understanding of the nature, scope, and purpose of comparison." The ancient use of the term is "divided between contexts describing the general act or a process of comparison and contexts in which a figure of comparison is present, and this process is concerned primarily with the latter." McCall observes differences between Greek and Latin attitudes, and between ancient and modern views.

0328   Murphy, James J., ed. *A Synoptic History of Classical Rhetoric.* Studies in Speech. New York: Random House, 1972. 199 pp.

Offers an overview of rhetorical theory as found in ancient Greek and Roman cultures. Each chapter is written by a different scholar and covers a specific historical period. Direct summaries of each of the major rhetorical works of the period are provided.

0329   Oravec, Christine. "'Observation' in Aristotle's Theory of Epideictic." *Philosophy and Rhetoric* 9 (1976): 162-174.

Argues against the view that epideictic is "trivial entertainment" by saying that Aristotle conceived of its juridical and educative functions as well. Oravec also says that "this perspective . . . suggests some audience-based theoretical principles for defining and explicating the genre."

0330   Perelman, Chaim, and Olbrechts-Tyteca, L. *The New Rhetoric: A Treatise on Argumentation.* Trans. by John Wilkinson and Purcell Weaver. Notre Dame: Notre Dame University Press, 1969. 566 pp.

Defines rhetoric and its strategies as argumentation rather than as style. Furthermore, Perelman and Olbrechts-Tyteca show that the persuasive power of an argument is influenced significantly by its situation. Rhetoric has social and political implications. The approach to rhetoric advanced in this extremely influential book is "new" in comparison to that taken by such studies as Booth's *The Rhetoric of Fiction* (0139), where rhetoric is treated as expressive style. But actually the linking of rhetoric to strategies of persuasion represents a re-discovery of classical theory that dates back to Aristotle. This book, then, brings rhetorical criticism (in the classical sense) into the twentieth century. This book has three main sections: "The Framework of Argumentation"; "The Starting Point of Argument"; and "Techniques of Argumentation." See also 0534, 0568, 1444, 1461, 1470.

0331   Richards, Ivor Armstrong. *The Philosophy of Rhetoric.* New York: Oxford University Press, 1936. 138 pp.

A classic study, now out-dated but still often quoted. Richards considers rhetoric to be "a study of misunderstanding and its remedies." He explores the ways in which "good communication can differ from bad." Topics considered are "The Aims of Discourse and Types of Context"; "The Interanimation of Words"; and "Metaphor."

0332   Thomson, James A. K. *Irony: An Historical Introduction.* London: George Allen and Unwin, 1926. Reprint. Folcroft, PA: Folcroft Library Editions, 1974. 242 pp.

Thomson begins with a look at the Greeks, from whom the concept of irony has come down. He deals with the great comic and tragic writers Aristophanes, Aeschylus, Euripides and Sophocles, as well as with the epic poet Homer. He also considers Herodotus, Thucydides and Plato, then turns to the development of the concept of irony by the ancient Romans, including Horace, Ovid and Tacitus.

0333   Welch, John. *Chiasmus in Antiquity*. Hildesheim: Gerstenberg, 1981.

A collection of essays that attest to the pervasive quality of the use of chiasmus in ancient literature. Chiasmus is a rhetorical device that consists of two main elements, inversion and balance, which combine to produce a third, climactic centrality. When elements occur in the stuctural pattern ABCB'A', the middle element (C) receives emphasis. The essays in this volume indicate that use of chiasmus flowed from other ancient literature into biblical western classical literature.

READER-ORIENTED APPROACHES: AFFECTIVE, PHENOMENOLOGICAL, PSYCHOANALYTICAL, ETC.

See also 0001, 0049, 0070, 0083-0085, 0100, 0102-0103, 0121-0122, 0259, 0283, 0495, 0500, 0508, 0512, 0528, 0555, 0587, 0714, 0860, 0907, 0952, 1054, 1114, 1143, 1183-1184, 1208-1215, 1293-1294, 1309, 1338, 1371, 1381, 1396-1397, 1417, 1420, 1446, 1486-1487, 1490-1491, 1536, 1541, 1597, 1606, 1611, 1615, 1617, 1620, 1640, 1656.

0334   Bachelard, Gaston. *The Poetics of Space*. New York: Orion Books, 1964. 240 pp.

Using as examples French lyric poems, Bachelard insists upon the non-rational interplay between the psyche of the reader and the image of the poem. Poetry must not be translated into rational terms or intellectualized as has been then the tendency in psychological criticism. Criticism must *be* a poem to have any validity. See also 0372.

0335   Barnouw, Dagmar. "Critics in the Act of Reading." *Poetics Today* 1,4 (1980): 213-222.

A brief commentary on Jauss' *Aesthetic Experience and Literary Hermeneutic*s (0099), and on Iser's *The Implied Reader* (0390) and *The Act of Reading* (0389). Iser works with American texts, while Jauss "draws on a broad . . . eclectic variety of German and French literary and philosophical texts." Barnouw says that Iser wants to present an aesthetic response theory but is dissatisfied with the notion of interpretation as an end in itself.

0336   Black, Stephen A. "On Reading Psychoanalytically." *College English* 39 (1977): 267-274.

Contends that we should regard literary meaning as inherent in "the relationship which occurs between a reader and a literary work." Black argues against both objective (new-critical) and subjective positions, preferring as his model the relationship that occurs in the analyst's consulting room. He discusses reading psychoanalytically with reference to a pedagogical experiment that he used in his own classroom.

0337   Bleich, David. "Epistemological Assumptions in the Study of Response." In *Reader Response Criticism*, ed. by Jane P. Tompkins, 134-163. Baltimore: Johns Hopkins University Press, 1980.

Originally published in 1978 in Bleich's book *Subjective Criticism* (0341). He evaluates the epistemologies of a succession of scholars and teachers (including Louise Rosenblutt, Norman Holland, and Stanley Fish) and discusses the ways in which they affect each scholar's assessment of the text-reader interplay. He concludes that when "knowledge is no longer viewed as objective, the purpose of pedagogical institutions . . . is to synthesize knowledge rather than to pass it along: schools become the regular agency of subjective initiative."

0338   Bleich, David. *Literature and Self-Awareness: Critical Questions and Emotional Responses*. New York: Harper and Row, 1977.

Describes the encounter of readers with literature in terms drawn from subjective psychology. Bleich distinguishes between "response," which is the initial process of symbolization through which a work is given meaning in the mind of an individual reader, and "interpretation," which is the process of resymbolization through which responses are given coherence.

0339   Bleich, David. "The Logic of Interpretation." *Genre* 10 (1977): 363-394.

Discusses Freud's method and practice in interpreting dreams, saying that "rather than interpretation discovering the motives of dreams, dreams are the motive for interpretation." Bleich applies these insights to interpretation of aesthetic objects. As in a therapeutic situation, the interpreter of an aesthetic object has the desire to create knowledge from the subjective experience of the work of art. The "logic of interpretation," then, "derives from the subjective paradigm."

0340   Bleich, David. *Readings and Feelings: An Introduction to Subjective Criticism*. Urbana, IL: National Council of Teachers of English, 1975. 114 pp.

Considers the interactions of feelings and knowledge in the encounter between reader and text in an academic context. The opening chapter discusses the classroom situation and the teacher's role in it. Then Bleich discusses affective and associative responses to literature, criteria for literary judgment, and interpretation within a community.

0341   Bleich, David. *Subjective Criticism*. Baltimore: Johns Hopkins University Press, 1978. 320 pp.

Suggests a "new paradigm" through which our present conception of language may be altered, and through which individual readers can be given due consideration. Bleich uses evidence taken from his actual classroom experience in using subjective forms of thought. He presents four specific contexts for the organized pursuit of literary and linguistic knowledge.

0342   Bleich, David.   "The Subjective Paradigm in Science, Psychology, and Criticism." *New Literary History* 7 (1976): 313-334.

Notes a recent decrease in the "orthodoxy" of the study of literature, due to a change in social consciousness.   The shift is from an objective paradigm to a subjective paradigm.   Models for scientific study are also changing and show evidence of influence by the subjective paradigm, as do philosophical enterprises.   Bleich sees the subjective paradigm as promising an ethical dimension to knowedge.   See also 0380.

0343   Bleich, David; Kintgen, Eugene R.; Smith, Bruce; and Vargyai, Sando J.   "The Psychological Study of Language and Literature: A Selected Annotated Bibliography." *Style* 12 (1978): 113-210.

A bibliography divided into two parts: Part I is devoted to the perception and cognition of language, while Part II consists of the affective and philosophical considerations in relation to literature and aesthetics.   Kintgen introduces the first part, and Bleich the second.

0344   Bloom, Harold.   *Anxiety of Influence: A Theory of Poetry*.   New York: Oxford University Press, 1973.

The initial presentation of Bloom's psychoanalytical theory of literature.   Bloom considers poetry from the viewpoint of literary history and describes the work of poets as being to overcome the influence of their precursors.   Every poem, therefore, presents a "misreading" of previous poetry.   For practical application of the theory see 0346, 0348.   See also 1571.

0345   Bloom, Harold.   *Kabbalah and Criticism*.   New York: Seabury Press, 1975.   126 pp.

Begins with a discussion of what Kabbalah is, comparing it to Gnosticism and Neoplatonism.   Kabbalah is "more a mode of intellectual speculation than a way of union with God . . . (The) Kabbalists sought *knowledge* in the Book."   The following two chapters, "Kabbalah and Criticism" and "The Necessity of Misreading," touch upon some secular poetry, but are concerned generally with the act of reading in a Kabbalistic way.

0346   Bloom, Harold.   *A Map of Misreading*.   New York: Oxford University Press, 1975.   206 pp.

Demonstrates how the theory of poetry proposed in *Anxiety of Influence* (0344) works in practice.   Bloom's "map" shows how English and American poets had to create their own psychic defenses against the two giants, Milton and Emerson.   Such poets as Wordsworth, Shelley, Keats, Tennyson, Whitman, Dickinson, Stevens, Warren, and

Ashberry can be placed on the map as "misreading" these two giants in an effort to overcome their inevitable influence.

0347   Bloom, Harold. *Poetics of Influence*. Ed. and introduced by John Hollander. New Haven, CT: Henry R. Schwab, 1988. 500 pp.

Collects essays from different periods of Bloom's writing, including pieces from larger works, arranged in chronological order.   The final three essays are previously unpublished. As well as famous essays on William Butler Yeats, Robert Browning and Sigmund Freud, this collection includes: "Martin Buber on the Bible"; "Jewish Culture and Jewish Identity"; "Apocalypse Then"; "'Before Moses Was, I Am': The Original and Belated Testaments"; and "Criticism, Canon Formation, and Prophecy: The Sorrows of Facticity."

0348   Bloom, Harold. *Ruin the Sacred Truths: Poetry and Belief from the Bible to the Present*. Cambridge, MA: Harvard University Press, 1989. 216 pp.

Applies the author's own brand of psychological literary criticism to the biblical book of Jeremiah as well as to Dante, Shakespeare, Milton, Blake, Wordsworth, Kafka, Freud, Beckett, and others. The central thesis is that original writers must transform their intellectual and spiritual heritage; a new work succeeds only if it distorts, misreads, and overpowers older works of tradition. Bloom proposes that what all of the writers he discusses have in common is a threatened and exhilarated sense of others' achievements (Dante overcomes Virgil; Shakespeare, Chaucer; Blake, the Hebrew Bible; and so on).

0349   Brinker, Menachem. "Indeterminacy, Meaning, and Two Phenomenologies of Reading: Iser and Ingarden." *Poetics Today* 1,4 (1980): 203-212.

Iser's 1978 book *The Act of Reading* (0389) uses Ingarden's earlier contribution (0387) as a point of departure.   Brinker summarizes Iser's critique of Ingarden, then describes Iser's approach to the act of reading.

0350   Bruss, Elizabeth W. "The Game of Literature and Some Literary Games." *New Literary History* 9 (1977): 153-172.

Says that certain literary works demand more than a reader who becomes "lost" in a book; they invite a "play-reader" who must be capable of seeing character, narrative suspense, sensuous language, and all the rest as mobile and highly problematical, as "just so many counters to be shifted about the board." The game is played between writer and reader. Bruss' article explores "the nature of these roles and the quality of their interaction."

0351   Crews, Frederick. *Out of My System: Psychoanalysis, Ideology, and Critical Method*. New York: Oxford University Press, 1975. 214 pp.

Contains four chapters dealing directly with critical theory based on Freud. The work is also fueled by political concerns, notably the author's protest of the Vietnam War.

0352   Crews, Frederick, ed. *Psychoanalysis and the Literary Process*. Berkeley and Los Angeles: University of California Press, 1970. 296 pp.

Collects six essays that grew out of a seminar in which participants "provisionally agreed to share psychoanalytic assumptions" and look together at literary texts. The book intends "to demonstrate the range and potential usefulness of psychoanalytic criticism" and to help others who would like to make use of a similar approach. The book contains a bibliography of psychoanalytic theories and of psychoanalytic criticism of literature.

0353   Crosman, Inge Karalus.   "Annotated Bibliography of Audience-Oriented Criticism." In *The Reader in the Text*, ed. by Susan R. Suleiman, 401-424. Princeton, NJ: Princeton University Press, 1980.

Categorizes the books and articles chosen as "most relevant" to the topic of the book as Rhetorical, Semiotic and Structuralist, Phenomenological, Psychoanalytic and Subjective, Sociological and Historical, Hermeneutic, and Special Volumes. Not all the entries are annotated.

0354   Crosman, Robert. "Do Readers Make Meaning?" In *The Reader in the Text*, ed. by Susan R. Suleiman, 149-165. Princeton, NJ: Princeton University Press, 1980.

Says that "meaning" can "stand for a speaker's intention, the common understanding, or an individual's subjective valuing of something." The understandings of this word will provide "different answers to the question of whether readers will make meaning." He discusses Hirsch's views (0096-0097) in depth, and concludes that "yes, readers make meaning."

0355   Culler, Jonathan.   "Prolegomena to a Theory of Reading." In *The Reader in the Text*, ed. by Susan R. Suleiman, 46-66. Princeton, NJ: Princeton University Press, 1980.

Claims that literary criticism is "a discipline which aims at knowledge." He warns against experimental situations that seek free associations in order to determine what the range of interpretation may be about a particular work. Rather, "one need only consult the spectrum of interpretation that literary history records for almost every major work." He uses Blake's poem "London" as an example.

0356 De Maria, Robert, Jr. "The Ideal Reader: A Critical Fiction." *Proceedings of the Modern Language Association* 93 (1978): 463-474.

Presents a history of critical interest in the reader's status, concentrating on Samuel Johnson and John Dryden from the eighteenth century, Samuel Taylor Coleridge from the nineteenth, and finally Northrop Frye. Johnson's reader, De Maria says, is an allegorical, archetypal figure. Dryden's reader is from "a certain class of men" and represents "particular conceptions of nature, and an authoritative, though not universal, community of judgments." Coleridge also calls "for an elite group of readers" who learn primarily by learning about themselves. Frye's reader "is a soul seeking salvation," and he is both creative and heroic.

0357   Detweiler, Robert, ed. *Reader Response Approaches to Biblical and Secular Texts. Semeia* 31 (1985). 230 pp.

Detweiler edits the 1985 issue of *Semeia*, which is wholly given over to this topic. In addition to Fowler's introduction (0367) and Detweiler's conclusion (1563), there are two major sections. The first, "Reading Biblical Texts," includes 0506, 0733, 1121, 1133, 1161. The second section, "Reading Secular Texts," contains essays on works by Vaughan, Pope, Melville, and Brecht.

0358   Fish, Stanley E. *Change, Rhetoric, and the Practice of Theory*. Durham, NC: Duke University Press, forthcoming.

Announced for publication.

0359   Fish, Stanley E. "How to Do Things with Austin and Searle: Speech Act Theory and Literary Criticism." *Modern Language Notes* 91 (1976): 983-1025.

Concludes that, "if Speech Act theory is itself an interpretation, then it cannot possibly serve as an all-purpose interpretive key." Fish reads Shakespeare's *Coriolanus* in the article, observing that its power "is a function of its limitations."

0360   Fish, Stanley E. "Interpreting the *Variorum*." In *Reader Response Criticism*, ed. by Jane P. Tompkins, 164-184. Baltimore: Johns Hopkins University Press, 1980.

In this essay from 1976, Fish begins by responding to the publication of Volumes I and II of the Milton Variorum commentary.   His interest, he says, is in the interpretive cruxes, seeking "not to solve . . . (them), but to make (them) signify," by seeing them as "evidence of an experience and then by specifying for that experience a meaning." He explores reader response to three sonnets and to some passages from *Lycidas*, showing the inadequacy of formalist response to poetry. The interpretive action, too, needs to be considered. Fish says, "This, then, is my thesis: that the form of the reader's experience, formal units, and the structure of intention are one, that they come into view simultaneously, and that therefore the questions of priority and independence do not arise."

0361   Fish, Stanley E. *Is There a Text in This Class? The Authority of Interpretive Communities*. Cambridge, MA: Harvard University Press, 1980. 408 pp.

This collection of essays traces Fish's journey from formalism to a belief that authoritative critical communities produce meaning. "A polemic that was mounted in the name of the reader and against the text has ended by the subsuming of both the text and the reader under the larger category of interpretation." Accessible, sensible, and self-critical, it provides fine examples of the practical application of Fish's evolving theory. See also 0409, 1054, 1549, 1617, 1698.

0362   Fish, Stanley E.   "Literature in the Reader: Affective Stylistics." In *Reader Response Criticism*, ed. by Jane P. Tompkins, 70-100. Baltimore: Johns Hopkins University Press, 1980.

Also published in Fish, *Is There a Text?* (0361), this article begins by addressing Wimsatt and Beardsley's "The Affective Fallacy" (0222) which claims that too much emphasis on a poem's "results" causes the poem itself to "disappear." Using a specific example, Fish makes an analysis of what a sentence *does* rather than what it *means*. He sees the text as an event in the reader, rather than as a thing. The event itself becomes the text's meaning.

0363   Fish, Stanley E.   "Normal Circumstances, Literal Languages, Direct Speech Acts, the Ordinary, the Everyday, the Obvious, What Goes Without Saying, and Other Special Cases." *Critical Inquiry* 4 (1978): 625-644.

This article opens with a story of a baseball player's new view of a baseball game following his religious conversion. Using Milton's *Samson Agonistes*, Fish argues "that there is always a text . . . but that what is in it can change, and therefore at no level is it independent of and prior to interpretation." Fish calls his position "neither subjective nor objective."

0364   Fish, Stanley E.   *Self-Consuming Artifacts*.   Berkeley and Los Angeles: University of California Press, 1972. 432 pp.

Fish deals with the works of Plato, Augustine, Donne, Bacon, Herbert, Bunyan, and others. This inviting book shows how the reader is transformed through encountering texts by these authors. The applied criticism is instructive, though not always in accord with Fish's more recent theories.

0365   Fish, Stanley E.   *Surprised by Sin: The Reader in Paradise Lost*. Berkeley and Los Angeles: University of California Press, 1971. 361 pp.

Fish describes this book in *Is There a Text?* (0361): "The thesis of that book is that *Paradise Lost* is a poem about how its readers came to be the way they are. It follows, I argue, that the difficulties one experiences in reading the poem are not to be lamented or discounted but are to be seen as manifestations of the legacy left to us by Adam when he fell."

0366   Fish, Stanley E.   "Why No One's Afraid of Wolfgang Iser." *Diacritics* 11,1 (1981): 2-13.

Reviews Iser's *The Art of Reading* (0389), asking why, if Iser is so influential, isn't he controversial as well? His major ideas--like the process of interaction between text and reader and the "gaps" that need creative, imaginative work on the reader's part --seem able to accomodate emphases that have often been perceived as contradictory in the writing of other theorists. Iser affirms both sides of a traditional opposition. But his theory falls apart, Fish says, because its crucial distinction "between the determinate and the indeterminate will not hold," a problem that the second half of the article elaborates. See also 0394, 0427.

0367   Fowler, Robert M.   "Who is 'the Reader' in Reader-Response Criticism?" *Semeia* 31 (1985): 5-23.

Discusses the distinction between the "reader" (who serves the text) and the "critic" (who acts as its judge and master), and between the real reader, the implied reader, and the narrative (along with their authorial counterparts). Fowler also discusses the rhetorical stance of the "ideal reader" and the rediscovery of reading as "a rich and dynamic temporal experience." The author is a biblical scholar, best known for his work on the Gospel of Mark (1208-1215).

0368   Freund, Elizabeth. *The Return of the Reader: Reader-Response Criticism*. New York: Methuen and Co., 1987. 192 pp.

Touts the merits of reader-oriented critical theory in conscious defiance of text-oriented approaches. Part I, "Precursors," has a chapter devoted to a reconsideration of the criticism of I. A. Richards and one on "New Criticism and the Avoidance of Reading." Part II, which deals with "Reader-Response Criticisms" has four chapters devoted to Jonathan Culler, Stanley Fish, Norman Holland, and Wolfgang Iser. This book is clearly written and provides a good introduction to contemporary theory.

0369   Gibson, Eleanor J., and Levin, Harry. *The Psychology of Reading*. Cambridge, MA: MIT Press, 1975. 630 pp.

Offers a thorough compendium of psychological inquiry into the relationship among reading, human development and pedagogy. The authors, who are psychologists, deal with perception, linguistic skills, systems of writing and other topics in their introduction, followed by an encyclopedic study of the psychology of reading.

0370   Gibson, Walker. "Authors, Speakers, Readers, and Mock Readers." In *Reader Response Criticism*, ed. by Jane P. Tompkins, 1-6. Baltimore: Johns Hopkins University Press, 1980.

This article from 1950 works upon the assumption that, as there exist an author and a speaker, there also exist a reader and a consciousness engaged by a text. This consciousness whom Gibson calls the "mock reader," interacts with the "speaker," both in advertising and in serious literature like *The Great Gatsby*.

0371   Gloversmith, Frank, ed. *The Theory of Reading*. Sussex: Harvester Press, 1984. 246 pp.

A collection of essays by authors who contend that the value of a novel depends as much on the individual reader as on the work itself, so that "our inherited notion of the novel must be an anachronism." The authors deny the possibility of an infallible theory of reading, but offer various alternatives to traditional theory. This approach, the editor says, represents an affirmation of "legitimate pluralism." The essays are "Renoving that Bible: The Absolute Text of (Post) Modernism" by Valentine Cunningham; "Author-Reader-Language: Reflections on a Critical Closed Circuit" by David Morse; "Representation and Colonial Text: A Critical Exploration of Some Forms of Mimeticism" by Homi Bhaba; "Bakhtin, Sociolinguistics and Deconstruction" by Allon White; "Autonomy Theory: Ortega, Roger Fry, Virginia Woolf" by Frank Gloversmith; "Contexts of Reading: The Reception of D. H. Lawrence's *The Rainbow* and *Women in Love*" by Alistair Davies; and "Making and Breaking the Novel Tradition" by Stuart Laing. See also 0414.

0372   Hans, James S. "Gaston Bachelard and The Phenomenology of the Reading Consciousness." *Journal of Aesthetics and Art Criticism* 35 (1977): 315-327.

Describes Bachelard's poetics (0334) as one of "epiphany," and as a theory that is "specifically subjective in viewpoint with an objective intent." Bachelard, he says, has provided us with a poetics that places the image in the forefront and distinguishes the image from both metaphor and concept.

0373   Harding, D. W. "Psychological Processes in the Reading of Fiction." *British Journal of Aesthetics* 2 (1962): 133-147.

Sees the mode of response made by the reader of a novel as an extension of the mode of response made by an onlooker at actual events. Reading is partly "imaginative or empathetic insight," but it is also the reader's "evaluation of the participants and what they do and suffer." Finally, the "sophisticated reader knows that he is in social communication of a special sort with the author."

0374   Hartman, Geoffrey H., ed. *Psychoanalysis and the Question of the Text.* Baltimore: Johns Hopkins University Press, 1978. 182 pp.

Contains a collection of theoretical essays on psychoanalytic literary criticism. Contributions include articles by Murray M. Schwartz, Cory Nelson, Neil Hertz, Jacques Derrida, and Barbara Johnson as well as the editor. These essays take up Freud's insights in ways that the older psychoanalytic criticism failed to do: to understand "from within the institutional development of psychoanalysis, and from the inner development of Freud's writings, what kind of event in the history of interpretation psychoanalysis is proving to be."

0375   Herméren, Göran. "Intention and Interpretation in Literary Criticism." *New Literary History* 7 (1975): 57-82.

Argues against Palmer (0014), who upholds Monroe Beardsley's and William Wimsatt's famous views on the "intentional fallacy" (0222).

0376   Holland, Norman. *The Dynamics of Literary Response.* New York: W. W. Norton and Co., 1968. 378 pp.

Proposes to talk about literature "primarily as an experience." Holland first describes works of literature objectively, as so many words on a piece of paper or spoken aloud. Then he describes his own psychological response to the objective stimulus and looks for points of correspondence between the text objectively understood and subjectively experienced.

0377   Holland, Norman. *Five Readers Reading*. New Haven, CT: Yale University Press, 1975. 418 pp.

The "five readers" are students who discuss on tape their responses to examples of twentieth-century short stories. Using psychological tests, Holland shows how their readings relate to their psychological makeup. He denies the autonomy of texts, positing that we must understand the transactions between readers and texts in order to understand texts themselves. He defines three stages of reader response and suggests finally that responses of various readers need to be shared.

0378   Holland, Norman. *The I*. New Haven, CT: Yale University Press, 1985.

A psychoanalytic study by an author who frequently devotes himself to phenomenological varieties of literary criticism. This ambitious volume, which is indebted to Freud but refers to a broad range of psychoanalytic theories, is divided into four sections: "The Aesthetics of I"; "A Psychology of I"; "A History of I" and "A Science of I."

0379   Holland, Norman.   "Literary Interpretation and Three Phases of Psychoanalysis." *Critical Inquiry* 3 (1976): 221-233.

Taking Wordsworth's short poem "A Slumber Did My Spirit Seal" as a "patient," Holland describes the three phases through which psychoanalytic criticism has moved. First, a critic will read the poem in the "early psychoanalytic vocabulary of the Oedipus complex." Then, in the "second phase, a literary critic would try to find ego strategies as they are apparently embodied in the language of a poem," gaining a reading that is "less bizarre." Finally, "the third phase of psychoanalysis looks toward the main current of twentieth-century scientific thought." This phase "is itself a scientific paradigm, but it is also the science that describes how people get such paradigms in their heads." This sort of criticism will have "as many readings as there are readers to write them . . . (risking) intimacy in order to restore individuality."

0380   Holland, Norman. "The New Paradigm: Subjective or Transactive?" *New Literary History* 7 (1976): 335-346.

Comments upon Bleich's essay, "The Subjective Paradigm in Science, Psychology, and Criticism" (0342). Holland agrees with Bleich that "a profound change has taken place in our expectations of objectivity, but he prefers the term "transactive" to "subjective" because "the *transaction* between self and other is paramount."

0381   Holland, Norman. *Poems in Persons: An Introduction to the Psychoanalysis of Literature*. New York: W. W. Norton and Co., 1973. 183 pp.

Contains three essays: "A Maker's Mind"; "Two Readers' Minds"; and "My Mind and Yours"; as well as "A Polemical Epilogue and Brief Guide to Further Reading." This book arises from modern phychoanalytic psychology that is concerned with individuals and their responses rather than with "universal symbolism." Specific poems and poets as well as readers are used as examples.

0382   Holland, Norman.   "Re-Covering 'The Purloined Letter': Reading as a Personal Transaction."   In *The Reader in the Text*, ed. by Susan R. Suleiman, 350-370.   Princeton, NJ: Princeton University Press, 1980.

In this leisurely, playful article, Holland writes about his own relationship to Edgar Allen Poe's "The Purloined Letter," bringing in other readings for contrast.   He calls his own method "transactive criticism" because he "works explicitly from his transaction of the text."   He seeks to "use human differences to add response to response, to multiply possibilities, and to enrich the whole experience."

0383   Holland, Norman.   "A Transactive Account of Transactive Criticism."   *Poetics* 7 (1978): 177-189.

Defines "transactive criticism" as one that explicitly makes its subject matter the critic's personal involvement with the text.   This article is chatty and personal, and it demonstrates that "the difference in response to the same text is as significant as the sameness of the text."

0384   Holland, Norman.   "Transactive Criticism: Re-Creation Through Identity."   *Criticism* 18 (1976): 334-352.

Argues against the old seventeenth-century belief that "true knowledge requires the splitting of the knower from the known."   Interpretation, says Holland, "re-creates identity through experience," and is "a function of identity."   That function is a matter of "defense, expectation, fantasy and transformation."   He gives examples of the transaction from his own reading, concluding that "there is, in short, not a Cartesian gap but a psychoanalytic bridge between you and what you experience--an interlocking, mutual creation."

0385   Holland, Norman.   "Unity   Identity   Text   Self."   In *Reader Response Criticism*, ed. by Jane P. Tompkins, 118-133. Baltimore: Johns Hopkins University Press, 1980.   Also published in *Proceedings of the Modern Language Association* 90 (1975): 813-22.

Begins by defining the four terms in the title, then proceeds to a discussion of the "white spaces between those big words."   The article's bent is psychological.   But, Holland says, "in establishing an inextricable proportionality among" the four terms, "and so denying claims of objectivity that would separate them, I am not positing an isolated, solipsistic self."

0386   Holub, Robert C.   *Reception Theory: A Critical Introduction*.   London: Methuen and Co., 1984.   189 pp.

Introduces German reception theory to an English-speaking audience.   The first two chapters review this theory, including "The Change in Paradigm and its Socio-Historical Function" and "Influences and Precursors" including Russian formalism, Roman Ingarden, Prague structuralism, Hans-Georg Gadamer and sociology of literature.   The third chapter considers "The Major Theorists," Hans Robert Jauss and Wolfgang Iser.   The author then turns to "Alternative Models and Controversies" including the "Communication Model"; "Marxist Reception Theory" and "Empirical Reception Theory." The final chapters point "to unresolved problems in reception theory in the context of modern criticism." See also 0414.

0387 Ingarden, Roman. *The Cognition of the Literary Work of Art*. Trans. by Ruth Ann Crowley and Kenneth Olson. Evanston, IL: Northwestern University Press, 1973. 466 pp.

Primarily concerned with three "attitudes in which one can encounter a literary work of art": "the aesthetic"; "the preaesthetic" and "the postaesthetic." Ingarden analyzes these in his introduction, where he also says that cognition of a literary work "will be composed of different but closely related processes" and "will necessarily take place in a temporal process." Five chapters follow. In the first, Ingarden treats functions or operations that contribute to the constitution of a literary work of art as an object of knowledge. The second makes the point that some strata in a work of art will not be fully realized, while others may be overemphasized, and the third distinguishes between the literary work of art and the scientific work. Chapter Four continues the descriptive analysis of cognitive activity with the literary work of art as object, and the fifth chapter poses questions concerning the epistemological value of the results of the various types of cognition of the literary work of art." See also 0349, 0386, 0393.

0388 Ingarden, Roman. *The Literary Work of Art: An Investigation of the Borderlines of Ontology, Logic and Theory of Literature*. Trans. by George Grabowicz. Evanston, IL: Northwestern University Press, 1973. 415 pp.

Approaches literature from a phenomenological and structuralist perspective and expresses a philosophical conviction that certain features of the literary work of art cannot be noticed outside the focus of a phenomenological illumination. Part I of the book defines literary works, providing an "essential anatomy" of them. Part II deals with "The Structure of a Literary Work," and Part III, "Supplementation and Conclusions," includes "Borderline Cases" like plays and films, "The Life of a Literary Work," and "The Ontic Position of a Literary Work."

0389   Iser, Wolfgang. *The Act of Reading: A Theory of Aesthetic Response*. Baltimore: Johns Hopkins University Press, 1978. 239 pp.

Focuses on the interaction between the "poles of text and reader," which "form the ground-plan on which a theory of literary communication may be built." Iser believes that, since reader and text are partners in a process of communication, our prime concern should not be with the *meaning* of a text, but with its *effect*. The book is divided into four parts. The first discusses the traditional norms of interpretation from the nineteenth century to New Criticism. Part II deals with the text, and Part III with reading. Part IV deals with "the spurs to interaction that are the necessary prerequisites for the reader to assemble the meaning of the text in a process of re-creative dialectics." See also 0335, 0349, 0366.

0390   Iser, Wolfgang. *The Implied Reader: Patterns of Communication in Prose Fiction from Bunyan to Beckett*. Baltimore: Johns Hopkins University Press, 1974. 309 pp.

Attempts "to lay the foundations for a theory of literary effects and responses based on the novel, since this is the genre in which reader involvement coincides with meaning production." This important book presents a clear and readable analysis of a number of novels. Especially interesting to the religious scholar might be the first chapter, "Bunyan's *Pilgrim's Progress*: The Doctrine of Predestination and the Shaping of the Novel." See also 0335, 0413.

0391   Iser, Wolfgang. "Interaction Between Text and Reader." In *The Reader in the Text*, ed. by Susan R. Suleiman, 106-119. Princeton, NJ: Princeton University Press, 1980.

Describes the reading process as an interaction between the text and the reader. These two are asymmetrical partners--the reader is constantly called upon to fill in gaps or blanks. "Gaps function as a kind of pivot on which the whole text-reader relationship revolves." Iser uses Fielding's *Tom Jones* as a sample text. The article is derived from 0389.

0392   Iser, Wolfgang. "Interview (by Norman Holland and Wayne Booth)." *Diacritics* 10,2 (1980): 57-74.

In this enlightening exchange, both interviewers ask Iser three questions. Holland's are: (1) "What evidence about the experience of literature can carry weight in both your and my psychological traditions?" (2) "If . . . differences in responses to literature are very substantial relative to the similarities, can you use a bi-active model to provide a comprehensive account of the literary transaction?" and (3) "Can you open your bi-active model toward other relations to a text besides the constituting of meaning, other texts besides fiction, other modes of seeing or hearing literature besides reading, and other non-literary acts of perception and cognition?" Booth asks: (1) "Do you see any use . . . in exploring the ways in which authors imply and often achieve such personal, powerfully dramatic bondings?" (2) "Would your conception of the implied reader be underlined, or destroyed, or enriched, by saying that the reader-in-the-text, at least when the text is what we call fictional, is *always* a double figure?" and (3) What "is *your* way of dealing with the fact . . . that who we are in 'real life' is in large part the result of the friendships we have made with various implied authors?"

0393   Iser, Wolfgang. "The Reading Process: A Phenomenological Approach." In *Reader Response Criticism*, ed. by Jane P. Tompkins, 50-69. Baltimore: Johns Hopkins University Press, 1980.

This article, originally published in *The Implied Reader* (0390) discusses the "virtual dimension" of the text, which "is not the text itself, nor is it the imagination of the reader: it is the coming together of text and imagination." Iser depends heavily upon the observations of Ingarden's *The Cognition of the Literary Work of Art* (0387). Departing from Ingarden, who sees anything that "blocks the flow of sentences" as thereby frustrating the reader, Iser views these interruptions as "gaps" that are instead significant for the reading process. The "unwritten part (of the text) . . . gives us the opportunity to picture things." Thus the gaps in the text enable us to use our imagination. By forming a "gestalt" of the text, readers form "illusions," which establish and disrupt consistency. During the reading process, readers formulate themselves "and so discover what had previously seemed to elude . . . (their) consciousness." See also 0349.

0394   Iser, Wolfgang. "Talk Like Whales." *Diacritics* 11,3 (1981): 82-87.

This article replies to Fish's "Why No One's Afraid of Wolfgang Iser" (0366). Iser responds to Fish's "attack" on his "distinction between determinacy and indeterminacy." Iser says that Fish does not understand that he draws, in fact, a threefold distinction "between the given, the determinate, and the indeterminate." See also 0427.

0395   Jauss, Hans Robert. "Levels of Identification of Hero and Audience." *New Literary History* 5 (1974): 283-317.

Discusses the various levels of reception on which the reader can identify with a hero. Through these identifications, "the transformation of aesthetic experience into symbolic or communicative action is accomplished." Jauss discusses Aristotle's concept of the effect of tragedy on the spectator, the "Christian aesthetics of pity," and other modes of identification.

0396   Jauss, Hans Robert. *Toward an Aesthetic of Reception*. Minneapolis: University of Minnesota Press, 1982. 300 pp.

Contains five articles by Jauss and an introduction by Paul de Man. The collection provides an historical appreciation of the literary enterprise, especially of readers' responses or "receptions." Jauss says that misreading is a possibility and suggests that texts be read more than once. Although his approach is largely phenomenological, he also takes insights from Marxism, linguistics, formalism and other approaches.

0397   Kintgen, Eugene R. "Reader Response and Stylistics." *Style* 11,1 (1977): 1-18.

Differentiates between "stylistics" and "linguistics." He surveys many critics' understanding of style from a reader-response perspective and concludes that "stylistics will have to incorporate the perceptions and responses of readers." The only real question for Kintgen is whether the best approach is idiosyncratic and anecdotal, or somewhat more rigorous and empirical, or both.

0398   Lategan, Bernard C. "Coming to Grips with the Reader in Biblical Literature." *Semeia* 48 (1989): 3-20.

Discusses basic aspects of reader-oriented research. The concept of the reader in the text is explained with reference to the distinction between theoretical and empirical research, different levels of reading, and the dynamic nature of the reading process. The article serves as an introduction to a collection of essays by biblical scholars that offer reader perspectives on the New Testament (0412, 1186, 1212, 1274, 1482, 1486-1487, 1491, 1666, 1676.

0399   Leenhardt, Jacques. "Toward a Sociology of Reading." In *The Reader in the Text*, ed. by Susan R. Suleiman, 205-224. Princeton, NJ: Princeton University Press, 1980.

Describes a survey of actual readers encountering two novels, in order to determine whether groups of readers belonging to different sociological categories will manifest uniform tendencies. Leenhardt describes several systems of reading, discovering that "the points of rupture" in these systems are "probably one of the means whereby structures of perception can be renewed."

0400   Mailloux, Steven. *Interpretive Conventions: The Reader in the Study of American Fiction*. Ithaca, NY: Cornell University Press, 1982. 232 pp.

Begins by analyzing five theories of reading, namely those of Stanley Fish, Norman Holland, David Bleich, Wolfgang Iser, and Jonathan Culler. Mailloux concludes that none of them is sufficient for the study of American fiction, which requires "a reader-response criticism based on a consistent social model of reading." Mailloux provides examples of the practical application of this method, and concludes the book with a chapter suggesting pedagogical applications.

0401   Mailloux, Steven. "Reader-Response Criticism?" *Genre* 10 (1977): 413-431.

Endeavors to place one reader-responose critic, Stanley Fish, in the context of four others--David Bleich, Norman Holland, Wolfgang Iser, and Jonathan Culler. Mailloux categorizes the work of the four under Subjectivism, Phenomenology, and Structuralism. Mailloux finds Fish's work to be closest to Culler's.

0402   Marshall, Donald G. "Reading as Understanding: Hermeneutics and Reader-Response Criticism." *Christianity and Literature* 33 (1983): 37-48.

Contends that, properly understood, reader-*response* implies an obligation laid upon the reader to make an effort to understand what the work says. To do this, we must admittedly begin with an understanding projected by our prejudices, but interpretation does not really start until we are struck by something in the work that makes us realize our own limitations. Thus, reading as understanding demands a conversation that puts the self at risk, but through which we discover what we most truly are.

0403   Martindale, Colin. "Psychological Contributions to Poetics." *Poetics* 7 (1978): 121-133.

An overview of psychology's contributions to aesthetics in general and to literary studies in particular. Martindale presents three paradigms: the psychodynamic, the psychobiological, and the cognitive. Next, he gives theories of the stages of aesthetic production and aesthetic response, and finally of aesthetic evolution. The article concludes with a helpful list of references.

0404   Poulet, Georges. "Criticism and the Experience of Interiority." In *Reader Response Criticism*, ed. by Jane P. Tompkins, 41-49. Baltimore: Johns Hopkins University Press, 1980.

Discusses the experience of reading, in which the book as object disappears and the reader becomes aware of "thinking the thoughts of another." This reader lives in "a certain identity with the work and the work alone," and thereby gives it "not only existence, but awareness of existence."

0405   Rabinowitz, Peter J. "Truth in Fiction: A Reexamination of Audiences." *Critical Inquiry* 4 (1977): 121-142.

Using the critical controversy about Nabokov's *Pale Fire* as an example, Rabinowitz asks, "How do we even begin to talk about truth in fiction?" He centers his model "less on the novel's text than on the novel's reader." He defines four audiences and two sorts of ambiguity.

0406   Rabinowitz, Peter J. "What's Hecuba to Us?" The Audience's Experience of Literary Borrowing. In *The Reader in the Text*, ed. by Susan R. Suleiman, 241-263. Princeton, NJ: Princeton University Press, 1980.

Inquires "into the ways an artist's technical procedures contribute to the work's effects: specifically, the way that the new work uses the audience's knowledge of the original." Rabinowitz devises schema for classification, interpretation and evaluation of literary borrowings.

0407   Ray, William. "Recognizing Recognition: The Intra-Textual and Extra-Textual Critical Persona." *Diacritics* 7,4 (1977): 20-33.

Indicates significant differences between the "implied reader" of Iser (0390) and the "narratee" described by Prince (0200) and Piwowarczyk (0192). These models "articulate almost diametrically opposed trajectories within the narrative act--and each disregards the other's premises."

0408   Reichert, John. *Making Sense of Literature*. Chicago: University of Chicago Press, 1977. 222 pp.

Sees literary criticism as dependent upon both the intention of the author and the response of the reader, and as properly dealing with each individual literary "event." Reichert's book is concerned, in part, with teaching people how to do literary study. Reichert writes clearly and convincingly and illustrates his points by using a number of specific examples of practical criticism.

0409   Rendall, Steven. "Fish vs. Fish." *Diacritics* 12,4 (1982): 49-57.

Reviews Stanley Fish's *Is There a Text in This Class* (0361), calling it the work of one who "thrives on opposition" as well as "a brilliant and virtually unprecedented exercise in self-criticism," demonstrating Fish's growth as a critic. Rendall cites Fish's major ideas and the charges that are brought against him.

0410   Rogers, Robert. "Amazing Reader in the Labyrinth of Literature." *Poetics Today* 3 (1982): 31-46.

After naming everybody else's reader model--the Implied Reader, Average Reader, and so on--Rogers describes his own "Amazing Reader" in the first section of this essay. In the second section, he illustrates some features of the Amazing Reader model by describing experiences a set of actual readers have had with Wallace Stevens' "The Snow Man." They include Rogers, some students, and other critics. The Amazing Reader is "coequal with author and text as distinct from one who dominates over them."

0411   Roland, Alan, ed. *Psychoanalysis, Creativity, and Literature: A French-American Inquiry*. New York: Columbia University Press, 1978. 368 pp.

Begins with two essays studying the "sociocultural milieu" of recent French and American psychoanalysis. The second section contains essays by followers of Jacques Lacan, Sigmund Freud, and Heinz Kohut, allowing the reader additional insight into French psychoanalytical thought. The third section deals with American conceptions of creativity and includes essays by Kenneth Burke and others. Finally, the fourth section contains essays on literary criticism and psychoanalysis by Norman N. Holland, Alan Roland, André Green, René Girard, and others.

0412   Schenk, Wolfgang. "The Roles of the Readers or the Myth of *the* Reader." *Semeia* 48 (1989): 55-82.

Distinguishes the reader of a text from the addressee of the text on the one hand and from the research scholar who interprets the text on the other. Insights of reception theory and reader-response criticism are touted at the expense of tradition-history.

0413   Scholes, Robert. "Cognition and the Implied Reader." *Diacritics* 5 (1975): 13-15.

Reviews Iser's *The Implied Reader* (0390) differentiating that reader from the "ideal reader" of structuralism. Scholes "overstates" Iser's case, saying that between "the Reformation and the Second Coming we seem doomed to read texts which offer us more and more cognitive activity with less and less satisfying cognition," which seems to be "as good a definition of hell as any that I can conceive."

0414   Shepherd, David. "The Authority of Meanings and the Meanings of Authority: Some Problems in the Theory of Reading." *Poetics Today* 7 (1986): 129-145.

Reviews and discusses Holub's *Reception Theory* (0386) and Gloversmith's collection of essays, *The Theory of Reading* (0371). Shepherd concentrates on Holub's discussions of the "relationship between literature and history" and on the "disabling ahistoricity of reception theory."

0415   Sherman, Carol. "Response Criticism: 'Do Readers Make Meaning?'" *Romance Notes* 18 (1977): 288-292.

Reports to Romance literature scholars on a forum that Sherman attended at the Modern Language Association in 1976. She briefly describes reader-centered criticism and says critical theory is going "from the text as artifact to the reader as text."

0416   Slatoff, Walter. *With Respect to Readers: Dimensions of Literary Response.* Ithaca, NY: Cornell University Press, 1970. 211 pp.

Endeavors "to point out some inadequacies of our usual ways of studying and teaching literature, to insist that books exist primarily to be read and that they must be read by individual human beings, and to explore some of the questions which arise when we do seriously acknowledge that books require readers." Slatoff believes that "detachment" is not the be-all and end-all in reading: involvement is also needed. An appendix contains two student papers.

0417   Steiner, G. "'Critic'/'Reader'." *New Literary History* 10 (1979): 23-52.

Says that the reader's contiguities to the text are ontological, whereas those of the critic are epistemological. The reader does not encounter or aim at objectivization --authentic reading momentarily fixes transcendence. Steiner concludes that we need more and better "readers," rather than more "critics."

0418   Stierle, Karlheinz. "The Reading of Fictional Texts." In *The Reader in the Text*, ed. by Susan R. Suleiman, 83-105. Princeton, NJ: Princeton University Press, 1980.

Differentiates between "quasi-pragmatic" and "centripetal" responses to fictional texts and between the types of texts that invite these different responses. Stierle's position differs from Wolfgang Iser's because it asserts that the construction of meaning is not a creative achievement by the reader. This article makes use of Edmund Husserl's concepts of "theme" and "horizon."

0419   Suleiman, Susan R. "Ideological Dissent from Works of Fiction: Toward a Rhetoric of the *roman à thèse*." *Neophilologus* 60 (1976): 162-177.

Indicates two points at which a reader might dissent from a novel: when the reader has seen through one of the "formal tricks" of the author, and when the reader refuses to assent to the vision or ideology of the author.

0420 Suleiman, Susan R. "Introduction: Varieties of Audience-Oriented Criticism." In *The Reader in the Text*, 3-45. Princeton, NJ: Princeton University Press, 1980.

Suleiman distinguishes "six varieties of (or approaches to) audience-oriented criticism." Under each topic she presents the perspectives of the chief or clearest spokespersons, including Wayne Booth for rhetorical theory; Roland Barthes for structuralism; Wolfgang Iser for phenomenological criticism; Norman Holland for psychoanalytic criticism; Lucien Goldmann and H. R. Jauss for sociological and historical criticism; and Geoffrey Hartman, Jacques Derrida and J. Hillis Miller for hermeneutical criticism. This clearly-conceived and clearly-presented introduction gives the reader an excellent preparation for encountering the essays collected in *The Reader in the Text* (see 0421).

0421 Suleiman, Susan R., and Crosman, Inge, eds. *The Reader in the Text: Essays on Audience and Interpretation.* Princeton, NJ: Princeton University Press, 1980. 441 pp.

This collection, along with Jane Tompkin's (0424), presents an important group of essays that introduce one to reader-oriented critical theory. The book includes a helpful introductory essay (0420) in addition to 0039, 0199, 0232, 0303, 0354-0355, 0382, 0391, 0399, 0406, 0418, 0472 and an annotated bibliography (0353). The collection is arranged in order of increasing specificity, going from broadly theoretical statements to readings of individual works from various national literatures, genres, and periods.

0422 Tompkins, Jane P. "Criticism and Feeling." *College English* 39 (1977): 169-178.

Tompkins says that "few reader-response critics have paid attention to what individual readers feel." This weakness she finds in Stanley Fish and Wolfgang Iser, and "even Norman Holland, who recognizes the necessity for dealing with personal feeling." David Bleich, she says, "takes cover in the Freudian stronghold. Walter Slatoff has another sort of failing: he is "unpersuasive" because of his writing's "too hasty intimacy" and "moral agenda that is never openly addressed." Finally, she boldly provides her own response to *The Sun Also Rises*, saying that her understanding of it "grows directly out of my outrage at Hemingway's treatment of Robert Cohn."

0423 Tompkins, Jane P. "The Reader in History: The Changing Shape of Literary Response." In *Reader Response Criticism*, 201-232. Baltimore: Johns Hopkins University Press, 1980.

A helpful, insightful survey of the western literary critical tradition. Tompkins says that in both New Criticism and reader-response criticism, the search for "meaning is the aim of the critical act." Thus they are similar to each other and different from the "long history of critical thought in which the specification of meaning is not a central concern." Both New Criticism and reader-response defend literature against scientific bias and positivism. "The difference is not one of goals but of tactics."

0424   Tompkins, Jane P., ed. *Reader-Response Criticism: From Formalism to Post-Structuralism*. Baltimore: Johns Hopkins University Press, 1980. 275 pp.

Gathers essays from as far back as Walker Gibson's contribution from 1950 (0370) and traces the course of reader-response criticism through essays by Prince (0196), Fish (0360, 0362), Bleich (0337) and others. The articles are exceptionally well chosen, and Tompkin's own Introduction and final essay (0423) are outstanding in clarity and perceptiveness. Tompkins includes a useful annotated bibliography. See also 0013, 0237, 0283, 0385, 0393, 0404.

0425   Verdaasdonk, H., and Van Rees, C. J. "Reading a Text vs. Analyzing a Text." *Poetics* 6 (1977): 55-76.

Concentrates "on the assumptions about the nature of the reading process underlying nearly all works done in literary theory." The authors offer two representative attempts to develop a theory of the "reception" of literary texts. Finally, they suggest a concept of the reading process that makes it possible to avoid the problems they have brought forward.

0426   Watkins, Evan. *The Critical Act: Criticism and Community*. New Haven, CT: Yale University Press, 1978.

Seeks a new theory of literature that can appreciate how poetry is "critical as well as creative without at the same time turning poems into nothing more than engines of critical deconstruction." The book has two major sections, "Dialectic and the Myth of Structure" and "Dialectic as Creation and Critique." Watkins is convinced that "while it is impossible to read recent poetry by extrapolating from what one already knows, an ability to understand new literature offers a genuine way into understanding literature of the past."

0427   Weber, Samuel. "Caught in the Act of Reading." In *Demarcating the Disciplines: Philosophy, Literature, Art*, 181-214. Minneapolis: University of Minnesota Press, 1986.

A study of Wolfgang Iser that begins by alluding to Fish's "Why No One's Afraid of Wolfgang Iser?" (0366). Weber asks, "what, then, of the *wound* that Iser, no less than Fish claims to treat?" For Iser, he says, "it is the text that controls and defines the possibility of its totalization by readers. The only question is: *who--or what--controls the text?*"

POSTSTRUCTURALISM/DECONSTRUCTION

See also 0009, 0011, 0083, 0085, 0091, 0102-0103, 0110, 0116, 0121, 0240, 0298, 0500, 0511, 0516, 0522, 0550, 0564, 0652, 0694, 0740, 0764, 0894-0895, 0919, 1089, 1131, 1161, 1186, 1225, 1292, 1541, 1547, 1549, 1565, 1571, 1579, 1594, 1603, 1611, 1615, 1617-1619, 1630-1633, 1640, 1656, 1658-1659, 1677, 1684, 1691-1692, 1694, 1706, 1714, 1719-1722, 1730-1731, 1737, 1740, 1746-1748.

0428   Abrams, M. H. "The Deconstructive Angel." *Critical Inquiry* 3 (1977): 425-538.

Responds to criticisms by Wayne Booth (0138) and by J. Hillis Miller, who says that Abrams "like other traditional historians can never be right" in interpretation. Abrams goes on to present what he makes out to be "the elected linguistic premises" of Jacques Derrida and of Miller, saying that he does not believe "their radically skeptical conclusion from these premises are wrong. On the contrary, . . . their conclusions are *infallibly* right, and that's where the trouble lies." See also 0459.

0429   Arac, Jonathan; Godzich, Wlad; and Martin, Wallace, eds. *The Yale Critics: Deconstruction in America*. Minneapolis: University of Minnesota Press, 1983. 259 pp.

Contains eight essays, providing insight into the theories of Paul de Man, J. Hillis Miller, Geoffrey Hartman and Harold Bloom. The philosophical background of this "Yale School" in the writings of Martin Heidegger, Friedrich Nietzsche, Jacques Derrida and others is explored. Martin's introduction carefully considers the subjects of the book, and the lengthy Afterword draws some interesting conclusions.

0430   Atkins, G. Douglas. *Reading Deconstruction/Deconstructive Reading*. Lexington: University Press of Kentucky, 1983. 168 pp.

Describes and analyzes deconstruction. Part One provides an exposition of deconstructive principles and practices. Part Two offers a deconstructive reading of two texts. Part Three compares traditional and deconstructive reading, saying that, "each requires the other and indeed contains the other within itself." Atkins also sees a third entity to whom the author and the deconstructionist are related. This entity is "sometimes called the trace, *differance*, supplementarity, and occasionally God."

0431   Attridge, Derek; Bennington, Geoff; and Young, Robert, eds. *Post-Structuralism and the Question of History*. Cambridge: Cambridge University Press, 1987. 328 pp.

Claims that, contrary to the belief of scholars like Frank Lentricchia (0103), deconstructive literary criticism brings historical issues back into the discipline. This collection includes essays by Jonathan Culler, Rodolphe Gasché and others. Texts considered by the authors include philosophical works by Karl Marx, Michel Foucault, Jacques Derrida, and so on, in addition to literary works.

0432   Bloom, Harold; de Man, Paul; Derrida, Jacques; Hartman, Geoffrey; and Miller, J. Hillis. *Deconstruction and Criticism*. New York: Seabury Press, 1979. 256 pp.

A collection of varied and weighty essays. Bloom's essay, "The Breaking of Form," is especially significant; Miller's phenomenological essay, "The Critic As Host," is the most accessible. In part, this book seeks to defend P. B. Shelley's "The Triumph of Life" and other romantic works which were held in lower esteem by the New Critics. The preface (written by Hartman) describes Derrida, de Man, and Miller as "merciless deconstructors" and Hartman and Bloom as "barely deconstructors."

0433   Buttigieg, Joseph A., ed. *Criticism Without Boundaries: Directions and Crosscurrents in Postmodern Critical Theory*. Ward-Phillips Lectures in English Language and Literature, 12. Notre Dame, IN: University of Notre Dame Press, 1987. 251 pp.

A collection of nine essays by speakers associated with the journal *boundary 2*. The essays all consider the possibilities, implications, and significance of postmodernism. They are "The Function of the Literary Critic in the Postmodern World" by Paul A. Bové; "De-struction and the Critique of Ideology: A Polemical Meditation on the Margin" by William V. Spanos; "Critical Communities" by Donald Peases; "Heidegger, Holderin, and Politics" by Fred R. Dallmayer; "Contemporary Issues in Feminist Theory" by Donna Przbylowicz; "Rhetoric and Realism; or Marxism, Deconstruction, and the Novel" by Jonathan Arac; "The Reality of Theory: Freud and His Critics" by Daniel T. O'Hara; "From Structures of Meaning to the Meaning of Structures" by Michael Hays; and, "When the Sorcerer's Apprentice Becomes the Defeated Master: Frankfurtians" by Fabio B. Dasilva."

0434   Caputo, John D. *Radical Hermeneutics: Repetition, Deconstruction, and the Hermeneutic Project*. Bloomington: Indiana University Press, 1987. 332 pp.

Focuses on Husserl, Heidegger and Derrida. Part II of the book takes "up the deconstructive critique of hermeneutics issuing from Derrida," which fires "the steel of hermeneutics, 'radicalizing' it, making it ready for the worst." Finally, Caputo attempts to show "that pursuing such radical intentions does not abandon us to the wolves of irrationality, moral license, and despair and does not succumb to nihilism and anarchism. The point is to make life difficult, not impossible."

0435 Culler, Jonathan. *On Deconstruction: Theory and Criticism After Structuralism*. Ithaca, NY: Cornell University Press, 1982. 312 pp.

Discusses Jacques Derrida, Paul de Man, Jacques Lacan, Harold Bloom, Stanley Fish, and others, showing how they approach texts. Culler shows the importance of feminism in the post-New Critical mode of reading, as well as the role of psychoanalytic approaches. This book is written in a manner that the traditional reader will find inviting and convincing. See also 1748.

0436   Culler, Jonathan. *The Pursuit of Signs: Semiotics, Literature, Deconstruction.* Ithaca, NY: Cornell University Press, 1981. 256 pp.

Investigates the problems of producing a semiotics of literature, especially with regard to disagreements within semiotics about how to proceed. The book has three parts: Part One offers overviews of recent criticism and of semiotics, outlining two major questions: the role or status of interpretation, and the relation of semiotics to deconstruction. Part Two assesses "various ways of approaching literary signification and argues for a distinction between interpretive criticism and poetics. Part Three is concerned with the implications for semiotics of the aspects of literary meaning that deconstruction has brought to the fore.

0437   De Man, Paul. *Blindness and Insight: Essays in the Rhetoric of Contemporary Criticism.* 2nd ed. Minneapolis: University of Minnesota Press, 1983. 308 pp.

A collection of essays that examine the writings of a number of other literary critics, including Ludwig Binswanger, Georg Lukac, Maurice Blanchot, Georges Poulet, and Jacques Derrida. In every case, de Man attempts to show that a paradoxical discrepancy appears between general statements made about the nature of language and actual results of interpretation. Yet, de Man continues, these critics seem to thrive on this unrecognized discrepancy and, in fact, owe their best insights to the assumptions that these insights disprove.

0438   De Man, Paul. *The Resistance to Theory.* Introduction by Wlad Godzich. Minneapolis: University of Minnesota Press, 1986. 160 pp.

A posthumous collection of five essays, a long lecture, and an interview with de Man by Stefano Rosso. It contains a bibliography of de Man's writing. The title essay is one of the most influential in American deconstruction. The book is dense and philosophical, but it is important for its critique of traditional interpretation. On de Man's ideas, see also 0103, 0113, 0240, 0429, 0435, 0461, 0467, 0516.

0439   Derrida, Jacques. *The Archeology of the Frivolous: Reading Condillac.* Trans. by John P. Leavey, Jr. Pittsburgh: Duquesne University Press, 1980. 143 pp.

A deconstructive reading by the master of deconstruction. Derrida considers *An Essay on the Origin of Human Knowledge,* which may be regarded as "frivolity itself." Along the way, he considers Metaphysics and Imagining.

0440   Derrida, Jacques. *Dissemination.* Trans. by Barbara Johnson. Chicago: University of Chicago Press, 1981. 366 pp.

A beautifully translated and introduced work, *Dissemination* contains four essays that demonstrate the polyvalence of texts. The four essays include a pre-preface, which is his musings on the preface; an essay on Plato's "phaedrus"; an essay on mimesis; and the title essay, which presents an alternative to the usual patterns of western thought.

0441   Derrida, Jacques. *Glas*. Trans. by John P. Leavey, Jr. and Richard Rand. Lincoln: University of Nebraska Press, 1986. 262 pp.

This book is written with two columns on every page, one of which centers upon Hegel while the other contains Derrida's reflections. Other writings appear in various places on the pages. This construction is playful, and original, though baffling. The work itself is like what Northrop Frye calls a Menippean Satire (0088), and as such breaks down the barriers between literature and philosophy. See also 0454.

0442   Derrida, Jacques. *Margins of Philosophy*. Trans. by Alan Bass. Chicago: University of Chicago Press, 1982. 330 pp.

This collection of essays contains: "Tympan," an essay in two columns, with notes and diagrams; "Différance"; "Ousia and Grammé: Note on a Note from *Being and Time*"; "The Pit and the Pyramid: Introduction to Hegel's Semiology"; "The Ends of Man"; "The Linguistic Circle of Geneva"; "Form and Meaning: A Note on the Phenomenology of Language"; "The Supplement of Copula: Philosophy before Linguistics"; "White Mythology: Metaphor in the Text of Philosophy"; "Qual Quelle: Valéry's Sources"; and "Signature Event Context," which concludes with the author's signature.

0443   Derrida, Jacques. *Of Grammatology*. Trans. by Gayatri Chakravorty Spivak. Baltimore: Johns Hopkins University Press, 1976. 446 pp.

This extremely influential book has a lengthy, helpful introduction by its translator. Many of Derrida's important concepts are elaborated in this work, as well as his readings of other writers like Claude Lévi-Strauss and Ferdinand de Saussure.

0444   Derrida, Jacques. *Positions*. Trans. by Alan Bass. Chicago: University of Chicago Press, 1981. 114 pp.

In interviews with Henri Ronse, Julia Kristeva, Jean-Louis Houdebine and Guy Scarpetta, Derrida presents his opposition to western thought. This difficult work becomes increasingly dense as it progresses. It aims to break into the reader's comfortable, usual ways of thinking, especially "logocentrism."

0445 Derrida, Jacques. *Speech and Phenomena and Other Essays on Husserl's Theory of Signs*. Trans. by David B. Allison. Evanston, IL: Northwestern University Press, 1973.

Contains three essays: "Speech and Phenomena"; "Form and Meaning"; and "Difference." This book is most helpful to those with some prior acquaintance with Husserl and his followers (including Heidegger, Nietzsche, Saussure, Freud, and Levinas). Derrida studies Husserl's linguistic philosophy and attempts to go beyond it via his contemporaries and the later thinkers. A crucial work in the deconstructive canon.

0446   Derrida, Jacques. *Writing and Difference*. Trans. by Alan Bass. Chicago: University of Chicago Press, 1978. 342 pp.

A collection of essays on philosophical writers including Freud, Lévi-Strauss, Husserl and Levinas. In this demanding work, Derrida goes beyond the boundaries set by Ferdinand de Saussure, whom he claims does not adequately distinguish the signifier from the signified. Derrida shifts the linguist's focus from speech to writing and discerns the possibilities of philosophy for the future.

0447   Felperin, Howard. *Beyond Deconstruction: The Uses and Abuses of Literary Theory*. New York: Oxford University Press, 1985. 226 pp.

The core of this book is Felperin's grappling with Marxism, structuralism, and deconstruction, which he feels "exemplify, perhaps even . . . exhaust, the distinctive possibilities of thought available to contemporary theoretical discourse . . . (and correspond to) the discursive models outlined by Sextus Empiricus . . . (which are) dogmatists, academics, and sceptics." The first chapter, "Leavisism Revisited," introduces the reader to Felperin's own "perplexities" with literary criticism. In "Toward a Poststructuralist Practice: A Reading of Shakespeare's *Sonnets*," Felperin says that he will, as he is "duty-bound" to do, participate in the reading and re-reading of "an ever negotiable canon of texts with all the resourcefulness available to it." The final chapter "attempts to account for" the "recent paradigm-shift toward theory" that makes possible a new way of reading.

0448   Frank, Manfred. *What Is Neostructuralism?* Trans. by Sabine Wilke and Richard Gray. Theory and History of Language, 45. Minneapolis: University of Minnesota Press, 1989. 482 pp.

Discusses deconstruction from a hermeneutical point of view. Frank looks at three issues (history, subjectivity, and semiotics) with reference to five representative authors: Jacques Lacan, Michel Foucault, Jacques Derrida, Gilles Deleuze, and Jean-Francois Lyotard. Frank challenges the antirationalism of deconstruction and attempts to build a new hermeneutical program of "reconceived subjectivism based on decenteredness and subservience to forces other than its own."

0449   Gasché, Rodolphe. *The Tain of the Mirror: Derrida and the Philosophy of Reflection*. Cambridge, MA: Harvard University Press, 1986. 384 pp.

This philosophical exposition focuses on Jacques Derrida's "relation to the philosophical tradition, and emphasizes the manner in which his writings address not only particular philosophical problems and their traditional formulations, but, more important, the philosophical itself." Gasché sees deconstructionist literary criticism as "the offspring of a heritage that has little in common with that of Derrida's thought. (It) must be understood as originating in New Criticism." This book has three parts: first, says the author, "I situate and interpret Derrida's philosophy with respect to . . . criticism of the notion of reflexivity. Second, . . . I also link together a multitude of motifs in Derrida's oeuvre in order to demonstrate the consistent nature of this philosophical enterprise, and to attempt to systematize some of its results. Third, I further develop these concerns, especially insofar as they impinge on the problem of universality, by analyzing a series of Derridean concepts that have been absorbed into deconstructionist criticism."

0450   Harari, Josué V., ed. *Textual Strategies: Perspectives in Post-Structuralist Criticism*. Ithaca, NY: Cornell University Press, 1979. 464 pp.

Contains sixteen articles by such eminent poststructuralists as Roland Barthes, Jacques Derrida, Paul de Man, Michel Foucault, Edward W. Said, René Girard, Michael Riffaterre, Gérard Genette and others. These essays are mostly exercises in applying theory to literary texts, rather than in abstract theorizing. The book also contains an annotated bibliography.

0451   Harland, Richard. *Superstructuralism: The Philosophy of Structuralism and Post-Structuralism*. New York: Methuen and Co., 1987. 213 pp.

Defines "superstructuralism" as a larger intellectual phenomenon over and above structuralism, one which covers "the whole field of Structuralists, Semioticians, Althusserian Marxists, Foucaultians, Post-structuralists, etc." The book has three sections: "The Superstructuralist Way of Thinking"; "Superstructuralism Becomes Philosophical"; and "Post-Structuralist Philosophy."

0452   Hartman, Geoffrey H. *Criticism in the Wilderness: The Study of Literature Today*. New Haven, CT: Yale University Press, 1980. 336 pp.

Provides a historical and evaluative look at the "wilderness of critical positions" that has ensued from the collision of what Hartman regards as Anglo-American practical criticism and European philosophic criticism. The book is an example of "metacriticism" (criticism of criticism), in that it provides close readings not only of literary works (by Yeats, Wordsworth, Dickinson, and others), but also of critical texts by Harold Bloom, Jacques Derrida, Northrop Frye, Kenneth Burke, and others. Hartman's proposal for mediation recognizes the "pastoral" value of explication, but favors the poststructuralist agenda of allowing criticism to develop as a genre in its own right. Literary critics need to drop the distinction between "primary" and "secondary" literature and recognize that, while criticism helps readers with other texts, it is also composed of texts of its own.

0453 Hartman, Geoffrey H. "Literary Criticism and Its Discontents." *Critical Inquiry* 3 (1976): 203-220.

Says that literary criticism is itself a genre of literature, concerned with its own style. The post-New Critical critics are a "group which crosses the line into philosophy, theology, linguistics, sociology, and psychoanalysis." The newest criticism, "revisionism," takes upon itself the hermeneutic task: "to understand understanding through the detour of the writing/reading experience." The concept that works of literary criticism are literature, and therefore subject to critique brings Hartman near to the relativism of poststructuralism and to the notion that critics "play" with texts rather than interpreting them.

0454   Hartman, Geoffrey H. *Saving the Text: Literature/Derrida/Philosophy.*
Baltimore: Johns Hopkins University Press, 1981. 190 pp.

This book studies Derrida's *Glas* (0441) and provides insight into Derrida's debt to
Martin Heidegger and relationship to Jacques Lacan. The book also contains a
number of plates, which are illustrations from mostly mid-twentieth-century art.

0455 Harvey, Irene. *Derrida and the Economy of Difference.* Bloomington: Indiana
University Press, 1986. 304 pp.

Gives Derrida's major ideas a concise and thorough treatment. Harvey discusses
Derrida's work both within philosophical tradition and in contrast to it. Her writing
on Derrida's debt to Kant is helpful, as is her thought on his ethic.

0456 Hutcheon, Linda. *A Poetics of Postmodernism: History, Theory, Fiction.* New
York: Routledge, Chapman, and Hall, 1988. 304 pp.

Envisions a "poetics of postmodernism" that can be comprehended only through
paradox. This poetics would "enact the metalinguistic contradiction of being inside
and outside, complicitous and distanced, inscribing and contesting its own provisional
formulations." This difficult book sees postmodernism's relationship to modernism,
but believes that it rejects the modernist anti-historical and anti-contextual stances.

0457 Johnson, Barbara. *The Critical Difference: Essays in the Contemporary Rhetoric
of Reading.* Baltimore: Johns Hopkins University Press, 1980. 156 pp.

Has as its pervasive theme "the importance of the functioning of *what is not known*
in literature and theory." Johnson grapples with the theory of deconstruction,
structuring each chapter according to a series of "differences into which the reader is
lured with a promise of comprehension." These differences include: masculine and
feminine; prose and poetry; poetry and theory; science and literature; naive and ironic;
and literature, psychoanalysis, and philosophy.

0458   Kermode, Frank. *The Art of Telling: Essays on Fiction.* Cambridge, MA:
Harvard University Press, 1983. 240 pp.

Expresses reservations about deconstruction, but seeks to moderate here between the
"dangerous" newest criticism and the entrenched conservatism of older models.
Especially interesting is Chapter 7, "Can We Say Absolutely Anything We Like?"

0459 Kincaid, James R. "Coherent Readers, Incoherent Texts." *Critical Inquiry* 3
(1977): 781-802.

This rather dense essay asserts that Wayne Booth (0138) and M. H. Abrams (0428)
are more right about readers; but J. Hillis Miller is more right about texts and
language generally.

0460   Krupnik, Mark, ed. *Displacement: Derrida and After*. Bloomington: Indiana University Press, 1983. 212 pp.

Collects seven essays by writers including Paul de Man (on Hegel); Tom Conley (on Derrida); and Gayatri Spivak (on "Displacement and the Discourse of Woman"). The editor's Introduction discusses "displacement" and its importance, as do most of the essays contained within this volume.

0461   Leitch, Vincent B. *Deconstructive Criticism: An Advanced Introduction and Survey*. New York: Columbia University Press, 1983. 256 pp.

A difficult work that takes on the stylistic character of deconstruction, while offering summaries of some of the most important deconstructive critics. It studies in depth the writing of Jacques Derrida, Paul de Man, J. Hillis Miller, Harold Bloom, Michel Foucault, and Roland Barthes. Leitch also attempts to provide insight into their methodologies and theories. See also 1748.

0462   Llewelyn, John. *Derrida on the Threshold of Sense*. London: Macmillan Press, 1986. 137 pp.

Explicates Derrida's readings of some of the texts of Hegel, Husserl, and Heidegger, as well as Ferdinand de Saussure, Claude Lévi-Strauss, John Austin and John Searle, which both "because of themselves and in spite of themselves . . . deconstruct themselves." See also 1541.

0463   Merrell, Floyd. *Deconstruction Reframed*. West Lafayette, IN: Purdue University Press, 1985. 261 pp.

A discussion of deconstruction that focuses primarily on its implications for fields other than literary study. Merrell summarizes the thought of Jacques Derrida, emphasizing its relationship to the philosophy of C. S. Peirce. He then relates this system of thinking to physics, philosophy of science, and mathematics.

0464   Miller, J. Hillis. *The Disappearance of God: Five Nineteenth-Century Writers*. Cambridge, MA: Harvard University Press, 1963. 367 pp.

An early work by a literary critic who would later become a proponent of deconstruction (cf. 0081, 0083, 0116, 0429, 0432, 0461). Miller here analyzes the works of five authors (De Quincey, R. Browning, E. Brontë, Arnold, and Hopkins) who believe in God but who also are aware of God's distance and are desperate to reestablish contact. The method of analysis is to consider individual works within the entire corpus of the author's work.

0465   Norris, Christopher. *The Contest of Faculties: Philosophy and Theory after Deconstruction*. New York: Methuen and Co., 1985. 247 pp.

A collection of essays concerned with the question of "how theory can justify its claims when faced with various forms of sceptical or relativist argument." The point of deconstruction is not to argue that "textualist" readings are inevitably irrational; rather the point of deconstruction is to argue that conclusions which may be at odds with consensual wisdom may nevertheless be rational.

0466   Norris, Christopher. *Deconstruction: Theory and Practice*. New York: Methuen and Co., 1982. 200 pp.

Helps the reader to understand the nature of deconstruction, especially in Derrida's major texts. Norris also cites reasons why deconstruction has become so central in American critical thought and considers the contributions of both the American deconstructionists and their dissenters. He describes with clarity the relationship of deconstruction to linguistics and philosophy. This book is a good starting point for readers approaching the works of Derrida. See also 1748.

0467   Norris, Christopher. *The Deconstructive Turn: Essays in the Rhetoric of Philosophy*. London: Methuen and Co., 1983. 201 pp.

Exposes certain philosophical writings to the deconstructive kind of reading practiced by Jacques Derrida, Paul de Man and others in their criticism of literary works. Norris deconstructs works by Ludwig Wittgenstein, John Austin, Søren Kierkegaard, Walter Benjamin, and Livingston Lowes. Such deconstruction begins by questioning the deep laid assumptions that philosophy has to do with certain kinds of truth that are not to be found in literature.

0468   Norris, Christopher. *Derrida*. Cambridge, MA: Harvard University Press, 1987. 271 pp.

Introduces Derrida, showing his place within the philosophical and literary critical traditions. This clearly-written book contains a chronology of Derrida's life and writings, and chapters on "Derrida on Plato: Writing as Poison and Cure"; "Speech, Presence, Origins: from Hegel to Saussure"; "Rousseau: Writing as Necessary Evil"; "Derrida and Kant: the Enlightenment Tradition"; "Letters Home: Derrida, Austin and the Oxford Connection"; and "Nietzsche, Freud, Levinas: on the Ethics of Deconstruction."

0469   Norris, Christopher. *Paul de Man: Deconstruction and the Critique of Aesthetic Ideology*. New York: Routledge, Chapman, and Hall, 1988. 200 pp.

Defends de Man's assessment of rhetoric, believing that his work does not in fact avoid political engagement to its detriment. This book provides a sympathetic treatment of an influential critic.

0470   Rorty, Richard. "Deconstruction and Circumvention." *Critical Inquiry* 11 (1984): 1-21.

Differentiates two senses of "deconstruction." The first sees breaking down the distinction between philosophy and literature as essential. The other refers "to a method of reading texts." The article concentrates on Jacques Derrida and Martin Heidegger.

0471   Ryan, Michael. *Marxism and Deconstruction: A Critical Articulation.* Baltimore: Johns Hopkins University Press, 1982. 272 pp.

Attempts to mediate between Marxist and deconstructionist criticism, which have often been suspicious of one another. Deconstruction can help Marxism to avoid the failures of the Soviet system, especially by avoiding unhelpful dichotomies like theory-practice. One example of an enhanced Marxism which Ryan gives is radical feminism.

0472   Schor, Naomi. "Fiction as Interpretation -- Interpretation as Fiction." In *The Reader in the Text*, ed. by Susan R. Suleiman, 165-182. Princeton, NJ: Princeton University Press, 1980.

Sets Barthes' *S/Z* (0229) against Sontag's essay "Against Interpretation" (0120) and suggests that interpretation is something "done *in* fiction" rather than *to* it. Thus, interpretation itself becomes a fiction. Schor takes as examples the tasks of interpreting Henry James, Marcel Proust, and Franz Kafka. The article concludes by returning to Sontag and suggesting a feminine mode of interpretation.

0473   Spanos, William V. *Repetitions: The Postmodern Occasion in Literature and Culture.* Baton Rouge: Louisiana State University Press, 1987. 376 pp.

Suggests a hermeneutics that remembers or retrieves the occasion that engaged it. The sequence of the essays discloses the author's coming to understand the postmodern occasion not merely as a chronological but also as an ontological phenomenon. Spanos' effort to thematize the cultural and sociopolitical implications of the old logocentric measure and the new occasional measure distinguishes his "destructive hermeneutics" from the exegetical procedures of deconstruction as it is now practiced in America.

0474   Staten, Henry. *Wittgenstein and Derrida.* Lincoln: University of Nebraska Press, 1984. 182 pp.

Tries to redirect discussion of Jacques Derrida by two maneuvers: First, Staten attempts to show how we work through philosophical texts to find what we find in Derrida's work; then, he brings Derrida's project into relation with that of Ludwig Wittgenstein, in order to suggest an Anglo-American context within which deconstruction makes philosophical sense.

0475   Stout, Jeffrey. "What Is the Meaning of a Text?" *New Literary History* 14 (1982): 1-12.

Aims to undermine the widespread assumption that the question in the title "either requires or deserves an answer." Stout claims that "Meanings, if they exist, could turn out to be the *least* interesting thing about texts."

0476   Taylor, Mark C. "Deconstruction: What's the Difference?" *Soundings* 66 (1983): 387-403.

Sketches an outline of deconstruction, filling in first some of its philosophical background. It is "on the border that simultaneously separates and joins Phenomenology and Existentialism." Taylor also describes "logocentrism's" method of interpretation, which looks beneath appearances for "a truth which can be discovered, uncovered, or disclosed." Jacques Derrida calls this approach Platonic, although it also has Judeo-Christian roots. Taylor calls "Romantic hermeneutics, phenomenology, archetypal analysis and structuralism" extensions "of the philosophical and theological doctrine of the logos." Derrida reinterprets interpretation, and "his work can be understood as an effort to affirm that hopelessness need not be despair."

0477   Taylor, Mark C., ed. *Deconstruction in Context: Literature and Philosophy.* Chicago: University of Chicago Press, 1986. 446 pp.

An anthology that suggests "*one* way to deconstruction." After a long introduction by the editor, a number of important essays follow, including Edmund Husserl's "Phenomenology"; Friedrich Nietzshe's "The Will to Power"; Martin Heidegger's "The End of Philosophy and the Task of Thinking" and "The Origin of the Work of Art"; Jean-Paul Sartre's "Being and Nothingness"; Georges Bataille's "The Labyrinth"; and Jacques Derrida's "Différance." The introduction is clearly written and helps to make the essays in the collection more accessible.

0478   Ulmer, Gregory. *Applied Grammatology: Post(e)-Pedagogy from Jacques Derrida to Joseph Beuys.* Baltimore: Johns Hopkins University Press, 1985.

A dense, difficult book that presumes its readers already have a thorough understanding of Jacques Derrida's work. Ulmer's radical approach to pedagogy is based upon grammatology, and his ideas spring from Jacques Derrida, Jacques Lacan, and Joseph Beuys.

0479   Waters, Lindsay, and Godzich, Wlad, eds. *Reading de Man Reading.* Minneapolis: University of Minnesota Press, 1988. 300 pp.

Collects fourteen essays by J. Hillis Miller, Geoffrey Hartman, Rodolphe Gasché and others on the topic of Paul de Man's theory and practice of reading. These essays by his disciples show his exalted place in the academy and attempt to understand his writings through his own method of understanding texts.

0480   Weedon, Chris. *Feminist Practice and Poststructuralist Theory.* London: Basil Blackwell, 1987. 187 pp.

Argues that poststructuralism is useful to feminism, and considers "its implications for feminist critical practice." Weedon is interested in "ways of understanding social and cultural practices which throw light on how gender power relations are constituted, reproduced and contested." The second chapter "outlines the key principles of poststructuralist theory," and the following chapters focus on psychoanalysis, "language and subjectivity," and on "discourse and power." The final chapter suggests implications for "a possible direction for future feminist cultural criticism." The bibliography at the end lists a number of feminist as well as poststructuralist resources.

0481 Wood, David, and Bernasconi, Robert, eds. *Derrida and Différance.* Evanston, IL: Northwestern University Press, 1988. 114 pp.

A collection of essays intended to bring out the subtlety and complexity of strategic movements that "converge in this term *différance*." In addition to essays by Walter Brogan, Gayle Ormiston and others, the book contains a letter from Derrida to a Japanese friend, "An Interview with Derrida," and "The Original Discussion of 'Différance' (1968)," newly translated.

PART THREE: METHOD

See also 0107, 0130, 0580, 0583, 0585, 0594, 0601, 0607, 0637, 0660, 0668, 0825, 1048, 1062-1063, 1067-1068, 1247, 1557, 1599, 1611, 1615-1616, 1620, 1628, 1670, 1743.

0482   Bar-Efrat, Shimon. *Narrative Art in the Bible*. Journal for the Study of the Old Testament Supplement Series, 70/Bible and Literature Series, 17. Trans. by Dorothy Shefer-Vanson. Sheffield: Almond Press, 1989. 295 pp.

A narratology applied to the Hebrew Bible (Old Testament) that focuses on techniques and forms as "the principal means whereby narrative impresses itself upon the reader." Concepts discussed include the role of a covert, omniscient narrator, depiction of characters, development of plot, shaping of time within space, and the stylistic devices of sentences and chapters. These topics are clarified with examples from a variety of Old Testament narratives; the most extensive exposition is of the Ammon and Tamar story in 2 Samuel 13.

0483   Barton, John. "Classifying Biblical Criticism." *Journal for the Study of the Old Testament* 29 (1984): 19-35.

Attempts to adapt Abram's model (0076) for classifying modes of literary criticism (mimetic, pragmatic, expressive, objective) for a typology of approaches to the Bible. Barton considers historical criticism and structuralism, but notes that there are no pragmatic or reader-oriented approaches being practiced in biblical studies. The latter statement became quickly outdated.

0484   Barton, John. *Reading the Old Testament: Method in Biblical Study*. Philadelphia: Westminster Press, 1984. 256 pp.

An introduction to several methods of Old Testament study, including source criticism, form criticism, redaction criticism, canonical criticism, structuralism, and New Criticism. The presentation of the newer literary approaches side by side with the more traditional historical-critical ones facilitates comparative evaluation.

0485   Beardslee, William A. *Literary Criticism of the New Testament*. Guides to Biblical Scholarship. Philadelphia: Fortress Press, 1969. 86 pp.

A series of essays that concentrate on religious functions of the narrative form of various New Testament writings. An early work, the book now appears somewhat uneven. Some of the essays use the term "literary criticism" to refer to what today is called source criticism or form criticism. Beardslee breaks new ground, however, when he insists on a need to pay closer attention to the larger forms of books as narrative wholes and when he suggests that the rhetoric of New Testament writings can only be understood if they are treated "just like any other books." The volume is interesting today precisely for its transitional focus--it offers testimony to the manner in which the need for a more literary approach to the Bible grew out of historical criticism and was first expressed by the historical critics themselves. One chapter is devoted to New Testament proverbs (including beatitudes) and another to the book of Revelation.

0486   Beardslee, William A. "Recent Literary Criticism." In *The New Testament and Its Modern Interpreters*, ed. by Eldon Jay Epp and George W. MacRae, 175-198. Philadelphia: Fortress Press, 1989.

Surveys developments and trends in the application of modern literary-critical methods to the New Testament. Beardslee focuses on parable interpretation, discussing recent developments under three categories: phenomenological interpretation, aesthetic-rhetorical interpretation, and structural analysis. He notes that biblical literary critics are divided in their assessment of the value of older historical criticism. He also observes a movement away from the aesthetic-rhetorical criticism typified by Amos Wilder toward methods that are more rigorous and less intuitive. Finally, he lists areas in which literary criticism impinges on hermeneutics.

0487   Bergen, Robert D. "Text as a Guide to Authorial Intention: An Introduction to Discourse Criticism." *The Journal of the Evangelical Theological Society* 30 (1987): 327-336.

Commends discourse criticism as a methodology appropriate for use in biblical studies, especially as a guide to discerning the authorial intention of texts. Bergen identifies key assumptions of discourse criticism and explains how it can discern emphatic points in a text through its attention to order of information, quantity of information, and type of information presented. Many discourse critics would regard their approach as text-oriented rather than author-oriented as Bergen seems to assume.

0488   Berlin, Adele. *Poetics and Interpretation of Biblical Narrative*. Sheffield: Almond Press, 1983. 180 pp.

An in-depth study of two features of narrative criticism (characterization and point of view) as they are used in Old Testament narrative, followed by an extended narrative analysis of the book of Ruth. Berlin believes that poetics should be distinguished from interpretation--it offers a kind of recipe that tells what the cake is made of but not how it tastes. She discerns literary devices within the text without attempting to explicate meaning for present readers.

0489   Bertram, Michael. "Semiotics: The Structural Approach." *The Bible Today* 26 (1988): 26-30.

Explains semiotics and structural analysis in three steps: (1) surface analysis of the text to define its literary contours; (2) narrative analysis to note transformations in the characters; and (3) discursive analysis to examine the thematic oppositions that seem to characterize the story. Bertram advocates structural analysis as a method that will bring new vitality for preachers to the study of biblical texts.

0490   Black, C. Clifton, III.   "Rhetorical Criticism and the New Testament." *Proceedings: Eastern Great Lakes Biblical Society* 8 (1988): 77-92.

Introduces the method of rhetorical criticism and commends its usefulness and significance for interpretation of the New Testament. The method laid out is that proposed by Kennedy (0529). A bibliography of over 100 works is included.

0491   Bland, Kalman P. "The Rabbinic Method and Literary Criticism," in *Literary Interpretations of Biblical Narratives*, ed. by Kenneth R. R. Gros Louis with James S. Ackermann and Thayer S. Warshaw, 16-25. Nashville: Abingdon Press, 1974.

Prizes midrashic interpretation of the Bible as instructive for today, since the Torah has a different face for every one who reads it. To appreciate the meaning and beauty of the Bible, we must be attentive to the latent significance of every word.

0492   Boers, Hendrikus. "From Syntax to Semantics: A Review of Robert Funk, *The Poetics of Biblical Narrative*." *Forum* 5,3 (1989): 61-68.

Faults Funk (0513) for not distinguishing clearly between syntax and semantics, or between cohesion (which is a function of syntax) and coherence (which is a function of semantics). Still, the "grammar of discourse" Funk provides will be useful for any reader who is interested in finding out why she or he enjoys reading a story.

0493   Boomershine, Thomas E. *Story Journey: An Invitation to the Gospel as Storytelling*. Nashville: Abingdon Press, 1988. 220 pp.

Encourages and helps to facilitate memorization of biblical stories for oral presentation. Boomershine stresses that biblical stories were originally written to be heard, not read, and proposes that greater attention to this orality component aids in understanding of the texts as stories.

0494   Bovon, François. "French Structuralism and Biblical Exegesis." In *Structural Analysis and Biblical Exegesis*, by R. Barthes, F. Bovon, F.-J. Leenhardt, R. Martin-Achard, and J. Starobinski; trans. by A. M. Johnson, 4-20. Pittsburgh Theological Monograph Series, 3. Pittsburgh: Pickwick Press, 1974.

Surveys the development of French structuralism and its introduction as a method in biblical studies. Bovon concentrates especially on the work of Lévi-Strauss and Barthes. In conclusion, he notes two benefits to be gained from structuralist exegesis:

(1) turned too long toward diachrony, exegesis will find its bearings in synchrony; and, (2) structuralism will serve as a balance to existential analysis.

0495   Brown, Schuyler. "Reader Response: Demythologizing the Text." *New Testament Studies* 34 (1988): 232-237.

Identifies historical reading, doctrinal reading and literary reading as alternative strategies favored by different reading communities. Reaffirming the legitimacy of the latter approach, Brown advises a "Copernican revolution" in interpretive theory that accepts the fact that meaning is generated by the experience of reading rather than residing in a text or in the intention of the author.

0496   Bruns, Gerald L. "Midrash and Allegory." In *The Literary Guide to the Bible*, ed. by Robert Alter and Frank Kermode, 625-646. Cambridge, MA: Belknap Press, 1987.

A hermeneutical essay that describes midrashic and allegorical modes for interpreting scripture and struggles with the challenge to modern interpretation posed by them. These methods represented a concern for the reciprocity between text and history. A truly historical view of scripture is a view that appreciates the dialectical relationship between the text and its interpreters.

0497   Bucher, C. "New Directions in Biblical Interpretation." *Brethren Life and Thought* 28 (1983): 21-28.

Surveys new approaches to the Bible, including literary criticism, structuralism, anthropological and sociological approaches, and canonical criticism. Some of these methods extend previously uttered critiques of the historical-critical paradigm and further hermeneutical challenges offered by black, feminist, and liberation theologians.

0498   Camary-Hoggatt, Jerry Allan. "On Bridges and Abutments: A Review of Robert Funk, *The Poetics of Biblical Narrative*." *Forum* 5,3 (1989): 69-78.

Attempts to place Funk's work (0513) within the wider milieu of literary studies. Funk is conversant with structuralists, but is not a structuralist himself. He is concerned almost exclusively with what is visible on the surface of the text. He is more interested in the textual signals themselves than in reader responses to those signals. Camary-Hoggatt feels a second volume is necessary, one that deals with such matters as the repertoire of the reader, the difference between orality and textuality, and the problem of polyvalence.

0499   Chevallier, M. A. "L'analyse littéraire des textes du Nouveau Testament (Conseils aux étudiants)." *Revue d'histoire et de philosophie religieuses* 57 (1977): 367-378.

Describes synchronic analysis of a New Testament text as a process that involves determining the literary genre (narrative or discourse) and studying the system of significants and its functioning. Texts treated for illustrative purposes include 1 Corinthians 13, Luke 2:1-20, and Luke 3:21-22.

0500   Clévenot, Michel. *Materialist Approaches to the Bible.* Trans. by William J. Nottingham. Maryknoll, NY: Orbis Books, 1985. 148 pp.

Describes and encourages approaches to scripture that take as their departure the consciousness of readers produced by the social class to which they belong. Readers are invited to re-read texts in ways that free them from the interpretations given by those who use them to legitimize social power. Materialist approaches to the Bible are more informed by Marxist ideology and by sociology than by literary criticism, but they do draw from concepts of reader-response and deconstruction theories. Clevenot's book is largely an introduction to the less accessible work of Belo (1185).

0501   Combrink, H. J. Bernard. "The Changing Scene of Biblical Interpretation." In *A South African Perspective on the New Testament*, ed. by J. H. Petzer and P. J. Hartin, 9-17. Leiden: E. J. Brill, 1986.

Surveys the recent influx of literary methods in biblical studies. Combrink notes the emphasis on rhetoric, on narrative theology, and on reception theory. New advances in sociological studies are noted as well.

0502   Craddock, Fred B. "The Gospels as Literature." *Encounter* 49 (1988): 19-35.

Explains basic concepts of narrative and reader-response criticism: that a Gospel is to be read as a literary unit, that understanding the text means being attentive to literary mechanisms and strategies, and that the reader is an active participant in the generation of meaning.

0503   Crossan, John Dominic. "Waking the Bible: Biblical Hermeneutic and Literary Imagination." *Interpretation* 23 (1978): 269-285.

Traces a trend in biblical scholarship from historical criticism to literary criticism, and then from classical literary criticism to structural literary criticism. The article is referenced to a bibliography and remains a useful survey even today, though the idea that formalist approaches would be but a way station on the road to structuralism has proved incorrect.

0504   Culley, Robert C., ed. *Studies in the Structure of Hebrew Narrative.* Philadelphia: Fortress Press, 1976. 122 pp.

A form-critical work that anticipates and prepares for certain formalist and structuralist studies of Old Testament narrative. Culley examines the relation between oral and written tradition and, in the process, notes repeated uses of common structures that give cumulative force to patterns in individual stories.

0505 Daube, David. "Rabbinic Methods of Interpretation and Hellenistic Rhetoric." *Hebrew Union College Annual* 22 (1949): 239-264.

Submits the thesis that rabbinic methods of interpretation derive from Hellenistic rhetoric, which is at the bottom both of the fundamental ideas from which the rabbis proceeded and of the manner in which these ideas were translated into practice. Daube examines in detail Hillel's rules of interpretation.

0506 Dauber, Kenneth. "The Bible as Literature: Reading Like the Rabbis." *Semeia* 31 (1985): 27-48.

Proposes that reading the Bible as literature means reading it according to certain relational models long utilized by rabbis. Traditional criticism and deconstruction both miss the mark, the former because of its existentialization of relationality and the latter because of its skepticism, which denies relationality. The Bible resists the philosophical project of knowing Being, and instead establishes a certain relation. Rabbis understand the Bible not as a text to be interpreted, but as a text that is itself interpretation.

0507 Davis, Charles Thomas, III. "A Multidimensional Criticism of the Gospels." In *Orientation By Disorientation*, ed. by Richard A. Spencer, 87-98. Pittsburgh: Pickwick Press, 1980.

Argues for a wedding of historical (extrinsic) and literary (intrinsic) approaches to texts. Biblical studies must continue to utilize historical criticism, but must cease to absolutize historical method. Intrinsic approaches stress such elements as rhythm, organization, symbol, and the ability of the text to define its own world. A multidimensional approach to texts can be developed that correlates with Origen's view of scripture as historical, symbolic, and spiritual.

0508 Detweiler, Robert. *Story, Sign, and Self: Phenomenology and Structuralism as Literary-Critical Methods*. Philadelphia: Fortress Press, 1978. 224 pp.

Provides "a general overview of phenomenology and structuralism as critical methods." Detweiler considers "literary critical phenomenology and structuralism together and in interaction with each other." The author hopes to create "an arena where interpreters of secular and religious texts can meet." The introductory chapter, "Basic Concepts of Phenomenology and Structuralism" introduces both systems of thought for readers unfamiliar with either. See also 1586.

0509 Dornisch, Loretta. "Symbolic Systems and the Interpretation of Scripture: An Introduction to the Work of Paul Ricoeur." *Semeia* 4 (1975): 1-26.

Provides a background and overview of Ricoeur's work and its relevance for biblical interpretation. The study offers (1) a description of the evolution of Ricoeur's thought from a theory of symbol to a theory of language; (2) an analysis of his theory of the world of the text and the relationships of sets of symbols; (3) a theory of symbolic language; (4) a suggestion of the importance of Ricoeur's work for biblical interpretation; and, (5) a selected bibliography. See also 0558

0510 Fischer, James A. *How To Read the Bible*. Rev. ed. New York: Dodd, Mead, and Co., 1987. 165 pp.

An introduction to Bible reading for the non-specialist. Fischer invites persons who may already have some acquaintance with the Bible through their religious upbringing to come to a new appreciation of the Bible as literature. Chapters are devoted to the dynamics of reading stories, legal material, reflective passages, psalms, prophets, and prayers.

0511 Fowler, Robert M. "Post-Modern Biblical Criticism." *Forum* 5,3 (1989): 3-30.

Cites a number of "indexes" of postmodern biblical criticism, including the following: discovery that we must live without definitive explications; distrust of claims to have found the center; shift from meaning as content to meaning as event; and conviction that all reading is inevitably skewed and incomplete. Fowler believes that the changes occurring in biblical criticism reflect changes occurring in our culture. He concludes that postmodern biblical criticism may turn out to be occasional criticism, that is, dependent on the particular occasion and especially useful in particular (occasional) ways. Responses by George Aichele, Jr. (1055) and Stephen D. Moore (1619) follow the article.

0512 Fowler, Robert M. "Using Literary Criticism on the Gospels." *The Christian Century* 99 (1982): 626-629.

A personal account of the author's own movement (under the guidance of Norman Perrin) from historical-critical study of the Gospels to an embracing of new literary approaches, especially reader-response criticism. Modern literary-critical analysis is presented as a logical methodological outgrowth of form and redaction criticism.

0513 Funk, Robert W. *The Poetics of Biblical Narrative*. Sonoma, CA: Polebridge Press, 1988. 318 pp.

A narratology based specifically on data derived from biblical texts. Funk's work is similar in certain respects to the secular studies of Propp (0202), Chatman (0150), Genette (0247), and Rimmon-Kenan (0206). But rather than simply reproducing their categories and applying them to the Bible, he starts with biblical narrative, discovers patterns and rules inherent in the texts, and then attempts to organize these into meaningful categories. The resulting poetics covers the entire narrative transaction: the relationship of narrator to narratee, the process of focalization, the shaping of narrative units sequentially, the devices of showing and telling, and the significance of temporal ordering are only a few of the topics discussed. Funk approaches narrative poetics here as a language scholar would approach grammar. The work is clearly conceived as an introduction to what must be a further-reaching project, but it represents a monumental achievement in its own right--indispensable for narrative criticism of the Bible. This book was the subject of three articles in *Forum* 5,3 (1989). See 0492, 0498, 0549. It contains a brief study of the Markan passion narrative.

0514 Fuerst, Wesley J. "Literary, Rhetorical Criticism," *The Bible Today* 26 (1988): 20-24.

Commends rhetorical criticism as a method that looks at an entire literary work as a whole and takes into account literary connections that appear in the text. The primary focus is on the text as an act of communication. By way of example, Fuerst offers a rhetorical critical study of Psalm 22:12-21.

0515 Gottwald, Norman K. *The Hebrew Bible: A Socio-Literary Introduction.* Philadelphia: Fortress Press, 1985. 766 pp.

A basic introduction to the Old Testament that incorporates three approaches: traditio-historical methodology, new literary criticism (including structuralism), and socio-historical research. Although Gottwald himself is best known for his work in the latter field, this book stresses the contributions that all three approaches offer and insists on the need for use of all three. See also 0524.

0516 Greenwood, D. S. "Poststructuralism and Biblical Studies: Frank Kermode's *The Genesis of Secrecy.*" In *Gospel Perspectives: Studies in Midrash and Historiography,* ed. by R. T. France and David Wenham, 3:263-88. Sheffield: JSOT Press, 1983.

Provides a brief and general introduction to poststructuralism for New Testament scholars, with frequent reference to Kermode's work on Mark (1225). The discussion, however, is theoretical rather than exegetical and also takes into account the ideas of Jacques Derrida, John Dominic Crossan, and Paul de Man.

0517 Greenwood, David C. *Structuralism and the Biblical Text.* Religion and Reason, 32. Berlin: Mouton Publishers, 1985. 155 pp.

Traces the development of structuralism from its roots in the linguistic theories of Ferdinand de Saussure to its current usage in biblical studies. One chapter is devoted to the methodology of Claude Lévi-Strauss, one to that of Roland Barthes, one to A. J. Greimas, and one to Erhardt Güttgemanns. Another chapter treats Claude Chabrol, Jean Starobinski, Louis Marin, Dan Via, and Umberto Eco. Greenwood concludes with an assessment of structuralism as a method for biblical exegesis and presents two structural analyses of his own: Genesis 22:1-19 (the ordeal of Isaac) and Luke 15:11-32 (the parable of the prodigal son).

0518 Gunn, David M. "New Directions in the Study of Biblical Hebrew Narrative." *Journal for the Study of the Old Testament* 39 (1987): 67-75.

Surveys the development of contemporary literary approaches to the Old Testament, from early influences (form criticism, canonical criticism) through text-oriented, reader-oriented, and deconstructive studies. Gunn believes that modern literary-critical study has almost become the "new orthodoxy" in biblical studies.

0519   Güttgemanns, Erhardt. *Erhardt Güttgemanns' "Generative Poetics."* Ed. by Norman R. Petersen. *Semeia* 6 (1976). 220 pp.

A collection of four significant papers by Güttgemanns. Taken together, the essays outline an approach to exegesis called "generative poetics" and demonstrate several applications of the approach to Gospel texts. The approach is defended with reference to modern structuralist theory and by comparison to traditional historical exegesis. The significance of the method for the shaping of a "linguistic theology" (as opposed to Bultmann's existentialist theology) is also noted. Responses to these articles are collected in *Semeia* 10 (0266, 1561, 1610, 1625).

0520   Hartman, Geoffrey H., and Budick, Sanford, eds. *Midrash and Literature.* New Haven, CT: Yale University Press, 1986. 424 pp.

A collection of essays on the topics "Bible and Midrash"; "Midrash and Aggadah"; "From Midrash to Kabbalah"; "Literature and Midrash"; and "Contemporary Midrash." The "Literature and Midrash" section considers the relationship of midrash to secular western literature and contains an essay by Frank Kermode. The three preceding sections are more directly related to critical study of the Bible. The Introduction says that there are "ways in which midrash cannot possibly coincide with any secular poetics." There are significant constraints and restraints upon the freedom of midrash. On the other hand, "the passwords into our era," that Jacques Derrida and others began to trace out twenty years ago have lain inscribed in midrash for two millenia. See also 1541.

0521   Heyer, C. J. den. "Struktuur-analyse." *Gereformeerd Theologisch Tijdschrift* 79 (1979): 86-110.

Characterizes new approaches to literary analysis as movements toward autonomy. Special attention is paid here to the method (popular in South Africa) of dividing a text into colas or syntactical units constituting independent sentences. John 2:13-22 is treated as a test case. The purpose of structural analysis, which aims to replace historical criticism, is to elucidate the text's relevance for today.

0522   Hunter, J. H. "Deconstruction and Biblical Texts: Introduction and Critique." *Neotestamentica* 21 (1987): 125-140.

A critical introduction to deconstruction as a poststructuralist literary practice. The chief benefit of deconstruction is that it requires a reassessment of the roots of interpretation.

0523   Jackson, Jared, and Kessler, Martin, eds. *Rhetorical Criticism: Essays in Honor of James Muilenburg.* Pittsburgh Theological Monographs, 1. Pittsburgh: Pickwick Press, 1974. 287 pp.

A collection of essays by students of Muilenburg, who is largely credited with moving Old Testament scholarship beyond form-criticism to a more literary-oriented rhetorical criticism (see 0541). The volume opens with an introduction by Bernhard Anderson on "The New Frontier of Rhetorical Criticism" exemplified in Muilenburg's own work.

A select bibliography of Muilenburg's writings is also included. For annotations of some of the essays, see 0707-0708, 0741, 0852-0853, 0915, 0955-0956, 0962.

0524   Jobling, David. "Sociological and Literary Approaches to the Bible: How Shall the Twain Meet?" *Journal for the Study of the Old Testament* 38 (1987): 85-93.

A review of Gottwald's "Socio-Literary" introduction to the Old Testament (0515). Jobling holds that, while Gottwald is good in the areas of sociological and political theory, his literary treatment of the Bible leaves much to be desired. First, he is more interested in using documents as sources than as texts to be read in their final form. Second, he employs a conservative theoretical approach that views the function of literature as basically representational.

0525   Johnson, Alfred M., Jr. "Structuralism, Biblical Hermeneutics, and the Role of Structural Analysis in Historical Research." In *Structuralism and Biblical Hermeneutics: A Collection of Essays*, ed. and trans. by Alfred M. Johnson, Jr., 1-28. Pittsburgh Theological Monograph Series, 22. Pittsburgh: Pickwick Press, 1979.

Serves as an introduction to the volume in which it appears (0527). Johnson explains that the type of structuralism associated with Roland Barthes and A. J. Greimas is but one variety. Another stream, deriving from the work of Claude Lévi-Strauss and Edmund Leach, owes more to anthropology than to linguistics. This latter type of structuralism is not guilty of what Robert Scholes calls the "formalist fallacy," namely, the charge that structural analysis is unconcerned with history or with the cultural world beyond the literary work that it studies. It also avoids objections that Paul Ricoeur has raised to the appropriateness of structuralism for biblical studies.

0526   Johnson, Alfred M., Jr., ed. *The New Testament and Structuralism: A Collection of Essays by Corina Galland, Claude Chabrol, Guy Vuillod, Louis Marin, and Edgar Haulotte*. Pittsburgh Theological Monograph Series, 11. Pittsburgh: Pickwick Press, 1976. 338 pp.

Contains English translations of articles that originally appeared in *Langages* 22, which also included the essay "Genesis as Myth" by Edmund Leach (0593). The heart of this collection consists of three structuralist interpretations of Gospel texts (1058, 1154-1155). In addition, the book contains two methodological essays: "Problems of the Narrative Semiology of the Biblical Texts" by Claude Chabrol and "The Legibility of the Scriptures" by Edgar Haulotte. Guy Vuillod offers "Exercises on Some Short Stories," which analyzes contractual arrangements in a number of selections from Old and New Testament books. The book is further enhanced by "An Introduction to the Method of A. J. Greimas" by Corina Galland, by a glossary of formalist and structuralist terms, and a fairly extensive bibliography.

0527   Johnson, Alfred M. Jr., ed. *Structuralism and Biblical Hermeneutics: A Collection of Essays*. Pittsburgh Theological Monograph Series, 22. Pittsburgh: Pickwick Press, 1979. 228 pp.

A collection of essays translated by the editor from French originals. The essays offer theoretical reflections on structuralism and its use in biblical studies and provide examples of structuralist exegesis, to which responses are offered by Alain Bancy and X. Leon-Dufour. The tone for the collection is set by the editor's introductory essay (0525) and by a contribution from A. J. Greimas. Jean Pouillon offers "Structuralism: A Definitional Essay." Also included are a presentation of structuralist theses by Alain Blancy, an appendix on how to do structuralist readings by Corina Galland, and a 15-page bibliography.

0528   Keegan, Terence. *Interpreting the Bible: A Popular Introduction to Biblical Hermeneutics*. New York: Paulist Press, 1985. 177 pp.

Provides a basic introduction to the methods and principles of three approaches to biblical interpretation: structuralism, reader-response criticism, and canonical criticism. A separate chapter treats "narrative criticism" as a variety of reader-response, and one chapter offers a test-case study of "the reader of Matthew's Gospel." Keegan also addresses the relationship of scripture and the church from a Roman Catholic perspective.

0529 Kennedy, George A. *New Testament Interpretation Through Rhetorical Criticism*. Chapel Hill: University of North Carolina Press, 1984. 165 pp.

A basic handbook for the application of classical rhetorical criticism to New Testament texts. Kennedy, a classicist, details concepts of rhetoric as understood in antiquity, drawing primarily on the works of Aristotle. The Sermon on the Mount is interpreted as an example of deliberative rhetoric, John 13--17 as exemplary of epideictic rhetoric, and 2 Corinthians as illustrative of judicial rhetoric. Additional chapters consider the rhetoric of the Gospels, of the speeches in Acts, and of three Pauline epistles (1 Thess, Gal, and Rom). One of the best books on this subject, though it can be augmented by 0534, which considers more recent theories of rhetoric. See also 0490, 0577, 1492, 1498, 1515, 1522-1523, 1595.

0530   Kessler, Martin. "An Introduction to Rhetorical Criticism of the Bible: Prolegomena." *Semitics* 7 (1980): 1-27.

Offers a bibliography and some commentary on contemporary literary criticism, structuralism, and the different schools of literary theory as a guide for biblical scholars who wish to become acquainted with these materials.

0531 Kessler, Martin. "A Methodological Setting for Rhetorical Criticism." In *Art and Meaning: Rhetoric in Biblical Literature*, ed. by David J. A. Clines, David M. Gunn, and Alan J. Hauser, 1-19. Sheffield, England: JSOT Press, 1982.

Locates rhetorical criticism in the spectrum of methodological approaches to the Bible, both diachronic and synchronic. Kessler believes that rhetorical criticism deserves to be considered the leading synchronic approach, if it is defined in a way that includes both classical rhetoric and new rhetoric.

0532   Kovacs, Brian W., ed. "A Joint Paper by the Members of the Structuralism and Exegesis SBL Seminar." In *Society of Biblical Literature 1982 Seminar Papers*, ed. by Kent Harold Richards, 251-270. Chico, CA: Scholars Press, 1982.

A structuralist manifesto, offering a basic statement of the principles and goals that govern structuralist exegesis. Authors are Daniel Patte, Mark Ellingsen, James B. Harrod, Arno Hutchinson, Jr., David Jobling, Elizabeth Struthers Malbon, Gail O'Day Preston, Hugh C. White, and Brian Kovacs.

0533   Louw, J. P. "Primary and secondary reading of a text." *Neotestamentica* 18 (1984): 18-25.

Describes the process of interpretation as consisting of two readings: the primary reading corresponds to what the syntactic features and semantic features of the text allow. Normally, or at least ideally, only one such reading will be regarded as the most probable or correct. A secondary reading of the text involves semantic reinterpretation of the vocabulary, the discourse structure, and the pragmatics of the text. This takes place within a new frame of reference not substantiated by the restrictions of the text.

0534   Mack, Burton L. *Rhetoric and the New Testament*. Guides to Biblical Scholarship. Minneapolis: Fortress Press, 1989. 110 pp.

A basic guide to the use of rhetorical criticism in New Testament studies. The book goes beyond an earlier handbook by Kennedy (0529) in drawing on recent theories of rhetoric, especially those of Perelman and Olbrecht-Tyteca (0330). As such, New Testament rhetoric is consistently discussed not simply in terms of its stylistic qualities or aesthetic effects, but as designed to enhance argumentation. In addition, the importance of the situation or speech context for determining the persuasive force of any given rhetorical argument is emphasized. Selections of texts from all four Gospels, from Acts, from Paul's letters to Corinth and Galatia, and from Hebrews are included in an exegetical section that demonstrates practical application of the theories. A final chapter discusses the place of the discipline in the total configuration of critical scholarship.

0535   Man, R. E. "The Value of Chiasm for New Testament Interpretation." *Bibliotheca Sacra* 141 (1984): 146-157.

Encourages recognition of chiastic structural devices by biblical exegetes. Such recognition can help exegetes to appreciate comparisons and contrasts, identify the point of emphasis in a passage, understand the point being made, clarify the meaning of a statement, and determine the major purpose or theme of a book.

0536   Marin, Louis. "Du corps au texte: Propositions métaphysiques sur l'origine du récit." *Esprit* 41 (1973): 913-928.

Offers metaphysical propositions for a structuralist approach to New Testament resurrection texts.

0537   Martin, James P.   "Toward a Post-Critical Paradigm." *New Testament Studies* 33 (1987): 370-385.

Draws on analogous revolutions in physics, cosmology and other fields to describe current changes in theology and biblical hermeneutics as movement from a Mechanical Paradigm toward a Holistic Paradigm.   In so doing, Martin tries to describe the differences between classical historical criticism and postmodern historical criticism, emphasizing the need for the latter.

0538   McKnight, Edgar V. *Meaning in Texts: The Historical Shaping of a Narrative Hermeneutics*. Philadelphia: Fortress Press, 1978. 332 pp.

Relates the structural study of narrative to New Testament hermeneutics. Part One discusses the philosophical hermeneutics of Schliermacher, Dilthey, Heidegger, and Gadamer and the New Testament hermeneutics of Bultmann, Fuchs, and Ebeling. Part Two traces the development of structuralism from its birth in Russian formalism to its current usage in biblical studies. Part Three advocates and outlines a program for the use of structuralism in New Testament studies. See 1586, 1624.

0539   Milne, Pamela Jeanne. *Vladimir Propp and the Study of Structure in Hebrew Biblical Narrative*. Bible and Literature Series, 13. Sheffield: Almond Press, 1988. 325 pp.

Provides an extensive examination of Propp's *Morphology of the Folktale* (0202) and considers the implications of his study for biblical research. Milne also discusses the work of structuralist critics whose thinking is influenced by Propp (e.g., Claude Lévi-Strauss, A. J. Greimas) and the work of biblical scholars (e.g., Heda Janson, Robert Culley) who have used his model in exegesis. She then applies Propp's model to Daniel 1--6, but finds it insufficient for describing any of the stories contained there. See also 0989.

0540   Morgan, Robert, with Barton, John. *Biblical Interpretation*.   Oxford Bible Series. Oxford: Oxford University Press, 1988. 342 pp.

A history of approaches to biblical interpretation and a survey of approaches that are used most widely today. One chapter is devoted to "Literary Study of the Bible."

0541 Muilenburg, James. "Form Criticism and Beyond," *Journal of Biblical Literature* 88 (1969): 1-18.

Suggests that form-critical studies of the Old Testament ought to be supplemented by rhetorical criticism, which can aid in defining the limits of literary units in recognizing their structure, and in discerning the configuration of their component parts. Delivered as a Presidential Address by Muilenburg to the Society of Biblical Literature, this speech is considered by many to have been instrumental in opening the way to rhetorical and other literary approaches to the Bible.

0542   Parsons, Mikeal C. "Reading Talbert: New Perspectives on Luke-Acts." In *Society of Biblical Literature 1987 Seminar Papers*, ed. by Kent Harold Richards, 687-720. Atlanta: Scholars Press, 1987.

A survey of the work of Charles Talbert, who began his career as a redaction critic but more recently has tried to incorporate elements of modern literary criticism (along with genre criticism) into his studies of Luke-Acts. See 1347-1349.

0543   Patrick, Dale, and Scult, Allen. *Rhetoric and Biblical Interpretation*. Journal for the Study of the Old Testament Supplement Series, 82/Bible and Literature Series, 26. Sheffield: Almond Press, 1990.

Integrates Muilenberg's vision of rhetorical criticism (0541) with ideas from classical rhetorical tradition and contemporary hermeneutics. The authors define rhetoric as "the means by which a text establishes and manages its relationship to its audience in order to achieve a particular effect."

0544   Patte, Daniel. *Structural Exegesis for New Testament Critics*. Guides to Biblical Scholarship. Minneapolis: Fortress Press, 1989. 144 pp.

Not merely a revision of 0545, but a reconceptualization of how to apply structuralist principles in New Testament exegesis. The book presents a clear six-stage method for doing structural exegesis and illustrates the method by application to three texts: John 3:1-21; 4:4-42; Luke 10:21-24. Patte goes beyond the tendency for structuralism to limit its concern to detection of underlying (deep or abstract) structures and attempts to employ knowledge of underlying structures as a guide in reading the surface structure of the text.

0545   Patte, Daniel. *What is Structural Exegesis?* Guides to Biblical Scholarship. Philadelphia: Fortress Press, 1976. 90 pp.

An account, more readable than most, of structuralist theory and method, and of how structuralist principles and techniques may be used for exegesis of New Testament texts. The book served its purpose but has since been supplanted by a better volume by the same author in the same series (0544). See also 0278, 1562.

0546   Patte, Daniel, and Patte, Aline. *Structural Exegesis: From Theory to Practice. Exegesis of Mark 15 and 16. Hermeneutical Implications*. Philadelphia: Fortress Press, 1978. 134 pp.

A follow-up to 0545 that presupposes what is presented there. This volume offers a method of structural analysis that probes beneath narrative roles to discover the deep values that lie beneath a narrative's surface. These are expressed in the fundamental oppositions that the narrative mediates. The method is then applied to a study of Mark 15--16. A final chapter devoted to the hermeneutical implications of structuralist method discusses the distinctions between "secular" and "sacred" texts. See also 1586.

0547 Perrin, Norman. "The Evangelist As Author: Reflections on Method in the Study and Interpretation of the Synoptic Gospels and Acts." *Biblical Research* 17 (1972): 5-18.

Traces the development of how the role of the evangelists has been viewed in different critical approaches: source criticism viewed the evangelists as compilers; form criticism viewed them as collectors and editors; and redaction criticism, through its increasing emphasis on the freedom and creativity exercised by these evangelists, has come at last to view them as authors. This means that the discipline of general literary criticism must now be applied to study of the gospels, including study of characters, plot, and theme.

0548 Petersen, Norman R. *Literary Criticism for New Testament Critics*. Guides to Biblical Scholarship. Philadelphia: Fortress Press, 1978. 92 pp.

A basic introductory guide to literary criticism of New Testament narrative. Petersen, the premier theorist of narrative criticism, begins by pointing out problems with the evolutionary model that forms a paradigm for historical-critical scholarship. Next, he sketches a convincing rationale for the addition of literary-critical methods based on communication models. He argues for the co-existence of both historical and literary modes of criticism. The book also contains two exegetical chapters that have become classic studies in their own right: "Story-Time and Plotted Time in Mark's Narrative" and "Narrative World and Real-World in Luke-Acts."

0549 Phillips, Gary A. "Discourse of Biblical Narratology: A Review of Robert Funk, *The Poetics of Biblical Narrative*. *Forum* 5,3 (1989): 79-86.

Critiques Funk's work (0513) from a postmodern perspective. His book is a monument to formalism and, as such, brings all the insights and problems of formalism to the biblical text. Phillips offers a deconstructive critique not of Funk's work specifically, but of formalism in general. He views Funk's narratology as helpful, but notes that Michel Foucault and Mieke Bal have indicated the possibility of a "deconstructive narratology," which Funk's work is not.

0550 Polzin, Robert M. *Biblical Structuralism: Method and Subjectivity in the Study of Ancient Texts*. Philadelphia: Fortress Press, 1977. 216 pp.

Offers a brief description of structuralism, presents a structural analysis of the book of Job, and then assesses classic biblical studies by Julius Wellhausen, Gerhard von Rad, and Martin Noth from a structuralist perspective. Polzin regards structuralism as more of "an imaginative approach" than a distinctive methodology. The hermeneutic of structuralism differs from that of other approaches in that the interpreter is aware of his or her own subjectivity. Many structuralists would not agree with Polzin on this point, but would hold that the structures of language offer a more objective basis for analysis of texts than he claims. Although this study touts structuralism, its real interest (in retrospect) seems to be in what has since become known as post-structuralism or deconstruction.

0551 Powell, Mark Allan. "The Bible and Modern Literary Criticism." In *Summary of Proceedings: Forty-Third Annual Conference of the American Theological Library Association*, ed. by Betty A. O'Brien, 78-94. Evanston, IL: American Theological Library Association, 1990.

Contrasts modern literary criticism of the Bible with traditional historical-critical study. Literary criticism is distinguished in four ways: (1) a focus on the finished form of the text; (2) an emphasis on the unity of the text as a whole; (3) a perspective that views the text as an end in itself; and, (4) an interest in readers over authors. A ten-page bibliography is included.

0552 Powell, Mark Allan. *What is Narrative Criticism?* Guides to Biblical Scholarship. Minneapolis: Fortress Press, 1990. 144 pp.

A comprehensive guide to the principles and methods of narrative criticism as they are currently being applied to the New Testament Gospels. The book provides a brief historical overview of the development of the discipline and clearly distinguishes it from both historical-critical methodologies and from other literary approaches (rhetorical criticism, reader-response criticism, and structuralism). Principles and concepts are discussed in relation to three categories (events, characters, settings), with a special chapter devoted to the pervasive issues of point of view, narration, irony, symbolism, and use of narrative patterns. The final chapter lists objections to the use of narrative criticism, indicates the promise that the method holds for biblical studies, and discusses the hermeneutical implications of a continued use of this approach. Topics treated as "case studies" include the plot of Matthew's Gospel, the role of the religious leaders in the synoptic Gospels, and narrative settings in the Gospel of Mark.

0553 Pregeant, Russell. "Where is the Meaning? Metaphysical Criticism and the Problem of Indeterminacy." *Journal of Religion* 63 (1983): 107-124.

Recognizes that texts are relatively indeterminate until rendered determinate by readers, and commends Alfred North Whitehead's metaphysics as a helpful perspective from which readers can do this. Pregeant presents an example of how Jesus' sayings about the Kingdom might be understood from a Whiteheadian perspective.

0554 Reese, James M. *Experiencing the Good News: The New Testament as Communication*. Wilmington, DE: Michael Glazier, 1984. 203 pp.

An introduction for students of the New Testament to the world of modern linguistic analysis. In part one, "Language as a System of Communication," Reese traces the theories of Roman Jakobson, Umberto Eco, Paul Ricoeur, and others. In part two, "Religious Language and Imagination," the theories are applied to biblical studies and the work of such exegetes as Amos N. Wilder and John Dominic Crossan is considered. To the extent that linguistic analysis has fueled the development of modern theories of literature, this book will be useful to those interested in literary criticism of the New Testament.

0555   Resseguie, James L.   "Reader-Response Criticism and the Synoptic Gospels."
Journal of the American Academy of Religion 52 (1984): 307-324.

Identifies critical assumptions and key strategies of various schools of reader-response
criticism and illustrates these with references to the synoptic Gospels. Resseguie
classifies reader-response approaches according to whether they view the reader as
encoded "in the text," as dominant "over the text," or as interactive "with the text." He
identifies two ways in which reader-response approaches differ from traditional forms
of biblical criticism: (1) they focus on dynamics of anticipation and retrospection as
determined from the perspective of "successive reading" (i.e., beginning-to-end); (2)
they attempt to show how the author "educates" the reader by building and then
shattering expectations or by encouraging reader identification with a particular
character.

0556   Rhoads, David.   "Narrative Criticism and the Gospel of Mark." *Journal of the
American Academy of Religion* 50 (1982): 411-434.

A classic article that inaugurates the approach to biblical studies known as "narrative
criticism" by outlining the way in which such a program might be applied to the
Gospel of Mark. Rhoads calls attention to the need for consideration of plot, conflict,
characters, settings, narrator, point of view, standards of judgment, implied author,
ideal reader, style, and rhetorical technique. The article concludes with questions
that narrative criticism poses for biblical research in general, questions that for the
most part have still not been answered.

0557   Richter, Wolfgang.   *Exegese als Literaturwissenschaft: Entwurf einer
alttestamentlichen Literatur Theorie und Methodologie*. Göttingen: Vandenhoeck and
Ruprecht, 1971. 211 pp.

Outlines a step-by-step approach for developing a "science of literature" appropriate
for study of the Old Testament. Richter's approach is firmly text-oriented; he claims
it will produce "a completely unbiased and neutral analysis" of the Old Testament, one
that will guard against the abuses of allegorizing. Texts are to be studied in terms of
the following aspects: (1) small units; (2) form; (3) genre; (4) tradition; (5)
composition or redaction; (6) content. This approach differs from modern literary
studies in its concentration on units discernible through source analysis rather than on
the text in its final form. Nevertheless, Richter's model emphasizes the connection
between form and meaning and has been especially influential in rhetorical criticism.
He also draws heavily on modern linguistic theory in ways that often parallel
structuralism.

0558   Ricoeur, Paul.   "Biblical Hermeneutics." *Semeia* 4 (1975): 27-148.

A philosopher of language, who admits he is neither a theologian nor an exegete,
attempts to draw conclusions from his studies that will be relevant for the study of
biblical literature, especially parables. The essay is divided into three parts: (1) "The
Narrative Form" attempts to clarify the formal structures of biblical parables on the
basis of structural semiotics applied to nonbiblical texts by such scholars as Vladimir
Propp, A. J. Greimas, and Roland Barthes; (2) "The Metaphorical Process" considers
the poetic approach that allows for identification of an intermediary between formal

explanation and existential interpretation; and, (3) "The Specificity of Religious Language" asks what makes parables specifically religious forms of discourse and offers a hypothesis based on a comparison of the way in which several modes of discourse point toward the meaning of the phrase "kingdom of God."

0559 Riva, Franco. "L'esegesi narrativa: dimensioni ermeneutiche." *Revista Biblica* 37 (1989): 129-160.

Surveys narrative exegesis as a method of biblical interpretation, with particular interest in German scholarship. The three dimensions of narrative exegesis are (1) *theological* (narrative theology, political theology, post-critical theology, theology of experience, and so on); (2) *philosophical* (structuralism and hermeneutic, analytical, philosophy of history and narrative tradition); and (3) *linguistic* (performance, narrative logic, tolerance and innocence).

0560 Riva, R. "Analisi strutturale ed esegesi biblica. Lingua e parola. Costrizioni di sistema e opzioni nella produzione e interpretazione segnica." *Revista Biblica* 28 (1980): 243-284.

Enjoins biblical exegetes to make use of structuralism in their studies and provides an introduction to the method. Riva defines signification in terms of the relation between signifier and signified, discusses language as a system of signs, and offers various theories of discourse and structuralist analysis. The same issue of this journal also contains a lexicon of terms used in structuralist analysis, prepared by Riva (pp. 375-379).

0561 Robbins, Vernon K. and Patton, John H. "Rhetoric and Biblical Criticism." *Quarterly Journal of Speech* 66 (1980): 327-337.

An extended book review, which lists and briefly discusses the significance of more than a dozen works related to rhetorical study of the Bible.

0562 Ryken, Leland, ed. *How To Read the Bible as Literature and Get More Out of It.* Academie Books. Grand Rapids, MI: Zondervan Publishing House, 1984. 208 pp.

A popular introduction by a conservative scholar who wishes to call attention to the literary artistry of the Bible. Ryken discusses "types of biblical stories" (heroic narrative, epic, comedy, tragedy), "types of biblical poetry" (encomium, love lyrics, and the various types of psalms), and the literary aspects of proverbs, Gospels, parables, epistles, satire, and visionary literature. His goal is to enable readers to approach the Bible with renewed appreciation and excitement and to thus obtain a more profound grasp of its truths.

0563   Sanders, E. P., and Davies, Margaret. *Studying the Synoptic Gospels*. London: SCM Press; Philadelphia: Trinity Press International, 1989. 374 pp.

A general textbook for introduction to Gospel studies that incorporates new literary approaches. One chapter is devoted to "Structuralism and De-Construction" and another to "Rhetorical Criticism and the 'Implied Reader'."

0564   Seeley, David. "Poststructuralist Criticism and Biblical History." In *Art/Literature/Religion: Life on the Borders*, ed. by Robert Detweiler, 157-171. Journal of the American Academy of Religion Thematic Studies Series, 49,2. Chico, CA: Scholars Press, 1983.

Summarizes the ideas of Jacques Derrida and Michel Foucault and indicates how poststructuralism might be applied to the New Testament. The new approach poses an uncomfortable challenge to biblical studies insofar as it demonstrates that texts cannot be read only as expressions of a theological position but must also be considered as "cultural artifacts." Hence, biblical scholarship needs "to cast its net more widely."

0565   Servotte, Herman, and Verbeek, Ludo. "De structuralistische Bijbellezing." *Collationes* 10 (1980): 426-441.

Describes the structuralist method and recommends its use as a supplement to other approaches to the Bible. A structuralist analysis of the Good Samaritan story (Luke 10:25-37) is offered as an example. A bibliography is included.

0566   Sheppard, G. T. "'Blessed Are Those Who Take Refuge in Him': Biblical Criticism and Deconstruction." *Religion and Intellectual Life* 5,2 (1988): 57-66.

Examines the implications of deconstruction for biblical interpretation, focusing on its denial of any objective means for settling interpretation. Sheppard believes the approach may have some pragmatic value, which he seeks to demonstrate with reference to Psalm 2:11.

0567   Sider, John W. "Nurturing Our Nurse: Literary Scholars and Biblical Exegesis." *Christianity and Literature* 32,1 (1982): 15-21.

Calls on Christian literary critics to devote themselves more intentionally to rendering aid in biblical exegesis, noting that "theologians and exegetes badly need our help with the Bible." What biblical scholars need, however, is not literary theory but knowledge of "old-fashioned critical concepts," such as plot, character, setting, and point of view.

0568   Snyman, Andreas H. "On Studying the Figures (*schemata*) in the New Testament." *Biblica* 69 (1988): 93-107.

Traces the significance of Perelman and Olbrecht-Tyteca's book on rhetorical criticism (0330) for New Testament studies. Figures, that is, instances in which language is used in an unusual way to achieve a striking result, must be studied with reference to their role in argumentation and with sensitivity to the rhetorical situation in which they were to function.

0569 Spencer, Richard, ed. *Orientation by Disorientation: Studies in Literary Criticism and Biblical Literary Criticism Presented in Honor of William A. Beardslee*. Pittsburgh Theological Monograph Series, 35. Pittsburgh: Pickwick Press, 1980. 270 pp.

A collection of articles organized into three categories: definition and history of literary criticism and biblical literary criticism (0084, 1628); description and analysis of various aspects and methods (1088, 1587, 1609, 1638); and exemplary applications of literary analysis to biblical materials (0812, 1079, 1129, 1174, 1370).

0570 Sternberg, Meir. *The Poetics of Biblical Narrative: Ideological Literature and the Drama of Reading*. Bloomington: Indiana University Press, 1985. 580 pp.

A major contribution to narratology with specific reference to the Hebrew Bible (Old Testament). The author is an established literary critic (0212), who approaches the Bible through accepted literary conventions, but who does not simply regard it as any other book. Literature such as the Bible demands a poetics attuned to the workings of ideological art. Concepts explored include omniscient narration, point of view, gaps and ambiguities, suspense, characterization, redundancy, and the rhetoric of persuasion. Against deconstruction, Sternberg says the Bible is a "foolproof composition" that is "proof against counterreading except by ignorance, willfulness, preconception or tendentiousness" (p. 50). Against traditional historical criticism, he examines the Masoretic text only, without regard for documentary hypotheses. See also 1552, 1645, 1654.

0571 Traina, Robert A. *Methodical Bible Study: A New Approach to Hermeneutics*. New York: Ganis and Harris, 1952. 262 pp.

A devotional but scholarly guide to "the joyous adventure to be found in studying the great variety of literature in the Old and New Testaments." Traina's articulation of rhetorical principles to be observed in biblical literature has been expanded elsewhere by Bauer (1127).

0572 Tuckett, Christopher. *Reading the New Testament. Methods of Interpretation*. Philadelphia: Fortress Press, 1987. 200 pp.

An introduction to critical methods of exegesis that, for its date, gives surprisingly short shrift to literary approaches. One chapter out of eleven is devoted to structuralism, and another to "other approaches," which include "canonical criticism" and "literary criticism." The author's evaluative comments confirm the suspicion that he does not think much of the literary approaches.

0573 Vorster, Willem S. "Readings, Readers, and the Succession Narrative: An Essay on Reception." *Zeitschrift für die alttestamentliche Wissenschaft* 98 (1986): 351-362.

An article on reception theory that draws on 2 Samuel 9--20 and 1 Kings 1--2 for its illustrations. Vorster appreciates the complexity of readers both "inside and outside" the text. Texts invite readers to produce their own understandings of what is written, and so allow a wide variety of acceptable responses. Responses that are prompted by factors outside the text, however, are judged inadequate.

0574 Watson, Duane F. "The New Testament and Greco-Roman Rhetoric: A Bibliography." *The Journal of the Evangelical Theological Society* 31 (1988): 465-472.

A classified bibliography of works that exemplify or facilitate rhetorical criticism of the New Testament. Watson lists ancient primary sources, modern theoretical works, and almost 100 rhetorical-critical studies of New Testament literature.

0575 White, Hugh C., ed. *Speech Act Theory and Biblical Criticism. Semeia* 41 (1988). 178 pp.

This volume of the journal *Semeia* is devoted to the relevance of certain developments in the field of linguistics for literary study of the Bible. The issue opens with an excellent survey of "Speech Act Theory and Literary Criticism" by the editor that deals primarily with the ideas of Austin (0042) and Searle (0069). Additional essays examine "Performative Utterance, the Word of God, and the Death of the Author" (Michael Hancher); "The Value of Speech Act Theory for Old Testament Hermeneutics" (Hugh C. White); "Speech Act Theory and Biblical Exegesis" (Daniel Patte); and "Infelicitous Performances and Ritual Criticism" (Ronald L. Grimes). An example of speech act theory in application to a particular text is offered by Susan Lanser (0711). Evaluative responses to the above articles include "The Contributions of Speech Act Theory to Biblical Study" by Martin J. Buss and "Philosophy of Language in the Service of Religious Studies" by Charles E. Jarrett. Bibliographies are included.

0576 Wittig, Susan. "A Theory of Multiple Meanings." *Semeia* 9 (1977): 75-103.

Wittig begins by asking, "What is the source of the phenomenon of multiple meanings?" She proposes "a semiotic model of analysis" where "plurisignification is the product of a duplex sign system which operates denotatively and connotatively at the same time, and which has at least two signifieds: . . . a *denotatum* and a *designatum*." Further, she says that parable "with its intentionally incomplete signification pattern, is not to convey a single meaning, but to direct our attention to the nature of meaning itself, and to the meaning systems out of which we generate signification." See also 1115.

0577   Wuellner, Wilhelm. "Where Is Rhetorical Criticism Taking Us?" *Catholic Biblical Quarterly* 49 (1987): 448-463.

Reviews Kennedy's classical model for rhetorical criticism (0529) and indicates ways in which theories of rhetorical criticism are in transition. Newer studies do not limit their focus to the rhetoric of religious persuasion but also examine the dynamics of personal and social identification and transformation inherent in texts. Rhetorical critics are interested now in the whole range of appeals embraced and provoked by rhetoric: not only the rational and cognitive dimensions, but also the emotive and imaginative ones.   As a result, rhetorical criticism is taking its practitioners increasingly into interdisciplinary studies.

PART FOUR: CRITICISM

THE BIBLE

0578   Alter, Robert, and Kermode, Frank, eds. *The Literary Guide to the Bible.*
Cambridge, MA: Belknap Press, 1987. 678 pp.

A comprehensive collection of articles on every section of the Bible by an
international team of 26 scholars, some well-known in secular literary circles and some
established biblical critics.   The essays vary greatly in quality and intent.   On
publication, this book received widespread media attention (cf. 1673) and is frequently
cited as evidence of the new interest in literary study of the Bible. See 0496, 0609,
0638, 0690, 0739, 0751, 0753, 0764, 0766, 0801, 0855, 0858, 0867, 0871, 0873, 0883,
0905, 0926, 0935, 0943, 0946, 0977, 0980, 0990, 1000, 1041, 1146, 1206, 1230, 1299,
1343, 1393, 1433, 1510, 1536.

0579   Bach, Alice. *Sighs and Whispers: Dialogue and Silence in Biblical Narrative.*
Literary Currents in Biblical Interpretation. Louisville, KY: Westminster/John Knox
Press, forthcoming.

Announced for publication.

0580   Barthes, R.; Bovon, F.; Leenhardt, F. J.; Martin-Achard, R.; and Starobinski,
J. *Structural Analysis and Biblical Exegesis.* Pittsburgh Theological Monograph Series
3. Trans. by A. M. Johnson. Pittsburgh: Pickwick Press, 1974. 164 pp.

A collection of five essays by French scholars. The first provides a critical survey of
the use of French structuralism in biblical exegesis (0494).   The remaining four
contrast structuralist studies of biblical texts with other methodological approaches.
A structuralist analysis of Genesis 32:23-33 by Barthes (0683) is presented alongside
a form-critical study of the same passage by Robert Martin-Achard. A structuralist
look at Mark 5:1-20 by Starobinski (1259) is similarly paired with a social-
psychoanalytical reading of the story by Leenhardt (1231).

0581   Breck, John. "Biblical Chiasmus: Exploring Structure for Meaning." *Biblical Theology Bulletin* 17 (1987): 70-74.

Explores the rhetorical device of chiasmus as illustrative of the manner in which literary form is determinative of meaning in biblical literature. Breck insists that genuine chiasmus does not consist simply of inverted parallelism (ABB'A') but is organized around a thematic center (ABCB'A'). The chiasm thus functions to reveal the center of the passage. Passages from psalms, Gospels, and epistles are considered.

0582   Cahill, P. Joseph. "The Unity of the Bible." *Biblica* 65 (1984): 404-411.

A review of Frye's *The Great Code* (0586). Cahill says that Frye shows the Bible is unified by intricately woven literary relationships. His book commends the unity of the Testaments, the primacy of a literary orientation toward the Bible, and appreciation for polysemous meaning.

0583   Caird, G. B. *The Language and Imagery of the Bible.* Philadelphia: Westminster Press, 1980. 288 pp.

A study in three sections: Part 1 considers the hermeneutical question of how meaning is conveyed through language, with special consideration of Hebrew idiom and thought forms; Part 2 offers an analysis of figurative speech in the Bible--similes, metaphors, parables, allegories, anthropomorphisms, and so on; Part 3 addresses the issue of language as it relates to history, myth, and eschatology.

0584   Clines, D. J. A.; Fowl, S. E.; and Porter, S. E. *The Bible in Three Dimensions: Essays in Celebration of Forty Years of Biblical Study in the University of Sheffield.* Journal for the Study of the Old Testament Supplement Series, 87. Sheffield: JSOT Press, 1990. 240 pp.

A collection of essays on the Bible organized under three categories: "Modern Criticism"; "Social World Studies of Israel and Early Christianity"; and "Questions of Interpretative Method." The first part includes the following essays: "Reading Esther from Left to Right: Contemporary Strategies for Reading a Biblical Text" by D. J. A. Clines; "Zion in Transformation: A Literary Approach to Isaiah" by B. G. Webb; "Lot as Jekyll and Hyde: A Reading of Genesis 18--19"; and "The Parable of the Unjust Steward: Irony *is* the Key" by S. E. Porter.

0585   Diel, Paul. *Symbolism in the Bible: The Universality of Symbolic Language and Its Psychological Significance.* Trans. by Nelly Marans. San Francisco: Harper and Row, 1986. 175 pp.

Applies a method of translating symbolic language based on psychological theory to three biblical texts: Genesis 1--3, John 1, and selected passages from the epistles of Paul. Diel, known in literary circles for his work in Greek mythology, treats these texts, respectively, in terms of three themes: the myth of Fall, the myth of Incarnation, and the myth of Resurrection.

0586   Frye, Northrop. *The Great Code: The Bible and Literature.* New York: Harcourt Brace Jovanovich, 1982. 261 pp.

Frye presents the Bible and literature from the perspective of an English teacher. He says that literature students need to know about the Bible since it has had tremendous influence on Western writers up to the eighteenth century and to some extent even beyond. He never claims to be a biblical scholar or linguist, but deals with the Bible as the Western creative mind has dealt with it--in canonical order, and from the 1611 Authorized Version (KJV). He begins by discussing "the language that people use in talking about the Bible," then proceeds to discussions of myth and metaphor that should be helpful to scholars whose first area of expertise is not literary theory and practice. See also 0088. For reviews, see 0582, 1570, 1637, 1645, 1668, 1727.

0587   Gottcent, John H. *The Bible: A Literary Study.* Boston: Twayne Publishers, 1986. 120 pp.

Examines Bible passages from a literary perspective that accents the role of the reader in finding meaning. The passages are examined in three stages: (1) a close reading of the text; (2) a search in the text for patterns of human experience applicable to the reader's own world; and (3) use of those patterns in clarification of the readers' own experiences. Chapters are devoted to The Flood; Moses; Jephthah; Samson; Saul; David; Elijah and Ahab; Jonah; Psalm 23; Job; Ruth; Ecclesiastes; the Good Samaritan; the Prodigal Son; Acts; and Revelation.

0588   Gottcent, John H. *The Bible as Literature: A Selected Bibliography.* Boston: Twayne Publishers, 1979. 170 pp.

An annotated bibliography of works considered useful for scholars who interpret the Bible as literature. The bibliography includes a large number of works that are not themselves literary-critical (e.g., historical-critical studies, and translations and editions of the Bible itself), but which literary critics may want to consult.

0589   Gros Louis, Kenneth R. R.; Ackerman, James S.; and Warshaw, Thayer S., eds. *Literary Interpretations of Biblical Narratives.* Nashville: Abingdon Press, 1974. 352 pp.

A collection of essays (continued in 0590) originally developed for the purpose of aiding secondary school teachers of English in teaching the Bible as literature. The essays vary in their concerns. A few are devoted to methods or issues that must be considered when understanding the Bible in this way, but most offer examples of how particular biblical passages can be understood as literature. Many, though not all, of the authors appear to conceive of reading the Bible "as literature" as an alternative to reading it "as scripture." The idea that the two approaches are somehow exclusive has been largely rejected in more recent biblical literary criticism. For annotations of several articles, see 0491, 0614, 0697-0698, 0727, 0735, 0783, 0800, 0823, 0884, 0928, 0954, 1014, 1180, 1218, 1531, 1648.

0590   Gros Louis, Kenneth R. R., and Ackerman, James S., eds. *Literary Interpretations of Biblical Narratives, Volume II*. Nashville: Abingdon Press, 1982. 320 pp.

A collection of articles similar to those brought together in an earlier volume (0589). The perspective of the authors is basically the same as in that volume: literary criticism of the Bible is viewed as a field distinct from (though complementary to) biblical scholarship. The purpose of studying the Bible as literature is not primarily to elucidate its theological message, but to appreciate its aesthetic and artistic quality. See 0681, 0689, 0695-0696, 0699, 0754, 0781, 0803, 0817, 0824, 0839, 0933, 1036, 1305, 1360, 1416.

0591   Josipovici, Gabriel. *The Book of God: A Response to the Bible*. New Haven, CT: Yale University Press, 1988. 350 pp.

A literary study of the Bible by a professor of English literature. Josipovici places himself in the tradition of Alter (0607), Auerbach (0128), Frye (0586), and Kermode (1225), with one distinction: he attempts to respond to the entire Christian Bible (Genesis to Revelation) as a narrative and poetic whole. Rejecting virtually all historically oriented biblical scholarship as irrelevant, he views the Bible as a work to be encountered, not interpreted. Rhythm, speech, character, and distance are topics given extensive treatment and close readings are provided for Genesis 1--3, the Joseph story, the book of Judges, and the letter to the Hebrews. Three chapters are devoted to the characters of David, Jesus, and Paul. Selected prayers, psalms, and genealogies are also discussed.

0592   Kreuziger, Frederick A. *Apocalypse and Science Fiction: A Dialectic of Religious and Secular Soteriologies*. American Academy of Religion Academy Series, 40. Chico, CA: Scholars Press, 1982. 247 pp.

Observes that two genres, apocalyptic literature and science fiction, lie on the margins, respectively, of the fields of religious and literary studies. The majority of the book is devoted to a treatment of science fiction as a literary category: its origins and genre. Both science fiction and apocalyptic are studied together, however, as examples of popular literature that is "user-oriented," determined by the hopes and expectations of their readers. The tension between future expectation and present response, and the conviction that history is not wholly dependent on human instrumentality are two dynamics in both genres that allow for dialogue between them.

0593   Leach, Edmund. *Genesis as Myth and Other Essays*. London: Jonathan Cape, 1969. 124 pp.

Contains three essays on biblical themes by a structural anthropologist. In the title work, Leach traces structural patterns in Genesis, concentrating on the issue of sexual rules and transgressions. He considers the presence of such patterns in diverse forms of mythology to be of psychological, sociological, and scientific significance. A second essay, "The Legitimacy of Solomon" employs an explicitly Lévi-Straussian procedure to observe some structural aspects of Old Testament history. The third essay, "Virgin

Birth," contends that the first chapter of Matthew's Gospel should be treated seriously by anthropologists as a record of theological doctrine. See also 1581.

0594   Leach, Edmund, and Aycock, Alan. *Structuralist Interpretations of Biblical Myth.* Cambridge: Cambridge University Press, 1983. 176 pp.

Applies the authors' own modified version of Lévi-Strauss' structuralist methodology to selected biblical texts and themes. The book begins with a historical survey by Leach of anthropological approaches to the Bible that was originally published in 1961 and, unfortunately, is not updated here. Leach then presents structuralist readings of the Moses-Miriam story, of the Christ-Melchizedek theme found in Hebrews and in Christian art, and of the parables of Jesus. Aycock presents studies on Lot's wife and on the mark of Cain.

0595   Licht, Jacob. *Storytelling in the Bible.* 2nd ed. Jerusalem: Magneso Press, 1986. 154 pp.

A discussion of the craft of storytelling, as displayed in the Bible. The book examines both mimetic and aesthetic qualities and especially emphasizes techniques of scene-writing and the use of repetition. Chapters are also devoted to "Time" and to "Complex Structures." A useful book, the volume is not well-known and has been largely ignored in most literary studies of scripture.

0596   Macky, Peter W. "The Multiple Purposes of Biblical Speech Acts." *Princeton Seminary Bulletin* 8 (1987): 50-61.

Draws on speech-act theory to suggest seven possible purposes that might lie behind the words of biblical writers: presentative, expressive, evaluative, performative, exploratory, dynamic, and relational. Macky thinks that the ultimate purpose was probably relational--to enable readers in their relationship with God.

0597   Parunak, H. Van Dyke. "Oral Typesetting: Some Uses of Biblical Structure." *Biblica* 62 (1981): 153-168.

Discusses the structural devices of chiasm (ABCC'B'A') and alternation (ABCABC), with regard to three functions: dividing text, unifying text, and emphasizing text. All examples cited are from the Old Testament, but the principles discussed are applicable to New Testament literature as well.

0598   Parunak, H. Van Dyke. "Transitional Techniques in the Bible." *Journal of Biblical Literature* 102 (1983): 525-548.

Identifies and discusses key transitional techniques in biblical literature: key words, links, and hinges. All three techniques may be used to establish concurrence at various levels (morphological, lexical, syntactical, rhetorical).

0599   Placher, William C. "Scripture as Realistic Narrative: Some Preliminary Questions." *Perspectives in Religious Studies* 5 (1978): 32-41.

Suggests that much of the Bible can be better described as "realistic narrative" (i.e., "truth-telling anecdote") rather than as accurate history or as myth. Realistic narrative conveys true information, although it need not be historically accurate. The truth conveyed by realistic narrative, however, is generally not reducible to nonnarrative form.

0600   Rossow, F. C. "Dramatic Irony in the Bible--With a Difference." *Concordia Journal* 8 (1982): 48-52.

Compares biblical irony with irony in secular literature. Dramatic irony in secular literature is usually grim, painful, and shattering, but in the Bible irony highlights God's grace and goodness. The "surprise" of biblical irony is typically an accent on blessing rather than tragedy, gospel rather than law.

0601   Ryken, Leland. *Words of Delight: A Literary Introduction to the Bible*. Grand Rapids, MI: Baker Books, 1987. 382 pp.

An introduction to various forms of biblical literature with emphasis on the literary artistry and craftsmanship employed by the writers. The author explains what it means to read the Bible as literature, lists distinctive characteristics of biblical narrative and poetry, and explains the artistic means through which the stories and poems of the Bible produce their intended effects. Several literary forms are discussed, with fairly extensive literary analyses provided for representative material: hero stories (Daniel, Gideon, Esther, Ruth), epic (Exodus, David, Revelation), tragedy (Samson, Saul), satire (parables, Amos, Jonah), and drama (Job). Other studies include comments on the stories of Abraham, Jacob, and Joseph, on Genesis 1--3, on examples of encomium, on the Song of Solomon, and on various types of psalms and proverbs. A companion volume dealing exclusively with the New Testament has also been published (1047).

0602   Savran, George. *Telling and Retelling: Quotation in Biblical Narrative*. Bloomington: Indiana University Press, 1988. 192 pp.

An in-depth study of the phenomenon of quotation as it relates to the poetics of dialogue in biblical literature. Quotation is at once direct speech and recollection of prior words. Savran considers quotation as speech within speech, as a phenomenon that brings one set of words into contact or conflict with another. He analyzes the functions of quotation on levels of story and discourse and discusses the types of effects created by the resultant interplay of the points of view represented. He distinguishes between verifiable and unverifiable quotations and discusses the role that quotation can play as repetition, as interpretation, and as reformulation of memory.

0603   Williams, James G. "The Beautiful and the Barren: Conventions in Biblical Type-Scenes." *Journal for the Study of the Old Testament* 17 (1980): 107-119.

Discusses episodes in both Old and New Testament narrative that demonstrate varied use of established conventions in the literature of ancient Israel. Four kinds of type scenes are treated: (1) the wife as sister; (2) the betrothal; (3) the *agon* (contest) of the barren wife; and (4) the promise to the barren wife.

0604   Williams, James G. *Those Who Ponder Proverbs: Aphoristic Thinking and Biblical Literature*. Sheffield: Almond Press, 1981. 128 pp.

A sweeping study of the literary and conceptual characteristics of proverbs and aphorisms in several writings (Proverbs, Ecclesiastes, Sirach, and the synoptic Gospels). Proverbs and Sirach are seen to exemplify the "aphoristic wisdom of order," which emphasizes self-control, a retributive principle of justice, and a conservative adherence to tradition. Ecclesiastes and the synoptic teachings of Jesus exemplify the "aphoristic wisdom of counter-order," which is skeptical of tradition and emphasizes disorientation and paradox. "Proverb" is distinguished from "aphorism" as using a collective voice rather than an individual voice.

0605   Williams, James G. *Women Recounted: Narrative Thinking and the God of Israel*. Bible and Literature Series, 6. Sheffield: Almond Press, 1982. 150 pp.

Investigates stories about key female characters in the Bible in order to indicate and clarify the interrelationship of biblical images of the feminine with thinking about the nature of language and about the God of Israel. Williams first considers type-scenes involving what he calls the "arche-mother" figure. He then goes on to look at the following models: the mother of all living (Eve); the aggressive or warrior woman (Deborah, Jael, Judith); the dependent heroine (Esther, Mary); the reversal of the patriarchal mode (Ruth); and the temptress (Delilah, Potiphar's wife, the alien woman of Proverbs).

THE OLD TESTAMENT

See also 0482, 0488, 0504, 0515, 0523, 0541, 0570, 0845, 1043, 1654.

0606   Alonso-Schökel, Luis. *A Manual of Hebrew Poetics*. Studia Biblica, 11. Rome: Editrice Pontifico Instituto Biblico, 1988. 228 pp.

A study of the techniques of biblical poetry. First, Alonso-Schökel surveys the study of biblical poetry. Next, he devotes a chapter to the enumeration of genres. The rest of the book is devoted to discussion of techniques: rhythm; parallelism; synonymy; repetition; merismus; antithesis and polarized expression; images; figures of speech; dialogue and monologue; and, development and composition.

0607   Alter, Robert. *The Art of Biblical Narrative*. New York: Basic Books, 1981. 195 pp.

Sets out to "illuminate the distinctive principles of the Bible's narrative art" and suceeds to an extent that surpasses any previous work. Alter contends that we can only receive the full impact of biblical narratives when we come to appreciate them as stories, that is, from the perspective of literary style. In his first chapter, he demonstrates that Genesis 38, long regarded by traditio-historians as an interpolation, is ingeniously related to its context. In chapter 2, he shows that narrative literature in the Bible runs the gamut from historicized fiction to fictionalized history. Chapter 3 uses betrothal stories to illustrate the concept of "type scenes." Chapter 4 deals with the interplay of narrative and dialogue and Chapter 5 treats techniques of repetition. Chapter 6 analyzes the relationship beteen David and Michal as a key to understanding the art of reticence in characterization. Chapter 7 argues that what historians have often regarded as sloppy patchwork in composition is more often evidence of literary montage. Chapter 8 treats the story of Joseph in terms of the knowledge of the characters and the omniscience of the narrator. One of the single most influential books in the development of modern literary study of the Bible, this book was the subject of several articles in *Journal for the Study of the Old Testament* and in *Biblical Research*. See 0885, 1539, 1552, 1567, 1585, 1672.

0608   Alter, Robert. *The Art of Biblical Poetry*. New York: Basic Books, 1985. 228 pp.

A comprehensive treatment of Hebrew poetry by a renowned literary critic. The point that has received the most attention is Alter's argument (also presented in 0609) that so-called parallelism in Hebrew poetry actually involves intensification or refinement: the second statement of each parallel may be characterized as "how much more so." See also Kugel (0642) on this point. Alter's book contains chapters devoted to Job, Psalms, Prophecy, Proverbs, and Song of Songs.

0609   Alter, Robert. "The Characteristics of Ancient Hebrew Poetry." In *The Literary Guide to the Bible*, ed. by Robert Alter and Frank Kermode, 611-624. Cambridge, MA: Belknap Press, 1987.

Emphasizes two dominant characteristics of Hebrew poetry: parallelism of intensification and narrative development within lines. Alter notes that the celebrated parallelism of Hebrew poetry only rarely implies synonymity. More often, an advancement in meaning occurs, from the general to the specific, from the literal to the metaphorical, and so on. Also, though there is scant narrative verse in Israel, narrative developments are often assumed between the lines, from one verse to the next. These two features of Hebrew poetry both exemplify a dynamic movement characteristic of the religious and visionary ends served by this distinctive poetics.

0610   Alter, Robert. "How Convention Helps Us Read: The Case of the Bible's Annunciation Type-Scenes." *Prooftexts* 3 (1983): 115-130.

Explores the range of variations in the annunciation type scene as an illustration of how the use of a literary convention can indicate thematic propositions and tone in literary texts. Alter offers a helpful distinction between the identification of narrative motifs in a type scene and the study of recurrent patterns in form criticism. The latter looks for the function of the text in culture (*Sitz im Leben*) while the former views the text as a mediated portrayal of reality that is itself a transformation of culture. Alter analyzes five occurences of the annunciation type scene (Genesis 18:9-15; 25:19-25; Judges 13; 1 Samuel 1; 2 Kings 4:8-17) and identifies a tripartite schema in each: initial barrenness, divine promise, birth of a son.

0611 Alter, Robert. "Sacred History and the Beginnings of Prose Fiction." *Poetics Today* 1 (1980): 143-162.

Contends that "prose fiction is the best general rubric for describing biblical narrative." The Bible is deliberately written in prose, that is, non-epic form. He uses Genesis 2 and 25 and the David narrative as examples.

0612 Bal, Mieke. *Lethal Love: Feminist Literary Readings of Biblical Love Stories.* Bloomington: Indiana University Press, 1987. 141 pp.

Various readings of "biblical love stories" by a noted narratologist (0133). Bal demonstrates the possibilities of multivalent interpretation by taking five different approaches to five different stories: David and Bathsheba is studied from the perspective of narratology; Samson and Delilah, from psychoanalytic theory; Ruth and Boaz, from historical criticism; Judah and Tamar, from plot-oriented interpretation; and Adam and Eve, from formalism (cf. 0711). Thus, Bal deconstructs traditional, patriarchal interpretations that view the women in these stories as victimizers by demonstrating the possibilities of new readings. The book is a revision of a former French work (0130).

0613 Bal, Mieke, ed. *Anti-Covenant: Counter-Reading Women's Lives in the Hebrew Bible.* Journal for the Study of the Old Testament Supplement Series, 81/Bible and Literature Series, 22. Sheffield: Almond Press, 1989. 243 pp.

Presents readings of several biblical stories from a perspective that intentionally enhances the roles of female characters. Included are "The Legacy of Abraham" by Carol Delaney; "Anti-Covenant" by Ann Marmesh; "Desire and Danger: The Drama of Betrayal" by Betsy Merideth; "Deborah the Woman Warrior" by Rachael C. Rasmussen; "Narrative Theory, Ideology, and Transformation in Judges 4" by Stephen Hanselmann; "Constructions of Women in Readings in the Story of Deborah" by Jane Shaw; "Tamar and the Limits of Patriarchy: Between Rape and Seduction" by Fokkelien van Dijk-Hemmes; "An Ideology of Expendability: Virgin Daughter Sacrifice" by Anne Michele Tapp; "A Ritual Processed" by Beth Gerstein; "Pseudo-Philo and the Transformation of Jephthah's Daughter" by Cynthia Baker; and "Between Altar and Wandering Rock: Toward a Feminist Philology" by Mieke Bal.

0614 Barzel, Hillel. "Moses: Tragedy and Sublimity." In *Literary Interpretations of Biblical Narratives,* ed. by Kenneth R. R. Gros Louis with James S. Ackerman and Thayer S. Warshaw, 120-140. Nashville: Abingdon Press, 1974.

Interprets the character of Moses as portrayed in the Bible, viewing the latter as a work of literature issuing uniformly from a single narrator. Moses is a sublime figure, who comes into the presence of the Almighty and becomes the national leader of his people. But Moses is also a tragic figure, denied the privilege of seeing God's face and the opportunity of entering the Promised Land.

0615   Beentjes, Pancratius C. "Inverted Quotations in the Bible: A Neglected Stylistic Pattern." *Biblica* 63 (1982): 506-523.

Calls attention to several examples of inverted quotations (e.g. Genesis 27:29 and Numbers 24:9; Leviticus 26:4 and Ezekiel 34:27; Psalm 23:6 and Psalm 27:6). An inverted quotation is one in which lines from one text are quoted in another, but in reverse order. Beentjes attempts to catalogue certain types of the stylistic figure and suggests that the intentional deviation may be an attention-getting device.

0616   Berlin, Adele. *The Dynamics of Biblical Parallelism*. Bloomington: Indiana University Press, 1985. 192 pp.

Discusses parallelism in terms of its grammatical, lexical, semantic, and phonological aspects. Parallelism consists of a network of equivalences and/or contrasts involving many aspects and levels of language.

0617   Bird, Phyllis. "The Harlot as Heroine: Narrative Art and Social Presupposition in Three Old Testament Texts." *Semeia* 46 (1989): 119-140.

Deals with Genesis 38:1-26; Joshua 2:1-24; and 1 Kings 3:16-27, three texts that have a harlot or assumed harlot as major actor. Bird seeks to combine literary and social-historical methods to determine the way the narrator constructs the character of the harlot within the context of social presuppositions. The article argues that all three texts presuppose a view of harlots as marginal figures in society who are tolerated but despised. This ambivalent attitude is found in literature as in life and is resolved in neither.

0618   Blenkinsopp, Joseph. "Biographical Patterns in Biblical Narrative." *Journal for the Study of the Old Testament* 20 (1981): 27-46.

Applies a model similar to that used by Propp for Russian folktales (0202) to two Old Testament stories: the story of Tobit, and the story of Jacob in Genesis 25:19--50:14. Blenkinsopp regards his story as an example of how narrative structure can be taken seriously as a bearer of meaning and message.

0619   Brenner, Athalya. *The Israelite Woman: Social Role and Literary Type in Biblical Narrative*. Biblical Seminar Series, 2. Sheffield: JSOT Press, 1985. 144 pp.

A double study on the roles of women, first in ancient Israelite society, and then in biblical literature. In the first part of her book, Brenner surveys what can be known about the social roles of women in this patriarchal society (queens, wise women, poets and authors, prophetesses, magicians, sorcerers and witches, and prostitutes). In the second part, she highlights four roles that women assume in biblical literature: mother of the hero, temptress, foreigner, and ancestress. In general, the literary type is more domestic than that which women appear to have sometimes exercised in society.

0620 Brettler, Marc Zvi. *God Is King: Understanding an Israelite Metaphor.* Journal for the Study of the Old Testament Supplement Series, 76. Sheffield: JSOT Press, 1989. 239 pp.

Applies recent literary research into the theory of metaphor to the prominent biblical metaphor that identifies God as "king." Brettler finds that the metaphor is avoided in some instances, and care is taken not to limit God by it in others. For instance, royal characteristics that have a diminutive connotation are not projected on to God. The metaphor also changes as Israelite kingship changes. Still, the metaphor has sufficient force to influence, in turn, Israel's notion of kingship.

0621   Burns, John Barclay.   "Pharaoh in the Old Testament: A Literary Degradation." *Proceedings: Eastern Great Lakes Biblical Society* 7 (1987): 17-26.

Examines Genesis 12:10-19; 37--50; Exodus 1--15; and Ezekiel 31--32 to show how the figure of pharaoh is degraded and ridiculed as the enemy of Yahweh. Ultimately, pharoah assumes a quasi-comic dimension. Burns uses literary criticism without divorcing interpretation from the historical purposes of the writers.

0622   Chadwick, H. Munro, and Chadwick, N. Kershaw. *The Growth of Literature, Volume II*. Cambridge: Cambridge University Press, 1936.

This seminal work on the origins of literature includes a discussion of "Early Hebrew Literature." The Chadwicks consider both heroic and non-heroic elements, historical and nonhistorical features, and other topics from a scholarly, comparativist view of ancient writings, both Eastern and Western.

0623   Clines, David J. A. *What Does Eve Do to Help? and Other Readerly Questions in the Old Testament.* Journal for the Study of the Old Testament Supplement Series, 94. Sheffield: JSOT Press, 1990. 178 pp.

A collection of six essays that take a reader-response approach to Old Testament texts. A preface introduces reader-response criticism and rejects the possibility of objective reading as a chimaera. Then, Clines considers "'What Does Eve Do to Help?' and Other Irredeemable Androcentric Orientations in Genesis 1--3"; "What Happens in Genesis"; "The Ancestor in Danger: But Not the Same Danger"; "The Old Testament Histories: A Reader's Guide"; "Deconstructing the Book of Job"; and "The Nehemiah Memoir: The Perils of Autobiography." The essays were all originally presented as papers at the Society of Biblical Literature and have a tendency to be humorous.

0624   Clines, David J. A.; Gunn, David M.; and Hauser, Alan J. *Art and Meaning: Rhetoric in Biblical Literature*. Journal for the Study of the Old Testament Supplement Series, 19. Sheffield: JSOT Press, 1982. 266 pp.

A collection of papers, most of which were originally presented at the Society of Biblical Literature section on Rhetorical Criticism, and all of which focus on the verbal artistry (rhetoric) through which biblical writers create meaning. See 0531, 0701, 0740, 0744, 0749, 0755, 0876, 0914-0915, 0950, 1295, 1428.

0625   Cloete, W. T. W. "Verse and Prose: Does the Distinction Apply to the Old Testament?" *Journal of Northwest Semitic Languages* 14 (1988): 9-15.

Argues, against Kugel (0642), that there is a dichotomy--not a spectrum--between prose and verse in the Bible. Cloete attempts to distinguish the two.

0626   Culley, Robert C. "Themes and Variations in Three Groups of Old Testament Narratives." *Semeia* 3 (1975): 3-13.

Examines miracle stories, deception stories, and punishment stories in the Old Testament and determines that the most prevalent theme common to all three is that of movement between life and death.

0627   Damrosch, David. *The Narrative Covenant: Transformations of Genre in the Growth of Biblical Literature*. San Francisco: Harper and Row, 1987. 352 pp.

Attempts to integrate historical and literary criticism by insisting on the importance of genre in literary studies. Damrosch says that literary analysis can only be fruitful after source criticism has established the developmental history of a text and comparisons with other ancient literature have established its genre.   The most relevant genres for biblical narratives are epic, chronicle, and history.   Texts considered include Genesis 2--11 (in comparison with Gilgamesh epic), the David story, and the book of Leviticus.

0628   Eslinger, Lyle M. *Into the Hands of the Living God*. Journal for the Study of the Old Testament Supplement Series, 84/Bible and Literature Series, 24. Sheffield: Almond Press, 1989. 272 pp.

Draws on narratology to present new readings of the Deuteronomistic history. The book begins with an extended introduction to "narrative ontology," with examples drawn from Genesis 1; Nehemiah 1; 1 Samuel 8--12; and Judges 2. Chapter 2 looks at a particular problem, the supposed discrepancies between Joshua and Judges concerning the success of Israel's conquests (Eslinger relates them to different points of view). Chapter 3 studies the first two chapters of Judges, and chapter 4 presents a verse-by-verse analysis of 1 Samuel 12. Chapter 5 examines King Solomon's prayers in 1 Kings 1--11, chapter 6 analyzes irony in 2 Kings 17, and chapter 7 reflects on the use of explicit evaluation in the Deuteronomistic narrative.

0629   Exum, J. Cheryl. "Murder They Wrote: Ideology and the Manipulation of Female Presence in Biblical Narrative." *Union Seminary Quarterly Review* 43 (1989): 19-39.

A feminist-deconstructionist reading of two texts that focuses on the characters of Michal (2 Samuel 6) and Jephthah's daughter (Judges 11). Exum demonstrates that both texts traditionally serve patriarchal interests--the first punishes a woman who speaks her mind, and the second glorifies the obedience of a woman who sacrifices herself for a man. But feminists can read the texts in such a way as to "expose the valorization of submission and the glorification of the victim as serving phallocentric interests."

0630   Exum, J. Cheryl, ed. *Signs and Wonders. Biblical Texts in Literary Focus.* Semeia Studies. Atlanta: Scholars Press, 1988. 247 pp.

A collection of essays on biblical texts that present different reading strategies and, so, underscore the importance of using various literary approaches. Each essay is followed by a critical response, written by another scholar. See 0710, 0771, 0780, 0828, 0868, 0984.

0631   Exum, J. Cheryl, and Whedbee, J. William. "Isaac, Samson, and Saul: Reflections on the Comic and Tragic Visions." *Semeia* 32 (1984): 5-40.

Examines the stories of these three persons as illustrative of comic and tragic patterns in the Old Testament. The discussion takes into account three perspectives: (1) plot; (2) stylistic and thematic pattern; and (3) characterization of heroes. Noting that comedy and tragedy reflect decidedly different views of reality, the authors conclude that the dominant vision in the Bible is comic. But tragic vision, exemplified here in the story of Saul, is present also and serves to highlight by contrast the themes of the comic stories.

0632   Fisch, Harold. *Poetry With A Purpose: Biblical Poetics and Interpretation.* Indiana Studies in Biblical Literature. Bloomington: Indiana University Press, 1988. 218 pp.

Examines several of the Old Testament's finest literary passages from a view that regards the Bible not only as literature but also as "anti-literature." The texts exhibit a self-negating factor that encourages the reader to see the hollowness of the very patterns that the text exhibits. "Imagination and distrust of imagination go together." Passages considered in some detail include Esther, Job, the song of Moses (Deuteronomy 31), Song of Solomon, Psalms, Hosea, and Ecclesiastes.

0633   Follis, Elaine R., ed. *Directions in Biblical Hebrew Poetry.* Journal for the Study of the Old Testament Supplement Series, 40. Sheffield: JSOT Press, 1987. 312 pp.

A collection of papers on poetry in the Old Testament. Four of the essays are on the characteristics of Hebrew poetry in general: "Another Look at Biblical Hebrew Poetry" by David Noel Freedman; "Alternating (ABA'B') Parallelism in the Old

Testament Psalms and Prophetic Literature" by John T. Willis; "The Parallelism of Greater Precision" by David J. A. Clines, and "The Pseudosorties: A Type of Paradox in Hebrew Verse" by Michael Patrick O'Connor. Another deals with the common poetic reference to "daughter of Zion" found throughout the Old Testament: "The Holy City as Daughter" by Elaine R. Follis. Other essays treat individual texts (0881, 0901, 0906, 0917, 0963, 1003, 1019).

0634   Fuchs, Esther. "The Literary Characterization of Mothers and Sexual Politics in the Hebrew Bible." *Semeia* 46 (1989): 151-168.

Offers a feminist-critical reading of motherhood in the Hebrew Bible. The Bible repeatedly ascribes to female figures an invincible desire for sons and intimates that "good" women eventually become fertile. Thus, a narrative closure is achieved that encircles the mother figure with the male figure of the husband and the son. Fuchs considers this effect to be an expression of sexual politics, whereby the subversive power of motherhood is contained within the genealogical economy of patriarchy.

0635   Gamzu, Yossi. "The Semitic and the Hellenic types of narrative." *Semitics* 9 (1984): 58-85.

Reflects upon the different narrative styles evident in the Old Testament and in the works of Homer, with frequent reference to Auerbach's *Mimesis* (0128). Conflict is given more prominence in the Hebrew narratives than in the Greek ones. Also, Homer tended to deal only with the ruling class, while the biblical materials are more democratic in their representation. The result is that the biblical legends create a historical element not found in the Homeric material.

0636   Geller, Stephen A. *Parallelism in Early Biblical Poetry.* Harvard Semitic Monographs, 20. Missoula, MT: Scholars Press, 1979. 389 pp.

Presents a thorough and precise analysis of the grammatical and semantic aspects of parallelism in a study inspired by the work of Roman Jakobson. Geller tries to work from patterns detected in the smallest units of texts (micro-units) toward conclusions that may hold true on a larger scale (macro-units). His main contribution is to move scholarship away from thinking of parallelism simply in terms of such semantic relationships as synonym/antonym. He shows that parallelism also encompasses such factors as meter, phonetics, grammar and, on the semantic level, patterns of rhetorical relationships.

0637   Good, Edwin M. *Irony in the Old Testament.* Philadelphia: Westminster Press, 1965. 256 pp.

An early study of one important literary concept with reference to various Old Testament writings. Good believes the recognition of irony and its rhetorical effects is significant not only for appreciation of the Bible as literature but also for understanding the character of biblical faith. Individual chapters focus on Jonah, Saul, Genesis, Isaiah, Qoheleth (Ecclesiastes), and Job.

0638   Greenfield, Jonas C. "The Hebrew Bible and Canaanite Literature." In *The Literary Guide to the Bible*, ed. by Robert Alter and Frank Kermode, 545-560. Cambridge, MA: Belknap Press, 1987.

Briefly traces the contributions that Ugaritic literary texts have made to our knowledge of Canaanite culture and then focuses on the poetic and rhetorical devices that the Hebrew poets apparently inherited from their Canaanite neighbors. Chief among these is a distinctive use of word pairs, but other devices including parallelism and simile are also discussed. Greenfield concludes with a discussion of the Baal epic and the importance of its imagery for understanding Hebrew literature.

0639   Jobling, David. *The Sense of Biblical Narrative: Three Structural Analyses in the Old Testament*. Sheffield: JSOT Press, 1978. 102 pp.

Draws on structuralism to present three studies: Jonathan in 1 Samuel 13--31; the quail story and its aftermath in Numbers 11--12; and Ahab's quest for rain in 1 Kings 17--18.

0640   Jobling, David. *The Sense of Biblical Narrative II: Structural Analyses in the Hebrew Bible*. Sheffield: JSOT Press, 1986. 153 pp.

A collection of three studies: (1) "Myth and Its Limits in Genesis 2.4b--3:24" was originally published in 0720. It contends that a folktale model underlies the "Creation and Fall" myth and focuses on the ambiguity of Yahweh's role as both Sender and Opponent. (2) "Deuteronomic Political Theory in Judges and 1 Samuel 1-12" continues the study on Jonathan in Vol. 1 (0639). (3) "'The Jordan a Boundary': Transjordan in Israel's Ideological Geography" (see 0757).

0641   Korpel, Marjo, and de Moor, Johannes C. "Fundamentals of Ugaritic and Hebrew Poetry." In *The Structural Analysis of Biblical and Canaanite Poetry*, ed. by Willem van der Meer and Johannes C. de Moor, 1-61. Journal for the Study of the Old Testament, 74. Sheffield: JSOT Press, 1988.

Identifies the basic units of ancient Ugaritic and Israelite poetry: (1) the *foot* is a word containing at least one stressed syllable; (2) the *colon* is composed of from one to five feet; (3) the *verse* is composed of from one to nine cola; (4) the *strophe* is composed of verses that are usually connected by external parallelism; (5) the *canticle* is a unit consisting of one or more strophes that are held together, usually by external parallelism; (6) canticles may be further combined to form larger structural units such as *sub-cantos* and *cantos*.

0642   Kugel, James L. *The Idea of Biblical Poetry: Parallelism and its History*. New Haven, CT: Yale University Press, 1981. 351 pp.

A groundbreaking study of parallelism as the chief characteristic of biblical poetry by a historical critic who is also a historian of scholarship. Kugel refutes the traditional idea that parallelism consists of saying the same thing twice and argues rather that the second line of parallel verses typically advances or intensifies the meaning of the first verse. The pattern may be summarized as "A, and what's more B." The same thought has been developed in somewhat different terms by Alter (0608-0609) Kugel also advances the thesis that, because parallelism is a common feature in much of what we would call prose, the difference between poetry and prose in the Bible should be viewed as a continuum. See also 0646, 0649, 0673.

0643   Kugel, James L. *In Potiphar's House: The Interpretive Life of Biblical Texts.* New York: Harper and Row, 1990. 208 pp.

An account of how central texts retain their vitality through retelling by their interpreters. Kugel takes the Joseph story in Genesis, as well as other texts from the Old Testament, and demonstrates how different versions of the stories develop from "innocent looking details" in the text.

0644   Kugel, James L. "Some Thoughts on Future Research into Biblical Style: Addenda to *The Idea of Biblical Poetry*." *Journal for the Study of the Old Testament* 28 (1984): 107-117.

Responds to criticisms of the author's influential book (0642) and outlines matters requiring further study with regard to parallelism, syntax, Ancient Near Eastern parallels, and meter.

0645   LaCocque, André. *The Feminine Unconventional: Four Subversive Figures in Israel's Traditions.* Overtures to Biblical Theology. Minneapolis: Fortress Press, 1990. 144 pp.

Reflects on the stories of four biblical heroines--Susanna, Judith, Esther, and Ruth. All four stories present women who transcend typical male-female polarities by breaking stereotypes of femininity. These stories offer sharp criticism of an ideology incapable of generosity and sensitivity. All four feature women who save their people via "substitutional self-offering." Thus these texts function to subvert themes in other Old Testament texts. LaCocque makes reference to modern literary theory but also draws heavily on traditional historical-critical scholarship.

0646   Landy, Francis. "Poetics and Parallelism: Some Comments on James Kugel's *The Idea of Biblical Poetry*." *Journal for the Study of the Old Testament* 28 (1984): 61-87.

Summarizes and evaluates certain key ideas in Kugel's influential work on parallelism (0642).   Landy is largely approving of Kugel's arguments, but feels the latter overreacts in his insistence that the Bible is not what we call literature or accessible to literary analysis. Landy also argues, against Kugel, that parallelism is analogous to meter as a formal characteristic of biblical poetry, which must be understood on a literary continuum with prose. He thinks that Kugel has ignored considerations of genre and of larger structural units.

0647 Long, Burke O., ed. *Images of Man and God: Old Testament Short Stories in Literary Focus.* Bible and Literature Series, 1. Sheffield: Almond Press, 1981. 179 pp.

A collection of six literary studies on Old Testament short stories (0680, 0716, 0788, 0829, 0841, 1028). The book is written for pastors and students, with sensitivity to the vision of religious truth embodied in these tales.

0648 Luke, Helen M. *The Inner Story: Myth and Symbol in the Bible and Literature.* New York: Crossroad Publishing Co., 1982. 118 pp.

A Jungian interpretation of symbolic dimensions of the human psyche as these are portrayed in literature. The stories of the Exodus, Saul, and Jacob are considered alongside *The Bacchae, The Little Prince*, and *The Lord of the Rings*. Another chapter is devoted to "The Symbolism of Water in the Bible."

0649 Miller, Patrick D., Jr. "Meter, Parallelism, and Tropes: The Search for Poetic Style." *Journal for the Study of the Old Testament* 28 (1984): 99-106.

Outlines the basic concepts of Kugel's book, *The Idea of Biblical Poetry* (0642) and compares these with the views of other scholars, including Michael O'Connor.

0650 Milne, Pamela Jeanne. "Folktales and Fairy Tales: An Evaluation of Two Proppian Analyses of Biblical Narratives." *Journal for the Study of the Old Testament* 34 (1986): 35-60.

Surveys and evaluates two attempts at applying Vladimir Propp's work on folktales (0202) to Old Testament literature--Sasson's study on Ruth (0802) and Blenkinsopp's on the Jacob and Tobit stories (0618). Milne maintains the potential benefit of Propp's work for biblical analysis, but argues that neither Sasson nor Blenkinsopp have been successful in their applications.

0651 Miscall, Peter D. "Literary Unity in Old Testament Narrative." *Semeia* 15 (1979): 27-44.

Builds on an earlier article by Polzin (0721) by modifying his approach somewhat and extending his conclusions. Whereas Polzin discovered a constant theme in three Genesis texts to be the role that personal observation plays in discernment of the divine will, Miscall takes the main point to be that divine revelation must have a physical and observable aspect. His study moves beyond the three Genesis texts discussed by Polzin to include comments on 1 Samuel 25 and 2 Samuel 11--12. Thus, the context for the argument is broadened from an already controversial assumption of literary unity of the Pentateuch to an assumption of literary unity of the Old Testament in general. The article is followed by a response by Polzin himself (1639).

0652   Miscall, Peter D. *The Workings of Old Testament Narrative.* Semeia Studies.
Philadelphia: Fortress Press, 1983. 150 pp.

A deconstructive approach to two Old Testament texts (Genesis 12; 1 Samuel 16:22).
Miscall submits these passages to "close readings" that note everything the texts say
and also much of what they leave out. The result is an accentuation on the multiple
meanings that either text might legitimately have. Miscall regards his study as a
demonstration of the deconstructive principle that meaning in texts is undecidable.

0653   Niditch, Susan, ed. *Text and Tradition: The Hebrew Bible and Folklore.*
Semeia Studies. Atlanta: Scholars Press, 1990. 243 pp.

A collection of papers from a conference on the Hebrew Bible and Folklore. Most
of the studies are attentive to the patterned repetition in the language, content, and
structures of texts, as well as attention to context and to the use of tradition. See
0700, 0712, 0756, 0769-0770, 0775, 0792.

0654   Niditch, Susan, and Doran, Robert. "The Success Story of the Wise Courtier:
A Formal Approach." *Journal of Biblical Literature* 96 (1977): 179-193.

Measures three stories, Daniel 2, Genesis 41 and Ahiqar 5--7 against a type of
folklore discerned in Finnish studies. The basic type involves a story in which a
person of lower status is capable of solving a problem at the request of a person of
higher status. Genesis 41 veers from the type slightly through the introduction of a
divine helper, and Daniel 2 veers still further by also introducing the motif of prayer.

0655   Polzin, Robert M. *Moses and the Deuteronomist: A Literary Study of the
Deuteronomistic History.* New York: Seabury Press, 1980. 224 pp.

A literary investigation of Deuteronomy, Joshua, and Judges that pays special
attention to the conflict of voices detectable on various compositional planes. Polzin
makes much use of Uspensky's typology (0305). He discerns a voice of authoritarian
dogmatism on the surface of the Deuteronomistic history that speaks of unconditional
election and the absolute immutability of God's word. Beneath the surface, however,
a voice of critical traditionalism is detectable that speaks of election conditioned by
Israel's disobedience and the need for ongoing reinterpretation of the word.
Ultimately, neither voice is able to explain the fate of Israel, which must be regarded
by the reader as mysterious.

0656   Polzin, Robert M., and Rothman, Eugene, eds. *The Biblical Mosaic: Changing
Perspectives.* Chico, CA: Scholars Press, 1982. 236 pp.

A collection of essays that focus on the changing perspectives derived from dialogue
between biblical scholars and literary critics as they interpret the Hebrew Bible (Old
Testament). See 0726, 0734, 0763, 0821, 0854, 0972-0973, 1557.

0657   Preminger, Alex, and Greenstein, Edward L., eds. *The Hebrew Bible in Literary Criticism*. New York: Frederick Ungar Publishing Company, 1986. 619 pp.

A compilation of excerpts from hundreds of different works on the Old Testament representing a wide variety of concerns and approaches. The excerpts are organized topically into over a hundred categories. One set of categories highlights "literary features" such as character, dialogue, humor, metaphor, parallelism, plot, and so on. Another focuses on individual writings and texts. Some of the excerpts are from renowned authors, including Melville, Tolstoy, and D. H. Lawrence. Others are from modern literary critics, including New Critics, formalists, structuralists, reader-response critics, and deconstructionists. See also 1046.

0658   Radday, Yehuda T., and Brenner, Athalya, eds. *On Humor and the Comic in the Hebrew Bible*. Journal for the Study of the Old Testament Supplement Series, 92/Bible and Literature Series, 23. Sheffield: Almond Press, 1990.

A collection of articles by the editors and ten other authors that testify to the plentiful representation of humor in Old Testament literature. Studies include concentrations on parody in Jonah, word-play in Samuel, and other varieties of humor in Ecclesiastes, Esther, and Job. Another study focuses on humor in proper names, and still another on the surprising lack of humor directed against women in the Bible.

0659   Randall, C. Corydon. "Satire in the Bible." Ph.D. diss., Hebrew Union College - Jewish Institute of Religion. 1969. 138 pp.

Catalogues and analyzes uses of satire as a literary form in the Old Testament. Three major types of satire include invective, sarcasm, and irony. Satirical devices include fable, parable, proverb, riddle, metaphor, simile, symbolic act, naming, paronomasia, and parody, though the latter does not appear to be used in the Bible. The rhetorical function of satire is to expose, criticize, and persuade in order to bring about a resolution of an incongruity between what is and what ought to be.

0660   Robertson, David. *The Old Testament and the Literary Critic*. Guides to Biblical Scholarship. Philadelphia: Fortress Press, 1977. 86 pp.

Opens with a chapter on "The Bible as Literature" and then presents studies on selected Old Testament texts. In the opening chapter, Robertson defines and delimits the work of the literary critic in approaching the Bible, distinguishing between "pure literature" (which has no ulterior purpose) and "applied literature" (which does). Subsequent chapters compare Exodus 1--15 to Euripides' *Bacchae*, and Psalm 90 to Shelley's "Hymn to Intellectual Beauty" (0920). Another chapter is devoted to Job. The most unusual chapter, "The Prophets and Poets," treats the prophets as part of a fictional plot involving the story of the Word of God, a story that extends into the New Testament. See also 1562, 1587.

0661   Rosenberg, Joel W. *King and Kin: Political Allegory in the Hebrew Bible*. Indiana Studies in Biblical Literature. Bloomington: Indiana University Press, 1986. 270 pp.

Examines the shape, style, and argument of three narrative complexes in the Old Testament and attempts to show their interrelationship. The three complexes are the Garden story, the Abraham cycle and the Davidic history. Traditional scholarship has discerned independent literary histories for these materials, but Rosenberg finds that they work together to sustain a single integrated argument. He reads Genesis as a companion volume to 2 Samuel, if not as a "midrash" upon it. The study depends on literary analysis for its identification of symbolic, allegorical, and typological qualities essential to the author's thesis.

0662   Savran, George. "The Character as Narrator in Biblical Narrative." *Prooftexts: A Journal of Jewish Literary History* 5 (1985): 1-17.

Explains that, although the narrator of biblical stories is always authoritative, omniscient, and reliable, this does not hold true when characters function as narrators. Events described by characters are presented from that particular point of view. Savran cites two examples of characters retelling past events (Genesis 24:34-49; 44:18-34).

0663   Schneidau, Herbert N. *Sacred Discontent: The Bible and Western Tradition*. Baton Rouge: Louisiana State University Press, 1976. 331 pp.

A study of the Hebrew Bible by a scholar of English literature best known for his work on Ezra Pound. Schneidau works from the English text and demonstrates incomplete understanding of certain Old Testament concepts, but his insights, drawn not only from literary criticism but also from linguistic analysis and anthropology, are often surprising and fresh. Though he treats only Old Testament writings, he makes occasional reference to the New Testament also, in the belief that the two are organically related. See also 1562.

0664   Thompson, John A. "The 'Response' in Biblical and Non-Biblical Literature with Particular Reference to the Hebrew Prophets." In *Perspectives on Text and Language*, ed. by Edgar W. Conrad and Edward G. Newing, 255-268. Winona Lake, IN: Eisenbrauns, 1987.

Identifies uses of a formal response in several biblical writings--Psalms, Job, Ecclesiastes, Lamentations, Amos, Jeremiah, and Deutero-Isaiah. The use of this response is compared to its function in such non-biblical works as Greek tragedy, Handel's *Messiah*, and Gilbert and Sullivan operas.

0665   Toker, N. "The Narrator's Voice in Etiological Passages." *Beth Mikra* 27 (1981): 31-39.

Examines the impact of comments by the narrator (e.g., "therefore to this day . . .") that interrupt the narrative flow of etiological passages in the Old Testament. Various stylistic features that may affect the impression this device creates are also included. The article is in Hebrew.

0666   Trible, Phyllis. *God and the Rhetoric of Sexuality*. Overtures to Biblical Theology. Philadelphia: Fortress Press, 1978. 206 pp.

Studies in the Hebrew Bible (Old Testament) informed by modern literary theory and a feminist hermeneutic. Trible tries to accent what she believes to be neglected themes and counterliterature. Texts considered include Genesis 2--3 ("a love story gone awry"), Ruth ("a human comedy"; see 0803), Song of Songs ("love's lyrics redeemed"), and Jeremiah 31:15-22.

0667   Trible, Phyllis. *Texts of Terror: Literary-Feminist Readings of Biblical Narratives*. Overtures to Biblical Theology. Philadelphia: Fortress Press, 1984. 128 pp.

Studies four "sad stories" regarding the abuse of women from the same literary-feminist perspective that informed *God and the Rhetoric of Sexuality* (0666). Trible considers the stories of Hagar (Genesis 16--21), Tamar (2 Samuel 13), the unnamed concubine (Judges 19), and the daughter of Jephthah (Judges 11).

0668   Tsmudi, Y. "Parallels and Opposites (Methods of Characterization in Biblical Narrative)." *Beth Mikra* 31 (1985-1986): 371-380.

Examines the use of contrast as a method of characterization in biblical narrative. Characters or important figures may be juxtaposed with other characters in similar situations so as to accent certain qualities. Examples drawn from the book of Genesis include Jacob and Esau and the offerings of Cain and Abel. The article is in Hebrew.

0669   Van der Lugt, Pieter. *Strofische structuren in de bijbels-hebreeuwse poëzie*. Ph.D. diss., Theological University of the Reformed Churches in the Netherlands (Kampen), 1980.

Proposes a new method for analyzing the structure of biblical poetry. Van der Lugt emphasizes the role of "external parallelism" in the construction of strophes. Strophes are composed of several verses, held together by repetitive devices. The outer borders of the strophes are indicated by markers securing the renewed interest of the audience--for example, deictic particles, imperatives, vocatives, tautological parallelism, extra long verses, and so on. Cf. 0670.

0670   Van der Meer, Willem, and De Moor, Johannes C., eds. *The Structural Analysis of Biblical and Canaanite Poetry*. Journal for the Study of the Old Testament Supplement Series, 74. Sheffield: JSOT Press, 1988. 422 pp.

A collection of studies intended to introduce a new method for analyzing the structure of biblical poetry. The method is essentially that developed by van der Lugt (0669), and most of the contributors are Dutch scholars. An introductory essay elaborates on a number of principles underlying the studies (0641). The rest of the articles are mainly concerned with analyses of specific texts. See 0768, 0902, 0922, 0958, 0982, 1008, 1016, 1023.

0671   Van Dyk, P. J. "The Function of So-Called Etiological Elements in Narratives." *Zeitschrift für die alttestamentliche Wissenschaft* 102 (1990): 19-33.

Claims that many supposed etiological elements in Old Testament narratives are actually rhetorical devices--rather than functioning to explain historical origins of certain phenomena, they function to legitimate and affirm the symbols of the narrative and to heighten its entertainment value. Van Dyk uses Genesis 16:11, 14 as an example.

0672   Van Grol, Harm W. M. *De versbouw in het klassieke hebreeuws*. Ph.D. diss., Catholic Theological University of Amsterdam, 1986.

Suggests that classical Hebrew poetry may have utilized a metrical system based on word accents. Texts considered include Numbers 23:7-10; 2 Samuel 1:19-27; Isaiah 1:21-26; 5:1-7; 62; Joel 1:5-14; 4:9-17; Psalms 6; 121; 130; and Proverbs 8; 30:10-33.

0673   Watson, Wilfred G. E. "A Review of Kugel's *The Idea of Biblical Poetry*." *Journal for the Study of the Old Testament* 28 (1984): 89-98.

Compares certain ideas in Kugel's influential work (0642) with the author's own (cf. 0674). Kugel's definition of parallelism is more narrow than that preferred by Watson. Kugel argues that there is no meter in Hebrew poetry, while Watson argues for a metrical system based on stress. Kugel thinks that distinctions between prose and poetry in the Bible constitute an imposition of modern categories, but Watson believes such distinctions are possible.

0674   Watson, Wilfred G. E. *Classical Hebrew Poetry: A Guide to Its Techniques*. Journal for the Study of the Old Testament Supplement Series, 26. Sheffield: JSOT Press, 1984. 455 pp.

A comprehensive study on the characteristics and style of biblical poetry. Watson includes chapters on meter, parallelism, stanzas and strophes, verse patterns, sound (assonance, alliteration, rhyme, onomatopoeia, wordplay), imagery, poetic devices, and secondary techniques (expansion, lists, inversion).

0675   White, Hugh C. "A Theory of the Surface Structure of the Biblical Narrative." *Union Seminary Quarterly Review* 34 (1979): 159-173.

Notes how the central role of the divine voice in Old Testament narrative subverts a typical pattern in literature according to which first-person speech is contained within third-person narration. The effect of attributing a central role to direct discourse of the divine voice is to elevate the illocutionary mode of meaning above the logical. The ambiguous position of the divine voice, both inside the narrative as a character and outside the narrative like the narrator, sets up a semantic tension between the closed meaning of logical discourse and the open meaning of performative speech.

This theory is applied in a study on Genesis 2--3 contained in *Semeia* 18, edited by Patte (0720).

THE PENTATEUCH

See also 0614, 0698, 0866, 1550, 1608.

0676   Bloom, Harold. "From J to K, or The Uncanniness of the Yahwist." In *The Bible and the Narrative Tradition*, ed. by Frank McConnell, pp. 19-35. New York: Oxford University Press, 1986.

Describes the "uncanniness" of the stories attributed by biblical scholars to the Yahwist tradition (called "J" for short) and compares these to the uncanny elements of Kafka (whom Bloom decides to call "K" for short). In this article, Bloom still refers to J as a "he" (cf. 0677). The quality of the stories is such that their acceptance by later traditions is remarkable, due perhaps only to the strength (or "facticity") of their author.

0677   Bloom, Harold, and Rosenberg, David. *The Book of J.* New York: Grove/Weidenfeld, 1990. 340 pp.

A reading of the Yahwist material in Genesis by the reader-oriented critic who authored *Anxiety of Influence* (0344). The material is translated by Rosenberg. An introduction and comments follow by Bloom. For the most part, Bloom ignores traditional biblical scholarship, at least since Wellhausen. His interpretation of J tries to be controversial, if not trendy. The writing is, in Bloom's mind, a completely secular text that has been misunderstood, revised, censored, and mutilated by countless editors and theologians throughout the ages. The original book of J presents Yahweh as a god who is not to be loved or feared. And the author of the book was a woman.

0678   Clines, David J. A. *The Theme of the Pentateuch*. Journal for the Study of the Old Testament Supplement Series, 10. Sheffield: JSOT Press, 1978. 152 pp.

Argues that the Pentateuch is a unity, not in its origin, but in its final shape. The Pentateuch is essentially a narrative, one that tells a coherent story. The unifying conceptual theme is one of promise, which evokes hope.

0679   Mann, Thomas W. *The Book of the Torah: The Narrative Integrity of the Pentateuch*. Atlanta: John Knox Press, 1988. 178 pp.

Applies concepts derived from narratology to present a comprehensive interpretation of the Pentateuch as a whole. Mann does not deny the validity of documentary hypotheses that identify literary sources behind the current text, but he prefers to emphasize the coherence of the books as they now exist and their interrelationships with each other. The study moves beyond literary-critical exegesis to consider theological, ethical, and hermeneutical issues as Mann describes the Pentateuch as an open-ended narrative that presents a "story-shaped" model for reality.

0680   Nohrnberg, James. "Moses." In *Images of Man and God: Old Testament Stories in Literary Focus*, ed. by Burke O. Long, 35-57. Bible and Literature Series, 1. Sheffield: Almond Press, 1981.

Examines Moses as a "hero figure" in Old Testament literature. Unlike Jacob (a selfish hero) or Samson (a hero who is more vulnerable because of his gift), Moses is a hero "whose individuality is almost completely dissolved in his office."

GENESIS

See also 0128, 0316, 0517, 0580, 0584-0585, 0587, 0591, 0593-0594, 0601, 0605, 0607, 0610-0613, 0617-0618, 0621, 0628, 0631, 0637, 0650, 0652, 0654, 0666-0668, 0671, 0735, 0739, 0796, 0804, 1642, 1670, 1682.

0681   Ackerman, James S. "Joseph, Judah, and Jacob." In *Literary Interpretations of Biblical Narratives, Volume II*, ed. by Kenneth R. R. Gros Louis with James S. Ackerman, 85-113. Nashville: Abingdon Press, 1982.

Discusses the role of "doubling" in the Joseph story, interpreting the repetitions not as evidence of source conflation but as a literary device intended to emphasize certain ironies within the plot. Special attention is directed to the parallels between what happens to Joseph at the hands of his brothers and what happens later to the brothers themselves, and to parallels of contrast between Reuben and Judah.

0682   Aharoni, R. "Jacob and Esau: A Play in Three Acts." *Beth Mikra* (1978): 327-340.

Considers the struggle between Jacob and Esau as developing in three stages: birth (Genesis 25:21-28), birthright (Genesis 25:29-34), and blessing (Genesis 27). God has the primary role in the first stage. In the second, Esau appears to be to blame. Only in the third stage, does Jacob emerge as a cheater. The article is in Hebrew.

0683   Barthes, Roland. "Wrestling with the Angel: Textual Analysis of Genesis 32:23-33." In *The Semiotic Challenge*, ed. and trans. by Richard Howard, 246-260. New York: Hill and Wang, 1988. Also published as "The Struggle with the Angel: Textual Analysis of Genesis 32:23-33." In *Structural Analysis and Biblical Exegesis* by R. Barthes, F. Bovon, F-J. Leenhardt, R. Martin-Achard, and J. Starobinski, trans. by A. M. Johnson, 21-33. Pittsburgh Theological Monograph Series, 3. Pittsburgh: Pickwick Press, 1974.

Presents first a sequential and then a structural analysis of the story of Jacob and the angel. The sequential analysis examines the story in three stages: crossing the Jabbok, the struggle, and the change of names. In examining these stages, Barthes seeks to inventory the actions of the characters. The structural analysis that follows pays more attention to classifying the functions of the characters in the narrative. Barthes draws parallels between the functions of the characters in this story and those attributed to characters in Russian folk tales by Propp (0202). In the 1974 volume, this essay is paired for comparative purposes with a traditional form-critical study of the same passage. See also 1581, 1670.

0684   Bratcher, Margaret Dee. "The Pattern of Sin and Judgment in Genesis 1--11." Ph.D. diss., The Southern Baptist Theological Seminary, 1984. 281 pp.

Studies the plots of the narratives in Genesis 1--11 to discover a pattern of sin and judgment. The pattern consists of episodes of sin, discovery of sin by Yahweh, judgment speech, mitigation of the judgment, and execution of the judgment. In all but the flood narrative, an episode of temptation precedes the commission of the sin.

0685   Brisman, Leslie. *The Voice of Jacob: On the Composition of Genesis*. Indiana Studies in Biblical Literature. Bloomington: Indiana University Press, 1990. 144 pp.

Explores Genesis as the scene of conflict between a pious and a revisionary spirit. Although Brisman is concerned with the process of composition and with establishing the original text (matters on which he stands outside the mainstream of biblical criticism), he takes seriously the idea of the Bible as literature.

0686   Caspi, Mishael Maswari. "The Story of the Rape of Dinah: The Narrator and the Reader." *Hebrew Studies* 26 (1985): 25-45.

Approaches the story of the rape of Dinah in Genesis 34 in light of the procedure of the narrator and the role of the reader. The narrator imposes his values on the reader.

0687   Cohn, Robert L. "Narrative Structure and Canonical Perspective in Genesis." *Journal for the Study of the Old Testament* 25 (1983): 3-16.

Attempting to study the book of Genesis in its "canonical" form, this study makes certain observations about how the book can be read as a unified narrative. Two progressions in particular are noteworthy: (1) a progression from single one-episode stories in the early part of the book to the fuller, more tightly constructed cycles of episodes in the latter part; and (2) a progression toward more subtle indications of divine presence and greater allowance of human autonomy as the book develops.

0688   Crenshaw, James L. "Journey Into Oblivion: A Structural Analysis of Gen. 22:1-19." In *Structuralism: An Inter-disciplinary Study*, ed. by Susan Wittig, 99-112. Pittsburgh: Pickwick Press, 1975.

Presents a structuralist interpretation of the story of the sacrifice of Isaac that accepts and builds on historical-critical observations.   Crenshaw is interested in the syntagmatic structures and the mythic structures.   The latter are discerned (in a comparison with Isaiah 7) to involve such elemental conflicts as father vs. son; parental love vs. fear of the gods; intention vs. actual deed.

0689   Dahlberg, Bruce. "The Unity of Genesis." In *Literary Interpretations of Biblical Narratives, Volume II*, ed. by Kenneth R. R. Gros Louis with James S. Ackerman, 126-134. Nashville: Abingdon Press, 1982.

Contends (against the view of traditional biblical scholarship) that the book of Genesis, taken as a whole and by itself, is a unified work of literary art.   The relationship of Genesis to the Pentateuch is analogous to that of an overture to a dramatic opera: it serves as an introduction to a larger work, but also as a work of art complete in itself.   Genesis celebrates a divine deliverance that takes place in Egypt before the exodus, in a narrative that is meaningful and self-contained.

0690   Fokkelman, Jan P. "Genesis." In *The Literary Guide to the Bible*, ed. by Robert Alter and Frank Kermode, 36-55. Cambridge, MA: Belknap Press, 1987.

Argues that the reader of Genesis must respect the multiformity and discord of the book while also looking for means of integration that give it unity.   Examples of the former include the alternation between poetry and prose and the variety in length of episodes. Means of integration are used at the levels of genre, theme, plot, content, and key words. Fokkelman concludes with a discussion of structure that places special emphasis on elements of repetition.

0691   Fokkelman, Jan P. "Time and the Structure of the Abraham Cycle." *Oudtestamentische Studiën* 25 (1989): 96-109.

Argues that the organization of time in the Abraham narrative provides the key to understanding its structure.   Specific references to persons' ages are set in a chiastic structure, with Abraham's one hundredth year as the center of the chiasm.

0692   Gammie, John G. "Theological Interpretation By Way of Literary and Tradition Analysis: Genesis 25--36." In *Encounter with the Text: Form and History in the Hebrew Bible*, ed. by Martin J. Buss, 117-134. Philadelphia: Fortress Press, 1979.

Utilizes motif analysis, structural analysis, and stylistic analysis in a study of the Jacob-Esau narrative.   Motif analysis focuses on the predominance of strife.   Structural analysis highlights concentric arrangements and ironic reversals. Stylistic analysis notices word plays on proper names.

0693 Fox, Everett. "Can Genesis Be Read as a Book?" *Semeia* 46 (1989): 31-40.

Examines Genesis for structural coherence and seeks to demonstrate narrative unity of the book in its canonical form. Fox notes progressive development of characters and of style. The book may be organized into four subdivisions (Primeval history, Abraham cycle, Jacob cycle, Joseph story), but common theme words and motifs bind the four parts together. Balanced and chiastic structural arrangements also argue for the unity of the work in its present form. The unifying message of the entire work concerns selection and survival amidst struggle and disaster.

0694 Furman, Nelly. "His Story Versus Her Story: Male Genealogy and Female Strategy in the Jacob Cycle." *Semeia* 46 (1989): 141-150.

Discusses the role that garments play as signifiers in the Jacob and Joseph stories from the perspective of semiotics and deconstruction theory. For men in the stories, the garments have a fixed symbolic value, but for women they are open to a variety of meanings. The result is that the stories can be read from both androcentric and gynocentric viewpoints and can serve as metaphors for either patriarchalism or feminism.

0695 Greenstein, Edward L. "An Equivocal Reading of the Sale of Joseph." In *Literary Interpretations of Biblical Narratives, Volume II*, ed. by Kenneth R. R. Gros Louis with James S. Ackerman, 114-125. Nashville: Abingdon Press, 1982.

Takes the account of the sale of Joseph in Genesis 37 as an example of a composite and inconsistent text, of which there are many in the Bible, and discusses how literary criticism should deal with such texts. Traditional scholarship has denied the narrative unity of such passages and attempted to explain the inconsistencies rather than to expose them. Following Roland Barthes' proposal for structural analysis, Greenstein insists that a literary reading must allow the inconsistencies to remain--the reader is presented with conflicting accounts of what happened and must regard these conflicts as intrinsic to the text's meaning.

0696 Gros Louis, Kenneth R. R. "Abraham." In *Literary Interpretations of Biblical Narratives, Volume II*, ed. by Kenneth R. R. Gros Louis with James S. Ackerman, 53-84. Nashville: Abingdon Press, 1982.

A combination of two short essays. The first presents a close reading of the Abraham story in light of the choice made by Lot in Genesis 13. As the narrative continues, Lot, concerned primarily for himself, is seen to shrink as an individual, while the destiny of Abraham expands. The second essay is more interesting: Gros Louis interprets the sacrifice of Isaac (Genesis 22) as not only God's testing of Abraham but also as Abraham's testing of God. This interpretation is presented in dialogue with the different view of Erich Auerbach presented in his classic literary study, *Mimesis* (0128).

0697   Gros Louis, Kenneth R. R. "The Garden of Eden." In *Literary Interpretations of Biblical Narratives*, ed. by Kenneth R. R. Gros Louis with James S. Ackerman and Thayer S. Warshaw, 52-58. Nashville: Abingdon Press, 1974.

Provides a short narrative reading of the Adam and Eve story that calls attention to the different facets of sin: against God, against other humans, and against self. Eden is interpreted metaphorically in a timeless sense of order, harmony, and security. Gros Louis follows Milton in speculating that if Adam had not been cast out of the garden, he would not have died and, so the story goes, would still be present as a semi-divine Father of all today.

0698   Gros Louis, Kenneth R. R. "Genesis 1--2." In *Literary Interpretations of Biblical Narratives*, ed. by Kenneth R. R. Gros Louis with James S. Ackerman and Thayer S. Warshaw, 41-51. Nashville: Abingdon Press, 1974.

Contrasts the presentations of God as creator in the two creation accounts. In the first, God works according to a predetermined plan, while in the second, God works experimentally. The first account is "conservative," emphasizing order and hierarchy; the second is "liberal," emphasizing innovation and philanthropy.

0699   Gros Louis, Kenneth R. R. "Genesis 3--11." In *Literary Interpretations of Biblical Narratives, Volume II*, ed. by Kenneth R. R. Gros Louis with James S. Ackerman, 37-52. Nashville: Abingdon Press, 1982.

Continues the theme of earlier essays on Genesis 1--2 (0698) and on the Garden of Eden (0697). Genesis 3--11 presents a poetic interpretation of history that is united by different kinds of disobedience: Adam and Eve against God, Cain against his brother and neighbor, Adam's descendants against their own nature, Ham against his father, and the workers at Babel against art. Yet there is hope: the serpent will be bruised, Cain will not be killed, the rainbow will signify the covenant. Humanity strives to recreate Eden (metaphor for security and harmony), but, unable to do so, must rely on God's mercy.

0700   Hasan-Rokem, Galit. "And God Created the Proverb . . . Inter-generic and Inter-textual Aspects of Biblical Paremiology--or the Longest Way to the Shortest Text." In *Text and Tradition: The Hebrew Bible and Folklore*, ed. by Susan Niditch, 107-120. Semeia Studies. Atlanta: Scholars Press, 1990.

Analyzes Genesis 2:18 and 2:24 as instances of proverbs in narratives. The proverbs, in keeping with folk-narrative style, appear at points of the most extreme ambivalence in the text. They are therefore hermeneutic keys to the interpretation of the narrative. This article is followed by a response from Roland Murphy.

0701   Hauser, Alan Jon. "Genesis 2--3: The Theme of Intimacy and Alienation." In *Art and Meaning: Rhetoric in Biblical Literature*, ed. by David J. A. Clines, David M. Gunn, and Alan J. Hauser, 20-36. Sheffield, England: JSOT Press, 1982.

Examines the motif of intimacy and alienation in Genesis 2--3. Intimacy is depicted in Genesis 2 by God's care in forming man; God's creation of the garden for man;

God's efforts to create a companion for man; God's creation of such a companion from a part of man himself; and man and woman's mutual presence in the garden, naked and unashamed. Alienation is depicted in Genesis 3 by human striving to be like God; the making of clothes to cover nakedness; the attempt to hide from God; and the man and woman's attempts to blame each other or others for their failings.

0702 Helyer, Larry R. "The Separation of Abram and Lot: Its Significance in the Patriarchal Narratives." *Journal for the Study of the Old Testament* 26 (1983): 77-88.

Calls attention to an important motif in Genesis 13 that serves to link the account of Abram and Lot's separation to the plot of the Abraham cycle as a whole. Lot's choice of pasturage outside the land of Canaan eliminates him as potential heir to the covenant promise; after Lot's separation, Abram has no heir. This motif links Genesis 13 to the entire Abraham cycle as one of eight such crises that threaten fulfillment of the promise.

0703 Humphreys, W. Lee. *Joseph and His Family: A Literary Study.* Columbia: University of South Carolina Press, 1988. 233 pp.

Examines the Joseph "novella" from two perspectives. The first half of the book presents a synchronic analysis of Genesis 37--50 that emphasizes genre, plot, characterization, and rhetorical technique. The second half takes up a diachronic analysis that considers how the material developed into its present form.

0704 Jeansonne, Sharon Pace. "The Characterization of Lot in Genesis." *Biblical Theology Bulletin* 18 (1988): 123-129.

Examines the narrator's presentation of Lot in Genesis as a character who increasingly falls away from righteous behavior. Lot's actions and dealings with Abraham, his response to divine messengers, and his treatment of his daughters are used in a way that enables the narrator to present the theme of God as a merciful judge.

0705 Jeansonne, Sharon Pace. *The Women of Genesis: From Sarah to Potiphar's Wife.* Minneapolis: Fortress Press, 1990. 158 pp.

Examines the function of key female characters in the narrative of Genesis 12--50. Jeansonne demonstrates that the role of the women is not simply secondary to that of the men--the women play key roles in the shaping of Israel's history. Many of the women come across as strong characters, able and willing to act on their own.

0706 Kennedy, James M. "Peasants in Revolt: Political Allegory in Genesis 2--3." *Journal for the Study of the Old Testament* 47 (1990): 3-14.

Reads the story of Adam and Eve as an "ideology-bound model of reality" that describes allegorically the struggle between Judah's royal elite and the peasant class. The narrator sides with the royal elite by depicting Adam and Eve as peasants who must submit to the centralized authority represented in the character of Yahweh.

0707 Kessler, Martin. "Rhetorical Criticism of Genesis 7." In *Rhetorical Criticism*, ed. by Jared J. Jackson and Martin Kessler, 1-17. Pittsburgh Theological Monograph Series, 1. Pittsburgh: Pickwick Press, 1974.

A synchronic study of Genesis 7 in its present form that places special emphasis on the use of repetition. The account is "not poetry with its particular demands for a certain quality of artistry, but theological narrative." Still, a certain artistic sophistication can be detected in which "every single detail seems not only to serve its purpose formally and materially, but also to express the concerns of the narrative."

0708 Kikawanda, Isaac M. "A Quantitative Analysis of the 'Adam and Eve,' 'Cain and Abel,' and 'Noah' Stories." In *Perspectives on Text and Language*, ed. by Edgar W. Conrad and Edward G. Newing, 195-204. Winona Lake, IN: Eisenbrauns, 1987.

Makes three observations about the stories in Genesis 1--11: (1) the greatest portion of the Adam and Eve story is devoted to its beginning, the greatest portion of the Cain and Abel story to its middle, and the greatest portion of the Noah story to its ending; (2) the proportionate quantity of humanity destroyed in each of the stories increases from the first story to the third, while the proportionate quantity of people saved decreases; and (3) the quantity of appreciation for salvation by the reader increases as the number of humans saved decreases.

0709 Kikawanda, Isaac M. "The Shape of Genesis 11:1-9." In *Rhetorical Criticism*, ed. by Jared J. Jackson and Martin Kessler, 18-32. Pittsburgh Theological Monograph Series, 1. Pittsburgh: Pickwick Press, 1974.

Identifies rhetorical features and structural devices in the story of the tower of Babel in order to recover the underlying scheme that organizes the story. Kikawanda considers quantitative balance, chiasmus and introversion, inclusion, linear progression, sequential repetition, broken symmetry, and irony.

0710 Landy, Francis. "Narrative Techniques and Symbolic Transactions in the Akedah." In *Signs and Wonders: Biblical Texts in Literary Focus*, ed. by J. Cheryl Exum, 1-40. Atlanta: Scholars Press, 1989.

Examines narrative techniques in the story of the sacrifice of Isaac in Genesis 22. Special attention is devoted to point of view and to redundancy, which emphazise Abraham's unvoiced subjectivity. Also considered are spatial and temporal modes, the subversion of narrative sequence through anticipation and retardation, and "the mystification of the place that thus attains a symbolic dimension." Contradictory demands are accomodated in the narrative through deception involving the mediating term, Isaac. The story is finally understood as a symbolic transaction and is related to other such transactions involving child sacrifice or the wife-sister motif in Old Testament literature. The article is followed by a response from Jan P. Fokkelmann.

0711   Lanser, Susan Sniader. "(Feminist) Criticism in the Garden: Interring Genesis 2--3." *Semeia* 41 (1988): 67-84.

Explores tensions in the interpretation of Genesis 2--3 that result from different understandings of language. Traditional interpretations, which think the text inscribes male supremacy, assume a speech act theory that emphasizes the power of inference. Revisionist interpretations, such as those put forward by Trible (0666) and Bal (0612), assume a theory of language as formal code and read this text as inscribing sexual equality. Lanser proposes a third reading that appreciates this tension and views the text as an expression of patriarchy that is uncomfortable with itself.

0712   Lord, Albert B. "Patterns of Lives of the Patriarchs from Abraham to Samson to Samuel." In *Text and Tradition: The Hebrew Bible and Folklore*, ed. by Susan Niditch, 7-18. Semeia Studies. Atlanta: Scholars Press, 1990.

Examines the reappearance throughout Old Testament narrative of patterns and elements associated with the lives of the patriarchs.   One such example is the "miraculous birth" pattern found in the stories of Isaac and Ishmael; Jacob and Esau; and the succession from Jacob to Joseph. The pattern reappears in the story of Samson, and again in that of Samuel. This article is followed by a response from David M. Gunn.

0713   Maxwell-Mahon, W. D. "'Jacob's Ladder': A Structural Analysis of Scripture." *Semitics* 7 (1980): 118-130.

Examines five codes that structure the narrative of Genesis 28:10-22: (1) the proairetic code of action; (2) the hermeneutic code or code of questioning; (3) the semic code or semantic items defining names and characters; (4) the symbolic code or code of motif; and (5) the referential code or code of cultural knowledge.

0714   Mazor, Yair. "Genesis 22: The Ideological Rhetoric and the Psychological Component." *Biblica* 67 (1986): 81-88.

Presents a literary reading of the story of Isaac's binding, with special attention to implicit psychological characterization.   Mazor first discusses certain rhetorical phenomena in the text, such as the narrator informing the reader that God's demand is but a temptation in the first verse, and the allusion to Genesis 12:1 in verse 2. Then Mazor attempts the psychological reading by proposing reasons for Abraham's procrastination, evasion of truth, and so on.

0715   McEvenue, Sean E. "A Comparison of Narrative Styles in the Hagar Stories." *Semeia* 3 (1975): 64-80.

Compares the narrative styles of J, E, and P traditions in Genesis 16 and 21. The J account dramatizes the interior conflicts of Sarah to provide a setting for Yahweh's decision about the tribe of Ishmael. The E account is concerned with human emotion (grief) even apart from action. The P account removes conflictual and dramatic aspects in favor of genealogical material.

0716   McGuire, Erol. "The Joseph Story: A Tale of Son and Father." In *Images of Man and God: Old Testament Stories in Literary Focus*, ed. by Burke O. Long, 9-25. Bible and Literature Series, 1. Sheffield: Almond Press, 1981.

Briefly traces the Joseph story in Genesis as one of the most carefully composed, imaginatively provocative, and structurally unified short works in the Bible. McGuire graphs the downward and upward patterns of action in the story, demonstrating its near perfect symmetry. Above all, however, the twin peaks in Joseph's career represent his loving relationship with his father.

0717   Miscall, Peter D. "The Jacob and Joseph Stories as Analogies." *Journal for the Study of the Old Testament* 6 (1978): 28-40.

Describes the Jacob and Joseph stories in Genesis as "narrative analogies" that provide oblique commentary on each other. Both stories feature treachery between brothers, a twenty-year separation, and a subsequent reunion. In different ways, both texts indicate that divine intervention is not a constant process. In both, the reunions are marked by forgetting the past and returning towards the present and future (in neither reunion is there need for forgiveness or atonement).

0718   Niditch, Susan. *Underdogs and Tricksters: A Prelude to Biblical Folklore*. San Francisco: Harper and Row, 1987. 186 pp.

Applies the methodologies of modern folklorists to a set of biblical narratives featuring unlikely heroes. The study treats the Bible as literature, but as "traditional literature," with no single originator. Accordingly, Niditch's study has more in common with Hermann Gunkel than with Robert Alter--she compares the biblical tales to other examples of ancient folklore rather than to modern literature. The stories considered include the wife-sister tales of Genesis 12:10-20; 20:1-18; 26:1-17; the two cycles about successful younger sons in Genesis 25--36 (Jacob) and Genesis 37--50 (Joseph); and the book of Esther.

0719   O'Callaghan, Martin. "The Structure and Meaning of Genesis 38: Judah and Tamar." *Proceedings of the Irish Biblical Association* 5 (1981): 72-88.

Examines, first, the thematic structure of this story and determines the fundamental theme to be the opposition of life/death. Next, O'Callaghan uncovers points of comparison and contrast concerning the two main actants, Judah and Tamar. In addition, he examines the consistent use of chiasm and elements of irony.

0720   Patte, Daniel, ed. *Genesis 2 and 3: Kaleidoscopic Structural Readings. Semeia* 18 (1980). 164 pp.

Presents several studies on Genesis 2--3, all of which make use of some variety of structural exegesis. The editor opens the volume with an essay on the several levels at which structures for the text can be discerned. The essays that follow explore structures at these various levels. Contributors include Robert C. Culley, David Jobling, Daniel Patte and Judson F. Parker, Hugh C. White, and Thomas Boomershine. All of the articles are followed by responses from other scholars.

Finally, responses to all of the studies are offered by Robert Detweiler, Brian Watson Kovacs, and Clarence H. Snelling.

0721   Polzin, Robert M.   "'The Ancestress of Israel in Danger' in Danger." *Semeia* 3 (1975): 81-97.

Looks for synchronic relationships between three texts (Genesis 12:10-13:1; 20; 26:1-11) that traditional scholarship has regarded as variants of the same tradition. Polzin finds that transformations occur within the stories that concern how God's will comes to be known.   The stories present three possible modes for divine revelation (especially with regard to determining whom God has blessed or cursed): the Act of God, the Word of God, and personal observation.   The latter is singled out as the most consistently reliable.   This article evoked further discussion concerning the literary unity of the Old Testament (see 0651, 1639).

0722   Prewitt, Terry J.   *The Elusive Covenant: A Structural-Semiotic Reading of Genesis*. Bloomington: Indiana University Press, 1990. 160 pp.

Unites studies of literary form, sign theory, and kinship structures to demonstrate the close relationship between the unfolding genealogies and the narrative structures of Genesis.

0723   Robinson, Robert B.   "Literary Function of the Genealogies of Genesis." *Catholic Biblical Quarterly* 48 (1986): 595-608.

Studies the tension in Genesis between the fixed, deterministic tendency of the genealogies and the autonomous disorder of the narrative.   It is the two elements in combination that define the genre of the book.

0724   Rosenberg, Joel W.   "The Garden Story Forward and Backward: The non-narrative dimension of Gen. 2--3." *Prooftexts: A Journal of Jewish Literary History* 1 (1981): 1-27.

Discerns three types of non-narrative elements in Genesis 2--3: (1) parenthetic descriptions (2:10-14; 3:14-19a); (2) namings (2:23-3:20); and (3) explicit etiological statements (2:24; 3:19b).   By paying attention to redactional features in the composition of this narrative, Rosenberg tries to present the story as an art of quotation, of verbal irony, and of allegory.

0725   Roth, Wolfgang.   "The Text is the Medium: An Interpretation of the Jacob Stories in Genesis." In *Encounter with the Text: Form and History in the Hebrew Bible*, ed. by Martin J. Buss, 103-116. Philadelphia: Fortress Press, 1979.

Applies Paul Ricoeur's methodological synthesis of structural linguistics, phenomenology of speech, and ontology of discourse to a study of the Jacob tradition in Genesis. The text is viewed as an invitation that becomes contextualized through actualization here and now.

0726 Saldarini, Anthony J., and Ben-Amos, Dan. "'Interpretation of the Akedah in Rabbinic Literature' and 'The Akedah: A Folklorist's Response.'" In *The Biblical Mosaic: Changing Perspectives*, ed. by Robert Polzin and Eugene Rothman, 149-167. Philadelphia: Fortress Press, 1982.

Offers a dialogue between rabbinic and folkloric interpretations of Genesis 22. Saldarini shows how ancient commentators expressed admiration at Abraham and Isaac's obedience to God but were also defensive with regard to God's command and Abraham's intention. Ben-Amos finds the rabbinic readings to be merely thematic and synchronic. He stresses a need for interpreting texts in their relationship to the culture, ideas, and events of distinct historical periods.

0727 Seybold, Donald A. "Paradox and Symmetry in the Joseph Narrative." In *Literary Interpretations of Biblical Narratives*, ed. by Kenneth R. R. Gros Louis with James S. Ackerman and Thayer S. Warshaw, 59-73. Nashville: Abingdon Press, 1974.

Delineates the literary forms of repetition, pattern and character that operate in Genesis 37--50. Structure is created and controlled by (1) the three sets of dreams; (2) the four sets of analogous relationships into which Joseph enters--at home, in Potiphar's household, in prison, and in Pharoah's household; and (3) the variations on the pit episode and the paradox of prison/refuge that they suggest. Seybold recognizes that the Judah/Onan/Tamar story in Genesis 38 intrudes into the narrative, but does not think it ultimately disturbs the pattern or symmetry. An interesting sub-theme in this article concerns the use of Joseph's clothing as symbol and as structuring device.

0728 Steinberg, Naomi. "The Genealogical Framework of the Family Stories in Genesis." *Semeia* 46 (1989): 41-50.

Uses Todorov's system of structural analysis (cf. 0300, 0302) to examine the relationship between genealogy and narrative in Genesis 12--50. The genealogies serve to organize the family histories of Abraham, Isaac, and Jacob into three parallel cycles. Narrative serves as a transitional device between genealogies; all three of the narrative cycles focus on resolving disequilibrium mentioned in the genealogies preceding the stories.

0729 Steinmetz, Devora. *From Father to Son: Kinship, Conflict, and Continuity in Genesis*. Literary Currents in Biblical Interpretation. Louisville, KY: Westminster/John Knox Press, 1991. 208 pp.

Views kinship in the Genesis narratives as a symbolic structure representing the ability of the emerging culture to survive despite conflict that threatened society's existence. Steinmetz focuses especially on word patterns and on narrative structure evident in passages where family leadership is transferred from father to son.

0730   Thompson, Thomas L. "Conflict of Themes in the Jacob Narratives." *Semeia* 15 (1979): 5-26.

Argues against the traditional understanding of the conflict narratives in the Jacob cycle as historiographical. Thompson thinks the historiographical elements present in the tales are limited and are built on a fictional base.

0731   Turner, Laurence A. *Announcements of Plot in Genesis*. Journal for the Study of the Old Testament Supplement Series, 96. Sheffield: JSOT Press, 1990. 210 pp.

Examines statements in Genesis that open major narrative blocks and, ostensibly, suggest ways in which the stories that follow are likely to develop. Turner discovers that, in fact, the announcements are misleading indicators. Genesis is more concerned with the ironies of human motive and divine providence than with the working out of any pre-ordained divine plan.

0732   Van Wolde, E. J. *A Semiotic Analysis of Genesis 2--3: A Semiotic Theory and Method of Analysis Applied to the Story of the Garden of Eden*. Assen: Van Gorcum, 1989. 224 pp.

Applies semiotic theories of A. J. Greimas and C. S. Peirce to this biblical account. Van Wolde begins with an extended description of Greimas' theory, which she believes must be augmented by Peirce's insights into the role of the reader. She then lays out a four-stage analytical model (narrative, semantic, discursive, communicative) and analyzes the Genesis account with regard to the first three stages.

0733   White, Hugh C. "The Joseph Story: A Narrative Which 'Consumes' Its Content." *Semeia* 31 (1985): 49-69.

Addresses the tension in the Joseph story between the semantic world presented through the direct discourse of the characters and the referential world presented through the indirect discourse of the narrative framework. White shows that in the Joseph story the referential world is ultimately subordinated to the semantic world of direct discourse and that this subordination prevents the story from attaining closure.

0734   White, Hugh C. "Word Reception as the Matrix of the Structure of the Genesis Narrative." In *The Biblical Mosaic: Changing Perspectives*, ed. by Robert Polzin and Eugene Rothman, 61-83. Philadelphia: Fortress Press, 1982.

A structuralist interpretation of Genesis. The book develops as it does out of semiological necessity--the nature of language dictates, for instance, the sequence of the key events. The movement from prohibition (1--11) to promise (12--50) corresponds to the progress of human awareness from closed to an open semiology.

EXODUS

See also 0587, 0594, 0601, 0614, 0621, 0660, 0792, 0925, 1580, 1591, 1743.

0735   Ackerman, James S. "The Literary Context of the Moses Birth Story." In *Literary Interpretations of Biblical Narrative*, ed. by Kenneth R. R. Gros Louis with James S. Ackerman and Thayer S. Warshaw, 74-119. Nashville: Abingdon Press, 1974.

Relates the first two chapters of Exodus to themes expressed elsewhere in the Pentateuch. The events here are a prelude to the exodus, which is conceived of as a new act of God's creation; therefore, they contain repeated allusions to the primeval stories of Genesis 1--11.   The Joseph story also serves as a prototype for understanding the exodus: themes of descent and bondage figure prominently in both and yet, in both, symbols of death and evil are transformed into means of deliverance. God is "hidden" in Exodus 1--2 only because God has descended into the pit of Egypt and so is totally identified with the people in their powerlessness and suffering.

0736   Boyarin, Daniel. *Intertextuality and the Reading of Midrash*. Indiana Studies in Biblical Literature. Bloomington: Indiana University Press, 1990. 176 pp.

Uses passages from the *Mekilta*, an early midrash on Exodus, to illuminate the study of midrashic texts through application of modern literary theory.

0737   Chirichigno, G. C. "The Narrative Structure of Exod 19-24." *Biblica* 68 (1987): 457-479.

Uses a model for structural poetics adapted from Tzvetan Todorov to analyze the narrative structure of the Sinai account. Chirichigno finds that the sequence structure of the narrative's propositions explains its awkward surface structure, which presents a non-linear temporal ordering of events. The literary device of "resumptive repetition" is used to present the theophany on Sinai twice, once from the perspective of Yahweh, and once from the perspective of the people.

0738   Dozeman, Thomas B. "Spatial Form in Exod 19:1-8a and in the Larger Sinai Narrative." *Semeia* 46 (1989): 87-101

Assesses the effect on the reader of spatial form devices inserted by redactors into the account of Exodus 19:1-8a. Spatial form devices are defined as techniques that subvert the chronological sequence inherent in narrative. Redactors insert such devices as means for linking distant traditions, but in the canonical form of the text, the effect is to halt the forward movement of the narrative. In the book of Exodus, the movements of Moses do not establish a clear temporal sequence for the narrative but create scenes that must be juxtaposed to each other.

0739   Fokkelman, Jan P. "Exodus." In *The Literary Guide to the Bible*, ed. by Robert Alter and Frank Kermode, 56-65. Cambridge, MA: Belknap Press, 1987.

Presents a scheme for understanding the overall structure of Exodus, emphasizes continuity between the book and its predecessor (Genesis), and suggests that the book is unified internally by its portrayal of Israel as a spiritual entity and by its accent on the divine Name.

0740   Gunn, David M. "The 'Hardening of Pharaoh's Heart': Plot, Character and Theology in Exodus 1--14." In *Art and Meaning: Rhetoric in Biblical Literature*, ed. by David J. A. Clines, David M. Gunn, and Alan J. Hauser, 72-96. Sheffield, England: JSOT Press, 1982.

Discusses the element of divine causality in the plot of Exodus 1--14. Not only Pharaoh, but also Moses, the people, and all characters in this story act within a framework of divine causality. No one escapes God's control or its repercussions: "the story is about freedom, but freedom turns out to involve varieties of servitude."

0741   Hamlin, E. John. "The Liberator's Ordeal. A Study of Exodus 4:1-9." In *Rhetorical Criticism*, ed. by Jared J. Jackson and Martin Kessler, 33-42. Pittsburgh Theological Monograph Series, 1. Pittsburgh: Pickwick Press, 1974.

Interprets the three signs to Moses in Exodus 4 from a reader-oriented perspective informed by sociological-anthropological study. Hamlin reads the passage in light of contemporary liberation ideologies, encouraging every interpreter to locate the oppressing forces in his or her own life as a means of "finding the thrust of God's word in the contemporary world."

0742   Holbert, John C. "A New Literary Reading of Exodus 32, The Story of the Golden Calf." *Quarterly Review* 10,3 (1990): 46-68.

Attempts to read the story of the golden calf taking seriously the words of the biblical text in its current form, without trying to decide how and from where we got them. The story presents Moses as hero and Aaron as anti-hero. The leadership exemplified by Moses consists of total zeal for Yahweh coupled with unstinting compassion for the people he has been called to lead. The story in its current form emphasizes Aaron's culpability in the making of the calf and so presents him as only a provisional leader who becomes a rebel against Yahweh's will.

0743   Howell, Marieth. "Exodus 15, 1b-18: A Poetic Analysis." *Ephemerides Theologicae Lovanienses* 65 (1989): 5-42.

Divides the poem into two stanzas (1b-12, 13-18), identifies strophes, and isolates poetic devices in a line-by-line analysis. Two tables are presented, one with repeated roots and synonyms and the other with rare words.

0744   Isbell, Charles. "Exodus 1--2 in the Context of Exodus 1--14: Story Lines and Key Words." In *Art and Meaning: Rhetoric in Biblical Literature*, ed. by David J. A. Clines, David M. Gunn, and Alan J. Hauser, 37-61. Sheffield, England: JSOT Press, 1982.

Examines the structure of Exodus 1--2 as a prelude to Exodus 1--4. Isbell divides the first two chapters into two major units, 1:8--2:22 and 2:23-25. Each of these units is then discussed with reference to story lines and to key words that function either within or between units. 2:24-25 establishes a tight connection to the narrative that follows.

0745   Magonet, Jonathan. "The Bush That Never Burned (Narrative Technique in Exodus 3 and 6)." *The Heythrop Journal* 16 (1975): 304-311.

Discerns a concentric pattern for Exodus 3:7-10 based on the key words, "my people" (7a, 10), "seen" (7a, 9b), "cry" (7b, 9a), and "land" (8a, 8b). The center of the passage contrasts the land of slavery with the land of promise, while the external ring emphasizes God's concern for the suffering of God's people. Magonet relates the passage to Exodus 6:2-8 in a manner expounded further in 0746.

0746   Magonet, Jonathan. "The Rhetoric of God: Exodus 6:2-8." *Journal for the Study of the Old Testament* 27 (1983): 56-67.

Diagrams Exodus 6:2-8 according to a concentric pattern related to that discerned previously for Exodus 3:7-10 (0745). The passage moves from outward themes of covenant and freedom to the theme of redemption represented in verse 6, the center of the diagram. The article is followed by a response from Pierre Auffret and by Magonet's response to Auffret's remarks.

0747   Moberly, R. W. L. *At the Mountain of God: Story and Theology in Exodus 32 --34*. Journal for the Study of the Old Testament Supplement Series, 22. Sheffield: JSOT Press, 1983. 258 pp.

A narrative reading of the Sinai story. The heart of the book is a verse-by-verse exegetical analysis built on presuppositions of narrative criticism. But Moberly is also aware of traditional concerns, and so devotes a chapter to analyzing the story, from a historical-critical perspective, as a "cult legend."

0748   Robinson, Bernard P. "Symbolism in Exod. 15:22-27 (Marah and Elim)." *Revue biblique* 94 (1987): 376-388.

Says that symbolic exegesis of this passage such as that practiced by rabbis and early Christian communities is justified on the basis of the story's literary features. These include a pervasive use of paronomasia, echoes of preceding passages, and anticipations of later ones. The tree cast into the waters of Marah is the Torah, the seventy palms represent the collective immortality of the people, and the twelve springs, the gift of life and salvation.

0749   Vater, Ann M. "'A Plague on Both our Houses': Form-and Rhetorical-Critical Observations on Exodus 7--11." In *Art and Meaning: Rhetoric in Biblical Literature*, ed. by David J. A. Clines, David M. Gunn, and Alan J. Hauser, 62-71. Sheffield, England: JSOT Press, 1982.

Proposes that consideration of the story of the plagues in Exodus as a "Living Oracle" story resolves certain problems in interpretation that have beset both form-critical and stylistic-rhetorical investigations.   Primary emphasis on the commissioning scene legitimates the authority of the human oracle such that the display of God's power over death must be understood as a response to the refusal to accept this authority.

0750   Waring, Dawn Elizabeth. "The Nature of Yahweh's Relationship with His People: A Literary Analysis of Exodus 32--34." Ph.D. diss., Fuller Theological Seminary, School of Theology, 1985. 269 pp.

Demonstrates the basic unity that underlies the highly complex and, from a source-critical perspective, composite text of Exodus 32--34.   Despite its complicated prehistory, the text functions in its current form as a meaningful whole, emphasizing that from the beginning the people of God stand as a forgiven people.

LEVITICUS

See also 0889.

0751   Damrosch, David. "Leviticus." In *The Literary Guide to the Bible*, ed. by Robert Alter and Frank Kermode, 66-77. Cambridge, MA: Belknap Press, 1987.

Discusses the literary meaning of Leviticus from the perspective of authorial intent --specifically, the intent of the priestly writers who shaped the final form of the Pentateuch. By interweaving law and history, these writers sought to set the law within a narrative context and also to subsume the narrative within a larger symbolic order. The effect is to bring out the redemptive potential of exile.

0752   Schwartz, Baruch J. "Selected chapters of the Holiness Code - A Literary Study of Leviticus 17--19." Ph.D. diss., Hebrew University of Jerusalem, 1988. 358 pp.

Proposes that the legal material in the book of Leviticus be read as literature, in the same way that poems, narrative, prophetic oracles, and wisdom teaching are read. The goal of such study is to discern the literary art employed and the expressive function of every detail. Schwartz attempts to illustrate the effectiveness of such an approach through analysis of the material in Leviticus 17, 18, and 19.

NUMBERS

See also 0639, 0672.

0753   Ackerman, James S. "Numbers." In *The Literary Guide to the Bible*, ed. by Robert Alter and Frank Kermode, 78-91. Cambridge, MA: Belknap Press, 1987.

Divides Numbers into three sections (1:1-10:10; 10:11-25:18; 26:1-36:13) and discusses thematic concerns that give literary unity to the work. The latter include: reflection on the wilderness as an ordeal similar to the diaspora; the establishment of spatial structures and hierarchies of personnel that permit certain groups to approach God's presence; divine guidance and protection; the need to remain separate from surrounding nations; and the anticipation of life in the Promised Land. Ackerman notes the presence of symbolic oppositions, such as that between meat and manna, which he believes parallels a more significant juxtaposition of spirit and word.

0754   Clark, Ira. "Balaam's Ass: Suture or Structure?" In *Literary Interpretations of Biblical Narratives, Volume II*, ed. by Kenneth R. R. Gros Louis with James S. Ackerman, 137-144. Nashville: Abingdon Press, 1982.

Notes that apparent inconsistencies in the story of Balaam do not have to be explained as the crude sutures of a bumbling redactor, but, rather, can be read as providing structural emphasis to the main issue of the tale. Why does God grant Balaam permission to go to Moab and then get mad at him for making the journey? Since God's omnipotent control of human events is the main point of this narrative, God's manipulation of Balaam appears as a joke. God's jokes display all-powerful providence no less than potent commands and sublime visions.

0755   Coats, George W. "Humility and Honor: A Moses Legend in Numbers 12." In *Art and Meaning: Rhetoric in Biblical Literature*, ed. by David J. A. Clines, David M. Gunn, and Alan J. Hauser, 97-107. Sheffield, England: JSOT Press, 1982.

Proposes that a pattern of unity attends to Numbers 12 in its current form, despite the complex literary history discernible to tradition critics. The story in its present shape is not so concerned with a rebellion against Moses as it is with the unusual status of Moses among all the people of the world. Thus, while 12:3 is viewed as disruptive vis à vis the old narrative tradition, it is now seen to be pivotal for reading the story as a unit.

0756   Culley, Robert C. "Five Tales of Punishment in the Book of Numbers." In *Text and Tradition: The Hebrew Bible and Folklore*, ed. by Susan Niditch, 25-34. Semeia Studies. Atlanta: Scholars Press, 1990.

Offers some general comments about the nature of folklore and then considers five stories from Numbers (11:1-3; 11:4-35; 12; 20:1-13; and 21:4-9). The repetition of the punishment motif found in all these stories is intended to reinforce the notion that Yahweh may not be crossed or provoked. This essay is followed by a response from Dan Ben-Amos.

0757   Jobling, David. "'The Jordan A Boundary': A Reading of Numbers 32 and Joshua 22." In *Society of Biblical Literature 1980 Seminar Papers*, ed. by Paul J. Achtemeier, 183-208. Chico, CA: Scholars Press, 1980.

Attempts a structuralist analysis of the geographical and social settings depicted in these texts, focusing on the role of the Jordan as a boundary. The region across the Jordan has an ambiguous role in this literature and becomes the object of paradoxical attitude--a desire for a more formalized relationship with this territory on the one hand and a wish that it would just go away on the other. As a boundary, the Jordan functions both to limit and to mediate the conflicts and compromises of Israel's narrative history.

0758   Jobling, David. "A Structural Analysis of Numbers 11 and 12." In *Society of Biblical Literature 1977 Seminar Papers*, ed. by Paul J. Achtemeier, 171-204. Missoula, MT: Scholars Press, 1977.

Lays out the narrative programs of this material according to recent form-criticism and then engages the material in semantic analysis according to the methodology of A. J. Greimas and Claude Lévi-Strauss. Nine "codes" are discussed (e.g., geographical, topographical, kinship) by which key oppositions may be identified. Finally, the message of the myth is discussed with regard to its transformational relations to other Old Testament passages.

0759   Newing, Edward G. "The Rhetoric of Altercation in Numbers 14." In *Perspectives on Text and Language*, ed. by Edgar W. Conrad and Edward G. Newing, 211-229. Winona Lake, IN: Eisenbrauns, 1987.

Studies the altercation between Moses and Yahweh over the latter's plan to destroy Israel in Numbers 14:11-25. Key words in the three speeches are used in varying interrelationships. The linkages are intricate and are clearly defined uniquely for each speech. The text is a fine example of prose rhetorical writing.

0760   Wilson, Johnny Lee. "A Rhetorical Critical Analysis of the Balaam Oracles." Ph.D. diss., Southern Baptist Theological Seminary, 1981. 173 pp.

Examines the use of various features in the Balaam oracles. Wilson finds instances of assonance, repetition, parallelism, anaphora, and other stylistic devices. He investigates the rhythm, syntax, and imagery of the oracle, with particular attention to systems of irony.

DEUTERONOMY

See also 0632.

0761   Christenson, Duane L. "Prose and Poetry in the Bible: The Narrative Poetics of Deuteronomy 1,9-18." *Zeitschrift für die alttestamentliche Wissenschaft* 97 (1985): 179-189.

Analyzes the "prose" text of Deuteronomy 1:9-18 in terms of its poetic qualities: meter, symmetrical design, concentric framing devices, inversion, and parallelism. Christenson questions whether the distinction between "prose" and "poetry" is always clear in biblical literature and suggests that this passage might better be described as "narrative poetry."

0762   Geller, Stephen A. "The Dynamics of Parallel Verse--A Poetic Analysis of Deut. 32:6-12." *Harvard Theological Review* 75 (1982) 35-56.

Examines this passage as exemplary of the theory regarding nuclear relationships of parallel verse laid out in 0636.   Geller sees the passage as composed of twelve couplets, most of which form quatrains. Geller's understanding of parallelism stresses the necessity to combine both lines of the verse to obtain the meaning: the second line is not simply a repetition of the first, and neither line is to be considered an independent statement.

0763   Gold, Joseph. "Deuteronomy and the Word: The Beginning and the End." In *The Biblical Mosaic: Changing Perspectives*, ed. by Robert Polzin and Eugene Rothman, 45-59. Philadelphia: Fortress Press, 1982.

A philosophical, semiological investigation of Deuteronomy. Gold argues that the emergence of Mosaic monotheism coincides with a new awareness concerning the centrality of language in human life. Deuteronomy represents the earliest example of "popular, universal, and compulsory education."

0764   Polzin, Robert M. "Deuteronomy." In *The Literary Guide to the Bible*, ed. by Robert Alter and Frank Kermode, 92-101. Cambridge, MA: Belknap Press, 1987.

Argues that Deuteronomy presents a dialogue between the words of Moses and the words of the narrator, which divert the reader's attention from Moses' speech and force the contemporary audience to focus on their temporal distance from Moses' words.   Even Moses' own words draw us in two directions concerning his self-awareness as the pre-eminent teacher of God's word. This dialogue extends ultimately to include variety in perspective on God's relationship to Israel and on God's motivation for giving Israel the Promised Land.

JOSHUA

See also 0188, 0628, 0655.

0765   Culley, Robert C. "Stories of the Conquest: Joshua 2, 6, 7, and 8." *Hebrew Annual Review* 8 (1984): 25-44.

Concentrates on the narrative action in these stories, which moves from expectation to fulfillment. All four stories are viewed as "fairly coherent narrative texts" in their current form. Juxtaposition of divine and human perspectives is significant for all the stories, especially Judges 8.

0766   Gunn, David M. "Joshua and Judges." In *The Literary Guide to the Bible*, ed. by Robert Alter and Frank Kermode, 102-121. Cambridge, MA: Belknap Press, 1987.

Treats these two books under three categories: "Formal Connection and Plot," "Thematic Connection: Joshua--Judges 3," and "Thematic Connection: Judges 3--21." Gunn places special emphasis on rhetorical connectives, framing passages, and the narrator's refrains. In his second section, he struggles with the gap between the rhetoric of fulfillment and the rhetoric of incompletion and the question this raises concerning the supposedly unconditional nature of God's covenant.

0767   Koopmans, William T. *Joshua 24 as Poetic Narrative*. Journal for the Study of the Old Testament Supplement Series, 93. Sheffield: Sheffield University Press, 1990. 522 pp.

Uses structural analysis of Judges 24 to demonstrate the text's literary unity, which has been questioned by source-critical theory. Attention is also paid to relationships between Judges 24 and both the Pentateuch and the Deuteronomistic history.

0768   Koopmans, William T. "The Poetic Prose of Joshua 23." In *The Structural Analysis of Biblical and Canaanite Poetry*, ed. by Willem van der Meer and Johannes C. de Moor, 83-118. Journal for the Study of the Old Testament Supplement Series, 74. Sheffield: JSOT Press, 1988.

A structural analysis of poetic structures in the supposedly prose text of Joshua 23. These structures rely on repetitive and external parallelism rather than on internal parallelism at the level of the verse. Nevertheless, Koopmans holds that the structural symmetry evident at the level of cola, verses, strophes, and the like reveals a narrative structure as carefully crafted as most classical Hebrew poetry.

0769   Zakovitch, Yair. "Humor and Theology or the Successful Failure of Israelite Intelligence: A Literary-Folkloric Approach to Joshua 2." In *Text and Tradition: The Hebrew Bible and Folklore*, ed. by Susan Niditch, 75-98. Semeia Studies. Atlanta: Scholars Press, 1990.

Unveils the humor invested in the story of Rahab and the spies by comparing it with similar stories in the Bible and thus highlighting its distinctive features. The story is compared with tales of two types: spy stories (Numbers 13--14; Joshua 1:22-26; 18:2-11; 2 Samuel 17:17-22); and stories of a woman who rescues a man (1 Samuel 19:9-17; 2 Samuel 17:17-22; cf. Judges 4:17-21; Judges 16:1-3). One instance of such humor is the predicament of the bungling spies who find themselves in the shadow of the Canaanite harlot. This article is followed by a response from Frank Moore Cross.

JUDGES

See also 0188, 0587, 0591, 0601, 0605, 0610, 0612-0613, 0617, 0628-0629 0631, 0655, 0667, 0712, 0757, 0766, 0844, 1743.

0770 Alter, Robert. "Samson Without Folklore." In *Text and Tradition: The Hebrew Bible and Folklore*, ed. by Susan Niditch, 47-56. Semeia Studies. Atlanta: Scholars Press, 1990.

Examines subtle ways in which traditional folkloric material has been given literary articulation in the story of Samson. These include: the use of thematic key words; variation in near verbatim repetition; nuanced dialogue; and, especially, a distinctive treatment of the term "time." This article is followed by a response from David E. Bynum.

0771 Amit, Yairah. "The Story of Ehud (Judges 3:12-30): The Form and the Message." In *Signs and Wonders: Biblical Texts in Literary Focus*, ed. by J. Cheryl Exum, 97-123. Atlanta: Scholars Press, 1989.

Demonstrates how the reader is guided to make a connection between human action and divine salvation in Judges 3:12-30. The fact that Ehud is able to execute his plan without any disruptions and is, in fact, helped along the way convinces the reader that 3:15 is to be taken literally and that the success of these plans is brought about by the divine will. The article is followed by a response from David Jobling.

0772 Bal, Mieke. *Death and Dissymmetry: The Politics of Coherence in Judges*. Chicago: University of Chicago Press, 1988. 392 pp.

Applies the transdisciplinary method developed in 0773 to a gendered reading of stories involving female characters throughout the book of Judges. The guiding principle throughout is "the dissymmetry of power" as displayed in oppositions within the text--oppositions, for instance, between man and woman, mother and daughter, or killer and victim.

0773 Bal, Mieke. *Murder and Difference: Gender, Genre and Scholarship on Sisera's Death*. Bloomington: Indiana University Press, 1988. 160 pp.

Analyzes the two accounts of Sisera's death in Judges 4:18-22; 5:24-30 according to four different approaches ("codes") and evaluates these approaches according to their ability to deal with the differences between the accounts. Particularly interesting are the historical and literary codes, which Bal views as diametrically opposed (the remaining two are the theological and the anthropological). The historical code receives the harshest criticism, but all four are exposed as displaying an ideological gender bias that gives preference to the account in 4:18-22. Accordingly, Bal proposes a new transdisciplinary "gender code" that allows for a feminist reading. This project continues in 0772.

0774   Brenner, Athalya. "A Triangle and a Rhombus in Narrative Structure: A Proposed Integrative Reading of Judges IV and V." *Vetus Testamentum* 40 (1990): 129-138.

Compares the prosaic account of the death of Sisera in Judges 4 with the poetic account in Judges 5, with emphasis on the operating structure of the cast of characters in each. The relationships of the characters in Judges 4 can be diagrammed as a triangle, for there are three groups of two members: Deborah and Barak, God and Jael, and Jabin and Sisera. But Judges 5 must be diagrammed as a rhombus, containing two sets of interrelated triangular relationships: Deborah-Jael-Sisera's mother, and Barak-God-Sisera. The significance of the latter story lies in its gender differentiation: female characters belong to one triangle and male characters to another.

0775   Camp, Claudia V., and Fontaine, Carole R. "The Words of the Wise and Their Riddles." In *Text and Tradition: The Hebrew Bible and Folklore*, ed. by Susan Niditch, 127-152. Semeia Studies. Atlanta: Scholars Press, 1990.

A study of Samson's riddle in Judges 14 using the tools of folkloristic performance analysis. The story is examined from three perspectives: the interaction situation, the riddle situation, and the context situation. Attention is given to differences in point of view between the narrator and the characters. The article is followed by a response from Edgar Slotkin.

0776   DeWitt, Dale Sumner. "The Jephthah Traditions: A Rhetorical and Literary Study in the Deuteronomistic History." Ph.D. diss., Andrews University, 1987. 406 pp.

Examines the literary structure and arrangement of the five Jephthah narratives and the book of Judges as a whole. The Jephthah narratives are shown to be symmetrically arranged with the central piece containing a diplomatic speech of Jephthah that embodies the traditional kerygma of Israel. The remainder of the book of Judges is also seen to have been composed according to this symmetry of corresponding pairs.

0777   Exum, J. Cheryl. "Aspects of Symmetry and Balance in the Samson Saga." *Journal for the Study of the Old Testament* 19 (1981): 3-29.

Considers three aspects of narrative art in the Samson saga: (1) Thematic symmetry --common literary motifs and thematic parallels between chapters 14--15 and 16 are noted; (2) Structural symmetry--organizational patterns are explicated that show correspondence between chapters 13 and 16 on one hand, and between 14 and 15 on the other; (3) Contribution to theological purpose--narrative artistic devices in 15:9-19 are investigated as accenting the message that deliverance and life are ultimately in the hands of Yahweh.

0778   Exum, J. Cheryl. "Literary Patterns in the Samson Saga: An Investigation of Rhetorical Style in Biblical Prose." Ph.D. diss., Columbia University, 1976. 232 pp.

Investigates Judges 13--16 from the perspective of rhetorical criticism. A chapter on "Thematic Symmetry" examines literary motifs that determine the theme. Another, on "External Design," focuses on stylistic techniques, and one on "Internal Structures" looks at the relation between form and meaning in the units that make up the overall structural arrangement. Chapters 13, 14, 15, and 16 have their own individual structures, themes, and plots, as do the episodes and elements of which they are composed.

0779   Exum, J. Cheryl. "Promise and Fulfillment in Narrative Art in Judges 13." *Journal of Biblical Literature* 99 (1980): 43-59.

Studies literary characteristics of this biblical chapter in order to demonstrate how the form of a passage is determinative of its meaning. Formally, the character Manoah is central to the chapter, yet within the sections that feature him, attention is also diverted away from him to either his wife or to Yahweh. One point of the story of the birth of Samson is that the mother is as important as the father. Another is the accent on Yahweh as the giver of blessing.

0780   Exum, J. Cheryl. "The Tragic Vision and Biblical Narrative: The Case of Jephthah." In *Signs and Wonders: Biblical Texts in Literary Focus*, ed. by J. Cheryl Exum, 59-83. Atlanta: Scholars Press, 1989.

An inductive reading of the Jephthah story that demonstrates how Jephthah is presented as a "tragic hero" who acts against his will in taking the life of his child. The tragic elements lie primarily in the conjuncture of "chilling coincidence" with divine silence, that is, with the refusal of the deity to take a position regarding what transpires. The paper is followed by a response from W. Lee Humphreys.

0781   Freeman, James. "Samson's Dry Bones: A Structural Reading of Judges 13 --16." In *Literary Interpretations of Biblical Narratives, Volume II*, ed. by Kenneth R. R. Gros Louis with James S. Ackerman, 145-160. Nashville: Abingdon Press, 1982.

Presents an outline for reading Judges 13--16 as a carefully constructed narrative. The story consists of eleven major sections, each of which contains four elements: a crude muscular display, a more specialized sensory activity, a sophisticated act of mind, and a betrayal. This repeated pattern exposes certain truths about people and their relationships.

0782   Greenstein, Edward L.   "The Riddle of Samson." *Prooftexts: A Journal of Jewish Literary History* 1 (1981): 237-260.

Proposes that the entire Samson story must be read like a riddle, with its meaning compressed into a select set of symbols whose latent meanings must be exposed. The story is a kind of allegory, an epitomization of Israel that has no exact analogue elsewhere in biblical narrative.

0783   Gros Louis, Kenneth R. R. "The Book of Judges." In *Literary Interpretations of Biblical Narratives*, ed. by Kenneth R. R. Gros Louis with James S. Ackerman and Thayer S. Warshaw, 141-162. Nashville: Abingdon Press, 1974.

Surveys the stories of the judges as illustrative of the variety and paradoxical nature of human experiences. The judges have nothing in common with each other except that God uses them to achieve redemption of repentant Israel. Furthermore, the book delights in the peculiar, unexpected character of its heroes: Ehud is left-handed, Deborah and Jael are women, Gideon is a simple farmer, Jephthah is an outcast son of a prostitute, Samson is easily out-witted. Implicit in these stories is a democracy of spirit that affirms every kind of human gift and characteristic, including those that might be cast as weak or worthless.

0784   Halperin, Sarah. "Tragedy in the Bible." *Semitics* 7 (1980): 28-39.

Traces the Aristotelian components of tragedy in the Samson story, discovering that this story fits the classical definition of tragic literature. The story symbolizes the plight of humanity in the world, hovering between poles of greatness and weakness, splendor and fallibility, heroism and failure.

0785   Klein, Lillian R. *The Triumph of Irony in the Book of Judges*. Journal for the Study of the Old Testament Supplement Series, 68/Bible and Literature Series, 14. Sheffield: Almond Press, 1988. 260 pp.

Argues against the notion that contradictions within Judges result from clumsy editing by proposing that they represent an intentional use of irony in a well-constructed, unified narrative.   Klein distinguishes carefully between those statements that represent the point of view of the reliable narrator and those that represent the less reliable points of view of characters who may wrongly claim God's support for their actions. She draws heavily from Paul Ricouer, Meir Sternberg, and other literary theorists in presenting an interpretation that tries to take the book seriously as literature, but she also remains sensitive to the interests of historical criticism, with which she is clearly in dialogue.

0786   Niditch, Susan. "Samson as Culture Hero, Trickster, and Bandit: The Empowerment of the Weak." *Catholic Biblical Quarterly* 52 (1990): 608-624.

Analyzes the story of Samson in Judges 13--16 from the perspective of folkloric and comparative literature studies. Samson may be viewed as culture hero, as trickster, or as bandit, but in any case, the overriding theme of the story is marginal confrontation with oppressive authority. Samson's birth, adventures with women and assailants, and death all emphasize victory of the weak over seemingly implacable forces.

0787   Oren, E. "The Samson Stories." *Beth Mikra* 25 (1980): 259-262.

Notes several features of the Samson stories, such as the repetition of God's coming to Samson's aid, and the linking of the room to salvation. The narrative mocks the Philistines, by showing that every success rebounds ultimately to their disadvantage. The article is in Hebrew.

0788   Vickery, John B. "In Strange Ways: The Story of Samson." In *Images of Man and God: Old Testament Short Stories in Literary Focus*, ed. by Burke O. Long, 58-73. Bible and Literature Series, 1. Sheffield: Almond Press, 1981.

Compares and contrasts the story of Samson with more modern short stories and "tall tales" in which "narrative invention refuses to be shackled by plausibility." The Samson story differs from such tales in its appeal to divine intervention and also in its presentation of the hero as a less than sympathetic figure. But tracing the story's narrative and thematic development reveals that ultimately the desire of the hero and the purpose of the Lord are the same--deliverance from bondage.

0789   Waldman, Nahum M. "Concealment and Irony in the Samson Story." *Dor le Dor* 13 (1984-1985): 71-80.

Examines the motif of concealment, deception, and irony in the Samson story, highlighting the circumstances of Samson's birth, his stratagems, his restricted grasp of the Nazirite role, his relations with Philistine men and women, and so on. The greatest irony is found in the riddle of Judges 14:14, which refers to Samson himself, although Samson does not realize it.

0790   Webb, Barry G. *The Book of Judges: An Integrated Reading.* Journal for the Study of the Old Testament Supplement Series, 46. Sheffield: Sheffield University Press, 1987. 280 pp.

A detailed literary reading of Judges that pays special attention to stylistic and structural devices (chiasms, concentric structures, inclusios, and so on). After outlining his method, Webb presents a line-by-line close reading of Judges 10:6--12:7 (Jephthah) in order to demonstrate his points pragmatically. The rest of the work examines Judges from beginning to end, in three sections: 1:1--3:6; 3:7--16:31; 17:1--21:25. Webb regards the first section as an "overture" and the final section as a "coda." He stresses the unity of ideas and themes that pervade all three parts and so bind the book together as a literary unit.

RUTH

See also **0488, 0587, 0601, 0605, 0612, 0645, 0650, 0666.**

0791   Coxon, Peter W. "Was Naomi a Scold? A Response to Fewell and Gunn."
Journal for the Study of the Old Testament 45 (1989): 25-37.

A rebuttal of the interpretation provided by the scholars named in the title concerning
characterization of Naomi in the book of Ruth (0795). Coxon offers a point-by-point
argument, suggesting at almost every instance a more traditional interpretation of
Naomi as altruistic and of Ruth as self-sacrificing. The article is followed by a
strongly-worded response by Fewell and Gunn that supports their interpretation and
implies that sexist prejudices prevent Coxon from accepting it.

0792   Feeley-Harnik, Gillian. "Naomi and Ruth: Building Up the House of David."
In *Text and Tradition: The Hebrew Bible and Folklore*, ed. by Susan Niditch, 163-184.
Semeia Studies. Atlanta: Scholars Press, 1990.

Explores the transition from Judges to Kings depicted in the book of Ruth against the
background of the transition from bondage to freedom depicted in Exodus. The birth
of the monarchy out of Moab parallels the birth of Israel out of Egypt, but David's
monarchy is not just a re-creation of Egypt in Canaan. The article is followed by a
response from Edward L. Greenstein.

0793   Fewell, Danna Nolan, and Gunn, David M. "Boaz, Pillar of Society: Measures
of Worth in the Book of Ruth." *Journal for the Study of the Old Testament* 45 (1989):
45-59.

Continues the study begun in 0795 by evaluating the character of Boaz in Ruth from
a reader-oriented, feminist perspective. Fewell and Gunn's analysis reveals Boaz to
be less than the hero traditional interpretations have typically made him out to be.
His interest in Ruth is primarily sexual, and his demand for the public confirmation
is a ploy to turn a dubious marriage into a social triumph. Boaz is trapped by the
same patriarchy as Naomi, though he is trapped in privilege and she in dependency.

0794   Fewell, Danna Nolan, and Gunn, David M. *Compromising Redemption:
Relating Characters in the Book of Ruth*. Literary Currents in Biblical Interpretation.
Louisville: Westminster/John Knox Press, 1990. 142 pp.

Challenges idealized readings of the book of Ruth by focusing on the distinctive
viewpoints of characters and of the compromises that their world forces them to
make. The story reveals the confining power of gender, class, race and religion but
also affirms the promise of human relationship and its power to redeem. Chapters
are devoted to the characters of Naomi (cf. 0795), Boaz (cf. 0793) and Ruth.

0795   Fewell, Danna Nolan, and Gunn, David M.   "'A Son is Born to Naomi':
Literary Allusions and Interpretation in the Book of Ruth." *Journal for the Study of
the Old Testament* 40 (1988): 99-108.

Presents a reader-oriented, feminist interpretation of Ruth that views Naomi in a less-
than-positive light.   Fewell and Gunn first call attention to the several silences of
Naomi at key points in the story and offer suggestions as to what the reader might
conjecture at each point (e.g., the silence at 1:18 is interpreted as implying that Naomi
would prefer to be free of Ruth's company).   Fewell and Gunn also identify allusions
in the story to other biblical tales, comparing Naomi's manipulations to those of
Sarah, Lot's daughters, Laban, and Tamar.   The study is written in dialogue with one
by Trible (0803) and is continued in 0793.   For a response, see 0791.

0796   Fisch, A. H.   "A Structuralist Approach to the Stories of Ruth and Boaz." *Beth
Mikra* 24 (1979): 260-265.

Points to a common sequence of events that contribute to the stories of Lot's
daughters (Genesis 19), Judah and Tamar (Genesis 38), and Ruth.   The sequence is
descent, disaster, woman without husband, redeemer, trick, celebration, marriage,
blessing.   The article is in Hebrew.

0797   Garsiel, M.   "Literary Structure, Plot Development, and Narrative Technique
in the Book of Ruth." *Beth Mikra* 23 (1978): 444-457.

Discerns a common short-story pattern in the book of Ruth: background, problem,
complications, climax, resolution.   Expectations of resolutions are repeatedly aroused
but then postponed.   Success is finally achieved only because each of the major
characters is willing to act unselfishly.   The article is in Hebrew.

0798   Green, Barbara.   "The Plot of the Biblical Story of Ruth." *Journal for the Study
of the Old Testament* 23 (1982): 55-68.

Traces the plot of Ruth by starting with what Green regards as the climactic scene
(4:1-12), and working backwards through the tale to notice by what steps and hints the
pathway to this climax was laid.   Ruth is more than a simple love story--it is a story
of the liberation of God's people from the land of oppression and death, a story of
the "re-seeding" of God's people and their land.

0799   Radday, Y. T., and Welch, G. W.   "Structure in the Book of Ruth." *Beth Mikra*
24 (1979): 180-187.

Demonstrates a widespread use of chiasm as a structuring device for both setting and
character development in Ruth.   The story's main theme is expressed in the story's
center (3:1-3), which stresses that God is present in the thoughts and deeds of the
righteous.   The article is in Hebrew.

0800   Rauber, D. F. "The Book of Ruth." In *Literary Interpretations of Biblical Narratives*, ed. by Kenneth R. R. Gros Louis with James S. Ackerman and Thayer S. Warshaw, 163-176. Nashville: Abingdon Press, 1974.

Examines the literary craft of Ruth, by which the book is formally structured according to the recurring theme of emptiness and fullness. Rauber argues that, since Ruth is a piece of high literary art, critics should not attempt to define its significance in terms limited to a particular historical application.

0801   Sasson, Jack M. "Ruth." In *The Literary Guide to the Bible*, ed. by Robert Alter and Frank Kermode, 320-328. Cambridge, MA: Belknap Press, 1987.

Briefly surveys the four episodes of this folktale, with reference to the narrator's skill in handling the tale. For a more complete account of the same approach, see 0802.

0802   Sasson, Jack M. *Ruth: A New Translation with a Philological Commentary and a Formalist-Folklorist Interpretation*. 2nd ed. Biblical Seminar Series, 10. Sheffield: JSOT Press, 1990. 300 pp.

An updated version of a seminal 1979 commentary that integrated literary insights drawn from folkloric studies with linguistic data and historical concerns. Sasson is concerned with the formal features of the book of Ruth and with highlighting the artistry of the narrator. See also 0650.

0803   Trible, Phyllis. "A Human Comedy: The Book of Ruth." In *Literary Interpretations of Biblical Narratives, Volume II*, ed. by Kenneth R. R. Gros Louis with James S. Ackerman, 161-190. Nashville: Abingdon Press, 1982.

Interprets the story of Ruth as a comedy in which the brave and bold decisions of women embody and bring to pass the blessings of God. Trible notes that, although the story reflects the patriarchal climate of "a man's world," this is subverted by the women of Jerusalem's identification of the child as the son of Naomi rather than of Elimelech (4:17); thus the language of a man's world is reinterpreted to preserve the integrity of a woman's story. The article is also featured as one chapter of 0666. See also 0795.

0804   West, Ramona Faye. "Ruth: A Retelling of Genesis 38?" Ph.D. diss., The Southern Baptist Theological Seminary, 1987. 189 pp.

Provides a literary analysis of the Judah-Tamar story in Genesis 38 and a literary analysis of the book of Ruth, which West believes is a "retelling" of that story. Ruth, like Tamar, is viewed as a woman who acts intentionally to determine her own future and the futures of Naomi and Boaz.

1, 2 Samuel; 1, 2 Kings

See also 0188, 0482, 0573, 0587, 0591, 0593, 0601, 0605, 0607, 0610-0612, 0617, 0628-0629, 0631, 0637, 0639, 0651-0652, 0667, 0672, 0712, 1287, 1550, 1580, 1597, 1599.

0805   Bar-Efrat, Shimon. "Literary Modes and Methods in the Biblical Narrative." *Immanuel* 8 (1978): 19-31.

Examines narratives in 2 Samuel 10--20 and 1 Kings 1--2 with the use of tools and categories developed in modern literary theory. Bar-Efrat considers the role of the "omniscient narrator," direct and indirect ways of character shaping, the handling of time and space, and the subtleties of style.

0806   Berlin, Adele. "Characterization in Biblical Narrative." *Journal for the Study of the Old Testament* 23 (1982): 69-85.

A study in the characterization of four women in the books of Samuel and Kings. Michal and Bathsheba in 1 Kings 1--2 are full characters, realistically portrayed; Abigail is more of a "type" than an individual; Abishag and Bathsheba in 2 Samuel 11--12 are merely "agents" who function as part of the setting. Berlin also notes interesting parallels between David's responses to his wives and his public life--for example, lust for Bathsheba corresponds to his expansionist policies and impotence with Abishag corresponds to his loss of control over the empire.

0807   Bowman, Richard Gene. "The Crises of King David: Narrative Structure, Compositional Technique, and the Interpretation of II Samuel 8:15--20:26." Ph.D. diss., Union Theological Seminary in Virginia, 1981. 363 pp.

Attempts to delineate the organizational structure of the narrative in 2 Samuel 8:15 --20:26 in terms of its component narrative scenes. After laying out his methodology, which includes a proposal of four criteria by which a unit may be labeled a "scene," Bowman finds that the Samuel narrative is organized into four such scenes: 2 Samuel 9; 10--12; 13--14; and 15--20. The second and third parts are given a detailed analysis.

0808   Brueggemann, Walter. "Narrative Intentionality in 1 Samuel 29." *Journal for the Study of the Old Testament* 43 (1989): 21-35.

Attempts to understand the rhetoric of David's "trial before Achish" from the perspective of the narrative's intended Israelite audience. David is acquitted by Achish, although the audience knows that David is in fact guilty. Still, from the perspective of this particular intended audience, David's guilt may be dismissed as treachery against Israel's enemies--David may be regarded as truly innocent, though not in the way that Achish intended. Brueggemann concludes with some suggestions for reading the rhetorical intentionality of the trial of Jesus in Luke and in John in a similar fashion.

0809   Campbell, Anthony F.   "The Reported Story: Midway between Oral Performance and Literary Art." *Semeia* 46 (1989): 77-86.

Suggests that a number of Old Testament texts are intended to serve as memory aids for storytellers who would present fuller versions of the stories orally. These "reports of stories" contain the basic elements of character and plot, but also leave out much that could be supplied by the storyteller's imagination. Evidence for the thesis focuses on instances in which the reported stories omit elements that, though easily supplied through imagination, are in fact essential to the unfolding of the plot. Specific texts discussed include 1 Samuel 18:20-27; 19:1-7; 11-17; 20:1-42; 22:6-19; 24:1-22; 2 Samuel 3:12-16.

0810   Ceresko, Anthony. "A Rhetorical Analysis of David's 'Boast' (1 Samuel 17:34-37): Some Reflections on Method." *Catholic Biblical Quarterly* 47 (1985): 58-74.

Presents a rhetorical analysis of this passage that is attentive to such features as sound patterns, inclusion, parallel pairs, key words, and concentric structures. The "reflections on method" trace implications of the rhetorical analysis for text criticism, source criticism, and socio-cultural analysis.

0811   Cohn, Robert L. "Literary Technique in the Jeroboam Narrative." *Zeitschrift für die alttestamentliche Wissenschaft* 97 (1985): 23-35.

Demonstrates a rough chiastic shape to the Jeroboam narrative, which has as its center the story of the man of God being killed by the lion. This story, illustrating how God's chosen instrument can become God's victim, underscores the theological dynamic in the broader story of the rise and fall of Jeroboam.

0812   Culley, Robert C. "Punishment Stories in the Legends of the Prophets." In *Orientation By Disorientation*, ed. by Richard A. Spencer, 167-182. Pittsburgh: Pickwick Press, 1980.

Using a formalist method similar to that applied by Propp to Russian folktales (0202), Culley analyzes six Old Testament stories: 2 Kings 2:23-24; 2 Kings 1:2-17; 2 Kings 5:20-27; 1 Kings 21:1-29; 1 Kings 20:33-42; and 1 Kings 13:21-24. The stories all exhibit the same action sequence, "wrong-wrong punished," but the potential for filling out this sequence is exploited in different ways so as to draw our attention to different things in each story.

0813   Deeley, Mary Katharine. "The Rhetoric of Memory in the Stories of Saul and David: A Prospective Study." In *Society of Biblical Literature 1988 Seminar Papers*, ed. by David J. Lull, 285-292. Atlanta: Scholars Press, 1988.

Examines the use of remembrance of past specific events by characters in the books of Samuel as a rhetorical device that furthers plot developments and reader understanding of the places of Saul and David in Israel's history.

0814   Eslinger, Lyle M. *The Kingship of God in Crisis: A Close Reading of 1 Samuel 1--12*. Bible and Literature Series, 10. Sheffield: Almond Press, 1985. 515 pp.

Draws on narratology to present a close reading of these twelve chapters. Eslinger challenges conventional interpretations regarding the role of the ark and the choosing of Saul. The book is presented in commentary style, progressing through the text, verse by verse.

0815   Eslinger, Lyle M. "Viewpoints and Point of View in 1 Samuel 8--12." *Journal for the Study of the Old Testament* 26 (1983): 61-76.

Demonstrates that 1 Samuel 8--12 can be read, from a literary perspective, as a coherent narrative, without being dissected into pro-monarchic and anti-monarchic source strata as is traditionally done. The narrator remains neutral toward the idea of monarchy, and the differing opinions pro and con represent the viewpoints of various characters within the story.

0816   Fischer, Alexander. "David und Batseba: Ein literarkritischer und motivgeschichtlicher Beitrag zu II Sam 11." *Zeitschrift für die alttestamentliche Wissenschaft* 101 (1989): 50-59.

Describes the story of David and Bathsheba as a "circular composition." Fischer calls attention to literary motifs in the story and says that their presence casts doubt upon the story's historicity.

0817   Fishbane, Michael. "I Samuel 3: Historical Narrative and Narrative Poetics." In *Literary Interpretations of Biblical Narratives, Volume II*, ed. by Kenneth R. R. Gros Louis with James S. Ackerman, 191-203. Nashville: Abingdon Press, 1982.

Analyzes the formal structure and narrative stylistics of 1 Samuel 3 (the call of Samuel), noting the manner in which formal phonemic repetitions complement levels of meaning achieved by chiastic arrangements and other means. Fishbane draws a lesson from his study for interpretation of Old Testament history in general: biblical history is mediated by language and its effects and so must be understood in terms of the deployment of language that produces the received history.

0818   Fokkelman, Jan P. "A Lie Born of Truth, Too Weak to Contain It: A Structural Reading of 2 Samuel 1:1-16." *Oudtestamentische Studiën* 23 (1984): 39-55.

Treats the apparently conflicting traditions of Saul's death in 1 Samuel 31 and 2 Samuel 1 according to techniques laid out in *Narrative Art and Poetry in the Books of Samuel* (0219). 2 Samuel 1:1-16 are held to be a story within a story.

0819   Fokkelman, Jan P. *Narrative Art and Poetry in the Books of Samuel. A Full Interpretation Based on Stylistic and Structural Analyses.* 2 vols. Studia semitica neerlandica, 20. Assen: Van Gorcum, 1981, 1986. 534, 744 pp.

A close, line-by-line reading of most of the narrative material in the books of Samuel (vol. 1 deals with 2 Samuel 9--20 and 1 Kings 1--2; vol. 2 deals with 1 Samuel 3--31 and 2 Samuel 1). The most impressive aspect of this work is its attention to detail. Observations about plot structure and characterization are made throughout, but the major focus is on such textual particulars as word sounds, word patterns, and modes of repetition. Numerous diagrams, lists, charts, and symbolizations are also used to highlight structural patterns. In addition, Fokkelmann delineates thematic oppositions in the narrative, such as piety-sin, illusion-truth, and unity-duality in the narrative. His study ultimately moves from words and sentences to propose overall structures of scenes and acts for the work as a whole.

0820   Fokkelman, Jan P. "Saul and David: Crossed Fates." *Bible Review* 5,3 (1989): 20-32.

Focuses on the narrative art of the storyteller in 1 Samuel. Saul is presented as a tragic hero. Fokkelman traces the story of Saul sequentially to its conclusion in 2 Samuel 1.

0821   Goldenberg, Robert. "The Problem of False Prophecy: Talmudic Interpretations of Jeremiah 28 and 1 Kings 22." In *The Biblical Mosaic: Changing Perspectives*, ed. by Robert Polzin and Eugene Rothman, 87-103. Philadelphia: Fortress Press, 1982.

Surveys various rabbinic attempts to deal with the problematic implication of the Micaiah ben Imlah story, namely that "the divine gift of prophecy can be more dangerous than anyone had ever imagined." Goldenberg shows that the rabbis went beyond trying to understand the text on its own terms--midrashic interpretations explored potential meanings as well as plausible ones, in an effort to produce a meaning that was religiously acceptable. This ancient practice corresponds in certain ways to reader-oriented approaches in modern literary study. See also 0854.

0822   Gregory, Russell Inman. "Elijah's Story Under Scrutiny: A Literary-Critical Analysis of 1 Kings 17--19." Ph.D. diss., Vanderbilt University, 1983. 245 pp.

Studies the narrative of 1 Kings 17--19 as an ironic account of a prophet who resigns his commission when he deems he is the best judge of how the mission should be performed. The irony at the structural level is magnified by dramatic and episodic irony throughout the narrative. A third level of irony is implanted in Elijah's treatment of the prophets of Baal. Gregory also shows how this story relies upon earlier biblical motifs and serves as the basis for later accounts.

0823   Gros Louis, Kenneth R. R. "Elijah and Elisha." In *Literary Interpretations of Biblical Narratives*, ed. by Kenneth R. R. Gros Louis with James S. Ackerman and Thayer S. Warshaw, 177-190. Nashville: Abingdon Press, 1974.

Discusses the characterization of Elijah and Elisha in the books of Kings, with frequent references to Shakespeare's Hamlet. The prophets are presented as channels for the powerful workings of God, yet also as human. In the context of the great clashes about them, they are ultimately still, small voices speaking the word of the Lord in a way that goes unheard.

0824   Gros Louis, Kenneth R. R. "King David of Israel." In *Literary Interpretations of Biblical Narratives, Volume II*, ed. by Kenneth R. R. Gros Louis with James S. Ackerman, 204-219. Nashville: Abingdon Press, 1982. Also published as "The Difficulty of Ruling Well: King David of Israel." *Semeia* 8 (1977): 15-33.

Surveys briefly the presentation of David in the Hebrew Bible as both a public and private character.   Gros Louis compares David in the Bible to Prince Hal in Shakespeare's Henry V. Both narratives deal with what it means to be a king, that is, with what it means for a man with his own personal desires and needs to be entrusted with the public welfare.

0825   Gross, Walter. "Lying Prophet and Disobedient Man of God in 1 King 13: Role Analysis." *Semeia* 15 (1979): 97-135.

Applies role analysis to 1 Kings 13 in order to demonstrate paradigmatically what this method can contribute to interpretation. Argues that in this text the reason for the man of God's disobedience or for the nabi's lie are unimportant; all that is important is that the man of God did disobey and that the nabi changes roles from false intermediary to genuine intermediary. Gross thinks that role analysis can deepen insight into the structure and meaning of a text, though he cautions that form criticism should always precede role analysis as a methodological step and he admits that few texts will succumb to the method of role analysis as easily as the one discussed here.

0826 Gunn, David M. "David and the Gift of the Kingdom (2 Sam 2--4, 9--20, 1 Kgs 1--2)." *Semeia* 3 (1975): 14-45.

Discusses the engaging portrait of David in these texts as representative of a narrative vision that is artistic rather than propagandistic or didactic. The central theme of the accession-rebellion-succession narrative is giving and grasping. David is presented as a complex figure who is willing to allow the kingdom to be a gift to others but who is also willing to use violence to seize the wife of Uriah. The artistic quality of the story derives from the author's ability to present human frailty sympathetically and to offer a complex vision of life that is often comic and ironic in its contrasting perspectives and conflicting norms.

0827   Gunn, David M. *The Fate of King Saul: An Interpretation of a Biblical Story.*
Sheffield: University of Sheffield Press, 1980. 181 pp.

A successful application of narrative criticism to the story of Saul in 1 Samuel 8:1--
2 Samuel 2:7. Gunn interprets the entire text as a unified narrative in its final form,
regarding the competing perspectives that might derive from compositional history as
now enhancing the work as literature. The book abounds with insight into the literary
meaning of symbols and conflicts that comprise this classic tale of an ill-fated
protagonist (Saul) and a well-favored antagonist (David). Ultimately, Gunn concludes
that Saul's downfall is due not only to his own weakness but also to fate. Saul
functions as a scapegoat--his failure expiates God's hostility over the people's desire
for a king and paves the way for David.

0828   Gunn, David M. "In Security: The David of Biblical Narrative." In *Signs and
Wonders: Biblical Texts in Literary Focus*, ed. by J. Cheryl Exum, 133-151. Atlanta:
Scholars Press, 1989.

Considers the various portraits of David offered in 1 Samuel 16--1 Kings 2, in 1
Chronicles 10--29, and in Ezra-Nehemiah. At least three pictures present themselves:
"the sweet psalmist of Israel"; "the man after God's own heart" (that is, the model man
and ideal king); and "the man of blood" (that is, the conquering warrior). Gunn
refuses to judge between these portraits, but affirms only a shifting image of David
in a story that "refuses to be tamed, secured, or neatly ordered." This article is
followed by a response from Peter D. Miscall.

0829   Gunn, David M. "A Man Given Over to Trouble: The Story of King Saul."
In *Images of Man and God: Old Testament Short Stories in Literary Focus*, ed. by
Burke O. Long, 89-112. Bible and Literature Series, 1. Sheffield: Almond Press,
1981.

A short survey of the story of Saul by a literary critic who has also given the story a
book-length treatment elsewhere (0827). Here, Gunn considers the story in the
following parts: Prologue (1 Samuel 8); Saul's Rise (1 Samuel 9--12); Saul the King:
the Philistines (1 Samuel 13--14); Saul the King: the Amalekites (1 Samuel 15); Saul
and his Rival: David at Court (1 Samuel 16:1--19:17); Saul and his Rival: David at
Large (1 Samuel 19:18--23:29); Saul and his Rival: Failure (1 Samuel 24:1--27:4);
Saul's End (1 Samuel 27:5--31:7); and Epilogue (1 Samuel 31:8--2 Samuel 7). Saul
is viewed as a tragic figure who engenders sympathy.

0830   Gunn, David M. *The Story of King David: Genre and Interpretation.* Sheffield:
University of Sheffield Press, 1978. 164 pp.

Argues for consideration of the Succession Narrative as "story" (i.e., "a work of art and
entertainment") rather than as history writing, political propaganda, or wisdom
literature. Gunn's literary interpretation reveals complex interaction of the political
and personal aspects of David's life. Central to each of these aspects are the themes
of gaining, displacement, and bequeathal of status and authority. This book was an
early and important example of narrative criticism applied to the Old Testament.
Traditional historical-critical methods are employed throughout, but are transcended
by literary interpretations.

0831 Hauser, Alan Jon, and Gregory, Russell Inman. *From Carmel to Horeb: Elijah in Crisis*. Journal for the Study of the Old Testament Supplement Series, 85/Bible and Literature Series, 19. Sheffield: Almond Press, 1990. 180 pp.

Two separate studies contained in one volume. In the first, "Yahweh Versus Death --The Real Struggle in 1 Kings 17--19," Hauser seeks to demonstrate that the conflict that gives these chapters their literary dynamic and shape is not that between Yahweh and Baal, but a deeper struggle between Yahweh and death in which Yahweh must prove his power as the god of fertility. In a second study, "Irony and the unmasking of Elijah," Gregory maintains that Elijah is portrayed ironically in 1 Kings 17--19 as a man driven by his own ambitions, that is, as one who has not yet answered the call to serve God that he urges others to accept.

0832 Humphreys, W. Lee. "The Tragedy of King Saul: A Study of the Structure of 1 Samuel 9--31." *Journal for the Study of the Old Testament* 6 (1978): 18-27.

Demonstrates the narrative unity of 1 Samuel 9--31 by analyzing the structure of the tale as a tragic story centering on Saul. The story is divided into three parts: "Saul becomes king over Israel" (9--14); "The disintegration of Saul and his kingship" (15--27); and "The last days of King Saul" (28--31). The figure of Samuel serves a distinctive literary function, appearing at the outset of each part to announce privately what is to be worked out publicly.

0833 Jackson, Jared Judd. "'David's Throne': Patterns in the Succession Story." *Canadian Journal of Theology* 11 (1965): 183-195.

A rhetorical study of the succession narrative that focuses on the relationship between David and Joab. According to Jackson's analysis, David is presented as a weak and vacillating ruler who is manipulated by the stronger Joab. The climax of this characterization comes in 2 Samuel 18--19, where Joab flagrantly disobeys the king by murdering Absalom and then humiliating the distraught father.

0834 Janzen, J. Gerald. "'Samuel Opened the Doors of the House of Yahweh' (2 Samuel 3:15)." *Journal for the Study of the Old Testament* 26 (1983): 89-96.

Suggests a literary parallel between chapters one and three of 1 Samuel in which the temple of Yahweh (in 1 Samuel 3) is to be taken as the "architectural analogue" to the womb of Hannah (in 1 Samuel 1). The reference in 3:15 to Samuel "opening the doors of the house of Yahweh" recalls his earlier emergence from the closed womb of Hannah.

0835 Klaus, N. "Bad News for David--A Literary Analysis (2 Sam 18:19-32)." *Beth Mikra* 28 (1982-1983): 358-367.

A detailed study of the story of Joab informing David of his son Absalom's death. Klaus notes the chiastic structure and the prominence of certain key words. The article is in Hebrew.

0836   Kleven, Terence. "Rhetoric and Narrative Depiction in 2 Samuel 1:1-16."
Proceedings: Eastern Great Lakes Biblical Society 9 (1989): 59-73.

Analyzes stylistic characteristics of this pericope to indicate that its rhetorical purpose
within the narrative is to demonstrate David's regard for the anointed of the Lord.
Thus, a rhetorical examination does not permit an interpretation of the passage that
posits David as secretly delighted to hear of Saul's death.

0837   Lasine, Stuart. "Judicial Narratives and the Ethics of Reading: the Reader as
Judge of the Dispute between Mephibosheth and Ziba." *Hebrew Studies* 30 (1989):
49-69.

Discusses 2 Samuel 19 as a judicial narrative that draws the reader into evaluating and
judging the characters through the presentation of ambiguous evidence. Lasine
believes that, on the basis of what the narrator reveals, the reader is expected to judge
Mephibosheth negatively and to recognize that David is precipitous and self-
interested in this pericope.

0838   Lasine, Stuart. "Melodrama as Parable: The Story of the Poor Man's Ewe
Lamb and the Unmasking of David's Topsy-Turvy Emotions." *Hebrew Annual Review*
8 (1984): 101-124.

Describes Nathan's story of the ewe lamb as a one-dimensional melodrama, which
elicits from David a melodramatic response. Yet the parable fails to right David's
topsy-turvy emotions, for later in the narrative he is still portrayed as ruled by
fluctuations between excessive emotion and callous indifference.

0839   Levenson, Jon D. "I Samuel 25 as Literature and History." In *Literary
Interpretations of Biblical Narratives, Volume II*, ed. by Kenneth R. R. Gros Louis with
James S. Ackerman, 220-242. Nashville: Abingdon Press, 1982.

Describes the literary craft of the narrator in 1 Samuel 25 in a way that denies
generalizations made about the Hebrew Bible by Auerbach in his *Mimesis* (0128).
The narrator functions differently in 1 Samuel than in Genesis 22, which formed the
basis for Auerbach's observations. Here, characters are presented as personifications
of character types prominent in wisdom literature: Nabal represents the fool (as his
name suggests) and Abigail, the wise. Levenson concludes with some comments on
the episode's pivotal function within the narrative as a whole and with some
observations on the historical events that may lie behind the tale.

0840   Long, Burke O. "Historical Narrative and the Fictionalizing Imagination."
Vetus Testamentum 35 (1985): 405-416.

Analyzes fictional elements in 1 Kings 20 as a demonstration of how Israelite
historians presented their picture of Israel's past with creative imagination. The
account here is structured rather artificially as a chiasm with negotiations between
Ben-hadad and Ahab forming the outer parameters (1-11, 31-34), two battles forming
the inner ones (12-21, 23-30), and the prophet's council forming the transitional center
(22).

0841   Long, Burke O. "Wounded Beginnings: David and Two Sons." In *Images of Man and God: Old Testament Short Stories in Literary Focus*, ed. by Burke O. Long. Bible and Literature Series, 1. Sheffield: Almond Press, 1981.

Considers the story of Amnon, Tamar, David, and Absalom in 2 Samuel 13--14 as an episode in the larger narrative that is in itself satisfying and complete. The archetypal pattern of the story (harmony--disruption--restoration) parallels that of the Genesis creation story (cosmos--chaos--cosmos). In this sense, the events of this human tragedy enact the deeply biblical and human pattern--the struggle to make whole what continues to be disrupted.

0842   Long, V. Philips. *The Reign and Rejection of King Saul: A Case for Literary and Theological Coherence*. Society of Biblical Literature Dissertation Series, 118. Atlanta: Scholars Press, 1989. 276 pp.

A narrative-critical reading of 1 Samuel 9--15 that hopes, by examining the literary dynamics of the story, to also shed new light on its historical and theological difficulties. Long discovers a greater degree of narrative coherence throughout the material than is usually recognized. For example, he argues that the Gilgal episode in 13:7b-15a is *not* out of place. This leads to a reading of chapters 13--14 as a description and defense of the rejection of Saul.

0843   Martin, John A. "The Literary Quality of 1 and 2 Samuel." *Bibliotheca Sacra* 141 (1984): 131-145.

Notes two literary devices used in presenting the material in the books of Samuel: (1) juxtaposition of characters in order to show conflicts resolved by the care of God in exalting those faithful to the covenant; and (2) stress on a reversal-of-fortune motif to show that Yahweh lifts the needy.

0844   McConville, J. G. "Narrative and Meaning in the Books of Kings." *Biblica* 70 (1989): 31-49.

A survey of key passages in the books of Kings that attempts to show their development of common themes. McConville thinks the literary approach, which treats the books of Kings as a coherent document, has turned up evidence that calls for re-consideration of theories involving multiple authorship of the books. He also compares Kings to Judges, viewing the former as a "mirror image" of the latter.

0845   Miscall, Peter D. *1 Samuel: A Literary Reading*. Indiana Studies in Biblical Literature. Bloomington: Indiana University Press, 1986. 256 pp.

A commentary on 1 Samuel that makes use of a variety of literary-critical methodologies. Miscall's eclectic approach treats the book as part of a larger entity, Genesis--Kings, which he believes is held together by plot, characters, and theme. His commentary discovers literary and thematic patterns within the text of 1 Samuel, as well as pointing out gaps, ambiguities, and contradictions that must be regarded as deliberate and so left unresolved. Tensions in the characterization of David (devout shepherd vs. calculating warrior) are especially notable. See also 1616.

0846   Moore, Rick Dale. *God Saves: Lessons from the Elisha Stories*. Journal for the Study of the Old Testament Supplement Series, 95. Sheffield: JSOT Press, 1990. 175 pp.

Studies the stories in 2 Kings 5; 6:8-23; and 6:24--7:20 as "didactic salvation stories." Moore's methodology is basically that of form criticism, enhanced by appreciation for literary artistry.

0847   Nelson, Richard D. "The Anatomy of the Book of Kings." *Journal for the Study of the Old Testament* 40 (1988): 39-48.

A study in point of view in the book of Kings that makes use of Boris Uspensky's typology of four planes on which point of view might be expressed (ideological, phraseological, spatial/temporal, and psychological). Nelson concludes that the reader may be encouraged to distrust the point of view of the narrator.

0848   Parker, Kim Ian. "Narrative Tension in 1 Kings 1--11: A Study of the Structural and Thematic Unity of the Solomonic Narrative." Ph.D. diss., McMaster University (Canada), 1988.

Attempts to show that the narrative tension between the portrayal of Solomon as both Israel's ideal and apostate king can be explained through a holistic reading without recourse to historical or source hypotheses. The two dream theophanies (1 Kings 3:4-15; 9:1-10) function as fulcrums that balance the narrative in two sections. The unifying theme of both sections is Solomon's relationship with Torah and Wisdom.

0849   Parker, Kim Ian. "Repetition as a Structuring Device in 1 Kings 1--11." *Journal for the Study of the Old Testament* 42 (1988): 19-27.

Provides a close reading of the first eleven chapters of 1 Kings, which has traditionally been viewed as a heterogenous mix of materials, in order to demonstrate narrative coherence. Parallels exist between introductory (1--2) and concluding (11:14-43) frame stories. Two major sections begin with a dream (3:1-15, 9:1-10a) and end with an episode concerning Solomon's attitude toward God (6--8, 11:1-3). Each section consists of four internal episodes with parallels between the first two of the first section and the last two of the second section, and between the last two of the first section and the first two of the second section.

0850   Perdue, Leo G. "'Is There Anyone Left of the House of Saul . . .?': Ambiguity and Characterization of David in the Succession Narrative." *Journal for the Study of the Old Testament* 30 (1984): 67-84.

Proposes that the narrator's characterization of David is intentionally ambiguous, so that two different interpretations of David emerge: (1) a dynamic character who attempts to rule his kingdom with compassion and forgiveness, but changes at the end of his life to an embittered old man who relies on ruthless force, and (2) a static figure who is consistently ruthless, demanding loyalty and promoting only his own self interests. Such ambiguity may reflect the ambiguity with which Israel regarded the institution of the monarchy in general.

0851   Polzin, Robert M. *Samuel and the Deuteronomist: A Literary Study of the Deuteronomistic History: 1 Samuel.* San Francisco: Harper and Row, 1989. 296 pp.

A sequel to 0655. Polzin studies 1 Samuel as part of a larger, anti-monarchical narrative that extends from Deuteronomy through 2 Kings. He is especially adept at pointing out parallels and repetitions within 1 Samuel, or between 1 Samuel and the larger work. Polzin regards the Deuteronomistic Historian as a creative author and proposes "a parabolic reading" of the work. One particularly interesting aspect of this study is its suggestion that "sons" serve as metaphors for kings.

0852   Ridout, George. "The Rape of Tamar: A Rhetorical Analysis of 2 Sam. 13:1-22." In *Rhetorical Criticism*, ed. by Jared J. Jackson and Martin Kessler, 75-84. Pittsburgh Theological Monograph Series, 1. Pittsburgh: Pickwick Press, 1974.

Studies the phenomenon of repetition in the account of 2 Samuel 13:1-22 and notes a chiastic structure for the passage. Ridout stresses especially the repetitive use of the words "brother" and "sister," and the contrast between "love" and "hate" that appears at the extremes (13:1, 22) and center (13:15) of the chiasm.

0853   Ritterspach, A. D. "Rhetorical Criticism and the Song of Hannah." In *Rhetorical Criticism*, ed. by Jared J. Jackson and Martin Kessler, 68-74. Pittsburgh Theological Monograph Series, 1. Pittsburgh: Pickwick Press, 1974.

Considers the form, internal structure and key words of 1 Samuel 2:1-10 in a manner that reveals the passage to be a profound theological statement that is, at the same time, intensely personal and human.

0854   Robertson, David. "Micaiah ben Imlah: A Literary View." In *The Biblical Mosaic: Changing Perspectives*, ed. by Robert Polzin and Eugene Rothman, 139-146. Philadelphia: Fortress Press, 1982.

Presents a literary reading in 1 Kings 22, paying special attention to the role of the narrator. The text sets up expectations that are not fulfilled in any straightforward way, so that the narrator is effectively distanced from the characters of the story and from some of its conclusions. This essay shows how a modern literary critic might deal with problematic implications in this text--it is juxtaposed in the volume *Biblical Mosaic* with two other essays, one by Goldenberg that demonstrates how ancient rabbis treated the text (0821) and one by Wolfgang Roth that surveys traditional historical-critical interpretations.

0855   Rosenberg, Joel W. "1 and 2 Samuel." In *The Literary Guide to the Bible*, ed. by Robert Alter and Frank Kermode, 122-145. Cambridge, MA: Belknap Press, 1987.

Surveys the account of Israel's history provided in these two books and concludes that the books are a work of national self-criticism. The Samuel collection recognizes that Israel could not have survived without a dynastic royal house, but that house and its subjects are held accountable to standards of prophetic justice.

0856   Rosenberg, Joel W.   "The Institutional Matrix of Treachery in 2 Samuel 11." *Semeia* 46 (1989): 103-118.

Seeks to show the role that the story of David and Bathsheba plays in the political history of the larger narrative (the Succession Document). Attention to several details in the story ascribe weight to the institutional factors that form a portrait of this political history of Israel. Such details include the king's interaction with his servants, his court's relation to the distant battlefield, his relation to the institutions of holy war and mercenary combat, his sense of protocol and priorities, his manner of conveying and receiving information, and his vulnerability to manipulation, public scrutiny, and court gossip. Together, these factors build a tragic situation in which David is the criminal and the nation is both his accomplice and his victim.

0857   Roth, Wolfgang.   "You are the Man! Structural Interaction in 2 Samuel 10 --12." *Semeia* 8 (1977): 1-13.

Applies Crossan's method of phenomenological-structural analysis (1690) to this text. Whereas Crossan's approach dealt primarily with parable, Roth expands the method to deal here with myth and polemic as other types of story. What is characteristic about 2 Samuel 10--13 is interaction of parable, polemic, and myth. The study suggests that, while the final redactors of the Deuteronomistic History may have been "myth makers," they preserved parable and polemic in a dialectic tension with myth and so kept the jagged edges and disturbing limits that those elements of story provide.

0858   Savran, George.   "1 and 2 Kings." In *The Literary Guide to the Bible*, ed. by Robert Alter and Frank Kermode, 146-164. Cambridge, MA: Belknap Press, 1987.

Proposes an overall chiastic structure for these two books and discusses the narrator's techniques for characterization, especially with regard to moral judgments. Extended treatment is given to the character of Solomon and to the treatment of three themes: the covenant with David, the Temple, and the fulfillment of oracles.

0859   Shea, William H.   "Chiasmus and the Structure of David's Lament." *Journal of Biblical Literature* 105 (1986): 13-25.

Examines both the poetic form and the thematic elements of 2 Samuel 1:19-27 and determines that both are structured chiastically. In terms of form, the lines of the poem consist of increasingly longer couplets until, at the center, the process reverses and the couplets become progressively shorter. Chiastic ordering of thematic elements complements this intricate formal design.

0860   Sternberg, Meir, and Perry, Menakhem.   "The King through Ironic Eyes: Biblical Narrative and the Literary Reading Process." *Poetics Today* 7 (1986): 275-322.

Analyzes "gaps" in the biblical story of David and Bathsheba and proposes ways in which the reader may try to fill these. The story calls for multiple systems of gap-filling in a manner analogous to Henry James' novel, *The Turn of the Screw*.

Questions left unanswered as a result of the narrator's reticence can be answered in mutually exclusive ways. Such questions include, "Does Uriah know about his wife's doings?" and "What does David think Uriah thinks?" The article focuses on narrative structure as a basis for reader construction (or deconstruction) of a text.

0861   Viviano, Pauline Antoinette. "A Literary Study of 2 Kings 17:7-41." Ph.D. diss., Saint Louis University, 1981. 210 pp.

A literary analysis of 2 Kings 17:7-14. Viviano determines that the text is an emphatic statement of sin and punishment followed by a story and comment, equally emphatic, about the necessity of exclusive worship of Yahweh.

0862   Waldman, Nahum M. "Two Biblical Parables: Irony and Self-Entrapment." *Dor le Dor* 15 (1986-1987): 11-18.

Analyzes the parable told by the wise woman of Tekoa and the parable told by Nathan as examples of entrapment: the parable is designed to engage the listener, but the ficticity of the story is not disclosed until after that listener has responded.

0863   Wicke, Donald W. "The Structure of 1 Sam. 3: Another View." *Biblische Zeitschrift* 30 (1986): 256-258.

Notes a chiasm in this chapter of 1 Samuel: A--Samuel's career in the shadow of Eli (1); B--Eli and Samuel in darkness (2-3); C--Yahweh breaks through (4-10); C'--Yahweh speaks (11-14); B'--Samuel and Eli in light (15-18); A'--Samuel's career as a prophet.

1, 2 CHRONICLES

See also 0828.

0864   Dillard, Raymond B. "The Literary Structure of the Chronicler's Solomon Narrative." *Journal for the Study of the Old Testament* 30 (1984): 85-93.

Explores the Chronicler's presentation of Solomon (2 Chronicles 1--9) as a chiastic narrative. The center of the chiasm focuses on the divine response in 2 Chronicles 7:11-22, in which God speaks to Solomon (12-18) and to the people (19-22).

0865   Duke, Rodney K. *The Persuasive Appeal of the Chronicler: A Rhetorical Analysis*. Journal for the Study of the Old Testament Supplement Series, 88/Bible and Literature Series, 25. Sheffield: Almond Press, 1990. 240 pp.

A rhetorical-critical examination of three modes of persuasion in Chronicles: "logos" (appeal based on logical reasoning); "ethos" (appeal based on character of narrator);

and "pathos" (appeal to emotions of audience). The Chronicler retells the history of Israel with rhetorical skill that moves from an inductive presentation of his thesis to a more propositional form of argumentation.

0866 Solomon, Anne M. "The Structure of The Chronicler's History: A Key to the Organization of the Pentateuch." *Semeia* 46 (1989): 51-64.

Looks for a common grid for narrative organization of traditions that may undergird both the Chronicler's history and the Pentateuch. The Chronicler's history betrays a structural pattern of five units: (1) Genealogical Introduction (1 Chronicles 1--9); (2) David (1 Chronicles 10--29); (3) Solomon (2 Chronicles 1--9); (4) Four Generations of Struggle (2 Chronicles 10--36); (5) Four Generations to Restoration (Ezra-Nehemiah). The Pentateuch exhibits a parallel scheme: (1) Introduction; (2) Abraham; (3) Isaac; (4) Four Generations of Strife from Jacob to Moses; (5) Four Generations from Exodus to Inheritors of the Land. Thus the basic outline for both is (1) Introduction; (2) Covenant; (3) Sanctuary; (4) Affliction in Four Stages; (5) Return in Four Stages. Further evidence that such generational thinking contributed to the structuring of traditions can be seen by the fact that the five-fold pattern is also present within Exodus 16--Deuteronomy 34 in a manner superfluous to its overall presence in Genesis 1--Deuteronomy 34.

0867 Talmon, Shemaryahu. "1 and 2 Chronicles." In *The Literary Guide to the Bible*, ed. by Robert Alter and Frank Kermode, 365-374. Cambridge, MA: Belknap Press, 1987.

Though included in a "literary guide," this article treats 1 and 2 Chronicles from the traditional perspective of historical criticism. Discussion of "content," "historical scope," "structure," "authorship and date," and "place in the canon" do not touch on issues uncovered by traditional introductions.

EZRA, NEHEMIAH

See also 0628, 0828.

0868 Eskenazi, Tamara C. "Ezra-Nehemiah: From Text to Actuality." In *Signs and Wonders: Biblical Texts in Literary Focus*, ed. by J. Cheryl Exum, 165-197. Atlanta: Scholars Press, 1989.

Shows how Ezra-Nehemiah programmatically and pervasively combines form and content to articulate a central theme, namely "the actualization of the written text in the life of the community." The book exemplifies the primacy of written texts by its overall structure and by its use of letters and memoirs. This article is followed by a response from David J. A. Clines.

0869   Eskenazi, Tamara C. *In an Age of Prose: A Literary Approach to Ezra-Nehemiah*. Society of Biblical Literature Monograph Series, 36. Atlanta: Scholars Press, 1988. 211 pp.

Divides Ezra and Nehemiah into three sections (Ezra 1:1-4; Ezra 1:5--Nehemiah 7:72; Nehemiah 8:1--13:31) and shows how each part contributes to the development of three central themes: centrality of the community as a whole; expansion of the "house of God" to encompass the city as a whole; centrality of written texts as a source of authority. Eskenazi also studies the characters of Ezra and Nehemiah and compares the two-volume work to 1 Esdras.

0870   Eskenazi, Tamara C. "The Structure of Ezra-Nehemiah and the Integrity of the Book." *Journal of Biblical Literature* 107 (1988): 641-656.

Studies the contribution that repetition of lists makes to reading Ezra-Nehemiah as a narrative whole. As a literary critic working with the Masoretic text, Eskenazi assumes unity of Ezra-Nehemiah (and the separation of both from Chronicles). His structural analysis demonstrates that the work possesses a certain internal logic when read this way.

0871   Talmon, Shemaryahu. "Ezra and Nehemiah." In *The Literary Guide to the Bible*, ed. by Robert Alter and Frank Kermode, 357-364. Cambridge, MA: Belknap Press, 1987.

Treats the books of Ezra and Nehemiah as exemplary of biblical historiography. Describes the structure of the current two-volume complex as organized in three constituent blocks, each of which is composed of the same types of sub-units. Structural devices include closing invocations, summary notations, and resumptive repetition.

ESTHER

See also 0584, 0601, 0605, 0632, 0645, 0658, 0718, 1550.

0872 Goldman, Stan. "Narrative and Ethical Ironies in Esther." *Journal for the Study of the Old Testament* 47 (1990): 15-31.

Identifies three types of irony found in the book of Esther--rhetorical, generative, and intuitive--and traces their influence for an ethical reading of the book. The ironies reveal the ethical and unethical assumptions behind the Jewish attack against the Persians, generate a vision of how to live with dual loyalties (Jewish and Gentile), and depict a demystification of the Jews that includes Jewish solidarity and self-criticism.

0873   Sasson, Jack M.   "Esther."   In *The Literary Guide to the Bible*, ed. by Robert Alter and Frank Kermode, 335-342.   Cambridge, MA: Belknap Press, 1987.

A short, narrative reading of this tale, attentive to such matters as characterization and point of view.   The story features unambiguously drawn characters and fully resolved situations.   Originally, it served to explain the Jewish festival of Purim, but now can be read for pleasure, as a story in which brutal villains receive their due while the proud and the lovely are vindicated.

JOB

See also 0601, 0608, 0632, 0637, 0658, 0660.

0874   Bezuidenhout, L. C.   "Struktuur en strekking van Job 38:39--39:30 (The Structure and Meaning of Job 38:39--39:30)."   *Hervormde Teologiese Studies* 43 (1987): 709-722.

Approaches Job as a literary work of art, noting the codes that function in the work as points of departure.   In particular, the systematic presentation of aspects of the animal kingdom in Job 38:39--39:30 is examined.   They draw attention to God's providence without forcing God's actions into a system of mechanical causality.

0875   Brenner, Athalya.   "Job the Pious?:   The Characterization of Job in the Narrative Framework of the Book."   *Journal for the Study of the Old Testament* 43 (1989): 37-52.

Combines modern literary analysis with source criticism to describe the relationship between the prosaic and poetic portions of Job.   Brenner supposes that the current work represents a traditional folktale (the prosaic portion) that is transformed by the poetic dialogues.   The dialogues challenge and demolish the naive thinking of what now serves as the framework of the story.

0876   Clines, David J. A.   "The Arguments of Job's Three Friends."   In *Art and Meaning: Rhetoric in Biblical Literature*, ed. by David J. A. Clines, David M. Gunn, and Alan J. Hauser, 199-214.   Sheffield, England: JSOT Press, 1982.

Discusses the rhetoric of the speeches in Job in two stages.   First, Clines comments on tonality, nodal sentences, topoi, and verb modality, especially as these elements are significant for coherence.   Second, he demonstrates the distinctive viewpoints of each of Job's friends by signaling coherence in each set of speeches by a single character, and differences between each set of speeches and those offered by the other characters.

0877   Clines, David J. A. "False Naivety in the Prologue of Job." *Hebrew Annual Review* 9 (1985): 127-136.

Proposes a reading of the prologue to Job that allows it to be read as consistent with the poetic part of the book that follows. Clines suggests that the prologue is cunningly wrought in order to give an "appearance of artlessness." The prologue beguiles naive readers into finding a reflection of their own shallowness in the text. This subtle conveyance of "a false naivety" serves as an entrance to the dialogues, in which the questions raised by the prologue are explored in depth. See also 0879.

0878   Cooper, Alan. "Narrative Theory and the Book of Job." *Studies in Religion* 11 (1982): 35-44.

Offers a diagram of the plot structure of Job. The story exhibits a chiastic arrangement as follows: Order-Curse-Argument-Accusation-Disorder-Accusation-Argument-Curse-Order.

0879   Cooper, Alan. "Reading and Misreading the Prologue to Job." *Journal for the Study of the Old Testament* 46 (1990): 67-79.

Attempts to bolster Clines' argument for regarding the prologue to Job as a subtle portion of the narrative intended to play off of the reader's initial false assumptions (0877). Cooper notes that the text contains no causal connection between Job's piety and his prosperity, but that such a connection is typically provided by the reader's presuppositions. Ultimately, the prologue to Job lures the reader into grappling with profound questions by offering diverse leads but no definitive answers. Readers are forced to come up with their own answers and, so, to learn something about themselves.

0880   Crossan, John Dominic, ed. *The Book of Job and Ricoeur's Hermeneutics.* *Semeia* 19 (1981). 123 pp.

Presents four exegetical studies of Job 38 by scholars who consciously follow the hermeneutic of Ricoeur's *Interpretation Theory* (0017). The studies are "Job or the Impotence of Religion and Philosophy" by André Lacocque; "Job 38 and God's Rhetoric" by Michael V. Fox; "Satanic Semiotics, Jobian Jurisprudence" by Richard Jacobson; and "Reading Ricoeur Reading Job" by David Pellauer. Six more essays are then presented that comment on the first four: "The Sense of the Text and a New Vision" by Frederick J. Bolton; "Three Ways in Text Interpretation" by Donald R. Buckey; "Speech and Silence in Job" by Robert Paul Dunn; "Cosmos and Covenant" by Walter James Lowe; "The *Silence* of Job as the Key to the Text" by Alan M. Olson; and "Deconstruction, Plurivocity, and Silence" by Allan Patriquin. An introduction to the hermeneutic of Ricoeur and a bibliography compiled by Loretta Dornisch is also included.

0881   Fontaine, Carole R.   "Folktale Structure in the Book of Job."   In *Directions in Biblical Hebrew Poetry*, ed. by Elaine R. Follis, 205-232. *Journal for the Study of the Old Testament Supplement Series*, 40.   Sheffield: JSOT Press, 1987.

Takes a formalist approach, analyzing the "morphology of Job" according to the thirty-one functions of a folktale discerned by Propp in his classic study of Russian stories (0202).   Fontaine concludes that the work does meet the criteria adequately to be considered a "poeticized folktale."   Taken together, the narrative and poetic portions form a tale of the "victim-hero" type, though admittedly one of considerable complexity.

0882   Girard, René.   *Job: The Victim of His People*.   Trans. by Yvonne Freccero. Stanford, CA: Stanford University Press, 1987.   173 pp.

A biblical study by an eminent scholar of social anthropology (0031-0034).   Girard applies his theory of victimization to the book of Job.   The theory holds that the only irreducible dichotomy is that between victim and persecutor.   Scapegoating represents a common but unsuccessful attempt at reducing this dichotomy, one that tries to disguise the role of the victim.   This attempt is evident in the book of Job, but scripture refuses the disguise.   The reader must choose either to accept the arguments of Job's friends or to accept Job's arguments and regard him as genuine victim. Girard encourages the second option, for to accept the first makes the reader an accomplice of the persecutors.   See also 0889, 0898.

0883   Greenberg, Moshe.   "Job."   In *The Literary Guide to the Bible*, ed. by Robert Alter and Frank Kermode, 283-304.   Cambridge, MA: Belknap Press, 1987.

Surveys the book of Job as "the classic expression in world literature of the irrepressible yearning for divine order, baffled but never stifled by the disarray of reality."   Greenberg especially appreciates the poetry of the book, which is "continually astonishing in its power and inventiveness."

0884   Gros Louis, Kenneth R. R.   "The Book of Job."   In *Literary Interpretations of Biblical Narratives*, ed. by Kenneth R. R. Gros Louis with James S. Ackerman and Thayer S. Warshaw, 226-266.   Nashville: Abingdon Press, 1974.

Surveys the book of Job as a unified narrative and lists the themes that it develops: the book insists that righteousness and obedience must be based on personal integrity rather than on a desire for reward, since even the innocent suffer and one cannot expect happiness whatever one does.   Job also demonstrates the limits of religious dogma and the ultimate impossibility of understanding God.

0885   Habel, Norman C.   "The Narrative Art of Job: Applying the Principles of Robert Alter."   *Journal for the Study of the Old Testament* 27 (1983): 101-111.

Demonstrates the usefulness of Alter's literary approach to the Old Testament (0607) by applying it to the book of Job.   Habel demonstrates the literary unity of Job (long doubted by historical scholars) in a manner similar to that which Alter uses to demonstrate the coherence of the Joseph story.   He also finds an internal dialectic between narration and dialogue, an artistic use of repetition in the technique of type scenes, and an application of reticence and absence in characterization. See also 1539.

0886   Hoffman, Yair. "Irony in the Book of Job." *Immanuel* 17 (1983-1984): 7-21.

Identifies various types of irony to be found in the book of Job--on the part of Job himself, his friends, and God, and especially on the part of the author. The mythical character of the dialogue is interpreted as a final irony of the author.

0887   Johns, Donald Arvid. "The Literary and Theological Function of the Elihu Speeches in the Book of Job." Ph.D. diss., Saint Louis University, 1983. 213 pp.

Considers the contribution that the speeches of Elihu make to the book of Job. Elihu combines characteristics of the wise man and the prophet, drawing heavily on traditions of his namesake, Elijah. Elihu not only corrects Job, but also his three friends, providing a needed transition to the speeches of the Lord.

0888   Lacocque, André. "Job and the Symbolism of Evil." *Biblical Research: Journal of the Chicago Society for Biblical Research*. 14-15 (1979-1980): 7-19.

Provides a reading of the symbolism of evil in Job informed by Paul Ricoeur's books *The Symbolism of Evil* and *Conflict of Interpretations* (0016). Lacocque moves from consideration of retribution to discussion of the radical demoralization of the universe manifested in Job 38. At the end, Job's suffering is less in need of being compensated by God than is God's creation in need of being vindicated by humanity. The story shows that humans fear God for nought, but that, to our astonishment, it is also for nought that God loves humans.

0889   Levine, Baruch. "René Girard on Job: The Question of the Scapegoat." *Semeia* 33 (1985): 125-133.

A response to the first few chapters of 0882, which were published in this journal. Levine argues that Job's "heroic dissidence" cannot be considered illustrative of the scapegoat phenomenon as conceived in the Ancient Near East because there is no connection between Job's suffering and the well-being of the community. He draws on Leviticus 16 and Isaiah 52--53 and insists on the need to understand literature within the context of the culture and society in which it was written.

0890   Lichtenstein, Aaron. "Irony in the Book of Job," *Dor le Dor* 13 (1984): 41-42.

Says that the whole book of Job is built on a basic irony: the reader is informed in the prologue of something that Job does not understand, namely that there is a partial contradiction between the doctrine of retribution and the doctrine of freedom of choice. Hence the reader recognizes the irony in the words of the four messengers ("I alone escaped to tell you") and in the words of Elihu (33:12), but Job does not.

0891   Lichtenstein, Aaron. "Toward a Literary Understanding of the Book of Job." *Hebrew Studies* 20/21 (1979-1980): 34-35.

Says that, from a literary standpoint, the reader of Job is not party to the revelation Job receives from the whirlwind, and so must rely on the prologue to find an answer to the question of why this just man has been tormented.

0892   Loyd, Douglas Emory. "Patterns of Interrogative Rhetoric in the Speeches of the Book of Job." Ph.D. diss., The University of Iowa, 1986. 328 pp.

Examines the use of interrogatives in the speeches of Job. Two types of questions are identified: "propositional questions," which call for a yes or no response; and "wh-questions," which call for something more (who, what, where, why). The study reveals a distinctive structure in the speeches of the friends of Job and demonstrates dramatically the central significance of chapter 21.

0893   Miller, Ward S. "The Structure and Meaning of Job." *Concordia Journal* 15 (1989): 103-120.

Analyzes the literary style and structure of Job, which Miller regards as "a masterpiece of literary skill." The study focuses particularly on the use of antithesis and contrast, on six themes that interact throughout the narrative, and on the symmetry of the book.

0894   Penchansky, David. *Betrayal of God: Ideological Conflict in Job*. Literary Currents in Biblical Interpretation. Louisville, KY: Westminster/John Knox Press, 1990. 124 pp.

Examines inconsistencies between Job's beliefs and actions from the perspective of neo-Marxist postmodern literary criticism. The book offers a positive response to the experience of undeserved suffering by affirming the validity of human pain and rejecting common theological explanations for it.

0895   Penchansky, David. "Dissonance in Job: The Weight of Literary and Theological Conflict." Ph.D. diss., Vanderbilt University, 1988. 207 pp.

Explores three aspects of literary dissonance in Job: the portrayal of Job as both blasphemous and pious, the representation of Yahweh as both approving and disapproving of Job, and the absence of Satan in the text after the text has established his importance in the prologue. These are considered with reference to formalist, Marxist, and deconstructive theories, and with regard for the work of Fredric Jameson and Pierre Macherey.

0896   Perdue, Leo G. *Wisdom in Revolt: Metaphorical Theology in the Book of Job*. Journal for the Study of the Old Testament Supplement Series, 112/Bible and Literature Series, 29. Sheffield: Almond Press, 1990. 290 pp.

A comprehensive study of wisdom materials in the Bible, with accent on Job. Perdue seeks to synthesize narrative criticism with research into anthropology, myth, and metaphor. His ultimate interest is in giving wisdom its rightful place in a historical reconstruction of ancient Israelite religion.

0897   Polzin, Robert, and Robertson, David, eds. *Studies in the Book of Job*. *Semeia* 7 (1977). 154 pp.

Contains three major articles that offer literary perspectives on the book of Job, and a number of responses to these articles by other scholars. The three articles are (1) "The Comedy of Job," by J. William Whedbee, which proposes that the most apt generic description for the book in its final form is comedy; (2) "Toward a Dramatic Reading of the Book of Job," by Luis Alonso-Schökel, which first explores the interplay of the characters among themselves and with the audience and then discusses the creative tension in the work between the two conceptions of God's justice presented there; and (3) "Gagging on Job, or the Comedy of Religious Exhaustion" by John J. Miles, which discusses Job as exemplary of the inadequacy of both religion and literature to enculturate values for the modern world.

0898   Radzinowicz, Mary Ann. "How and Why the Literary Establishment Caught Up With the Bible: Instancing the Book of Job." *Christianity and Literature* 39 (1989): 77-89.

Uses examples of studies on the book of Job to indicate the manner in which secular and non-Christian literary critics have recently "seized scripture back as their own best exegetical proving-ground." Radzinowicz concentrates on Richards' *Beyond* (0899) and on Girard's *Job: The Victim of His People* (0882), with some reference also to Frank Kermode, Geoffrey Hartman, Moshe Greenberg, and Gabriel Josipovici.

0899   Richards, Ivor Armstrong. *Beyond*. New York: Harcourt Brace Jovanovich, 1974.

Contends that the meaning of Job is indeterminate, if the poetic center and folk-tale frame are read together. The interchangeable moral seriousness of Job and Shaddai (God) give the poetic drama its unified focus. Job's protests are to be read as Shaddai's self-criticism, a reading that requires the reader's "liberated mind" to go beyond the words that Shaddai speaks from the whirlwind, to go beyond them in the direction of Job's intuition. See also 0898.

0900   Rodd, Cyril. *The Book of Job*. Narrative Commentaries. Philadelphia: Trinity Press International, 1990.

Announced for publication.

0901   Scholnick, Sylvia Huberman. "Poetry in the Courtroom: Job 38--41." In *Directions in Biblical Hebrew Poetry*, ed. by Elaine R. Follis, 185-204. Journal for the Study of the Old Testament Supplement Series, 40. Sheffield: JSOT Press, 1987.

Analyzes the poetic response of God in Job 38--41 to determine the nature of its connection to the charges Job brought against God earlier. The force of God's queries is to discredit Job's accusation that God has unlawfully appropriated his property. Job charged God with being an unjust Judge, but the divine response casts God in the role not of Judge, but of King. By responding to the charges, God accepts accountability to the human system of justice but also reveals that divine justice is inherent in the Lord's sovereignty over the universe.

0902   Van der Lugt, Pieter. "The Form and Function of the Refrains in Job 28: Some Comments Relating to the 'Strophic' Structure of Hebrew Poetry." In *The Structural Analysis of Biblical and Canaanite Poetry*, ed. by Willem van der Meer and Johannes C. de Moor, 265-293.   Journal for the Study of the Old Testament Supplement Series, 74. Sheffield: JSOT Press, 1988.

Takes the famous "Hymn to Wisdom" in Job 28 as an example for the investigation of strophic structures in Hebrew poetry (cf. 0669). Van der Lugt finds that the hymn exhibits a very rigid poetic framework, constructed in three uniform stanzas of eight verse-lines, preceded by an introductory section of four lines. Each of the three stanzas, furthermore, is composed of two uniform sub-stanzas of four lines, similar to the introductory section. This article is presented in tandem with another by Van der Lugt that presents a historical survey of research on strophes and stanzas in Job.

PSALMS

See also 0510, 0514, 0562, 0564, 0587, 0591, 0601, 0608, 0632, 0642, 0672, 1550, 1599.

0903   Allen, Leslie C. "The Value of Rhetorical Criticism in Psalm 69." *Journal of Biblical Literature* 105 (1986): 577-598.

A rhetorical analysis of the psalm that lays special emphasis on structural and stylistic features. Allen notes major and minor "pauses" in the psalm's composition that both emphasize its textual integrity and indicate a different structural outline than has been suggested previously. Light is also shed upon the individual flair given to traditional forms in the rhetorical style of this psalm.

0904   Alonso-Schökel, Luis. "The Poetic Structure of Psalm 42--43." *Journal for the Study of the Old Testament* 1 (1976): 4-11.

A structural analysis of the two psalms, read as one, on three levels: image structure, dialogue, and dynamic structures. The dynamic movement of the psalm from nostalgia to the future is noted, along with the interplay between the sense of God's absence and the sense of God's presence (which is created by the awareness of God's absence).

0905   Alter, Robert. "Psalms." In *The Literary Guide to the Bible*, ed. by Robert Alter and Frank Kermode, 244-262. Cambridge, MA: Belknap Press, 1987.

Includes observations under the subheadings, "Genre," "Style," "Structure," and "Themes." The two most prominent genres are supplication and praise, but genre should not be considered a fixed entity or viewed as a reliable index of *Sitz im Leben*. The psalms are more traditional stylistically than other kinds of biblical poetry: figurative language is abundant, but word plays are scarce. Structure was improvised to meet the needs of the individual poem, though a certain penchant for "envelope structure" (returning at the end to words or ideas expressed at the beginning) is discernible. Themes cut across genre distinctions: death and rebirth, e.g., is equally prominent in the supplications and the thanksgivings.

0906   Berlin, Adele. "On the Interpretation of Psalm 133." In *Directions in Biblical Hebrew Poetry*, ed. by Elaine R. Follis, 141-147. *Journal for the Study of the Old Testament Supplement Series*, 40. Sheffield: JSOT Press, 1987.

Interprets Psalm 133 as a work that contains a "word chain"--a particularly cohesive literary device whereby each line of a poem is linked to the next by the recurrence of a common word: word A occurs in lines 1 and 2, word B in lines 2 and 3, and so on. According to Berlin, the word chain in Psalm 133 has not been recognized as such and this has led to misperceptions about the psalm's structure and meaning. Berlin does not read it as a wisdom psalm, but as an ode to Zion with religious and national meaning.

0907   Berry, Donald Kent. "Traditional Approaches and a Reader-Oriented Analysis of Psalm 18." Ph.D. diss., The Southern Baptist Theological Seminary, 1987. 223 pp.

Offers interpretations of Psalm 18 from the perspectives of textual, form, rhetorical, and reader-response criticism. The reader-response approach discusses networks of signals for the reader, isolates and typifies the text's speech acts, and examines ancient and contemporary contexts for reading the psalm.

0908   Brueggemann, Walter. *Abiding Astonishment: Psalms, Modernity, and the Making of History*. Literary Currents in Biblical Interpretation. Louisville, KY: Westminster/John Knox Press, 1991. 96 pp.

Examines the social-political function of the psalms, focusing on Psalms 78, 105, 106, and 136. Brueggemann attempts to read these psalms in relation to "voices of marginality," experiencing their message as both liberating affirmation and as controlling censure.

0909   Ceresko, Anthony R. "A Poetic Analysis of Ps 105, with Attention to Its Use of Irony." *Biblica* 64 (1983): 20-46.

Attempts to redeem literary appreciation for this psalm by calling attention to subtle literary devices, especially irony. For example, the psalm notes ironically that Joseph becomes a "servant" of the Lord by being sold as a "slave," and it refers repeatedly to the land that belongs to various nations, after first asserting that the earth is

Yahweh's. Ceresko is also concerned with implications of his analysis for consideration of the psalm's structure.

0910   Collins, Terrence. "Decoding the Psalms: A Structural Approach to the Psalter." *Journal for the Study of the Old Testament* 37 (1987): 41-60.

A structuralist study of the entire book of Psalms which is viewed as an integrated system. The study discovers different types of hidden structures that reveal an inherent cohesion despite the random surface arrangement of elements. The underlying message of the book is encoded within an implicit story framework that operates at the subconscious level of assumptions and patterns of thinking. Collins attempts to delineate this underlying story framework according to an actantial model.

0911   Curtis, Adrian. *The Book of Psalms*. Philadelphia: Trinity Press International, forthcoming.

Announced for publication.

0912   Durlesse, James Arthur. "A Rhetorical Critical Study of Psalm 19, 42, and 43." *Studia Biblica et Theologia* 10 (1980): 179-197.

Proposes that Psalm 19A and 19B were not separate compositions later joined together (as the traditional theory holds), but that 19B was composed to conform to the already existing 19A. This thesis is bolstered by analysis of rhetorical criteria and internal structure of the two sections of Psalm 19. Psalms 42--43 appear to have been composed in the same fashion and should be read together.

0913   Grossberg, Daniel. "The Disparate Elements of the Inclusio in Psalms." *Hebrew Annual Review* 6 (1982): 97-104.

Examines a particular kind of inclusion whereby the closing words of a psalm parallel the opening words, but do not repeat those words verbatim (as in Psalm 8). Grossberg studies Psalms 26, 29, 47, 82, and 97. He suggests that the alterations are a guard against monotony. They introduce an element of surprise into an overall impression of symmetry.

0914   Kselman, John S. "'Why have you abandoned me?': A Rhetorical Study of Psalm 22." In *Art and Meaning: Rhetoric in Biblical Literature*, ed. by David J. A. Clines, David M. Gunn, and Alan J. Hauser, 172-198. Sheffield, England: JSOT Press, 1982.

A translation of Psalm 22, with notes on its rhetorical features. Kselman views the structure of the psalm as tripartite: a lament in 2-22, a thanksgiving in 23-27, and a universal chorus of praise in 28-32. Vertical and horizontal perspectives mark all three sections.

0915   Kuntz, J. Kenneth. "The Canonical Wisdom Psalms of Ancient Israel: Their Rhetorical, Thematic and Formal Dimensions." In *Rhetorical Criticism*, ed. by Jared J. Jackson and Martin Kessler, 186-222. Pittsburgh Theological Monograph Series, 1. Pittsburgh: Pickwick Press, 1974.

Identifies nine rhetorical or stylistic features of wisdom psalms: (1) comparative proverbs making use of "better sayings"; (2) numerical sayings; (3) admonitions (with or without motive clauses; (4) addresses to pupils as "sons"; (5) formulas using words such as "Happy are those who . . . "; (6) rhetorical questions; (7) similies; (8) acrostic arrangements of colas; and (9) second-person discourse aimed horizontally toward humanity rather than vertically toward deity.

0916   Kuntz, J. Kenneth. "Psalm 18: A Rhetorical-Critical Analysis." *Journal for the Study of the Old Testament* 26 (1983): 3-31.

A rhetorical-critical analysis of Psalm 18 that includes attention to the following: (1) strophic structure; (2) style and vocabulary; (3) essential unity of the composition; (4) use of diverse divine names and epithets; and, (5) spatial imagery.

0917   Lenowitz, Harris. "The Mock-*śimha* of Psalm 27." In *Directions in Biblical Hebrew Poetry*, ed. by Elaine R. Follis, 153-159. *Journal for the Study of the Old Testament Supplement Series*, 40. Sheffield: JSOT Press, 1987.

Suggests that the "song" (*simha*) that the captors request in Psalm 27 is a song of joy and goes on to demonstrate that a mock song of joy lies at the heart of Psalm 27. Lenowitz's definition of *simha* as a song of joy may have implications for the interpretation of other passages in the Old Testament where this term is used.

0918   McCann, J. Clinton, Jr. "Psalm 73: An Interpretation Emphasizing Rhetorical and Canonical Criticism." Ph.D. diss., Duke University, 1985. 274 pp.

A study of Psalm 78 from three perspectives: form criticism, rhetorical criticism, and canonical criticism. The section on rhetorical criticism notes significant repetitions and reversals, which emphasize contrasts between the psalmist and the wicked.

0919   McCarthy, David Paul. "A Not-So-Bad Derridean Approach to Psalm 23." *Proceedings: Eastern Great Lakes Biblical Society* 8 (1988): 177-192.

Offers a deconstructive, almost tongue-in-check reading of the 23rd Psalm, by which the sheep is viewed as ultimately to be placed on the table (altar) as a sacrifice. The reading illustrates the Derridean principle that texts ultimately embarrass their own ruling system of logic because they are filled with *aporia* that allow for infinite, contradictory readings.

0920   Robertson, David. "Literary Criticism of the Bible: Psalm 90 and Shelley's 'Hymn to Intellectual Beauty.'" *Semeia* 8 (1977): 35-50.

Regards Psalm 90 as more exemplary of "pure literature" than of "religious literature" because the thought-emotions experienced in reading this psalm are brought about primarily by literary rather than religious means. By comparing the psalm to a masterpiece by Shelley, Robertson shows that it is an aesthetic object that can be evaluated and appreciated independently of religious belief.

0921   Ryken, Leland. "Metaphor in the Psalms." *Christianity and Literature* 31,3 (1982): 9-29.

Considers metaphor in the psalms from four perspectives: as a rhetorical figure (the metaphor itself); metaphor and the reader (the obligations that metaphor imposes on a reader); metaphor and the poet (why poets speak metaphorically); and, metaphor and reality (the ontological question of whether metaphor expresses truth).

0922   Van der Meer, Willem. "Psalm 110: A Psalm of Rehabilitation." In *The Structural Analysis of Biblical and Canaanite Poetry*, ed. by Willem van der Meer and Johannes C. de Moor, 207-234. Journal for the Study of the Old Testament Supplement Series, 74. Sheffield: JSOT Press, 1988.

A comprehensive structural analysis of the psalm, with discussion of its exegetical treatment in both Old and New Testament studies. Van der Meer finds that attention to both structure and content bring out the same theme: expulsion from rulership and subsequent restoration.

Proverbs

See also **0562, 0601, 0604-0605, 0608, 0642, 0672.**

0923   Camp, Claudia V. *Wisdom and the Feminine in the Book of Proverbs*. Bible and Literature Series, 13. Sheffield: Almond Press, 1985. 352 pp.

Examines six literary motifs in the Bible that can be brought to bear on the female figures in Proverbs: (1) the wife as household manager and as counselor to her husband; (2) the lover; (3) the harlot and adulteress; (4) the wise woman; (5) the use by women of indirect means to achieve divine ends; (6) the activity of women as authenticators of tradition. Each of these images illuminates some aspect of personified Wisdom in Proverbs. Camp integrates her literary analysis with socio-historical concerns.

0924 Lichtenstein, Murray H. "Chiasm and Symmetry in Proverbs 31." *Catholic Biblical Quarterly* 44 (1982): 202-211.

Points out stylistic and structural analogies between the two poems in Proverbs 31, "The Words of Lemuel" (1-9) and "The Excellent Wife" (10-31). Though once independent units, the two now complement each other. Each of the poems considered separately exhibits an internal chiasm.

0925 Silberman, Lou H. "Toward A Rhetoric of Midrash: A Preliminary Account." In *The Biblical Mosaic: Changing Perspectives*, ed. by Robert Polzin and Eugene Rothman, 15-26. Philadelphia: Fortress Press, 1982.

Offers an example of midrashic interpretation, by which reflections on the concluding verses of Proverbs are linked progressively to passages from Genesis, Exodus, Deuteronomy, and Jeremiah. The ultimate meaning of Proverbs 31:29-31 is explicated in light of Exodus 19:1-2.   This study forms part of a collection of essays demonstrating various literary approaches to the Bible--the ancient practice of midrashic interpretation is considered to be similar in some respects to modern literary analyses.

0926 Williams, James G. "Proverbs and Ecclesiastes." In *The Literary Guide to the Bible*, ed. by Robert Alter and Frank Kermode, 263-282. Cambridge, MA: Belknap Press, 1987.

Reflects on the contributions of these two works as representative of a distinctive way of looking at the world, a way that depicts a "vital order informed by retributive justice." The proverbs are presented as poetic compositions, exalted speech that is better captured in the King James Version of the Bible than in modern English translations. Proverbs are of different kinds and make use of such literary elements as riddles, intensification, narrativity, and metaphoric play. The distinctive feature of Ecclesiastes is its appeal to the rhetoric of argumentation and individual experience rather than to ancient tradition.

ECCLESIASTES

See also **0587, 0604, 0632, 0637, 0658.**

0927 Fox, Michael V. *Qoheleth and His Contradictions*. Journal for the Study of the Old Testament Supplement Series, 71/Bible and Literature Series, 18. Sheffield: Almond Press, 1989. 384 pp.

A commentary on Ecclesiastes that emphasizes the book's rhetorical structures and literary features.   Fox formulates systematically the implicit assumptions and convictions that are present in Ecclesiastes, drawing special attention to the numerous self-contradictions. Central issues discussed are life's meaning, toil and pleasure, wisdom, and justice.

0928 Gros Louis, Kenneth R. R. "Ecclesiastes" In *Literary Interpretations of Biblical Narratives*, ed. by Kenneth R. R. Gros Louis with James S. Ackerman and Thayer S. Warshaw, 267-282. Nashville: Abingdon Press, 1974.

Distinguishes between the author of Ecclesiastes and "the Preacher" as a created character. The Preacher's comments on life find a sympathetic response on the part of the reader, but the Preacher himself is less appealing. The Preacher regards order in the world as depressing because it is not centered in humanity. Ultimately, though, the reader need not find pessimism in this work, but only blunt and painful self-awareness.

0929 Johnson, Raymond Eugene, Jr. "The Rhetorical Question as a Literary Device in Ecclesiastes." Ph.D. diss., Southern Baptist Theological Seminary, 1986. 333 pp.

Seeks to determine the impact of rhetorical questions in Ecclesiastes on the structure, argument and mood of the book. Also, the questions are examined as a literary device in order to determine their impact on the reader.

0930 Ogden, Graham S. "The 'Better'-Proverb (*Tob Spruch*), Rhetorical Criticism, and Qoheleth." *Journal of Biblical Literature* 96 (1977): 489-505.

Examines the particular use of the comparative ("better than") proverb in Ecclesiastes. It serves as a specifying statement for an introductory admonition, as well as "providing a fulcrum about which complementary values move."

0931 Viviano, Pauline Antoinette. "The Book of Ecclesiastes: A Literary Approach." *The Bible Today* 22 (1984): 79-84.

Analyzes the literary patterns in Ecclesiastes 1--2 as providing the paradigm for reading the remainder of the book. The key is 1:2, repeated in 12:8 and thus forming an inclusio.

SONG OF SOLOMON

See also 0601, 0608, 0632, 0666, 0996, 1599.

0932 Falk, Marcia. *Love Lyrics from the Bible: A Translation and Literary Study of the Song of Songs*. Sheffield: Almond Press, 1982. 142 pp.

Presents Song of Solomon as a collection of 31 independent love poems. Falk also identifies four basic contexts, five recurring themes, and six central motifs that are found in several of the poems.

0933 Gros Louis, Kenneth R. R. "The Song of Songs." In *Literary Interpretations of Biblical Narratives, Volume II*, ed. by Kenneth R. R. Gros Louis with James S. Ackerman, 243-258. Nashville: Abingdon Press, 1982.

Interprets the Song as a statement of perspective or point of view. The poet has created a world where beauty is sensual and where sensuality is beautiful. The reader is permitted to perceive the world through the senses of two lovers. The lyrics of the poem are not so much about love as they are about what love thinks it sees.

0934 Landy, Francis. *Paradoxes and Paradise: Identity and Difference in the Song of Songs*. Bible and Literature Series, 7. Sheffield: Almond Press, 1983. 410 pp.

Attempts to read the Song of Solomon with appreciation for its ability to appeal to the senses as much as to the intellect. Landy intends to free the Song from biblical criticism that would adapt it doctrinally or provide it with "a safely distant historical niche." Rather, the Song concerns human intimacy and so must be understood through the processes of imagination and with critical tools sharpened by psychoanalysis. Landy's reading finds that the theme of the book is the process of fusion and differentation. With references to Genesis, the Song speaks of paradise in terms of imaginative transcendence: paradise exists in the world only through being inaccessible to it.

0935 Landy, Francis. "The Song of Songs." In *The Literary Guide to the Bible*, ed. by Robert Alter and Frank Kermode, pp. 305-319. Cambridge, MA: Belknap Press, 1987.

Analyzes the imagery of the Song as a metaphor for "the discovery of a common identity between discrete terms." The Song is not simply about human love but about sign and referent--ultimately, it is about the poetic process. The lovers are two persons, but the poem is their composite speech. Each of them represents an aspect of the poet. The most astonishing characteristic of the poem is the dominance and initiative of the female, who is metaphorically aligned with the feminine aspect of divinity. Thus, the Song reverses the predominantly patriarchal theology characteristic of much of the Bible.

0936 Segal, Benjamin J. "Four Repetitions in the Song of Solomon." *Dor le Dor* 16 (1987-1988): 32-39.

Notes the use of repeated "guide words" in the Song of Solomon that convey the meaning of the work as a whole. Most of the words treated here have clear sexual implications.

0937 Shea, William H. "The Chiastic Structure of the Song of Songs." *Zeitschrift für die alttestamentliche Wissenschaft* 92 (1980): 378-396.

Proposes that the entire Song of Songs is structured chiastically into six sections (1:2 --2:2; 2:3-17; 3:1--4:16; 5:1--7:10; 7:11--8:5; 8:6-14), an arrangement that suggests it is a unified composition rather than a collection of miscellaneous love songs.

THE PROPHETS

See also 0510, 0608, 0660.

0938   Dick, Michael Brennan. "Prophetic *Poiesis* and the Verbal Icon." *Catholic Biblical Quarterly* 46 (1984): 226-246.

Proposes that the demise of prophetic literature in Israel was due, ironically, to a self-contradiction inherent in the prophetic critique of idol-making. The prophets railed against the idea that human craft could produce any representation of the divine but, as the writing prophets honed their literary skill, they became vulnerable to their own critique.

0939   Geller, Stephen A. "Were the Prophets Poets?" *Prooftexts: A Journal of Jewish Literary History* 3 (1983): 211-221.

Explores the tension between the roles of "prophet" as a mouthpiece of God and "poet" as one who crafts one's own speech. Israel's prophets would be considered false prophets if they were suspected of molding their own prophecies. Nevertheless, an examination of the levels of meaning apparent in Isaiah 40:6-8 reveals that this prophet displays poetic ability and so may be regarded as a poet today.

0940   Gottwald, Norman K. "Tragedy and Comedy in the Latter Prophets." *Semeia* 32 (1984): 83-96.

Contends that, although prophetic books themselves are not coherent narratives, they can be read in terms of the "implied narrative" that lies behind them. The implied narrative behind the books of the latter prophets concerns the destruction of both northern and southern kingdoms, but also the national identity that continued in restoration and dispersion. Thus, these books are structured as comedy rather than as tragedy, for salvation has the final word over judgment.

0941   House, Paul R. *The Unity of the Twelve.* Journal for the Study of the Old Testament Supplement Series, 97/Bible and Literature Series, 27. Sheffield: Almond Press, 1990. 262 pp.

A close reading that demonstrates an essential unity of the twelve "minor prophets," which in the Hebrew canon are grouped as one book. House identifies common literary motifs and literary themes.

0942   Jumielity, Thomas. *Satire in the Hebrew Prophets* (title tentative). Literary Currents in Biblical Interpretation. Louisville, KY: Westminster/John Knox Press, forthcoming.

Announced for publication.

0943   Marks, Herbert. "The Twelve Prophets." In *The Literary Guide to the Bible*, ed. by Robert Alter and Frank Kermode, 207-233. Cambridge, MA: Belknap Press, 1987.

Struggles with the heterogeneous character of the "Book of the Twelve Prophets." Many of the books contained within this collection are themselves products of redaction, so that the text "challenges our common habit of construing meaning with reference to the intentions of an imagined author." Ultimately, Marks comments on the various books individually, emphasizing the interplays of "voice and text" and of "vision and revision" that are found there.

0944   Murray, D. F. "The Rhetoric of Disputation: Re-Examination of a Prophetic Genre." *Journal for the Study of the Old Testament* 38 (1987): 95-121.

Attempts to define a genre of prophetic oracles in terms of a basic rhetorical strategy. Oracles that utilize the rhetoric of "disputation" may be grouped together, even though they differ in structural pattern. The rhetoric of disputation involves three steps, which must be present or implied: thesis, counter-thesis, and dispute.

0945   Williams, James G. "Irony and Lament: Clues to Prophetic Consciousness." *Semeia* 8 (1977): 51-74.

Investigates irony as a means of expression for the biblical prophets, with special reference to the *hôy*-form employed by Amos, Isaiah, and Micah. Primary focus is placed on the form of lament itself, with consideration also of such poetic devices as paranomasis, attribution, exaggeration, and repetition of images. Ironic poetry is seen as indicative of the existential tensions of the prophets, a tension that results from being caught between God and people.

ISAIAH

See also 0584, 0637, 0672, 0889, 0945, 1283, 1308.

0946   Alonso-Schökel, Luis. "Isaiah." In *The Literary Guide to the Bible*, ed. by Robert Alter and Frank Kermode, 165-183. Cambridge, MA: Belknap Press, 1987.

Regards the book of Isaiah as a "collection of collections" and does not attempt to find unity of form or content in the diverse material. The focus, rather, is on the literary qualities of the various poets represented. Attention is given to such devices as parallelism, onomatopoeia, and personification. Alonso-Schökel considers the most interesting aspect of the poets found in the first part of Isaiah to be their ability to transform experienced reality into a new, coherent, poetic universe. Deutero-Isaiah, he claims, ranks among the great religious poets of history.

0947 Clines, David J. A. *I, He, We, They: A Literary Approach to Isaiah 53.* Journal for the Study of the Old Testament Supplement Series, 1. Sheffield: JSOT Press, 1976. 65 pp.

An early attempt at reading an Old Testament text not only in terms of what it says, but also in terms of what it does *not* say. In addition, Clines draws on rhetorical criticism to describe how Isaiah 53 says what it does, and he describes the poem as a "language event."

0948 Exum, J. Cheryl. "Isaiah 28-32: A Literary Approach." In *Society of Biblical Literature 1979 Seminar Papers*, ed. by Paul J. Achtemeier, 2 vols., 1:123-152. Missoula, MT: Scholars Press, 1979.

Attempts to read Isaiah 28--32, which is usually regarded as an editorial collection of independent oracles, as a literary whole. Interpretation of the text as it now stands focuses on interrelations of key themes, the function of tropes, and the employment of rhetorical devices. Exum's study looks primarily at chapter 28, discovering that this chapter establishes patterns and themes that also hold for 28--32 as a whole. For example, 28:1-6 moves from judgment to promise, as does 28--32 as a unit. Also the whole collection in 28--32 demonstrates a development from confusion to clarity that parallels a similar development in chapter 28 alone. The central concern of 28--32 is to demonstrate the wisdom of Yahweh.

0949 Exum, J. Cheryl. "Of Broken Pots, Fluttering Birds, and Visions in the Night: Extended Simile and Poetic Technique in Isaiah." *Catholic Biblical Quarterly* 43 (1981): 331-352.

Presents a close reading of three texts from Isaiah (30:12-14; 31:4-5, and 29:1-14) in demonstration of the premise that the meaning of an image cannot be reduced to what it signifies. Figurative language derives its power from the capacity to suggest multiple meanings, but this lack of precision does not prevent it from conveying meaning with deftness.

0950 Exum, J. Cheryl. "'Whom will he teach knowledge?': A Literary Approach to Isaiah 28." In *Art and Meaning: Rhetoric in Biblical Literature*, ed. by David J. A. Clines, David M. Gunn, and Alan J. Hauser, 108-139. Sheffield, England: JSOT Press, 1982.

Emphasizes the rhetorical unity of Isaiah 28 and its relationship to the larger context of Isaiah 28--32. Exum is less interested in the editorial arrangement of the individual oracles than in the meaning that they take on when read in their present context. Cf. 0948.

0951 Geller, Stephen A. "A Poetic Analysis of Isaiah 40:1-2." *Harvard Theological Review* 77 (1984): 413-424.

Examines these two verses of Isaiah as an example of Geller's views on parallelism (0636). Parallelism is not simply redundant prose, but a sophisticated device that "activates all levels of language." Biblical verse attains through parallelism what other poetics attain through metaphor. In the case of the Isaiah passage, two planes of meaning are established--syntactic and allusive. The parallelism contributes to ambiguity, opening up simultaneous possibilities of meaning.

0952   Gitay, Yehoshua. "Isaiah and His Audience." *Prooftexts: A Journal of Jewish Literary History* 3 (1983): 223-230.

A reader-response analysis of Isaiah 1--39, with attention to structure and to theories of multiple authorship. The rhetoric of Isaiah's speeches in 1--9 receives the most attention.

0953   Gitay, Yehoshua. *Prophecy and Persuasion. A Study of Isaiah 40--48.* Forum Theologiae Linguisticae, 14. Bonn: Linguistica Biblica, 1981. 242 pp.

A rhetorical-critical study of Deutero-Isaiah. Gitay uses categories of classical rhetoric to determine the individual rhetorical units of which this book is composed. Each unit is organized according to an established pattern: introduction, thesis, statement of facts, confirmation, refutation, and conclusion. The type of persuasive strategy of each unit is classified in terms of the types of argument used (e.g., rational, emotive, ethical).

0954   Gros Louis, Kenneth R. R.   "Isaiah: Chapters 40--55."   In *Literary Interpretations of Biblical Narratives*, ed. by Kenneth R. R. Gros Louis with James S. Ackerman and Thayer S. Warshaw, 208-225. Nashville: Abingdon Press, 1974.

Describes Second Isaiah as analogous to a song or poem written for an army returning from battle. The themes are not new, but the tone is celebrative, written to encourage, revitalize, and renew.

0955   Holmgren, Frederick. "Yahweh the Avenger. Isaiah 63:1-6." In *Rhetorical Criticism*, ed. by Jared J. Jackson and Martin Kessler, 133-148. Pittsburgh Theological Monograph Series, 1. Pittsburgh: Pickwick Press, 1974.

Establishes points of unity between the oracles in Isaiah 63:1-6 and Isaiah 60--62 by identifying the role of Yahweh in the oracle as that of a blood avenger for the nation. Holmgren is primarily interested in the historical question of authorship, but he makes numerous observations about the rhetorical character of the oracle in his study. He discerns a double chiastic structure for Isaiah 63:1-6.

0956   Jackson, Jared Judd. "Style in Isaiah 28 and a Drinking Bout of the Gods (RS 24.258)". In *Rhetorical Criticism*, ed. by Jared J. Jackson and Martin Kessler, 85-98. Pittsburgh Theological Monograph Series, 1. Pittsburgh: Pickwick Press, 1974.

Discusses the poetic diction of Isaiah 28 with emphasis on stylistic devices and structure. Jackson also compares the passage with the satirical account of a banquet for the gods found in the Ugaritic Ras Shamra text.

0957   Johnston, Ann. "The Concept of Waiting in the Isaianic Corpus: A Rhetorical Critical Study of Selected Texts." Ph.D. diss., Boston University, 1986. 311 pp.

Examines stylistic and rhetorical features, as well as specific literary forms, images, and allusions in order to explicate the meaning of "waiting" in the Isaianic literature. Waiting is understood as "a call to enter actively into the creative activity of God."

0958   Korpel, Marjo C. A. "The Literary Genre of the Song of the Vineyard (Isa 5:1-7)." In *The Structural Analysis of Biblical and Canaanite Poetry*, ed. by Willem van der Meer and Johannes C. de Moor, 119-155. Journal for the Study of the Old Testament Supplement Series, 74. Sheffield: JSOT Press, 1988.

Analyzes the poetic structures of Isaiah 5:1-7 in order to determine the literary genre of the song. Particular attention is paid to rhyme and assonance. Korpel concludes that the song is best ascribed to the genre of allegory, although it makes slight use of the genres of love song and lawsuit as well.

0959   Kuntz, J. Kenneth. "The Contribution of Rhetorical Criticism to Understanding Isaiah 51:1-16." In *Art and Meaning: Rhetoric in Biblical Literature*, ed. by David J. A. Clines, David M. Gunn, and Alan J. Hauser, 140-171. Sheffield, England: JSOT Press, 1982.

Cites seven ways in which Isaiah 51:1-61 emphasizes that deliverance is near: presentation of Yahweh in the first-person; use of the divine imperative; deft use of imagery; repetition of key words and phrases; use of contrast; employment of rhetorical questions; and use of direct quotation. Kuntz also provides a verse-by-verse rhetorical analysis of the individual strophes in this poem.

0960   Lewis, Dale James. "A Rhetorical Critical Analysis of Isaiah 24--27." Ph.D. diss., The Southern Baptist Theological Seminary, 1985. 220 pp.

Examines the "Isaiah apocalypse" from the perspective of rhetorical criticism. Lewis attempts to determine the genre, form, and function of the literature, and pays special attention to the external literary structure of the unit.

0961   Nielsen, Kirsten. *There is Hope for a Tree: The Tree as Metaphor in Isaiah.* Journal for the Study of the Old Testament Supplement Series, 65. Sheffield: JSOT Press, 1989. 301 pp.

Studies the use of the tree image in Isaiah 1--39, demonstrating the manner in which images become available for re-use and re-interpretation in biblical texts. She considers both the "informative" and "performative" functions of the metaphor, and says the use of metaphorical language encourages continual reinterpretation of the original proclamation. She also tries to extrapolate historical conclusions from her essentially literary study, relating the development of the image to hypotheses concerning dating of the relevant material.

0962   Sacon, Kiyoshi K.   "Isaiah 40:1-11.   A Rhetorical-Critical Study."   In *Rhetorical Criticism*, ed. by Jared J. Jackson and Martin Kessler, 99-116.   Pittsburgh Theological Monograph Series, 1.   Pittsburgh: Pickwick Press, 1974.

Represents, with complex diagrams, the rhetorical structure of this passage, using sentence units as the basis for the analysis.   Sacon finds that "an exceedingly high structure is efficiently handled . . . along with various techniques of poetical and phonological artristry."

0963   Walsh, Jerome T.   "The Case for the Prosecution: Isaiah 41:21--42:17."   In *Directions in Biblical Hebrew Poetry*, ed. by Elaine R. Follis, 101-118.   *Journal for the Study of the Old Testament Supplement Series*, 40.   Sheffield: JSOT Press, 1987.

Investigates the stylistic and logical structure of this section of Isaiah to demonstrate its coherence as a literary unit.   The unit can be divided into three sections (41:21-29; 42:1-8; 42:9-17), each of which displays a careful symmetry, as does the passage as a whole.   Logical coherence is provided when the passage is read as a "case for the prosecution in a trial scene," that is, as Yahweh's challenge to the claim of other gods.

0964   Watts, John D.   "The Characterization of Yahweh in the Vision of Isaiah."   *Review and Expositor* 83 (1986): 439-450.

Offers six suggestive roles that may partially represent the way Yahweh is portrayed by the titles, metaphors, images, adjectives, and so on in Isaiah 1--66: Heavenly King, Practical Strategist, Prudent Owner/Cultivator of the Land, Possessive Patron of Jerusalem, Covenant God of Israel, and The Eternal One: High and Holy.   Thus, Yahweh is presented as a well-rounded, open, and complex character.

0965   Webster, Edwin C.   "The Rhetoric of Isaiah 63--65."   *Journal for the Study of the Old Testament* 47 (1990): 89-102.

Outlines the poetic structures of Isaiah 63:7--64:11 and of Isaiah 65, using the same approach as in 0966.   The first poem (63:7--64:11) has three pairs of clusters, each of which is marked by repeated use of a key word or phrase.   The second poem (65), also has a triadic structure, with common themes linked by verbal repetitions.

0966   Webster, Edwin C.   "A Rhetorical Study of Isaiah 66."   *Journal for the Study of the Old Testament* 34 (1986): 93-108.

Proposes a rhetorical structure for Isaiah 66 based, not on metrical considerations, but on concentric arrangement and repetition of *Leitworte* (characteristic terms).   The chapter divides into three units: an oracle (1-6), a riddle and a song praising Jerusalem (7-14), and another oracle (15-24).   Each of the three units displays a concentric pattern.

JEREMIAH

See also 0348, 0666, 0821, 1459.

0967   Clendenen, E. Ray. "Discourse Strategies in Jeremiah 10:1-10." *Journal of Biblical Literature* 106 (1987): 401-408.

Uses rhetorical criticism to identify the discourse strategy of this passage in its current form, even though the passage is traditionally regarded as having a complex textual history. Clendenen identifies three devices or strategies by which the present text achieves its effect: contrast, chiasmus, and code-switching (shifting from one language to another in order to generate conversational inferences). The latter device is seen in v. 11, where Aramaic prose is used in an otherwise Hebraic text.

0968   Cole, Ronald Dennis. "The Idolatry Polemics in the Book of Jeremiah: A Study in Prophetic Rhetoric." Ph.D. diss., New Orleans Baptist Theological Seminary, 1984. 242 pp.

Analyzes rhetorically the passages in Jeremiah that address worship of gods other than Yahweh. Chapter 1 contains a rhetorical analysis of terms related to deity. Chapter 2 considers terms for the cult. Chapter 3 looks at the forms of Jeremiah's polemic, which are largely traditional forms adapted through chiasmus, inclusio, repetition, ellipsis, and expansion. Chapter 4 summarizes motifs related to deity, to humanity, and to nature in these passages.

0969   Diamond, A. R. *The Confessions of Jeremiah in Context: Scenes of Prophetic Drama.* Journal for the Study of the Old Testament Supplement Series, 45. Sheffield: JSOT Press, 1987. 308 pp.

A contextual study of the "confessions" passages in Jeremiah (11:18--12:6; 15:10-21; 17:14-18; 18:18-23; 20:7-18). Diamond interprets the passages within their literary context and with regard for the dynamics of "dramatic dialogue" between the prophet and God, and between the prophet and God versus Israel.

0970   Dorn, Luis. "The Unexpected as a Speech Device: Shifts of Thematic Expectancy in Jeremiah." *The Bible Translator* 37 (1986): 216-222.

Notes the use in Jeremiah of figures and standard expressions that usually convey well-being but that are shifted to convey themes of evil, punishment, or doom. Such a device is also used in Amos (1:3--2:3), Hosea (9:14) and Isaiah (5:1-7). Examples in Jeremiah include 2:2-3; 4:29-31; 6:1-5; 11:16; 12:13; 13:12-14.

0971   Edlin, James Oliver. "Literary Design in Jeremiah 30--33." Ph.D. diss., Southern Baptist Theological Seminary, 1985. 189 pp.

Demonstrates the literary design of Jeremiah 30--33 created by the interplay of verbal elements. First, Edlin studies the small units of paragraphs, poems, and oracles. Next, he demonstrates networks of relationships that exist between the various units, describing how the small units combine to form divisions, sections, blocks, and eventually the whole composition.

0972   Fishbane, Michael, and Hartman, Geoffrey.   "'A Wretched Thing of Shame, A Mere Belly: An Interpretation of Jeremiah 20:7-12' and 'Jeremiah 20:7-12:   A Literary Response.'"   In *The Biblical Mosaic: Changing Perspectives*, ed. by Robert Polzin and Eugene Rothman, 169-195.   Philadelphia: Fortress Press, 1982.

Juxtaposes two distinct literary readings of Jeremiah's prayer.   Fishbane uncovers the prayer's dynamic structure and tries to establish a connection between this structure and Jeremiah's renewed hope and confidence.   Hartman regards the prayer as belonging to the genre of "crying or shouting" rather than to the "modalities of speech with which we usually associate literature."   Hartman's essay also outlines issues that he sees as significant for biblical scholarship in general.

0973   Heinemann, Joseph.   "A Homily on Jeremiah and the Fall of Jerusalem."   In *The Biblical Mosaic: Changing Perspectives*, ed. by Robert Polzin and Eugene Rothman, 27-41.   Philadelphia: Fortress Press, 1982.

Considers the midrashic interpretation of Jeremiah offered in *Pesquita Rabbati, Pisqa* 26.   The interpretation presents Jeremiah as a complex figure torn by conflicting emotions, and thereby revolves all discrepancies in his behavior.   Heinemann notes that, even in ancient times, the question of creativity in interpretation was significant.   Rabbis, like modern scholars, debated the relative value of metaphorical and literal readings.

0974   Holladay, William L.   *The Architecture of Jeremiah 1--20*.   London: Associated University Presses, 1976.   204 pp.

A study of the formal structure of the book of Jeremiah that uses rhetorical criticism.   This book was one of the earliest attempts to move beyond form criticism in an effort to apply rhetorical criticism to large units of material (as opposed to smaller units).   Rhetorical criticism identifies the distinctive features of units (repetitions, parallels, contrasts, and so on) and thereby allows for inductive structural analysis.

0975   Lewin, Ellen Davis.   "Arguing for Authority: A Rhetorical Study of Jeremiah 1:4-19 and 20:7-18."   *Journal for the Study of the Old Testament* 32 (1985): 105-119.

Explores the rhetorical connection between the call narrative in Jeremiah 1:4-19 and the final "confession" in Jeremiah 20:7-18, two passages that have been identified as forming an inclusio.   Lewin shows that the second passage not only completes the argument at one level, but also advances it to the next stage.   The passage in chapter 20 points forward, as well as back, citing the evidence of previous oracles to establish the prophet's authority as firmly as possible.   Lewin's understanding of rhetorical criticism is more in line with modern literary theory than that of many biblical scholars, for she is interested not only in how Jeremiah might have affected his audience, but also in how his message is determined and affected by his audience.

0976 Lundbom, Jack R. *Jeremiah. A Study in Ancient Hebrew Rhetoric*. Society of Biblical Literature Dissertation Series, 18. Missoula, MT: Scholars Press, 1975. 195 pp.

Primarily a study of two rhetorical devices in the book of Jeremiah: inclusio and chiasmus. These are found both within the individual speeches and within the organization of the book as a whole. The former instances may be attributed to the prophet's own use of well-known homiletical devices and the latter to Baruch's preparation of the manuscript for use in temple worship. See also 0979.

0977 Rosenberg, Joel W. "Jeremiah and Ezekiel." In *The Literary Guide to the Bible*, ed. by Robert Alter and Frank Kermode, 184-206. Cambridge, MA: Belknap Press, 1987.

Holds that the key to a literary reading of these books is making sense of the interplay between prophecy and traditionary memory--both works contain not only the words of their alleged authors, but also reflections of others. In Jeremiah, the distinction between prophecy and tradition corresponds largely to that between poetry and prose. Ezekiel is more homogeneous. With regard to Jeremiah, Rosenberg also discusses chiastic structures for the book and the implications these have for making sense of its confusing chronology.

0978 Trible, Phyllis. "The Gift of a Poem: A Rhetorical Study of Jeremiah 31:15-22." *Andover Newton Quarterly* (1977): 271-280.

Analyzes this poem as a chiasm of five strophes with the following pattern: words of a woman (Rachel), words to a woman (Yahweh to Rachel), words of a man (Ephraim), words of a woman (Yahweh), and words to a woman (Jeremiah to Israel).

0979 Willis, John T. "Dialogue Between Prophet and Audience as a Rhetorical Device in the Book of Jeremiah." *Journal for the Study of the Old Testament* 33 (1985): 63-82.

Supplements Lundbom's identification of the two chief rhetorical devices in Jeremiah as chiasm and inclusio (0976) by indicating a third: dialogue between the prophet and his audience. Willis analyzes six pericopes (3:21--4:4; 5:12-17; 8:13-17; 8:18-23; 14:1-10; 14:17--15:4) in order to illustrate the presence of the device and its significance for the structure of the book.

LAMENTATIONS

0980 Landy, Francis. "Lamentations." In *The Literary Guide to the Bible*, ed. by Robert Alter and Frank Kermode, 329-334. Cambridge, MA: Belknap Press, 1987.

Treats the five laments, each with its own perspective, as literature tied to historical circumstance and as literature that must communicate its own inadequacy in order to succeed. The "obtrusively formal" pattern of the acrostic structures used here represent an attempt to mitigate catastrophe by housing it in a familiar literary framework.

0981   Mintz, Alan. "The Rhetoric of Lamentations and the Representation of Catastrophe." *Prooftexts: A Journal of Jewish Literary History* 2 (1982): 1-17.

Examines the skillful use of language in the book of Lamentations as expression of the traumatized relations of God and Israel after the destruction of Jerusalem. Personification of the experiences of the individual in the collective entity serves to preserve the emotive power of pity and anger. Shifts of speaker and of point of view effectively portray lamentation as the discourse of Israel and consolation as the discourse of God.

0982 Renkema, Johan. "The Literary Structure of Lamentations." In *The Structural Analysis of Biblical and Canaanite Poetry*, ed. by Willem van der Meer and Johannes C. de Moor, 294-396. Journal for the Study of the Old Testament Supplement Series, 74. Sheffield: JSOT Press, 1988.

A comprehensive analysis of the poetic structure of the book of Lamentations. Renkema divides the entire work into cantos, canticles, sub-cantos, and strophes and notes the interconnections between these various units.

EZEKIEL

See also 0621, 0977.

0983   Allen, Leslie C. "Ezekiel 24:3-14: A Rhetorical Perspective." *Catholic Biblical Quarterly* 49 (1987): 404-414.

Discusses these verses as a rhetorical unit, marked by an inclusio that consists of wordplay in 3a and 14b. The unit divides into three sections (3-5; 6-8; 9-14), each of which has distinctive rhetorical features. The third, climactic section stresses Yahweh's direct involvement in Jerusalem's fate.

0984   Davis, Ellen Frances. "Swallowing Hard: Reflections on Ezekiel's Dumbness." In *Signs and Wonders: Biblical Texts in Literary Focus*, ed. by J. Cheryl Exum, 217-237. Atlanta: Scholars Press, 1989.

Contends that it was through Ezekiel that Israelite prophecy first moved into a primary textual mode. Ezekiel's patterns of thought and public speech are shaped by habits of reading and writing. His eating of the scroll and consequent dumbness symbolize the new constraints imposed upon the prophetic tradition by the textualization of communication. This article is followed by a response from Katheryn Pfisterer Darr.

0985   Davis, Ellen Frances. *Swallowing the Scroll: Textuality and the Dynamics of Discourse in Ezekiel's Prophecy.*   Journal for the Study of the Old Testament Supplement Series, 78/Bible and Literature Series, 21. Sheffield: Almond Press, 1989. 184 pp.

Argues that Ezekiel represents the creation of a new literary idiom for prophecy-- one less oriented toward current events than toward reshaping tradition. Davis studies Ezekiel in terms of the dynamics of orality and textuality. She finds that he has made the medium of prophecy not the prophet, but the text.

0986   Durlesser, James Arthur. "The Rhetoric of Allegory in the Book of Ezekiel." Ph.D. diss., University of Pittsburgh, 1988. 420 pp.

Investigates the rhetoric of ten oracles in the book of Ezekiel in which the prophet uses allegory as a means of address (Ezekiel 15; 17; 19; 34; 16; 23; 27; 31; 29:1-6a; 32:1-16). Examination is made of the poetic and narrative techniques, such as catchwords, chiasm, inclusio, paronomasia, shifts in theme, and syntactic anomalies.

DANIEL

See also 0539, 0592, 0601, 0654.

0987   Fewell, Danna Nolan. *Circle of Sovereignty: A Story of Stories in Daniel 1-- 6.* Journal for the Study of the Old Testament Supplement Series, 72/Bible and Literature Series, 20. Sheffield: Almond Press, 1988. 207 pp.

A close reading of Daniel 1--6 informed by reader-response and deconstructive theory. Fewell reads the story as presenting a progression of conflict between divine and human sovereignty. The king's repeated affirmations of God represent an attempt to control divinity. The question raised is, how bound is God's sovereignty to human acknowledgement?

0988   Good, Edwin M. "Apocalyptic as Comedy: The Book of Daniel." *Semeia* 32 (1984): 41-70.

Presents Daniel as mainly (though not entirely) comic in the sense in which Northrop Frye uses the term (0088, 0586), that is, as a form of *mythos* in which the plot moves from happiness through disaster to a resolution of renewed happiness. The stories in Daniel 1--6 are comic individually and exhibit an overall comic plot line when taken together. Comic elements are less evident in the visions, especially those of Daniel 9--12.

0989   Milne, Pamela Jeanne. "Narrative Structure in Daniel 1--6: An Analysis of Structure in a Group of Old Testament Texts, Based on Vladimir Propp's 'Morphology of the Folktale.'" Ph. D. diss., McGill University (Canada), 1982.

Examines narrative structure in Daniel 1--6 using a method of analysis developed by Propp in his study of Russian folktales (0202). The tales in Daniel 1--2 and 5 exhibit a similar structure and so constitute a group. The tales in Daniel 3 and 6 constitute a second group. Daniel 4 is structurally dissimilar to the other tales in 1--6. See also 0539.

0990   Talmon, Shemaryahu. "Daniel." In *The Literary Guide to the Bible*, ed. by Robert Alter and Frank Kermode, 343-356. Cambridge, MA: Belknap Press, 1987.

Despite some treatment of style and imagery, this "literary" treatment of Daniel does not differ markedly from traditional historical-critical analyses. Talmon discusses the book's linguistic and literary diversity, its historical origins and use of traditions, and its affinities with other examples of diaspora literature. The work is regarded as a variant of late biblical historiography that presents a fictional tale embodying the theme of "successful exile."

HOSEA

See also 0632, 0943.

0991   Buss, Martin J. "Tragedy and Comedy in Hosea." *Semeia* 32 (1984): 71-82.

Discusses the interplay of tragic and comic impulses in the prophecy of Hosea. A tragic mood expresses sympathy for the downfall of the nation, while comic elements make fun of the people's foolishness and express joy in a new relation with God.

0992   Catlett, Michael Lee. "Reversals in Hosea: A Literary Analysis." Ph. D. diss., Emory University, 1988. 308 pp.

Examines the use of repeated lexemes and imagery in Hosea. These often occur in quite dissimilar contexts--for example, pronouncements of salvation and judgment often share the same vocabulary. Theologically, these reversals point to the power of Yahweh to transform judgment into salvation.

0993   Kruger, P. A. "Prophetic Imagery: On Metaphors and Similes in the Book of Hosea." *Journal of Northwest Semitic Languages* 14 (1988): 143-151.

Discusses a few characteristics of Hosea's use of imagery, such as word plays, images of plants and animals, descriptions of the characteristics of evildoers, and so on.

Metaphors are consistently avoided in comparisons involving the Lord--similes are used instead.

0994   Lundbom, Jack R.   "Poetic Structure and Prophetic Rhetoric in Hosea." *Vetus Testamentum* 29 (1979): 300-308.

Reflects on the purpose of the inclusio that can be discerned in Hosea 4:11-14 and 8:9-13. Lundbom surmises that the inclusio serves to captivate the audience, creating expectation through postponement of resolution until, at the end of the discourse, the prophet returns to the point made earlier. Beyond this, the inclusio serves as an argumentative device, used to convey the terrible message of divine judgment.

0995   Mazor, Yair.   "Hosea 5:1-3:   Between Compositional Rhetoric and Rhetorical Composition." *Journal for the Study of the Old Testament* 45 (1989): 115-126.

A structuralist investigation of patterns that contribute to the rhetorical argument of Hosea 5, especially the first three verses. Mazor finds in the chapter a gradually diminishing momentum, starting with two patterns that contain "paratactic-extircating characteristics," followed by a third pattern that is incomplete.

0996   Van Dijk-Hemmes, Fokkelien.   "The Imagination of Power and the Power of Imagination: An Intertextual Analysis of Two Biblical Love Songs: the Song of Songs and Hosea 2." *Journal for the Study of the Old Testament* 44 (1989): 75-88.

Deconstructs Hosea 2 from a feminist perspective that draws also from the Song of Solomon. The Hosean metaphor of a harlot-wife contradicts the prophet's own vision of justice. The wife's version of love can be found in the Song, but love songs created by women are distorted in the Hosean text. Van Dijk-Hemmes suggests that the prophet's call for justice be repackaged in terms of the wife's love song, the Song of Songs that is "a celebration of the relation of Goddess with her people."

AMOS

See also 0601, 0943, 0945, 1580.

0997   Garrett, Duane A.   "The Structure of Amos as a Testimony to its Integrity." *Journal of the Evangelical Theological Society* 27 (1984): 275-276.

Identifies Amos 5:10-13 as a chiasm and demonstrates parallelism between 8:7-14 and 9:1-15. Garrett claims that recognition of these rhetorical features argues against the idea that Amos 5:13 or 9:11-15 are later additions to the text.

0998   Gitay, Yehoshua. "A Study of Amos's Art of Speech: A Rhetorical Analysis of Amos 3:1-15." *Catholic Biblical Quarterly* 42 (1980): 293-309.

Examines this pericope from the perspective of rhetorical criticism, determining the situation or exigency that called for the appeal, the structure and style of the appeal, and the rhetorical techniques employed. Gitay believes that consideration of all these features demonstrates that the passage is a rhetorical unit.

0999   Tromp, N. "Amos 5:1-17. Towards a Stylistic and Rhetorical Analysis." *Oudtestamentische Studiën* 23 (1984): 56-84.

Utilizes rhetorical analysis to understand this passage from Amos, arguing for a deliberate chiastic structure in the text. Tromp is concerned with identifying the current text as redacted literary unit based on a primary oral stratum.

JONAH

See also 0078, 0587, 0637, 0658, 0943, 1550, 1743.

1000   Ackerman, James S. "Jonah." In *The Literary Guide to the Bible*, ed. by Robert Alter and Frank Kermode, 234-243. Cambridge, MA: Belknap Press, 1987.

Briefly surveys this unique entry in the prophetic collection, with special emphasis on the author's use of irony to distance us from the hero and to keep the story on a "narrow path between invective and farce." The book has similarities with satire: incongruous, distorted events; a mixture of literary genres; an image of violence at the heart of the story; a journey as a typical setting; and relatively little emphasis on plot or character development.

1001   "An Approach to the Book of Jonah: Suggestions and Questions." *Semeia* 15 (1979): 85-96.

An anonymous study contributed to *Semeia* by "a group from Rennes, France." The article attempts to provide a semiotic analysis of Jonah. The structuralist methodology looks first at a syntactic analysis of the opposition between God and Jonah in the narrative. Next, an attempt is made at discursive analysis of oppositions that can be listed according to various codes: spatial, legal, and vital. The first part of the study is more successful than the second.

1002   Bacher, S. "The Book of Jonah--The Author vs. His Hero." *Beth Mikra* 28 (1982/83): 39-43.

Proposes that the author of the book of Jonah is a different sort of prophet than the character of Jonah in the story. The author is a prophet like Moses who emphasizes God's mercy and grace. The character of Jonah, however, is a prophet like Elijah or

Nahum who regards God as committed to carrying out the demands of justice. The article is in Hebrew.

1003   Christensen, Duane L. "Narrative Poetics and the Interpretation of the Book of Jonah." In *Directions in Biblical Hebrew Poetry*, ed. by Elaine R. Follis, 29-48. *Journal for the Study of the Old Testament Supplement Series*, 40. Sheffield: JSOT Press, 1987.

Presents a "metrical reading" of the book of Jonah, analyzing the entire work line by line and counting the phonetic morae and syntactic-accentual units for each line. Thus, even the sections of the book normally designated as prose are studied here as verse. The language soars to its most lyrical heights in the so-called "psalm of Jonah" (2:3-10), which must be regarded as an integral part of structural design of the book as a whole.

1004   Craig, Kenneth M., Jr. "Jonah and the Reading Process." *Journal for the Study of the Old Testament* 47 (1990): 103-114.

Emphasizes the need to read Jonah with a strategy that avoids the "hindsight fallacy" of interpreting the whole work on the basis of its conclusion. In providing insufficient, even misleading information, the author invites the reader to stabilize the action as it unfolds. The text, then, must be viewed as a continuum. Its meaning encompasses all that develops in the mind of the reader as impressions are drawn and re-drawn throughout.

1005   Goodhart, Sandor. "Prophecy, Sacrifice and Repentance in the Story of Jonah." *Semeia* 33 (1985): 43-63.

Analyzes the final parable of the gourd in Jonah 4 in terms of the diachronic identity established between Israel and Nineveh. The parable reveals that Jonah's reluctance to prophesy to Nineveh is not only lacking in compassion, but is in fact anti-Jewish. By making an idol of the law itself, Jonah would subvert the anti-idolatry center of the Torah. Goodhart attempts to interpret the story within the scriptural and liturgical contexts in which it is read, that is within the social context that construes the essence of Judaism as a collection of rituals and within the individual context that views the essential condition of Jewish life as repentance.

1006   Hauser, Alan Jon. "Jonah: In Pursuit of the Dove." *Journal of Biblical Literature* 104 (1985): 21-37.

Analyzes the element of surprise as the key structural device employed by the writer of Jonah. Before 3:10--4:1, the writer misdirects the reader into thinking Jonah flees either out of fear of God's wrath or because he does not wish to be the agent of the city of Nineveh's destruction. This misdirection is aided by the meaning of the prophet's name (Jonah means "dove"), which connotes flight or passivity. The surprising revelation that Jonah fears God will relent and forgive Nineveh reverses the reader's expectations concerning both the prophet and God in a way that is a mark of effective storytelling.

1007 Holbert, John C. "'Deliverance Belongs to Yahweh!': Satire in the Book of Jonah." *Journal for the Study of the Old Testament* 21 (1981): 59-81.

Describes the book of Jonah as "a short story characterized by the use of satire" and identifies satirical elements in the book. Holbert first explores the literary definition of satire, which he explicates in terms of five aspects. He then examines the first two chapters of Jonah, noting instances in which these five aspects are present.

1008 Hoop, Raymond de. "The Book of Jonah as Poetry: An Analysis of Jonah 1:1-16." In *The Structural Analysis of Biblical and Canaanite Poetry*, ed. by Willem van der Meer and Johannes C. de Moor, 119-171. Journal for the Study of the Old Testament Supplement Series, 74. Sheffield: JSOT Press, 1988.

Analyzes Jonah 1:1-16 as a canto composed of three sub-cantos, each of which in turn comprises two canticles composed of two strophes. Three characteristic indicators of Hebrew poetry--parallelism, responsion, and inclusion--are noted.

1009 Magonet, Jonathan. *Form and Meaning: Studies in Literary Technique in the Book of Jonah*. Bible and Literature Series, 8. Sheffield: Almond Press, 1983. 184 pp.

Analyzes Jonah in terms of its language, structure, quotations, and themes. Magonet hopes to find an explanation for the contrast between the apparent simplicity of the narrative and the vast range of interpretations it has produced. He discovers a complex structure beneath the evident simplicity. The analysis focuses especially on repetitions (of words, phrases, and sentences), which produce patterns of interrelationships throughout the book.

1010 Mather, Judson. "The Comic Art of the Book of Jonah." *Soundings* 65 (1982): 280-291.

Proposes that the comic reversals in the book of Jonah are not secondary elements, but the very point of story. The reader is "taken in by the author" just as Jonah is "taken in by God."

1011 Pelli, Moshe. "The Literary Art of Jonah." *Hebrew Studies* 20/21 (1979-1980): 18-28.

Highlights some of the more subtle aspects of literary artistry in Jonah, such as what is left unsaid and allusions to the prophecy of Joel. Suggestions are also offered for an overall understanding of the book.

1012 Potgieter, Johan Hendrik. "A Narratological Approach to the Book of Jonah." Ph.D. diss., University of Pretoria (South Africa), 1989.

Examines the book of Jonah in three stages: (1) the structure of the book in its present form is analyzed, with particular significance ascribed to the three prayers (1:14; 2:3-10; 4:2-3); (2) the narratological criteria of actants, actions, time, and space are described; and (3) the communicative functions of these narrative conventions are determined in order to ascertain the message of the book. Potgieter concludes that the book of Jonah is a short story and should be read and interpreted as such.

1013   Walsh, Jerome T. "Jonah 2, 3-10: A Rhetorical Critical Study." *Biblica* 63 (1982): 119-229.

Studies the psalm of Jonah from a literary perspective. A close reading of the text pays special attention to formal features and structural patterns. Motif analysis discerns two motifs (spatial movement and the presence/absence of Yahweh), which are developed in parallel fashion. Interpretation on the level of the text calls attention to Yahweh's salvation as a gift and as an act of faithfulness; interpretation on the level of the reader involves an invitation to join the psalmist in thankful praise.

1014   Warshaw, Thayer S. "The Book of Jonah." In *Literary Interpretations of Biblical Narratives*, ed. by Kenneth R. R. Gros Louis with James S. Ackerman and Thayer S. Warshaw, 191-207. Nashville: Abingdon Press, 1974.

Examines Jonah as exemplary of a story in which the reader learns a lesson that is taught to the protagonist. The story uses such literary devices as satire and suspense to develop two themes: mercy as superior to law and order, and the universal character of love. Ultimately, the story leaves the reader to supply his or her own meaning to questions about human nature.

1015   West, Mona. "Irony in the Book of Jonah: Audience Identification with the Hero." *Perspectives in Religious Studies* 11 (1984): 233-242.

Interprets the irony, exaggerations, and sarcasm of the book of Jonah as these may be related to post-exilic Israel's empathy with the character of Jonah. The intended effect is for Israel to turn its attention away from pitying itself to the love and concern of God for all humanity.

MICAH

See also 0943, 1599.

1016   De Moor, Johannes C. "Micah 1: Structural Approach." In *The Structural Analysis of Biblical and Canaanite Poetry*, ed. by Willem van der Meer and Johannes C. de Moor, 172-185. Journal for the Study of the Old Testament Supplement Series, 74. Sheffield: JSOT Press, 1988.

Examines the two sub-cantos of Micah 1 to find that they form a well-balanced literary whole, in spite of probable composition at least twenty years apart. Even if the two sub-cantos have different compositional histories, de Moor concludes, they appear to have been chosen for their matching poetical structures.

1017   Hagstrom, David Gerald. *The Coherence of the Book of Micah: A Literary Analysis*. Society of Biblical Literature Dissertation Series, 1988. 152 pp.

Examines the literary features that make Micah a unified, coherent whole, rather than simply the collection of independent units that it has often been thought to be. Hagstrom considers continuity and discontinuity, repetitions of vocabulary, the structure of various sections, thematic continuities, and so forth.

HABAKKUK

See also 0943.

1018   Bratcher, Dennis Ray. "The Theological Message of Habakkuk: A Literary-Rhetorical Analysis." Ph.D. diss., Union Theological Seminary in Virginia, 1984. 392 pp.

Concentrates on the literary and rhetorical features of the book of Habakkuk in order to elucidate its theological message. Patterns by which the book is organized are examined, as are literary devices used to produce various effects. The message of the book affirms doubt as a way of approaching God and the future as a source of hope. Response to evil in the world cannot come from within the individual but must come from God who provides strength in human weakness.

1019   Hiebert, Theodore. "The Use of Inclusion in Habakkuk 3." In *Directions in Biblical Hebrew Poetry*, ed. by Elaine R. Follis, 119-140. *Journal for the Study of the Old Testament Supplement Series*, 40. Sheffield: JSOT Press, 1987.

Sets out the text of Habakkuk in four stanzas, as indicated by the presence of inclusive features in the poem. The stanzas are of uneven length, consisting of verses 2; 3-7; 8-15; and 16-19. Hiebert finds that stanzas 2 and 3 contain a theophany, which is enclosed within the literary framework of stanzas 1 and 4. The primary stylistic device by which this structure is achieved is inclusion, which is employed at multiple levels to produce concentric structures, and which involves every aspect of literary structure: phonemes, syntax, verse structure, key words and phrases, themes, and motifs.

ZEPHANIAH

See also 0943.

1020   Ball, Ivan J., Jr. "The Rhetorical Shape of Zephaniah." In *Perspectives on Language and Text*, ed. by Edgar W. Conrad and Edward G. Newing, 155-166. Winona Laka, IN: Eisenbrauns, 1987.

Attempts to demonstrate the unity of Zephaniah by way of rhetorical analysis. The book is divided into rhetorical units, each of which is seen to exhibit distinctive features.   Taken together, these units present a definite pattern that would be destroyed by deletion or rearrangement of any constitutive parts.

1021   Ball, Ivan J., Jr. "A Rhetorical Study of Zephaniah." Ph.D. diss., Graduate Theological Union, 1972. 313 pp.

Uses rhetorical criticism to study the literary structure of the book of Zephaniah. The first and last sections of the book are found to form an inclusio, with the first section of chapter two serving as the kernel of the entire book.   Chapters one and three evince a parallel structure.

1022   House, Paul R. *Zephaniah: A Prophetic Drama*. Journal for the Study of the Old Testament Supplement Series, 69/Bible and Literature Series, 16. Sheffield: Almond Press, 1988. 146 pp.

A literary study of Zephaniah that assigns the book to the genre of drama, in distinction from epic and lyric. The third chapter consists of a close reading of the text with consideration given to structure, dialogue, plot, characterization, themes, point-of-view, and time sequence.

1023   Van Grol, Harm W. M. "Classical Hebrew Metrics and Zephaniah 2--3." In *The Structural Analysis of Biblical and Canaanite Poetry*, ed. by Willem van der Meer and Johannes C. de Moor, 186-206. Journal for the Study of the Old Testament Supplement Series, 74. Sheffield: JSOT Press, 1988.

Presents a new thesis concerning Hebrew versification and metrics (cf. 0672), with illustrations drawn from four poems in Zephaniah (2:13-15; 3:1-5; 6-8; 14-17). Van Grol seeks to describe Hebrew rhythm patterns in terms of a "pure stress meter" determined by the word accents.

ZECHARAIAH

See also 0943.

1024   Bergdall, Chaney R.   "Zechariah's Program of Restoration: A Rhetorical Critical Study of Zechariah 1--8. Ph.D. diss., Fuller Theological Seminary, School of Theology, 1986. 302 pp.

A synchronic analysis that uses rhetorical criticism to investigate the literary structure of Zechariah 1--8. A chiastic structure for the cycle of eight visions is noted, with 1:1-6 and 7:1--8:23 providing the framework. Other chiasms and key-word structures are also observed. The literary structure enables the work to hold in tension seemingly contradictory ideas (cult responsibility vs. ethical responsibility, divine agency vs. human agency, and so on).

1025   Clark, David J.   "Discourse Structure in Zechariah 7.1--8.23."   *The Bible Translator* 36 (1985): 328-335.

Analyzes the discourse structure of this section of Zechariah to reveal that it possesses its own unity and is not, as sometimes thought, a motley collection of oracles that serves as an appendix to the book. The section is also related to the rest of the book of Zechariah, with 7:1 beginning a new section in a manner comparable to 1:1 and 1:7.

MALACHI

See also 0943.

1026   Blake, Richard Dudley.   "The Rhetoric of Malachi." Ph.D. diss., Union Theological Seminary, 1988. 402 pp.

A rhetorical-critical study of Malachi that examines the text in terms of categories for interpretation derived from Paul Ricoeur. Blake highlights the use of character archetypes and notes the manner in which the question-and-answer motif holds the text together. The alien element within Israel that leads to poor management of the cult is treated metaphorically.

1027   Wendland, Ernst.   "Linear and Concentric Patterns in Malachi."   *The Bible Translator* 36 (1985): 108-121.

Identifies instances of parallelism, chiasm, simile and metaphor, synecdoche and metonymy, rhetorical question, antithesis, exclamatory utterance, graphic diction, verbal shift, closure, linear patterning, and concentric patterning in the book of Malachi.

1 Esdras

See also 0869.

1028 Crenshaw, James L. "The Contest of Darius' Guards." In *Images of Man and God: Old Testament Short Stores in Literary Focus*, ed. by Burke O. Long, 74-88. Bible and Literature Series, 1. Sheffield: Almond Press, 1981.

Examines the dialogue attributed to Darius' guards in 1 Esdras 3:1--5:3 as an example of the rhetorical question-and-answer device in literature. The device allows for a question to be posed and several answers with varying degrees of adequacy to be presented in response. The device not only enables the reader to evaluate the relative merits of the proposed solutions, but also permits an element of humorous entertainment that prevents the rhetoric from being weighed down by the seriousness of its subject.

Tobit

See also 0618, 0645.

1029 Nowell, Irene. "The Book of Tobit: Narrative Technique and Theology." Ph.D. diss., Catholic University of America, 1983. 319 pp.

A literary study of the book of Tobit. Nowell begins with a review of literary works that have been influential in the development of her approach. Tobit is then analyzed according to genre, plot and structure, characterization, and stylistic techniques (narrator, dialogue and reticence, irony, imagery, and key words). Implications for understanding the theology of the work are presented also.

1030 Nowell, Irene. "The Narrator in the Book of Tobit." In *Society of Biblical Literature 1988 Seminar Papers*, ed. by David J. Lull, 27-38. Atlanta: Scholars Press, 1988.

Presents a study of the narrator in Tobit in two parts: (1) narrative technique is analyzed in four categories derived from Friedman (0164)--speaker, angle, channels of information, and distance; (2) narrative functions are described in categories proposed by Alter (0607)--chronicle of public events and context of meaning, textual contrast, essential actions, expository data, and dialogue-bound narration. Nowell concludes that the narrator of Tobit is unobtrusive, reliable, omniscient, and powerfully economical.

1031   Saito, T. "The Structure of Folktales in the Book of Tobit." *Seishogaku Ronshu* 19 (1985): 44-72.

Shows that the universal structures of folktales as identified by Vladimir Propp, Claude Lévi-Strauss, A. J. Greimas, and others are present in the Book of Tobit. Saito identifies the "motifeme sequence," analyzes the story in terms of Propp's seven spheres of action and Greimas' actantial model, and confirms the presence of the basic semantic opposition common to folktales ("own" vs. "foreign"). The article is in Japanese.

1032   Soll, William.   "Tobit and Folklore Studies, with Emphasis on Propp's Morphology." In *Society of Biblical Literature 1988 Seminar Papers* 3, ed. by David J. Lull, 39-53. Atlanta: Scholars Press, 1988.

Analyzes the plot of Tobit in terms of the constant functions discerned in folktales by Propp (0202) and decides that the story has a fairy tale for its source. Although the book in its current form belong to a subsequent genre, the fairy tale remains present, discernible in the basic structure of the plot.

JUDITH

See also 0605, 0645.

1033   Alonso-Schökel, Luis. "Narrative Structures in the Book of Judith." In *Protocol Series of the Colloquies of the Center for Hermeneutical Studies in Hellenistic and Modern Culture* 11 (March, 1974): 1-20.

Attempts to read the book of Judith in its present form as a coherent narrative, drawing on insights of text-oriented theory. The study focuses on composition, irony, dénouement, characters, and the function of the story for its original audience.

1034   Craven, Toni. "Artistry and Faith in the Book of Judith." *Semeia* 8 (1977): 75-101.

A rhetorical study of the parallel structures of the two parts of the book of Judith (1--7 and 8--16). Both parts are chiastically structured and in each half thematic repetition is the major stylistic feature--repetition of fear in the first part and repetition of Judith's great beauty in the second. Other corresponding features of form and content between the two parts are also noted.

1035   Craven, Toni. *Artistry and Faith in the Book of Judith.* Society of Biblical Literature Dissertation Series, 70. Chico, CA: Scholars Press, 1983. 139 pp.

Treats the book of Judith as the product of the storyteller's imagination. The book is entirely deserving of the high praise it has received for its literary artistry. Craven rejects the claim that the first seven chapters are a faulty introduction to the story proper, and contends that the work in its current form functions as a narrative whole.

1036   Gros Louis, Delores. "Narrative Art in the Book of Judith." In *Literary Interpretations of Biblical Narratives, Volume II*, ed. by Kenneth R. R. Gros Louis with James S. Ackerman, 259-272. Nashville: Abingdon Press, 1982.

A study of plot, characterization, and two major themes (power and fear) in this self-contained narrative. The book of Judith is realistic fiction, a pseudo-history that is also a religious story, emphasizing one woman's triumph through faith in God. The story is didactic in that it emphasizes the need for prayer, fasting, tithing, purification, and observance of dietary laws, but it is also a good popular story, embodying elements of irony and suspense. It teaches as it delights.

2 BARUCH

1037   Murphy, Frederick J. *The Structure and Meaning of 2 Baruch*. Society of Biblical Literature Dissertation Series, 78. Atlanta: Scholars Press, 1985. 148 pp.

Builds on the work of Sayler (1038) to discuss the structure of 2 Baruch as a clue to the intentions of the work's historical author. Murphy believes the book can be divided into seven sections, each of which concludes with a pertinent address. The seventh section provides a summary of the author's main points. The intention of the author discernible from such a structure is to present a two-world scheme that relativizes the importance of the Temple and the land and reorients the people from a this-worldly attitude to an other-worldly one.

1038   Sayler, Gwendolyn B. *Have the Promises Failed? A Literary Analysis of 2 Baruch*. Society of Biblical Literature Dissertation Series, 72. Chico, CA: Scholars Press, 1984. 171 pp.

Devotes one chapter to an analysis of the literary structure of 2 Baruch, which Sayler considers as an integrated literary whole. Departing from traditional theories regarding source, she finds that the work is structured to tell a story that moves from grief to consolation. This story is carried by units of narrative prose, into which are inserted non-narrative elements such as laments, prayers, visions, and conversations. The rest of the book is occupied with historical concerns, such as reconstructions of the world of the real author and comparisons with other ancient documents. See also 1037.

THE NEW TESTAMENT

See also 0490, 0493, 0529, 0534, 0544-0545, 0845, 1582-1583, 1604.

1039   Aune, David E. *The New Testament in Its Literary Environment*. Philadelphia: Westminster Press, 1987. 260 pp.

Describes the major genres and forms of literature found in the New Testament, comparing the documents to other Jewish and Hellenistic writings. In doing this, Aune hopes to shed light on the conventions that the New Testament writers chose to follow in a way that will provide a firmer base for rhetorical and literary-critical studies.

1040   Barr, David L. *New Testament Story: An Introduction*. Belmont, CA: Wadsworth Publishing Co., 1987. 379 pp.

The first textbook-style introduction to the New Testament to incorporate the insights of rhetorical and narrative approaches to the Bible. While the book remains faithful to typical redactional and historical concerns, it also includes attention to such matters as the employment of literary devices and the creation of particular effects (such as irony).

1041   Elsom, Helen. "The New Testament and Greco-Roman Writing." In *The Literary Guide to the Bible*, ed. by Robert Alter and Frank Kermode, 545-560. Cambridge, MA: Belknap Press, 1987.

Compares the synoptic Gospels, Acts, and Paul's epistles to contemporary Greco-Roman literature. The synoptics are formally analogous to Hellenistic biographies, but claim a different significance. Acts resembles Greco-Roman romance literature. Paul's epistles follow general conventions of ancient epistolary art.

1042   Funk, Robert W. *Parables and Presence: Forms of the New Testament Tradition*. Philadelphia: Fortress Press, 1982. 206 pp.

A collection of previously published essays exploring how language serves as an event that gives presence. Parables are studied as an event of language that gives presence to Jesus and letters as an event of language that gives presence to Paul.

1043   Jónsson, Jakob. *Humour and Irony in the New Testament: Illustrated by Parallels in Talmud and Midrash*. Reykjavik: Bokautgafa Menningarsjoda, 1965. 314 pp.

A fairly comprehensive survey of the use of humor in early Christian homiletics, including the preaching of Jesus. A broad background for the study is established through chapters on humor in the Greek and Roman world, in the Old Testament, and in the Talmud and midrashic literature. The heart of the book focuses on Jesus' humor as portrayed in the synoptic Gospels, but chapters are also devoted to John,

Acts, Paul, and other New Testament writings. The book is a predecessor to more recent studies that focus on irony as a significant concept for biblical literature.

1044   Kelber, Werner H. *The Oral and Written Gospel: The Hermeneutics of Speaking and Writing in the Synoptic Tradition, Mark, Paul, and Q.* Philadelphia: Fortress Press, 1983. 254 pp.

Studies the hermeneutical significance of transforming oral speech into text with reference to the gospel tradition. The New Testament was produced in a culture that stood on the threshold of crossing over from orality to textuality. Signs of transition appear, for instance, in Paul's preference for the spoken word over "the letter" of written texts. Rather than viewing the literary Gospels as natural products of antecedent tradition, Kelber suggests they offer radical alternatives to it. Thus, the quality of the Gospels "as literature" is itself hermeneutically significant. See also 1282.

1045   Petzer, J. A., and Hartin, P. J., eds. *A South African Perspective on the New Testament: Essays by South African New Testament Scholars Presented to Bruce Manning Metzger during His Visit to South Africa in 1985.* Leiden: E. J. Brill, 1986. 271 pp.

A collection of essays, several of which focus on literary methods of analysis, reception theory, semiotics, and recent theories of rhetoric, metaphor, narrative structure, and point of view. See 0501, 1170, 1379, 1431, 1475.

1046   Ryken, Leland, ed. *The New Testament in Literary Criticism.* New York: Frederick Ungar Publishing Co., 1984. 349 pp.

An anthology of comments by various literary critics on topics related to the New Testament. The topics, arranged alphabetically, include headings for several biblical books (Matthew, Mark, Luke, John, Acts, Hebrews, and James) and for several types of literature (epistle, humor, hymn, parable, poetry, proverb, and satire). In addition, whole sections are devoted to 1 Corinthians 13 and to the parables of the Good Samaritan, the Prodigal Son, and the Sower. Two other sections highlight "Jesus as Poet" and "Paul as Letter Writer." A companion volume has been published on the Old Testament (0657).

1047   Ryken, Leland. *Words of Life: A Literary Introduction to the New Testament.* Grand Rapids, MI: Baker Books, 1987. 182 pp.

An introduction to the various forms of literature within the New Testament, with emphasis on the literary artistry and crastsmanship of the writers. An introductory chapter asks, "How literary is the New Testament?" and lists several distinctive features of the New Testament as literature. Subsequent chapters are devoted to the Gospels, the parables, the book of Acts, the epistles, and the book of Revelation. Also included are sections on poetry, proverbs and hymns in the New Testament and on the rhetorical features of oratory evident in the Sermon on the Mount, in the address of Paul at Athens, and in 1 Corinthians 13. The book is a companion volume to a work on biblical literature in general (0601).

1048   Via, Dan O., Jr. *Kerygma and Comedy in the New Testament: A Structuralist Approach to Hermeneutics*. Philadelphia: Fortress Press, 1975. 179 pp.

This book has four parts. Part One presents an overview of the development of structuralism and suggests a synthesis of structuralist, phenomenological, and existential modes of interpretation that will be useful for biblical studies. The proposed synthesis brackets out diachronic relationships and focuses instead on synchronic transformations. Part Two attempts to relate Paul's concept of death and resurrection (1 Corinthians 1:17-2:5; Romans 9:30-10:21) to images in Greek religion and Part Three makes a similar attempt with the Gospel of Mark. Via regards Paul, Mark, and Greek writings (such as Aristophanes) as all being comic, though they cannot be said to belong to the genre of comedy as traditionally defined. Part Four presents a brief structural analysis of the Gospel of Mark, in terms of its sequential, actantial, and indicial elements.

1049   Via, Dan O., Jr.   *Self-Deception and Wholeness in Paul and Matthew*. Minneapolis: Fortress Press, 1990. 173 pp.

Draws on psychoanalytical theory and modern literary criticism to exegete passages from Paul's letters and Matthew's Gospel in terms of what they teach about self-deception and the recovery of wholeness. Paul relates self-deception primarily to the misdirected notion that righteousness can be achieved apart from grace, and Matthew relates it primarily to the lack of correspondence between internal conviction and external action.

1050   Watson, Duane F., ed. *Persuasive Artistry: Studies in New Testament Rhetoric in Honor of George A. Kennedy*. Journal for the Study of the New Testament Supplement Series, 50. Sheffield: JSOT Press, 1990. 500 pp.

A collection of essays that apply the methods of rhetorical-critical interpretation to various New Testament texts. Seventeen scholars are represented, including Yehoshua Gitay, John R. Levison, Rollin Grams, C. Clifton Black, Wilhelm Wuellner, Richard B. Vinson, Vernon K. Robbins, Frank Thielman, Duane F. Watson, Michael R. Cosby, Robert Jewett, Frank Witt Hughes, Frederick W. Danker, James D. Hester, Robert G. Hall, Clarice Martin, and Stephen Mark Pogoloff. Portions of the New Testament considered include the Gospels, Acts, Romans, 2 Corinthians, Galatians, and Ephesians.

1051   Wieser, Thomas. "Community--Its Unity, Diversity and Universality." *Semeia* 33 (1985): 83-95.

Examines a number of New Testament passages from the perspective of René Girard's thesis that human communities develop out of an act of violence that unites all against one. Jesus' message is examined first with reference to his own ministry through which he confronts and dissolves human communities. Further study focuses on the founding of a new community in the book of Acts, on divisions in the community faced by Paul in 1 Corinthians, and on the notion of unity and universality developed in John 17.

1052   Wilder, Amos N. *Early Christian Rhetoric: The Language of the Gospel.*
Cambridge, MA: Harvard University Press, 1971. 143 pp.

A reprint of *The Language of the Gospel: Early Christian Rhetoric* (New York: Harper
and Row, 1964). Wilder examines early Christian proclamation that is concerned "not
so much with what the early Christians said as how they said it." Wilder emphasizes
the novelty of Christian speech, maintaining that the four chief literary types in the
New Testament (gospel, epistle, acts, apocalypse) are essentially unique.   More
convincing arguments attend his discussions of small literary units (dialogue, story,
parable, poem). The book concludes with a hermeneutical essay, "Image, Symbol,
Myth," which attempts to refine the Bultmannian program for an existential encounter
with texts. See also 1111.

1053   Wilder, Amos N. *Jesus' Parables and the War of Myths: Essays on Imagination
in the Scriptures.* Ed. by James Breech. Philadelphia: Fortress Press, 1982. 168 pp.

A collection of previously published essays by one of the most significant figures in
the development of New Testament rhetorical criticism. Some of the essays are also
found in 1052 or in 1728. The focus of attention is on imaginative language, including
myth, parable, and apocalyptic. The volume begins with two prefaces, one by Breech
(pp. 1-14) and another by Wilder (pp. 15-38), which clarify Wilder's rhetorical
approach and its significance for theological studies.

THE GOSPELS

**See also 0507, 0512, 0519, 0529, 0547, 0552, 0555, 0591, 0604, 1041, 1043-1044, 1047,
1050, 1052, 1098, 1100, 1214, 1589, 1608, 1614-1615, 1620, 1680.**

1054   Adam, A. K. M. "The Sign of Jonah: A Fish-eye View." *Semeia* 51 (1990):
177-191.

Surveys various interpretations that have been offered for the "sign of Jonah" prophecy
in the synoptic Gospels as emblematic of Fish's thesis regarding interpretive
communities (0361). The variety of both synchronic and diachronic interpretations
offer evidence that an interpretation is only correct relative to particular interests and
contexts.

1055   Aichele, George, Jr. "Literary Fantasy and the Composition of the Gospels."
Forum 5,3 (1989): 42-60.

A response to 0511, this article is primarily concerned with source theories by which
the Gospels came to be written. It also contains interesting reflections on the role of
fantasy in the Gospels, especially Mark. "Fantasy" resides between the referential
genres of the "marvelous," for which only a supernatural explanation is possible, and
the "uncanny," which, though strange, permits a natural explanation. The implied

reader who encounters fantasy is unable to determine to which of these two incompatible poles the narrative points.

1056 Brewer, Derek. "The Gospels and the Laws of Folktale: A Centenary Lecture, 14 June 1978." *Folklore* 90 (1979): 37-52.

A lecture delivered to Great Britain's Folklore Society commending greater attention to biblical materials, especially the synoptic Gospels. The synoptic Gospels are products of oral tradition that have much in common with other folkloric literature, yet they have only rarely been studied from this perspective by either biblical or literary scholars. At the same time, Brewer notes an anti-folkloric tendency in the Gospels that defies the expectations of traditional narrative.

1057 Butts, James R. "The Chreia in the Synoptic Gospels." *Biblical Theology Bulletin* 16 (1986): 132-138.

Identifies three types of chreiai that can be found in the synoptic Gospels, drawing on information found in the progymnasmata (rhetorical handbook) of Theon. A chreia, according to Theon, is "a concise statement or action attributed with aptness to some specified character or to something analogous to a character." The passages that Butts identifies as chreiai in the Gospels correspond to what biblical scholars have typically called "pronouncement stories."

1058 Chabrol, Claude. "An Analysis of the 'Text' of the Passion." In *The New Testament and Structuralism*, ed. by Alfred M. Johnson, 145-186. Pittsburgh: Pickwick Press, 1976.

A structuralist analysis of a Gospel "metatext," of which the passion narratives in Matthew, Mark, and Luke are presumed to be "substitutable variants." The primary concern is with developing an operational model with which the three gospel texts can later be compared. The central part of the essay is actually taken up with a structuralist analysis of Peter's meeting with Cornelius (Acts 10:1-48), which serves as a testing ground for developing the model. A representational grid built on the oppositions between Alterity and non Alterity, is identified in the Cornelius story and then found to be applicable to the passion narrative as well. See also 1581.

1059 Crossan, John Dominic. "Literary Criticism and Biblical Hermeneutics." *Journal of Religion* 57 (1977): 76-80.

A review of Perrin's *Jesus and the Language of the Kingdom* (1072). Crossan praises the work as an "excellent review of a major turning point in New Testament studies," but faults Perrin for ignoring the work of Erhardt Güttgemanns.

1060   Entrevernes Group, The. *Signs and Parables: Semiotics and Gospel Texts*. Trans. by Gary Phillips. Pittsburgh Theological Monograph Series, 23. Pittsburgh: Pickwick Press, 1978. 323 pp.

Applies semiotic methods to the interpretation of Luke 10:25-34; Mark 6:30-53; Luke 15; and Luke 5:1-11. The latter study is the work of Jacques Geninasca. The others are the work of a group of interpreters including Jean Calloud, Georges Combet, Jean Delorme, Corina Galland-Combet, François Génuyt, Jean-Claude Girard, Louis Panier, and Annie Perrin. A section of the book is also devoted to discussion of the formal aspects, function, and strategy of actors in parable and miracle stories in general. A "postface" is offered by A. J. Greimas, whose semiotic theory forms the basis for the methods this group employs. See also 1590.

1061   Freyne, Sean. *Galilee, Jesus, and the Gospels: Literary Approaches and Historical Investigations*. Philadelphia: Fortress Press, 1988. 311 pp.

Presents, in the first half of the book, a literary perspective on how Galilee is to be understood within the context of each of the Gospel narratives. Significant differences are to be found, but all four present Galilee as an antithesis to Jerusalem.

1062   Frye, Roland Mushat. "A Literary Perspective for the Criticism of the Gospels." In *Jesus and Man's Hope*, vol. 2, ed. by Donald G. Miller and Dikran Y. Hadidian, 193-221. Pittsburgh: Pittsburgh Theological Seminary, 1971.

A historian of literature reflects on the field of biblical studies from the perspective of nonbiblical literary analysis. The existentialist demythologizing of Bultmann is attacked on two grounds: (1) the notion of "modern man" assumed by this approach is a fallacy that ignores the plurality of modern culture; (2) demythologizing inevitably substitutes inadequate paraphrases for superior originals. Frye then presents his view of the Gospels as "dramatic histories," similar in some respects to works of Shakespeare, Shaw, and Sherwood, and recommends that biblical scholars consider treating the Gospels in the same fashion that these secular works are treated.

1063   Frye, Roland Mushat. "The Synoptic Problem and Analogies in Other Literatures." In *The Relationships Among the Gospels: An Inter-Disciplinary Dialogue*, ed. by William O. Walker, 261-302. San Antonio: Trinity University Press, 1978. Republished, in part, as "Literary Criticism and Gospel Criticism." *Theology Today* 36 (1979): 207-219.

Expresses the view of a prominent literary historian that the methods by which historical criticism attempts to reconstruct source histories would be unacceptable in secular fields. Frye suggests that the confidence biblical scholars place in historical-critical methodology is misplaced and proposes that attention should instead be directed toward literary analysis of the symbolic and rhetorical meanings communicated in the Gospel narratives.

1064   Galbreath, Paul Harold. "The Christology of the Gospels and Abraham Maslow's Characteristics of Self-Actualization." Ph.D. diss., Baylor University, 1984. 181 pp.

Discovers through a narrative-critical reading of the Gospels that parallels can be drawn between the portraits of Jesus offered there and the fourteen characteristics of the self-actualized or fully-integrated person in Abraham Maslow's psychological model.

1065   Güttgemanns, Erhardt. "Narrative Analyse Synoptischer Texte." *Linguistica Biblica* 25/26 (1973): 50-73.

Applies the author's method of "generative poetics" (cf. 0519) to 14 texts from the synoptic Gospels (mostly parables). Güttgemanns finds that the narratives are based on combinations of 16 binary semantic-narrative elements. The study is analogous to work on folktales by Propp (0202).

1066   Kelber, Werner H. "Narrative As Interpretation and Interpretation As Narrative." *Semeia* 39 (1983): 107-133

Seeks to draw connections between the first-century narrators of the Gospels and twentieth-century interpreters of Gospel narratives. First, Kelber investigates the hermeneutical status of Mark's Gospel in the context of early Christian tradition, with special attention to orality/literacy dynamics. Next, he reflects on the hermeneutical presuppositions of literary criticism, which recognizes that Gospel composition works out of tradition and in response to an audience. The conclusion is that, inasmuch as the Gospels themselves constitute interpretation, readers and scholars who interpret the Gospels continue hermeneutical practices pursued by the evangelists.

1067   Mack, Burton L. *Anecdotes and Arguments: The Chreia in Antiquity and Early Christianity*. Occasional Papers, 10. Claremont, CA: Institute for Antiquity and Christianity, 1987.

Outlines the process by which chreiai (succinct, anecdotal sayings) are to be elaborated according to the progymnasmata of Hermogenes (an ancient rhetorical handbook) and applies this to a study of pronouncement stories in the synoptic Gospels. See also 1068.

1068   Mack, Burton L., and Robbins, Vernon K. *Patterns of Persuasion in the Gospels*. Foundations and Facets: Literary Facets. Sonoma, CA: Polebridge Press, 1989. 230 pp.

An examination of aphoristic sayings and pronouncement stories in the Gospels, in light of the rhetorical theories of Theon (*Progymnasmata*) and Hermogenes (*Progymnasmata* and *Peri ton Staseon*). Mack and Robbins compare aphoristic speech to chreai and discuss pronouncement stories as elaborations of chreai. As such, these gospel forms are examined for their strategy of argumentation. Specific texts studied include the sayings about foxes and furrows (Matthew 8:19-22; Luke 9:57-60); the story of the anointing of Jesus (Mark 14:3-9; Matthew 26:6-13; Luke 7:36-50; John

12:1-8); the story of plucking grain on the sabbath (Mark 2:23-28; Luke 6:1-6; Matthew 12:1-8); the parables of Mark 4:1-34; and the account of the Beelzebub controversy (Matthew 9:32-34; 12:22-37; Mark 3:19-30; Luke 11:18-28). The authors note both similiarities and differences between the Christian rhetoric of elaboration and that of the Hellenistic world at large.

1069   Marin, Louis. *Sémiotique de la Passion: Topiques et figures*. Bibliothéque de Sciences Religieuses. Paris: Aubier, Cerf, Delachaux, and Niestlé, 1971. 252 pp.

A semiotic analysis of two aspects of the Gospel passion narratives. The first part of the book concentrates on proper names, especially place names. Marin shows that these names are neutralized in the course of the narrative and transformed into common nouns that are invested with new meaning through their relations to individual characters in the narratives. The second part, on characters, focuses particularly on Judas. Judas plays not only a meta-narrative role as traitor, but also a supplementary role as a non-necessary element that effects transformations. See also 1572.

1070   Navone, John, and Cooper, Thomas. *The Story of the Passion*. Rome: Gregorian University Press, 1986. 415 pp.

Draws ethical and devotional insights from the story of Jesus' passion, which Navone reads as the story of God's unconditional love. The four Gospels present four faces of God's love in Jesus Christ manifested as "costly (Mark), fraternal (Matthew), universally compassionate (Luke), and inhabiting (John)."

1071   Patte, Daniel. *Kingdom and Children: Aphorism, Chreia, Structure. Semeia* 29 (1983). 130 pp.

Presents one structuralist and two form-critical studies of the aphorisms regarding "kingdom and children" found in the canonical Gospels (Matthew 18:3; 19:14; Mark 10:14-15; Luke 18:16-17; John 3:3, 5) and the Gospel of Thomas (22). Patte submits the texts to a structural exegesis and both Vernon K. Robbins and John Dominic Crossan analyze the aphorisms as rhetorical chreiai. Responses to the articles by Ronald F. Hock, Robert C. Tannehill, Lou H. Silberman, and Bernard Brandon Scott are also offered.

1072   Perrin, Norman. *Jesus and the Language of the Kingdom: Symbol and Metaphor in New Testament Interpretation*. Philadelphia: Fortress Press, 1976. 225 pp.

Argues that the expression "Kingdom of God" is a symbol (as opposed to a conception) and attempts to delineate the meaning of the symbol in the language of Jesus. Perrin studies explicit "kingdom sayings," in addition to the Lord's prayer, proverbial sayings, and parables. He regards the kingdom of God as a tensive symbol (one that has a plurality of referents) rather than as a steno-symbol (one that has a one-to-one relationship to its referent). See also 1059.

1073   Resseguie, James L. "Defamiliarization and the Gospels." *Biblical Theology Bulletin* 20 (1990): 147-153.

Applies the Russian formalist Victor Shklovsky's concept of defamilarization to the Gospels. The concept consists of a "creative distortion of the world of ordinary perception to renew the reader's diminished capacity for fresh perception." Resseguie catalogues various "estranging devices" identified by the formalists as producing defamiliarization and observes their operation in the Gospels at the levels of rhetoric, characterization, and plot.

1074   Robbins, Vernon K. "Pronouncement Stories From a Rhetorical Perspective." *Forum* 4,2 (1988): 3-32.

Distinguishes pronouncement stories from other stories on the basis on their internal rhetoric, and discusses the use of epideictic, deliberative, and judicial rhetoric in them. Robbins views pronouncement stories as a type of chreai, one that presents an apt and aptly-attributed response by a person in a situation. He also devotes a portion of this essay to the way pronouncement stories are elaborated in accord with the rules of ancient rhetorical handbooks, a subject given further treatment in 1068.

1075   Robinson, James M. "The Gospels as Narrative." In *The Bible and The Narrative Tradition*, ed. by Frank McConnell, 97-112. New York: Oxford University Press, 1986.

Considers the development of the Gospels as narratives from a basic perspective of redaction criticism, in order to introduce a dialogue between that discipline and literary criticism. Robinson compares the four Gospels and their predecessor "Q" in terms of the narrative qualities discernible in each and in terms of the apparent tension between orality and textuality that typified early Christianity.

1076   Schneidau, Herbert N. "Literary Relations among the Gospels: Harmony or Conflict?" *Studies in the Literary Imagination* 18 (1985): 17-32.

Emphasizes the differences between the four Gospels and the need to read each of the four on its own terms. Schneidau is a professor of English literature and he writes for colleagues who also teach the Bible as literature. His point has been widely-accepted among Bible scholars for years, but apparently cannot be taken for granted among literary critics who are demonstrating new interest in biblical literature.

1077   Scott, Bernard Brandon. *Jesus, Symbol-Maker for the Kingdom*. Philadelphia: Fortress Press, 1981. 182 pp.

Attempts to study the sayings of the historical Jesus through semantic and structural analysis to determine the underlying model or world that they evoke. Scott discovers a pre-discursive "grammar" for the parables, which can be confirmed through structural study of other sayings material--notably, the beatitudes, the Lord's Prayer, and several proverbs--and which can even be seen in the deep structures underlying Jesus' deeds. Special attention is given to reversal of expectation. Recurrent motifs include comedy-through-tragedy, extreme grace, and the religious in the secular.

Throughout this literary study, Scott continues to read the texts as referential, hoping to contribute in some way to the "new quest" of the historical Jesus by discovering how Jesus used symbols, especially the master-symbol, "Kingdom of God."

1078 Stegner, William Richard. *Narrative Theology in Early Jewish Christianity*. Louisville, KY: Westminster/John Knox, 1989. 141 pp.

A historical-critical study that analyzes four New Testament narratives (the baptism of Jesus, the temptation of Jesus, the transfiguration, and the feeding of the 5000) according to a method devised by Birger Gerhardsson. Stegner stresses that his study is *not* an example of "narrative criticism" in the sense that the term is now used in literary analysis. Still, his "genetic analysis" of early Christian narratives demonstrates that even historical-critical studies can respect the narrative character of certain New Testament texts.

1079 Tannehill, Robert C. "Attitudinal Shift in Synoptic Pronouncement Stories." In *Orientation By Disorientation*, ed. by Richard A. Spencer, 183-198. Pittsburgh: Pickwick Press, 1980.

Lists six types of pronouncement stories found in the synoptic Gospels and illustrates how each of these may call for a movement from one attitude to another on important issues of religion and life. The six types are correction stories, objection stories, commendation stories, quest stories, test stories, and inquiry stories. All of these present movement from a provoking occasion to a response. The stories are inherently interesting and for this reason involve the reader sufficiently to succeed in changing attitudes.

1080 Tannehill, Robert C. *The Sword of His Mouth: Forceful and Imaginative Language in Synoptic Sayings*. Semeia Studies. Philadelphia: Fortress Press, 1975. 224 pp.

A rhetorical and poetic study of the language of Jesus as depicted in synoptic sayings material. Jesus' words embody a forceful, imaginative, and "tensive" quality that distinguishes them from casual speech. His sayings use a "depth rhetoric" that challenges the hearers' fixed structures of meaning and value.

1081 Tannehill, Robert C. "Tension in Synoptic Sayings and Stories." *Interpretation* 34 (1980): 138-150.

Emphasizes the importance of rediscovering the "tensive language" of the synoptic Gospels. Tensive language is that which embodies a tension and expresses a conflict with ordinary ways of acting and thinking. The Gospel stories are structured in ways that differ sharply from the assumptions that govern our lives, although these points of tension are often lost on readers for whom the language of the Gospels has become familiar. Tannehill calls attention to tensive language in sayings of Jesus, pronouncement stories, and the Gospel of Mark (as a narrative unit).

1082 Winton, Alan P. *The Proverbs of Jesus: Issues of History and Rhetoric*. Journal for the Study of the New Testament Supplement Series, 35. Sheffield, England: JSOT Press, 1990. 236 pp.

Critiques historical-critical treatments of Jesus' wisdom sayings and attempts a fresh assessment that evaluates them in terms of their rhetorical effectiveness. Winton distinguishes between "sense" and "force" in proverbial speech and tries to account for the rhetorical strategies behind numerous sayings in the synoptic Gospels.

THE PARABLES OF JESUS

See also 0517, 0558, 0562, 0568, 0576, 0584, 0587, 0594, 1042, 1046-1047, 1052-1053, 1065, 1072, 1077, 1153, 1227, 1263, 1282, 1590, 1627, 1688, 1697.

1083 Bailey, Kenneth. *Poet and Peasant and Through Peasant Eyes: A Literary-Cultural Approach to the Parables of Luke*. Grand Rapids: Wm. B. Eerdmans Publishing Co., 1976-80. 238 pp, 187 pp.

Combines two previously published books in one volume. Bailey's main interest and greatest contribution lies in his elucidation of parables in terms of cultural mores and customs of the ancient world. He is also sensitive, however, to the poetic qualities of the texts, diagramming their literary structures, and reflecting on particular literary features.

1084 Beardslee, William A. "Parable Interpretation and the World Disclosed by the Parable." *Perspectives in Religious Studies* 3 (1976): 123-139.

Traces the trend in parable research toward viewing "reduction of the world" as a primary function of the parable and suggests that a more adequate description of this function would be "the shattering of cultural security." Parables intend to disrupt the social world of their hearers but they do so with the expectation that this world will continue in spite of the disruption.

1085 Beardslee, William A. "Parable, Proverb, and Koan." *Semeia* 12 (1978): 151-177.

Argues for a middle route for interpreting the parables and proverbs of Jesus between what the author regards as two mistaken extremes. In need of correction are, on the one hand, the traditional view that assumes Jesus' words relate to God as an ordering principle, and, on the other, the new view that his sayings are like koans of Zen Buddhism, intended only to produce creative disruption. The paper concludes that it is proper to understand God as the referent and ordering principle for Jesus' words, if God is not understood in as static a sense as has often been done in the past. See also 1088.

1086   Beavis, Mary Ann. "Parable and Fable." *Catholic Biblical Quarterly* 52 (1990): 473-498.

Calls for a re-examination of the relationship between Jewish parables and Greek fables. Beavis contends that some of the synoptic parables are much like the Greek fables and were probably meant to be intrepreted in this way. She finds support in recent literary studies that have opened the parables to multiple interpretations rather than limiting them to distinctive eschatological and ethical emphases.

1087   Boucher, Madeleine. *The Mysterious Parable: A Literary Study*. Catholic Biblical Quarterly - Monograph Series, 6. Washington D.C: Catholic Biblical Association of America, 1977. 101 pp.

Applies certain insights of literary theory to the parables in order to discern their "structure of meaning." Boucher determines that every parable is intended to have both a surface meaning and a deeper meaning. Historical criticism (particularly Adolf Jülicher) has sought only the literal meaning, rejecting indirect or tropical meanings as "allegorizing." But Boucher claims to the contrary that the parables are tropical narratives with rhetorical purpose. Furthermore, she views this double nature of parable as the key to understanding the entire Gospel of Mark, which is built on the theme of mystery intrinsic to the parables.

1088   Cobb, John B., Jr. "A Theology of Story: Crossan and Beardslee." In *Orientation By Disorientation*, ed. by Richard A. Spencer, 151-166. Pittsburgh: Pickwick Press, 1980.

Summarizes positions on the parables of Jesus advanced by John Dominic Crossan and William A. Beardslee and argues for the superiority of the latter. Crossan rightly notes the disruptive character of the parables, but focuses too narrowly on this aspect. Beardslee notes that the parables maintain continuities with ordinary human life as well as challenging established habits.

1089   Crossan, John Dominic. *Cliffs of Fall: Paradox and Polyvalence in the Parables of Jesus*. New York: Seabury Press, 1980. 120 pp.

A study of the parables of Jesus in general, and of the parable of the Sower in particular which contends that parables are by nature polyvalent and can have no single meaning. Parables use primordial metaphoric language to create worlds and reality, but at the heart of every parable is paradox. Heavily influenced by Jacques Derrida's theories of deconstruction, Crossan contends that parables about God are meant to self-destruct because God has no image. The most an interpreter can do is to "play" with the parabolic language, accepting the lack of reality as a game to enjoy. Three papers offering different responses to this book are contained in *Society of Biblical Literature 1980 Seminar Papers*, ed. by Paul Achtemeier. See 1588, 1663, 1665. Also see 1635, 1704-1705.

1090   Crossan, John Dominic. *Finding Is the First Act: Trove Folktales and Jesus' Treasure Parable*. Missoula, MT: Scholars Press, 1979. 141 pp.

Compares Jesus' parable in Matthew 13:44 diachronically and synchronically to worldwide treasure tales and to Jewish treasure stories. The most distinctive aspect of Jesus' story is the identification of the treasure as being on land owned by someone other than the finder, hence the need to "sell all that one has to obtain it." Thus, Jesus' parable subverts the usual moral value of such stories and introduces an element of paradox not found in Jewish treasure folktales. Crossan offers this study as an example of the importance of considering synchronic elements as well as diachronic ones in literary analysis.

1091   Crossan, John Dominic. "A Metamodel for Polyvalent Narration." *Semeia* 9 (1977): 105-147.

Responds to three divergent interpretations of the prodigal son story in Luke 15 (1096) by offering a model that explain the principle underscoring these and other possible readings. Crossan's model describes polyvalent narration as "ludic" (as opposed to "mimetic") allegory--a paradox formed into a narrative, such that it "precludes canonical interpretation and becomes a metaphor for the hermeneutical multiplicity it engenders.

1092   Crossan, John Dominic. "Parable, Allegory, and Paradox." In *Semiology and Parables: An Exploration of the Possibilities Offered by Structuralism for Exegesis*, ed. by Daniel Patte, 247-281. Pittsburgh Theological Monograph Series, 9. Pittsburgh: Pickwick Press, 1976.

Relates Crossan's ideas about parable to structuralist theory. One question to be considered is whether the different interpretive possibilities offered by a parable are all manifestations of the same level of structure. Crossan concludes that the parable as literary genre characterized by paradox and the allegory as deep structure are parts of the same network--it is the structuring processes of the playful human imagination that are at work on all these levels. The article is followed by responses from John R. Donahue and John R. Jones and by the transcript of a panel discussion from the conference where the paper was first delivered.

1093   Crossan, John Dominic. "Parable as Religious and Poetic Experience." *Journal of Religion* 53 (1973): 330-358.

Notes the recent tendency to view Jesus' parables as literature with emphasis on their relationship to metaphor, and so explores more precisely the sort of metaphor that they might be. They are not didactic metaphors (examples, analogies, allegories), which are capable of being reduced to literal language. Rather, they are poetic metaphors, which can never be so reduced without losing their power. Crossan defines poetic metaphor as "language through which, by which, and in which the referent of the speaker's experience is experienced anew by the hearer." Jesus' parables represent his own experience of God verbalized poetically.

1094   Crossan, John Dominic. "Paradox Gives Rise to Metaphor: Paul Ricoeur's Hermeneutics and the Parables of Jesus." *Biblical Research: Journal of the Chicago Society of Biblical Research* 14-15 (1979-1980): 20-37.

Surveys and comments on Ricoeur's notion of parables in general and of the parables of Jesus in particular. Crossan understands Ricoeur to view parables in general as combining narrative form and metaphorical genre (Crossan himself would add the qualification of brevity). With regard to the parables of Jesus, however, a third element becomes relevant: paradox.

1095   Crossan, John Dominic, ed. *The Good Samaritan.* *Semeia* 2 (1974). 193 pp.

A collection of articles on the parable of the Good Samaritan from a variety of different literary perspectives. Included are "An Analysis of Narrative Structure and the Good Samaritan" by Daniel Patte; "The Parable of the Good Samaritan: An Essay in Structural Research" by Georges Crespy; "The Good Samaritan as Metaphor" by Robert W. Funk; and "The Good Samaritan: Towards A Generic Definition of Parable" by Crossan. Critical discussion of these articles is offered by Robert C. Tannehill, Patte, and Crossan. This issue of *Semeia* also includes other articles on parables not specifically related to the announced theme (see 1099, 1101, 1118).

1096   Crossan, John Dominic, ed. *Polyvalent Narration.* *Semeia* 9 (1977). 147 pp.

Explores the possibilities for multiple meanings in biblical texts by way of analyses of the story of the prodigal son in Luke 15. Mary Ann Tolbert presents a study of this parable from a (Freudian) psychoanalytical perspective, Dan O. Via, Jr. offers a Jungian reading, and Bernard B. Scott presents a structuralist interpretation. These three studies are followed by two theoretical works: "A Theory of Multiple Meanings" by Susan Wittig (0576) and "A Metamodel for Polyvalent Narration" by Crossan (1091).

1097 Davis, C. R. "Structural Analysis of Jesus' Narrative Parables: A Conservative Approach." *Grace Theological Journal* 9 (1988): 191-204.

Claims that structuralism, as an inherently neutral method, can be used by those who believe the Bible is inspired and inerrant. Davis then classifies 27 parables into four categories.

1098 Donahue, John R. *The Gospel in Parable: Metaphor, Narrative, and Theology in the Synoptic Gospels*. Philadelphia: Fortress Press, 1988. 256 pp.

Interprets selected parables within the literary contexts of the Gospels in which they are found. Donahue finds that numerous parables mirror their framing Gospel so as to present that Gospel in miniature. The prevailing concerns of the study are those of redaction criticism, but Donahue also understands the parables as narratives (with particular emphasis on characters and plot) and he ultimately discusses each of the synoptic Gospels as a parabolic narrative in itself.

1099   Doty, William G. "The Parables of Jesus, Kafka, Borges, and Others, with Structural Observations." *Semeia* 2 (1974): 152-193.

Suggests that the parables of Jesus should be considered along the same trajectory as other literary parables, including the dream stories of Kafka and the minor stories of Borges.   Characteristics on this trajectory include (sur/super)realism, reversal of expectation, humor, universality, non-application, mystery, and an interlocking of speaker and hearer.

1100   Drury, John. *The Parables in the Gospels. History and Allegory.* New York: Crossroad Publishing Co., 1985. 192 pp.

A study of selected parables within the contexts of their respective Gospels that makes use of a curious hybrid of methodologies. The book appeals to modern literary theory in its insistence in looking *at* the text rather than *through* it, and Drury's comments do in fact call attention to poetic features. Nevertheless, the real concern of the work is explicitly referential: to demonstrate what ancient texts meant to readers in the past rather than to explicate the meaning to readers now. As such, the work is eclectic, drawing here and there from narrative and rhetorical criticism, but remaining primarily concerned with redactional interests.

1101   Funk, Robert W. "Structure in the Narrative Parables of Jesus." *Semeia* 2 (1974): 51-73.

Divides the parables of Jesus into two groups, according to the sets of participants in them. Both groups feature two contrasting respondents as well as a Determiner to whom the response is made. In one group of parables, the two respondents are opposed to each other. In another group of parables, one respondent is clearly primary and the second serves only as a foil. Funk is most interested in the first group. Closer analysis reveals a consistent narrative structure, whereby expected destinies and fortunes are reversed: Jesus always sides with the respondent who offers the unexpected response. The article is followed by a critical response by Dan O. Via.

1102   Funk, Robert W., ed. *A Structuralist Approach to the Parables.* *Semeia* 1 (1974). 278 pp.

A collection of three essays that bring the insights of structuralist methodology to bear on the parables. In "The Servant Parables of Jesus," John Dominic Crossan relates the clash of structures in nine of Jesus' parables to the linguisticality of Jesus' teaching on permanent eschatology. In "Parable and Example in the Teaching of Jesus," Crossan looks at some parables peculiar to the Gospel of Luke and interprets them apart from (or in tension with) the interpretive frames provided by their current narrative setting. In "Parable and Example Story: A Literary-Structuralist Approach," Dan O. Via presents a detailed response to the two articles by Crossan. Briefer responses to both Crossan and Via are then provided by Norman Petersen and Robert Funk, and both Crossan and Via are allowed to answer the challenges raised in this critical discussion. A substantial bibliography on parable research rounds out the volume.

1103   Harnisch, Wolfgang. *Die Gleichniserzählungen Jesu: Eine hermeneutische Einführung.* Göttingen: Vandenhoeck and Ruprecht, 1985. 332 pp.

A study of the ten "genuine parables" in the Gospels, specified as such in distinction from metaphors and allegories. For Harnisch, parables are essentially narrative in form, and his interpretation of them shows an awareness of literary-critical concerns. Emphasis is given to the element of surprise, the semantic dissonance within these narratives that communicates in an unexpected way.

1104   McDaniel, Martin Calvert. "Parables in Context: Luke's Parables of the Minas and the Wicked Tenants and Their Literary Contexts." Ph.D. diss., Vanderbilt University, 1989. 381 pp.

Attempts to interpret Luke's parables of Minas (Luke 19:12-27) and of the Wicked Tenants (20:9-16) in terms of the accompanying actions of Jesus in the Gospel narrative. Drawing on Greimasian structuralism, McDaniel observes that a number of homologous actantial roles are attached to identical thematic roles in both the parables and their context.

1105   Noel, Timothy Lee. "The Parable of the Wedding Guest: A Narrative-Critical Interpretation." *Perspectives in Religious Studies* 16 (1989): 17-27.

Examines six connecting devices that establish the continuity of this parable in Luke 14:7-11 with its context (14:1-24): verbal keys; themes; persons; settings; values; and connecting phrases.

1106   Noel, Timothy Lee. "Parables in Context: Developing A Narrative-Critical Approach to Parables in Luke." Ph.D. diss., The Southern Baptist Theological Seminary, 1986. 211 pp.

Seeks to develop and apply a narrative-critical methodology for study of the parables in Luke's Gospel. Six connecting devices for use between parables are described and the functions of parables within their contexts are discussed under the categories of plot and characterization. Three parables are given extended treatment: the Sower, the Wedding Guest, and the Vineyard.

1107   Parsons, Mikeal C. "'Allegorizing Allegory': Narrative Analysis and Parable Interpretation." *Perspectives in Religious Studies* 15 (1988): 147-164.

Notes the resurgence that narrative criticism has brought to allegory in parable interpretation. Parsons considers the allegorizing of parables to be appropriate in literary criticism but faults literary approaches for failing to consider the roles of real author and real readers in their interpretive paradigm.

1108   Patte, Daniel. "Structural Analysis of the Parable of the Prodigal Son: Towards a Method." In *Semiology and Parables: An Exploration of the Possibilities Offered by Structuralism for Exegesis*, ed. by Daniel Patte, 71-150.   Pittsburgh Theological Monograph Series, 9. Pittsburgh: Pickwick Press, 1976.

Examines the parable from Luke 15 in terms of four models: narrative structure, mythical structure, elementary structure, and the interrelationship between these three structures. The essay is followed by formal responses from Robert C. Culley and William G. Doty and by notes from a panel discussion.

1109   Patte, Daniel. "Structural Network in Narrative: The Good Samaritan." In *Structuralism: An Inter-disciplinary Study*, ed. by Susan Wittig, 77-98. Pittsburgh: Pickwick Press, 1975.

A structuralist examination of the famous parable in Luke 10 according to models proposed by Claude Lévi-Strauss and, especially, A. J. Greimas. Patte considers the cultural structures, the structures of the enunciation, and the deep structures (which include narrative structure, mythic structure, and elmentary structure). "Structure" is defined in terms of the constraints that preside over the meaning of a narrative text. The semantic effect of the parable is discovered to be deeply offensive to the religious mind: it suggests that one can be truly religious only if one ventures outside of the religiously ordered world and becomes irreligious.

1110   Patte, Daniel, ed. *Semiology and Parables: Exploration of the Possibilities Offered by Structuralism for Exegesis*. Pittsburgh: Pickwick Press, 1976. 384 pp.

Contains five papers delivered at a conference on structuralist interpretation, along with responses and transcripts of panel discussions following each.   In addition, responses by Walburga von Raffler Engel and David Robertson to a paper by Robert Funk are included, even though Funk's paper was not available for publication. One of the papers, by Louis Marin, concerns "A Parable by Pascal," with responses by Larry H. Crist, Robert Detweiler, and Lou H. Silberman. For the others, see 1092, 1108, 1116, and 1119.

1111   Perrin, Norman. "The Parables of Jesus as Parables, as Metaphors, and as Aesthetic Objects: A Review Article." *Journal of Religion* 47 (1967): 340-347.

Discusses the parable research of Joachim Jeremias, Amos Wilder (1052), Robert Funk (1697), and Dan Via (1117) and traces the development of scholarly interest from historical exegesis to literary concerns.

1112   Praeder, Susan Marie. *The Word in Women's Worlds: Four Parables*. Wilmington, DE: Michael Glazier, 1988. 120 pp.

Brings literary concerns and sociological analysis to bear on four New Testament parables that feature women: the leaven, the lost coin, the judge and the widow, and the ten maidens.   Praeder considers these four stories exceptional to the general "invisibility" of women and their worlds in the parables of Jesus.

1113   Scott, Bernard Brandon. *Hear Then the Parable: A Commentary on the Parables of Jesus*. Philadelphia: Fortress Press, 1989. 465 pp.

A comprehensive treatment of 33 parables in the synoptic Gospels that draws upon a variety of critical methodologies. In addition to establishing an "originating structure" for each parable and then discussing each parable in terms of its redactional variation, Scott brings literary and social-scientific insights to bear on the parables. Scott's interpretations stress the relationship that the parabolic stories have to the mythological vision of the kingdom of God; he attempts in each case to discern how the story interacts with this vision to produce the "parabolic effect."

1114   Thiselton, Anthony C. "Reader-Response Hermeneutics, Action Models, and the Parables of Jesus." In *The Responsibility of Hermeneutics*, ed. by Roger Lundin, Anthony C. Thiselton, and Clarence Walhout, 79-126. Grand Rapids, MI: Wm. B. Eerdmans Publishing Co., 1985.

Utilizes insights of reader-response criticism to propose that different levels of linguistic or textual action in the parables of Jesus correspond to progressive levels of understanding. The article is part of a broader discussion that emphasizes right action as an important hermeneutical concern that should not be divorced from true knowledge.

1115   Tolbert, Mary Ann. *Perspectives on the Parables: An Approach to Multiple Interpretations*. Philadelphia: Fortress Press, 1978. 144 pp.

Attributes diversity of interpretations in parable studies to elements intrinsic to the form and structure of the parables. A parable is a story that means more than it says, that requires participation of its readers in creating meaning. Tolbert draws especially on Wittig's theory of multiple meanings (0576) and on Wheelwright's analysis of metaphor (0073). Affirmation of the need to recognize multiple interpretations does not result in anarchy: interpretations should be congruent with the logic of the narrative, they should be able to account for all of the elements of the story, and they should be internally consistent. Two interpretations of the prodigal son--one that passes these criteria and one that fails them--are presented as a test case.

1116   Via, Dan O., Jr. "The Parable of the Unjust Judge: A Metaphor of the Unrealized Self." In *Semiology and Parables: An Exploration of the Possibilities Offered by Structuralism for Exegesis*, ed. by Daniel Patte, 1-32. Pittsburgh Theological Monograph Series, 9. Pittsburgh: Pickwick Press, 1976.

Presents a structuralist and a Jungian interpretation of a parable from Luke 18. Via first offers functional and actantial analyses of the parable and then interprets its "irreducible diachronic element" in terms of Jungian concepts. The exercise is followed by responses from Norman R. Petersen, Edward McMahon, and James L. Crenshaw, and by a panel discussion featuring these and other participants. The real issue of concern is not Via's comments on this particular parable, but whether and how it is possible to integrate structuralist and psychological theory. See also 1662.

1117   Via, Dan O., Jr. *The Parables: Their Literary and Existential Dimension.* Philadelphia: Fortress Press, 1967. 217 pp.

Proposes a new methodology for interpreting the parables, based on an existential hermeneutic and on literary analysis. Via questions the validity of the "one-point" approach to parables, of allegorical interpretation, and of historical methods that view them in terms of their *Sitz im Leben*. He sees the parables as aesthetic objects, less about God than they are about the inter-relationships of humans encountered by God. The methodology, laid out clearly in the first half of the book, is subsequently applied to eight parables selected for analysis. These are considered in two literary categories: tragic (the Talents, the Ten Maidens, the Wedding Garment, the Wicked Tenants, and the Unforgiving Servant) and comic (the Workers in the Vineyard, the Unjust Steward, and the Prodigal Son). One of the most influential studies on parables in this century--a book that opened the door to increased attention to the aesthetic qualities of biblical texts. See also 1111, 1635.

1118   Wilder, Amos N. "The Parable of the Sower: Naiveté and Method in Interpretation." *Semeia* 2 (1974): 134-151.

Interprets the parable as a literary medium with universal human appeal. The story of the sower is related to the gestalt and signals of its language. It engages primordial responses concerning the relationship of humanity to nature. Central to the parable is the anguish of human effort and the hope of fruition through miscarriage.

1119   Wittig, Susan. "Meaning and Modes of Signification: Toward a Semiotic of the Parable." In *Semiology and Parables: An Exploration of the Possibilities Offered by Structuralism for Exegesis*, ed. by Daniel Patte, 319-347. Pittsburgh Theological Monograph Series, 9. Pittsburgh: Pickwick Press, 1976.

Discusses the semiotics of parables in terms of the varied elements of a communication model: sender, sign, receiver, referent. Wittig concludes that structural studies cannot help us to define *the* meaning of a parable, for the meaning of a parable (or of any text) depends upon the reader's own act of structuration.

THE GOSPEL OF MATTHEW

See also 0528-0529, 0534, 0552, 0593, 1046-1047, 1049, 1054, 1061, 1063, 1065, 1067-1072, 1074-1078, 1080, 1089-1090, 1098, 1100, 1102-1103, 1112-1113, 1211, 1305.

1120   Akin, D. L. "A Discourse Analysis of the Temptation of Jesus Christ as Recorded in Matthew 4:1-11." *OPTAT* (Dallas) 1 (1987): 78-86.

Examines participants, event-line, cohesive devices within the text, non-events (setting, background, evaluation, and collateral), and peak/climax in Matthew's narrative of the temptation.

1121 Anderson, Janice Capel. "Double and Triple Stories, the Implied Reader, and Redundancy in Matthew." *Semeia* 31 (1985): 71-89.

Shows how double and triple stories chart the role of the implied reader in Matthew. The repetition, arrangement, and location of the stories shapes the reading process. The use of redundancy for rhetorical effect is discussed within the context of information theory.

1122 Anderson, Janice Capel. "Mary's Difference: Gender and Patriarchy in the Birth Narratives." *Journal of Religion* 67 (1987): 183-202.

A literary analysis of the Matthean and Lukan birth narratives from the intentional perspective of a feminist reader. Both stories are shown to project and undermine versions of a male ideology that defines female gender and legitimates patriarchal control. Mary's female difference and extraordinary conception are incorporated into a patriarchal framework in a way that continues to subvert that framework. Luke even more than Matthew emphasizes Mary's freedom from patriarchal control and direct relationship to God.

1123 Anderson, Janice Capel. "Matthew: Gender and Reading." *Semeia* 28 (1983): 3-27.

Explores the usefulness of certain literary approaches for a feminist exegesis of the Gospel of Matthew. Two tentative analyses are offered: an analysis of the symbolic significance of gender in the Gospel and an analysis of the role of the implied reader in relationship to a feminist reading of the Gospel.

1124 Anderson, Janice Capel. "Matthew: Sermon and Story." In *Society of Biblical Literature 1988 Seminar Papers*, ed. by David J. Lull, 496-507. Atlanta: Scholars Press, 1988.

A reader-response approach to Matthew 5--9, focusing on the interrelationship of the Sermon on the Mount and the miracle stories that follow. Anderson notes the various possible interpretations that have been given, especially with regard to identification of the false prophets in 7:15-20. Her main interest is not in solving this dilemma, but in examining the reading strategies that have led individuals or communities to interpret the text in particular ways. She concludes that text, reader(s), and community must be viewed as partners in interpretation.

1125 Barta, Karen A. "Mission in Matthew: The Second Discourse as Narrative." In *Society of Biblical Literature 1988 Seminar Papers*, ed. by David J. Lull, 527-535. Atlanta: Scholars Press, 1988.

Suggests that the discourse of Jesus in Matthew 10:5b-42 is structured not only by themes, but by a narrative framework of mission and mission life. Two events, the exclusive mission to Israel in 10:5b-6 and the continuing Jewish persecution after that mission ends (10:23-25) form the "kernels" of this narrative frame. The remaining Jesus sayings incorporated into the discourse function as "satellites," filling in circumstances and consequences.

1126   Bauer, David Robert. "The Literary Function of the Genealogy in Matthew's Gospel." In *Society of Biblical Literature 1990 Seminar Papers*, ed. by David J. Lull, 451-468. Atlanta: Scholars Press, 1990.

Considers the literary function of the first seventeen verses of Matthew's Gospel within the story world of the Gospel as a whole. Matthew 1:1 is viewed as the general heading, 1:2-16 as the genealogical list itself, and 1:17 as a concluding summary. 1:16 represents a climax, signifying that Israel's history is incomprehensible outside of Jesus Christ as he is presented in Matthew's Gospel. The functions of interruptions at key points are also noted (e.g., the mention of women in verses 3, 5, 6, and 16 accents the inclusion of Gentiles and of the marginalized in God's plan). Bauer concludes by noting ways in which the genealogy serves as an introduction to the narrative. These include establishing Matthew's point of view concerning Jesus and introducing major categories according to which Jesus is to be understood.

1127   Bauer, David Robert. *The Structure of Matthew's Gospel: A Study in Literary Design*. Journal for the Study of the New Testament Supplement Series, 31/Bible and Literature Series, 15. Sheffield: Almond Press, 1988. 180 pp.

Examines the structure of Matthew's Gospel from the perspective of rhetorical criticism. Bauer introduces and defines 15 categories of compositional relationships that help to define literary structure and then determines how these function in the Gospel of Matthew. Repetitions of comparison and repetitions of contrast are especially significant, in addition to particularization, climax, preparation, and causation. The analysis reveals that Matthew's narrative divides into three sections (1:1-4:16; 4:17-16:20; 16:21-28:20), each of which climaxes with an affirmation of Jesus as the Son of God.

1128   Black, C. Clifton, III. "Depth of Characterization and Degrees of Faith in Matthew." In *Society of Biblical Literature 1989 Seminar Papers*, ed. by David J. Lull, 604-623. Atlanta: Scholars Press, 1989.

Dialogues with Kingsbury's presentation of characterization in Matthew (cf. 1150), suggesting that the latter's working definition of "character," regard for the relation of character to theology, assessment of "roundness" and "flatness," and concentration on traits are all matters open to reassessment. Black proposes that more attention needs to be paid to the choices that characters make within the narrative. Through such choices (narrated or implied), the reader is confronted with varying and conflicting degrees of fidelity to God.

1129   Boers, Hendrikus. "Language Usage and the Production of Matthew 1:18--2:23." In *Orientation By Disorientation*, ed. by Richard A. Spencer, 217-234. Pittsburgh: Pickwick Press, 1980.

A brief examination of the nativity stories in Matthew intended to demonstrate that Matthew (unlike Mark) does not handle traditions as a redactor but as an author. Matthew makes use of materials to give expression to the meaning he intends, producing a new coherent whole. Boers indicates that this characteristic of Matthew is illustrative of Saussure's theory that every speech act is a new realization of possibilities (0067).

1130   Boonstra, Harry. "Satire in Matthew." *Christianity in Literature* 29,4 (1980): 32-45.

Studies Jesus' polemic against the Pharisees in Matthew's Gospel as an instance of literary satire. Boonstra considers questions involving target (how accurate is the portrayal?), audience (Pharisees themselves, disciples, crowds), and technique (irony, incongruous juxtaposition, hyperbole, parable, counterquestion, name-calling, and so on). The latter part of the study is the most fruitful.

1131   Burnett, Fred W. "Characterization and Christology in Matthew: Jesus in the Gospel of Matthew." In *Society of Biblical Literature 1989 Seminar Papers*, ed. by David J. Lull, 588-603. Atlanta: Scholars Press, 1989.

Examines the role that the proper name "Jesus" plays in Matthew's narrative, deciding that the name serves as a signifier for which there are numerous possible signifieds, all of which deconstruct when used as keys to understanding the christology of Matthew as a whole. The signified of the proper name "Jesus" remains an undecidable in Matthew, even though 28:16-20 gives the reader an illusion of decideability.

1132   Burnett, Fred W. "Characterization in Matthew: Reader Construction of the Disciple Peter." *McKendree Pastoral Review* 4 (1987): 13-43.

Traces several facets of Matthew's characterization of Peter that encourage the reader to be interested in the personality of this character even apart from his function within the plot. The reader is given more information about this character than is pertinent for the plot, including his two names and indications of his emotions and opinions.

1133   Burnett, Fred W. "Prolegomenon to Reading Matthew's Eschatological Discourse: Redundancy and the Education of the Reader in Matthew." *Semeia* 31 (1985): 91-109.

Investigates the effect of redundancy at both narrative and discourse levels on Matthew's implied reader. The name "Jesus" is presented as a redundant reinforcement of the Gospel's initial presentation of Jesus as "God with us." In the eschatological discourse, reader expectations about Jesus are unfulfilled, but the overall effect of redundancies is to create a narrative world in which stability is primary.

1134   Calloud, Jean. *Structural Analysis of Narrative: Temptation of Jesus in the Wilderness*. Trans. by Daniel Patte. Semeia Supplements. Philadelphia: Fortress Press, 1976. 108 pp.

Introduces the biblical student to the structural analysis of A. J. Greimas. The bulk of the book is devoted to an analysis of Matthew 4:1-11 illustrative of this method.

1135   Clark, D. J., and Waard, J. de. "Discourse Structure in Matthew's Gospel." *Scriptura* Special 1 (1982): 1-97.

Discusses the alternative sections of narrative and discourse in Matthew's Gospel as forming three acts: 1--9; 10--18; 19--28. Three appendixes are included.

1136   Combrink, H. J. Bernard. "The Structure of the Gospel of Matthew as Narrative." *Tyndale Bulletin* 34 (1983): 61-90.

Approaches the structure of Matthew in two ways--textual indicators and narrative plot--and notes the essential congruence of the results. Textual indicators suggest a chiastic outline: A (1:1--4:17) B (4:18--7:29) C (8:1--9:35) D (9:36--11:1) E (11:2--12:50) F (13:1-53) E' (13:54--16:20) D' (16:21--20:34) C' (21:1--22:46) B' (23:1--25:46) A' (26:1--28:20). Analysis of narrative plot yields a compatible three-part outline: setting (1:1--4:17), complication (4:18-25:46), resolution (26:1-28:20).

1137   De Villiers, Pieter G. R., ed. *Structure and Meaning in Matthew 14--28.* Neotestamentica, 16. Stellenbosch: The New Testament Society of South Africa, 1983.

Continues the collection of essays in 1138 by applying the same methodological approach used there to the second half of Matthew's Gospel. This collection, published five years later than the first, exhibits a conspicuous development toward more diversity in approach, an indication that "discourse analysis" is still undergoing refinement as a method.

1138   De Villiers, Pieter, G. R., ed. *The Structure of Matthew 1--13: An Exploration into Discourse Analysis.* Neotestamentica, 11. Stellenbosch: The New Testament Society of South Africa, 1978.

A collection of essays that apply a form of structural exegesis known as "discourse analysis" to sections of the first half of Matthew's Gospel. Discourse analysis is to be distinguished from French structuralism, though its goal of discovering the deepest level of a text's meaning through analysis of its literary and linguistic structure is the same. Methodologically, discourse analysis is similar to types of rhetorical criticism. See also 1139.

1139   Edwards, Richard A. *Matthew's Story of Jesus.* Philadelphia: Fortress Press, 1985. 95 pp.

Interprets Matthew's narrative from the perspective of a "first-time" reader, emphasizing the narrative flow of the plot. Special attention is given to the manner in which the narrator guides the reader by revealing or concealing information as the narrative progresses. An early attempt at treating this Gospel as a story, rather than simply as an essay in story form. See also 1616.

1140 Edwards, Richard A. "Uncertain Faith: Matthew's Portrait of the Disciples." In *Discipleship in the New Testament*, ed. by Fernando F. Segovia, pp. 47-61. Philadelphia: Fortress Press, 1985.

Briefly analyzes the role of the disciples in Matthew's narrative from the perspective of reader-response criticism. The reader's attention is drawn to the ambivalence of the disciples in contrast to the stability of Jesus and of his Father in heaven. The narrative flow of the story, however, culminates in stories that focus on the disciples' understanding of Jesus' teaching, on their "unsure worship," and on their reception of a commission to "disciplize." At the end of the story, these matters remain foremost in the reader's attention.

1141 Fenton, J. C. "Inclusio and Chiasmus in Matthew." In *Studia Evangelica*, ed. by Kurt Aland, F. L. Cross, Jean Danielou, Harold Risenfeld, and W. C. van Unnik, 174-179. Berlin: Akademie Verlag, 1959.

Identifies instances of these two literary devices in Matthew's Gospel and speculates as to their significance.

1142 Hill, David. "The Figure of Jesus in Matthew's Story: A Response to Professor Kingsbury's Literary-Critical Probe." *Journal for the Study of the New Testament* 21 (1984): 37-52.

Argues with Kingsbury's contention that God's evaluative point of view (which identifies Jesus pre-eminently as "Son") must be regarded as normative for Matthew's narrative (1148). Hill thinks more attention should be given to Jesus' point of view concerning himself (as "Son of man") and to the hints and allusions found throughout the narrative to Jesus as the Servant of the Lord. Actually, Hill's argument is not only with Kingsbury's use of narrative criticism but with the method itself, which he regards as "undeniably subjective." For Kingsbury's reply, see 1149.

1143 Howell, David B. *Matthew's Inclusive Story: A Study in the Narrative Rhetoric of the First Gospel.* Journal for the Study of the New Testament Supplement Series, 42. Sheffield, England: JSOT Press, 1990. 292 pp.

Uses narrative and reader-response criticism to bridge the gap between the two horizons in Matthew's story. Matthew tells the past story of Jesus, but addresses the contemporary Christians of his own community. The link between these two horizons can be found in the literary concept of the implied reader. Howell seeks to define this implied reader by examining the narrative rhetoric of the Gospel, observing interpretive moves the reader is encouraged to make. He assumes a "naive reader" who is hearing the story for the first time.

1144 Jones, Ivor H. *The Gospel of Matthew.* Narrative Commentaries. Philadelphia: Trinity Press International, forthcoming.

Announced for publication.

1145 Kea, Perry V. "Discipleship in the Great Sermon: A Literary-Critical Approach." Ph.D. diss., University of Virginia, 1983.

Interprets the Sermon on the Mount (Matthew 5--7) from the perspective of a literary theory informed by Paul Ricoeur and Wolfgang Iser. Poetic devices such as parallelism, metaphor, irony, hyperbole, paradox, and aphorism are discussed with reference to individual sayings. An overriding concern is the semantic confluence of indicative and imperative in the sermon, which Kea relates to Matthean eschatology.

1146 Kermode, Frank. "Matthew." In *The Literary Guide to the Bible*, ed. by Robert Alter and Frank Kermode, 387-401. Cambridge, MA: Belknap Press, 1987.

This reading of Matthew by a renowned literary critic emphasizes the need to recognize the logic of the evangelist's imagination. The latter may be revealed in his treatment of the Old Testament: he grants the old text its sanctity but always assumes it must be fulfilled in something new. Likewise, Matthew's narrative presents Jesus as the new Israel, as can be seen in examination of certain phases of the story: the Nativity, the Temptation, the Transfiguration, the Triumphal Entry, and the Cleansing of the Temple. See also 1177.

1147 Kingsbury, Jack Dean. "The Developing Conflict Between Jesus and the Jewish Leaders in Matthew's Gospel: A Literary-Critical Study." *Catholic Bible Quarterly* 49 (1987): 57-73.

Describes Matthew's characterization of the Jewish leaders and delineates the role that the latter play in the plot of this Gospel. The leaders are a character group, whose chief trait is "evil" and whose evaluative point of view is consistently aligned against the true point of view of God. The story line of the leaders develops in three stages that parallel those of the story line of Jesus. The conflict between Jesus and the Jewish leaders is central to Matthew's story and heightened intensity of this conflict marks major movements in the development of the story's plot.

1148 Kingsbury, Jack Dean. "The Figure of Jesus in Matthew's Story: A Literary-Critical Probe." *Journal for the Study of the New Testament* 21 (1984): 3-36.

A study in Matthean christology utilizing the insights of narrative criticism. Kingsbury extrapolates the story line of Jesus as presented in Matthew's narrative in three stages (1:1--4:16; 4:17--16:20; 16:21--28:20). Although the article contains numerous insights (see also 1150), the most important point is that Matthew's narrative presents Jesus pre-eminently as the Son of God. Kingsbury argues that God's evaluative point of view is established as normative in this narrative; accordingly, God's identification of Jesus as "Son" (3:17; 17:5) takes precedence over all other descriptions of Jesus offered in the narrative. For further discussion of this point, see 1142 and 1149.

1149 Kingsbury, Jack Dean. "The Figure of Jesus in Matthew's Story: A Rejoinder to David Hill." *Journal for the Study of the New Testament* 25 (1985): 61-81.

A response to criticisms of an earlier Kingsbury article (1148) made by Hill (1142). Kingsbury restates and bolsters the arguments set forth in his initial article and then faults counter-views presented by Hill: Matthew's narrative does not present a peculiar category of Servant christology, though it does present Jesus as one who serves, and the title Son of man never functions to designate "who Jesus is" for any of the characters in this narrative.

1150   Kingsbury, Jack Dean. *Matthew As Story*. 2nd rev. ed. Philadelphia: Fortress Press, 1988.   171 pp.

A comprehensive treatment of Matthew's Gospel from the perspective of narrative criticism.   An opening chapter discusses the story of Matthew in terms of its events, characters, and settings, and the discourse of the Gospel in terms of its implied author, point of view, and implied reader.   The heart of the volume is devoted to extrapolations of the story lines of Jesus, of the religious leaders, and of the disciples. Special chapters are devoted to Jesus' use of the title "Son of man," to the great speeches, and to the community of Matthew.   Kingsbury emphasizes the role that conflict plays in the development of Matthew's plot.   The best book on Matthew from this perspective.   See also 1128.

1151   Kingsbury, Jack Dean.   "The Parable of the Wicked Husbandmen and the Secret of Jesus' Divine Sonship in Matthew: Some Literary-Critical Observations." *Journal of Biblical Literature* 105 (1986): 643-655.

Argues that the secret of Jesus' divine sonship constitutes a major motif in Matthew's story and that the parable in 21:33-46 plays a critical role in the development of this motif.   In general, human characters in Matthew's narrative do not know that Jesus is the Son of God and those who do discover this secret (the disciples) keep the knowledge to themselves.   In the parable of the wicked husbandmen, Jesus discloses the secret, but the Jewish leaders are unable to comprehend the truth of what he says and ultimately judge his claim to be that of a "deceiver" (27:63).

1152   Kingsbury, Jack Dean.   "Reflections on 'the Reader' of Matthew's Gospel." *New Testament Studies* 34 (1988): 442-460.

Discusses models of readership that have been envisioned by historical-biographical, redactional, and literary approaches to Matthew, indicating the contribution that the concept of an implied reader endorsed by narrative criticism has to offer.   Kingsbury demonstrates specific exegetical and hermeneutical problems that arise when Matthew's Gospel is interpreted from the perspective of a reader who is construed as a contemporary of the historical Jesus or a member of the evangelist's first-century community.   The implied reader favored by narrative criticism is the reader of Matthew as he or she can be inferred from or reconstructed on the basis of the text. Following this model alerts one to the world of the story but does not commit one to an anti-historical bias.

1153   Marin, Louis.   "Essai d'analyse structurale d'un récit-parabole: Matthieu 13, 1-23."   *Etudes Theologiques et Réligieuses* 46 (1971): 35-74.

Examines Matthew 13:1-23, which includes the parable of the Sower, in terms of its syntagmatic   correlations: exterior/interior;   crowds/disciples;   clear-obscure parable/private-enlightening explanation. Marin charts the successive movements of Jesus (house, lakeside, boat) and the successive audiences. The fourfold rhythm of repetitive-inverse symmetry detectable there can also be found within the parable itself. The paradigmatic dimension of the text is discernible in such schemas as gift/non-gift and now/time.

1154 Marin, Louis. "Jesus before Pilate: A Structural Analysis Essay." In *The New Testament and Structuralism*, ed. by Alfred M. Johnson, 97-144. Pittsburgh: Pickwick Press, 1976.

Examines the surface structures of Matthew 27:1-2, 11-31 with a model derived from A. J. Greimas. Marin segments the text into twelve parts and studies the relationships that can be discerned between them. He is particularly interested in "couplings" of segments where semantic relationships are comparable and parallel. In addition, he notes the dynamic oppositions that are inherent in the text, especially with regard to character relationships.

1155 Marin, Louis. "The Women at the Tomb: A Structural Analysis Essay of a Gospel-Text." In *The New Testament and Structuralism*, ed. by Alfred M. Johnson, Jr., 73-96. Pittsburgh: Pickwick Press, 1976. 338 pp.

A structuralist study of the "surface structures" of the short story found in Matthew 28:1-8. The conclusion is that there is within the narrative an apparent narrative in which another story is secretly told--that of the passage from a discursive figure focused on the natural human or supernatural event. See also 1581.

1156 Matera, Frank J. "The Plot of Matthew's Gospel." *Catholic Biblical Quarterly* 49 (1987): 233-253.

Investigates the plot of Matthew's Gospel from a particular literary point of view that understands plot in terms of "narrative logic." Matera determines that Matthew's plot is organized into six narrative blocks organized around kernel events (the birth of Jesus, the beginning of Jesus' ministry, the question of John the Baptist, the conversation at Caesarea Philippi, the cleansing of the temple, and the great commission). The climax of the entire narrative in 28:16-20 indicates that the cumulative affective response the narrative seeks to produce is worship (28:17) and confidence (28:20).

1157 O'Donnell, Patrick James. "A Literary Analysis of Matthew 8: Jesus' First Gentile Mission." Ph.D. diss., The Iliff School of Theology, 1979. 223 pp.

Examines questions of structure, rhetoric, plot, characterization, point of view, and setting in the eighth chapter of Matthew. Plot is seen to provide the unifying force in the chapter, and that plot is concerned with a Gentile mission by Jesus. The most notable indicator of plot is Jesus' prophecy of eschatological reversal in Matthew 8:11-12.

1158 Panier, Louis. *Récit et commentaries de la tentation de Jésus au désert*. Paris: Cerf, 1984. 381 pp.

An analysis of the temptation narrative in Matthew's Gospel (4:1-11) following the method of structural analysis developed by A. J. Greimas, who served as advisor of the doctoral dissertation on which this study is based. Panier approaches the text in terms of what he regards as the three aspects of biblical commentary: the narrative component, the discursive component, and enunciation.

1159 Patte, Daniel. "Bringing Out of the Gospel-Treasure What is New and What is Old: Two Parables in Matthew 18--23." *Quarterly Review* 10,3 (1990): 79-108.

Examines two lectionary texts (18:21-35; 21:28-32) in terms of three possible lessons that preachers might derive from them. In each case, Patte interprets the lessons (1) from a traditional perspective that attempts to discern to what they refer; (2) from a new perspective that focuses on interrelationships of the characters within the text; and (3) from a contextual perspective that examines the role that this pericope plays in the larger narrative.

1160 Patte, Daniel. *The Gospel According to Matthew: A Structural Commentary on Matthew's Faith*. Philadelphia: Fortress Press, 1987. 432 pp.

A systematic investigation of Matthew from the perspective of structuralism. The Gospel is examined by sections, with particular attention to semantic and narrative oppositions (e.g., "new" vs. "old," "good" vs. "evil") that reveal convictions the author held to be self-evident. The work is accessible to those who are unfamiliar with the theory and method of structuralism.

1161 Phillips, Gary A. "History and Text: The Reader in Context in Matthew's Parables Discourse." *Semeia* 31 (1985): 111-138.

Interprets the parable discourse of Matthew 13 according to the post-structuralist paradigms of Jacques Derrida and Michel Foucault. The resultant reading attempts to balance attention to the text with attention to the reader and to historical context.

1162 Powell, Mark Allan. "Direct and Indirect Phraseology in the Gospel of Matthew." In *Society of Biblical Literature 1991 Seminar Papers*, ed. by Eugene H. Lovering, Jr., 405-417. Atlanta: Scholars Press, 1991.

Proposes a new distinction for studying point of view on the phraseological plane (cf. 0305) and illustrates the significance of this distinction with reference to characterization in the Gospel of Matthew. Phraseology may be described as either direct or indirect depending on whether the subject of the speech is addressed or simply referred to in speech addressed to another. No distinction can be observed between the point of view of Jesus revealed through direct phraseology and that revealed through indirect phraseology in Matthew's Gospel, but with regard to Jesus' opponents, such a distinction is not only noticeable but striking. Matthew uses this distinction to supplement his more explicit characterization of these opponents as hypocrites.

1163   Powell, Mark Allan.   "The Plot and Subplots of Matthew's Gospel."   To appear in *New Testament Studies* 38,2 (1992).

Surveys three views of Matthew's plot presented previously by Edwards (1139), Matera (1156), and Kingsbury (1150) and seeks to expand on these studies by synthesizing the three elements they consider most significant (narrative flow, narrative logic, and conflict).   Powell decides that the main plot of Matthew's Gospel concerns God's saving activity enacted through Jesus in opposition to Satan.   Conflicts between Jesus and the disciples on the one hand and between Jesus and the religious leaders on the other form significant subplots that are tangential to the main plot line, though they ultimately serve to advance its interests.   Only the main plot line is resolved favorably within the narrative: Jesus loses his conflicts with both the disciples and the religious leaders in order that God might win the greater conflict with Satan.

1164   Powell, Mark Allan.   "The Religious Leaders in Matthew's Gospel: A Literary-Critical Approach."   Ph.D. diss., Union Theological Seminary in Virginia, 1988.   264 pp.

A comprehensive literary examination of every passage in Matthew's Gospel concerning the religious leaders, with particular interest in character traits, evaluative point of view, and the role that the leaders play in the story.   Three traits, "evil," "hypocritical," and "spiritually blind," are found to be especially pertinent, and the first of these is shown to be foundational for the other two.   The leaders' point of view is consistently aligned with that of Satan rather than with that of God.   The conflict between the leaders and Jesus and its development within the narrative is described in terms of the threats that these characters pose to each other.

1165   Reeves, Keith H.   "The Resurrection Narrative in Matthew: A Literary-Critical Examination."   Ph.D. diss., Union Theological Seminary in Virginia, 1988.   165 pp.

Analyzes Matthew 27:55--28:20 in terms of the structure of the narrative, the characters portrayed within the narrative, and the scenes that comprise the narrative. Particular attention is given to themes that unify the narrative and to plot development.   The three most important themes are (1) resolution of conflict between Jesus and his disciples and renewal of conflict between Jesus and the religious leaders; (2) prophecy and fulfillment; and (3) the universal mission to the nations.

1166   Stanton, Graham.   *The Gospel for a New People: Studies in Matthew*.   London: T and T Clark, 1990.   320 pp.

Essentially a historical investigation into the origin and purpose of Matthew's Gospel, this book also discusses in its first section the new literary-critical and social-scientific approaches to Matthew.   Stanton believes that these new methodologies help to clarify Matthew's purposes and the circumstances of the Christian communities for whom he wrote.

1167   Stock, Augustine. "Is Matthew's Presentation of Peter Ironic?" *Biblical Theology Bulletin* 17 (1987): 64-69.

Provides an English summary of Van Iersel's article on Matthew 16:18 (1171) and adds some comments on implications for Roman Catholic views of the primacy of Peter today.

1168   Stramare, T. "L'annunciazione a Giuseppe in Mt. 1,18-25: Analisi letteraria e significato teologico." *Biblica et orientalia* 31 (1989): 3-14.

A literary analysis of the annunciation to Joseph in Matthew's Gospel. Stramara focuses on narrative patterns, including the use of chiasmus and inclusion. He is also interested in the text's redactional history, and attempts a brief semiotic analysis.

1169   Thiemann, Ronald F. "The Unnamed Woman at Bethany." *Theology Today* 44 (1987): 179-188.

Describes the character role of the unnamed woman at Bethany in Matthew's narrative (26:6-13) as being to open the concept of disciple to persons other than the original twelve.

1170   Van Aarde, A. G. "Plot as Mediated through Point of View: Mt. 22:1-14-- A Case Study." In *A South African Perspective on the New Testament*, ed. by J. H. Petzer and P. J. Hartin, 62-75. Leiden: E. J. Brill, 1986.

Studies the "plotted time" in Matthew's Gospel, particularly as depicted in the parable of the wedding banquet (Matthew 22:1-14). The plotting of Matthew's Gospel employs two equivalent narrative lines, namely that of the pre-Easter Jesus-commission and that of the post-Easter disciples-commission. The conjunction of these two lines can be seen in 22:1-14, which illustrates Matthew's idea of "plotted time" in a nutshell.

1171   Van Iersel, Bas. "Matteus 16,18: Simôn, Petros, petra, prôtos. Reflectie op woordspelingen rond Simon, de steenrots." *Tijdscrift voor Theologie* 25,4 (1985): 402-409.

Asks whether the wordplay between Peter's name (*petros*) and the Greek word for rock (*petra*) in Matthew 16:18 might be ironic, since Peter is not characterized as providing a strong foundation in Matthew's narrative as a whole. Van Iersel decides it is not, in light of another word play between *petros* and *protos* ("first"), which emphasizes not his strength but his primacy. See also 1167.

1172   Via, Dan O., Jr. "The Gospel of Matthew: Hypocrisy as Self-Deception." In *Society of Biblical Literature 1988 Seminar Papers*, ed. by David J. Lull, 508-516. Atlanta: Scholars Press, 1988.

Contends that Matthew's narrative presents hypocrisy as a form of self-deception by which the hypocrite is both the victimizer who lies and the victim who is lied to. Key texts discussed include 7:15-20; 6:1-18; and 18:23-25. Hypocrisy is cured by the gospel or word of the kingdom, which gives understanding or insight.

1173   Via, Dan O., Jr. "Narrative World and Ethical Response: The Marvelous and Righteousness in Matthew 1--2." *Semeia* 12 (1978): 123-149.

Focuses on Matthew 1-2 in an investigation of the significance that the narrative element of atmosphere has for defining what is ethically obligatory and possible. The relationship of eschatological well-being and ethical performance is especially noted. The broad concern of the article is to determine the proper autonomy for the literary, the religious, and the ethical, as these are expressed in the New Testament and elsewhere.

1174   Via, Dan O., Jr.   "Structure, Christology, and Ethics in Matthew."   In *Orientation By Disorientation*, ed. by Richard A. Spencer, 199-216.   Pittsburgh: Pickwick Press, 1980.

Uses structural analysis to expose tensions in Matthew's understanding of christology, salvation, and ethics. In terms of christology, Matthew presents the Son as the embodiment of divine freedom (grace), but also as Wisdom-Torah (demand). Salvation is based both on the divine forgiveness demonstrated through the Son and on good works, which include the human extension of forgiveness to others. The ethical life is presented both as a response to the presence of salvation and as a condition for the receipt of salvation.

1175   Vigen, Larry Allan. "To Think the Things of God: A Discourse Reading of Matthew 16:13--18:35." Ph.D. diss., Vanderbilt University, 1985. 429 pp.

Develops a "discoursive reading" (i.e., a reading that converses about itself) of Matthew 16:13--18:35. The discoursive reading deconstructs the naturally synthetic reading process and reconstructs it as logical, in the direction that a reader might be expected to proceed. The study is based on the work of A. J. Greimas and of Daniel Patte, who supervised it.

1176   Weaver, Dorothy Jean. *Matthew's Missionary Discourse: A Literary Critical Analysis*. Journal for the Study of the New Testament Supplement Series, 38. Sheffield: Sheffield Academic Press, 1990. 260 pp.

Attempts to resolve the apparent discrepancies and interpretive difficulties attending Matthew 9:35--11:1 by interpreting the passage from the perspective of its implied reader. The narrator locates the missionary discourse within the framework of Jesus' own ministry in order to establish the significance of the disciples' task. Parallels are drawn between the disciples' ministry and Jesus' own, but the narrator omits any account of the fulfillment of the disciples' mission. The implied reader is ultimately drawn into fulfilling the task of the commission as set forward in 9:35--11:1 and transformed in 28:16-20.

1177   Williams, James G.   "Paraenesis, Ethics, and Excess: Matthew's Rhetoric in the Sermon on the Mount." *Semeia* 50 (1990): 163-187.

Draws on sociological/anthropological studies and on literary-rhetorical criticism to discuss the Sermon on the Mount as an example of paraenetic literature. Williams picks up on a suggestion by Frank Kermode (1146) to the effect that the Sermon utilizes a "rhetoric of excess." The shocking statements of Jesus (in the antitheses, for instance) are not to be taken literally but express rhetorically the need for transformation.

1178   Witherup, Ronald D.   "The Cross of Jesus: A Literary-Critical Study of Matthew 27." Ph.D. diss., Union Theological Seminary in Virginia, 1985. 395 pp.

A comprehensive narrative-critical analysis of Matthew 27 that presents this chapter as playing a climactic role in bringing together four central themes in Matthew's Gospel: (1) salvation history; (2) prophecy and fulfillment; (3) discipleship; and (4) Jesus' identity as the royal, obedient, and faithful Son of God.

1179   Witherup, Ronald D.   "The Death of Jesus and the Raising of the Saints: Matthew 27:51-54 in Context." In *Society of Biblical Literature 1987 Seminar Papers*, ed. by Kent Harold Richards, 574-585. Atlanta: Scholars Press, 1987.

Proposes that the unique account of the earthquake and of the raising of saints in Matthew 27:51-54 has a climactic role in the structure of chapter 27 and carries both christological and salvation-historical significance. The events are an expression of God's point of view and serve to elicit the divine perspective on Jesus' identity, namely that he is the Son of God. They also serve as eschatological signs that signal the beginning of the new age.

1180   Wojcik, Jan.   "The Two Kingdoms in Matthew's Gospel." In *Literary Interpretations of Biblical Narratives*, ed. by Kenneth R. R. Gros Louis with James S. Ackerman and Thayer S. Warshaw, 283-295. Nashville: Abingdon Press, 1974.

Presents a close reading of Matthew 14 and 26, emphasizing the manner in which scene shifts juxtapose the actions of those who are opposed to God with those who are on God's side. These scene shifts are illustrative of Jesus' preaching in Matthew concerning the two kingdoms. The theme and its manner of literary presentation are unique to Matthew.

1181   Wolthuis, Thomas Ray.   "Experiencing the Kingdom: Reading the Gospel of Matthew." Ph.D. diss., Duke University, 1987. 374 pp.

Analyzes the structure of Matthew's Gospel and the theme of the kingdom of heaven from a literary-critical perspective. A detailed thematic outline of the Gospel is defended, yet it is recognized that in the reading process these thematic divisions are governered by the process of exposition, rising action with impediments, crisis, falling action, catastrophe, and dénouement. The crisis (or key turning point) of the narrative is chapter 13. The symbol of the kingdom of heaven unifies all the thematic sub-structures.

THE GOSPEL OF MARK

See also 0128, 0513, 0516, 0534, 0546, 0548, 0552, 0556, 1046-1048, 1054-1055, 1060-1061, 1063, 1065, 1067-1072, 1075-1076, 1078, 1080-1081, 1087, 1089, 1098, 1100, 1102-1103, 1113, 1118, 1248, 1441, 1597, 1650, 1693.

1182 Barber, Raymond Carl. "Mark as Narrative: A Case for Chapter One." Ph.D. diss., Graduate Theological Union, 1988. 390 pp.

Studies the poetic function of the first two chapters of Mark's Gospel. Barber is interested in Mark's selection and arrangement of his message along the linear axis of grammar, semantics, technique of poetic arrangement, plot, and characterization mediated through point of view. He finds that 1:1-11 establishes the ideological point of view from which and through which the rest of the story of Mark is told.

1183 Bassler, Jouette M. "The Parable of the Loaves." *Journal of Religion* 66 (1986): 157-172.

Uses reader-response criticism to interpret the two feeding stories as "parables," that is, as metaphors for an implied reader. By the end of Mark's narrative, the reader is to realize that the loaves in these stories referred "on some inchoate level" to Jesus' broken body on the cross. But this is realized only in retrospect: Mark's text generates puzzlement at the point where this christological message is emphasized and this puzzlement is set into a broader narrative context that emphasizes misunderstanding.

1184 Beavis, Mary Ann. "The Trial Before the Sanhedrin (Mark 14:53-65): Reader Response and Greco-Roman Readers." *Catholic Biblical Quarterly* 49 (1987): 581-596.

Compares the Markan account of Jesus' trial before the Sanhedrin to four other pericopes that bear a structural resemblance to this passage (7:31-37; 8:22-26; 8:27-33; 15:1-5). The main interest of the article is in exposing the inadequacy of reader-response criticism to recognize structural clues to interpretation that would have been clear to ancient readers.

1185 Belo, Fernando. *A Materialist Reading of the Gospel of Mark.* Trans. by Matthew J. O'Connell. Maryknoll, NY: Orbis Books, 1981. 384 pp.

Originally published in 1974 as *Lecture Matérialiste de l'evangile de Marc.* Belo presents a reading of Mark's Gospel from the perspective of a Marxist hermeneutic, informed by structuralist literary principles. Belo also draws heavily from social scientific studies to emphasize the role that social/class dynamics have in determining the reading process. See also 0500.

1186   Berg, Temma F. "Reading In/to Mark." *Semeia* 48 (1989): 187-206.

Discusses why biblical critics seek to avoid poststructuralism in their reading methodologies and then offers a poststructuralist reading of Mark's Gospel. Berg wonders whether Christian readers will ever be able to embrace poststructuralism, given their predilection for reading the New Testament as a revelation of Christ. Her study of Mark reveals gaps and discontinuities in the text and argues that the reader cannot be defined uniformly.

1187   Best, Ernest. "Mark's Narrative Technique." *Journal for the Study of the New Testament* 37 (1989): 43-58.

Describes Mark's ability to tell a story, with emphasis on what may be regarded as conscious technique. Best emphasizes the oral character of Mark's story, which makes repetition and a strong story line important. He also notes characteristic devices, such as the "sandwiching" of incidents and the element of surprise.

1188   Bilezikian, Gilbert G. *The Liberated Gospel: A Comparison of the Gospel of Mark and Greek Tragedy.* Grand Rapids, MI: Baker Books, 1977. 159 pp.

Contends that Mark imitated the model of Greek tragedy to give his Gospel shape and notes several similarities between the Gospel and Greek tragedies. The plot of Mark's Gospel contains the elements for tragedy as outlined in Aristole's *Poetics*: a complication (1:1-8:26), a recognition scene (8:27-30), and a dénouement (8:31-16:8).

1189   Blackwell, John. "Myth, Meaning and Hermeneutic: The Method of Claude Lévi-Strauss Applied to Narrative in Mark." Ph.D. diss., School of Theology at Claremont, 1981. 112 pp.

Describes the structuralist method of Claude Lévi-Strauss and applies it to the exegesis of two stories from Mark: the parable of the Sower and the story of the woman with the hemorrhage. Each story is interpreted in light of the fundamental oppositions it assumes.

1190   Blackwell, John. *The Passion As Story: The Plot of Mark.* Philadelphia: Fortress Press, 1988. 96 pp.

Interprets the passion narrative in Mark's Gospel as story (i.e., as "imaginative communication of truth") rather than as "mere representation of historical fact." Blackwell notes the singling out of particular characters, times, and places, and the contrasts that are produced with regard to these (e.g., Pilate vs. high priest; leper's house vs. tomb). Attention is also directed to Mark's use of selected Old Testament passages. What gives the story of the passion its authority is that it conveys the human condition and provides for its transformation.

1191   Boers, Hendrikus. "Reflections on the Gospel of Mark: A Structural Investigation." In *Society of Biblical Literature 1987 Seminar Papers*, ed. by Kent Harold Richards, 255-267. Atlanta: Scholars Press, 1987.

The stated purpose of this article is to discover the unity of the gospel of Mark on the basis of its internal text-syntactic structure. Actually, it is a collection of miscellaneous insights regarding various themes and motifs in Mark's narrative. Boers considers the place that several key passages (the Gospel heading, its ending, the first passion prediction, and so on) have in determining the internal structure. He also discusses the roles of key characters and character groups and the significance of such themes as the messianic secret and the meaning of suffering.

1192   Boomershine, Thomas E. "Mark 16:8 and the Apostolic Commission." *Journal of Biblical Literature* 100 (1981): 225-239.

Surveys traditional interpretations of Mark 16:8 and then proposes a new understanding based on suggestions for how the passage would have been read orally. Boomershine proposes that the scandalous actions of the woman's flight and silence would have been reported in a tone of judgment, while the reasons for these would be explained with sympathy. Thus, the hearers would understand the women's actions but also realize how wrong they were. Accordingly, 16:8 reverses the motif of the messianic secret in favor of an apostolic commission to proclaim the gospel.

1193   Boomershine, Thomas E. "Mark, the Storyteller: A Rhetorical-Critical Investigation of Mark's Passion and Resurrection Narrative." Ph.D. diss., Union Theological Seminary (New York), 1974. 380 pp.

Examines Mark's passion narrative in light of three central hypotheses: (1) Mark reorganized traditional materials into new literary units; (2) the narrative was written for oral presentation; (3) the passion narrative is integrally related to the Gospel's over-all meaning. Boomershine draws not only on the concepts of rhetorical criticism but also on those that would later be associated with narrative criticism (point of view, characterization, plot development, and so on). In these matters, as well as in the attention to orality, this work was a seminal study, anticipating concerns that would dominate scholarship a decade or more later.

1194   Boomershine, Thomas, and Bartholomew, Gilbert. "Narrative Technique of Mark 16:8." *Journal of Biblical Literature* 100 (1981): 213-223.

Demonstrates the likelihood that 16:8 is the intended ending of Mark's Gospel by comparing the literary style of this verse with verses that end stories elsewhere in the Gospel. Three features are discussed: the use of extensive narrative commentary, the use of intensive inside views, and the use of short sentences. With regard to all three matters, Mark can be seen to employ the same narrative techniques in 16:8 as in endings of other stories in the Gospel.

1195 Calloud, Jean. "Toward A Structural Analysis of the Gospel of Mark." *Semeia* 16 (1980): 133-165.

Provides samples of structuralist research with regard to Mark 2. As a first step, the method is applied to individual episodes. Next, the semantic relations disclosed within those episodes are progressively extended to series of episodes. As a result, a level of coherence and continuity emerges for the Gospel as a totality, based on the correlations discovered between the individual episodes.

1196 Camery-Hoggatt, Jerry Alan. "Word Plays: Evidence of Dramatic Irony in the Gospel of Mark." Ph.D. diss., Boston University, 1985.

Proposes a rhetoric for understanding the narrative irony of Mark's Gospel based on two fields of research: sociological study that examines the verbal and conceptual "life world" assumed by the text, and literary study that explores the strategies by which the text generates new understanding. One chapter is devoted to the theme of the messianic secret.

1197 Cassel, Jay Frank. "The Reader in Mark: The Crucifixion." Ph.D. diss., University of Iowa, 1984.

Proposes a theory for reading Mark based on the work of Wolfgang Iser. Cassel emphasizes the effect on readers of perspectives formed by other texts on which the primary text draws for allusions and generic patterns. The study analyzes expectations formed in readers of Mark's crucifixion narrative by Daniel 6, Wisdom of Solomon 2--5, and Psalm 22. Mark raises these expectations only to contradict them.

1198 Chu, Samuel Wing-Wah. "The Healing of the Epileptic Boy in Mark 9:14-29: Its Rhetorical Structure and Theological Implications." Ph.D. diss., Vanderbilt University, 1988. 276 pp.

A narrative/rhetorical study of Mark 9:14-29 in its context. The text is tied closely to the two preceding pericopes (9:2-8, 9-13). The central theme appears to be discipleship, and this is addressed through illustrations of success and failure. Jesus himself is presented as the "powerful/powerless" one who is able to drive out demons but still must deal with human limitations.

1199 Culpepper, R. Alan. "Mark 10:50: Why Mention the Garment?" *Journal of Biblical Literature* 101 (1982): 131-132.

Suggests that Bartimaeus' casting off his garment is part of a chain of references to garments in Mark's Gospel (2:21; 11:7-8; 13:16) that constitute a literary motif. In Mark, the old garment represents that which the disciple must leave behind to follow Jesus.

1200   Dewey, Joanna. "The Literary Structure of the Controversy Stories in Mark 2:1--3:6." In *The Interpretation of Mark*, ed. by William Telford, 109-118. Issues in Religion and Theology, 7. Philadelphia: Fortress Press, 1985.

Diagrams a concentric structural pattern for the conflict stories presented in Mark 2:1 --3:6. Mark 2:1-12 and 3:1-6 display similar formal arrangements, such that they may be identified as the external circle. Mark 2:13-17 and 2:23-28 also display a similar form, though in content 2:13-17 points back to 2:1-12 and 2:23-28 points ahead to 3:1-6. The center of the concentric pattern, then, is 2:18-22, with its statement about new wine and allegorical reference to Jesus as the bridegroom.

1201   Dewey, Joanna. "Mark as Interwoven Tapestry: Forecasts and Echoes for a Listening Audience." *Catholic Biblical Quarterly* 53 (1991): 221-236.

Argues that the Gospel of Mark does not possess a single structure composed of sequential units but, rather, an "interwoven tapestry" made up of overlapping structures. Mark uses a nonlinear recursive compositional style characteristic of aural narrative. Dewey notes forecasts of what is to come and echoes of what has already been said.

1202   Dewey, Joanna. *Markan Public Debate: Literary Technique, Concentric Structure, and Theology in Mark 2:1--3:6.* Society of Biblical Literature Dissertation Series 48. Chico, CA: Scholars Press, 1980. 277 pp.

A rhetorical analysis that demonstrates this passage has been structured concentrically both as a whole and in parts. Techniques of chiasm, ring composition, and extended concentric structure are employed in order to shape materials into narrative units. Dewey also discovers examples of concentric structure elsewhere in Mark, indicating that this is a Markan literary technique rather than a peculiarity of a particular source.

1203   Dewey, Joanna. "Oral Methods of Structuring Narrative in Mark." *Interpretation* 43 (1989): 32-44.

Compares the Gospel of Mark to the structural characteristics of oral narrative, as described primarily by Eric Havelock, who has studied the shift from oral to written media in Greek culture. Having determined that Mark fits the characteristics of narrative designed for a listening (not reading) audience, Dewey discusses the implications of this insight for understanding the negative portrayal of the disciples and the open ending of the Gospel.

1204   Dewey, Joanna. "Point of View and the Disciples in Mark." In *Society of Biblical Literature 1982 Seminar Papers*, ed. by Kent Harold Richards, 97-106. Chico, CA: Scholars Press, 1982.

Discusses Mark's ambiguous portrait of the disciples in light of categories for mood and voice developed by Genette (0249) and in light of a theory of opposing textual authorities (diegetic vs. mimetic) proposed by Lanser (0177). Dewey concludes that, though the implied reader will identify in some ways with Jesus in Mark's Gospel, that reader will also identify in certain ways with the disciples.

1205   Dols, William Ludwig, Jr. "Toward a Field Critical Hermeneutic of the Phrase *'Ho huios tou anthropou'* in the Narrative World of Mark: Interreadings from Literary Criticism, Analytical Psychology, and Cultural Anthropology." Ph.D. diss., Graduate Theological Union, 1988. 421 pp.

Draws on insights from literary criticism, analytical psychology, and cultural anthropology to examine Jesus' identification of himself as the "Son of man." Dols contends that the phrase identifies a vocation exemplified by but not exclusive to Jesus as a paradigmatic person. Jesus' use of the term in Mark's narrative calls readers to inner transformation and social change.

1206   Drury, John. "Mark." In *The Literary Guide to the Bible*, ed. by Robert Alter and Frank Kermode, 402-417. Cambridge, MA: Belknap Press, 1987.

Assigns Mark to the genre of folktale and then offers miscellaneous reflections on its literary interpretation: the story is lean, almost formulaic, and allows little digression; it is probably intended to be read aloud; the first 15 verses offer ciphers and codes used in the rest of the book; characters tend to lose their individuality in favor of communal roles; social boundaries drawn in the narrative are frequently transgressed. The essay concludes with an attempt at solving the riddle of bread in Mark 8:14-21.

1207   Edwards, James R. "Markan Sandwiches: The Significance of Interpolations in Markan Narratives." *Novum Testamentum* 31,3 (1989): 193-216.

Studies the typically Markan device of inserting one story into the middle of another. Edwards identifies nine instances of this device. In some instances, the inserted story illustrates the surrounding narrative; in others, it creates a contrast. Themes highlighted through such sandwich motifs include the necessity of suffering and discipleship, the meaning of faith, bearing witness, judgment, and the dangers of apostasy.

1208   Fowler, Robert M. "Irony and the Messianic Secret in the Gospel of Mark." *Proceedings: Eastern Great Lakes Biblical Society* 1 (1981): 26-36.

Interprets the theme of the messianic secret in Mark as a construct of the book's readers, motivated by its ironic presentation of Jesus as a messiah whose messiahship is hidden. The messianic secret is not to be found in the text of Mark, but in the experience of reading that text. The fact that so many readers think they find this theme in Mark is testimony to the effectiveness of the author's use of irony. See also 1213.

1209   Fowler, Robert M. *Let the Reader Understand: Reader-Response Criticism and the Gospel of Mark*. Minneapolis: Fortress Press, 1991.

Attempts to define reader-response criticism and to apply it thoroughly to the Gospel of Mark. Fowler's vision of reader-response criticism draws on the work of Stanley Fish and Wolfgang Iser, as well as on the ideas of more text-oriented theorists, such as Wayne Booth and Seymour Chatman. He is particularly interested in the rhetoric of Mark's Gospel.

1210 Fowler, Robert M. *Loaves and Fishes: The Function of the Feeding Stories in the Gospel of Mark.* Society of Biblical Literature Dissertation Series, 54. Chico, CA: Scholars Press, 1981. 258 pp.

Proposes that doublets in Mark's Gospel and their placement should be attributed to Mark's literary skill as an author rather than to the incorporation of various sources. Specifically, Fowler suggests that Mark composed 6:30-44 (feeding of 5000) on the basis of an earlier story found in 8:1-10 (feeding of 4000). Mark intentionally created tensions between the stories, manipulating how the reader will perceive one story by stationing a comparable story as a backdrop for it. In the case of the feeding stories, Mark develops a strong ironic tension by having the disciples show their lack of understanding not once but twice.

1211 Fowler, Robert M. "Reading Matthew Reading Mark: Observing the First Steps toward Meaning-as-Reference in the Synoptic Gospels." In *Society of Biblical Literature 1986 Seminar Papers*, ed. by Kent Harold Richards, 1-16. Atlanta: Scholars Press, 1986.

Critique's Hans Frei's description of the Bible as "realistic narrative" and proposes a need for biblical scholars to consider alternatives to the hermeneutic of meaning-as-reference. Discussion of linguistic studies by Ludwig Wittgenstein, John Austin, John Searle, Paul Hernadi, and Roman Jakobson leads Fowler to recognition of at least one such alternative: meaning as the experience of the pragmatic or rhetorical force of an utterance. The latter portion of the paper demonstrates that preference for the meaning-as-reference model began very early in biblical studies--Mark's Gospel was apparently interpreted according to such a model when used as a source by Matthew.

1212 Fowler, Robert M. "The Rhetoric of Direction and Indirection in the Gospel of Mark." *Semeia* 48 (1989): 115-134.

Discusses the experience of reading the Gospel of Mark from the perspective of reader-response criticism, examining passages in which rhetorical strategies of direction or indirection are employed by the narrator. Parenthetical comments (e.g., 10:22; 12:12 and perhaps 2:10, 28) exemplify direction; indirect narrative strategies of opacity, intertextual allusion, ambiguity, verbal and dramatic irony, and unanswered questions exemplify indirection. The author concludes that Mark's Gospel is designed less to say something to the reader than to do something to the reader. A subsidiary aim of the article is to sharpen the critical vocabulary of reader-response criticism; attention is paid to definition of such terms as "story," "discourse," "reliable commentary," "inside view," and "uptake."

1213 Fowler, Robert M. "The Rhetoric of Indirection in the Gospel of Mark." *Proceedings: Eastern Great Lakes Biblical Society* 5 (1985): 47-56.

Expands upon an earlier article concerning irony in Mark (1208) by suggesting that irony serves (along with ambiguity, opacity, and paradox) as part of an overall rhetoric of indirection in Mark. See also 1212.

1214   Fowler, Robert M. "Thoughts on the History of Reading Mark's Gospel." *Proceedings: Eastern Great Lakes Biblical Society* 4 (1984): 120-130.

Discusses the relationships between the Gospels in terms of "intertextuality," i.e., the process by which a text implicates or includes other texts within itself. Fowler notes several instances in which Mark's Gospel presents ambiguities that are resolved in one way or another in the other Gospels. From the perspective of reception theory, then, the other Gospels appear as reading grids that obscure our vision of Mark. The article is intended to serve as part of a larger program, namely a necessary shift of focus in biblical studies from issues of Gospel production to Gospel reception.

1215   Fowler, Robert M. "Who is 'the Reader' of Mark's Gospel?" In *Society of Biblical Literature 1983 Seminar Papers*, ed. by Kent Harold Richards, 31-54. Chico, CA: Scholars Press, 1983.

An early attempt at defining the reader of Mark according to standards of reader-response criticism. Fowler distinguishes between critic and reader and between implied reader, real reader and narratee, before focusing his discussion on the concept of an ideal reader and on the temporality of the reading process. He decides that the reader of Mark has an individual persona, a communal persona, and a textual persona, the interaction of which is exploited through Mark's rhetoric of indirection.

1216   Genest, Olivette. *Le Christ de la Passion: Perspective Structurale. Analyse de Marc 14,53--15,47, des paralleles bibliques et extra bibliques.* Recherches Theologie, 21. Tournai: Desclee, 1978. 220 pp.

Explains the three textual levels discerned by Roland Barthes (functions, actions, narrations) and applies this structuralist methodology to three scenes in the Markan passion narrative: the seer veiled (14:65); the king mocked (15:16-20b), and the savior lost (15:29-32c). Genest draws comparisons from the theme of the mocked just person in other biblical and extrabiblical literature.

1217   Girard, René. "Scandal and the Dance: Salome in the Gospel of Mark." *New Literary History* 15 (1984): 311-324.

A study of Mark 6:14-29 by a prominent social anthropologist (0031-0034). Girard interprets Salome's request for John the Baptist's head as a classic example of "the mimetic genesis of desire." The text portrays Salome as first not knowing what to ask, but as then adopting the suggestion of her mother and making it her own. The text illustrates Girard's literary and social theories insofar as the beheading of John results from a process of scapegoating that owes its distinctive character to mimetic desire.

1218   Gros Louis, Kenneth R. R. "The Gospel of Mark." In *Literary Interpretations of Biblical Narratives*, ed. by Kenneth R. R. Gros Louis with James S. Ackerman and Thayer S. Warshaw, 296-329. Nashville: Abingdon Press, 1974.

Presents a close reading of the first four chapters of the Gospel of Mark and discusses seven themes presented in these chapters: (1) the mystery of Jesus; (2) the healing power of Jesus; (3) the secrecy of Jesus; (4) Jesus as the breaker of rules; (5) Jesus as bridegroom; (6) the lack of understanding of people who hear Jesus; (7) the development of Jesus' disciples. Light is shed on all of these themes in the parables and in the placement of scenes within the Gospel. Gros-Louis concludes with a discussion of what value the Gospel of Mark might have aside from its specifically religious considerations: the Gospel affirms that life is meaningful though puzzling, and warns that concern for self leads to fear of nonconformity.

1219 Hedrick, Charles W. "Narrator and Story in the Gospel of Mark: *Hermeneia and Paradosis.*" *Perspectives in Religious Studies* 14 (1987): 239-258.

Explicates the role of the narrator in the telling of Mark's story. The narrator uses asides, "footnotes," parentheses, and explanatory comments to clarify aspects of the plot, draw morals, indicate theological interpretations, and convey the implied author's comments. Hedrick thinks that the value of Mark as a historical text must be reconsidered in light of the author's apparent use of literary devices (one example: the positive characterization of women).

1220 Hedrick, Charles W. "What Is a Gospel? Geography, Time and Narrative Structure." *Perspectives in Religious Studies* 10 (1983): 255-268.

Proposes that the episodes in the first 13 chapters of Mark are organized on a geographical frame, while those in the last 3 are organized on a chronological frame. Hedrick also comments on the clusters of John the Baptist material in 1:1-14; 6:17-29; 11:27-33; and on the effect of the ending of the Gospel in light of 14:28 and 16:7.

1221 Howcroft, Kenneth. *The Gospel of Mark.* Narrative Commentaries. Philadelphia: Trinity Press International, forthcoming.

Announced for publication.

1222 Ireland, William Johnson, Jr. "'By What Authority?': Toward the Construction of a Symbolic World in Mark." Ph.D. diss., Southern Baptist Theological Seminary, 1987. 220 pp.

Investigates the function of "authority passages" in Mark (1:21-38; 2:1-12; 3:13-19; 6:7-13, 30; 10:35-45; 11:27-33; 14:53-65). One chapter indicates the role that these passages play in characterization, plot, and setting, by means of a technique of reversal. The overall thesis is that the passages aid in the construction of a symbolic world, a system of meaning that imposes order on experience.

1223 Kelber, Werner H. *Mark's Story of Jesus.* Philadelphia: Fortress Press, 1979. 96 pp.

An influential first-attempt at reading Mark as a unified narrative. Although the work retains typical historical concerns throughout, the emphasis on literary unity points in the direction of increased attention to the character of Mark's Gospel as "a story." Kelber also anticipates the interests of literary critics in his attention to such elements as conflict, tension, suspense, and surprise.

1224   Kelber, Werner H.   "Narrative and Disclosure: Mechanisms of Concealing, Revealing, and Reveiling." *Semeia* 43 (1988): 1-20.

Explores the literary devices of secrecy and disclosure in the Gospel of Mark and argues that this narrative seeks to overcome secrecy more than to enforce it. Consideration of the role of the reader reveals a hermeneutical dynamic that is unfriendly toward secrecy. The reader has access not only to what is communicated to characters in the narrative but also to what is concealed from them. Thus the commands to keep Jesus' identity a secret are enjoined only to be revealed. A response to this article by Dan Via is included in the same issue.

1225   Kermode, Frank. *The Genesis of Secrecy: On the Interpretation of Narrative.* Cambridge, MA: Harvard University Press, 1979. 169 pp.

A book on literary theory by a renowned scholar of English literature that focuses on interpretation of large sections of the Gospel of Mark. As a self-described "secular critic" who is unconcerned with matters of faith, Kermode nevertheless approaches Mark in terms of discerning the "spiritual sense" as opposed to the carnal. His main concern is with the enigmatic character of the Markan narrative--he applies 4:11-12 to the book as a whole. Mark depicts an "unfollowable world" in which meaning is ultimately not determinable. In this very sense, it is true to the riddling character of the real world, a world in which enigmas are preferred to muddles, in which it is impossible to live without repeated, though futile, attempts at interpretation. See also 0516, 1270, 1545, 1673, 1675.

1226   Kingsbury, Jack Dean. *The Christology of Mark's Gospel.* Philadelphia: Fortress Press, 1983. 203 pp.

Approaches the subject of christology in Mark from the perspective of narrative criticism. The first two chapters survey understandings of Mark's christology that derive from research into the messianic secret theme or that ascribe a corrective approach to the evangelist. Kingsbury offers critical reappraisals of these views and then, in chapter three, traces a new approach to Markan christology based on the characterization of Jesus in the Gospel narrative. This approach leads to an emphasis on Mark's presentation of Jesus as the Davidic Messiah-King and, pre-eminently, as the Son of God. A final chapter also treats Mark's presentation of Jesus as Son of man.

1227   Kingsbury, Jack Dean. *Conflict in Mark: Jesus, Authorities, Disciples.* Minneapolis: Fortress Press, 1989. 150 pp.

A narrative-critical study of the Gospel of Mark that concentrates on the story lines of the three principal characters, whose interactions comprise the plot. The first chapter discusses the world of the story and makes introductory comments concerning settings, characters, and events (plot). The next three chapters focus, respectively, on the story of Jesus, the story of the authorities, and the story of the disciples. Kingsbury calls attention to "authority" as the critical issue in Jesus' conflict with the authorities and to the notion of discipleship as servanthood as the central motif in the conflict between Jesus and his own disciples.

1228   Kingsbury, Jack Dean. "The Religious Authorities in the Gospel of Mark: A Literary-Critical Study." *New Testament Studies* 36 (1990): 42-65.

Discusses the role that the religious authorities play as a character group in Mark's narrative. The root issue in Jesus' conflict with this character group is the issue of authority: Jesus has authority while the religious leaders do not (Mark 1:22). In Mark's story world, to be without authority is to think the things of humans rather than the things of God. Mark's characterization of the religious authorities, in terms of the point of view and traits ascribed to them, can be understood in this light.

1229   Klauck, Hans-Josef.   "Die erzählerische Rolle der Jünger im Markusevangelium: Eine narrative Analyse." *Novum Testamentum* 24 (1982): 1-26.

Assesses the role of the disciples in Mark in terms of an analytic model that takes into account various narrative levels: that of the characters in the narrative, of the narrator and narratee, of the implied author and narratee, and of the real author and narratee. A polemical interpretation is ruled out, while historical and paraenetic interpretations are given some validity.

1230   Leach, Edmund. "Fishing for Men on the Edge of the Wilderness." In *The Literary Guide to the Bible*, ed. by Robert Alter and Frank Kermode, 579-599. Cambridge, MA: Belknap Press, 1987.

A sample of anthropological, structuralist exegesis applied ostensibly to Mark 1:9-11. Leach ultimately decides that the mythological trope of the apostolic fishermen suggests the role that the latter have in saving souls from damnation as they cross over from this world into the next. He draws freely from Old Testament stories, Greek mythology and references in the other Gospels, sometimes mixing these all together and departing on digressions unrelated to the announced theme.

1231 Leenhardt, Franz-J. "An Exegetical Essay: Mark 5:1-20." In *Structural Analysis and Biblical Exegesis*, by R. Barthes, F. Bovon, F. J. Leenhardt, R. Martin-Achard, and J. Starobinski; trans. by A. M. Johnson, 85-109.   Pittsburgh Theological Monograph Series, 3. Pittsburgh: Pickwick Press, 1974.

Interprets the story of the Gerasene demoniac from a social-psychoanalytical perspective. The tale is not primarily a miracle story, but one of deliverance from tyranny within. The notations in 5:15 indicate reintegration of the healed man into the social body and into his own humanity. This essay was commissioned to demonstrate an alternative reading to the structuralist exegesis of this passage presented by Starobinski (1259). By taking the approach he does, Leenhardt shows that structuralist and historical-critical approaches are not the only options for Bible scholars.

1232 Lull, David J. "Interpreting Mark's Story of Jesus' Death: Toward a Theology of Suffering." In *Society of Biblical Literature 1985 Seminar Papers*, ed. by Kent Harold Richards, 1-13. Atlanta: Scholars Press, 1985.

Reads Mark's story of Jesus' "ignominous and repulsive" death as an attempt to deal with the problem of suffering. Mark tells the story with "protesting faith" and with an artistry that shuns accepted religious explanations for why people suffer. Three elements are lifted up in Mark's story: obedient endurance, faith in God's deliverance, and the outcry of protest--these elements may guide those who raise the question of suffering, though they do not themselves provide an answer.

1233 Mack, Burton L. *A Myth of Innocence: Mark and Christian Origins*. Philadelphia: Fortress Press, 1988. 432 pp.

A book with a stated historical objective--to discover the original purpose and function of Mark's Gospel--that nevertheless contains numerous insights into the literary character of the Gospel. Mack attributes far more creativity to the author of Mark's Gospel than would most scholars--for example, he credits Mark with inventing the story of Judas' betrayal. The material in Mark's Gospel is all examined as having been composed to meet particular needs of the community. Thus, Mack moves beyond the arena of redaction criticism to consider the Gospel more from a socio-rhetorical perspective.

1234 Magness, J. Lee. *Sense and Absence: Structure and Suspension in the Ending of Mark's Gospel*. Atlanta: Scholars Press, 1986. 136 pp.

Considers the ending of Mark's Gospel in light of both modern literary theory and ancient literary practice. Magness discusses literary theories about "absent endings" with reference to such scholars as Wolfgang Iser, Frank Kermode, Alan Friedman, Wayne Booth, and Eric Rabkin. He then details numerous examples of absent or suspended endings in ancient literature in general and in biblical literature in particular. He suggests that, through foreshadowing and the use of synechdocal elements, the Markan author gives enough clues to enable his readers to make sense of the ending as it is.

1235 Malbon, Elizabeth Struthers. "Disciples/Crowds/Whoever: Markan Characters and Readers." *Novum Testamentum* 28 (1986): 104-130.

Demonstrates that Mark characterizes both Jesus' disciples and the crowds of followers as having both strong and weak points, so as to facilitate identification of real readers with these followers of Jesus.

1236 Malbon, Elizabeth Struthers. "Fallible Followers: Women and Men in the Gospel of Mark." *Semeia* 28 (1983): 29-48.

Focuses attention on women characters in the Gospel of Mark, especially the hemorrhaging woman, the Syro-Phoenician woman, the poor widow, and the anointing woman. Malbon concludes that the portrait of these female characters contributes to the complex and composite portrait of followers in Mark's Gospel and helps to score a twofold point: anyone can be a follower, but no one finds it easy.

1237 Malbon, Elizabeth Struthers. "Galilee and Jerusalem: History and Literature in Marcan Interpretation." *Catholic Biblical Quarterly* 44 (1982): 242-255.

Presents the author's view of Mark's geopolitical settings as revelatory of a fundamental opposition between chaos and order (cf. 1241) in contradistinction to more traditional interpretations stemming from historical concerns.

1238 Malbon, Elizabeth Struthers. "The Jesus of Mark and the Sea of Galilee." *Journal of Biblical Literature* 103 (1984): 363-377.

Discusses the topographical opposition between land and sea in Mark's narrative. The sea functions as a barrier to foreign lands, but is mediated by Jesus who crosses the barrier and who teaches beside or even on the sea. See also 1241.

1239 Malbon, Elizabeth Struthers. "Mark: Myth and Parable." *Biblical Theology Bulletin* 16 (1986): 8-17.

Summarizes the ideas of scholars who have viewed Mark as myth or as parable and proposes that the Gospel integrates both of these distinctive impulses. The identification of Mark as "parable-myth" recognizes what Malbon views as an underlying opposition of narrative structure.

1240 Malbon, Elizabeth Struthers. "Mythic Structure and Meaning in Mark: Elements of A Lévi-Straussian Analysis." *Semeia* 16 (1980): 97-132.

Seeks to elucidate the mythic structures that underlie the Gospel of Mark as a literary and theological entity. The method of investigation is derived from the structuralist approach of Claude Lévi-Strauss. Three orders of the Markan narrative are sequentially and schematically outlined: geographical, calendrical, and theological. Two central conflicts identified as moving towards mediation in Mark's narrative are order vs. chaos and expectation vs. surprise.

1241 Malbon, Elizabeth Struthers. *Narrative Space and Mythic Meaning in Mark*. San Francisco: Harper and Row, 1986. 212 pp.

Applies structuralist theories of Claude Lévi-Strauss to an investigation of spatial settings in Mark's Gospel. Malbon determines that Mark's spatial settings can be grouped into three categories, each of which assumes its own particular narrative opposition: (1) Geopolitical space exhibits a basic contrast between "familiar" and "strange"; (2) Topographical space exhibits a basic contrast between "promise" and "threat"; and (3) Architectural space exhibits a basic contrast between "sacred" and "profane."

1242   Malbon, Elizabeth Struthers. "The Religious Leaders in the Gospel of Mark: A Literary Study of Markan Characterization." *Journal of Biblical Literature* 108 (1989): 259-281.

A literary study of the Jewish leaders as characters in Mark's narrative. The article briefly surveys prior historical studies by Theodore Weeden and Michael Cook and then delves into a narrative-critical investigation. The leaders fall into two sub-groups: (1) the scribes and Pharisees, and (2) the chief priests, scribes, elders and others. Both sub-groups are united, however, in their opposition to Jesus--though the Markan narrative also allows for significant "exceptions." Malbon's study also notes an interesting parallel between the distinctions between the groups of Jewish leaders in Mark and the distinctions between spatial settings (cf. 1241).

1243   Marshall, Christopher D. *Faith As A Theme in Mark's Narrative.* Society for New Testament Studies Monograph Series, 64. New York: Cambridge University Press, 1989. 262 pp.

Uses narrative criticism to study the theme of faith in Mark's Gospel. First, individual pericopes in which faith is a prominent theme are studied with regard to such matters as plot, characterization, and a variety of literary devices (repetition, intercalation, irony and paradox, riddles, rhetorical questions, and so on). Next, Marshall examines the way in which Mark integrates the faith pericopes into the narrative as a whole: reiteration of key words and concepts, prospective and retrospective references, framing devices, and so on. The importance of the concept for Mark's work and the theological integrity with which it is developed suggests that consideration of the faith theme should balance concern for the secrecy motif in finding a hermeneutical key for understanding this Gospel.

1244   Matera, Frank J. *What Are They Saying About Mark?* New York: Paulist Press, 1987. 115 pp.

Contains one chapter on "The Narrative of Mark's Gospel," which surveys works by Bilezekian (1188), Standaert (1258), Robbins (1252), Petersen (0548), and Rhoads and Michie (1250).

1245   Noble, David. "An Examination of the Structure of St. Mark's Gospel." Ph.D. diss., University of Edinburgh, 1972.

This dissertation has ostensibly historical goals ("clearer understanding of Jesus and traditions of the early Church about him") but makes observations important for a poetic reading of Mark as well. Pushing beyond form-criticism, Noble studies the stories in Mark's Gospel in terms of their narrative structure. A full pattern is discerned that includes seven elements (setting, situation, reply to situation, problem, reply to problem, result, and consequence) and five common variations or abbreviations of the full pattern are noted. Comparisons with Matthew and Luke indicate the pattern is distinctively Markan. Nobles concludes that Mark was an orderly writer who composed the stories himself. Thematic structures are also noted and compared to the narrative ones.

1246   Petersen, Norman R. "The Composition of Mark 4:1--8:26." *Harvard Theological Review* 73 (1980): 194-217.

Examines the structure of this section of Mark's Gospel as a series of three triadically composed cycles (4:1--5:20; 6:30-56; 8:1-20), which are separated by triadically composed intervals. The theme of the section is the unfolding of incomprehension, by which it becomes apparent that the so-called recipients of revelation (Jesus' disciples) understand no better than those from whom the mysteries of God's kingdom are concealed.

1247 Petersen, Norman R. "Point of View in Mark's Narrative." *Semeia* 12 (1978): 97-121.

Discusses the literary concept of point of view as it applies to Mark's narrative, with frequent reference to the categories of Uspensky (0305). At the time when this article was written, Petersen found it important to argue for the unity of Mark as a bona fide narrative--he devotes some space, therefore, to demonstrating how the coherence of point of view on various levels throughout the work guarantees the integrity of the Gospel as narrative rather than as redaction. This point rarely needs to be argued today. Petersen's study has continued to be very influential, however, for its contributions to understanding the role of the narrator in Mark's Gospel and for its numerous insights regarding the attribution of point of view as one aspect of characterization. Especially pertinent is the recognition that "thinking the things of God" and "thinking the things of humans" forms a fundamental distinction in Mark's Gospel for discerning point of view on the ideological plane. This observation has been the starting point for most subsequent studies on point of view not only in Mark, but in the other Gospels as well. The article has come to be regarded as a classic, almost definitive statement of the issues involved in treating this aspect of biblical literature.

1248 Petersen, Norman R. "The Reader in the Gospel." *Neotestamentica* 18 (1984): 38-51.

Addresses, first, the relationships among readers, texts, works, and worlds as these are considered in general literary theory. Then, Petersen turns to the Gospel of Mark to explore these relationships. His main focus is on the pivotal significance of Mark 13 for identifying the implied reader and the flow of the narrative. Petersen also considers how these considerations of the implied reader of Mark affect views on the historical context of the Gospel.

1249 Petersen, Norman R. "When Is the End Not the End? Literary Reflections on the Ending of Mark's Narrative." *Interpretation* 34 (1980): 151-166.

Presents a rather complex narrative understanding of the abrupt ending of Mark's Gospel at 16:8. The reader must regard this ending as providing closure to the story and must take it either literally or ironically. Petersen argues for the superiority of an ironic reading, which allows the reader to recognize the closure here as penultimate. The ultimate closure is to be imagined by the reader as occurring at a reunion in Galilee, as predicted by Jesus in Mark 13. Thus, Petersen goes on to discuss Mark 13 as the "embedding" of Jesus' story within Mark's story, and to emphasize the ironic effect that such embedding produces.

1250   Rhoads, David, and Michie, Donald. *Mark As Story: An Introduction to the Narrative of a Gospel*. Philadelphia: Fortress Press, 1982. 159 pp.

The first and, thus far, most influential study of an entire Gospel narrative from the perspective of modern literary criticism. Using the eclectic methodology of "narrative criticism" (cf. 0556), these scholars discuss the rhetoric of Mark's narrative with reference to the narrator, to point of view and standards of judgment, to style, to narrative patterns, and to other literary features such as riddles (parables), quotations, prophecies, and irony. The narrative itself is then investigated in terms of its settings, plot and characters. Rhoads and Michie discover that the Gospel can be read as a coherent narrative and that, as such, it offers a dynamic story told so as to create powerful effects on the reader. If some of these conclusions seem basic today, it is partly because Rhoads and Michie established them so well. One of the most important books in biblical studies to appear in recent years, this volume demonstrates the usefulness of a literary approach to the Gospels in a manner that remains inviting and fresh.

1251   Phelan, John Edward, Jr. "Rhetoric and Meaning in Mark 6:30--8:10." Ph.D. diss., Northwestern University, 1985. 276 pp.

Proposes that Mark 6:30--8:10 is organized as a chiasm. The outside parameters of this chiasm are the two feeding miracles, the inner parameters are the two stories of people finding faith and understanding (Syrophoenician woman; deaf and dumb man); and the central section concerns the theme of "cleansing the unclean." Thus, the rhetorical arrangement of the passage highlights the universal character of Jesus' mission and enables the reader to compare and contrast several responses to Jesus.

1252   Robbins, Vernon K. *Jesus the Teacher: A Socio-Rhetorical Interpretation of Mark*. Philadelphia: Fortress Press, 1984. 238 pp.

Proposes that Mark's Gospel takes the form of a biography of a disciple-gathering teacher who transmits his system of thought to his disciples and then demonstrates its worth by dying for it. In building this hypothesis, Robbins insists on reading Mark as a unified narrative constructed according to the canons of ancient rhetoric. The book contains insights into the rhetoric of Mark's Gospel--whole chapters are devoted to its formal structure and to conventional repetitive forms used in Mark.

1253   Robbins, Vernon. "Summons and Outline in Mark: The Three-Step Progression." *Novum Testamentum* 23 (1981): 97-114.

Notes that the three-step progression evident in the three passion prediction accounts in Mark (8:27-9:1; 9:30-50; 10:32-45) is also observable in scenes in which Jesus calls disciples (1:14-20; 3:7-19; 6:1-13; 10:46--11:1; 13:1-37). These passages portray Jesus as an authoritative teacher who embodies the content of his own teaching (cf. 1252) and serve as interludes in the overall structure of the Gospel.

1254   Scott, M. Philip. "Chiastic Structure: A Key to the Interpretation of Mark's Gospel." *Biblical Theology Bulletin* 15 (1985): 17-26.

Diagrams several rather complex chiasms that the author believes can be identified in Mark's Gospel. One such arrangement identifies Mark 9:7 as the pivotal passage of the entire work.   Scott reflects upon the implications of his diagrams for considerations of the structure of Mark's Gospel, as well as for its meaning. Mark's Gospel is not to be viewed as a historical narrative, but as one that produces a gradual development of implicit meaning through its chiastic structures.

1255   Shepherd, Tom. "The Definition and Function of Markan Intercalation as Illustrated in a Narrative Analysis of Six Passages." Ph.D. diss., Andrews University Seventh-day Adventist Theological Seminary, 1991.

A study of the prominent rhetorical device of intercalation in Mark's Gospel. Shepherd examines six "classic cases" of intercalation in Mark (3:20-35; 5:21-43; 6:7-32; 11:12-25; 14:1-11; 14:53-72) with reference to settings; characters; action and plot; time; narrator and implied reader; and stylistic features. He discovers a series of narrative characteristics that recur in intercalation and concludes that these characteristics combine to produce dramatized irony.

1256   Smith, Stephen H. "The Role of Jesus' Opponents in the Markan Drama." *New Testament Studies* 35 (1989): 161-182.

Examines how the various groups of Jewish opponents are presented in Mark's Gospel as instances of foreshadowing Jesus' crucifixion. Smith discerns two cycles of conflict (Galilean and Judean) prior to the Jerusalem passion cycle itself. Continuities and contrasts are discussed with regard to Mark's characterization of these character groups.

1257   Standaert, Benoit. *L'Evangile selon Marc: Commentaire.* Lire la Bible, 61. Paris: Les Editions du Cerf, 1983. 141 pp.

A popular version of 1258, focusing especially on the rhetorical structure of the Gospel.

1258   Standaert, Benoit. *L'Evangile selon Marc: Composition et Genre Litteraire.* Nijmegen: Stichting Studentenpers, 1978. 679 pp.

Argues that the Gospel of Mark was originally written to be read as a Christian Haggadah at an Easter vigil. Literary interest in the study concerns its strong focus on rhetorical technique in Mark. Standaert notes a pattern of prologue (1:1-13), narrative (1:14--6:13), argument (6:14--10:52), dénouement (11:1--15:47), and epilogue (16:1-8), and relates this to the rhetoric of Greek drama. He also calls attention to Mark's use of chiastic patterns. See also 1257.

1259   Starobinski, Jean. "The Struggle with Legion: A Literary Analysis of Mark 5:1-20." Trans. by Dan O. Via, Jr. *New Literary History* 4 (1973): 331-356. Also published as "The Gerasene Demoniac: A Literary Analysis of Mark 5:1-20." In *Structural Analysis and Biblical Exegesis*, by R. Barthes, F. Bovon, F.-J. Leenhardt, R. Martin-Achard, and J. Starobinski; trans. by A. M. Johnson, 57-84. Pittsburgh Theological Monograph Series, 3. Pittsburgh: Pickwick Press, 1974.

Presents a structuralist interpretation of Mark 5:1-20 that tries to decipher the internal temporality of the text that arises from its own wording. Special attention is paid to the spatial information provided (particularly that with regard to movement), to the role of quotation (of scripture, of John, and of Christ), and to oppositions between the state of possession and the state of healing and between Jesus recognized and Jesus rejected. Starobinski wanders from discussion of this text to discuss the opposition of insiders and outsiders perceived elsewhere in Mark's Gospel (especially in the parable of the Sower), and then returns to propose a parabolic interpretation for this text. In the 1974 volume (0580), this essay is paired with one by Leenhardt that takes a different approach to the same passage (1231).

1260   Stock, Augustine. *Call to Discipleship: A Literary Study of Mark's Gospel.* Good News Studies, 1. Wilmington, DE: Michael Glazier, 1982. 208 pp.

A reading of Mark's Gospel from beginning to end with sensitivity to narrative development and other literary concerns. Stock is consistent in his view of the Gospel as "a book" and of the evangelist as "an author," but his primary concern is what has traditionally been the goal of redaction criticism: definition of the theological perspective of the writer.

1261   Stock, Augustine. "Chiastic Awareness and Education in Antiquity." *Biblical Theology Bulletin* 14 (1984): 23-27.

Defends the presence of chiasm in Mark's Gospel by demonstrating that the use of chiasm was widely taught in antiquity, from Homeric times through classical Hellenism. It is not unlikely, then, that Mark's Gospel would make use of this rhetorical device, which can be seen in the conflict stories of Mark 2:1--3:6.

1262   Stock, Augustine. "Hinge Transitions in Mark's Gospel." *Biblical Theology Bulletin* 15 (1985): 27-31.

Provides a summary, in English, of an article by Van Iersel (1271) with comments on the transitional techniques discerned in biblical literature by Parunak (0598).

1263   Swanson, Richard W. "Parables and Promises Not Kept." Th. D. diss., Luther-Northwestern Theological Seminary, 1991.

Examines the parable of the Sower in terms of the force and flow of Mark's narrative, considering the parable in light of its interpretation, in light of other parables, and in light of the oddly abrupt way in which Mark ends. The parable is understood as providing an imaginative paradigm that shapes the reader's understanding of the end of Mark's narrative.

1264 Szarek, Eugene Carl. "Markan Ecclesiology and Anthropology: A Structural Analysis of Mark 3:7-12." Ph.D. diss., Marquette University, 1975. 291 pp.

An extended study of structural and linguistic features in the summary passages of Mark (1:28, 34, 3:7-12; 6:6b, 12-13, 56), which discovers that these summaries offer an interpretation of the rest of the Gospel. Their contributions include the presentation of a Galilean ecclesiology and an anthropology constructed on the themes of christology and discipleship.

1265 Tannehill, Robert C. "The Disciples in Mark: The Functions of a Narrative Role," in *The Interpretation of Mark*, ed. by William Telford, 134-157. Issues in Religion and Theology, 7. Philadelphia: Fortress Press, 1985.

A narrative-critical study of the disciples in the Gospel of Mark that concentrates on the changing relationship between the disciples and Jesus--a relationship that moves from concord to expanding and intensifying conflict. The role of the disciples reflects the concerns of the author and represents an indirect communication with the reader --the author assumes there will be similiarities between the disciples and his anticipated readers so that what he reveals about the disciples may become a revelation about the readers and so enable them to change.

1266 Tannehill, Robert C. "The Gospel of Mark as Narrative Christology." *Semeia* 16 (1980): 57-96.

Investigates the components of Mark's Gospel that make it a continuous, developing story. The accent is on the narrative role of the central character Jesus, and on his relationships to disciples, demons, supplicants, and opponents. Tannehill discusses the use of repetition, of surprise, and of patterns built on paradox, irony, and enticement to false hope.

1267 Tannehill, Robert C. "Reading It Whole: The Function of Mark 8:34-35 in Mark's Story." *Quarterly Review* 2 (1982): 67-78.

Discusses (with homiletical intent) the place that these two verses occupy in the narrative flow of Mark's story. Tannehill emphasizes the effect of Jesus' words on readers who, by this point in the story, have come to identify with the disciples but who, before the story is through, will have been brought by that identification to realize their own inadequacy.

1268 Thompson, Mary R. *The Role of Disbelief in Mark: A New Approach to the Second Gospel.* New York: Paulist Press, 1989. 188 pp.

Examines apparently contradictory (positive and negative) literary devices in Mark's Gospel, particularly with regard to the portrayal of the disciples. Mark's story presents a level of negation that is as important to its literary structure as its positive level. The result is a realistic narrative world in which faith and disbelief are allowed to coexist.

1269   Tolbert, Mary Ann. *Sowing the Gospel: Mark's World in Literary-Historical Perspective*. Minneapolis: Fortress Press, 1989. 352 pp.

A literary and rhetorical interpretation of Mark's Gospel that treats the work as popular fiction, similar to the Hellenistic erotic romance. Tolbert's interpretation focuses especially on negative responses to Jesus presented in Mark's narrative. The parable of the sower (4:1-9) describes four possible responses and all of these except that typified by seed falling on good soil are exemplified by characters in the narrative. The parable of the wicked tenants (12:1-12) stresses the inevitable rejection and death that was to be Jesus' lot. At the end of the narrative, the responsibility for sowing the gospel abdicated by characters within the story (including the frightened women) falls ultimately to the audience.

1270   Tolbert, Mary Ann, and Lawler, J. G. "Review of Frank Kermode's *The Genesis of Secrecy*." *Religious Studies Review* 8 (1982): 1-10.

Tolbert (pp. 1-6) finds Kermode's work (1225) "frustrating and disappointing" as literary theory, but "intriguing and delightful" as practical criticism. Lawler (pp. 6-10) thinks what Kermode does with the Gospel of Mark is remarkable, but also typical of exegesis by people who examine the Bible without believing it.

1271   Van Iersel, Bas. "De betekenis van Marcus vanuit zijn topografische stuctuur." *Tijdschrift voor Theologie* 22 (1982): 117-138.

Proposes a five-part concentric and topographical outline for Mark's Gospel: Wilderness (1:2-13); Galilee (1:14--8:26); The Way (8:27--10:52); Jerusalem (11:1--15:41); The Tomb (15:42--16:8). Tomb and Wilderness are linked by continuity (both are uninhabited, considered a dwelling place of demons, and, here, a place where new life is heralded); Galilee and Jerusalem are linked by contrast; The Way receives emphasis as the heart of the Gospel. See also 1262.

1272   Van Iersel, Bas. "Locality, Structure, and Meaning In Mark." *Linguistica Biblica* 53 (1983): 45-54.

Presents a literary analysis of Mark's structure in terms of a semiotic square. The Gospel can be outlined in five parts, which consist of concentric structure built around the lexemes "desert" (1:2-13), "Galilee" (1:16-8:21), "way" (8:27-10:45), "Jerusalem" (11:1-15:39, and "tomb" (15:42-16:8).

1273   Van Iersel, Bas. *Reading Mark*. Trans. by W. H. Bisscheroux. Edinburgh: T and T Clark, 1989. 312 pp.

Draws on insights of structuralism and narrative criticism to provide a popular reading of Mark's Gospel from a literary perspective. Special attention is paid to the structure of the Gospel, to the main lines of the story, to the development and relationships of characters, to the guidance of the narrator, and to the function of questions within the narrative (discussion of the latter point makes especially original contributions.)

1274   Van Iersel, Bas.   "The Reader of Mark as Operator of a System of Connotations." *Semeia* 48 (1989): 83-114.

Discusses the secrecy motif in Mark's Gospel according to Roland Barthes' model for denotative and connotative meaning in order to determine how the reader of Mark produces a coherent system of connotative meaning from the text. Iersel believes the eucharistic words of Jesus spoken at the last supper offer the key for decoding the system of connotative meanings related to the secrecy theme in the parables of the seed and the vineyard and in the two stories of feeding miracles.

1275   Via, Dan O., Jr.   *The Ethics of Mark's Gospel in the Middle of Time.* Philadelphia: Fortress Press, 1985. 242 pp.

Approaches the subject of ethics in Mark in light of structuralist theories and paradigms. Via begins his study of Mark's ethics in a novel way, with an examination of the Gospel's "plot." Particular attention is paid to the idea of time incorporated into this narrative: Mark thinks of time as having a beginning, middle, and end. The beginning possesses a special power and meaning that is to be recaptured at the end, but Mark wants also to assert that the power and meaning of primordial time has broken into the present. Applying this temporal principle to the Gospel narrative, Via finds that the middle of the plot (chapter 10) symbolizes the middle of time and offers ethical instruction for living in that period. The bulk of Via's book examines Mark 10 in this light, accenting the paradoxical quality of ethics to be lived in a time when eschatological power and meaning both are and are not present.

1276   Via, Dan O., Jr.   "Mark 10:32-52 -- A Structural, Literary, and Theological Evaluation." In *Society of Biblical Literature 1979 Seminar Papers*, 2 vols., ed. by Paul J. Achtemeier, 2:187-204. Missoula, MT: Scholars Press, 1979.

Compares a structural analysis of this passage with the views of five representative historical-critical scholars.   Via discovers the heart of the passage to be the paradoxical offering of repeated eschatological opportunities, a theme that is also demonstrated elsewhere in this Gospel.   According to this theme, moments of opportunity arrive in which everything hinges on one momentous decision, but (in the paradoxical view of Mark) such moments may be repeated: the "last chance" occurs again.

1277   Vorster, Willem S.   "Characterization of Peter in the Gospel of Mark." *Neotestamentica* 21 (1987): 57-76.

Views Peter as a literary character in Mark's story whose fallibility invites reader identification. It is not possible to tell which aspects of Mark's characterization of Peter are historical and which are created to serve the literary purposes of the narrative.

1278   Vorster, Willem S.   "Literary Reflections on Mark 13:5-37: A Narrated Speech of Jesus." *Neotestamentica* 21 (1987): 203-224.

Proposes that more attention needs to be paid to literary consideration of Mark 13 as a "narrated speech." The relationship of this speech to the problem of time in this narrative should be considered, as well as the presentation of the speech from the point of view of a reliable but not totally omniscient character. Such concerns can be distinguished from the usual scholarly agenda that approaches this text with questions of source theory and extratextual reference.

1279   Walsh, Richard G.   "Tragic Dimensions in Mark." *Biblical Theology Bulletin* 19 (1989): 94-99.

Discusses affinities with tragic literature in the Gospel of Mark: the plot's emphasis on the passion as Jesus' fate and the roles of such characters as the disciples and the opponents.   Walsh finds, however, that there are significant differences in these elements in Mark's story and in tragedy as usually conceived. The Gospel cannot be regarded as a pure tragedy, but it does embody the tragic vision of characters who choose not to accept the comic perspective of Jesus.

1280   Waybright, Gregory Lee.   "Discipleship and Possessions in the Gospel of Mark: A Narrative Study." Ph.D. diss., Marquette University, 1984. 331 pp.

Examines the theme of possessions in Mark's Gospel by tracing the development of the disciples as characters throughout the narrative and observing the relationship between each disciple and his or her possessions. It is discovered that in Mark's narrative the importance of possessions is relativized by the dawning of the messianic age and by the prominence of the church's mission.

1281   Weeden, Theodore J.   *Mark - Traditions in Conflict*. Philadelphia: Fortress Press, 1971. 182 pp.

A basic redactional study of Mark's project that anticipates certain literary motifs by focusing on the roles of "key characters in the Markan drama." Although Weeden attempts to explain Mark's characterization of the disciples in terms of historical reference rather than as a literary device, his study serves to call attention to the importance of characterization for making sense of the Gospel.

1282   Williams, James G.   *Gospel Against Parable: Mark's Language of Mystery*. Sheffield: Almond Press, 1985. 246 pp.

Reads the Gospel of Mark as a combination of the genres of biography and parable, that is, as a biography in parable form. Williams sees an equation in Mark between the suffering of the Son of man (the central theme of the Gospel as a whole) and the mystery of the kingdom of God (the central theme of the parables). The result is that the narrative Gospel controls the polyvalence of the parables, while the parables "open up" the Gospel, disallowing it to be read as a literal narrative. An excursus discusses Kelber's book on orality (1044).

1283 Wright, John. "Spirit and Wilderness: The Interplay of Two Motifs within the Hebrew Bible as a Background in Mark 1:2-13." In *Perspectives on Text and Language*, ed. by Edgar W. Conrad and Edward G. Newing, 269-298. Winona Lake, IN: Eisenbrauns, 1987.

Traces the background for two symbolic models brought together in Mark's story of Jesus and John the Baptist. Drawing especially on the development of these symbols in Deutero-Isaiah, Wright shows that the wilderness is an image of desolation and destruction that maintains its own possibility of re-creation, while the Spirit is an image of re-creation that maintains its own possibility of destruction.

1284 Zeller, D. "Die Hanlungsstruktur der Markuspassion. Der Ertrag strukturalistischer Literaturwissenschaft für die Exegese." *Theologische-praktische Quartalschrift* 159 (1979): 213-227.

An analysis of Mark 14--16 using French semiotic structuralism. Zeller investigates the external conditions of the plot (time, place, configuration of characters, microstructure), the sequence of the plot, the meaning of the plot, the underlying paradigmatic and semiotic models, and the pragmatic aspect of the text.

THE GOSPEL OF LUKE AND THE BOOK OF ACTS

See also 0499, 0516, 0529, 0534, 0542, 0548, 0565, 0587, 0591, 0808, 1041, 1043, 1046-1047, 1050-1051, 1054, 1058, 1060-1061, 1063, 1065, 1067-1072, 1075-1078, 1080, 1083, 1089, 1091, 1095-1096, 1098, 1100, 1102-1106, 1108-1109, 1112-1113, 1115-1117, 1122, 1302, 1441, 1590, 1626, 1651.

1285 Ades, J. I. "Literary Aspects of Luke." *Papers on Language and Literature* 15 (1979): 193-199.

Treats three aspects of Luke's literary skill: (1) his capacity to expand material into great dramatic episodes (as seen by comparison of certain episodes with their counterparts in Mark or Matthew); (2) his inclusion of unique literary units, such as the parable of the prodigal son; (3) his rhetorical skill evidenced in the account of Paul's trial before Agrippa in Acts 26.

1286 Barthes, Roland. "The Structural Analysis of Narrative: Apropos of Acts 10 --11." In *The Semiotic Challenge*, ed. and trans. by Richard Howard, 217-245. New York: Hill and Wang, 1988. Also published as "A Structuralist Analysis of a Narrative from Acts X-XI." In *Structuralism and Biblical Hermeneutics: A Collection of Essays*, ed. and trans. by A. M. Johnson, 109-143. Pittsburgh Theological Monograph Series, 22. Pittsburgh: Pickwick Press, 1979.

Uses the Cornelius story in Acts to demonstrate the process by which structural analysis interrogates (as opposed to interprets) a text. Barthes begins by stating three principles of structural analysis: formalization (the analysis seeks forms, not content); pertinence (pertinent features are those which permit us to postulate a code); and plurality (the analysis does not seek to establish meaning but to locate the site of possible meanings). The text of Acts is then considered by a process that involves segmentation, inventory of codes, and coordination of identified functions. The analysis determines that one outstanding feature of this text is the multiplicity of summaries, each of which allows a different destination of the message. Barthes regards this as a diagramatic image of the limitless character of grace. See also 1581.

1287 Brawley, Robert L. *Centering on God: Method and Message in Luke-Acts.* Literary Currents in Biblical Interpretation. Louisville, KY: Westminster/John Knox Press, 1990. 256 pp.

Considers Luke-Acts with reference to what Roland Barthes calls the five "literary voices": the hermeneutic voice, the voice of semes, the proairetic voice, the cultural voice, and the symbolic voice. Brawley's comprehensive study includes attention to point of view, levels of reliability, strategies for reformulating reader response, narrative structure, textual gaps, cultural repertoire, and redundant antithesis. Chapters are devoted to characterization of God and Jesus, and of Peter and Paul. Brawley also considers the logic of the stories, "truth in the narrative world," and "shared presumptions." The book aims at a synthesis of literary methods and insights.

1288 Brawley, Robert L. "Paul in Acts: Aspects of Structure and Characterization." In *Society of Biblical Literature 1988 Seminar Papers*, ed. by David J. Lull, 90-105. Atlanta: Scholars Press, 1988.

Utilizes structuralism and modern literary theory in order to localize the characterization of Paul in the antitheses of the narrative of Acts. Paul typifies Jews who maintain the hope of Israel by becoming messianists, who accept the extension of God's salvation to Gentiles, and who align with the twelve tribes judged by the Twelve.

1289 Brodie, Thomas L. "The Departure for Jerusalem (Luke 9, 51-56) as a Rhetorical Imitation of Elijah's Departure for the Jordan (2 Kgs 1, 1--2:6)." *Biblica* 70 (1989): 96-109.

Notes similarities and dissimilarities between these two biblical accounts, concluding that the story in Luke is a deliberate imitation of the Elijah story, adapted so as to demonstrate the superiority of Jesus over Elijah. Brodie makes some use of modern literary analysis, though his approach is most similar to historically based "composition criticism."

1290 Carroll, John T. "Literary and Social Dimensions of Luke's Apology for Paul." In *Society of Biblical Literature 1988 Seminar Papers*, ed. by David J. Lull, 106-118. Atlanta: Scholars Press, 1988.

Probes both literary and social aspects of the defense of Paul in Acts. Carroll analyzes accusations lodged against Paul in Acts and discusses the roles played by Roman officials, Agrippa II, James, Peter, and other legitimating agents in order to demonstrate that the key claim of the apology is that Paul is a faithful Jew.

1291 Carroll, John T. "Luke's Portrayal of the Pharisees." *Catholic Biblical Quarterly* 50 (1988): 604-621.

Analyzes Luke's characterization of the Pharisees as distinct from that of other Jewish groups. Luke depicts an evolution of hostility between Jesus and the Pharisees that sets before the reader two conflicting understandings of God's kingdom. The Pharisees also serve a legitimating function in the second part of Luke's story, where they affirm resurrection faith and unwittingly defend Christians against charges of undermining the Torah. Thus, the Pharisees serve both as antagonists of Jesus and as a link between Israel and the church.

1292 Craig, Kerry M., and Kristjansson, Margaret A. "Women Reading as Men/Women Reading as Women: A Structural Analysis for the Historical Project." *Semeia* 51 (1990): 119-136.

Presents feminist readings of Luke 11:14-32 based on the tools of structuralism and deconstruction. Drawing on a typology of feminist criticism provided by Jonathan Culler, the authors propose two different ways in which feminists might read these texts. One way involves a reading "as men" with suspicion and resistance to the inherent patriarchy. A second way involves reading "as women" in a deconstructive vein that challenges the whole patriarchal notion of rationality itself.

1293 Darr, John A. "Glorified in the Presence of Kings: A Literary-Critical Study of Herod the Tetrarch in Luke-Acts." Ph.D. diss., Vanderbilt University, 1986.

Seeks to develop a critical methodology for analysis of characters in New Testament narrative and to apply this methodology to Herod the Tetrarch in Luke-Acts. The method adopted is a variety of reader-response criticism. Herod is seen as an archetype for all political opponents in Acts and as a negative paradigm of recognition and response.

1294 Darr, John A. *Paradigms of Perception: The Reader and the Characters of Luke-Acts*. Literary Currents in Biblical Interpretation. Louisville, KY: Westminster/John Knox Press, forthcoming.

Announced for publication.

1295   Davis, Charles Thomas, III. "The Literary Structure of Luke 1--2." In *Art and Meaning: Rhetoric in Biblical Literature*, ed. by David J. A. Clines, David M. Gunn, and Alan J. Hauser, 215-229. Sheffield, England: JSOT Press, 1982.

Proposes that the first two chapters of Luke are structured around the three visits of the angel in 1:5-25; 1:26-38; and 2:1-20. The other events in the narrative represent completions of the events set in motion by the angelic announcements. The narrative is thus closely tied to certain Old Testament themes and to the unfolding of the narrative presented in the rest of Luke's Gospel.

1296   Dawsey, James M. *The Lukan Voice: Confusion and Irony in the Gospel of Luke*. Macon, GA: Mercer University Press, 1988. 198 pp.

Compares the voice of Jesus with that of the narrator in Luke's Gospel and concludes that the author ultimately sides with Jesus against his own narrator. The narrator speaks a language of worship, an oral type of speech that has its locus in the community of faith. Jesus speaks a language of prophecy, in words that depict the simple language of common people. Comparing the content of the two voices reveals numerous antitheses, which reveal the narrator to be less than reliable. With great irony, Luke portrays a narrator who sets out to convey in educated and cultic language (1:1-4) a knowledge of things that the wise and understanding cannot see (10:21). See also 1614.

1297   Dawsey, James M. "What's in a Name? Characterization in Luke." *Biblical Theology Bulletin* 16 (1986): 143-147.

Demonstrates that certain titles for Jesus (Son of man, Teacher, Lord, Son of God) are used in Luke to reveal not only Jesus but also other characters. Characters reveal something about themselves by their use or disuse of these titles. In addition, Dawsey describes the process through which third-person narration leads the reader to interpret the story.

1298   Dongell, Joseph R. "The Structure of the Gospel of Luke" (title tentative). Ph.D. diss., Union Theological Seminary in Virginia, 1991.

Examines the structure of Luke's Gospel according to the method of discourse analysis. Dongell first discusses and critiques types of structural analysis that have been proposed for Luke's Gospel, and then describes the semantic structures of discourse analysis that are to be employed in his examination of the Gospel. The new approach leads to a reassessment of the integrity and position of the so-called "travel narrative" in the Gospel.

1299   Drury, John. "Luke." In *The Literary Guide to the Bible*, ed. by Robert Alter and Frank Kermode, 418-439. Cambridge, MA: Belknap Press, 1987.

Interprets the literary quality of Luke's Gospel in comparison with the other three. Luke is the master of the "long view," that is, of articulating historical process and perspective. The humanism of Luke's Gospel contrasts with the theocentricity of John's. The Lukan parables are more lucid and realistic than those of Mark or

Matthew and offer a more realistic view of history. Luke's ethical view of goodness is also distinctive: it occurs "when a person copes realistically and resourcefully with what has come upon him."

1300   Edwards, Douglas R. "Acts of the Apostles and the Graeco-Roman World: Narrative Communication in Social Context." In *Society of Biblical Literature 1989 Seminar Papers*, ed. by David J. Lull, 362-377. Atlanta: Scholars Press, 1989.

Compares the narrative portrayals of human and divine characters in Acts with similar portrayals in pre-sophistic romances and evaluates why the respective authors of these works would use such narrative strategies to reach their particular audiences.

1301   Edwards, O. C., Jr. *Luke's Story of Jesus*. Philadelphia: Fortress Press, 1981. 96 pp.

Traces the story line of Jesus in the Gospel of Luke as a key to the theology of the Gospel.   Although this work makes only minimal use of modern literary-critical methods, it does reflect concern for regarding the book as a unit and shows appreciation for the author's literary skill.   Particular attention is called to the compositional structure of the book, with regard to both major sections and individual scenes. The basic theological category for understanding Luke's presentation for Jesus is fulfillment of prophecy.

1302   Gans, Eric. "Christian Morality and the Pauline Revelation." *Semeia* 33 (1985): 97-108.

Interprets the revelatory experience of Paul on the road to Damascus as essential to transformation of Christianity from a sect concerned primarily with morality to a religion concerned primarily with salvation. The essential lesson of that experience was that persecution of the moral doctrine espoused by Jesus' surviving disciples was tantamount to perecution of Jesus' own person. This "ineluctable persistence of Jesus" is proof of his divinity and forms the basis for claims to a soteriological role. The author is not a biblical scholar, but a communication theorist known for his "formal theory of representation."

1303   Gaventa, Beverly Roberts. "Toward a Theology of Acts: Reading and Re-reading." *Interpretation* 42 (1988): 146-157.

Suggests that typical approaches to the theology of Acts fail to take account of the narrative character of the book. Gaventa projects questions that should be answered by an approach that does take this quality of the book seriously (e.g., what world does the book create for its reader? what does the narrative repeat or omit?).

1304   Gowler, David B.   "Characterization in Luke: A Socio-Narratological Approach." *Biblical Theology Bulletin* 19 (1989): 54-62.

Seeks to combine literary sensitivities concerning characterization with the use of cultural scripts suggested by cultural anthropology, with the Gospel of Luke serving as a testing ground for applying the combined methodologies.   With regard to characters, direct definition is offered through the reliable voices of the narrator, Jesus, and God; indirect presentation may take the form of speech, action, external appearance, or environment.   With regard to cultural scripts, the pivotal value of honor and shame, the notion of dyadic personality, and the concept of limited good are studied in terms of their direct definition and indirect presentation in Luke.

1305   Gros Louis, Kenneth R. R.   "The Jesus Birth Stories."   In *Literary Interpretations of Biblical Narratives, Volume II*, ed. by Kenneth R. R. Gros Louis with James S. Ackerman, 273-284. Nashville: Abingdon Press, 1982.

Compares the two birth narratives in Matthew and in Luke and notes that they differ not only in details, but also in essentials--in structure, emphases, and point of view. Matthew's story is concerned to present the birth of Jesus as part of a predetermined plan in which human characters figure only as instruments of the divine will. Luke, however, dwells on individual choices and responses. For Matthew, Jesus' birth alters the course of history *per se*; for Luke, his birth alters the meaning of individual lives within history.

1306   Gueuret, Agnés. *La mise en discours.   Recherches sémiotique à propos de l'Evangile de Luc.* Paris: Cerf, 1987. 335 pp.

A semiotic analysis of selected portions of Luke's Gospel.   Gueuret begins with a detailed analysis of the temptation story in Luke 4:1-13, on the basis of which he develops a research methodology for the rest of the Gospel. This is then applied to other texts under the following headings: "spatial and temporal actors" (Luke 3; 4; 24); "cognitive distance and spatial-temporal isotopes" (Luke 8:1-21); "actorial and spatial time" (Luke 5; 13; 18; 24); and "actorial and temporal place" (Luke 19:28--23:49).

1307   Gueuret, Agnés. *L'Engendrement d'un Recit: L'Evangile de l'enfance selon Saint Luc.* Lectio Divina, 113. Paris: Cerf, 1983. 319 pp.

An analysis of Luke 1--2 according to the semiotic model for structural analysis developed by A. J. Greimas. Gueuret comments on the place of Luke 1:5--2:52 in the Gospel as a whole and examines the syntactic composition of three major sequences in the infancy narrative (1:5-80; 2:1-40; 2:41-52) and their sub-sequences. She also treats the expressive dimension of the passage, relates it to the preface (Luke 1:1-4), and discusses the value of semiotic analysis vis-à-vis historical criticism.

1308   Hamm, Dennis. "Paul's Blindness and Its Healing: Clues to Symbolic Intent (Acts 9; 22; and 26)." *Biblica* 71 (1990): 63-72.

Examines the way Paul's blindness is depicted in the three accounts of the Damascus road experience: (1) as a punitive act of God, (2) in muted and ambiguous language,

(3) as a metaphor. Luke's narrative draws on the symbolic world of Isaiah for its ironic imagery of physical blindness and its spiritual counterparts.

1309   Heil, John Paul. "Reader-Response and the Irony of Jesus Before The Sanhedrin in Luke 22:66-71." *Catholic Biblical Quarterly* 51 (1989): 271-284.

A narrative-critical study of this text that evaluates the irony of the scene from the perspective of the implied reader. The irony consists in the fact that the evidence for believing in Jesus as true messiah is the same as that for condemning Jesus to death as false messiah. In condemning Jesus, the Sanhedrin also condemn themselves for failure to believe in him. The experience of this irony urges the reader to supply the faith the Sanhedrin lacks.

1310   Johnson, Luke Timothy. *The Literary Function of Possessions in Luke-Acts*. Society of Biblical Literature Dissertation Series, 39. Missoula, MT: Scholars Press, 1977. 241 pp.

A study of the symbolic function that possessions may have in the Gospel of Luke and the book of Acts. Possessions serve as expressions for personal or communal identity. What people do with their possessions is revealing of character: acquisition, preservation, renunciation, and sharing are all responses that typify different characters and help to define their roles in the story.

1311   Karris, Robert J. *Luke: Artist and Theologian. Luke's Passion Account As Literature*. Theological Inquiries. New York: Paulist Press, 1985. 130 pp.

Draws on narrative criticism to study key motifs in Luke's "kerygmatic story" that come to a head in the passion narrative. The motifs on which Karris concentrates are justice, food, and faithfulness. Implications for soteriology and christology are explicated in a chapter that relates Luke 23 to the narrative as a whole.

1312   Karris, Robert J. "Windows and Mirrors: Literary Criticism and Luke's Sitz im Leben." In *Society of Biblical Literature 1979 Seminar Papers*, 2 vols., ed. by Paul J. Achtemeier, 1:47-58. Missoula, MT: Scholar's Press, 1979.

Encourages the use of literary criticism to answer a historical question--the *Sitz im Leben* (setting in life) of Luke's writings. Most of the article reviews what Karris calls "recent literary-critical studies of Luke-Acts," though in reality most of the works cited are historical-critical studies. Karris then suggests that more light could be shed on this issue by paying attention to the implied author and implied reader, the vision of life, and the inherent inconsistencies of the Lukan narratives.

1313   Kemmler, Dieter Werner. *Faith and Human Reason: A Study of Paul's Method of Preaching as Illustrated by 1-2 Thessalonians and Acts 17:2-4*. Novum Testamentum Supplements 40. Leiden: E. J. Brill, 1975. 225 pp.

Although the focus of this study is on the "intellectual element" in Paul's preaching rather than on its rhetorical character, the book has been thought important by some rhetorical critics. The bulk of the book is devoted to Acts, with examination of the Thessalonian correspondence used as a test case for certain hypotheses developed with reference to the Acts passage. The main thesis is that the two functions of preaching are identification of Christ and identification of the hearer and that these identifications are made through appeals based on human reason. Sixty pages are devoted to a word study of *peithein* (to persuade).

1314   Kingsbury, Jack Dean.   *Conflict in Luke: Jesus, Authorities, Disciples.* Minneapolis: Fortress Press, 1991.

A narrative-critical study of Luke's Gospel that traces the story lines of the three most important characters: Jesus, the religious authorities, and Jesus' disciples. Kingsbury emphasizes the elements of conflict that result from the intertwining of these story lines. The principal conflict occurs between Jesus and the religious authorities and focuses on the question of whom God has chosen to rule Israel. A subsidiary conflict concerns Jesus and his disciples, who are loyal but also uncomprehending. As with his books on Matthew (1150) and Mark (1227), Kingsbury also offers a brilliant opening chapter that summarizes the principal literary features of Luke as narrative: settings, characters, and plot.

1315   Kurz, William S.   "Hellenistic Rhetoric in the Christological Proof of Luke-Acts."   *Catholic Biblical Quarterly* 42 (1980): 171-195.

Contends that Luke follows commonly known rules of Hellenistic rhetoric in constructing arguments for the main protagonists of his story. A number of rhetorical conventions are noted, with the main emphasis being on the form and function of christological proofs presented in key speeches in Luke's Gospel and in Acts. These proofs, Kurz believes, represent a Christian adaptation of the Aristotelian enthymeme.

1316   Kurz, William S.   "Narrative Approaches to Luke-Acts." *Biblica* 68 (1987): 195-220.

Illustrates, with examples from Luke-Acts, how literary criticism can enrich biblical studies by shedding light on passages that are otherwise difficult to interpret. Kurz offers some cautions for applying contemporary literary criticism (especially structuralist or deconstructionist varieties) to biblical texts, but also lists literary-critical correctives to historical criticism: the recognition that the writer's audience is always a fiction warns against using texts to reconstruct historical communities; recognition of the artful function of gaps warns against jumping from so-called seams to sources; and so on. Three problems in Luke-Acts are considered: the prologue and narrative transition in Luke 1; the ending of Acts; and the "we" passages.

1317   LaHurd, Carol Joan Schersten.   "The Author's Call to the Audience in the Acts of the Apostles: A Literary-Critical-Anthropological Reading." Ph.D. diss., University of Pittsburgh, 1987. 286 pp.

Examines the author-audience relationship in Acts with the aid of rhetorical criticism. LaHurd is primarily concerned with the original, intended audience of the work.

Primary texts considered include representative speeches in Acts, the Peter-Cornelius episode of 10--11, and the repetition of Paul's call narrative in Acts 9, 22, and 26.

1318 Long, William R. "The Trial of Paul in the Book of Acts: Historical, Literary, and Theological Considerations." Ph.D. diss., Brown University, 1980.

This work is largely a historical study, but one chapter is devoted to literary analysis of the defense speeches of Paul in light of ancient rhetorical handbooks. It is argued that the strategy of the speeches seeks to define the main issue in terms of Paul's faithfulness to Judaism.

1319   Marin, Louis. "A Structural Analysis Essay of Acts 10:1--11:18." In *Structuralism and Biblical Hermeneutics: A Collection of Essays*, ed. and trans. by Alfred M. Johnson, Jr., 145-177. Pittsburgh Theological Monograph Series, 22. Pittsburgh: Pickwick Press, 1979.

A study of the Cornelius episode by a prominent structuralist. The story is notable for its repetitions: Cornelius' vision is reported four times, and Peter's twice. Marin charts the "sequences" in each of these accountings, noting which are missing or emphasized in each case. He then compares the two visions to each other, and notes the manner in which the text is organized as an "articulation of two narrative pairs." Examination of the text's "deep structures" reveals potential oppositions between verbality and orality and between speaking and eating. Marin appeals to eucharist imagery as one way of understanding this relationship of word and table.

1320 Martin, Clarice Jannette. "The Function of Acts 8:26-40 within the Narrative Structure of the Book of Acts: The Significance of the Eunuch's Provenance for Acts 1:8c." Ph.D. diss., Duke University, 1985. 281 pp.

Considers two functions for the Ethiopian enunch pericope in the overall narrative: (1) the pericope represents a fulfillment of the mandate to take the Gospel to "the ends of the earth"; (2) the pericope foreshadows both the future Gentile mission and the ultimate geographical and cultural scope of the Christian church.

1321 Marlow, John Thomas Arthur. "A Narrative Analysis of Acts 1--2." Ph.D. diss., Golden Gate Baptist Theological Seminary, 1988. 106 pp.

Studies Acts 1--2 as both story and as discourse, with reference to the work of Seymour Chatman, Roman Jakobson, and Wayne Booth. Luke is shown to be a literary artist of considerable skill, especially with regard to point of view.

1322 McMahan, Craig Thomas. "Meals as Type-Scenes in the Gospel of Luke." Ph.D. diss., The Southern Baptist Theological Seminary, 1987. 340 pp.

Examines the numerous accounts of meals in Luke's Gospel as examples of the ancient literary convention known as a type scene ("a recurring event in a story by which the various occurrences of the event are narrated in conformity with a fixed pattern"). McMahan examines the meals of Jesus with women, the meals of Jesus with tax-collectors and outcasts, the meals at which Jesus is a guest of the Pharisees, and the meals at which he is host to his disciples.

1323   McMahan, Edward John, II. "The Death and Resurrection of Jesus in Luke 23:26--24:53: A Greimassian Analysis." Ph.D. diss., Vanderbilt University, 1984. 397 pp.

Seeks to elucidate the systems of convictions that give rise to and structure Luke's account of the death and resurrection of Jesus. The method followed is the structuralist approach of A. J. Greimas, as adapted by Daniel Patte, who supervised the dissertation.

1324   Moessner, David P. *Lord of the Banquet: The Literary and Theological Significance of the Lucan Travel Narrative.* Minneapolis: Fortress Press, 1989. 358 pp.

Explicates the meaning of the central portion of Luke's Gospel in terms of two literary phenomena: (1) the relationship of narrated speech to plot (in this case, the relationship of the sayings of Jesus to the story of his journey to Jerusalem); (2) intertextuality (in this case, allusions throughout the text to Deuteronomy). Moessner demonstrates that Luke presents Jesus' journey and eventual rejection as the consummation of the history of Moses and all the prophets.

1325   Moore, Stephen D. "Luke's Economy of Knowledge." In *Society of Biblical Literature 1989 Seminar Papers*, ed. by David J. Lull, 38-56. Atlanta: Scholars Press, 1989.

A wandering and rather strange study of Luke's epistemology of reading. Kernel scenes regarding seeing or knowing are investigated and various approaches to reading Luke-Acts are described in terms of political and psycho-sexual metaphors.

1326   Nelson, Edwin S. "Paul's First Missionary Journey as Paradigm: Literary-Critical Assessment of Acts 13--14." Ph.D. diss., Boston University, 1982. 178 pp.

Examines two chapters of Acts from a literary-critical perspective. Acts 13--14 is structured chiastically in a way that demonstrates Luke's literary artistry. The chapters function paradigmatically within the larger narrative, anticipating themes and types of material to occur later. The chapters also function to define the character of Paul and, specifically, to define his authority by way of determining his relationship with the twelve.

1327   Nuttall, Geoffrey F. *The Moment of Recognition: Luke as Story-Teller.* London: Athlone Press, 1978. 16 pp.

A brief lecture that calls attention to Luke's unusual skill at telling a story. Nuttall regards Luke as a poetic historian and describes his stories as ones that seek to transform the reader through education of the imagination.

1328   O'Reilly, L. "Chiastic Structures in Acts 1--7." *Proceedings of the Irish Biblical Association* 7 (1983): 87-103.

Demonstrates that the whole Jerusalem phase of Acts consists of two large chiasms (Luke 24:52--Acts 5:42 and Acts 6:1--8:1). Each of these chiasms focuses on the theme of the Mosaic prophet (Acts 3:22; 7:37).

1329   Parsons, Mikeal C. "Christian Origins and Narrative Openings: The Sense of a Beginning in Acts 1--5." *Review and Expositor* 87 (1990): 403-422.

Examines the first five chapters of Acts with attention to "first impressions" that the reader gains there. Parsons is sensitive to Meir Sternberg's notion of the primacy effect in literature (0212), that is, the effect that narrative beginnings convey in manipulating a reader's attitudes, sympathies, norms, and hypotheses.

1330   Parsons, Mikeal C. *The Departure of Jesus in Luke-Acts.* Journal for the Study of the New Testament Supplement Series, 21. Sheffield: JSOT Press, 1987. 301 pp.

Studies the ascension narratives in Luke 24:50-53 and Acts 1:1-11 in light of literary theory concerning beginnings and endings in literature. Discrepancies between the two accounts can be accounted for in terms of their different literary function: one closes out the Gospel while the other opens the story of Acts. The literary effect is to separate the two stories as distinct books, while also providing continuity between them.

1331   Pervo, Richard I. *Luke's Story of Paul.* Minneapolis: Fortress Press, 1990. 96 pp.

A popular reading of Acts from the perspective of a first-time reader.

1332   Pervo, Richard I. "Must Luke and Acts Belong to the Same Genre?" In *Society of Biblical Literature 1989 Seminar Papers*, ed. by David J. Lull, 309-316. Atlanta: Scholars Press, 1989.

Debates the critical assumption that canonical division of Luke and Acts into two separate books is erroneous, suggesting that the two works--though by the same author--belong to different literary genres. Luke, like the other Gospels, fits best into the genre of biography, while Acts belongs to the genre of Hellenistic romance (1333).

1333   Pervo, Richard I. *Profit with Delight: The Literary Genre of the Acts of the Apostles.* Philadelphia: Fortress Press, 1987. 224 pp.

Assigns Acts to the literary genre of Hellenistic romance and discusses the intention of the book as being to edify readers while entertaining them. As an ancient novel, Acts can be read as a book of adventurous, humorous, and exotic stories directed to a popular audience. Pervo offers numerous insights into the literary craft of Acts that can be appreciated even apart from the thesis on genre they are intended to support.

1334   Powell, Mark Allan.   "The Religious Leaders in the Gospel of Luke: A Literary-Critical Study." *Journal of Biblical Literature* 109 (1990): 103-120.

A narrative-critical study of the role the religious leaders play as a character group in the story of Luke's Gospel. The leaders are characterized as fundamentally "self-righteous" and as foolishly rejecting the point of view of God. The basic line of opposition between them and Jesus is drawn in terms of salvation history: they prefer the old age to the new age brought by Jesus. The story line of the religious leaders is traced in two stages and is said to be framed by introductory and concluding episodes involving exceptions (Zechariah and Joseph of Arimathea). The literary effect of Luke's portrayal is to highlight the nature of Jesus' ministry as a divine offer of grace, peace, and reconciliation.

1335   Powell, Mark Allan. *What Are They Saying About Acts?* New York: Paulist Press, 1991.

Contains one chapter on "Reading Acts as Literature," which surveys rhetorical and narrative-critical studies on Acts.

1336   Powell, Mark Allan. *What Are They Saying About Luke?* New York: Paulist Press, 1989. 151 pp.

Suggests that Luke is no longer viewed only as a historian and as a theologian but also as a literary artist. Literary studies on Luke by Karris (1311), Parsons (1330), Talbert (1348), Tannehill (1353), and others are surveyed.

1337   Praeder, Susan Marie. "Acts 27:1--28:16: Sea Voyages in Ancient Literature and the Theology of Luke-Acts." *Catholic Biblical Quarterly* 46 (1984): 683-706.

Discusses Luke's use of a sea voyage genre to conclude the book of Acts. The choice of a characteristically Gentile story-form is an appropriate way to end the narrative of how God's salvation came to be sent to Gentiles. The story accents Paul's (and God's) concern for the salvation of all from the storm in a way that symbolizes the offer of universal salvation available through the gospel.

1338   Praeder, Susan Marie. "Jesus-Paul, Peter-Paul, and Jesus-Peter Parallelisms in Luke-Acts: A History of Reader Response." In *Society of Biblical Literature 1984 Seminar Papers*, ed. by Kent Harold Richards, 23-39. Missoula, MT: Scholars Press, 1984.

Surveys various interpretations that have been given to the evident parallels between these characters in Luke-Acts. Praeder demonstrates that the parallels have been made to serve a number of different innterpretive schemes. She advises critics to regard their responses to the parallels as representative of particular reading strategies, rather than attempting to posit any one interpretation as normative.

1339   Praeder, Susan Marie. "Luke-Acts and the Ancient Novel." In *Society of Biblical Literature 1981 Seminar Papers*, ed. by Kent Harold Richards, 269-292. Chico, CA: Scholars Press, 1981.

Proposes that Luke-Acts as a whole should be identified as an ancient novel in genre and as a Christian ancient novel in subgenre. Praeder presents a narrative paradigm for definition of genre according to which Luke-Acts may be identified as a novel on the basis of narrative criteria. In Luke-Acts historical and fictional events are embedded in fictional sequences. Reading Luke-Acts as a novel means reading it in comparison to other ancient novels rather than in comparison to ancient histories.

1340   Praeder, Susan Marie. "The Narrative Voyage: An Analysis and Interpretation of Acts 27--28." Ph.D. diss., Graduate Theological Union, 1980.

Interprets the account of Paul's sea voyage in Acts according to a narrative paradigm that emphasizes the structure of narrative, typologies of narration, and the phenomenology of reading. The story is interpreted as a narrative representation of the salvation of God. Special attention is paid to patterns of reversal and reciprocity, to the structuring of sequential units, and to a recurrent movement within several units from God-language to Christ-language.

1341   Puskas, Charles B., Jr. "The Conclusion of Luke-Acts: An Investigation of the Literary Function and Theological Significance of Acts 28:16-31." Ph.D. diss., St. Louis University, 1980. 181 pp.

Proposes that the literary function of Acts 28:16-31 is to provide a triumphal resolution to the conflict with Judaism that has been developed throughout both of Luke's volumes. Jewish rejection of the gospel no longer matters because Gentiles are accepting the message. Thus, the final words of the narrative stress the triumph of Christianity over religious, racial, and political obstacles.

1342   Resseguie, James L. "Point of View in the Central Section of Luke (9:51--19:44)." *Journal of the Evangelical Theological Society* 25 (1982): 41-47.

Proposes that the central section of Luke's Gospel (especially 14:1-33) presents two diametrically opposed ways of looking at the world. Jesus advocates renunciation, humiliation, and no possessions, while his opponents advocate self-assertion, exaltation, and possessions.

1343   Robinson, James M. "Acts." In *The Literary Guide to the Bible*, ed. by Robert Alter and Frank Kermode, 467-478. Cambridge, MA: Belknap Press, 1987.

A curious entry in this collection of supposedly literary interpretations, this article offers a very traditional historical reading of Acts. Robinson surveys recent historical scholarship and proposes that Acts offers a political apology intended to establish the legitimacy of the new, predominantly Gentile, Christian religion.

1344   Sheeley, Steven M. "Narrative Asides and Narrative Authority in Luke-Acts." *Biblical Theology Bulletin* 18 (1988): 102-107.

Discusses the effect of narrative asides on the relationship between the narrator and the reader in Luke-Acts, suggesting that the narrators of Luke and Acts establish and cultivate relationships with their readers in which the narrators have authority. Asides are categorized according to function. See 1345.

1345   Sheeley, Steven M. "Narrative Asides in Luke-Acts." Ph.D. diss., Southern Baptist Theological Seminary, 1987. 314 pp.

Identifies, categorizes, and examines narrative asides in Luke-Acts. A taxonomy of these "parenthetical remarks addressed directly to the reader" reveals four major uses: to provide information necessary for the understanding of the story, to provide general information, to offer inside views of characters, and to give self-conscious narration. The use of narrative asides in Luke-Acts is examined alongside their use in other ancient literature and appropriate comparisons are offered. The asides are also examined with reference to three narrative-critical categories: plot, narrator, and audience.

1346   Smith, Dennis E. "Table Fellowship as a Literary Motif in the Gospel of Luke." *Journal of Biblical Literature* 106 (1987): 613-638.

Describes the literary motif of table fellowship in Luke's Gospel as related to a symposium tradition evident in Philo, Plutarch, and other ancient writers. The motif serves five themes: ranking at table as a symbol of status, table talk as a mode of teaching, eating and drinking as a symbol of luxury, table service as a symbol for community service, and table fellowship as a symbol for community fellowship.

1347   Talbert, Charles H. *Acts*. Atlanta: John Knox Press, 1984. 120 pp.

A brief commentary that, despite its overtly homiletical intentions, serves as a companion volume to the author's literary study of Luke (1349). Talbert employs modern literary theory only cautiously, insisting on interpretation that defines the work as a product of a particular historical milieu.

1348   Talbert, Charles H. *Literary Patterns, Theological Themes, and the Genre of Luke-Acts*. Missoula, MT: Scholars Press, 1974. 159 pp.

A predecessor to modern literary studies of biblical books, this groundbreaking work calls attention to the literary artistry with which Luke's two volumes are intentionally constructed. Talbert is especially interested in the patterns of parallelism evident between the books and within each volume. The book makes significant contributions to a historical-theological understanding of Luke-Acts but also fits loosely into the category of "composition analysis" that has served for some as a transition from redaction criticism to narrative criticism.

1349 Talbert, Charles H. *Reading Luke: A Literary and Theological Commentary on the Third Gospel.* New York: Crossroad Publishing Co., 1982. 246 pp.

A close reading of the text of Luke's Gospel that draws on the insights of modern literary criticism without forsaking traditional historical concerns. Talbert's brand of literary criticism represents a refinement of "composition analysis," which in turn derives from redaction criticism. He pays careful attention to the literary structure and rhetoric of the narrative, but does not regard it as a production to be understood in light of timeless literary concepts. Rather, the work is consistently interpreted as part of an ancient biography, with frequent comparison to similar works of ancient literature. See also 1347. For a review, see 1616.

1350 Tannehill, Robert C. "The Composition of Acts 3-5: Narrative Development and Echo Effect." In *Society of Biblical Literature 1984 Seminar Papers*, ed. by Kent Harold Richards, 217-240. Chico, CA: Scholars Press, 1984.

Discusses similarities between the early chapters of Acts and two portions of Luke's Gospel: the beginning of Jesus' ministry, and Jesus' temple teaching and passion story. Reduplication also occurs within Acts 1--5 itself, especially in the two stories of the arrests of the apostles. Tannehill concludes by listing eight literary functions served by the elaborate patterns of repetition in Luke-Acts.

1351 Tannehill, Robert C. "Israel in Luke-Acts: A Tragic Story." *Journal of Biblical Literature* 104 (1985): 69-85.

Proposes that commitment to understanding Luke-Acts as a unitary narrative leads to the conclusion that the story of Israel there recounted must be regarded as tragic. The episodes in Luke-Acts are related to a unifying purpose disclosed through "previews and reviews," scriptural references, commission statements, and interpretive statements by reliable characters. This purpose clearly includes the salvation of Israel, yet at the end of the story, it appears unlikely that the purpose will be fulfilled.

1352 Tannehill, Robert C. "The Magnificat as Poem." *Journal of Biblical Literature* 93 (1974): 263-275.

Analyzes the poetic quality of Luke 1:46-55 from the perspective of New Criticism's emphasis on organic unity. The text is tightly constructed with formal patterns of repetition that include but also go well beyond parallelism. Repetitive strophic patterns and internal links in meaning cause the poem to work only if the unity of the text is honored. When this unity is respected, a dynamic tension between power and humility emerges that is central to the poem's meaning.

1353 Tannehill, Robert C. *The Narrative Unity of Luke-Acts: A Literary Interpretation. Volume I: The Gospel According to Luke.* Philadelphia: Fortress Press, 1986. 334 pp.

A comprehensive narrative-critical study of Luke's Gospel written from a perspective that views both the Gospel and the book of Acts as two parts of a single narrative. Tannehill stresses literary qualities in the Gospel that connect it with Acts, but the scope of his contribution goes way beyond this. Entire chapters are devoted to Jesus' relationship with various character groups: the oppressed, the crowds, the authorities, and the disciples. The rhetorical use of type scene, echoes, reviews and previews, and the like is also considered. The entire narrative is considered in light of a unifying purpose revealed at key points: universal salvation. Tension in the story is introduced through Israel's rejection of this salvation. See also 1354. For reviews, see 1614, 1616.

1354   Tannehill, Robert C. *The Narrative Unity of Luke-Acts: A Literary Interpretation. Volume II: The Acts of the Apostles.* Minneapolis: Fortress Press, 1990. 352 pp.

Continues the detailed narrative-critical study of Luke's two-volume work begun in 1353. Tannehill shifts from the topical style of presentation used there to a format that studies the text of Acts from its beginning to end. The plot of Acts is therefore viewed as a progression of connected episodes. Tannehill calls attention to rhetorical and causal elements that create the narrative unity within which each episode is to be considered. Other literary concerns, such as characterization, narrative time, symbolism, point of view, and the role of conflict are considered throughout. The most comprehensive and best literary study of Acts to date.

1355   Tyson, Joseph B. "Conflict as a Literary Theme in the Gospel of Luke." In *New Synoptic Studies: The Cambridge Gospel Conference and Beyond*, ed. by William R. Farmer, 303-330. Macon, GA: Mercer University Press, 1983.

Explores a selected literary theme in Luke's Gospel in order to demonstrate the possibility of comprehending the work as a whole without recourse to a source hypothesis. Tyson discovers that early and less malevolent conflict in Luke is associated with the Pharisees and with issues of torah, while later, more bitter conflict is associated with the priests in Jerusalem and with the temple. The temple teaching of Jesus serves to mark the shift in the narrative.

1356   Tyson, Joseph B. *The Death of Jesus in Luke-Acts.* Columbia: University of South Carolina Press, 1986. 212 pp.

Essentially a study in "composition criticism" rather than modern literary criticism, this work nevertheless sheds light on literary facets of Luke's Gospel, especially the theme of conflict (cf. 1355). Distinctive features in Luke's presentation of Jesus' death include: (1) the prominence of the theme of initial acceptance and final rejection; (2) sharp distinction between Pharisaic opposition and priestly opposition to Jesus; (3) ascription to the chief priests of sole responsibility for Jesus' death; (4) the presence of positive images regarding the temple and Jerusalem to balance the negative ones; (5) the concept that Jesus was opposed by the chief priests because of his claim to have authority in the temple; (6) the emphasis on the political innocence of Jesus. See also 1651.

1357   Walworth, Allen J. "The Narrator of Acts." Ph.D. diss., The Southern Baptist Theological Seminary (Louisville), 1984.

Describes the narrator of Acts as a reliable guide who exerts both diegetic and mimetic authority over the reader. Special attention is given to the manner by which the narrator guides the reader's sympathies and distance toward various characters. One chapter is also devoted to the narratee of Acts, who is understood to be a Gentile Christian with some inclinations toward Judaism.

1358   Wolfe, K. R. "The Chiastic Structure of Luke-Acts and Some Implications for Worship." *Southwest Journal of Theology* 22 (1980): 60-71.

Detects a concentric composition in Luke-Acts: A--Galilee (Luke 4:14--9:50); B--Samaria and Judea (9:51--19:40); C--Jerusalem (19:41--24:49); D--ascension (Luke 24:50-51); C'--Jerusalem (Acts 1:12--8:1a); B'--Judea and Samaria (8:1b--11:18); A' --to the ends of the earth (11:19--28:31). Thus, the ascension forms the central panel.

1359   York, J. O. *The Last Shall Be First: The Rhetoric of Reversal in Luke.* Journal for the Study of the New Testament Supplement Series, 46. Sheffield: JSOT Press, 1990. 208 pp.

Uses rhetorical criticism for historical-critical purposes. York examines the feature of reversal (what Aristotle called *peripateia*) in individual texts in Luke and in the Gospel as a whole. His interest is in discovering what the use of this rhetorical strategy suggests concerning the original audience of the third Gospel and the historical intentions of its author.

THE GOSPEL OF JOHN

See also 0274, 0521, 0529, 0534, 0585, 0808, 1041, 1046-1047, 1051, 1061, 1068-1071, 1075-1076, 1608, 1693.

1360   Bishop, Jonathan. "Encounters in the New Testament." In *Literary Interpretations of Biblical Narratives, Volume II,* ed. by Kenneth R. R. Gros Louis with James S. Ackerman, 285-294. Nashville: Abingdon Press, 1982.

Takes the story of the cure of a blind man in John 9 as illustrative of the way in which New Testament anecdotes about encounters with Jesus function paradigmatically. The story is typical in that Jesus serves as a figure for the Christ of faith and the persons who encounter him serve as figures of ourselves.

1361 Boers, Hendrikus. *Neither on This Mountain Nor in Jerusalem: A Study of John 4.* Society of Biblical Literature Monograph Series, 35. Atlanta: Scholars Press, 1988. 230 pp.

Applies A. J. Greimas' semiotic theory to John 4. Boers presents a detailed, exhaustive analysis of the semantics and syntax of this chapter, complete with numerous diagrams indicating intertextual relationships. He singles out significant sets of opposed values, such as "factional security vs. human solidarity," "partisan salvation vs. universal salvation," and "sustenance vs. obedience." These may be examined in terms of an existential polarity between death and life or in terms of a social polarity between alienation and integration. The "generative trajectory" of John 4 is also presented, and a final chapter summarizes the results of the study for interpreation of the chapter's meaning, with more emphasis on *how* it achieves meaning than on *what* that meaning is.

1362 Born, J. B. "Literary Features in the Gospel of John (An Analysis of John 3:1-21)." *Direction* 17 (1988): 3-17.

Examines implicit commentary in John's Gospel--information conveyed "between the lines" through literary allusions, misunderstandings, irony, and symbolism. John 3:1-21 is used as a test case for demonstrating the presence of these features.

1363 Bridges, James L. "Structure and History in John 11: A Methodological Study Comparing Structuralist and Historical Critical Approaches." Ph.D. diss., Graduate Theological Union, 1988. 319 pp.

Compares two studies on the story of the raising of Lazarus in John's Gospel: a historical-critical study by Gerard Rochais and a structuralist study by John R. Jones. Bridges concludes that, in spite of certain hermeneutical contradictions, the two approaches can be complementary and mutually informative. Both approaches suffer, however, from a tendency to decontextualize the narrative of Lazarus from a holistic reading of the overall Gospel.

1364 Bridges, Linda McKinnish. "The Aphorisms in the Gospel of John: A Transmissional Literary, and Sociological Analysis of Selected Sayings." Ph.D. diss., Southern Baptist Theological Seminary, 1987. 290 pp.

Seeks to identify aphorisms in the Gospel of John and to study these from source-critical, literary, and sociological perspectives. The literary analysis presents a close reading of the aphorisms with attention to their relationships with the narrator, the plot, the characters, and the reader.

1365 Brown, Schuyler. "The True Light (Jn 1:9-12)." *Toronto Journal of Theology* 1 (1985): 222-226.

Discusses the mythological language of faith used in the hymn that opens the Gospel of John (1:1-18). Set within the context of John's entire narrative, this language, which is basic to world religions, serves to undercut the evangelist's own christological exclusivism.

1366   Cahill, P. Joseph. "Narrative Art in John IV." *Religious Studies Bulletin* 2 (1982): 41-48.

Proposes a chiastic structure for the fourth chapter of John: A--meeting of Jesus with Samaritan woman (1-4); B--dialogue on living water (5-9); C--dialogue on true worship (16-26); B'--dialogue on true food (27-38); A'--meeting of Jesus with Samaritans (39-42). The central portion indicates the theme of the whole: true worship.

1367   Cauthron, Halbert A., Jr. "The Meaning of Kingship in Johannine Christology: A Structuralist Exegesis of John 18:1--20:18." Ph.D. diss., Vanderbilt University, 1984. 222 pp.

Seeks to discover the categories of meaning that function within the Johannine passion narrative and to elucidate the semiotic significance of the title "King of the Jews" as applied to Jesus in that narrative. The method used is one of structuralist analysis developed by A. J. Greimas and elaborated by Daniel Patte, who directed the dissertation.

1368   Clavier, Henri. "L'ironie dans le quatriéme Evangile." In *Studia Evangelica. Vol. 1*, ed. by Kurt Aland, et al, 261-276. Texte und Untersuchungen, 73. Berlin: Akadamie Verlag, 1959.

An early study of irony in the Gospel of John. Clavier regards Johannine irony as being of a special and original quality, of a less Socratic form than that of the synoptic Gospels. The latter conclusion is contested by Duke (1377).

1369   Crossan, John Dominic. "It is Written: A Structuralist Analysis of John 6." *Semeia* 26 (1983): 3-21.

An expanded version of an earlier work (1370). Crossan adds an extended introduction on the unity of John 6 and appends a discussion on the issue of orality/textuality raised by comments within this text. These additions are more coherent and effective than the rest of the work and make contributions that may be found useful in their own right.

1370   Crossan, John Dominic. "A Structuralist Analysis of John 6." In *Orientation By Disorientation*, ed. by Richard A. Spencer, 235-252. Pittsburgh: Pickwick Press, 1980.

Analyzes the feeding miracle and attendant discourse in John's Gospel through the methodology of structuralism in an effort to determine how the text achieves its meaning. Crossan distinguishes between narrative and discourse and between the actants and actions in the text. He concludes with some observations on the process by which the Feeder becomes the Food in the language of John's Gospel. Cf. 1369.

1371 Culbertson, Diana. "Are You Also Deceived? Reforming the Reader in John 7." *Proceedings: Eastern Great Lakes Biblical Society* 9 (1989): 148-160.

Applies psychoanalytic reading theories of Marshall Alcorn and Mark Bracher to John 7 to show how that text calls for recognition and thus re-formation on the part of the reader. Culbertson finds that Nicodemus is distinct from other characters in John 7 in that he models for the reader a pliancy of conviction that can lead to belief. The reader is drawn to ask, with this potential believer, "Where is he?," an inquiry that pertains not only to Jesus' geographical location within the story, but also to his presence in the world of the reader.

1372 Culpepper, R. Alan. *Anatomy of the Fourth Gospel: A Study in Literary Design.* Foundations and Facets: New Testament. Philadelphia: Fortress Press, 1983. 266 pp.

A major narrative-critical study of the Gospel of John, focusing on such themes as narrator, point of view, narrative time, plot, characters, implicit commentary (i.e., use of misunderstanding, irony, and symbolism), and the implied reader. Culpepper applies literary theories of Seymour Chatman, Gérard Genette, and others, explaining them clearly and applying them insightfully to John's text. The best and most comprehensive literary study of John.

1373 Culpepper, R. Alan. "The Pivot of John's Prologue." *New Testament Studies* 27 (1980): 1-31.

Proposes a chiastic structure for John 1-18 for which the central and controlling verse is 12b ("he gave them authority to be children of God"). The theme articulated by these words also serves to integrate much of the material found throughout the Fourth Gospel.

1374 Deakle, David Wayne. "A Study of Literary Pairs in the Fouth Gospel." Ph.D. diss., New Orleans Baptist Theological Seminary, 1985. 172 pp.

Studies "literary pairs" in the Gospel of John. Literary pairs are the two-member units that occur in clauses, sentences, and pericopes throughout the Gospel. Four cateories are proposed: parallelisms, repetitions, couplets, and dualistic vocabulary. The possibility of paranomastic pairs and personified pairs is also acknowledged.

1375 Diel, Paul, and Solotareff, Jeannine. *Symbolism in the Gospel of John.* Trans. by Nelly Marans. San Francisco: Harper and Row, 1988. 222 pp.

A study by a literary critic of the symbolic message of Jesus portrayed in John's Gospel. Best known for work in Greek mythology, Diel interprets symbolism from a psychological perspective, noting its evocative power to arouse emotions at the deepest levels of human psyche. This book was assembled by Solotareff from manuscripts by Diel after his death. It has three parts: the first concerns the myth of the incarnation presented in the prologue (see also 0585), the second concerns illustrative episodes, and the third the teaching of Jesus. Diel's analysis is unabashedly introspective, and his interpretations repeatedly reveal John's symbolism as expressive of faith in life itself.

1376   Dockery, D. S. "John 9:1-41: A Narrative Discourse Study." *OPTAT* (Dallas) 2 (1988): 14-26.

Examines the features of narrative discourse in the story of the man born blind in John 9. The story is seen to consist of seven recognizable episodes. Dockery also considers characters and plot.

1377   Duke, Paul. *Irony in the Fourth Gospel*. Atlanta: John Knox Press, 1985. 222 pp.

A book-length study of an important literary device in John's Gospel.   Duke summarizes contemporary literary theory on irony, drawing especially from Muecke (0185-0186) and Booth (0140). He discusses applications of irony in John both with regard to individual passages and with regard to sustained scenes. He notes the function of irony both as appeal and as weapon and concludes with some historical reflections on irony and the Johannine milieu. See also 1368.

1378   Du Rand, J. A. "The Characterization of Jesus as Depicted in the Narrative of the Fourth Gospel." *Neotestamentica* 19 (1985): 18-36.

Builds on the author's understanding of plot in John (1379) to investigate the characterization of Jesus.   The readers' reponses to Jesus are swayed through demonstrations of the consequences of different responses by various characters. Jesus is certainly the protagonist of the narrative but, as in most good stories, he remains a somewhat mysterious figure.

1379   Du Rand, J. A. "Plot and Point of View in the Gospel of John." In *A South African Perspective on the New Testament*, ed. by J. H. Petzer and P. J. Hartin, 149-169. Leiden: E. J. Brill, 1986.

Sets out to elucidate the point of view and plot of John's Gospel by analyzing the cultural and linguistic codes that appear in the Gospel story. Point of view is analyzed according to the planes of expression suggested by Uspensky (0305): psychological, spatial, temporal, and ideological (Du Rand does not discuss phraseological). Plot development is discussed in terms of Setting (1:1-51), Complication (2:1--17:26), and Resolution (18:1--21:25). The theme that unifies this plot is witness to the identity of Jesus. Du Rand draws heavily on Culpepper (1372).

1380   Du Rand, J. A. "A Syntactical and Narratological Reading of John 9--10." In *The Shepherd Discourse of John 10 and Its Context*, ed. by J. Beutler and R. T. Fortna. Cambridge: Cambridge University Press, 1991.

Announced for publication.

1381   Eslinger, Lyle M. "The Wooing of the Woman at the Well: Jesus, the Reader and Reader-Response Criticism." *Literature and Theology* 1 (1987): 167-183.

Discusses reader response to the story of Jesus and the woman at the well in John 4 in light of three factors: (1) the intentional use of a betrothal type-scene to mislead readers; (2) the use of double entendres; (3) the structure of the discourse.

1382   Foster, Donald. "John Come Lately: The Belated Evangelist." In *The Bible and the Narrative Tradition*, ed. by Frank McConnell, 113-131. New York: Oxford University Press, 1986.

Reflects on the power assumed by the narrator of John's Gospel, a power that is almost divine. Not only are John's words remarkably similar to those of Jesus in the Gospel, but John presents his Gospel itself as an eternally present, infinitely creative word, through which a whole world has come into being. Aware that he writes belatedly (i.e., after the other evangelists), John presents Jesus as the one who comes late in time but remains prior to all that went before him.

1383   Giblin, Charles Homer. "Confrontation in John 18, 1-27." *Biblica* 65 (1984): 210-232.

Discusses the first two scenes of John's passion narrative from a literary perspective. Giblin believes that attention to entrances and exits allows the passion narrative to be divided into five scenes (18:1-11; 18:12-27; 18:28--19:16a; 19:16b-37; 19:38-42). In the first two scenes, Peter assumes a typological role, and Jesus' trial before Annas is presented as a "moment of truth." Giblin uses narrative-critical categories, but is primarily interested in discerning the theology of the author, which is described in ecclesiological and christological terms. The study continues in 1384.

1384   Giblin, Charles Homer. "John's Narrative of the Hearing Before Pilate (John 18, 28--19, 16a)." *Biblica* 67 (1986): 221-239.

A sequel to 1383, this article examines the structure of the "third scene" in John's passion narrative as disclosing the progression of encounters between Pilate, Jesus, and the Jews. Although Jesus is the main character, it is the physical movements of Pilate (e.g. inside and outside) that give the passage its structure. The encounters build to a climactic irony by which the Jews are manipulated by Pilate into submitting to Caesar and rejecting their messianic hope.

1385   Girard, M. "Analyse structurelle de Jn 1, 1-18: l'unité des deux Testaments dans la structure bipolaire du prologue de Jean." *Science et Espirit* 35 (1983): 5-31.

Tries to establish the unity of the Johannine prologue through synchronic analysis. In addition, Girard addresses the larger structural issue of unity between the two Testaments, reflected here in the perspective of perfect continuity between creation and redemption.

1386   Grayston, Kenneth. *The Gospel of John*. Narrative Commentaries. Philadelphia: Trinity Press International, 1990. 177 pp.

As the first in a new series of commentaries on the New Testament, this book tries to transcend arguments over source strata and redactional history by focusing on the narrative of John's Gospel. Grayston is particularly interested in matters pertaining to language and literary structure. He differs from most modern literary critics, however, in viewing his task as being to interpret the narrative in terms of the intentions of its author.

1387   Hartman, Lars. "An Attempt at a Text-Centered Exegesis of John 21." *Studia Theologica* 38 (1984): 29-45.

A close reading of John 21 that attempts to take into account literary organization (in two parts: 1-14 and 15-23), recurring motifs, character relationships (especially Peter and the beloved disciple), and narrative flow. The study also considers the relationship of this unit to John 20 and suggests possible reactions of first-century readers to the text.

1388   Johnson, Alfred Marion, Jr. "The Cultural Context of the Gospel of John - A Structural Approach." Ph.D. diss., University of Pittsburgh, 1978. 383 pp.

Approaches the Gospel of John from the perspective of anthropological structuralism, which specializes in the relationships between a text and the cultures mirrored in it. The conclusion is that the Gospel is a document written to unify an in-group that primarily considered itself related to the Rachel tribes of the "House of Joseph" but that included some Judeans and Galileans as well.

1389   Jones, John Richard. "Narrative Structures and Meaning in John 11:1-54." Ph.D. diss., Vanderbilt University, 1982. 366 pp.

A structuralist analysis on the story of the raising of Lazarus, using the method of A. J. Greimas that has been adapted for biblical studies by Daniel Patte, this dissertation's adviser. The analysis proceeds through five structural levels, yielding three coordinated sets of deep values. The first endorses acceptance of death's reality. The second presents interpretations of Jesus in the form of oppositions between faith and unbelief. The third extends these values into the life of the Johannine community through the device of narrative ambiguity.

1390   Jonge, Marinus de. "Nicodemus and Jesus: Some Observations on Misunderstanding and Understanding in the Fourth Gospel." *Bulletin of the John Rylands Library* 53 (1971): 337-359.

A study of the figure of Nicodemus in John's Gospel. De Jonge concludes that Nicodemus is representative of sympathizing Jews who may be "on their way to belief in Jesus" but who are not believers yet. Though de Jonge pays scant attention to literary-critical theories as such, the study will be relevant to those interested in characterization or in the literary motif of "misunderstanding" in John.

1391   Kelber, Werner H. "In the Beginning Were the Words: The Apotheosis and Narrative Displacement of the Logos." *Journal of the American Academy of Religion* 58 (1990): 69-98.

Describes the fourth Gospel as an attempt in the first century to deal with the same philosophical paradox faced in modern times by Friedrich Nietzsche, Sigmund Freud, Martin Heidegger, and Jacques Derrida. The paradox, for John, consists of the inevitable need to use written words in an attempt to reduce the opposition between orality and literacy. John's Gospel is "deeply informed by the double gesture of decentering and logocentrism." In de-centering the Logos, John's Gospel adminsters deconstruction of its own onto-theological origin. This article is a foretaste of what is to appear in 1392.

1392   Kelber, Werner H. *The Eclipse of Presence: Transparency and Opacity in the Fourth Gospel*. Madison: University of Wisconsin Press, forthcoming.

Announced for publication. See 1391.

1393   Kermode, Frank. "John." In *The Literary Guide to the Bible*, ed. by Robert Alter and Frank Kermode, 440-466. Cambridge, MA: Belknap Press, 1987.

A reading of John's Gospel by a scholar of secular literature. Kermode is impressed by the virtues of economy, connexity and depth in John's Gospel. The fourth evangelist assigns multiple meanings to single words (e.g., "glory"), gives his own emphasis to material from the common stock, and works always to represent the eternal in relation to the transient. Kermode emphasizes the need of a literary interpretation to read John as a narrative unity. The prologue, for instance, must not be separated from the narrative proper. An excursus on the passion narratives brings out the distinctive emphases of the Johannine account.

1394   Kermode, Frank. "St. John as Poet." *Journal for the Study of the New Testament* 28 (1986): 3-16.

An analysis of John 1:1-18 by a well-known literary scholar. Kermode's concern is with the meaning that this passage holds for contemporary readers who receive it as poetry. His analysis focuses on the poem's internal features, on the "axis" established by the ordinary words "being" and "becoming," and on the role that the poem plays as paradigm for the Gospel narrative that follows.

1395   Koester, Craig. "Hearing, Seeing, and Believing in the Gospel of John." *Biblica* 70 (1989): 327-348.

Studies the juxtaposition of accounts of coming to faith with accounts of people who do not come to faith in John's Gospel. Those who do manifest a genuine faith do so after an initial experience of *hearing*. Those whose initial perception of Jesus is one of *seeing* regularly fail to come to true faith.

1396   Kotzé, P. P. A. "Ironie in die Johannesevangelie." *Hervormde Teologiese Studies* (Pretoria) 43 (1987): 431-447.

Discusses the nature of irony and its function in involving the reader, and then reflects on particular instances of irony in Jesus' conversation with Nicodemus.

1397   Kotzé, P. P. A. "John and Reader's Response." *Neotestamentica* 19 (1985): 50-63.

Examines John 2--3 in light of Wolfgang Iser's theories concerning reader perception of gaps and ambiguities. Attention is given to indeterminate fields of reference, determinate fields of reference, imagination, anticipation, and retrospection, shifts in perception, negation, and repetition.

1398   Kowalski, Judith. "'Of Water and Spirit': Narrative Structure and Theological Development in the Gospel of John." Ph.D. diss., Marquette University, 1987. 270 pp.

Analyzes the structure of John's Gospel by noting a variety of linguistic characteristics, temporal indicators, and narrative modes. The dynamics of a motif concerning water are highlighted--water seems to communicate the comparison beween spiritual timing and physical timing, which do not always coincide. Furthermore, functions regularly ascribed to water, such as birth, purification, baptism (witness), drinking (nurturance), and healing are, in this Gospel, ascribed to the action of the Word.

1399   Kurz, William S. "The Beloved Disciple and Implied Readers." *Biblical Theology Bulletin* 19 (1989): 100-106.

Analyzes gaps in the narrative presentation of the beloved disciple as suggestive of a typological relationship between this character and the implied reader. Three gaps are studied: (1) the beloved disciple is never named; (2) the beloved disciple is not mentioned as such until the farewell discourse; and (3) the beloved disciple's knowledge of the betrayer does not affect the plot. In addition, later references to this figure confirm the paradigmatic significance as an ideal disciple.

1400   Kysar, Robert. *John's Story of Jesus*. Philadelphia: Fortress Press, 1984. 96 pp.

A "retelling" of the story of John's Gospel with emphasis on the structure of the plot line. Kysar realizes that the flow of the story is often abrupt, but he eschews source reconstructions here to make sense of the text as it is now preserved. Recognizing that the primary significance of John's Gospel is theological, Kysar demonstrates also the effectiveness of the work as a story, highlighting the subtle ways in which the evangelist communicates his message to the reader.

1401   Léon-Dufour, Xavier. "Towards a Symbolic Reading of the Fourth Gospel," *New Testament Studies* 27 (1981): 439-456.

Advocates symbolic reading as the approach that relates present Christian experience to the historical past referenced in John's Gospel. As evidence that the Fourth Gospel is intended to be read in this way, three texts are considered, ones which present the symbolism of temple (2:13-22), rebirth (3:5), and bread (6:53-58).

1402   Leroy, Herbert. *Rätsel und Missverständnis: Ein Beitrag zur Formgeschichte des Johannesevangeliums*. Bonner Biblische Beiträge, 30. Bonn: Peter Hanstein, 1968. 195 pp.

An extensive examination of ten instances in John's Gospel where Jesus is misunderstood. The author treats these scenes as instances of a riddle form and discusses the role that riddle plays in John's theology. Later studies, including ones by Culpepper (1372) and Duke (1377) have drawn on Leroy's work in discussing "misunderstanding" as a literary motif in John.

1403   MacRae, George W. "Theology and Irony in the Fourth Gospel." In *The Word in the World: Essays in Honor of Frederick L. Moriarty*, ed. by Richard J. Clifford and George W. MacRae, 83-96. Cambridge: Weston College Press, 1973.

Characterizes Johannine irony as "dramatic irony" in distinction from satirical, Socratic, tragic, and metaphysical types of irony. Special attention is paid to the account of the trial before Pilate and to Johannine symbols.

1404   Mlakuzhyil, George. *The Christocentric Literary Structure of the Fourth Gospel*. Analecta Biblica, 117. Rome: Pontifical Biblical Institute, 1987. 370 pp.

A major study of the structure of John's Gospel from a literary perspective. Chapter 3 provides a list of literary criteria, dramatic techniques, and structural patterns that must be considered in such an analysis. The chapter has worth even apart from the rest of the study, but Mlakuzhyil is primarily interested in noting how these criteria, techniques, and patterns converge to yield an intentional structural outline. The Gospel is divided into five parts (1:1--2:11; 2:1--12:50; 11:1--20:29; 20:30-31; 21:1-25), which correspond roughly to the five episodes of classical Greek tragedies. Furthermore, each of the main sections is found to contain a chiasmus of six parts.

1405   Moore, Robert Rood. "Soteriology and Structure: A Study of the Relation Between the Soteriology and Present Literary Structure of the Fourth Gospel." Ph.D. diss., Emory University, 1982. 268 pp.

Examines the literary structure of the Gospel of John and its relationship to soteriological themes. Moore finds that the book is arranged in sections according to contexts of Jewish festivals, with a miracle (or sign) that is particularly relevant to the context included in each section. The conclusion of the study is that the literary structure of the Gospel is intended to serve as its soteriological thesis.

1406 Myers, D. E. "Irony and Humor in the Gospel of John." *OPTAT* (Dallas) 2 (1988): 1-13.

Postulates a reader for John's Gospel who knows nothing about "higher criticism" or theological commentary but who does know something about literary analysis. Such a reading produces a narrative that is humorous, ironic, and unified.

1407 Nuttall, A. D. *Overheard by God: Fiction and Prayer in Herbert, Milton, Dante and St. John.* New York: Methuen and Co., 1980. 160 pp.

Proposes that certain ancient writers composed their works under the assumption that they would be read not only by people but also by God. Samples of writing by Herbert, Milton and Dante are tested against this hypothesis. Biblical scholars will be most interested in the "Coda" on John's Gospel. Nuttall makes two points: (1) the work resembles modern literature in its use of "discontinuous dialog," though John uses such a device for different purposes; (2) avoiding questions of faith in readings of John's Gospel is bad literary criticism, tantamount to critiquing *Romeo and Juliet* without acknowledging the play is about love.

1408 O'Day, Gail R. "Narrative Mode and Theological Claim: A Study in the Fourth Gospel." *Journal of Biblical Literature* 105 (1986): 657-668.

Suggests that studies of revelation in John's Gospel have failed to take account of the narrative characteristics of the book and have failed to consider the "how" of revelation. O'Day surveys the Bultmannian distinction of *Dass* and *Was* that has dominated discussions of revelation in John up to now and suggests the new category of *Wie* ("how"). An example of attention to the "how" of revelation is presented in a brief narrative analysis of John 4 that gives particular attention to the use of irony.

1409 O'Day, Gail R. *Revelation in the Fourth Gospel: Narrative Mode and Theological Claim.* Philadelphia: Fortress Press, 1986. 143 pp.

Attempts to show that the theological claim of John's Gospel cannot be understood apart from consideration of its character as narrative literature. As revelatory literature, the Gospel of John uses narrative devices, particularly irony, to communicate. The narrative of the Gospel makes available to the reader an experience of Jesus and of the God known in Jesus in ways that resist attempts to assimilate them into systematic categories.

1410 O'Day, Gail R. *The Word Disclosed: John's Story and Narrative Preaching.* St. Louis: CBP Press, 1987. 112 pp.

A literary-critical commentary on four Johannine texts: 3:1-15; 4:4-42; 9:1-41; and 11:1-53. The focus in each case is on the discourse of the narrative, that is on *how* the texts communicate their meaning. The four passages are lectionary texts and O'Day consciously tries to indicate how preachers might communicate the meanings of the texts to modern audiences. The intention, then, is to pursue a reading strategy that allows us to be drawn *into* the texts and then to draw *out* what we discover in the texts. Transformational dynamics of reading and preaching are emphasized.

1411 Owanga-Welo, Jean. "The Function and Meaning of the Footwashing in the Johannine Passion Narrative: A Structural Approach." Ph.D. diss., Emory University, 1980. 296 pp.

Analyzes the footwashing story in chapter 13 of John from a structuralist perspective that draws on Claude Bremond, Vladimir Propp, A. J. Greimas, Tzvetan Todorov, and Roland Barthes. Owanga-Welo argues that the Johannine passion story begins at 11:55-57 rather than at 13:1 as is usually thought. The meaning of the footwashing is the inner purification of the disciples, which is interpreted as the preparation/qualification for future enthronement (20:19-23).

1412 Pahk, Sung Sang. "Structural Analysis of John VI:1-58: Meaning of the Symbol 'Bread of Life.'" Ph.D. diss., Vanderbilt University, 1984. 262 pp.

Applies the semiotic-structuralist model of A. J. Greimas, as adapted by this dissertation's director, Daniel Patte, to the story of the miraculous feeding and the bread of life discourse in John's Gospel. The study favors a sapiential interpretation of the text, but also finds that interpretation to be overly intellectual and spiritual. The basic truth of the passage is that Jesus himself, as the bread of life, gives both his teaching and his flesh and blood (life and death) for the world.

1413 Pazdan, Mary Margaret. "Nicodemus and the Samaritan Woman: Contrasting Models of Discipleship." *Biblical Theology Bulletin* 17 (1987): 145-148.

Considers John 3:1-21 and 4:1-42 as dialogical narratives that complement each other, as well as the narratives surrounding them. Nicodemus provides a model of initial discipleship and the Samaritan woman, a model of mature discipleship.

1414 Phillips, Gary A. "'This is a Hard Saying. Who Can Be Listener to it?': Creating a Reader in John 6." *Semeia* 26 (1983): 23-56.

Describes the text of John 6 as an instance of "enunciation," that is, as a signifier whose nature and function is the production of discourse. John 6 accomplishes this effect by fashioning a reader for itself out of the interplay of different levels and types of speaking that take place within the text. The reading role emerges from an iconic patterning between the type of speaking/hearing that occurs within the text among the characters and the narrator and the speaking/reading that relates to the evangelist's discourse as a whole.

1415 Plunkett, Regina St. G. "The Samaritan Woman: Partner in Revelation." *The Anglican Theological Review* (forthcoming).

Announced for publication.

1416   Resseguie, James L.   "John 9:   A Literary-Critical Analysis."   In *Literary Interpretations of Biblical Narratives, Volume II*, ed. by Kenneth R. R. Gros Louis with James S. Ackerman, 295-304.   Nashville: Abingdon Press, 1982.

Presents a close reading of John 9 that demonstrates the interrelationship of form and content in the passage.   The structure is built on two opposing plot movements: the comic movement of the blind man from ill-being to well-being and a reverse or tragic movement of the religious authorities from well-being to ill-being.   This double movement and the ironic characterizations that accompany it bring out the themes of light and judgment that are also developed on a content level.   The passage is a superb piece of literature, one that shows what it also tells.

1417   Rheinhartz, A.   "Great Expectations: A Reader-Oriented Approach to Johannine Christology and Eschatology." *Journal of Literature and Theology* (Oxford) 3 (1989): 61-76.

Examines the pattern of suggestion, negative response, and positive action that is expressed in three of the Johannine sign-stories (2:1-11; 4:46-54; 11:1-44).   The main purpose of this pattern is to correct or modify christological and eschatological expectations of the implied reader.

1418   Richard, E.   "Expressions of Double Meaning and Their Function in the Gospel of John." *New Testament Studies* 31 (1985): 96-112.

Surveys several categories of double meanings in John's Gospel and makes general observations regarding their use.   Richard considers misunderstanding, irony, technical terms used in general contexts, ambiguous terms used in specific contexts, figurative expressions, christological titles, and double meanings that transcend particular literary techniques.   These serve well the goal and perspective of the fourth gospel, with its theme of signs that convey reality for those with faith but that take on a quality of irony or judgment for those without faith.

1419   Schneiders, Sandra M.   "History and Symbolism in the Fourth Gospel."   In *L'évangile de Jean: Sources, Rédaction, Théologie*, pp. 371-376.   Bibliotheca ephemeridum theologicarum lovaniensum, 44.   Louvain: Louvain University Press, 1977.

Studies the relationship between symbolism and history in the Gospel of John, concluding that no inverse proportion exists between the two.   Because history is used by John as symbolic material, the more historical the Gospel is seen to be, the more symbolic it will be seen to be.   Symbolism is not just an element in John's narrative, but the characteristic mode of revelation.   Symbolism is a function of the whole, not just of the parts.   Johannine symbolism has nothing to do with allegory.   Although the symbols are polyvalent, they are not subject to endless or arbitrary interpretations.

1420 Staley, Jeffrey Lloyd. *The Print's First Kiss: A Rhetorical Investigation of the Implied Reader in the Fourth Gospel.* Society of Biblical Literature Dissertation Series, 82. Atlanta: Scholars Press, 1988. 138 pp.

Brings together insights of rhetorical criticism and reader-response criticism with regard to the Gospel of John. After reviewing literary studies on John, Staley presents an analysis of rhetorical strategies (especially concentric structure) and of the implied reader. The latter is led (as are characters in the Gospel) to adopt a "journeying faith" that moves from one level of understanding through confusion ("victimization") to a deeper level of understanding.

1421 Staley, Jeffrey Lloyd. "The Structure of John's Prologue: Its Implications for the Gospel's Narrative Structure." *Catholic Biblical Quarterly* 48 (1986): 241-264.

Proposes a concentric structure for John 1:1-18: A--relationship of Logos to God, creation, humankind (1-5); B--John's witness (6-8); C--journey of the Light (9-11); D --gift of empowerment (12-13); C'--Journey of the Logos (14); B'--John's witness (15); A'--relationship of Logos to humankind, re-creation, and God (16-18). Implications are drawn from this arrangement for understanding the narrative structure of the Gospel as a whole in terms of four ministry tours (1:19--3:36; 4:1--6:71; 7:1--10:42; 11:1--21:25).

1422 Szlaga, J. "Struktura literacka perykopy o wskrzeszeniu Lazarza (J 11,1-44) i jej funkcja teologiczna." *Rockzniki Teologiczne-Kanoniczne* 27 (1980): 81-91.

A structural analysis of place names, terminology about Lazarus, reactions of witnesses, and deeds of Jesus in John 11:1-44. Szlaga discerns five sections in the account (1-6; 7-16; 17-27; 28-37; 38-44). The middle section, which portrays Jesus as the resurrection and the life, is central to the pericope.

1423 Talbert, Charles H. "Artistry and Theology: An Analysis of the Architecture of Jn. 1:19--5:47." *Catholic Biblical Quarterly* 32 (1970): 341-366.

Proposes that John's Gospel is composed of two parts, each of which consists of a chiastic introduction (1:1-18; 13:1-35) followed by long chiastic sections (1:19--5:47; 15:1--17:26). Most of the article elaborates the chiastic structure of 1:19-5:47: A--witnesses (1:19--2:11); B--feast (2:13-22); C--official's visit (2:23--3:21); D--ritual and life (3:22-36); D'--ritual and life (4:1-42); C'--official's visit (4:43-54); B'--feast (5:1-30); A'--witnesses (5:31-47).

1424 Vorster, Willem S. "The Gospel of John as Language." *Neotestamentica* 6 (1972): 19-27.

Argues that the language of John's Gospel must be studied on the *parole* level as being the language usage of the Gospel's redactor. The methodology for this approach derives largely from Erhardt Güttgemann's linguistic theory. Vorster thus recommends that exegetical methods based on modern structural linguistics be used complementarily with the historical-critical approach to New Testament writings.

1425   Wead, David W. "The Johannine Double Meaning." *Restoration Quarterly* 13 (1970): 106-120.

A study of what might be regarded as a literary device in John's Gospel--the intentional use of words that can have more than one meaning (e.g., *anothen* in 3:3 can mean either "from above" or "anew"). Wead notes several instances of such double meanings, including instances in which the double meaning is provided by a Semitic word that stands behind the Greek word in the text, and instances in which the double meaning is obtained because two tenses (e.g., indicative and imperative second person plurals) of a verb use the same form.

1426   Wead, David W. "Johannine Irony as a Key to the Author-Audience Relationship in John's Gospel." In *American Academy of Religion Biblical Literature: 1974*, comp. by Fred O. Francis, 33-50. Missoula, MT: Scholars Press, 1974.

A rhetorical-critical study of irony in John. Wead indicates that John uses a Sophoclean type of irony that was common in Greek drama. This type of irony arises from disparity between characters in the story and the audience. The use of such irony presupposes confidence on the part of the author at bringing the audience to acceptance of his understanding of events.

1427   Wead, David W. *The Literary Devices in John's Gospel*. Theologischen Dissertation, 4. Basel: Fredrich Reinhart Kommissionsverlag, 1970.   130 pp.

Treats four "literary devices" in John's Gospel: (1) signs, (2) double meanings (cf. 1425), (3) irony (cf. 1426), and (4) metaphor. The treatment of signs deals more with historical concerns than with symbolic significance--in fact Wead cautions against attribution of the latter. Old Testament background is emphasized for understanding all of John's literary moves.

1428   Webster, Edwin C. "Pattern in the Fourth Gospel." In *Art and Meaning: Rhetoric in Biblical Literature*, ed. by David J. A. Clines, David M. Gunn, and Alan J. Hauser, 230-257. Sheffield, England: JSOT Press, 1982.

Proposes that the Gospel of John, as a literary whole, is meticulously constructed on the basis of symmetrical designs analogous to Hebrew parallelism. Five such patterns are described and traced throughout the Gospel: (1) balancing of incidents and themes in paired complementary units; (2) triadic and quadratic arrangements of paired units; (3) parallel sequences within complementary units; (4) word or formula repetitions to mark units; and (5) close balance as to length between complementary units.

THE EPISTLES OF PAUL

See also 0562, 0585, 1037, 1041-1044, 1046-1047, 1049, 1697.

1429   Boers, Hendrikus. "The Meaning of Christ in Paul's Writings: A Structuralist-Semiotic Study." *Biblical Theology Bulletin* 14 (1984): 131-144.

A structuralist study of references to Christ in Paul's epistles. The meaning of Christ in these letters is that he "thematizes the gift of life as a feature of the opposition between life and death, irrespective of what happens on the plane of the opposition between good and evil." This means that, for Paul, Christ does not free the believer from engagement in the struggle between good and evil, but that struggle is no longer related to the issue of life and death. Good does not lead to life, nor evil to death.

1430   Castelli, Elizabeth. "Mimesis as a Discourse of Power in Paul's Letters." Ph.D. diss., Claremont Graduate School, 1987.

Studies the rhetorical strategy of Paul's exhortation for Christians to become his imitators (1 Thessalonians 1:6; 2:14; Philippians 3:17; 1 Corinthians 4:16; 11:1). Analysis of the concept in Greco-Roman history reveals mimesis (imitation) to represent a "valorization of sameness over difference, which is always articulated hierarchically." Paul appropriates this concept and applies it to gain a privileged position of authority within his communities.

1431   DuToit, A. B. "Hyperbolic Contrasts: A Neglected Aspect of Paul's Style." Colloquim Biblicum Lovaniense, 73. Leuven: Leuven University Press, 1985.

Defines "hyperbolic contrasts" as "referential sayings, the two constituents of which appear to be . . . strongly contrastive, but which, viewed semantically, are really comparatives." DuToit identifies two kinds of hyperbolic contrasts (dialectical negation and normal hyperbolic contrasts) that occur in Paul's writings. With regard to both, he says the meaning of the exaggerated element is not to be absolutized, but understood dialectically in relation to the contrasted part of the saying.

1432   Everts, Janet Meyer. "Testing A Literary-Critical Hermeneutic: An Exegesis of the Autobiographical Passages in Paul's Epistles." Ph.D. diss., Duke University, 1985. 229 pp.

Examines three "autobiographical passages" in Paul's letters (Galatians 1--2; 2 Corinthians 10--13; Philippians 3) from a literary perspective. The primary reference of Paul's autobiography is not to historical events, but to the world of the gospel that has shaped his experience. Because his life embodies the truth of the gospel, he can use autobiography in defense of the gospel.

1433   Goulder, Michael. "The Pauline Epistles." In *The Literary Guide to the Bible*, ed. by Robert Alter and Frank Kermode, 479-502. Cambridge, MA: Belknap Press, 1987.

Discusses the formal structure and rhetoric of the undisputed Pauline letters, with an emphasis on the Corinthian correspondence. The letters exhibit a five-part pattern: salutation, thanksgiving, discussion of the church's situation, practical holiness, pious conclusion. Paul's use of metaphors, scripture, forensic language, and business images are all discussed, along with general considerations for his pastoral tact and effective (though transparent) persuasive strategies.

1434   Hatfield, Stephen Gill. "The Rhetorical Function of Selected Vice/Virtue Lists in the Letters of Paul." Ph.D. diss., Southwestern Baptist Theological Seminary, 1987. 270 pp.

A rhetorical-critical study of six vice/virtue lists in Paul's letters: Romans 1:29-31; 1 Corinthians 5:10-11; 6:9-10; 2 Corinthians 12:10-11; Galatians 5:9-23; and Colossians 3:5, 8, 12. In each case, Hatfield attempts to determine the rhetorical situation; analyze the arrangement of the passage, with special focus on progression and cohesion; and analyze stylistically the rhetorical features. He concludes that vice/virtue lists function in four basic areas of communication: informative, emotive, imperative, and performative.

1435   Jeremias, Joachim. "Chiasm in den Paulusbriefen." *Zeitschrift für die neutestamentliche Wissenschaft* 49 (1958): 145-156.

Argues that Paul does make use of chiasms in his writing and notes several examples of chiasms that occur with regard to sentence structure and even with regard to ideas (Galatians 1:10-12; 1 Corinthians 9:1-27; 15:35-57; Romans 3:4-8). The article seems unusually contentious today, since the presence of this literary device is now widely recognized.

1436   Judge, E. A. "Paul's Boasting in Relation to Contemporary Professional Practice." *Australian Biblical Review* 16 (1968): 37-50.

Deplores the lack of knowledge concerning New Testament rhetoric in scholarship today and contends that scholars are unable to understand the style and content of much of this literature without a more adequate understanding of rhetorical practice. Even though Paul may have lacked professional training in rhetoric, his "boasting" displays one example of discourse that assumes common social expectations concerning rhetorical expression.

1437   Magee, Bruce Robert. "A Rhetorical Analysis of First Corinthians 8:1--11:1 and Romans 14:1--15:13. Ph.D. diss., New Orleans Baptist Theological Seminary, 1988.   321 pp.

Examines two passages from Pauline letters that both deal with the issue of dietary restrictions for the church. Rhetorical criticism allows the texts to be studied with sensitivity for the influence of the different audiences and situations. The study concludes that Paul did not follow the formal rules of ancient rhetoric, but was an effective communicator in his own right, arguing persuasively in ways that would increase the adherence of his readers to his values.

1438   Olson, Stanley N. "Pauline Expressions of Confidence in His Addresses." *Catholic Biblical Quarterly* 47 (1985): 282-295.

Identifies the rhetorical function of different types of confidence-expression in Paul's letters and other Hellenistic writings. Two types, confidence about compliance, and confidence as the reason for making the request, function to produce a sense of obligation regarding the letter's request. Another two types, confidence with apology, and confidence-expression as polity request or command do this also, but, in addition, function to avoid the appearance of temerity or harshness.

1439   Patte, Daniel. *Paul's Faith and the Power of the Gospel: A Structural Introduction to the Pauline Letters*. Philadelphia: Fortress Press, 1983. 408 pp.

The first and most comprehensive treatment of the undisputed Pauline letters from a structuralist perspective. Patte attempts to discover and systematize the convictions that constitute Paul's faith by focusing on (1) what Paul considers to be self-evident, (2) the motivations underlying his argumentation in the various letters, (3) what Paul regards as real or illusory, good or evil, and (4) the semantic universe of the letters, i.e., the pattern by which all these convictions are put together. Paul's system of convictions is first laid out from readings in Galatians, then contrasted with the Phariasic system of convictions, then augmented by readings from 1 Thessalonians, Philemon, and Philippians and finally integrated comprehensively in a study of Romans. Passages from the Corinthian correspondence are examined last, as a test case to see if the system holds.

1440   Spencer, Aída Besancon. *Paul's Literary Style: A Stylistic Comparison of 2 Corinthians 11:16--12:13, Romans 8:9-39, and Philippians 3:2--4:13.*   Evangelical Theological Society Monograph Series. Jackson, MI: Evangelical Theological Society, 1984. 338 pp.

Demonstrates by means of a stylistic analysis of the passages indicated that Paul varied his style to suit the audience being addressed. Spencer's method of stylistic analysis weds modern linguistic theory with ancient rhetorical criticism. The linguistic data of the passages is analyzed according to ten stylistic operations: sentence changes, complexity of writing, adverbs, adverb clauses, propositional reduction, logical diagrams, abstract vs. concrete, imagery, Spitzer's philological circle, verb density, and variety of sentence length.

1441 Standaert, Beno. "La rhetorique ancienne dans saint Paul." In *L'Apotre Paul: personalité, style et conception du ministere*, ed. by A. Vanhoye, 78-92. Bibliotheca ephemeridum theologicarum lovaniensium, 73. Leuven: Leuven University Press, 1986.

Examines rhetorical structures used in 1 Corinthians 12--14, in 1 Corinthians 15, and in the epistle to Galatians. Various components of classical rhetoric are discerned within these units. Standaert also wanders from his main topic to discuss the presence of concentric patterns in Mark 2:1--3:6; John 20, and Luke 24. See also 1465.

ROMANS

See also 0529, 1048, 1050, 1437, 1439-1440.

1442 Aletti, Jean-Noël. "La presence d'un modele rhetorique en Romains: Son role et son importance." *Biblica* 71 (1990): 1-24.

Shows that Paul uses the rhetorical model for composition in Romans in an original way--each section (1:18--4:25; 5:1--8:39; 9:1--11:36) forms a rhetorical unit and, at least in the first two sections, the units are linked to each other by relaying propositions. Romans 1:16-17 is the main *propositio*.

1443 Aletti, Jean-Noël. "L'argumentation paulinienne en Rm 9." *Biblica* 68 (1987): 41-56.

Studies the concentric model of Paul's argumentation in Romans 9, which is evident especially in verses 6-29. Aletti notes the logic of the passage and the reciprocal function of the statements consisting of mercy and hardening. The relationship of Romans 9 to Romans 8 is discussed as well.

1444 Elliott, Neil. *The Rhetoric of Romans: Argumentative Constraint and Strategy and Paul's Dialogue with Judaism.* Journal for the Study of the New Testament Supplement Series, 45. Sheffield: JSOT Press, 1990. 315 pp.

Applies Perelman and Olbrechts-Tyteca's "new rhetoric" (cf. 0330) to a study of Romans, identifying the letter as paraenetic persuasion aimed at securing "obedience of faith" among Gentile Christians. Concentrating on the first four chapters of the letter, Elliott argues that Paul utilizes dialogue with an interlocutory Jewish partner as a devise for teaching Gentiles a lesson.

1445 Fiore, Benjamin. "Romans 9--11 and Classical Forensic Rhetoric." *Proceedings: Eastern Great Lakes Biblical Society* 8 (1988): 117-126.

Presents these three chapters as a rhetorical defense of God's trustworthiness and traces Paul's argument in terms similar to those laid out by Quintillian in his *Institutio oratoria*. The argument is presented in terms of an exordium (9:1-5), proof (9:6--11:32), and conclusion (11:33-36). The proof develops in three stages, the central portion of which assumes a chiastic arrangement with its focus on Christ as the end of the law.

1446   Heil, John Paul. *Paul's Letter to the Romans: A Reader-Response Commentary*. New York: Paulist Press, 1987. 208 pp.

Examines Romans as "a literary-rhetorical argumentation aimed at persuading the audience to accept the viewpoint of the author." Heil calls attention to such rhetorical techniques as chiasm, plays on words, diatribe, "gradatio," and catchword connections. The commentary moves beyond rhetorical criticism, however, in examining the effect of the argumentation on an imaginary, implied audience rather than on the actual, historical audience to which the letter was first written.

1447   Jewett, Robert. "Romans as an Ambassadorial Letter." *Interpretation* 36 (1982): 5-20.

Refines Wuellner's suggestion that Romans fits into the category of epideictic or demonstrative rhetoric by examining sub-types of epideictic rhetoric defined by Theodore C. Burgess. Jewett proposes that Romans fits one of these sub-types, an "ambassador's speech." See also 1451.

1448   McDonald, Patricia Mary. "Romans 5:1-11: The Structure and Significance of a Bridge." Ph.D. diss., The Catholic University of America, 1989. 282 pp.

Describes Romans 5:1-11 as functioning as a bridge at three levels. Materially, the passage bridges Romans 1--4 and 5--8, containing key words from each section. Rhetorically, the passage is a bridge between Paul and his audience, a group mostly unknown to him. Theologically, the passage bridges the gap between God and humanity through its emphasis on God's loving initiative in Christ.

1449   Scroggs, Robin. "Paul as Rhetorician: Two Homilies in Romans 1--11." In *Jews, Greeks, and Christians*, ed. by R. Hamerton-Kelly and R. Scroggs, 271-320. Leiden: E. J. Brill, 1976.

Argues that Romans 1--11 is made up of two self-contained and completely different homilies. Romans 1--4; 9--11 is a homily on the meaning of Israel's history that utilizes Jewish models for persuasion. Romans 5--8 is a homily on new life in Christ that utilizes the Greek rhetorical model of the diatribe. Thus, Paul is exposed as a rhetorician capable of working within more than one milieu.

1450   Stowers, Stanley K. *The Diatribe and Paul's Letter to the Romans*. Society of Biblical Literature Dissertation Series, 57. Chico, CA: Scholars Press, 1981. 261 pp.

Examines the dialogical element of Paul's style in Romans in light of diatribal forms that are characterized by a similar element. In particular, Stowers focuses on Paul's "address to imaginary interlocutors," which indicts the addressees for their pretension and arrogance, and on the positing of objections and false conclusions, which serve a pedagogical intent. The importance of the study for rhetorical criticism is that it proposes (*contra* Rudolf Bultmann) that Paul consciously and intentionally made use of diatribal forms in order to present himself as a philosophical teacher.

1451   Wuellner, Wilhelm. "Paul's Rhetoric of Argumentation in Romans: an Alternative to the Donfried-Karris Debate over Romans." *Catholic Biblical Quarterly* 38 (1976): 330-351. Also published in *The Romans Debate*, ed. by K. Donfried, 152-174. Minneapolis: Augsburg Publishing House, 1977.

Draws on the insights of rhetorical criticism to propose an alternative to the question of whether Romans is a theological treatise (Robert Karris) or situational letter (Karl Donfried). Wuellner analyzes the relationships between speaker, speech content, and audience inherent in this composition to propose that the letter belongs to the genre of epideictic or demonstrative rhetoric. The purpose of the letter is to announce and prepare for an apostolic mission, and the rhetorical means employed to accomplish this purpose are designed to establish a sense of communion centered around particular values recognized by the audience. See also 1447.

1, 2 CORINTHIANS

See also 0499, 0529, 0534, 1046-1048, 1050-1051, 1430, 1433, 1436, 1439-1441.

1452   Betz, Hans Dieter. "The Problem of Rhetoric and Theology according to the Apostle Paul." In *L'Apotre Paul: Personalite, Style, et Conception du Ministere*, ed. by A. Vanhoye, 16-48. Bibliotheca ephemiridum theologicarum lovaniensium, 73. Leuven: Leuven University Press, 1986.

Examines the problem of the relationship of rhetoric and theology, as Paul sees it. Betz turns primarily to the Corinthian correspondence, for it is here that Paul must deal with the problem most intentionally--he has been challenged by critics to define whether the use of Hellenistic rhetoric ("worldly wisdom") clashes with proclamation of the Gospel.

1453   Betz, Hans Dieter. *2 Corinthians 8 and 9*. Ed. by George M. MacRae. Hermeneia. Philadelphia: Fortress Press, 1985. 288 pp.

An exercise in rhetorical criticism that views these two chapters of our canonical letter to the Corinthians as fragments of two advisory letters written by Paul on different occasions. Though such fragmentation of the Corinthian epistle is controversial and interesting in its own right, the primary interest for literary critics here is Betz's analysis of the deliberative rhetoric displayed in these passages. As in his rhetorical commentary on Galatians (1471), he adduces numerous parallels to classical literature and makes frequent reference to ancient letter-writing handbooks to show that Paul follows conventional rhetorical standards for the writing of letters of advice and uses the rhetorical strategies expected of such a letter-writer in his day.

(

1454 Bünker, Michael. *Briefformular und rhetorische Disposition im 1. Korintherbrief.* Göttingen: Vandenhoeck and Ruprecht, 1984. 169 pp.

Examines the influence of ancient "friendship letter" format on 1 Corinthians and Paul's use of classical rhetorical strategies in two passages, 1:10--4:21 and 15:1-58. A helpful appendix is devoted to the concept of rhetoric in Pauline epistles.

1455 Fiorenza, Elizabeth Schüssler. "Rhetorical Situation and Historical Reconstruction in 1 Corinthians." *New Testament Studies* 33 (1987): 386-403.

A rhetorical-critical study of 1 Corinthians with blatant historical goals. Fiorenza hopes, by discerning the rhetorical situation of the letter, to be able to reconstruct the historical circumstances of the early Christian community. She identifies the species of rhetoric in the letter as deliberative. She proposes that the rhetorical situation concerns questions about Christian identity (especially with regard to life in a patriarchal society) that have prompted the Corinthians to write to a number of missionaries, including Paul, to solicit their views.

1456 Forbes, Christopher. "Paul's Boasting and the Conventions of Hellenistic Rhetoric." *New Testament Studies* 32 (1986): 1-30.

Examines Paul's boasting in 2 Corinthinas 10--12 (especially 10:12-13) in light of Greco-Roman rhetorical conceptions concerning comparison, self-praise, and irony. Forbes presents Paul as a master of rhetoric who, in this passage, satirizes self-advertisement. In so doing, he portrays himself as representative of the appealing character type of the "ironic" and his opponents as representative of the unappealing character type of the "pretentious."

1457 Hamerton-Kelly, Robert. "A Girardian Interpretation of Paul: Rivalry, Mimesis and Victimage in the Corinthian Correspondence." *Semeia* 33 (1985): 65-81.

Discusses four aspects of the Corinthian correspondence that can be illuminated by René Girard's hermeneutical theory: (1) a community split by rivalry into factions; (2) calls by the apostle to his readers to imitate him as he imitates Christ; (3) the self-understanding of the apostle as victim and scapegoat; and, (4) the exposition of the nature of the Christian community as the body of the crucified victim.

1458 Humphries, Raymond Alexander. "Paul's Rhetoric of Argumentation in 1 Corinthians 1--4." Ph.D. diss., Graduate Theological Union, 1979. 160 pp.

A rhetorical analysis of 1 Corinthians 1--4 intended to discover the persuasive function of the structural and textual rhetoric of these chapters and the rhetorical genre in which Paul is working. The structure of the four chapters derives from the strategy Paul adopts to persuade the Corinthians that the answer to the problem of disunity is to accept him as a paradigmatic figure. Paul's basic strategy is that of praise and censure, characteristic of the epideictic genre of rhetoric.

1459   O'Day, Gail R. "Jeremiah 9:22-23 and 1 Corinthians 1:26-31: A Study in Intertextuality." *Journal of Biblical Literature* 109 (1990): 259-267.

Examines Paul's use of the Jeremiah passage in 1 Corinthians as an example of "intertextuality," which refers to "the ways a new text is created from the metaphors, images, and symbolic world of an earlier text." In 1 Corinthians, "Jeremiah's critique of wisdom, power, and wealth as false sources of identity that violate the covenant are re-imaged by Paul as a critique of wisdom, power, and wealth that impede God's saving acts in Jesus Christ."

1460   Patte, Daniel. "A Structural Exegesis of 2 Corinthians 2:14--7:4 with Special Attention on 2:14--3:6 and 6:11--7:4." In *Society of Biblical Literature 1987 Seminar Papers*, ed. by Kent Harold Richards, 23-49. Atlanta: Scholars Press, 1987.

Applies semiotic theories of A. J. Greimas to this passage, probing the text to discover the primary characteristics of the interaction of the points of view of the author and of the readers. The study focuses mainly on 2 Corinthians 2:14--3:6; 6:11--7:4. Patte concludes that Paul endeavors to convince the Corinthians that what they viewed as detrimental effects of a false ministry should in fact be viewed as marks of faithfulness--not only of his ministry, but also of their own lives.

1461   Plank, Karl A. *Paul and the Irony of Affliction.* Semeia Studies. Atlanta: Scholars Press, 1987. 150 pp.

A rhetorical-critical study of 1 Corinthians 4:9-13. Plank first deduces the "rhetorical situation" of Paul's audience and then describes how Paul uses a variety of rhetorical strategies to overcome the perceived problems. These include hyperbole (4:9), antithesis (4:10), polysyndeton (4:11-12a), asyndeton (4:12b-13), and repetition (4:10-13), but chief among Paul's rhetorical strategies is irony. Plank discusses contemporary studies in rhetoric with reference to Perelman and Olbrechts-Tyteca (0330), and studies in irony with reference to Booth (0140) and Muecke (0184-0186).

1462   Segalla, G. "Struttura letteraria e unita della 2 Corinzi." *Teologia Evangelica* 13 (1988): 189-218.

Indicates correspondences between the prologue (1:1-11) and the conclusion (13:11-13) of 2 Corinthians, and then examines a chiastic structure for the rest of the letter: B--apology for Paul's apostolic glory (1:12--7:16); C--the grace of the collection (8:1 --9:15); B'--apology for Paul's apostolic authority (10:1--13:10).

1463   Snyman, A. H. "Remarks on the Stylistic Parallelisms in 1 Cor. 13." In *A South African Perspective on the New Testament*, ed. by J. H. Petzer and P. J. Hartin, 202-213. Leiden: E. J. Brill, 1986.

Analyzes 1 Corinthians 13 according to a method of rhetorical criticism that emphasizes semantic relationships between the parts of the text and features that determine the impact of the text on its audience. Macrolevel and microlevel rhetorical structures are delineated, and possible meanings are suggested for stylistic parallelisms.

1464   Spencer, Aída Besancon. "The Wise Fool (and the Foolish Wise): A Study of Irony in Paul." *Novum Testamentum* 23 (1981): 349-360.

A study of stylistic devices used by Paul in 2 Corinthians, including: tone, rhetorical devices, adversative logic, images, adverbial clauses, sentence transformations, perspective, verbs and minimal use of value-laden adjectives, high use of polysyllables, and variety of sentence length. All of these contribute to an ironic, indirect stance of pretended weakness, through which the apostle demonstrates rhetorical strength.

1465   Standaert, Beno. "Analyse rhetorique des chapitres 12 à 14 de 1 Co." In *Charisma und Agape*, ed. by Lorenzo de Lorenzi, 23-50. Rome: Abbey of St. Paul-Outside-the-Wall, 1983.

Presents a rhetorical analysis of the structure of 1 Corinthians 12--14, with special attention given to the thirteenth chapter, which Standaert regards as a *digressio*. The article proper ends on p. 34 and is followed by a 16-page transcript of discussions between Standaert and three different international groups (English, French, German) who presented responses to the articles. These discussions focus not only on the text at hand but also on the legitimacy/efficacy of interpreting Paul from the perspective of ancient rhetorical handbooks in the first place. See also 1441.

1466   Talbert, Charles H. *Reading Corinthians: A Literary and Theological Commentary on 1 and 2 Corinthians*. New York: Crossroad Publishing Co., 1987. 224 pp.

Presents a "close reading" of the two letters to the Corinthians that focuses on major thought units and their relationship to Pauline thought as a whole. The work is written for the nonspecialist but the method followed is grounded in rhetorical criticism and in studies of classical techniques for letter writing.

1467   Watson, Duane F. "1 Corinthians 10:23--11:1 in the Light of Greco-Roman Rhetoric: The Role of Rhetorical Questions." *Journal of Biblical Literature* 108 (1989): 301-318.

Examines the nature and function of two rhetorical questions in 1 Corinthians 10:29b-30 in light of Greco-Roman rhetoric. After reviewing traditional arguments regarding the role of these questions, Watson identifies the following uses of rhetorical questions prescribed in Greco-Roman rhetoric as likely to be at work in this passage: recapitulation, anticipation, argumentation, figure of thought, ornament.

1468   Wire, Antoinette Clark. *The Corinthian Women Prophets: A Reconstruction through Paul's Rhetoric*. Minneapolis: Fortress Press, 1990. 320 pp.

Uses rhetorical criticism to reconstruct the audience of Paul's letters to Corinth, focusing especially on the nature and significance of the women prophets there.

1469   Wuellner, Wilhelm. "Greek Rhetoric and Pauline Argumentation." In *Early Christian Literature and the Classical Intellectual Tradition: in Honorem Robert M. Grant*, ed. by W. R. Schoedel and R. L. Wilken, 177-188. Théologie Historique, 54. Paris: Editions Beauchesne, 1979.

Examines three digressions in 1 Corinthians (1:19--3:21; 9:1--10:13; 13:1-13) in order to demonstrate that Paul's digressions are not irrelevant interruptions but rather serve as part of an overall rhetorical strategy to support his argument. The digressions are illustrative of accepted rhetorical practice and are functionally determined by the rhetorical situation.

1470   Wuellner, Wilhelm. "Paul as Pastor: The Function of Rhetorical Questions in First Corinthians." In *L'Apôtre Paul: personalité, style et concêption du ministère*, ed. by A. Vanhoye, 49-77. Bibliotheca ephemeridum theologicarum lovaniensium, 73. Leuven: Leuven University Press, 1986.

Argues that rhetorical questions in 1 Corinthians do not function primarily as stylistic figures but as argumentative ones; they are not mere embellishment but serve a discernible effect. Drawing on the insights of Perelman and Olbrechts-Tytecca (0330), Wuellner lists four factors that determine the functions of rhetorical questions (the framework, starting point, techniques, and sequence of Paul's argumentation). The essay concludes with observations on "the pastor (i.e., Paul) as rhetorician, educator, and politician" and on "the legacy and promise of rhetorical criticism for the interpretation of Paul."

GALATIANS

See also 0529, 0534, 1050, 1439, 1441.

1471   Betz, Hans Dieter. *Galatians: A Commentary on Paul's Letter to the Churches in Galatia*. Hermeneia. Philadelphia: Fortress Press, 1979. 384 pp.

An in-depth commentary on the epistle to the Galatians that consistently utilizes the insights of rhetorical criticism. Betz regards the letter as a tightly-woven composition that follows the patterns recommended in ancient rhetorical handbooks for use in a case of law (judicial rhetoric). He draws continually from his immense knowledge of philosophical and rhetorical traditions of the first-century to illuminate individual passages with reference to parallels in Plato, Plutarch, and other classical authors.

1472   Betz, Hans Dieter. "The Literary Composition and Function of Paul's Letter to the Galatians." *New Testament Studies* 21 (1975) 353-379.

Summarizes the author's views concerning the rhetorical function and structure of Paul's letter to the Galatians (cf. 1471). The letter presupposes a juridicial context and is organized according to ancient rhetorical guidelines: prescript (1:1-5); *exordium*

(1:6-11); *narratio* (1:12--2:14); *propositio* (2:15-21); *probatio* (3:1--4:31); paraenesis (5:1 --6:10); and postscript (6:11-18). See 1476, 1478, 1484.

1473   Brinsmead, Bernard H. *Galatians. Dialogical Response to Opponents.* Society of Biblical Literature Dissertation Series, 65. Atlanta: Scholars Press, 1982.

Makes use of a form of rhetorical criticism that is especially congnizant of genre analysis and identification of the intended audience. Brinsmead identifies the genre of Galatians as an apologetic letter and identifies the audience as Pauline Christians plagued by a single intruding theology: apocalyptic and sectarian Judaism, probably associated with Qumran. Paul's notion of justification by faith is considered, from a rhetorical perspective, to be a polemical doctrine.

1474   Cosgrove, Charles H. "Arguing Like a Mere Human Being: Galatians 3:15-18 in Rhetorical Perspective." *New Testament Studies* 34 (1988): 536-549.

Analyzes the rhetoric of Paul's argument in Galatians 3:15-18 as an *argumentum ad hominen*, in which Paul proceeds on the basis of premises borrowed from his opponents but turned against them. Basically the argument is as follows: Major premise (stated in 15)--it is illegal to nullify or amend a covenant; Minor premise (implied in 17)--the law represents an attempt (by God) to nullify or amend the Abrahamic covenant; Conclusion--the law itself is illegal.

1475   Cronjé, J. van W. "Defamiliarization in the Letter to the Galatians." In *A South African Perspective on the New Testament: Essays by South African New Testament Scholars*, ed. by J. H. Petzer and P. J. Hardin, 214-227. Leiden: E. J. Brill, 1986.

Summarizes the idea of "defamiliarization" and then illustrates how Paul uses this stylistic feature in Galatians. Defamiliarization consists of shifts in expected language patterns. Cronje follows a system that recognizes five major categories: shifts in expectancies of word order; shifts in expectancies of syntax; shifts in propositions; shifts with regard to the communication function; and, shifts between meaning and referent. Paul's use of rhetorical questions and metaphor, for instance, are representative of the fourth category (communication function).

1476   Hall, Robert G. "The Rhetorical Outline for Galatians: A Reconsideration." *Journal of Biblical Literature* 106 (1987): 277-287.

Proposes that Galatians is better classified as deliberative rhetoric than as judicial. Hall suggests the following outline: Salutation/Exordium (1:1-5); Proposition (1:6-9); Proof (1:10--6:10); and Epilogue (6:1-18). Hall's argument is an alternative to that of Betz (1471-1472) and Hester (1478).

1477   Hays, Richard B. *The Faith of Jesus Christ: An Investigation of the Narrative Substructure of Galatians 3:1--4:11*. Chico, CA: Scholars Press, 1983. 305 pp.

Proposes that the framework of Paul's thought is constituted neither by a system of doctrine nor by his personal religious experience, but by a "sacred story." Hays attempts to delineate this story with the aid of modern linguistic and literary theory (especially that of A. J. Greimas).   He decides that the gospel story, as Paul understands it, involves the sending of Christ by God to liberate humanity from sin and death by giving himself for others in faithful obedience. To construe Paul's gospel story in this way demands that the words *pistis tou christou* be translated "the faith of Christ," a reading that Hays defends in a pivotal chapter of his study.

1478   Hester, James D. "The Rhetorical Structure of Galatians 1:11-2:14." *Journal of Biblical Literature* 103 (1984): 223-233.

Presents a more finely-tuned outline for the rhetorical structure of the first part of Galatians than that offered by Betz (1472).   Hester proposes that 1:6-10 serves as *exordium* (or *prooemium*); 1:11-12, as *stasis*; 1:13-14 as *transitio*; 1:5--2:10, as *narratio*; and 2:11-14, as *digressio* (or *egressus*). See also 1478.

1479   Hester, James D. "The Use and Influence of Rhetoric in Galatians 2:1-14." *Theologische Zeitschrift* 42 (1986): 386-408.

Advocates greater attention by scholars to Paul's use of rhetorical devices and explicates the argument of Galatians 2:1-14 in light of five such devices: paralipsis, aposiopesis, antithesis, metonymy, and periphrasis. Galatians 2:1-10 uses the topoi of quality and order; 2:11-14 uses a mixed chreia.

1480   Hübner, Hans. "Der Galaterbrief und das Verhältnis von antiker Rhetorik und Epistolographie." *Theologische Literarzeitung* 109 (1984): 241-250.

Contends that Betz's rhetorical treatment of Galatians (1471) does not resolve the problem of the relationship between rhetoric and epistolography. Paul's epistles must be understood in terms of Greek models for letter writing.

1481   Kraftchick, Steven J. *Ethos and Pathos in Galatians Five and Six: A Rhetorical Analysis*. Ph.D. diss., Emory University, 1985.

Analyzes the last two chapters of Paul's letter to Galatia in light of the rhetorical argument of the entire epistle. Kraftchick finds that the chapters serve to advance Paul's appeal to his own character (ethos) and to his audience's emotions (pathos). Thus, these chapters function as the apex of the entire argument, giving persuasive force to the letter's theoretical and theological concerns.

1482 Lategan, Bernard C. "Levels of Reader Instructions in the Text of Galatians." *Semeia* 48 (1989): 171-186.

Recognizes four levels at which instructions to the readers are provided in the text of Galatians: (1) a syntacto-rhetorical level; (2) a level of cultural codes; (3) the semantic universe of the texts; and, (4) the development of a participatory ethics. Although it is not clear whether these instructions will be followed by real readers in specific actualizations of the text, Lategan argues that a "full reading" requires integration of the different directives on all of these levels.

1483 Panier, Louis. "Pour une approche sémiotique de l'épître aux Galates." *Foi et Vie* 84,5 (1985): 19-32.

Considers the "global organization" of the discourse at Antioch and then divides Galatians 2:14b-21 into three sequences (14b; 15-17; 18-21). Four figures offer possibility for the development of a thematic model: the Law on a directed course; separation and gift; the Law of faith; and the Law in the body or the status of the subject.

1484 Smit, Joop. "The Letter of Paul to the Galatians: A Deliberative Speech." *New Testament Studies* 35 (1989): 1-26.

Argues that Galatians is not, as Betz would have it (1471-1472), an example of judicial rhetoric but, rather, of deliberative. Smit lists a number of problems with Betz's construal of the letter and then sets out his own view, according to the following structure: *exordium* (1:6-12); *narratio* (1:13--2:21); *confirmatio* (3:1--4:11); *conclusio* (4:12--5:6; with *conquestio*, 4:12-20; *enumeratio*, 4:21--5:6; and *indignatio*, 5:7-12); and *amplificatio* (6:11-18). In this letter, Paul tries to persuade the Galatians to decide that they should cling to the religious practice taught by him rather than adopting that advocated by his opponents.

1485 Vouga, F. "Zur rhetorischen Gattung des Galaterbriefes." *Zeitschrift für die neutestamentliche Wissenschaft* 79 (1988): 291-292.

Argues that Galatians is an example of deliberative rhetoric, based on comparisons with Demosthenes' speech "On Peace." The structure of the letter is *exordium* (1:6-11); *narratio* (1:12--2:14); *propositio* (2:15-21); *probatio* (3:1--4:31); and *exhortatio* (5:2--6:10).

PHILIPPIANS

See also **1430, 1439-1440.**

1486 Combrink, H. J. Bernard. "Response to W. Schenk, Die Philipperbriefe des Paulus." *Semeia* 48 (1989): 135-146.

Faults Schenk's commentary on Philippians (1490) for its failure to distinguish adequately between different categories of readers or between text and work. Combrink attempts to remedy this by providing his own survey of relocations of the implied referential actions in the poetic sequence of the letter and a description of the effects these have on the reader.

1487 Dormeyer, Detlev. "The Implicit and Explicit Readers and the Genre of Philippians 3:2--4:3, 8-9: Response to the Commentary of Wolfgang Schenk." *Semeia* 48 (1989): 147-160.

A review of Schenk's influential work (1490) with interspersed discussion of the author's own views on the matters discussed. Dormeyer thinks it important to relate the linguistic distinctions recognized by Schenk to levels of author-reader relationships. Whereas Schenk does not distingish between explicit and implicit readers, Dormeyer believes such distinctions are significant for conclusions regarding genre. Dormeyer pays special attention to the store of knowledge assumed to be possessed by the Philippians--through Paul, the Philippians have been able to evolve to become explicit, critical readers.

1488 Robbins, Charles. "Rhetorical Structure of Philippians 2:6-11." *Catholic Biblical Quarterly* 42 (1980): 73-82.

Proposes a structural outline for Philippians 2:6-11 that conforms to the principles of classical rhetoric. Robbins divides the passage into two sentences, each of which divides itself into units of four cola (vs. 6-7; 9-10) and two cola (vs. 8; 11). The theme of the first sentence (6-8) is Christ's abasement; the theme of the second (9-11), his glorification.

1489 Robuck, Thomas Turward. "The Christ-Hymn in Philippians: A Rhetorical Analysis of its Function in the Letter." Ph.D. diss., Southwestern Baptist Theological Seminary, 1987. 247 pp.

Studies how Philippians 2:5-11 relates to the integrity of the letter as a whole and demonstrates that interpreting the hymn as offering an ethical example links it rhetorically and structurally to the rest of the letter. The rhetorical function of the hymn in the letter is described according to Greco-Roman rules for rhetoric.

1490   Schenk, Wolfgang. *Die Philipperbriefe des Paulus: Kommentar.* Stuttgart: Kohlhammer Verlag, 1984.

Adopts a reader-oriented approach to Paul's letter and attempts to interpret it through consistent application of semiotic theory. The linguistic emphasis of the commentary represents more than concern for semantic meaning--Schenk is most interested in the pragmatic function of semantic units. Thus the text is considered unit by unit in terms of its signals and appeals to the reader. This commentary has been recognized as breaking new ground in the application of semiotic theory to the epistles, but it has also been criticized for being too traditional in other respects. See 1486-1487, 1491.

1491   Voelz, James W. "Some Things Old, Some Things New: A Response to Wolfgang Schenk, *Die Philipperbriefe des Paulus.*" *Semeia* 48 (1989): 161-170.

Criticizes Schenk's work (1490) for assuming that texts contain meaning to be discovered by the reader rather than recognizing that readers make meaning through interaction with the text.

1492   Watson, Duane F. "A Rhetorical Analysis of Philippians and Its Implications for the Unity Question." *Novum Testamentum* 30 (1988): 57-88.

A thorough rhetorical-analysis of Philippians, according to the methodological procedures laid out by Kennedy in 0529. Watson identifies the exigence of the letter as the appearance of a rival gospel in Philippi, probably as the result of Judaizing Christian itinerants. The species of rhetoric is deliberative. The rhetorical structure is *exordium* (1:3-26); *narratio* (1:27-30); *probatio* (2:1--3:21; with *digressio* at 2:19-30; *peroratio* (4:1-20; with *repetitio*, 4:1-9, and *adfectus*, 4:10-20. The rhetorical completeness of the letter in its current form argues in favor of its unity.

COLOSSIANS

1493   Baugh, S. M. "The Poetic Form of Col 1:15-20." *The Westminster Theological Journal* 47 (1985): 227-244.

Cites Colossians 1:15-20 as a good example of Semitic chiasmus: A--15-16; B--17a; C --17b; B'--18a; A' 18b-20. The center of the chiasm stresses the confession that all things continue to exist in Christ.

1494   Botha, J. "A Stylistic Analysis of the Christ Hymn (Col. 1:15-20)." In *A South African Perspective on the New Testament*, ed. by J. H. Petzer and P. J. Hartin, 238-251. Leiden: E. J. Brill, 1986.

Discusses the "macrolevel of rhetorical structure" and the "microlevel of rhetorical structure" in Colossians 1:15-20, as well as instances of significant repetition within these structures. Botha then describes the possible meaning of these rhetorical features with regard to the relationship of parts of the text to one another, and with regard to the relationship of the text to its receptor.

1, 2 THESSALONIANS

See also 0529, 1313, 1430, 1439.

1495 Hughes, Frank Witt. *Early Christian Rhetoric and 2 Thessalonians.* Journal for the Study of the New Testament Supplement Series, 30. Sheffield: JSOT Press, 1988. 128 pp.

Argues that 2 Thessalonians is a Deuteropauline letter written as a refutation of the fulfilled eschatology present in two additional Deuteropauline letters, Ephesians and Colossians. Chapter 2 presents an analysis of the rhetoric of the Pauline corpus in general and chapter 3 analyzes the rhetoric of 2 Thessalonians in particular.

1496 Jewett, Robert. *The Thessalonian Correspondence: Pauline Rhetoric and Millenarian Piety.* Philadelphia: Fortress Press, 1986. 240 pp.

One chapter of this book (chapter 5) examines the rhetoric of the two Thessalonian letters. The first epistle is analyzed as exemplary of epideictic or demonstrative rhetoric and the second as examplary of deliberative rhetoric. The context for this discussion, worked out in the rest of the book, is Jewett's view that Paul wrote the first letter to respond to a sudden deflation of millenarian faith and the second to "set the record straight" after the first letter backfired and engendered antinomian millenarian radicalism.

1497 Johanson, Bruce Carl. "A Text-Linguistic and Rhetorical Approach to 1 Thessalonians." Ph.D. diss., Uppsala Universitett (Sweden), 1987. 244 pp.

Draws on text-linguistics, literary theory, and both ancient and modern rhetorical criticism to examine the capacity for meaning of 1 Thessalonians as an act of communication in its initial context. The study draws these conclusions: (1) the rhetorical-persuasive function dominates over other functions; (2) the integrity and unity of 1 Thessalonians is substantiated; and (3) the letter exhibits a high degree of structures and functions common to ancient Greek epistolary writing and to Old Testament-Jewish exhortatory discourse.

1498 Johanson, Bruce Carl. *To All the Brethren: A Text-Linguistic and Rhetorical Approach to 1 Thessalonians.* Coniectanea Biblica, 16. Stockholm: Almqvist and Wiksell International, 1987. 230 pp.

One section of this work (Part Three) interprets 1 Thessalonians as a persuasive act of communication, drawing on the methods of rhetorical criticism advanced by Kennedy (0529). Johanson thinks, however, that it is not possible to read 1

Thessalonians in terms of *exordium, narratio, argumentatio,* and *peroratio.* Rather, it is a thanksgiving request letter that uses a variety of rhetorical types.

1499   Malbon, Elizabeth Struthers. "'No Need to Have Any One Write'?: A Structural Exegesis of 1 Thessalonians." *Semeia* 26 (1983): 57-83.

Examines both syntagmatic and paradigmatic relationships in 1 Thessalonians, following Claude Lévi-Strauss' structuralist model for interpretation. One interesting observation concerns the apparent parallel between the "apostolic parousia" promised in the letter and the "parousia of the Lord" discussed in the letter. Both aim to re-establish relationships and to fill absence with presence. The article also offers a typology of structuralist approaches to texts and an outline of a framework within which structural criticism might be said to operate.

1500   Patte, Daniel. "Method for a Structural Exegesis of Didactic Discourses. Analysis of 1 Thessalonians." *Semeia* 26 (1983): 85-129.

Treats 1 Thessalonians as a test case for a method designed to determine the faith of authors of didactic texts. "Faith" is here defined as the system of convictions that the author held to be self-evident. Patte first considers the characteristics of didactic discourse, noting its essential differences from narrative. Then he proposes a structuralist method for analyzing such literature in a way that will reveal the convictions that underlie it. Application of the method to 1 Thessalonians is viewed as a first step in determining the validity of the method. See also 1439.

1501   Richardson, Neil. *I and II Thessalonians.* Narrative Commentaries. Philadelphia: Trinity Press International, forthcoming.

Announced for publication.

PHILEMON

See also 1439.

1502   Church, F. Forrester. "Rhetorical Structure and Design in Paul's Letter to Philemon." *Harvard Theological Review* 71 (1978): 17-33.

Examines the letter of Paul to Philemon as a masterpiece of rhetorical persuasion. Paul incorporates the traditional elements of deliberative rhetoric within the structure of his epistle: the thanksgiving serves as an exordium (4-7), the main body of the letter offers a proof (8-16), and the closing serves as a peroration (17-22).

1503   Petersen, Norman R. *Rediscovering Paul: Philemon and the Sociology of Paul's Narrative World*. Philadelphia: Fortress Press, 1985. 308 pp.

Unites two approaches--modern literary criticism and cultural anthropology--in a detailed study of Paul's brief letter to Philemon. First, Petersen transforms Paul's letter into a narrative by identifying the plot, point of view, and narrative world that the letter implies. Next, he discusses the social roles and relations important for that narrative world. Finally, he brings in observations from other Pauline letters to discuss the symbolic universe that Paul shared with those to whom the letters were addressed.

HEBREWS

See also 0534, 0591, 0594, 1046.

1504   Attridge, Harold W. *The Epistle to the Hebrews*. Hermeneia. Philadelphia: Fortress Press, 1988. 437 pp.

A comprehensive commentary on Hebrews, distinctive for its use of rhetorical criticism to shed light on the structure and strategy of the epistle.

1505   Attridge, Harold W. "Paraenesis in a Homily (*logos paraklesos*): The Possible Location of, and Socialization in, the 'Epistle to the Hebrews.'" *Semeia* 50 (1990): 211-226.

Proposes a social function for the epistle to the Hebrews, based on an analysis of its rhetoric. Attridge rejects aims typically associated with paraensis: socialization of new members, legitimation of structure or authority, and polemic against another social unit. Rather, Hebrews intends to reinforce the identity of a community suffering social ostracism in such a way as not to isolate it from its environment.

1506   Black, D. A. "Hebrews 1-1:4: A Study in Discourse Analysis." *The Westminster Theological Journal* 49 (1987): 175-194.

Identifies the structure of these four verses as a single colon made up of sixteen individual units. Several rhetorical devices that function within this text are also observed.

1507   Cosby, Michael R. "The Rhetorical Composition and Function of Hebrews 11 in Light of Example-Lists in Antiquity." Ph.D. diss., Emory University, 1985. 316 pp.

Examines the persuasiveness of the example list found in Hebrews 11 which, like other ancient example lists follows no definite form but uses rhetorical features to magnify the impression that the list is intended to make. Special attention is paid here to the use of anaphora in 11:3-31 to link the examples back to the introduction in 11:1-2. The rhetorical question in 11:32a and the appeal to time in 11:32b convey the impression that *ad infinitum* listing would be possible. 11:32-38 uses asyndeton, paronomasia, repetition of clausal structure, and polysyndeton to construct a sweeping summary statement.

1508   Cosby, Michael R. "The Rhetorical Composition of Hebrews 11." *Journal of Biblical Literature* 107 (1988): 257-273.

Demonstrates that Hebrews 11, like other ancient example lists, uses various rhetorical techniques to make the number of examples given appear representative of many more that could also be cited. The dominant techniques in Hebrew 11 are anaphora in 11:3-31; direct assertion in 11:32; asyndeton, isocolon, paronomasia, and chiasm in 11:32-34; and asyndeton, polysyndeton, and paronomasia in 11:35-38.

1509   Ellingworth, Paul. *The Epistle to the Hebrews*. Narrative Commentaries. Philadelphia: Trinity Press International, forthcoming.

Announced for publication.

1510   Josipovici, Gabriel. "The Epistle to the Hebrews and the Catholic Epistles." In *The Literary Guide to the Bible*, ed. by Robert Alter and Frank Kermode, 503-522. Cambridge, MA: Belknap Press, 1987.

Discusses Hebrews in terms of its place in the whole Bible, as an exposition of the relationship of Jesus to the Old Testament. The letter represents well the attempt of emerging Christian culture to retain the vocabulary of the Hebrew culture from which it sprang, while inevitably draining that vocabulary of its original meaning. Slight reference is made to the Catholic Epistles as giving expression to some of the same themes and arguments found in Hebrews. Hebrews is unique, however, in its powerful use of notions such as perfection and fulfillment as hermeneutical tools.

1511   Lindars, Barnabas. "The Rhetorical Structure of Hebrews." *New Testament Studies* 35 (1989): 382-406.

An essentially historical study that makes some use of rhetorical criticism in attempting to discern the setting for the book of Hebrews. Lindars praises the letter as "the most accomplished writing in the New Testament" and as "an outstanding example of the art of persuasion." He envisions the point at issue as being a question of whether certain Jewish practices should continue to be practiced in a community fo Jewish Christians whose faith is similar to that represented by Stephen in Acts 6. The climax of the argument, which consists of a defense of the apostolic kerygma of the sacrificial death of Christ, comes in 10:19--12:29.

1512   Neeley, L. L. "A Discourse Analysis of Hebrews." *OPTAT* (Dallas) 3-4 (1987): 1-147.

A lengthy exposition of the criteria for dividing Hebrews into embedded discourses and paragraphs, for recognizing the constituents of Hebrews and its embedded discourses, and for differentiating backbone from support material. Neeley displays the overall constitutent structure of Hebrews along with important aspects of its semantic structure. He analyzes the internal structure of the three embedded discourses (1:1--4:3; 4:14--10:18; 10:19--13:21).

JAMES

See also 1046.

1513 Gieger, Loren Glen. "Figures of Speech in the Epistle of James: A Rhetorical and Exegetical Analysis." Ph.D. diss., Southwestern Baptist Theological Seminary, 1981.

A rhetorical analysis of figures of speech in the epistle of James. Chapter 1 examines figures involving resemblance: similies, similitudes, metaphor, hypocatastasis, symbol, and type. Chapter 2 treats figures involving some rhetorical change in the use, meaning, application or order of words: metonymy, metalepsis, synecdoche, antonomasia, euphemism, personification, anthropopathea, ampliato, irony, oxymoron, hyperbation, hysteron, proteron, hystesis, and antimetathesis. Chapter 3 analyzes figures involving amplification: alliteration, homeoteleuton, epizeuxis, anaphora, polysyndeton, anadiplosis, dualiplosis, epibole, parallelism, pleonasm, hyperbole, periphasis, climax, epxegesis, hypotyposis, prosopographia, and protimesis. Chapter 4 discusses figures involving condensation: ellipsis, brachylogy, asyndeton, aposipesis, and erotesis.

CATHOLIC EPISTLES

1514 Calloud, Jean, and Genuyt Francois. *La première épître de Pierre: analyse sémiotique*. Paris: Cerf, 1982. 215 pp.

A commentary on 1 Peter that also serves as an introduction to a semiotic/structuralist approach to biblical reading. The authors say that their concern is with "what the text says and what it means rather than the concerns of classical exegesis." Their outline of the letter is address (1:1-2); benediction (1:3-12); sanctification (1:13-25); edification (2:1-10); subjection (2:11--3:12); deliverance (3:13--4:6); judgment (4:7--5:11) and final salutation (5:12-14).

1515 Watson, Duane F. *Invention, Arrangement, and Style: Rhetorical Criticism of Jude and 2 Peter*. Society of Biblical Literature Dissertation Series, 104. Atlanta: Scholars Press, 1988. 214 pp.

Applies a rhetorical-critical method similar to that used by Kennedy (0529) to the two short letters of Jude and 2 Peter. This book contains an excellent introductory chapter on the methodology of rhetorical criticism, which offers a clear step-by-step description of how the discipline is practiced. Following detailed analyses of the letters, a final chapter discusses implication of the study for questions of literary integrity and dependency.

JOHANNINE EPISTLES

1516   Du Rand, J. A. "A Discourse Analysis of 1 John." *Neotestamentica* 13 (1979): 1-42.

Applies discourse analysis to 1 John to reveal five major sections: introduction (1:1-4); fellowship (1:5--2:17); filiation (2:18--4:6); love (4:7--5:5); and conclusion and résumé (5:6-21).

1517   Du Rand, J. A. "Structure and Meaning of 2 John." *Neotestamentica* 13 (1979): 101-120.

Applies discourse analysis to 2 John to show that its argument concentrates on the confession of Jesus Christ becoming a human being, and on the ethical viewpoint of love for one another. The letter's structure is salutation (1-3), thanksgiving (4), petition (5-6),   appeal (7-11), and conclusion (12-13).

1518   Du Rand, J. A. "The Structure of 3 John." *Neotestamentica* 13 (1979): 121-131.

Applies discourse analysis to 3 John to show that its six sections are arranged chiastically: salutation (1-2), thanksgiving (3-4), appeal and motivation (5-8, 9-11), recommendation (12), and conclusion (13-15).

1519   Klauck, Hans-Josef. "Zur rhetorischen Analyse der Johannesbriefe." *Zeitschrift für die neutestamentliche Wissenschaft* 81 (1990): 205-224.

A rhetorical analysis of the structure of the three Johannine epistles. The "macro-structure" of the first epistle is discerned as *captatio benevolentiae* (1:5--2:17), *narratio* (2:18-27); *propositio* (2:28-29); *probatio* (3:1-24); *exhortatio* (4:1-21); and *peroratio* (5:1-12). The second and third epistles have a parallel structure: *exordium* (2 John 4; 3 John 2-4); *narratio* (2 John 5; 3 John 5-6); *probatio* (2 John 6-11; 3 John 7-12); and *peroratio* (2 John 12; 3 John 13-14).

1520   Loader, William.   *The Johannine Epistles.*   Narrative Commentaries. Philadelphia: Trinity Press International, forthcoming.

Announced for publication.

1521   Watson, Duane F. "1 John 2.12-14 as *Distributio, Conduplicatio,* and *Expolitio*: A Rhetorical Understanding." *Journal for the Study of the New Testament* 35 (1989): 97-110.

A rhetorical analysis of these six verses that finds three figures of speech at work. The grouping of three (little children, fathers, young men) exemplifies *distributio* (distribution), the repeat of the grouping exemplifies *conduplicatio* (reduplication), and the contrasts between the two groupings exemplifies *expolitio* (refining).

1522   Watson, Duane F. "A Rhetorical Analysis of 2 John According to Greco-Roman Convention." *New Testament Studies* 35 (1989): 104-130.

A thorough rhetorical-critical study of 2 John according to the methodology laid out by Kennedy in 0529. The exigence of the letter, discerned with the aid of 1 John, is the appearance of secessionists from the Presbyter's church in other areas of the community. The species of rhetoric is deliberative. The rhetorical structure is *exordium* (4); *narratio* (5); *probatio* (6-11); and *peroratio* (12). Watson also discusses the function of the prescript (1-3) as *exordium*, and of the closing statement (13) as *peroratio*.

1523   Watson, Duane F. "A Rhetorical Analysis of 3 John: A Study in Epistolary Rhetoric." *Catholic Biblical Quarterly* 51 (1989): 479-501.

Attempts an analysis of 3 John according to Kennedy's model of rhetorical criticism (0529). The exigence of the letter is Diotrephes' refusal to grant hospitality to traveling missionaries. John 3 is a mixed letter, combining aspects of friendly, requesting, advisory, commendatory, praising, encouraging, vituperative, and accusing letters. It exemplifies epideictic rhetoric, with a stasis of quality. Its arrangement is *exordium* (2-4); *narratio* (5-6); *probatio* (7-12); and *peroratio* (13-14), framed by a prescript (1) and postscript (15). Watson also discusses various stylistic features, emphasizing ones that use symmetry or repetition.

REVELATION

See also **0174, 0485, 0587, 0592, 0601, 1047, 1053.**

1524   Barr, David L. "The Apocalypse as a Symbolic Transformation of the World: A Literary Analysis." *Interpretation* 38 (1984): 39-50.

Examines the use of symbolism in Revelation and the plot structure of that book in order to determine how it functions to give courage and comfort to Christians in time of trouble. The study of symbolism reveals that, while John draws images from the traditional apocalyptic stock, he radically reverses the values of these symbols. The examination of plot structure reveals a drama in three acts, each of which involves realization of salvation and judgment. Barr concludes that Revelation "works" because it creates a new world for its readers in which they are able to see themselves as actors in charge of their own destiny who, by voluntary suffering, participate in the overthrow of evil.

1525   Barr, David L. "The Apocalypse of John as Oral Enactment." *Interpretation* 40 (1986): 243-256.

Argues that the orality of the Apocalypse is an essential element of its hermeneutic. After discussing oral techniques of the book, Barr proposes that the intended setting for the work is that of oral enactment in a liturgical, eucharistic context. This oral presentation mediates the coming of Jesus to his congregation in salvation and judgment, enabling them to carry on the realization of God's rule in their midst.

1526   Barr, David L. "Elephants and Holograms: From Metaphor to Methodology in the Study of John's Apocalypse." In *Society of Biblical Literature 1986 Seminar Papers*, ed. by Kent Harold Richards, 400-411. Atlanta: Scholars Press, 1986.

Proposes a "holographic model" for understanding the book of Revelation that combines literary data, historical data, and social data to obtain a vision of John's community that would not be suggested by any one set of data alone. Barr thinks that John writes a symbolic story in which the enemy revealed is not simply a historical enemy. Although actual persecution may have occurred at some point in the community's history, the symbolic story of Revelation addresses more the problem of Roman tolerance than that of persecution. The story provides the element of opposition that the community needs for its social legitimation.

1527   Barr, David L. "How Were the Hearers Blessed? Literary Reflections on the Social Impact of John's Apocalypse." *Proceedings: Eastern Great Lakes Biblical Society* 8 (1988): 49-60.

Suggests that the book of Revelation is intended, when performed orally, to perform the social function of providing a rhetorical response to various threats to the happiness of its hearers. Such threats apparently include modest persecution, relative deprivation, and desires for vengeance or justice, but these are less significant than the tensions of coming to grips with the new social identity demanded of Christian communities. The study is grounded in fundamentally historical/sociological concerns, but also makes use of rhetorical-literary analysis to determine the intended effect of the book.

1528   Derrida, Jacques.   "Of an Apocalyptic Tone Recently Developed in Philosophy." *Semeia* 23 (1982): 63-97.

Moves from a discussion of the philosophy of Immanuel Kant to a deconstructive reading of the book of Revelation. The invitation/imperative, "Come" does not announce this or that apocalypse--it is in itself the apocalypse of the apocalypse. Likewise, modern announcements that there has never been and never will be an apocalypse are in themselves apocalyptic, forecasting closure without end.

1529   Fiorenza, Elizabeth Schüssler. *The Book of Revelation: Justice and Judgment.* Philadelphia: Fortress Press, 1985. 211 pp.

A historical-critical study of the community and concerns behind the book of Revelation that makes some use of rhetorical criticism to determine the "rhetorical situation" of the writing. That situation may be described as one of persecution, harrassment, and hostility, similar to the picture described by Pliny in his letter to the emperor Trajan. The rhetorical strategy of the book, then, is to mobilize the readers' emotions through images of eschatological salvation that will persuade them to decide in favor of faithful worship of God in spite of governmental threats.

1530   Gnatkowski, Mel W. "The Implied Reader in the Book of Revelation." Ph.D. diss., New Orleans Baptist Theological Seminary, 1988. 137 pp.

Describes the implied reader of Revelation on the basis of the rhetoric of authorial commentary. The author of Revelation communicates with the reader through opening and closing statements (1:1-8, 22:6-21), through the letters to the seven churches, and through interpretations and explanations of visions. Other forms of silent communication between the author and the implied reader include symbolism, irony, and contrast.

1531   Gros Louis, Kenneth R. R. "Revelation." In *Literary Interpretations of Biblical Narratives*, ed. by Kenneth R. R. Gros Louis with James S. Ackerman and Thayer S. Warshaw, 330-345. Nashville: Abingdon Press, 1974.

Attempts to describe how Revelation might be taught as literature in a secular setting, deciding finally that its central theme is an artistic one, namely, the limits of human imagination.

1532   Güttgemanns, Erhardt. "Die Semiotik des Traums in apokalyptischen Texten am Beispiel von Apokalypse Johannis I." *Linguistica Biblica* 59 (1987): 7-54.

Classifies apocalyptic as "fantastic literature" and attempts to apply Freud's theories of dream interpretation to the dream narrative in Revelation 1:9-20. In addition, Güttgemann seeks to further structuralist study of this book by presenting a brief grammatology of apocalyptic literature and by discussing the "macrosyntax" of Revelation.

1533   Harris, Michael. "The Literary Function of Hymns in the Apocalypse of John." Ph.D. diss., The Southern Baptist Theological Seminary, 1989. 355 pp.

Applies the tools of narrative criticism to the book of Revelation, examining the hymns in that book from the perspectives of plot development, narrative commentary, focalisation/point of view, and reader response. The study determines that a major role of the implied reader of Revelation is to concretize generic and spatial/temporal gaps. When these gaps are filled, the implied reader is persuaded to assume the role of the suffering and martyred saints.

1534 Harris, Michael, and Pippin, Tina. *Death and Desire: Reading Conventions in the Apocalypse of John* (title tentative). Literary Currents in Biblical Interpretation. Louisville, KY: Westminster/John Knox Press, forthcoming.

Announced for publication.

1535 Kirby, John T. "The Rhetorical Situations of Revelation 1--3." *New Testament Studies* 34 (1988): 197-207.

Identifies three rhetorical situations for the book of Revelation, as displayed in the first three chapters: the vision of Christ addressing John in chapter one; Christ addressing the churches by letter in chapters 2--3; and John addressing his readers as a whole. The interplay of these situations is the key to the significance of each, and to the book overall. In his analysis, Kirby identifies the overall rhetorical species of Revelation as deliberative, and he proposes a four-part rhetorical arrangement (proem, narration, proposition, epilogue) for each of the seven letters in chapters 2--3.

1536 McGinn, Bernard. "Revelation." In *The Literary Guide to the Bible*, ed. by Robert Alter and Frank Kermode, 523-544. Cambridge, MA: Belknap Press, 1987.

Suggests that Revelation is a book whose literary interest has been transferred from the text to its readers. Accordingly, McGinn offers a survey of how the book has been read throughout history. He does not attempt to adjudicate between the variety of readings or to offer his own interpretation but, rather, declares that the history of the interpretation of a text constitutes, in large measure, its meaning.

1537 Shea, William H. "Chiasm in Theme and by Form in Revelation 18." *Andrews University Seminary Studies* 20 (1982): 249-256.

Offers support for a chiastic structure in Revelation 18 by demonstrating how such a pattern relates to the hymnic material and prosaic introductions that compose the chapter. The chiasm applies not only to the themes presented, but also to the alternation of forms.

1538 Thompson, Leonard. "The Mythic Unity of the Apocalypse." In *Society of Biblical Literature 1985 Seminar Papers*, ed. by Kent Harold Richards, 13-28. Atlanta: Scholars Press, 1985.

A study of the language of the book of Revelation that contests the assumption of structuralism that myth progresses from oppositions to their resolution. Thompson's analysis of boundaries in Revelation does not support the notion that such boundaries separate fundamental, existential conflicts; rather, these boundaries serve simply as social or psychological compensation. The sort of metaphysical dualism assumed by structuralist analysis of oppositions is foreign to John's Revelation. The mythic language of this book serves to differentiate elements within an essentially undifferentiated flow, rather than as a device for bringing into alliance elements that are in essential conflict with each other.

PART FIVE:
EVALUATION

See also 0107, 0485, 0488, 0494, 0506-0507, 0512, 0547-0548, 0551-0552, 0555, 0562, 0570, 0572, 0607, 0817, 1049, 1052-1053, 1062-1063, 1078, 1097, 1107, 1114, 1184, 1186, 1303, 1316, 1372, 1424, 1470.

1539   Alter, Robert. "A Response to Critics." *Journal for the Study of the Old Testament* 27 (1983): 113-117.

Responds to pieces by Jobling (1585), Habel (0885), and Whybray (1672). Most of the response is directed to Jobling, in explanation of why Alter does not employ "technological reading." According to Alter, the general enterprise of converting literary studies into a science has not yielded very encouraging results.

1540   Amerding, Carl. "Structural Analysis." *Themelios* 4 (1979): 96-104.

Surveys the recent history of structural analysis and its application to scripture. The author is primarily interested in explicating the potential and the challenge that this method may pose for conservative, evangelical Christians.

1541   Ash, Beth Sharon. "Jewish Hermeneutics and Contemporary Theories of Textuality: Hartman, Bloom, and Derrida." *Modern Philology* 85 (1987): 65-80.

Reflects on general Judeo-Christian themes that speak to possible interrelations among Geoffrey Hartman, Jacques Derrida, and Harold Bloom, both as Jewish readers and as critics who have placed themselves inside and outside Jewish literary history. Ash gives a brief historical sketch of Jewish sacred literature, analyzes Hartman, Bloom, and Derrida on the status, or "question" of the Book; discusses Jewish tradition as orthodoxy and heresy; and ponders the relation between rhetoric and "ontotheology." The book contains evaluations of 0462 and 0520.

1542   Barr, James. "Biblical Language and Exegesis--How Far Does Structuralism Help Us?" *Kings Theological Review* 7,2 (1984): 48-52.

An evaluation of the usefulness of structuralism in theological studies. One basic problem is that not much of religion or biblical literature lends itself to the binary oppositions or diagrams that structuralism seeks. Still, insofar as structuralism means seeing human life as a network of relations in which things have meaning as they stand within that network, this approach seems fundamentally correct.

1543   Barr, James. "Reading the Bible as Literature." *Bulletin of the John Rylands University Library of Manchester* 56 (1973): 10-33.

Says that the desire for a religious or theological understanding of the Bible only contradicts a literary reading of it in part and at certain limited levels. For the most part, religious and theological understanding of the Bible requires understanding of the myth function that belongs to literature generally.

1544   Berlin, Adele. "On the Bible as Literature". *Prooftexts* 2 (1982): 323-327.

A response to an earlier article by Kugel (1593). Berlin objects that Kugel does not define literature but equates it with fiction and folklore, setting up a false dichotomy between "scripture" and "literature." Berlin then goes on to commend midrashic and "new criticism" approaches to the Bible that accept it as a unified whole and allow it to transcend its immediate context. The article is followed by a response from Kugel that restates the arguments of his original piece in contradistinction to Berlin's views.

1545   Betz, Hans Dieter. "Is Hermes the Hierophant, or is Christ?" *Journal of Religion* 62 (1982): 178-185.

An extended review of Kermode's *Genesis of Secrecy* (1225). Much can be learned from Kermode's secular analysis, but the fact that he regards Mark's Gospel as nothing but fiction consisting of interpretations of interpretations must be kept in mind.

1546   Beuken, Wim; Freyne, Sean; and Weiler, Anton, eds. *The Bible and Its Readers. Concilium* (February, 1991). Philadelphia: Trinity Press International, 1991.

This issue of the journal, *Concilium* (available from Trinity Press International), looks at the new situation in biblical studies arising from increased use of literary criticism. The emphasis is on how the Bible can have different meanings. A historical perspective is provided by a survey of how the Bible has been read by ordinary believers in the past, and how it is read by believers in different parts of the world today.

1547   Blank, G. Kim.   "Deconstruction: Entering the Bible through Babel."
Neotestamentica 20 (1986): 61-67.

Describes the problem that deconstruction raises for exegesis: if belief depends on
textual interpretation, then the only belief possible can be belief in problematics and
in proliferation of meaning.

1548   Brown, Frank Burch, and Malbon, Elizabeth Struthers. "Parabling as a *Via
Negativa*: A Critical Review of the Work of John Dominic Crossan." *Journal of
Religion* 64 (1984): 530-538.

Notes a tendency in Crossan's work to view the world of language in terms of
polarities and to ascribe priority to the negative pole. The theoretical justification for
this tendency is unclear.

1549   Burnett, Fred W. "Postmodern Biblical Exegesis: The Eve of Historical
Criticism." *Semeia* 51 (1990): 51-80.

Argues that postmodern biblical exegesis does not signal the demise of historical
criticism but, rather, calls the historical critic to new horizons of political and ethical
responsibilities. Historical discourse remains the context within which the biblical
critic must work, but postmodern ways of reading are requiring the critic to rethink
"history" and how it should be written. Burnett discusses Fish's concept of interpretive
communities (0361) and plays with the text of his own article by organizing the type
in occasional parallel columns on the page.

1550   Clines, David J. A. "Story and Poem: The Old Testament as Literature and
as Scripture." *Interpretation* 34 (1980): 115-127.

Argues that the distinction between the Bible as literature and the Bible as scripture
is largely artificial--the church can only hear its Bible as scripture when it reads it as
literature.   The point is scored with examples from Jonah, David, Esther, the
Pentateuch, and Psalms 42--43.

1551   Coggins, R. J. "History and Story in Old Testament Study." *Journal for the
Study of the Old Testament* 11 (1979): 36-46.

Raises uncertainty as to the continuing validity and appropriateness of an essentially
historical-type introduction to Old Testament study. Coggins suggests that the first
need is approach the stories *as stories*.

1552   Cohn, Robert L. "On the Art of Biblical Narrative." *Biblical Research* 31
(1986): 13-18.

Reviews Alter's *Art of Biblical Narrative* (0607) in light of Sternberg's *Poetics of
Biblical Narrative* (0570). Positive features in Alter's work include his tendency to
question the text and his focus on foreground rather than background. His stress on

the final form of the text and his lack of appreciation for the character of early Mesopotamian literature are problems that Sternberg's work corrects.

1553   Collins, J. J. "The Rediscovery of Biblical Narrative." *Chicago Studies* 21 (1981): 45-58.

Declares that the last decade has produced a paradigm shift in biblical studies from "history" to "story." Collins attributes the new emphasis on the power of stories to the generally negative results of previous historical research. The texts are now read as predominantly fictions, and as deriving their power from our ability to identify with them.

1554   Combrink, H. J. Bernard. "Multiple Meaning and/or Multiple Interpretation of a Text." *Neotestamentica* 18 (1984): 26-37.

Explores the problems of polysemy, ambiguity, polyvalence, and indeterminacy in texts, with reference to semiotic theory and the role of the reader. Valid interpretation of texts demand consideration of the rhetorical axis of communication as well as the mimetic axis of representation. The possibility of multiple interpretations must be conceded, but the Bible also presupposes an implied reader who recognizes that illumination of the Holy Spirit and use of all available exegetical knowledge are prerequisites for interpretation.

1555   Comstock, Gary. "Truth or Meaning: Ricoeur versus Frei on Biblical Narrative." *Journal of Religion* 66 (1986): 117-140.

Contrasts the hermeneutic of Hans Frei with that of Paul Ricoeur. Comstock says that Frei thinks it is enough to ask whether the biblical narratives are meaningful, while Ricoeur insists that we also ask whether they are true. Frei may believe the stories are true, but he sees no point in trying to argue this publicly. Ricoeur sees the stories as making genuine, public, and revolutionary claims about what is true, and, accordingly, thinks it essential to attend to these claims.

1556   Crossan, John Dominic. *A Fragile Craft: The Work of Amos Niven Wilder*. Biblical Scholarship in North America, 3. Chico, CA: Scholars Press, 1981. 81 pp.

A book-length review of the published works of Wilder through 1980. Wilder was one of the earliest and most influential of Bible scholars who regularly employed literary criticism in their work. He was also widely published as a poet and as a critic of secular literature. Crossan considers his work under three headings: "Eschatology and Ethics"; "Literature and Bible"; and "Imagination and Religion."

1557   Crossan, John Dominic. "Ruth Amid the Alien Corn." In *The Biblical Mosaic: Changing Perspectives*, ed. by Robert M. Polzin and Eugene Rothman, 199-210. Chico, CA: Scholars Press, 1982.

A brief apologetic for the use of structuralist methodology in biblical studies. Crossan believes that the present influx into biblical studies of anthropological, sociological, and literary methods has necessarily transformed the discipline into a field of disciplines. The twin axes of biblical studies are the historical and structural methodologies--both are necessary but the latter has logical priority.

1558   Crotty, R. B. "Changing Fashions in Biblical Interpretation." *Australian Biblical Review* 33 (1985): 13-30.

Discusses the current debate between proponents of diachronic and synchronic approaches to biblical studies as indicative of a revolution. The perception among those advocating synchronic approaches is that the diachronic approach has failed. The outcome of this revolution is still uncertain: one or the other approach could pass from the scene or they could be joined in some sort of compromise mode.

1559   Culpepper, R. Alan. "Commentary on Biblical Narratives: Changing Paradigms." *Forum* 5,3 (1989): 87-102.

Reflects on the evolution of the genre of "biblical commentaries" and then offers proposals for commentaries on books of the Bible in the 1990s. A commentary should enable readers to realize the potential of the text, and this can be best accomplished through the methods of literary criticism. Future commentaries should minimize fragmentation of the texts under discussion by treating every pericope as an integral part of the work as a whole. Development of themes, conflicts, patterns, and symbols should be followed closely so as to enable the reader to respond sensitively to the text.

1560   Culpepper, R. Alan. "Story and History in the Gospels." *Review and Expositor* 81 (1984): 467-477.

Proposes that narrative criticism of the Gospels offers potential for interpretation not realized through historical-critical study and reflects on the hermeneutical implications of this view for scholarship and the church. Noting that "truth requires a larger field than history," Culpepper ascribes to literary criticism the task of interpretation and to historical investigation the task of determining the significance of interpretation. Historical investigation remains important, but the tasks of interpreting meaning and investigating accuracy remain distinct.

1561   Detweiler, Robert. "Generative Poetics as Science and Fiction." *Semeia* 10 (1978): 137-150.

Responds to Güttgemanns' four essays in *Semeia* 6 (0519) by expanding on issues also raised by Kovacs (0266) and McKnight (1610). The central concern is with Güttgemanns' conscious attempt to place theology on a scientific basis, an attempt that he believes the rigorous methodology of generative poetics fulfills. Detweiler distinguishes between logical science and empirical science and indicates that linguistic and literary analysis can belong only to the former.

1562   Detweiler, Robert. "Recent Religion and Literature Scholarship." *Religious Studies Review* 4 (1978): 107-117.

Surveys a wide variety of recent publications on the intersection of religious and literary interests, including books by Wilder (1729), Schneidau (0663), Ricoeur (0017), Patte (0545), McFague (1713), Kort (1742), Wicker (1749), and Robertson (0660), as well as certain books that discuss secular literature from a religious or theological perspective. Detweiler concludes with seven general observations on the "state of the art" in religion and literature scholarship.

1563   Detweiler, Robert. "What Is a Sacred Text?" *Semeia* 31 (1985): 213-230.

Addresses the question of what constitutes a "sacred" text within the contexts of canon, phenomenology, reader involvement, and philosophical-literary criticism. Examination of the process of canon reveals the importance of power and authority in formally designating certain texts as sacred. Phenomenological examination reveals seven traits that characterize sacred texts (e.g., the claim to transform lives). Readers who view a text as sacred tend to encounter it with an aggresively faithful attitude. Sacred texts tend to lose their all important "presence" when viewed in terms of current deconstructive practices of modern literary criticism.

1564   Detweiler, Robert, ed. *Art/Literature/Religion: Life on the Borders.* Chico, CA: Scholars Press, 1983. 208 pp.

A collection of several disparate essays on a very broad theme. The work contains four pieces that may be of interest to those looking for a theological critique of poststructuralism (0091, 0564, 0740, 1719). In addition see 1681.

1565   Detweiler, Robert, ed. *Derrida and Biblical Studies. Semeia* 23 (1982). 97 pp.

Considers the significance of Derrida's theories regarding textuality, difference, and deconstruction for biblical studies, with an emphasis on hermeneutics. Contains one article by Derrida (1528) plus the following three pieces: "The Word Against the Word: Derrida on Textuality," by Herbert N. Schneidau; "Difference and Divinity," by John Dominic Crossan; and "Four Protocols: Derrida, His Deconstruction," by John P. Leavey. See also 1748.

1566   Dockery, D. S. "Author? Reader? Text? Toward a Hermeneutical Synthesis." *Theological Education* 38 (1988): 7-16.

Describes hermeneutical approaches that locate the meaning of a text in the author's intention, in the perspective of the reader, or in the text itself. Dockery thinks interpretation should be determined by historical and canonical contexts. Communication of the text's meaning, however, must take account of the audience-as-context today.

1567   Edelman, Diana.   "An Appraisal of Robert Alter's Approach."   *Biblical Research* 31 (1986): 19-25.

Praises Alter's close readings of narrative texts in 0607, but faults Alter for neglecting to use comparative data from the ancient near East and for confusing historical and theological issues. Alter's book represents a much needed reintroduction to literary analysis of the Bible, but goes overboard in its presentation of literary criticism as the "be all and end all" of biblical studies.

1568   Edwards, Bruce L., and Woodward, Branson L.   "Wise as Serpents, Harmless as Doves: Christians and Contemporary Critical Theories."   *Christianity and Literature* 39 (1990): 303-315.

Argues that deconstruction fails to provide an adequate basis for understanding how "God's texts" convey meaning to us. Christian critics must deny that language systems are ultimately or essentially arbitrary; they must maintain that language works not only in differentiation and deferral, but also through identification and representation. Deconstruction may be likened to a modern gnosticism that replaces a theocentric universe with an anthropocentric one.

1569   Ellingsen, Mark.   "Luther as Narrative Exegete."   *Journal of Religion* 63 (1983): 394-413.

Notes affinities between new literary approaches to the Bible and the exegetical work of Martin Luther.   Ellingsen admits that, when Luther was engaged in polemical argument, he employed either a "letter-spirit" or "Law-Gospel" canon for interpreting scripture that sometimes ignored its narrative characteristics.   But in less polemical contexts, Luther's sermons and lectures displayed an endeavor to identify his hearers with the biblical world and an unwillingness to separate the meaning of the text from its narrative form.

1570   Fennell, W. O.   "Theology and Frye: Some Implications of *The Great Code*."   *Toronto Journal of Theology* 1 (1985): 113-121.

Sees the critical point for theology in Frye's work (0586) as being resistance to the idea that the Bible has any point of reference beyond itself.   Frye idealizes reality and has a simplistic understanding of history.

1571   Fisher, David H.   "Self in Text, Text in Self."   *Semeia* 51 (1990): 137-154.

Traces the history of post-Reformation exegesis as a series of defences against previous methods in a manner that illustrates what Bloom calls the "anxiety of influence" (0344). The article concludes by suggesting that postmodern interpretive strategies offer the possibility of "a sublime text" that will bring a halt to this process.

1572   Fossion, A. "Sémiotique du récit évangélique. Lecture de Louis Marin." *Nouvelle Revue Théologique* 97 (1975): 127-143.

Discusses the second part of Marin's work on *Sémiotique de la Passion* (1069), which deals with the semiotics of the traitor. Fossion is primarily interested in evaluating Marin's method, which is based on the functional model of A. J. Greimas. He discusses Marin's work as exemplary of the new perspectives that semiotic analysis may offer Christianity.

1573   Frei, Hans W. *The Eclipse of Biblical Narrative: A Study in Eighteenth and Nineteenth Century Hermeneutics.* New Haven, CT: Yale University Press, 1974. 355 pp.

Ostensibly a study in the history of ideas, this influential work also makes a major contribution to *twentieth-century* hermeneutics. In tracing the hermeneutical arguments of the period he discusses, Frei shows that, eventually, the interpretive options gathered around two poles: either the Bible could be read literally and accepted as historically reliable or it could be read through a process of historical-critical investigation that located meaning and truth in something outside of the texts to which the texts referred. This legacy has caused twentieth-century discussions to be shaped by what Frei regards as a limited dichotomy. A third option is that the texts might be read as literally true in a way that does not assume historical accuracy --meaning might be located within the text as interpreted in light of its realistic (history-like), narrative form. See also 1555, 1577, 1587, 1592, 1634-1635, 1650, 1657, 1669, 1679.

1574   Frei, Hans W. "The 'Literal Reading' of Biblical Narrative in the Christian Tradition: Does It Stretch or Will It Break?" In *The Bible and the Narrative Tradition*, ed. by Frank McConnell, 36-77. New York: Oxford University Press, 1986.

Considers the deconstructive challenge to Christianity's reliance on the literal sense of scripture. Frei recommends that Christianity learn from Judaism and its practice of midrash, to develop a program for reading scripture that allows the literal sense to "bend, but not break."

1575   Genest, Olivette. "Analyse sémiotique et Bible. Situation et questions disputées." *Laval Théologique et Philosophique* 36 (1980): 115-128.

Situates semiotic analysis of the Bible within the general process of explicating texts and explores problems and objections that have arisen in connection with this approach: the grid of reading, decoding, models, meaning, the author, structural analysis, fundamentalist reading, and the believer's reading.

1576   Gerhart, Mary. "The Restoration of Biblical Narrative." *Semeia* 46 (1989): 13-30.

Proposes that narrative is generically cognitive, historical, and theological, in an attempt to design a theory of narrative that will move biblical literary criticism out of "a thicket of unexamined assumptions."

1577   Green, Garrett. "'The Bible As . . .': Fictional Narrative and Scriptural Truth." In *Scriptural Authority and Narrative Interpretation*, 79-96. Philadelphia: Fortress Press, 1987.

Affirms Frei's distinction between literal meaning and historical reference (1573) and argues that assertions of biblical truth should be applied primarily to the former. The literal sense of biblical stories is not their historical reference but their narrative meaning--the meaning of texts is the story they tell and it is possible to affirm these stories as "true" even if they contain fictive elements.

1578   Green, Garrett, ed. *Scriptural Authority and Narrative Interpretation*. Philadelphia: Fortress Press, 1987. 208 pp.

A collection of articles dealing with hermeneutical and theological issues related to the interpretation of scripture. Five are especially related to the new literary methods in biblical studies: see 1577, 1657, 1659, 1674, 1732. In addition to these, the book contains "Hermeneutics and the Authority of Scripture" by Charles Wood; "Biblical Narrative and Theological Anthropology" by David Kelsey; "Following at a Distance: Ethics and the Identity of Jesus" by Gene Outka; "The Story-Shaped Church: Critical Exegesis and Theological Interpretation" by George Lindbeck; and "The Church as God's New Language" by Stanley Hauerwas.

1579   Handelman, Susan. *The Slayers of Moses: The Emergence of Rabbinic Interpretation in Modern Literary Theory*. Albany: State University of New York Press, 1982. 267 pp.

Suggests that certain modern psychoanalytical, philosophical, and literary theories utilize a similar hermeneutic to that which undergirds rabbinic exegesis. Handelman discusses rabbinic hermeneutics as an alternative tradition to Hellenistic/Christian interpretation and then examines the work of Sigmund Freud, Jacques Lacan, Jacques Derrida and Harold Bloom with reference to it. She contends that each of these thinkers, in his own way, appropriates the insights of rabbinic hermeneutics but then disavows the source and develops a "heretic hermeneutic" in dialectic with that scheme. Her allegations are most convincing with regard to Derrida and Bloom, whose deconstructive and revisionist work consciously sets out to subvert inherited norms.

1580   Jackson, Jared Judd. "Rhetorical Criticism and the Problems of Subjectivity." *Proceedings: Eastern Great Lakes Biblical Society* 2 (1982): 34-45.

Demonstrates that rhetorical criticism can be used as a control on otherwise subjective criteria for source and form critical analyses. By way of example, four passages are discussed: Amos 3; 2 Samuel 15; Exodus 6:2-13; and Exodus 23:2-33.

1581   Jacobson, Richard. "The Structuralists and the Bible." In *A Guide to Contemporary Hermeneutics*, ed. by Donald K. McKim, 280-296. Grand Rapids, MI: Wm. B. Eerdmans Publishing Co., 1986.

A critical survey of the manner in which certain secular literary critics have applied structuralist analysis to biblical texts. Jacobson discusses works by Leach (0593), Barthes (0683, 1286), Chabrol (1058), and Marin (1155).

1582   Jasper, David. *The New Testament and the Literary Imagination.* Atlantic Highlands, NJ: Humanities Press International, 1987. 111 pp.

Urges a reading of the New Testament that will appreciate its metaphorical language and will call for a continual exercise of imagination. Theologically, this idea is grounded in the belief that the central claim of the New Testament concerns the transforming power of the resurrection. Practically, it implies acceptance of plural interpretations for scripture. Jasper also emphasizes the need for recognition of the variety of literary forms in the New Testament--he is critical of the term "story" as representing too narrow a classification. An entire chapter is devoted to proverbs and aphorisms.

1583   Jasper, David. "The New Testament and Literary Interpretation." *Religion and Literature* 17 (1985): 1-10.

Argues cogently for the need to be sensitive to literary concerns in New Testament study, but maintains that historical criticism cannot be ignored. Theological convictions should be based on literary readings of texts that respect the historical medium through which the literature comes to us.

1584   Jenson, Robert W. "Can a Text Defend Itself? An Essay *De Inspiratione Scripturae*." *Dialogue* 28 (1989): 251-256.

Says that if texts are allowed to mean only what interpreters say they mean, then they cannot exercise authority over a continuing tradition of speech. The simultaneous development in the history of the church of a canon of scripture and an episcopacy of leadership demonstrate the necessity of communal text-reading.

1585   Jobling, David. "Robert Alter's *The Art of Biblical Narrative*." *Journal for the Study of the Old Testament* 27 (1983): 87-99.

Reviews Alter's influential book (0607) as a marker of the "paradigm shift" in biblical studies from predominantly historical studies to a more synchronic, literary approach. Jobling faults Alter for his avoidance of semiotic and structuralist studies. See also 1539.

1586   Jobling, David. "Structuralism, Hermeneutics, and Exegesis: Three Recent Contributions to the Debate." *Union Seminary Quarterly Review* 34 (1979): 135-147.

Reviews three works on structuralism: McKnight's *Meaning in Texts* (0538), Detweiler's *Story, Sign, Self* (0508), and the Pattes' *Structural Exegesis* (0546). Whereas McKnight and Detweiler suggest that phenomenological literary criticism should be a fitting "conversation partner" for structuralism in biblical studies, Jobling thinks the discussion should be broadened to include poststructuralism and hermeneutics of science. On the practical side, structuralist exegesis needs to move into non-narrative parts of the Bible and needs to deal with larger portions of biblical texts. The Pattes are on the way to the first viable technique for structural analysis, but are not there yet.

1587   Keck, Leander E. "Will the Historical-Critical Method Survive? Some Observations." In *Orientation By Disorientation*, ed. by Richard A. Spencer, 115-128. Pittsburgh: Pickwick Press, 1980.

Explores possible reasons for the current disenchantment with the historical-critical method and discusses challenges to this method posed by Walter Wink, Hans Frei (1573) and David Robertson (0660). Keck suggests that reconstruction of historical circumstances remains necessary for use of the Bible in communities of faith because this perpetuates the process by which the past becomes paradigmatic and also enables the community to distance itself from elements of its past that have become unsavory (e.g., anti-Semitism).

1588   Kee, Howard Clark. "Polyvalence and Parables: Anyone Can Play." In *Society of Biblical Literature 1980 Seminar Papers*, ed. by Paul J. Achtemier, 57-61. Chico, CA: Scholars Press, 1980.

Offers a theological critique of Crossan's deconstructive approach to the parables (1089) by one who does not share Jacques Derrida's penchant for negative theology. Kee finds Crossan's work inadequate in that it substitutes flight from the space/time continuum for biblical theology of creation, and it does not address in any satisfying way the perennial existential questions of identity, meaning or purpose.

1589   Kelber, Werner H. "Gospel Narrative and Critical Theory," *Biblical Theology Bulletin* 18 (1988): 130-136.

Inventories five different approaches to the Gospel narratives in terms of the epistemological concept of meaning assumed by each of them: historical-theological approaches construe meaning as reference; literary, formalist interpretations construe meaning as narrative; receptionist aesthetics construe meaning as consciousness; structuralism construes meaning as system; and postmodernism construes meaning as deferment.

1590 Kieffer, R. "Analyse sémiotique et commentaire. Quelques réflexions à propos d' études de Luc 10.25-37." *New Testament Studies* 25 (1979): 454-468.

Summarizes and evaluates the semiotic analysis of the Good Samaritan parable presented by the Entrevernes group (1060). Kieffer appreciates the contributions of this research, but contends that no method should be used in complete isolation. He favors a new form of commentary called "epistemological commentary" that will respect the multidimensionality of language, of texts, and of methods of reading.

1591 Kieffer, R. "Lingvistiken och Nya testamentet: En forsknigsöversikt." *Svensk Teologisk Kvartalskrift* 58 (1982): 139-147.

Surveys the development and accomplishments of semiotic/structuralist approaches to scripture in different parts of the world. The approach has made its mark primarily in France, Germany, the USA, and Sweden. Kieffer concludes that modern linguistic method has "come to stay." The approach has been most successful so far in application to small units, but will increasingly be applied to whole narratives.

1592 Klaaren, Eugene M. "A Critical Appreciation of Hans Frei's *Eclipse of Biblical Narrative*." *Union Seminary Quarterly Review* 37 (1983): 283-297.

Compares Frei's influential book (1573) to Albert Schweitzer's *Quest of the Historical Jesus*. Frei has brought order to the complicated field of the history of modern biblical hermeneutics. He is guided by a grand theme, the modern eclipse of narrative and realistic interpretation of the Bible. And, he has increased the pressure for a renewed understanding of scripture in Christian theology.

1593 Kugel, James L. "On the Bible and Literary Criticism." *Prooftexts* 1 (1981): 217-236.

A critical review of current attempts to read the Bible as literature. Kugel finds such efforts anachronistic in that methods designed for the appreciation of modern literary competence are applied to literature produced according to quite different standards and for quite different purposes than it is now asked to fulfill. See also 1544.

1594 LaFargue, Michael. "Are Texts Determinate? Derrida, Barth and the Role of the Biblical Scholar." *Harvard Theological Review* 81 (1988): 341-357.

Defends a version of textual determinancy in view of Jacques Derrida's critique of empiricist objectivism, conceptualist objectivism, and expressivist view of language. LaFargue does not deny Derrida's premises (he notes that Karl Barth offered similar critiques), but attacks the conclusion drawn from these premises to the effect that texts are subject to an infinite number of incompatible but equally valid readings. Derrida confuses complexity with indeterminancy and richness of implication with ambiguity. Rather, what is needed is a "competence" for reading, based on the mind-set (*not* conscious intent) of the author.

1595   LaHurd, Carol Shersten. "Rhetorical Criticism, Biblical Criticism and Literary Criticism: Issues of Methodological Pluralism." *Proceedings: Eastern Great Lakes Biblical Society* 5 (1985): 87-101.

Examines Kennedy's rhetorical-critical study of Matthew 5--7 (0529) by comparing it to studies on this same text from the perspective of "biblical criticism" (i.e., historical criticism à la Joachim Jeremias) and from the perspective of "literary criticism" (i.e., linguistic-narrative criticism à la Walter Ong and Wayne Booth). Lahurd concludes that, although methodological pluralism results in some clash of conclusions, the different methods can serve as "checks and balances" on each other and may provide complementary insights on specific issues, such as audience analysis.

1596   Lasine, Stuart. "Indeterminacy and the Bible: A Review of Literary and Anthropologial Theories and Their Application to Biblical Texts." *Hebrew Studies* 27 (1986): 48-80.

Considers the several different conceptions of indeterminacy held by such biblical literary critics as Robert Alter, Meir Sternberg, David Gunn, and Peter Miscall. Lasine finds Miscall's deconstructive concept the least helpful and thinks that literary studies in general evince a failure to consider adequately the social function of narratives during specific periods of history. The problem of indeterminacy will have to be solved by a team effort involving anthropological, sociological, and literary methods.

1597   Lategan, Bernard C., and Vorster, Willem S. *Text and Reality: Aspects of Reference in Biblical Texts*. Atlanta: Scholars Press, 1985. 123 pp.

A dialogue of essays on the question of how texts refer to reality. Vorster presents studies of the parables in Mark 4 and of the Nathan parable in 2 Samuel 12 that argue for recognition of narrative context as the key determiner of meaning. Lategan agrees that New Testament hermeneutics must find a method that attends to the text itself but finds Vorster's attention to textual reference too restrictive. Drawing on structuralist and reader-response theories, he seeks to demonstrate the capacity of texts to project new worlds of meaning.

1598   Leigh, David J. "Michel Foucault and the Study of Literature and Theology." *Christianity and Literature* 33,1 (1983): 75-85.

Summarizes the life of Foucault, offers a brief overview of his most significant writings, summarizes his "basic notions," and then lists eight contributions that the study of Foucault could provide to theological criticism. Foucault is difficult to locate within the spectrum of modern literary criticism: he demonstrates affinities with Marxist, structuralist, and poststructuralist schools but renounces allegiance to all of these.

1599   Longman, Tremper III. *Literary Approaches to Biblical Interpretation.*
Foundations of Contemporary Interpretation, 3. Grand Rapids, MI: Zondervan
Publishing House, 1987. 164 pp.

A conservative appraisal of modern literary approaches to the Bible. Longman
presents a historical survey of the interrelationship of biblical and literary studies, lists
pitfalls and promises he sees in the use of literary methods (1600), and then provides
several examples of application of literary criticism to selected prosaic and poetic
passages. The book cautions against any downplaying of the historical worth of the
Bible but encourages literary analysis as supplemental to appreciation of scripture's
historical witness. Passages treated include Exodus 15:1-5; 1 Kings 22:1-38; Psalm
51:3-6; Song of Songs 5:10-16; Micah 4:2-5; Luke 1:46-55; Acts 10:1--11:18.

1600   Longman, Tremper, III. "The Literary Approach to the Study of the Old
Testament: Promises and Pitfalls." *The Journal of the Evangelical Theological Society*
28 (1985): 385-398.

Notes five problems and three benefits that literary study of the Bible may bring to
theology. The problems are to be found in the divided nature of literary studies, the
obscurantist language, the imposition of modern concepts on ancient literature, the
rejection of determinacy of texts, and the lack of concern for referential functions of
literature. Benefits include a new understanding of the conventions of storytelling
used in the Bible, attention to whole texts, and assistance in understanding the reading
process. This article was included, in revised form, in 1599.

1601   Longman, Tremper III. "Storytellers and Poets in the Bible: Can Literary
Artifice Be True?" In *Inerrancy and Hermeneutic: A Tradition, A Challenge, A Debate*,
ed. by Harrie M. Conn, 137-150. Grand Rapids, MI: Baker Books, 1988.

A critical but positive evaluation of literary approaches to the Bible from the
perspective of a conservative hermeneutic that affirms inerrancy and infallibility of
scripture in the area of history. Longman concludes that the question of whether the
Bible is literature or history is based on a false dichotomy; the Bible can be read and
trusted as both.

1602   Lys, Daniel. "Analyse structurale et approche littéraire." *Etudes Théologiques
et Religieuses* 52 (1977): 231-253.

Examines premises and achievements of structuralist exegesis, drawing mainly on Old
Testament texts as examples. Structuralism and literary criticism must work together
to provide a rounded understanding of the text. Sixteen different publications that
utilize structuralist/literary approaches to scripture are surveyed.

1603   Mackey, Louis. "Slouching Toward Bethlehem: Deconstructive Strategies in
Theology." *Anglican Theological Review* 65 (1983): 255-272.

Attempts to define deconstruction (which Mackey regards as neither nihilistic nor
atheistic) and to suggest ways in which deconstructive method might be useful for
theology. Two techniques are especially significant: questioning the hierarchic

elevation of speech over writing, and becoming alert to the ways in which words (signifiers) generate meanings unintentionally.

1604   Macky, Peter W. "The Coming Revolution: The New Literary Approach to the New Testament." In *A Guide to Contemporary Hermeneutics*, ed. by Donald K. McKim, 263-279 Grand Rapids, MI: Wm. B. Eerdmans Publishing Co., 1986.

Alleges that the influx of new literary approaches to the Bible heralds a paradigm shift comparable to that which occurred earlier when dogmatic interpretation gave way to historical-critical scholarship.   While rejecting the "jargonized" approach of structuralism as unhelpful, Macky applauds the arrival of other text-centered approaches that view meaning as inseparable from form.

1605   Malbon, Elizabeth Struthers. "Structuralism, Hermeneutics, and Contextual Meaning." *Journal of the American Academy of Religion* 51 (1983): 207-230.

Compares and contrasts structuralism and biblical hermeneutics. The four "terminal goals of structuralism (ideology or philosophy, theory, structural exegesis, narrative hermeneutics) are analogous to the four terminal goals of hermeneutics (theology or philosophy, theory, biblical exegesis, existential understanding). But there are three differences: (1) structuralism is interested in "the historic" while hermeneutics is interested in historicity; (2) structuralism is interested in systems of language while hermeneutics is interested in language events (such as speech or writing); (3) structuralism focuses on meanings within texts while hermeneutics focuses on meanings within text-reader relationships.

1606   Malina, Bruce J. "Reader-Response Theory: Discovery or Redundancy?" *Creighton University Faculty Journal* (Omaha) 5 (1986): 55-66.

Contends that the insights offered by reader-response criticism are readily available from sociolinguistics and discourse analysis. The method is problematic for biblical texts in any case because it was developed for texts that are intended to be read by individual readers.

1607   McCaughey, J. D. "Literary Criticism and the Gospels--A Rumination." *Australian Biblical Review* 29 (1981): 16-25.

Describes the new attention to literary criticism as one effective way of understanding what the text as it stands discloses to us. This has always been one of the goals of biblical exegesis. New Testament scholars must take seriously both literary history and literary criticism and listen to what is being said by contemporary literary critics.

1608   McConnell, Frank, ed. *The Bible and the Narrative Tradition*. Oxford: Oxford University Press, 1986. 152 pp.

A collection of essays by biblical critics and literary scholars devoted to the general theme of what allows certain texts to be defined as "sacred" and whether texts so defined can or should be studied as general literature. Three essays are written from essentially deconstructionist perspectives outside the community of faith, including 0676 and 1718. Three others represent perspectives of noted biblical scholars with varying degrees of commitment to the new literary methods: see 1075, 1382, and 1574.

1609   McKnight, Edgar V. "The Contours and Methods of Literary Criticism." In *Orientation By Disorientation*, ed. by Richard A. Spencer, 53-70. Pittsburgh: Pickwick Press, 1980.

Attempts to find a place for biblical criticism within the current spectrum of contemporary literary approaches. McKnight surveys varieties of literary criticism current today with help from Abrams' system of categorization (0076) and Hernadi's "compass" (0093). Literary criticism of the Bible may be grafted onto historical study, but demands some expansion of goals: meaning must not be limited by intentions of an original author or by effects on an original audience, though the legitimacy of these in determining meaning is not to be denied. Motivations of the actual author assist in determining the perspective of the implied author.

1610   McKnight, Edgar V. "Generative Poetics as New Testament Hermeneutics." *Semeia* 10 (1978): 107-121.

Responds to articles by Güttgemanns published in *Semeia* 6 (0519). McKnight suggests a model for New Testament interpretation that distinguishes levels of meaning and syntax without one level or pole being given priority. He advocates a comprehensive approach to texts in which the historical meaning, the existential meaning, or the affective meaning might be the focus of attention, but in which the fullest benefit will be recognized as coming from attention to all of the levels that impinge upon the reader.

1611   McKnight, Edgar V. *Post-Modern Use of the Bible: The Emergence of Reader-Oriented Criticism*. Nashville: Abingdon Press, 1988. 288 pp.

Advocates a radical reader-oriented criticism that stresses the role of the individual reader in the process of making sense of texts. McKnight offers a concise overview of the evolution of biblical scholarship and of literary criticism, tracing developments in both fields that have led to the present need for a postmodern approach.

1612   McKnight, Edgar V. "Structure and Meaning in Biblical Narrative." *Perspectives in Religious Studies* 3 (1976): 3-19.

Examines the relationship between structural analysis and approaches that are either historical-critical or hermeneutical. McKnight hopes that the use of structuralism in New Testament studies will lead to literary, theological, and humanistic insights not attainable through other disciplines.

1613   Mohr, M., and Mohr, M. H. "Interpreting the Text and Telling the Story." *Dialogue* 21 (1982): 102-106.

Contends that there is a significant gap between the literary critic's understanding of the Gospel narratives and the biblical critic's understanding of those same narratives. The authors believe that the hermeneutical tendency toward viewing scripture as story --as perpetually "open" text--will free the Jesus-story to enter the domain of literary discourse.

1614   Moore, Stephen D. "Are the Gospels Unified Narratives?" In *Society of Biblical Literature Seminar Papers*, 443-459. Atlanta: Scholars Press, 1987.

Argues that narrative criticism has failed to demonstrate that the Gospels are unified narratives. Focusing specifically on works by Dawsey (1296) and Tannehill (1353), Moore alleges that their interpretations ignore the cracks and crevices that result from the conflation of sources and so fail to prove that the text is a narrative unit.

1615   Moore, Stephen D. *Literary Criticism and the Gospels: The Theoretical Challenge*. New Haven, CT: Yale University Press, 1989. 226 pp.

A critical introduction to certain literary approaches to the Gospels: narrative criticism, reader-response criticism, and deconstruction. Moore reviews much of the current literature reflecting these approaches and asks pertinent questions concerning conclusions to be drawn from them. Aware that the new methodologies are still undergoing development, Moore consistently pushes their implications to logical extremes and indicates the potentially revolutionary challenges that these methods may pose for theological studies.

1616   Moore, Stephen D. "Narrative Commentaries on the Bible: Context, Roots, and Prospects." *Forum* 3,3 (1987): 29-62.

Discusses the potential contributions that might be made through an announced series of "narrative commentaries" to be published on the Bible. The context for such a series is determined by the new emphasis in biblical studies on holistic reading in general and on narrative criticism in particular. Early examples of such commentaries can be seen in works by Kelber (1223) and Talbert (1349) but the real prospects for the series are to be seen in recent contributions from Tannehill (1353), Edwards (1139), and Miscall (0845).

1617   Moore, Stephen D. "Negative Hermeneutics, Insubstantial Texts: Stanley Fish and the Biblical Interpreter." *Journal of the American Academy of Religion* 54 (1986): 707-719.

Reflects on the significance of Fish's theory of interpretive communities (0361) for biblical interpretation. The theory holds that whatever seems to be obvious is only so within some institutional or conventional structure. Realization of the extent to which meaning is a product of reading strategy may cause biblical scholars to direct less attention to texts themselves and more attention to the interpretive rules, strategems, and traditions by which we appropriate texts. But this will not work either, for interpretive conventions are no more stable as objects of investigation than texts. Poststructuralist interpretation theory offers only the absence of epistemological theory as a perhaps unanswerable challenge to biblical scholarship.

1618   Moore, Stephen D.   "The 'Post-'Age Stamp: Does It Stick? Biblical Studies and Postmodern Debate." *Journal of the American Academy of Religion* 57 (1989): 543-559.

Argues for more precision in use of the term "postmodern." Moore thinks it is problematic to call the poststructuralism of Jacques Derrida and Roland Barthes "postmodern." Truly postmodern biblical criticism is more likely to be found among radical feminist and so-called Third World theologians.

1619   Moore, Stephen D.   "Postmodernism and Biblical Studies: A Response to Robert Fowler." *Forum* 5,3 (1989): 36-41.

Responds to an article by Fowler (0511), in which reader-response criticism; the philosophies of Ludwig Wittgenstein, Hans Georg Gadamer, and John Austin; the media criticism of Walter J. Ong; and the deconstructive criticism of Jacques Derrida are all cited as instances of the postmodern movement. Moore questions whether all (or any) of these fit that label.

1620   Moore, Stephen D.   "Stories of Reading: Doing Gospel Criticism As/With a Reader." In *Society of Biblical Literature 1988 Seminar Papers*, ed. by David J. Lull, 141-159.   Atlanta: Scholars Press, 1988.

Critically examines certain assumptions regarding the role of the reader in reader-response criticism as it has been applied to the Gospels. Moore notes that positing readers for the Gospels is somewhat anachronistic in that these texts were originally intended to be heard not read. He also challenges the practice of positing "virginal" readers by pointing out ways in which the texts themselves seem to presuppose extra-textual competence. The article concludes with discussion of the possibilities of incorporating the experiences of real readers in critical exegesis and with discussion of the limitations of institutionalized reading. See also 1615.

1621   North, Robert.   "Violence and the Bible: The Girard Connection." *Catholic Biblical Quarterly* 47 (1985): 1-27.

A basic review of René Girard's sociological, anthropological, and literary theories, with an emphasis on their relevance for biblical criticism. North first summarizes Girard's thesis that all human institutions (including religion) give rise to violence. Then he lists the Old and New Testament texts that Girard interprets as confirmation of this hypothesis. Finally, he summarizes what he regards as Girard's strongest points, as well as listing points that seem "unfinished."

1622 Ong, Walter J. "The Psychodynamics of Oral Memory and Narrative: Some Implications for Biblical Studies." In *The Pedagogy of God's Image: Essays on Symbol and the Religious Imagination.* ed. by Robert Masson, 55-73. Chico, CA: Scholars Press, 1982.

Reflects on the way that memory and narrative plot are related in a predominately oral culture (such as that which produced the Bible) as opposed to the way that they are related in chirographic, typographic, or electronic cultures (such as our own). The paper concludes with an exhortation to biblical scholars to come to terms with the Bible in terms of the transit from oral to literate mental processes.

1623   Patte, Daniel. *The Religious Dimensions of Biblical Texts: Greimas's Structural Semiotics and Biblical Exegesis.* Semeia Studies. Atlanta: Scholars Press, 1990. 293 pp.

Considers the implications of A. J. Greimas' metatheory on the production of meaning (see 0256) for biblical exegesis. Patte believes that Greimas' structuralist approach allows discovery of the religious dimensions of texts in a manner that historical-critical approaches do not. Part I presents an overview of Greimas' structural semiotics for those who may have no background in the field. Illustrations refer to the parable of the Good Samaritan. Part II discusses the phenomenon of believing from the perspective of semiotics. Part III offers a systematic presentation of Greimas' approach and some final thoughts (on "The Generative Trajectory in Certain Non-Western Cultures" written by Timothy B. Cargal).

1624   Patte, Daniel. "Structuralism and Hermeneutics: A Review Article." *Perspectives in Religious Studies* 71 (1980): 60-70.

Reviews McKnight's *Meaning in Texts* (0538). Patte compares McKnight's proposal for joining hermeneutics and structuralism to the system of A. J. Greimas. McKnight's theory is based on an extralinguistic view of reality and an immanent understanding of revelation, whereas Greimas' is based on a linguistic view of reality and a transcendent understanding of revelation.

1625   Patte, Daniel. "Universal Narrative Structures and Semantic Frameworks." *Semeia* 10 (1978): 123-135.

Responds to Güttgemanns' four essays in *Semeia* 6 (0519) by attempting to show the logic of presuppositions upon which Güttgemanns' discourse unfolds. Patte faults Güttgemanns for following a model of "basis grammar" that plots sequential relations and logical relations on the same graph. Patte suggests a more complete model would make a distinction between syntactic narrative structure and paradigmatic structure.

1626   Perpich, Sandra Wackman. "A Hermeneutic Critique of Structuralist Exegesis, with Specific Reference to Lk 10:29-37." Ph.D. diss., Marquette University, 1981. 282 pp.

Proposes that Karl Rahner's theology of mystery provides a framework for allowing structuralism and hermeneutics to work complementarily. Although they seem to be governed by conflicting presuppositions, structuralism's failure to elucidate texts exhaustively indicates its need for a hermeneutic complement. Categories from Paul

Ricoeur's philosophy that pertain to a correlation of structuralism and hermeneutics are examined also. The story of the Good Samaritan in Luke 10 is used as a model for testing the thesis.

1627   Perrin, Norman. "Historical Criticism, Literary Criticism, and Hermeneutics: The Interpretation of the Parables of Jesus and of the Gospel of Mark Today." *Journal of Religion* 52 (1972): 361-375.

Contends that these three aspects of interpretation must be interrelated, even though they are distinct. To score this point, Perrin takes the parables of Jesus in Mark's Gospel and compares the way these are read by Matthew and Luke with the way they are read by later Christian "allegorizers." The former offer a "literary criticism" of the parables that go beyond what Mark intended to say, but they do not do so in a way that does violence to the nature of the text. Allegorization, on the other hand, refuses to treat the parables as parables and so misses their point.

1628   Petersen, Norman R. "Literary Criticism in Biblical Studies." In *Orientation By Disorientation*, ed. by Richard A. Spencer, 25-52. Pittsburgh: Pickwick Press, 1980.

Describes the development of modern biblical literary criticism against the background of developments in biblical scholarship and in secular literary studies. In biblical circles, source, form, and redaction criticism were all products of a philological approach, that literary criticism seeks to transcend. Secular literary studies, such as Auerbach's *Mimesis* (0128) demonstrated the need for attention to textual compositeness. Modern biblical literary criticism also emphasizes the role of the receiver in the production of meaning--a bare text is not a communication in itself, but a work to be performed by readers. In addition, modern biblical literary criticism emphasizes the need to distinguish the poetic from the referential in adoption of a second naivete.

1629   Pfitzner, Victor C. "The Charm of Biblical Narrative." *Lutheran Theological Journal* (Australia) 17 (1983): 1-12.

Emphasizes that the Bible is not only a vehicle for the communication of serious revelation but also literature, meant for us to enjoy.

1630   Phillips, Gary A. *Biblical Exegesis in a Postmodern Age*. Minneapolis: Fortress Press, forthcoming.

Announced for publication.

1631   Phillips, Gary A. "Biblical Exegesis in a Postmodern Age: Hearing Different Voices." *Journal of the American Academy of Religion* (forthcoming).

Announced for publication.

1632 Phillips, Gary A. "Exegesis as Critical Praxis: Reclaiming History and Text from a Postmodern Perspective." *Semeia* 51 (1990): 7-49.

Identifies the present challenges to biblical exegesis being posed by postmodern cultural thought and poststructuralist literary theory. Phillips views these challenges positively, as providing opportunity for defining within a new discursive context the possibilities of a historical understanding of texts strategic to our culture's self-identity. The postmodern context (defined with references to Dominick LaCapra, Jacques Derrida, and Michel Foucault) compels recognition of interpretive control and the emergence of biblical exegesis that is agonistic, contestatory, and multi-voiced.

1633 Phillips, Gary A. "Intertextuality and the Reading of Biblical Texts: From Canon to Chaos." In *Intertextuality and the Human Sciences*, ed. by Heinrich Plett. Munich: Kaiser, forthcoming.

Announced for publication.

1634 Placher, William C. "Hans Frei and the Meaning of Biblical Narrative." *The Christian Century* 106 (1989): 556-559.

A memorial tribute to Hans Frei that traces his legacy for biblical and literary studies. Frei anticipated the new conversations between biblical and literary critics and foreshadowed modern interests in social-anthropology by realizing the role of narrative in discussion of personal identity. His work is also timely given recent work in Christian ethics and the ongoing attraction of "descriptive theology" (e.g., Karl Barth).

1635 Poland, Lynn M. *Literary Criticism and Biblical Hermeneutics*. American Academy of Religion Academy Series, 48. Chico, CA: Scholar's Press, 1985. 220 pp.

Criticizes formalist and "New Criticism" approaches to the Bible for their failure to provide movement from form to content. Such approaches--exemplified by Crossan (1089, 1690-1691), Frei (1573), and Via (1117)--rightly reject the Bultmannian existential separation of form and content, but fail to articulate how a reader moves from meaning within the text to meaning for themselves. Poland draws on Paul Ricoeur to propose a system by which the reader moves from preunderstanding to explication of the world of the text to possible adoption of that world as the reader's own.

1636 Poland, Lynn M. "The New Criticism, Neoorthodoxy, and the New Testament." *Journal of Religion* 65 (1985): 459-477.

Compares the development of formalism in literary studies with the development of neoorthodoxy in theology. Poland finds the comparisons between the two movements (both concerned with continuity/discontinuity) to be instructive as historical background for understanding the current turn toward literary methods in biblical studies today.

1637   Poland, Lynn M. "The Secret Gospel of Northrop Frye." *Journal of Religion* 64 (1984): 513-519.

Reviews Frye's *The Great Code* (0586). The book is neither biblical scholarship in the usual sense nor a study of the Bible as literature. It reads the Bible as the code to Western culture. Frye believes in literature as a religion that offers universal salvation.

1638   Polzin, Robert M. "Literary and Historical Criticism of the Bible: A Crisis in Scholarship." In *Orientation By Disorientation*, ed. by Richard A. Spencer, 99-114. Pittsburgh: Pickwick Press, 1980.

Argues that the real crisis in biblical scholarship today does not concern the question of whether the primary approach to biblical narrative should be historical or literary but, rather, the problem that both historical and literary approaches are built on hermeneutical principles that the Bible itself paradoxically denies. In particular, the biblical messages do not exhibit any concern to establish the sense that previous traditions had for their original audience.

1639   Polzin, Robert M. "Literary Unity in Old Testament Narrative: A Response." *Semeia* 15 (1979): 45-50.

Responds favorably to an article by Miscall (0651) that attempts to build on Polzin's own earlier work (0721) and reflects on the hermeneutical implications of the approach that he and Miscall have adopted. Argues for the necessity of adopting at least a formalist literary approach to scripture and of exploring the need to move beyond formalism.

1640   Powell, Mark Allan. "Types of Readers and their Relevance for Biblical Hermeneutics." *Trinity Seminary Review* 12 (1990): 67-76.

Discusses five different literary approaches to the Bible in terms of the concept of "the reader" employed in each: deconstruction posits a "real reader"; structuralism, a "competent reader"; reader-response criticism, an "implied reader"; rhetorical criticism, an "intended reader"; and narrative criticism, an "ideal reader." Powell indicates the implications that each system may have for hermeneutics and proposes that the differences are analogous to various conceptions of "the author" that characterize schools of historical criticism.

1641   Poythress, Vern S. "Structuralism and Biblical Studies." *Journal of the Evangelical Theological Society* 21 (1978): 221-237.

Examines structuralism with specific regard for its impact on conservative evangelical theology. Weaknesses of the approach include the possibility of an excessive humanizing of the text, a tendency to place biblical materials on the same level as other literature, and a temptation to denigrate history. But the synchronic approach also allows the exegete to focus without apology on the canonical text, and consideration of deep structures opens up possibilities for a fullness of meaning.

1642   Pratt, Richard L., Jr.   "Pictures, Windows, and Mirrors in Old Testament Exegesis." *The Westminster Theological Journal* 45 (1983): 156-167.

Demonstrates by way of exegesis of Genesis 12:10-20 that it is possible for readers to treat the text as a picture, as a window, or as a mirror. Pratt claims that conservative Old Testament scholarship must show more concern for establishing the impact of the reader on the process of interpretation.

1643   Prickett, Stephen.   "The Status of Biblical Narrative." *Pacifica* 2 (1989): 26-46.

Says that to ask whether a biblical narrative should be considered as history, fiction, fact-like story, or faith-narrative imposes modern and inappropriate categories. The dissatisfactory results of all traditional approaches to hermeneutics stem from our inability to enter into the conceptual and literary frameworks of the Bible.

1644   Prickett, Stephen.   *Words and the Word: Language, Poetics, and Biblical Interpretation.* Cambridge: Cambridge University Press, 1986. 305 pp.

Considers the question of ambiguity in the Bible and the manner in which this is dealt with in translation and in poetics. With regard to the former, Prickett opposes the attempts of Bible translators to use clear and unambiguous language, since there is much in the Bible that is not clear and unambiguous. In a similar fashion, the attempt to develop a biblical poetics can represent a denial of ambiguity. But Prickett finds hope for the attempt in scholars like Paul Ricoeur and Dennis Nineham, who allow poetics to retain its contradictory connotations "of primitiveness and sophistication, of falsification and insight, of picture-language and symbol-truth."

1645   Reed, W. L.   "A Poetics of the Bible: Problems and Possibilities." *Journal of Literature and Theology* (Oxford) 1 (1987): 154-166.

Considers Frye's *The Great Code* (0586) and Sternberg's *Poetics of Biblical Narrative* (0570), but decides that the concepts of system and norm inherent in these are too open-ended and inclusive to account for the centripetal and exclusionary ethos of the biblical canon. Reed proposes a dialogical rather than narratological approach.

1646   Robertson, David.   "Literature, The Bible As." In *The Interpreter's Dictionary of the Bible*, Supplementary Volume, ed. by Keith Crim, 547-551. Nashville: Abingdon Press, 1976.

Notes that the phrase in the title designates a point of view taken by a small but increasing number of biblical scholars who do not feel their work invalidates other approaches to the Bible, but who believe literary appreciation of the Bible is one more way of approaching God's Word. Discusses current literary research on the Bible in two categories (structuralist and nonstructuralist) and notes both the consequences of and objections to the paradigm shift implied in the development of these methodologies.

1647   Ryken, Leland. "The Bible As Literature." Four parts. *Bibliotheca Sacra* 147 (1990): 3-15, 131-142, 259-269, 387-398.

Commends the use of a literary-critical approach to the Bible for conservative evangelical Christians. In part one, Ryken considers obstacles discouraging such an approach, notes characteristics of a literary approach, and cites the benefits of a literary approach. Part two considers narrative--the narrative character of the Bible as a whole and the narrative quality of Christian life and doctrine. Part three is devoted to discussion of the poetry of the Bible. Part four is subtitled "The Imagination as a Means of Grace" and attempts to refute the heresy that God's work is not artistic.

1648   Ryken, Leland. "Literary Criticism of the Bible: Some Fallacies." In *Literary Interpretations of Biblical Narratives*, ed. by Kenneth R. R. Gros Louis with James S. Ackerman and Thayer S. Warshaw, 24-40. Nashville: Abingdon Press, 1974.

Indicates misconceptions in biblical "literary criticism," as that discipline was practiced a generation ago. Ryken notes that biblical scholars do not use the term "literary criticism" in the same sense that literary critics do--they use it to describe a search for original text and definition of original context. Inherent in such an approach are suppositions and procedures that would be considered fallacies in the study of other literature: a fragmentation of the text and a preoccupation with the process that produced it. Ryken's concerns have been largely rectified in modern literary study of the Bible, though a few of the fallacies he notes might be recognized as persistent, e.g., tendencies to view everything in the Bible as literary, to despise the supernatural, or to belittle the Bible's literary craftmanship.

1649   Schiwy, Günther. *Structuralism and Christianity*. Trans. by Henry J. Koren. Duquesne Studies--Theological Series, 11. Pittsburgh: Duquesne University Press, 1971. 105 pp.

Considers structuralism as an intellectual movement that presents an alternative world view to that of Christianity. Schiwy believes that, although most structuralists have no intention of making direct attacks on Christianity, structuralism as a movement nevertheless poses challenges to Christian theology as a science.

1650   Scuka, Robert Franc. "The Retrieval of Biblical Narrative: A Constructive Alternative to the Narrative Hermeneutics of Hans Frei." Ph.D. diss., Southern Methodist University, 1987. 567 pp.

Formulates a hermeneutical framework for narrative reading of the Gospels that takes Paul Ricoeur's hermeneutical reflections into account and corrects what are seen as problematic elements in the approach of Hans Frei. Most of the work is dedicated to a review and critique of Frei's work (1573). Scuka believes that Frei makes problematic assumptions about both language and narrative and inconsistently reintroduces empirical-historical considerations into his exegesis. A reading of the Gospel of Mark is offered as illustrative of the hermeneutical framework Scuka proposes.

1651   Shuler, Philip L. "Questions of an Holistic Approach to Luke-Acts." *Perkins Journal* 40 (April, 1987): 43-47.

An extended review of Tyson's *Death of Jesus in Luke-Acts* (1356) that focuses on two concerns raised by Tyson's literary approach: (1) the question of genre; and (2) the implications of construing dominant themes as literary motifs rather than as references to real historical patterns.

1652   Silberman, Lou H. "Listening to the Text." *Journal of Biblical Literature* 102 (1983): 3-26.

Silberman approaches the current "crisis" in the discipline of biblical studies. He takes Frank Kermode's idea of "fictions" and Don Ihde's idea of "lies" together, saying that biblical scholars currently suffer from the failure of a fiction, namely the "Documentary fiction, the Source Myth." He provides a genesis of the current situation. Then he suggests: (1) "suspend explanations; describe"; (2) recognize varying possibilities; and (3) "seek structures." Finally, he offers some examples of listening to the text.

1653   Spencer, Aída Besancon. "An Apologetic for Stylistics in Biblical Studies." *The Journal for the Evangelical Theological Society* 29 (1986): 419-427.

Commends the use of stylistics for biblical studies as an appropriate methodology for biblical studies, especially as practiced by conservative evangelical Christians. Stylistics is an approach similar to rhetorical criticism based on certain linguistic studies akin to structuralism. Spencer delineates five stages that will usually constitute a "thorough stylistics study."

1654   Sprinkle, Joe K. "Literary Approaches to the Old Testament: A Survey of Recent Scholarship." *The Journal of the Evangelical Theological Society* 32 (1989): 299-310.

Reviews the work of four Old Testament scholars who use literary approaches to the Bible: James Muilenberg, Robert Alter, Adele Berlin, and Meir Sternberg. Sprinkle thinks that the new approaches (especially Sternberg's) will be helpful to evangelicals in many ways--they facilitate communication with other Bible scholars, for instance, and they aid in defending the unity of the Bible against documentary hypotheses.

1655   Stendahl, Krister. "The Bible as a Classic and the Bible as Holy Scripture." *Journal of Biblical Literature* 103 (1984): 3-10.

Recognizes that the Bible has an important role to play both as a classic of literature and as Holy Scripture, but insists that with regard to both of these roles, normative interpretation of the Bible must be determined in terms of original intentions. Stendahl faults approaches to the Bible as "story" for failing to respect this standard of normative interpretation.

1656   Stock, Augustine.   "The Limits of Historical-Critical Exegesis." *Biblical Theology Bulletin* 13 (1983): 28-31.

Discusses structuralist, poststructuralist, and reader-oriented approaches to scripture as possible alternatives to historical criticism, which has failed to provide pastors with access to the existential meaning of texts.

1657   Tanner, Kathryn E.   "Theology and the Plain Sense."   In *Scriptural Authority and Narrative Interpretation*, ed. by Garrett Green, 59-78.   Philadelphia: Fortress Press, 1987.

Champion's Frei's linking of scriptural authority to its "plain sense" (1573) and argues that when the latter is defined in terms of narrative meaning, the way is opened for a flexible and self-critical use of the Bible.

1658   Taylor, Mark C.   "The Eventuality of Texts."   *Semeia* 51 (1990): 215-240.

Argues that different reading strategies assume different construals of time.   Jacques Derrida and Emmanuel Levinas propose a poststructural strategy for speaking about the event character of texts that avoid the idealist and reductive pitfalls of the view of temporality inherent in both structuralism and hermeneutics.

1659   Thiemann, Ronald F.   "Radiance and Obscurity in Biblical Narrative."   In *Scriptural Authority and Narrative Interpretation*, ed. by Garrett Green, 21-41.   Philadelphia: Fortress Press, 1987.

Responds to Frank Kermode and other deconstructionists who regard biblical texts as irreducibly obscure by producing examples that demonstrate how biblical narratives depict a "followable world." The stories are coherent and function to invite the reader into the world they present. The reader may regard that world as uninhabitable and so choose not to enter it, but that is another matter. The role of theology is to affirm the implications of biblical assertion, not to explain the movements by which persons come to accept those claims.

1660   Thiselton, Anthony C.   "Keeping Up With Recent Studies II: Structuralism and Biblical Studies--Method or Ideology?"   *Expository Times* 89 (1977-1978): 329-335.

Offers a brief account of the origins and aims of structuralism, describes the use of structuralist approaches in New Testament studies, and suggests some of the movement's strengths and weaknesses relative to biblical studies. Thiselton stresses that it is possible to use the method of structural analysis without subscribing to the ideology behind it. It is too soon at this point to assess the movement on the basis of its contributions to exegesis.

1661 Tihon, P. "Exégèse et analyse structurale. Quelques réflexions de théologien." *Nouvelle Revue Theologique* 97 (1975): 318-344.

Contends that structural approaches to texts are often linked to structuralist systems that are incompatible with a Christian perspective. Distinctions are drawn between biblical exegetes who may use structural methods for the study of texts and semioticians who may also examine biblical texts. The difference is not one of method, but of priority of objectives.

1662 Tilborg, Sjef van. "Het strukturalisme binnen de exegese: een variant van het burgerlijke denken." *Bijdragen: Tijdschrift voor Filosofie en Theologie* 40 (1979): 364-379.

Contends that the majority of structuralists borrow from bourgeois thinking, in spite of the claim the discipline makes to being nonhistorical and nonreferential. Tilborg points to specific studies where he thinks the bourgeois thinking is detectable, including one by Via on the parable of the unjust judge (1116).

1663 Tolbert, Mary Ann. "Polyvalence and the Parables: A Consideration of J. D. Crossan's *Cliffs of Fall*." In *Soceity of Biblical Literature 1980 Seminar Papers*, ed. by Paul J. Achtemeir, 63-87. Chico, CA: Scholars Press, 1980.

Reviews Crossan's work (1089), which exalts the concept of "play" as an alternative paradigm to mimesis in interpretation of parables. But Tolbert notes that Crossan's concern for establishing the text with reference to the words of the historical Jesus is inconsistent with his own theory: he seems to want the historical Jesus to supply some normative authority for multiple interpretations.

1664 Tomes, R. "Recent Developments in Biblical Studies." *Faith and Freedom* 35 (1982): 78-84.

Says that dissatisfaction with a purely historical-critical approach has led biblical scholars to adopt such new approaches as canonical, literary, structuralist, sociological, and ideological criticism. Tomes thinks there are some problems with these new approaches but, overall, they are breathing new life into biblical studies.

1665 Tracy, David. "Reflections on John Dominic Crossan's *Cliffs of Fall: Paradox and Polyvalence in the Parables of Jesus*." In *Society of Biblical Literature 1980 Seminar Papers*, ed. by Paul J. Achtemeier, 69-74. Chico, CA: Scholars Press, 1980.

Notes, correctly, that although Crossan describes his work as a structuralist approach, it is actually poststructural or deconstructive. Tracy also explores the issues involved in choosing a hermeneutical model based on "free play" (à la Jacques Derrida and Roland Barthes) as opposed to one based on the "play of dialogue" (à la Hans-Georg Gadamer and Paul Ricoeur). Tracy believes Crossan's own model would be better informed by the latter, though he seems to have drifted, perhaps unconsciously, onto the "shifting sands" of the former.

1666   Vorster, Willem S. "The Reader in the Text: Narrative Material." *Semeia* 48 (1989): 21-40.

Addresses the following questions: Is there a reader in the text? Who or what is the reader in the text? How is the reader in the text? These questions are confronted with regard to the interpretation of the New Testament, particularly the Gospels and Acts.

1667   Weder, H. "Der 'Strukturalismus' in der Theologie." *Kirchenblatt für die reformierte Schweiz* 130 (1974): 386-389.

Discusses and evaluates several structuralist approaches to the Bible. Acceptance of these theories raises questions regarding the understanding of history, the criterion of truth, the theory of knowledge, the hypostasizing of the text, and the nature of revelation.

1668   Wegner, M. "Literary Criticism and Biblical Religious Language: Insights from Northrop Frye." *Currents in Theology and Mission* 12 (1985): 100-105.

Reviews Northrop Frye's contributions to biblical scholarship (cf. 0586). Wegner says that Frye interprets the Bible in terms of its literary characteristics: poetic language, comic mythical plot, centripetal metaphoric images, and generic typological sequences. Frye also focuses on the rhetorical, linguistic, and thematic interplays that shape the reader of the biblical text.

1669   West, Cornel. "On Frei's *Eclipse of Biblical Narrative*." *Union Seminary Quarterly Review* 37 (1983): 299-302.

Calls attention to Frei's work (1573) as one that "demonstrates specific ways in which forms of supernaturalism, historicism, classism, moralism, and positivism have imposed debilitating constraints on the emergence of biblical hermeneutics." His profound achievement lies in calling our attention to the "path not taken" in theological studies.

1670   White, Hugh C. "French Structuralism and Old Testament Narrative Analysis: Roland Barthes." *Semeia* 3 (1975): 99-127.

Compares a structuralist analysis of Genesis 32:23-33 by Barthes (0683) with traditional-critical study of the same text, as exemplified in the work of Hermann Gunkel. Barthes' interest is in determining the manner in which the structure of the text produces meaning rather than in reconstructing the process through which the text was produced. White finds some difficulties with Barthes' approach but thinks that the questions and dilemmas he raises may provide access to new levels of meaning.

1671 White, Hugh C. "Structural Analysis of the Old Testament." In *Encounter with the Text: Form and History in the Hebrew Bible*, ed. by Martin J. Buss, 45-66. Philadelphia: Fortress Press, 1979.

Traces recent developments in structuralist theory as supportive of an approach to Old Testament studies that will be both possible and desirable. White concentrates on the work of Claude Lévi-Strauss, A. J. Greimas, and Roland Barthes.

1672 Whybray, R. N. "On Robert Alter's *The Art of Biblical Narrative*." *Journal for the Study of the Old Testament* 27 (1983): 75-86.

Summarizes the chief contributions of Alter's book on narrative criticism of the Old Testament (0607). Whybray questions what appears to be a tendency on Alter's part to regard the quality of Israel's art as a product of its developing monotheism. In 1539, Alter explains that this represents a misconstrual of his position, which is simply that Israel's faith and art reinforce and enrich each other.

1673 Wilder, Amos N. *The Bible and the Literary Critic*. Minneapolis: Fortress Press, 1991. 186 pp.

A collection of essays by one of the first theologians in America to appreciate and advocate literary criticism of the Bible. The book opens with two pieces that Wilder calls "New Soundings." The first responds to the *New Yorker* magazine's somewhat tentative review of Alter and Kermode's *Literary Guide to the Bible* (0578). The second is an extended review by Wilder of Kermode's approach to the Gospel of Mark (1225). The next section of the book is historical--it traces the development of a truly literary approach to the Bible out of the historical consciousness of the early twentieth-century. Wilder focuses on Norman Perrin as one figure whose evolution from historical to literary orientation influenced many. The third section of the book offers a variety of essays on the challenges of postmodern theology and poststructural theology. Wilder dialogues with John Dominic Crossan, discusses "Story and Story World," and considers "Post-Modern Reality and the Problem of Meaning."

1674 Wiles, Maurice. "Scriptural Authority and Theological Construction: The Limitations of Narrative Interpretation." In *Scriptural Authority and Narrative Interpretation*, ed. by Garrett Green, 42-58. Philadelphia: Fortress Press, 1987.

Warns against the dangers of using narrative to impose an unwarranted unity on the canon. Wiles questions, for instance, whether it is possible to derive from the Gospels a single "story of Jesus"; though it may be theoretically possible to do so, he avers, the story thus obtained would be a "very bad one." Wiles believes a hermeneutical position that regards scripture as an indispensable resource rather than a binding authority is necessary for the church to acknowledge the varied nature of the stories found within scripture.

1675   Wright, T. R.   "Regenerating Narrative: The Gospels as Fiction."   *Religious Studies* 20 (1984): 389-400.

An extended review of Kermode's *The Genesis of Secrecy* (1225).   Wright approves of Kermode's application of structuralist and poststructuralist criticism to the Gospel of Mark, but does not think that recognizing Mark's fictive nature means abandoning interest in its capacity to convey historical truth.

1676   Wuellner, Wilhelm.   "Is There an Encoded Reader Fallacy?"   *Semeia* 48 (1989): 41-54.

Raises several issues that dispute the prevailing notion in literary studies that reading experience can be shaped solely by indigenous textual qualities as defined by linguistic and literary theory.   Wuellner fears that the use of textually encoded readers as heuristic devices limits the special character of biblical texts as inspired or ideological. Also, to the extent that such readers are defined by members of a First World patriarchal culture, the view that a textually encoded reading is "normative" may perpetuate cultural and sexual imperialism.

1677   Yaghjian, Lucretia B.   "Hermetic Art, or The Holy Spirit and Us: Narrative Sense or Secrecy in the Hermeneutic of Frank Kermode."   *Christianity and Literature* 30,1 (1980): 64-79.

Presents a Christian critique of Frank Kermode's deconstructionist hermeneutic, which regards the interpretation of narrative as doomed from the start by the impenetrable secrecy of the text.   For the Christian critic, interpretation can only begin where Kermode says it can go no further--where life or art does not make sense.   Christians experience the discovery of meaning as a "resurrection," as the work of the Holy Spirit.

PART SIX:
IMPLICATIONS

HOMILETICS

See also 1159, 1267, 1347, 1410.

1678   Culpepper, R. Alan. "Narrative Criticism as a Tool for Proclamation: 1 Samuel 13." *Review and Expositor* 84 (1987): 33-40.

Suggests ways that narrative criticism can be helpful in preaching the biblical stories. Biblical preaching involves retelling the stories so that the reader is drawn into the narrative world of the Bible. To illustrate, Culpepper shows how the conflicts and struggles depicted in 1 Samuel 13 may offer opportunities for reader identification with conflicts faced by persons of faith today.

1679   Ellingsen, Mark. *The Integrity of Biblical Narrative: Story in Theology and Proclamation*. Minneapolis: Fortress Press, 1989. 128 pp.

Explores the homiletical implications of recent narrative approaches to the Bible. Ellingsen offers a discriminating review of the work of such scholars as Amos Wilder, Erich Auerbach, and Hans Frei and then provides a framework for developing narrative sermons on biblical texts.

1680   Scott, Bernard Brandon. *The Word of God in Words: Reading and Preaching the Gospels*. Philadelphia: Fortress Press, 1985. 94 pp.

Elucidates implications of modern linguistic and literary theory for homiletics. Tracing the manner in which Gospel stories operate to create meaning, Scott emphasizes the role of readers as performers of that meaning. He suggests that an incarnational understanding of scripture must take seriously the character of revelation as dialogue between God and people. The recognition that individual perspectives affect meaning leads to a series of theses on how scripture ought to be read and proclaimed.

1681 Shea, John. "Religious-Imaginative Encounters with Scriptural Stories." In *Art/Literature/Religion: Life on the Borders*, ed. by Robert Detweiler, 173-180. Journal of the American Academy of Religion Thematic Studies, 49,2. Chico, CA: Scholars Press, 1983.

Describes the role of scripture in postmodern times as being to offer a religious-imaginative encounter that links the sacred with the profane. Four elements are significant: (1) the psychic posture of the reader; (2) the revelatory moment itself; (3) the poetic retelling of the text, expressing what has been found; and (4) placement of this retelling within the convictions and values of the history of interpretation.

THEOLOGY

See also 0130, 0500, 0511, 0516, 0528, 0546, 0552, 0556, 0588, 0607, 0672, 1072, 1275.

1682 Aichele, George, Jr. *The Limits of Story*. Atlanta: Scholars Press, 1985.

This metaphysical approach to story attempts "a series of approximations to some central questions that must be answered by anyone wishing to explore what story is, or to use the concept of story to some other end." The second chapter, "Form and World," takes the Garden of Eden as its metaphor. Subsequent chapters deal with "Beliefs, Fictions and Facts," "Genre and Reality," "The Metaphor of Story" and "Exceeding the Limits." The book is a happy mixture of phenomenology, contemporary critical theory and theological insight. It also contains a helpful glossary.

1683 Alonso-Schökel, Luis. *The Inspired Word: Scripture and Tradition in the Light of Language and Literature*. Trans. by Francis Martin. New York: Herder and Herder, 1965. 418 pp.

A hermeneutical study that seeks to synthesize Roman Catholic doctrinal statements concerning the inspiration of scripture with insights drawn from philosophy of language and literary analysis. Although broad in scope, Alonso-Schökel's study does consider such subjects as the function of language and the role of reception, matters that did not usually figure in hermeneutical discussions at the time the study was released.

1684 Altizer, Thomas J. J., et al. *Deconstruction and Theology*. New York: Crossroad Publishing Co., 1982. 178 pp.

Does not deal with biblical interpretation *per se*, but with the broader issue of deconstructive theology as an intellectual movement. The book includes the following studies: "The Deconstruction of God" by Carl A. Raschke; "Body, Text, and Imagination" by Charles E. Winquist; "Text as Victim" by Mark C. Taylor; "The Being of God When God is Not Being God: Deconstructing the History of Theism" by

Robert P. Scharlemann; "Toward What is Religious Thinking Underway?" by Max A. Myers; and "History as Apocalypse" by Thomas J. J. Altizer.

1685   Barr, James. "Story and History in Biblical Theology." *Journal of Religion* 56 (1976): 1-17.

Analyzes the decline of the biblical theology movement as due to a failure of that movement to take seriously the character of biblical (specifically, Old Testament) narrative as story as well as history. Barr lists several ways in which the Old Testament narratives do function as history, but then lists ways in which they do not. The tendency of the biblical theology movement to treat these narratives only as history involved it in contradictions. Still, Barr is hopeful that a new enterprise today might both do justice to the valid emphases that biblical theology sought, while avoiding the antinomies into which it fell.

1686   Beardslee, William A. "Narrative Form in the New Testament and Process Theology." *Encounter* 36 (1975): 301-315.

Explores the relationship between narrative study of the New Testament and process theology. Beardslee thinks that process thought can be fruitful in interpreting New Testament narratives and, at the same time, grappling with the issues raised in the New Testament narratives may stimulate the continuing development of process theology.

1687   Boling, Robert G., ed. *Paul Ricoeur and Biblical Hermeneutics. Biblical Research: Journal of the Chicago Society of Biblical Research* 14-15 (1979-1980).

This double issue of an annual journal is devoted entirely to the implications of Ricoeur's writings for biblical hermeneutics. The issue includes papers by Lacocque (0888) and Crossan (1094) plus an introduction to Ricoeur's thought by Lewis Mudge (also published in 1717). Ricoeur responds to all three papers.

1688   Breech, James. *Jesus and Postmodernism*. Philadelphia: Fortress Press, 1989. 224 pp.

Uses postmodern readings of Jesus' parables as a basis for theological speculation on the nature and integrity of life. The parables are stories without endings: they present narrative decisions and moral choices without revealing the outcomes or consequences of those choices. As such, they call us to live, as did Jesus himself, in a mode of being human that is neither episodic nor moralizing, a mode that seeks integrity apart from consequences.

1689   Croatto, J. Severino. *Biblical Hermeneutics: Toward a Theory of Reading as the Production of Meaning*. Trans. by Robert R. Barr. Maryknoll, NY: Orbis Books, 1987. 96 pp.

Draws on Ricoeur's hermeneutics of reading (0016) to argue for the grounding of exegesis in liberation theology. Croatto stresses (with Ricoeur) that reading does not just discover meaning, but produces it--the role of an interpreter is not simply to understand the meaning of a text, but to enlarge upon it. Liberation theology provides the best basis for such interpretation of biblical literature because the Bible's origin was in a liberation process.

1690 Crossan, John Dominic. *The Dark Interval: Towards a Theology of Story*. Niles, IL: Argus Communications, 1975. 134 pp. Reprint. Sonoma, CA: Polebridge Press, 1988. 128 pp.

Identifies five kinds of stories, which are laid out on a continuum: *myth* establishes worlds; *apologue* defends established worlds; *action* discusses and describes worlds; *satire* attacks worlds; and *parable* subverts worlds. The author is clearly predisposed toward the latter. Drawing from many fields (structuralism, anthropology, theology, philosophy), this book has had a profound effect not only on parable research, but on literary theory and theology in general. See also 0857, 1635, 1705.

1691 Crossan, John Dominic. *Raid on the Articulate: Comic Eschatology in Jesus and Borges*. New York: Harper and Row, 1976. 207 pp.

Explores, from the perspective of structuralist philosophy, the idea that language rather than history might be used as the master paradigm for critical study. Crossan continues his reflection on the teachings of Jesus begun in *In Parables* and *The Dark Interval* (1690), suggesting that Jesus purposely used language to disrupt the sapiential and legal traditions of Israel. But Crossan also goes on to contend that language becomes idolatrous if we do not recognize the impossibility of ever attaining objective knowledge of reality. He crosses into *post*structuralist philosophy, insisting that all data is theory-laden and, accordingly, rejecting the possibility of having any real knowledge of the world or of God. See also 1635, 1705.

1692 Crossan, John Dominic. "Stages in Imagination." In *The Archaeology of the Imagination*, ed. by Charles E. Winquist, 49-62. Chico, CA: Scholars Press, 1981.

Identifies four stages of imaginative development (magical, literal, metaphorical, and paradoxical) and maintains that the paradoxical level is the highest and final stage. Crossan advocates development of a paradoxical theology that will accept construction without forgetting its deconstructive origins. He likes the parables of Jesus because they are "purely paradoxical and disorienting."

1693 Culbertson, Diana. *The Poetics of Revelation: Recognition in the Narrative Tradition*. Studies in American Biblical Hermeneutics, 4. Macon, GA: Mercer University Press, 1989. 189 pp.

Places the Gospels of Mark and John alongside classics of world literature in discussing the literary theme of "recognition." The centrality of narrative in the gospel tradition is emphasized as well as the subtlety of the evangelists' narrative techniques. The main focus of the study, however, is epistemological; Culbertson stresses the essential character of revelation as self-discovery and presents a hermeneutic of "recognition as salvation" that undergirds secular and religious literature alike.

1694   Dean, William. "Deconstruction and Process Theology." *Journal of Religion* 64 (1984): 1-19.

Considers the importance of two deconstructionists--Jacques Derrida and physicist John Wheeler--for empirical theologians who work out of the process philosophy of Alfred North Whitehead. Dean understands the contribution to be positive, if indirect. Both Derrida and Wheeler provide grounds for addressing the question, "What is history and what does it mean?," a question that remains essential for the task of empirical theology.

1695   Fawcett, Thomas. *The Symbolic Language of Religion.* Minneapolis: Augsburg Publishing House, 1971. 288 pp.

Argues that symbols (as distinct from signs, signals, parables, allegories, and myths) are primordial, universal, and therefore inherently religious. All religions are based upon primordial symbols and develop out of reactions against the deaths of myths. Religious symbols may continue to endow human existence with meaning even in a secular age if they are not taken literally.

1696   Frye, Roland Mushat. "Metaphors, Equations and the Faith." *Theology Today* 37 (1980): 59-67.

A theological essay written by a Christian literary critic on the need to reaffirm metaphor as a foundation for truth. Despite the rise of historicism, there is a growing recognition that our center of consciousness can never be coterminous with the universe; thus, we can never create accurate isometric projections of the most important realities or reduce those realities to formulas and equations. Metaphors are needed, and for the Christian the governing metaphor is that of the grace and providence of God ultimately expressed in Jesus Christ.

1697   Funk, Robert W. *Language, Hermeneutic, and Word of God: The Problem of Language in the New Testament and Contemporary Theology.* New York: Harper and Row, 1966. 317 pp.

Critiques contemporary theological approaches to the problem of language and then explores new possibilities by way of examining parables of Jesus and epistles of Paul. Parables embody language in its primordial sense of power or event and it is this element that theology needs to recover. Parabolic speech concentrates on the familiar in such a way as to shatter it, and founds a world without reflecting upon it. The letters, by contrast, exhibit the danger of fragmenting this "totality of signification" inherent in the parable, though Paul ameliorates this by promising an oral word to follow the written. See also 1111.

1698   Gill, B. B. "The Moral Implications of Interpretive Communities." *Christianity and Literature* 33 (1983): 49-63.

Contends that, ironically, postmodern and reader-response approaches to literature are opening the way for a new resurgence of "moral criticism," that is, for evaluation of literature according to its ability to promote moral values and to serve moral purposes. Stanley Fish's concept of interpretive communities (0361) acknowledges the engagement of criticism with the concerns of the culture that it intends to serve. Just as gay, feminist, Marxist, or black communities may offer self-conscious interpretations of texts, so also religious communities may claim the right to interpret texts according to their moral priorities.

1699   Goldberg, Michael. "God, Action, and Narrative World: *Which* Narrative? *Which* Action? *Which* God?" *Journal of Religion* 68 (1988): 39-56.

Critiques attempts at "narrative theology" by Thomas Tracy and by Ron Thiemann (1723) for their failure to deal with the question of whether a Christian narrative theology should be based on the narratives of God in the Hebrew Bible (Old Testament). The identification of narrative action as characteristically "divine" begs the question Goldberg raises in his title.

1700   Gunn, David M. *The Interpretation of Otherness: Literature, Religion, and the American Imagination.* London: Oxford University Press, 1979. 250 pp.

Interprets the relationship between religion and literature in terms of their common identity as cultural forms. Literature tends to employ the symbolic materials of culture heuristically and to test the validity traditionally ascribed to them. Religion typically uses the materials of culture paradigmatically to construct or preserve a model of reality.

1701   Gunn, Giles. "Threading the Eye of the Needle: The Place of the Literary Critic in Religious Studies." *Journal of the American Academy of Religion* 43 (1975): 164-184.

Observes a new role for literary criticism in religious studies--and a new openness to religion and philosophy in literary studies. The newer methodologies of literary criticism are based on philosophical concepts, including those of Hans-Georg Gadamer, Martin Heidegger, and Paul Ricoeur. Gunn sees the synthesis as natural, because much of the best work on religious elements in recent years has been done by literary critics, while much of the best work on aesthetic theory has been done by philosophers of religion.

1702   Güttgemanns, Erhardt. "Sensus historisticus und sensus plenior oder Über 'historische' und 'linguistische' Methode: Thesen und Reflexionen zur erkenntnis-theoretischen Funktion von Linguistik und Semiotik in der Theologie." *Linguistica Biblica* 43 (1978): 75-112.

Engages noetic problems within theology and linguistics as part of a continuing project to secure the scientific character of theology as a rational discipline. Güttgemanns relates problems concerning "sense," "understanding," "analogy," and "historicness" to linguistic and semiotic projects. He is in dialogue with Karl Barth and Rudolf Bultmann.

1703   Hauerwas, Stanley, and Jones, L. Gregory. *Why Narrative? Readings in Narrative Theology*. Grand Rapids, MI: Wm. B. Eerdmans Publishing Co., 1989. 392 pp.

An anthology of essays on the subject of "narrative theology." While the essays do not deal with literary criticism of the Bible *per se*, the broader hermeneutical and theological implications of using narrative as an intellectual paradigm are explored.

1704   Hoffman, John C. *Law, Freedom and Story: The Role of Narrative in Therapy, Society and Faith*. Waterloo, Ontario: Wilfred Lauier University Press, 1986. 164 pp.

A broad-based study that draws implications from study of narrative dynamics for psychotherapy and theology. Hoffman begins with Crossan's understanding of Jesus' parables as stories that provide a structure within which to live while at the same time inviting transcendence and disruption of that structure (1089). Since such stories have the capacity to transcend affirmation/disruption polarities, Hoffman thinks narrative dynamics can be used therapeutically. He is also led to reconsider the theological relationship of gospel, law, and freedom, and to recognize a need for the development of a mode of theological expression that "calls beyond the form of the expression."

1705   Hoffman, John C. "Story as Mythoparabolic Medium: Reflections on Crossan's Interpretation of the Parables of Jesus." *Union Seminary Quarterly Review* 37 (1983): 323-333.

Survey's John Dominic Crossan's work in order to raise particular issues for theology and religion in general. Hoffman looks not only at Crossan's interpretations of parables (1089), but also at the epistemology expressed in *Raid on the Articulate* (1691) and at the literary types described in *Dark Interval* (1690). With regard to the latter, however, Hoffman argues that all stories can have a parabolic quality insofar as they invite the reader's participation in a world that is not his or her own.

1706   Jobling, David. "Writing the Wrongs in the World: The Deconstruction of the Biblical Text in the Context of Liberation Theologies." *Semeia* 51 (1990): 81-118.

Commends the appropriation of deconstruction for liberation theology and its biblical interpretation. Jobling notes that, in literary discussions outside of biblical circles, a debate flourishes between liberation (Marxist and feminist) discourse and deconstruction. Jobling surveys critical issues that attend the bringing together of liberation, deconstruction, and biblical studies.

1707   Krieg, Robert A. *Story-Shaped Christology: The Role of Narratives in Identifying Jesus Christ*. Theological Inquiries. New York: Paulist Press, 1988. 169 pp.

Examines the role that different kinds of narratives (historical narrative, biblical story, biography) can play in the christological studies of systematic theologians today. Krieg focuses on the work of three scholars: Walter Kaspar, Edward Schilebeeckx, and Franz Josef van Beeck.

1708   LaCapra, Dominick. *History and Criticism*. Ithaca, NY: Cornell University Press, 1985. 175 pp.

Argues that documentary objectivism and relativistic subjectivism do not constitute genuine alternatives. It is as acceptable to join history and criticism as it is "to have description, dramatic dialogue, and reflective soliloquy in the same novel." The book calls for a rethinking of historiography in the light of current literary theories. Historical research and literary criticism should be mutually supportive parts of the same complex. The book is not specifically oriented toward biblical or theological concerns, but has been noticed by religious scholars who find its thesis applicable to their field.

1709   LaCapra, Dominick. *History, Politics, and the Novel*. Ithaca, NY: Cornell University Press, 1987. 217 pp.

Considers a number of classic novels from a perspective that attempts to join literary theory to political, historical criticism. LaCapra contends that classic texts are "not only worked over symptomatically by common contextual forces (such as ideologies) but also rework and at least partially work through those forces in critical and at times potentially transformative fashion." LaCapra's work is considered important by some biblical scholars who are looking for ways of integrating historical and literary approaches.

1710   LaCapra, Dominick. *Rethinking Intellectual History: Contexts, Language*. Ithaca: Cornell University Press, 1983. 350 pp.

A collection of essays that explore the problems in relating texts to contexts, with particular interest in the field of intellectual history. LaCapra believes that recent developments in philosophical and linguistic studies and in literary criticism demand a reconsideration of historiography. He calls for a more dialogical approach to historiography that will mitigate the opposition between the historical agent and the historian. The essays consider, specifically, the implications for historiography of the work of Hayden White, Ludwig Wittgenstein, Paul Ricoeur, Jürgen Habermas, Jean-Paul Sartre, Fredric Jameson, Karl Marx, and Mikhail Bakhtin.

1711   LaCapra, Dominick. *Soundings in Critical History*. Ithaca, NY: Cornell University Press, 1989. 213 pp.

Engages current issues in critical theory from the perspective of a student of intellectual history. LaCapra argues that the "critique of totalization" that has been so prominent in recent thought should not devolve into reliance on fragmentation, decentering, and associative "play." Rather, it should be brought into dialogue with aspects of culture and society. The articulation that LaCapra most favors joins three important intellectual tendencies--Marxism, psychoanalysis, and poststructuralism-- in a way that points toward the development of self-critical historiography.

1712 McFague, Sallie. *Metaphorical Theology: Models of God in Religious Language*. Philadelphia: Fortress Press, 1982. 225 pp.

Extends linguistic and literary discussions concerning the role of metaphor to a consideration of metaphorical language for God in Christian theology. McFague bemoans the fact that most biblical and traditional metaphors for God are paternal ones. She advocates the development of maternal and feminist imagery in theological language.

1713 McFague, Sallie. *Speaking in Parables: A Study in Metaphor and Theology*. Philadelphia: Fortress Press, 1975. 186 pp.

Suggests that Jesus' parables (as well as a consideration of Jesus himself as the parable of God) may serve as models for theological reflection today. McFague identifies parables as "extended metaphors and discusses the possibilities of using such metaphorical language in articulation of theological concerns. The work is only tengentially related to modern literary study of the Bible, but represents a development in theology that, to some extent, arises from the observations of such study.

1714 Messmer, Michael W. "Making Sense of/with Postmodernism." *Soundings* 68 (1985): 404-426.

Describes distinct but related categories into which analyses of postmodernism may be grouped. Although they overlap, Messmer labels them "aesthetic, epistemic, and the sociocultural." He concludes that the sociocultural sense best identifies the issues we must all address in our (postmodern) time and place.

1715 Migliasso, S. "Dal simbolo al linguaggio simbolico. L'interesse di una svolte nella teoria ermeneutica di Paul Ricoeur per un'ermeneutica biblica creativa." *Revista Biblica* 29 (1981): 187-203.

Describes Paul Ricoeur's philosophy of language and explores its significance for biblical hermeneutics. Particularly significant is Ricoeur's understanding of the transition from symbol to symbolic language and of the relation between symbol and structure.

1716 Reese, James M. "Inspiration: Toward a Sociosemiotic Definition." *Biblical Theological Bulletin* 21 (1991): 4-12.

Proposes that a model of semiotics derived from the philosophical writings of C. S. Peirce will provide the most reliable methodological tool for understanding inspiration in the postmodern world. The paper was originally presented as the Presidential address at the 1990 meeting of the Catholic Biblical Association. It is specifically concerned with post Vatican II discussions of inspiriation within Roman Catholicism.

1717   Ricoeur, Paul. *Essays on Biblical Interpretation*. Ed. by Lewis S. Mudge. Philadelphia: Fortress Press, 1981. 192 pp.

Four essays on hermeneutics by a renowned philosopher of language that focus specifically on biblical interpretation. The essays are titled "Preface to Bultmann," "Toward a Hermeneutic of the Idea of Revelation," "The Hermeneutic of Testimony," and "Freedom in the Light of Hope." The book begins with a 40-page introduction to Ricoeur's thought by Lewis Mudge (also in 1687). See also 0558.

1718 Schneidau, Herbert N. "Biblical Narrative and Modern Consciousness." In *The Bible and the Narrative Tradition*, ed. by Frank McConnell, 132-150. New York: Oxford University Press, 1986.

Begins by stressing that narrative, not doctrinal propositions, is the essence of the Bible, and goes on to elucidate the implications for this recognition with regard to modern understandings of history. The biblical narrators, unlike Homer, are not sustained by an underlying cosmic consciousness or blueprint. The God of the Bible is inexplicable, remote, and interventionist in such a way that no cosmic constitution can be envisioned. With the exception of the foreign-influenced Wisdom books, the Bible rejects the notion that things happen according to their natures; rather, things happen as Yahweh chooses.

1719   Scott, Nathan A. "The Rediscovery of Story in Recent Theology and the Refusal of Story in Recent Literature." In *Art/Literature/Religion: Life on the Borders*, ed. by Robert Detweiler, 139-156. Journal of the American Academy of Religion Thematic Studies, 49,2. Chico, CA: Scholars Press, 1983.

Traces the "narrative theology" movement and the resistance to it in postmodern thought that rejects the notion of "story" as an organizing principle in life or in literature. Scott says theology should develop a "comparative poetics" that seeks to understand the Christian story in relation to the kinds of stories about human existence that issue from the general imagination of our time.

1720   Taylor, Mark C. *Altarity*. Chicago: University of Chicago Press, 1987. 352 pp.

Attempts to probe the "postmodern crisis of *word*" by examining swings in the author's own thought from Søren Kierkegaard to G. W. F. Hegel, back and forth. Taylor uses the image of the mask of Bacchus/Dionysus/anti-Christ swinging in the wind to describe the nature of his study. He discusses contributions to rethinking "the difference and otherness that lie 'beyond absolute knowledge.'" Taylor considers, in turn, Martin Heidegger, Maurice Merleau-Ponty, Jacques Lacan, Georges Bataille, Julie Kristeva, Emmanuel Levinas, Maurice Blanchot, Jacques Derrida and then finally returns to Kierkegaard.

1721   Taylor, Mark C. *Deconstructing Theology*. New York: Crossroad Publishing Co., 1982. 129 pp.

Presents "a renewed modern Protestant or post-ecclesiastical theology, a theology fully situated in the world or worlds of modernity." Taylor leans heavily upon Paul Ricoeur, Martin Heidegger, Roland Barthes and Jacques Derrida. He admits that "writing books, after having absorbed the insights of Deconstruction, is as difficult as writing theology, after having interiorized the death of God," and he sees this book as a "pre-text to a text yet to be written . . . a postmodern atheology" (cf. 1722).

1722   Taylor, Mark C. *Erring: A Postmodern A/theology*. Chicago: University of Chicago Press, 1984. 232 pp.

Offers a deconstruction for concepts of God, self, and history, and then asks: What comes now? Taylor continues the discussion that he began in *Deconstructing Theology* (1721). His style is refreshingly clear and accessible, and this book has significant bearing upon studies in other disciplines besides literature and theology.

1723   Thiemann, Ronald F. *Revelation and Theology: The Gospel as Narrated Promise*. Notre Dame: University of Notre Dame Press, 1985. 198 pp.

An experiment in "narrative theology." The book contains one chapter on the character of God presented in the narrative of Matthew's Gospel. God is presented as the Father of Jesus Christ, as Yahweh, and as the prevenient God of promise. This presentation is tied in to the overall theme of the book under the assumption that the doctrine of revelation should be a subtheme under the doctrine of God. See also 1699.

1724   Tracy, David. *The Analogical Imagination: Christian Theology and the Culture of Pluralism*. New York: Crossroad Publishing Co., 1981. 467 pp.

A sequel to 1725. Tracy here discusses the task of articulating theology with reference to three "publics": the wider society, the academy, and the church. He draws on Hans-Georg Gadamer in his discussion of the Bible as the basic Christian "classic." The Bible remains a classic because we recognize truth and reality in it. The paradigmatic, focal meaning of scripture is "the always-already, not-yet reality of grace."

1725   Tracy, David. *Blessed Rage for Order: The New Pluralism in Theology*. New York: Seabury Press, 1975. 271 pp.

Proposes that Christian theology must proceed as an investigation and correlation of two sources: (1) common human experience and language, which are to be investigated by way of phenomenological analysis; and (2) Christian tradition, which is to be investigated through historical and hermeneutical analysis of "classic Christian texts." In Tracy's view, the Bible fits into the latter category. The book represents the beginning of a major enterprise in "story theology." See also 1724, 1726

1726 Tracy, David. *Plurality and Ambiguity: Hermeneutics, Religion, and Hope.* San Francisco: Harper and Row, 1987. 148 pp.

Develops an understanding of "conversation" as a model for interpretation. Tracy draws on Lloyd Wittgenstein, Martin Heidegger, Ferdinand de Saussure, and Jacques Derrida to demonstrate that language is never a neutral or ahistorical tool. There are no innocent interpretations or innocent texts, because language itself is not innocent. Thus, a model of interpretation that remains open to both the classics of theology (including the Bible) and to modern voices (e.g., of the oppressed) offers the best approach to theology in an age of pluralism and ambiguity.

1727 Wiebe, D. "The 'Centripetal Theology' of *The Great Code.*" *Toronto Journal of Theology* 1 (1985): 122-127.

Says that Frye's work (0586) is important for consideration by traditional theologians. A theology based on literary criticism, rather than on science or metaphysics is "centripetal"--that is, its focus is on the life of the individual and the community within the biblical story, rather than on extrabiblical physical, historical, or metaphysical states of affairs.

1728 Wilder, Amos N. *The New Voice: Religion, Literature, Hermeneutics.* New York: Herder and Herder, 1969. 269 pp.

A collection of essays on a wide range of subjects. In an introductory essay on "Theological Criticism and Rhetorical Criteria," Wilder challenges theologians to become competent literary critics. This sensitivity to literary concerns continues in three more lectures on "Biblical Epos and Modern Narrative," "From the Almanach de Gotha to the Old Testament: The Case of Marcel Proust," and "The Symbolics on the New Testament." Subsequent essays deal with what Wilder considers to be the "language crisis of our time" and with the need for theology to engage the modern world through an honest encounter with the arts, including modern literature.

1729 Wilder, Amos N. *Theopoetic: Theology and the Religious Imagination.* Philadelphia: Fortress Press, 1976. 106 pp.

Says that renewal of Christianity is, to some extent, dependent on renewal of language. Neither existentialism nor demythologizing are fit for the task for they deprive Christianity of the imaginative and mythological language that it needs. What is needed is a repossession of myth in a colloquial idiom at a level as basic as that which first created the myth.

1730 Winquist, Charles E. *Epiphanies of Darkness: Deconstruction in Theology.* Philadelphia: Fortress Press, 1986. 130 pp.

A book that is not so much concerned with deconstruction as a method of literary criticism to be applied in biblical studies as with the overall implications of deconstructive thought for postmodern theology. Deconstruction's claim regarding the indeterminancy of meaning and the deferral of presence in language require new strategies for theological argument.

1731 Winquist, Charles E., ed. *The Archaeology of the Imagination*. Journal of the American Academy of Religion Thematic Studies, 48,2. Chico, CA: Scholars Press, 1981. 117 pp.

A collection of papers dealing with such topics as the nature of revelation, problems of language and transcendence, and the role of the feminine in a masculine society, all written with sensitivity to deconstruction and poststructuralist thought. Contributions include "Theologia Imaginalis" by David L. Miller; "The Apocalyptic Identity of the Modern Imagination" by Thomas J. J. Altizer; "The Circle of Confusion: From Psychology Through Science to Metaphor" by Robert D. Romanyshyn; "Stages in Imagination" by John Dominic Crossan (1692); "The Archaeology of the Imagination: Preliminary Excavations" by Charles E. Winquist; "On Dandelions: The Problem of Language" by Robert W. Funk; "Revelation, the Poetic Imagination, and the Archaeology of the Feminine" by Carl Raschke and Donna Gregory; and "Imagination and the Re-Valorization of the Feminine" by Lynn Ross-Bryant.

LITERARY STUDIES

See also 0357, 0660, 1562-1564.

1732 Crites, Stephen. "The Spatial Dimensions of Narrative Truthtelling." In *Scriptural Authority and Narrative Interpretation*, ed. by Garrett Green, 97-120. Philadelphia: Fortress Press, 1987.

Inquires as to how stories might be evaluated as "truthtelling," with slight reference to biblical narrative. Crites rejects historical reference and authorial intention as dominant concerns in such evaluation. Rather, a story will be judged "true" when it is true to our experience of social space, especially when it helps to awaken us to that experience.

1733 Edwards, Michael. "The Project of a Christian Poetics." *Christianity and Literature* 39 (1989): 63-76.

Raises several questions apropos to the development of a specifically Christian poetics. Edwards believes that such a poetics should be biblical, that is, inferred from what the Bible teaches about the human condition. It should, for instance, consider language and literature in terms of their relation to the Fall, as forces that work against the Fall and in favor of the Re-creation. See also 1735.

1734 Edwards, Michael. *Towards a Christian Poetics*. Grand Rapids, MI: Wm. B. Eerdmans Publishing Co., 1984. 246 pp.

Tries to define the contours of what should typify a distinctively Christian approach to literature. Edwards is not primarily concerned with biblical interpretation, but with interpretation by Christians of literature in general. A Christian poetics seeks to define the meaning of language and literature in light of biblical teaching. Chapters are devoted to "The Dialectic of Tragedy," to "Comedy and Possibility," to "Story," to "Translating," and more.

1735   Finley, C. Stephen.   "Criticism and Prophecy." *Christianity and Literature* 39 (1990): 283-292.

Contends that Christian criticism of literature should be prophetic, participating "in an ongoing way in the life of the gospel." Finley points as an example to an appendix in the autobiography of Cardinal Newman by David DeLaura that maintains that we are "called into judgment by so Christian a text as that of Newman's." Finley opens his article by faulting an earlier piece by Edwards (1733) for its conspicuous "resistance to theory."

1736   Finley, C. Stephen.   "Hermeneutic and Aporia: Beyond Formalism Once More." *Christianity and Literature* 38,1 (1988): 5-17.

A response to 1744. Finley believes that Ryken's proposal is tainted by a "covert agenda of formalism." The tension between attention to hermeneutics (which remains convinced of a text's relative communicability) and aporia (which traces indeterminacy) is not one that Christian critics should find destructive or fearful.

1737   Gunn, Giles.   "Moral Order in Modern Literature and Criticism: The Challenge to the new New Criticism." In *Art/Literature/Religion: Life on the Borders*, ed. by Robert Detweiler, 45-60. Journal of the American Academy of Religion Thematic Studies Series, 49,2. Chico, CA: Scholars Press, 1983.

Considers the consequences of poststructural/deconstructive criticism for concepts regarding the relation of art and morality. Gunn traces two ways in which art and morality have been related in this century: (1) some critics have sought to interpret literature against what they have regarded as a more or less secure moral standard; (2) other critics have viewed the role of literature as being to criticize life covertly, by offering to the imagination possibilities not disclosed by reality. Both these conceptions are now "seriously endangered" by those who have "lost faith in our contemporary ways of making sense."

1738   Hesla, David H.   "Religion and Literature: The Second Stage." *Journal of the American Academy of Religion* 46 (1978): 181-192.

Surveys the relationship between literature and theology in academic studies since 1950. Hesla sees the New Criticism movement with its emphasis on the autonomy of texts as diametrically opposed to the Apologetic Theology (Bultmann, Tillich) movement with its emphasis on existential relevance. The defeat of formalism in literary circles appears to mean that the theologians have won the day; a second stage is now open for dialogical study of literature and religion. Hesla believes this stage will be sustained by the language and methods of social and behavioral sciences.

1739   Jasper, David. *The Study of Literature and Religion. An Introduction.* Minneapolis: Fortress Press, 1989. 160 pp.

An introduction to the inter-disciplinary study of literature and religion (especially Western Christianity). The first half of the book focuses on religious impulses in what is usually described as "secular literature." Such concepts as beauty, truth, and morality are considered. The second half of the book is introduced by a chapter on "Hermeneutics, Literary Theory, and the Bible." Subsequent chapters trace the movement beyond the limits of formalism toward reader-oriented and postmodern hermeneutics.

1740   Knedlik, Janet Blumberg. "Saussure, Derrida, and a 'Christian' Literary Criticism?" *Christianity and Literature* 39 (1990): 293-302.

Summarizes the arguments of a number of essays that have appeared in this journal concerning the question of whether a Christian literary criticism is possible or desirable (including 1736 and 1744). Knedlik regrets that the articles have tended to fall into either "formalist" or "antiformalist" categories. She suggests that a Christian literary criticism requires three qualities: vigorous eclecticism, patient close reading, and honest repect.

1741   Kort, Wesley A. *Modern Fiction and Human Time: A Study in Narrative and Time.* Tampa: University of South Florida Press, 1985. 227 pp.

Discusses the relationship of narrative time to time in real life, and shows how different concepts of time are assumed by different novelists: Hemmingway and Lawrence exemplify Mircea Eliade's concept of "rhythmic time"; Mann and Faulkner exemplify Alfred North Whitehead's concept of "polyphonic time"; and Woolf and Hesse exemplify Martin Heidegger's concept of "melodic time." Kort writes as a theologian, probing not only connections between narrative art and real life, but also between narrative art and faith.

1742   Kort, Wesley A. *Narrative Elements and Religious Meaning.* Philadelphia: Fortress Press, 1975. 118 pp.

Examines works by authors as diverse as Kafka, Camus, Sartre, and Greene to expose the essentially religious meaning of these tales. The study is significant for biblical studies in two ways: (1) the chapters begin with succinct discussion of concepts applicable also to narrative criticism of the Bible (atmosphere and otherness, character and paradigm, plot and process, tone and belief); and, (2) the discussions illustrate the author's thesis, further developed elsewhere (1743), that all literature, by virtue of its narrativity, is in some sense scriptural. See also 1562.

1743   Kort, Wesley A. *Story, Text, and Scripture: Literary Interests in Biblical Narrative.* University Park: Pennsylvania State University Press, 1988. 180 pp.

Examines two qualities of scripture considered to be basic: narrativity and textuality. The conclusion reached is that scripture and literature are intrinsically interrelated. If the Bible reveals something about religion and God, it does so through narrativity and textuality. But a literary doctrine of scripture also implies a more scriptural doctrine of literature--even so-called secular literature may have more moral and spiritual value than is generally recognized and should, therefore, be interpreted and evaluated for its scriptural role. At the heart of this book are four literary studies on biblical material: plot in Exodus, character in Judges, atmosphere in Jonah, and tone in the Gospel of Mark.

1744 Ryken, Leland. "The Contours of Christian Criticism in 1987." *Christianity and Literature* 37,1 (1987): 23-37.

Declares that Christian literary critics need to define themselves as a particular "interpretive community" over against other critical schools today. Many schools, Ryken believes, are characterized by subjectivism, radical pluralism, nihilism, and even hostility toward Christianity. Christian criticism is similar to other approaches in many respects but is self-consciously from a Christian ethical and theological perspective. A response by Clarence Walhout follows Ryken's article. See also 1736.

1745 Swanston, Hamisch. "Literature and Theology: A note on some suggestions of F. D. Maurice." *The New Blackfriars* 59 (1978): 200-212.

Recalls a notion propounded by Maurice in the middle of the 19th century regarding the conjunction of scripture and literature and suggests that this notion may still be helpful today. Maurice indicated that through the reading of scripture we enter into personal communion with the Word and that this communion becomes a paradigm for all reading.

1746 Underwood, Horace H. "Derrida and the Christian Critic: A Response to Clarence Walhout." *Christianity and Literature* 35,3 (1986): 7-12.

A response to 1747. The feature that links deconstruction and Christianity is paradox. Deconstruction calls us away from rationalist attempts to prove God or God's Word, and calls us to the paradox of faith: inquiry leads only to absence, while the presence of God is guaranteed only by faith.

1747 Walhout, Clarence. "Can Derrida Be Christianized?" *Christianity and Literature* 34,2 (1985): 15-22.

Argues that, although Derrida's radical epistemology is fundamentally at odds with Christian articles of faith, encounter and dialogue with Derrida's deconstructive principles may be fruitful for Christianity. In his conception of language and in his conception of history, Derrida stands opposed, as should Christian theorists, to formalist conceptions of textual autonomy. See also 1746.

1748 Ward, Patricia A. "Revolutionary Strategies of Reading: A Review Article." *Christianity and Literature* 33 (1983): 9-18.

Reviews Culler's *On Deconstruction: Theory and Criticism after Structuralism* (0435), Detweiler's *Derrida and Biblical Studies* (1565), Leitch's *Deconstructive Criticism: An*

Advanced Introduction (0461), and Norris' *Deconstruction: Theory and Practice* (0466). In addition to introducing each of these books, Ward invites readers to go beyond "rhetorical slogans of . . . contemporary theory" and to become engaged with the "variety of literary theories that exist today."

1749   Wicker, Brian. *The Story-Shaped World: Fiction and Metaphysics, Some Variations on a Theme.* Notre Dame: University of Notre Dame Press, 1975. 230 pp.

Wicker begins with the premise that literary and religious studies can benefit one another. Because the critic takes metaphor seriously, a metaphysics is implied; because religion is based upon narratives, books can profitably be studied *as* narrative. He then contrasts the works of Lawrence and Joyce--the one whose writings consciously seek the transcendent, and the other who rejects falsehood in the form of Christian religion. Biblical narratives are considered also. See also 1562.

INDEX OF
AUTHORS, EDITORS,
AND COMPILERS

Notations preceded by "p." or "pp." refer to page numbers in the introductory essay. All other notations refer to entry numbers for items listed in the annotated bibliography.

INDEX OF TITLES

Notations preceded by "p." or "pp." refer to page numbers in the introductory essay. All other notations refer to entry numbers for items listed in the annotated bibliography.

INDEX OF SUBJECTS

Notations preceded by "p." or "pp." refer to page numbers in the introductory essay. All other notations refer to entry numbers for items listed in the annotated bibliography.